MW01178008

# BRITAIN
# 1994

# 1994 Fielding Titles

Fielding's Australia 1994

Fielding's Belgium 1994

Fielding's Bermuda/Bahamas 1994

Fielding's Brazil 1994

Fielding's Budget Europe 1994

Fielding's Caribbean 1994

Fielding's Europe 1994

Fielding's Far East 1994

Fielding's France 1994

Fielding's The Great Sights of Europe 1994

Fielding's Hawaii 1994

Fielding's Holland 1994

Fielding's Italy 1994

Fielding's Mexico 1994

Fielding's New Zealand 1994

Fielding's Scandinavia 1994

Fielding's Spain & Portugal 1994

Fielding's Switzerland & the Alpine Region 1994

Fielding's Worldwide Cruises 1994

Fielding's Shopping Guide to Europe 1994

# BRITAIN 1994

## The Entertaining and Lively Guide to England, Scotland and Wales

**Joseph Raff**

Fielding Worldwide, Inc.
308 South Catalina Avenue
Redondo Beach, California 90277 U.S.A.

Fielding's Britain 1994

Published by Fielding Worldwide, Inc.

Text Copyright ©1994 Joseph Raff

Icons & Illustrations Copyright ©1993 FWI

Photo Copyrights ©1993 to Individual Photographers

## FIELDING WORLDWIDE INC.

| | |
|---|---|
| PUBLISHER AND CEO | **Robert Young Pelton** |
| DIRECTOR OF PUBLISHING | **Paul T. Snapp** |
| CO-DIR. OF ELECTRONIC PUBLISHING | **Larry E. Hart** |
| CO-DIR. OF ELECTRONIC PUBLISHING | **Tony E. Hulette** |
| PRODUCTION SUPERVISOR | **Michael Rowley** |
| PRODUCTION MANAGEMENT | **Beverly Riess** |
| EDITORIAL MANAGER | **Wink Dulles** |
| OFFICE MANAGER | **Christy Donaldson** |
| CUSTOMER SERVICE MANAGER | **Theresa Martin** |

### EDITORS

| | |
|---|---|
| **Linda Charlton** | **Kathy Knoles** |
| **Tina Gentile** | **Evelyn Lager** |
| **Loretta Rooney Hess** | **Jane M. Martin** |
| **Dixie Hulette** | **Peggy Plendl** |
| **Ann Imberman** | **Jeanne-Marie Swann** |
| **Forrest Kerr** | **Gladis R. Zaimah** |

### PRODUCTION

| | |
|---|---|
| **Norm Imberman** | **Harold Pierson** |
| **Bryan Kring** | **Kip Riggins** |
| **Lyne Lawrence** | **Munir Shaikh** |
| **Chris Medeiros** | **Chris Snyder** |

**Lillian Tse**

| | |
|---|---|
| COVER DESIGNED BY | **Pelton & Associates, Inc.** |
| COVER PHOTOGRAPHERS — Front Cover | **Chuck O'Rear/Westlight** |
| Background Photo, Front Cover | **Craig Aurness/Westlight** |
| Back Cover | **Chuck O'Rear/Westlight** |
| INSIDE PHOTOS | **British Tourist Authority and Robert Young Pelton/Westlight** |

Inquiries should be addressed to: Fielding Worldwide, Inc., 308 South Catalina Ave., Redondo Beach, California 90277 U.S.A., ☎ *(310) 372-4474*, Facsimile *(310) 376-8064*, 8:30 a.m. - 5:30 p.m. Pacific Standard Time.

### ISBN 1-56952-006-2

Printed in the United States of America

# Dedication

To Judith, my chum—
and much, much more.

### Judith Raff

Judith shares with Joe the demanding research schedule that goes into the preparation of the Fielding Britain and European guides. Her specialty is the evaluation of merchandise and current fashions for the Selective Shopping Guide, but still she is involved totally in the gathering, weighing, and reporting on every major field of activity covered in the Fielding guides to Europe and Britain.

Born in Philadelphia, she was educated at Connecticut College for Women, the University of North Carolina, and New York University. When there is time for leisure, it is usually answered through downhill skiing, golf, or sailing.

## Joseph Raff

For many years Joe and his wife, Judith, have lived in Europe and crisscrossed their beat annually by car, train, boat, and plane to report on the latest trends and developments for readers of the Fielding guides.

Born in New York, Joe was graduated from the University of North Carolina at Chapel Hill, studied at Harvard, Ohio, and Indiana Universities, and then reported for the *Associated Press* and *Sports Illustrated* before moving overseas to edit the *Rome Daily American*. Since 1961 he has worked on the Fielding guides to Britian and Europe.

Travel writing for the Fielding publications requires almost six months of road work each year. Between times Joe is an avid sailor, an ardent golfer, and an Alpine skier. He lives on Mallorca.

# Letter from the Publisher

In 1946, Temple Fielding began the first of what would be a remarkable new series of well-written, highly personalized guide books for independent travelers. Temple's opinionated, witty, and oft-imitated books have now guided travelers for almost a half-century. More important to some was Fielding's humorous and direct method of steering travelers away from the dull and the insipid. Today, Fielding Travel Guides are still written by experienced travelers for experienced travelers. Our authors carry on Fielding's reputation for creating travel experiences that deliver insight with a sense of discovery and style.

Joseph and Judith Raff have lived in Europe for more than 30 years, and their knowledge of England—from its physical layout to the deep and long cultural heritage of the nation's people—is unequaled by any travel writer today. Whether your style is the hustle-and-bustle of London, or a quiet country inn in the West Country, Fielding's *Britain* is the definitive source for discovering the country's most compelling sights and activities, as well as its most treasured hideaways.

In 1994, the concept of independent travel has never been bigger. Our policy of *brutal honesty* and a highly personal point of view has never changed; it just seems the travel world has caught up with us.

Enjoy your Britain adventure with Joseph and Judy Raff and Fielding.

Robert Young Pelton
Publisher and CEO
Fielding Worldwide, Inc.

# TEMPLE FIELDING
# TRAVEL AWARD

You might call it the cradle of our language and drama. The late director-actor Sam Wanamaker was the American visionary who tried to make Shakespeare live again with his inspired re-creation of the Globe Theatre. The rich Elizabethan replica—not just the stage but an entire architecturally faithful complex—is almost on the exact site where the original Globe premiered The Bard's works in 1599 and afterwards. This year Mr. Wanamaker's monument to imagination, intellect, and literature will raise the curtain on yet another season of Shakespeare beside the age-old Thames in Southwark. To commend his historic and gratifying achievement, this book is proud to dedicate the 1994 Fielding Travel Award to:

## *The Globe Theatre*

### Previous Recipients

| | |
|---|---|
| Concorde SST | International Herald Tribune |
| Freddie Laker | Spanish Parador System |
| Conrad N. Hilton | Pistlolstraede (Copenhagen) |
| Eurail | Frankfurt's Museum Bank |
| Greyhound | World Monuments Fund |
| American Express | Portuguese Pousada System |
| The "Other" Mallorca | Zermatt (Switzerland) |

The Temple Fielding Travel Award is a 64-pound sculpture of crystal created by Master Artist Vicke Lindstrand at the Kosta studios in Sweden.

Consultant: Eugene Raskin, Professor of Architecture, Columbia University, NYC.

# Fielding Rating Icons

The Fielding Rating Icons are highly personal and awarded to help the besieged traveler choose from among the dizzying array of activities, attractions, hotels, restaurants and sights. The awarding of an icon denotes unusual or exceptional qualities in the relevant category. We encourage you to create your own icons in the margin to help you find those special places that make each trip unforgettable.

| | | | | | |
|---|---|---|---|---|---|
| Fielding Selection | Author Selection | Money Saver | Expensive | Quality | Warning |
| Homey | Luxurious | Rustic | Simple | Scenic | Business |
| Great Scenery | Picturesque | Beaches & Resorts | Spectacular Cuisine | Romantic | Relaxing |
| Museum/ Art Gallery | Artistically Important | Architecturally Interesting | History | Book Reference | Musically Interesting |
| Shopping | Festivals | Nightlife | Wine Tasting | Crafts | etc. |
| Cycling | Hiking | Golf | Tennis | Strolling | Horseback Riding |
| Cross-country Skiing | Downhill Skiing | Deep-sea Fishing | Fresh-water Fishing | Snorkeling & Diving | Sailing |
| Arrival & Departure | By Bus/Local Transportation | By Air | By Road | By Water | By Rail |

# TABLE OF CONTENTS

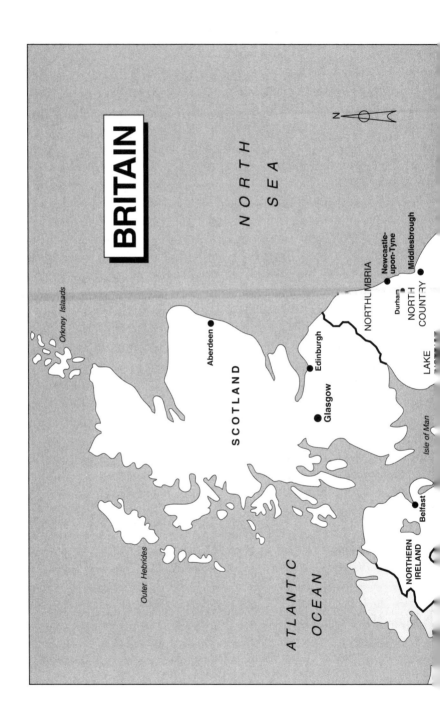

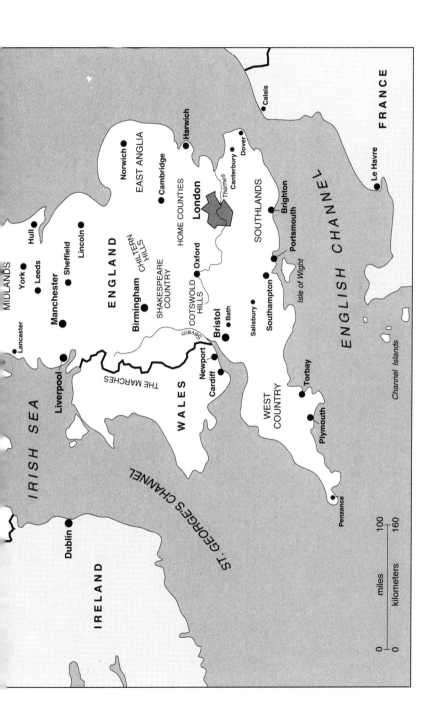

# THE BACKGROUND
# OF BRITAIN

*Souvenir stand in London*

In terms of size alone, Great Britain is not all that great. From north to south it is only about 600 miles long, and its girth is only about half of that at its widest point. Where it is narrow-waisted you can practically smell the salt air either to the west or to the east of you. (It is sometimes supposed this proximity is why the British have produced such formidable navies throughout a glorious military career.) Its 55,000,000 citizens find things pretty crowded. On average they bundle up into groups of practically 600 per square mile over a land mass that covers a mere 93,000 square miles. You still obtain a sensation of spaciousness (and sometimes even desolation) when you travel into the countryside because nearly half the Britons reside within five dozen cities or towns. Though the British raised the curtain on the Industrial Revolution, within a few minutes of any metropolis you'll find beautiful agricultural or forested terrain.

For such a relatively small area, there are tremendous variations in topography. Indeed, until 8,000 years ago, today's United Kingdom was physically united with the continent. This floating realm had no particular identity, and scientists suppose that the first organized culture may have come from the Mediterranean regions—a favor the British now return annually with their migrations to the beaches of Spain, Portugal, and Italy.

By the middle of the Stone Age, northern invaders swept in, along with other marauders from the western reaches of the Continent, causing the Iberians to flee into what is now Scotland. They had already left behind evidence of their megalithic propensities. The industrious construction of great stone circles and tombs was coupled with a progressive interest in mining. Soft and pliable copper gave way to the harder bronze, which carried trade and agriculture into the 15th and 14th centuries B.C. This could be considered the period of the world's first agro-biz, the extensive planting and reaping of grains. Sniffing prosperity, the Celts swept in, along with the Brythons, a Celtic band from which it is thought the word *Briton* has been derived. Bronze had now given way to iron, and this development not only enhanced the economic picture but seemed to activate the warring influences of the numerous tribes that were pouring into the British Isles. To exploit the wealth that was being generated and to establish a system of order in this morass of disparate interests, Julius Caesar sent his Roman Legions into England. Before the end of the first century in the Christian era, Latin was the dominant language from the southern shores of Oceanus Britannius to the northern waters of Oceanus Germanicus—in other words, from the South Downs to Scotland. Though the early Britons did not especially enjoy the Roman occupation, which continued for more than 400 years, they certainly benefited from the organization, the trade, and the leadership provided by the Legionnaires.

The foundations of Roman power crumbled at their base and through continuous efforts to economize, the outposts began to lose their potency. As control diminished, the Angles, Saxons, and Jutes rushed in to fill the vacuum. They established seven kingdoms and seemed to be well on the way to ensconcing themselves in to the seats of power vacated by the Romans.

# ANYONE HERE SEEN ARTHUR?

The legend of Camelot may only be that, a legend. Still, there are niggling suspicions that around 500 A.D. a talented Celt defeated the marauding Saxons and established a moment of peace over the land.

But which land?

Malory suggests Winchester was the enchanted venue, a city that at one point was more important than that upstart London. He was a poet of stature, so his *Morte d'Arthur* became sort of a document endorsing a convenient myth.

In a later chapter, "The West Country," you will read about Arthur's association with Glastonbury and mystic Avalon, which may have stood in the now-dry Somerset swamps. Here the commander who supposedly became a king, a statesman, and a peacemaker was carried (possibly by his knights) to a final resting place on the "Isle of Apples." Arthur is also believed to have died in battle on Salisbury Plain at a spot promisingly called Camlann. This belief, of course, has been disputed by loyalists of other theories and proponents of other Camelots. The River Cam certainly comes into the phonetic picture, suggesting that perhaps the neighboring Cadbury Castle was Arthur's headquarters. Evidently many died in an ancient battle within its shadows. Right in that district is the hamlet of Queen Camel, which has in its time been called Camalat. It's got a blood-soaked history, too, but is that yet enough?

Many also perished at Little Solsbury Hill, and that Arthurian slaughter took place far away in Avon, close to Bath.

Or how about Camulodunum? That's the name the Roman legions gave to present-day Colchester. Citizens of this oldest city in England believe here in Essex is where it (the legend) all started. Indeed, the Celts were here in great number. It was also a passage point for many battling tribes.

The Tintagel region farther west makes a claim on the elusive monarch too. It is nourished by the River Camel and supports a community named Camelford. Tennyson opined that Arthur was seen by the magician Merlin upon the banks of Cornwall. There are Celtic remains in the region to confirm the presence of such people during the time of Arthur's supposed reign. Bodmin Moor also enjoys a mythic association with Arthur.

There seems to be no shortage of claimants. On Scottish turf, the citizens of Stirlingshire insist Arthur was theirs. Merlin, they avow, was even interred at Drumelzier. There are further mists rising from the Eildon Hills that speak of these Knights of the Round Table. The Welsh, equally unwilling to be outdone by their northern neighbors, cite remote Caerleon as the king's magical palace grounds.

And so it goes. From Alderley Edge in Cheshire to Glamorgan to Yeovil and back again—north, south, east, and west—the land is alive with the ghosts of Arthur, Guinevere, Lancelot, and their favorite wizard. Whatever site you finally accept will be as sure as the verities surrounding the Loch Ness Monster, Alice's Wonderland, or the Land of Nod.

Were it not for this elusive, ectoplasmic monarch, the Jutes, the Angles, and the Saxons might have succeeded in suppressing the entire island nation. If, indeed, the legend of King Arthur and his Knights is true, here was their moment of glory in British history. World peace in those years, as today, was not very enduring. Raiders continued to find their way down to the rich territory of the Anglo-Saxons. In the fading hours of the eighth century, King Alfred the Great defeated the Danes and put his seal on a treaty that seemed to have secured the southern part of the nation for the British, leaving the northern counties to the Danes. By the end of the first millennium, the Vikings of the north had regrouped and redirected their efforts to control all of England. Tribute was demanded by the Danes—an act that was answered by the introduction of the first public tax to be imposed by any kingdom. The imaginative monarch to whom we must express everlasting gratitude for the bright idea of taxation was Ethelred the Unready. Ready or not, he died in 1016, leaving to mankind a legacy that will never be forgotten. Nor forgiven.

## 1066, ETC., ETC., ETC.

There is, of course, no other landmark date as prominent as this in English history. After numerous crossings of the Channel, on October 14, William the Conqueror engaged the enemy, King Harold and his troops, on the battlefield of Hastings. This event not only led to total control by the Norman barons over England but established the domination of French (Latin) as the court language for more than 200 years. Virtually everything Anglo-Saxon was suppressed during the ensuing reign of the Plantagenets; statecraft turned its primary focus on the conflict between man and divinity.

Monarchs heretofore had donned the mantle of godliness. Simultaneously the Church, aided by such personalities as Thomas Becket,

Archbishop of Canterbury, thought that institution was the appropriate custodian of God's will. In the gloom of a Canterbury night, a quartet of noble villains was dispatched by Henry II to murder Becket under the canopy of his own cathedral.

The Crusades were born, and religious controversy blanketed the civilized world from Caledonia to Jerusalem. King John had a difficult act to follow in his brother Richard the Lion Hearted. When he lost all of Normandy, John was given the pejorative nickname of Lackland—and he went on to lose a great deal more too. In 1215 (another monumental date in British annals), the English nobles forced John to sign the *Magna Carta*, which ended the special relationship that monarchs had had with Heaven and established the Rule of Law, the foundation of the English Constitution.

Apart from the *Magna Carta*, the English have no piece of paper or parchment to guarantee their liberty and civil rights. This oversight has been effectively rectified through a body of common law that has come down through the courts and the judgments of many wise jurists.

Though kings were reduced to largely titular power, the monarchy continues in its hereditary fashion, the scepter passing to the oldest son of the last sovereign. If there is no male heir, the crown then rests on the head of the female issue.

The British Parliament, of course, is the source of all bicameral systems of government. It consists of the House of Lords (upper house) and the House of Commons (lower house), which correspond roughly to the Senates and Houses of Representatives in other similar systems. Britain's House of Lords is populated mainly by the heirs to these aristocratic titles whereas members of the House of Commons are elected to office by the general public. Finally, the Commons usually utters the last word on all major legislation.

## ENCORE, THE FRENCH

In the latter part of the 13th century, the English sovereigns began to look north and west to consolidate their realm with the subjugation of Wales and Scotland. Feeling heady from his defeat of the Scots, Edward III next turned to the east with the tempting prospect of acquiring the French throne. Though he didn't realize it at the time, he was winding up the clock for the Hundred Years' War. Edward III's son, the Black Prince, had taken the French king as prisoner at the battle of Poitiers.

In the last year of the 14th century, the House of Lancaster, symbolized by a red rose, took command of the British throne. As control was dwindling on the French front, the Lancastrians began a canny program of repossession. This was disputed by the House of York, symbolized by the white rose. By the middle of the next century York was leading over Lancaster. But still the War of the Roses persisted and ground down the energies of the respective factions. Edward V, who took the crown in his boyhood, was declared illegitimate and was murdered with his younger brother, allowing their wicked uncle, Richard III, to take over the realm—all great material for the future William Shakespeare.

## ENTER THE TUDORS

Time seemed to calm the troubled waters, but not for long. The betrothal of Elizabeth of York to Henry VII drew the final curtain on the War of the Roses. But there was Henry VIII waiting in the wings. Again trouble with the Church, more trouble with his wives (six), and the precipitous Dissolution of the Monasteries, which essentially opened the ecclesiastical floodgates to allow Church treasure to flow to the crown and its obeisant cronies. The furious pugnacity of Henry VIII's reign was followed by the pacific sagacity of his intelligent and able daughter, Elizabeth I. Moreover, it was the Age of Discovery, so new horizons—indeed, New Worlds—were being revealed to Old World cultures. Elizabeth's masterly diplomacy and shrewdness in alliances secured her borders and led to a period of pride and prosperity. Being her father's daughter, she also had her ruder moments, such as when she ordered the execution of her cousin Mary, Queen of Scots, on the chopping block. Mary's demise must have had some influence on the conscience of the childless Elizabeth because her son eventually became James I of England, simultaneously James VI of Scotland—the same person but with different titles (and numbers). With the closing of the 16th century, the Spanish Armada had been defeated, the trade routes to the world had been opened and England was enjoying a flourishing moment on the world stage.

## A PAUSE TO REGROUP

In the early years of the 17th century, the doors to the House of Tudor were closed and the portals opened upon the Stuarts. England and Scotland were united under James I, but that sentimental gesture was not enough to hold the country together. There was great unrest, related in particular to the persecution of certain religious followings. The Puritans looked west for their religious freedom. Catholic orders appeared to have undue influence on the court. Charles I was beheaded by the middle of the century, and a new representative of the people, called a Lord Protector instead of a King, came to power. Oliver Cromwell became the standard bearer of the Parliamentarians against the Royalists. Civil War enveloped the nation for more than a decade. It was Cavaliers against Roundheads, and Cromwell's Roundheads took the day. It was a disturbed moment filled with vain hope, and, as the Lord Protector's ability to form a cohesive government gradually ebbed, the succession to his son Richard finally resulted in another Stuart, Charles II, resuming the position of state sovereign. Plague, fire, and poor leadership are an unhappy mixture, but that was the formula in the mid-60s of the 17th century. Under the reign of William and Mary—she was a Stuart, daughter of James II—Parliament achieved its shining hour. The Declaration of Rights was given the seal of approval by William and Mary, finally stating that the crown held office by the grace of Parliament and not by grace of God.

A review of the wars that took place during the Hanoverian rule focuses less on the monarchs than on the heroes of those battles. Admiral Nelson won victory and immortality at Trafalgar. Wellington dampened Napoleonic hubris at Waterloo. Meanwhile, a brash young fry of colonies across the sea had broken the yoke of the British Empire and decided to go it alone.

## A VICTORIAN LEGACY

Fortune did not shine so brightly on England again until the reign of Queen Victoria. From her assumption of power in 1837 until her death in the first year of the 20th century, her tumultuous energy charged England with new purpose. The most important civic institutions of modern times were formed under her reign. Steam power and rails spread to all corners of the nation. Trade routes were secured to the distant harbors of the globe. Colonizers supplied the world with British skills, schools were improved, and the disciples of the Industrial Revolution carried trade and Pax Britannica to the remotest islands and outposts of the planet. Gratefully and appropriately, Victoria was not only a monarch but became by Act of Parliament an Empress, whose influence was felt in every sphere of human activity. By the time of her death in 1901, England had been given a crucial boost into the 20th century.

The guiding light of the English people became mercantilism. Britain did not have resources to power an enjoyable worldwide influence, but it could get the minerals, agriculture, and products through the acquisition of colonies. India was in the bag. Burma became another asset. Africa was falling into line and Egypt represented a prize in a key position to effect easy flow of goods to British ports. The mercantile philosophy spread to the Pacific so that, by the early half of this century, the British dominion included Australia, New Zealand, Malaya, Borneo, New Guinea, down to South Africa, up to Newfoundland and Canada—a spread of sisterly exploitation that led to the timeworn truism that the sun never set on British territory. The fact of such widespread conglomeration was recognized officially in 1931 by the creation of the British Commonwealth of Nations.

## IT HAD A NICE RING TO IT

The myriad states were independent, yet they pledged fealty to the British monarchy. That loyalty didn't hold for long, however. Family squabbles were inevitable. India and Ireland had their own views, as did Pakistan and Burma. Most colonies everywhere entertained visions of unbridled riches and allegiance to no one but themselves. Many of the states and variform protectorates that could have fueled vast prosperity for Britain under continued administration withdrew; the mother country seemed obliged to carry the holdovers at least for a little while, a costly maneuver at best and a politically unsettling denouement that was riddled with Catch 22 situations.

Black ink was turning to red, and to administer such a far-flung skein seemed to be an overwhelming vanity. Through the Second World War—a time of coming together again—only Ireland of all the British realm and dominions chose not to bear arms in support of the U.K. During 1948-49, global fracturing became manifest once more. Asia was following its own agonizing course, accompanied by relentless bloodletting throughout India and Pakistan. The romantic links with Ceylon were cut. African states followed the *Uhuru* path to independence. Britain's patronage over Palestine ended, and the Suez once again became one of the world's choke points. The majestic legacy of Victoria the Empress was reduced to garden party handshakes and fraternal arrangements based on mutually beneficial commerce.

Almost as a symbol of the winding down of Britain's historic diplomat machinery, three short years from now an agreement will end nearly a century of British dominance at an administrative hub that is officially called Victoria. Today's world knows that crown colony better as Hong Kong.

# THE COURSE OF ENGLISH RELIGION

Later on you will read about the martyr named Alban (St. Albans), who met his death at the Anglo-Roman site called Verulamium. Such ardent faith, which established the roots of Christianity, came early and forcefully to the British Isles, perhaps from what is now France or possibly from the north. In any case, by early in the fourth century, there were already bishops functioning in an organized fashion in London, Lincoln, and York. Their network was extensive and powerful, amply predating England itself as a national entity.

Today's Church of England has an archbishop each in Canterbury and York, with a third seat held exclusively in Wales. At its genesis, Pope Gregory the Great gave England his papal seal of approval, and Augustine was to be the emissary of Rome. Berthra was already a Christian when she came from France to marry the king of Kent. Religion styled itself on a missionary pattern, the authority coming from Rome via an ecclesiastical chain of command that was highly effective in a teaching vernacular. Northumbria had become a center of learning, but, after generations of British cultural development, the Danes swooped down on these monastic communities and almost eradicated every vestige of Christian following. By the time King Alfred extended his influence over the land late in the ninth century, much of England had been recaptured from the Nordics and many of the intruders themselves—former pagans—had been converted. Fortunately for the church, William the Conqueror crossed the Channel and strode across the map of England to guarantee its continuity—provided it danced to the Cluny tune.

It did.

And it prospered. Enormously.

Royalty and Church reigned together—perhaps "reined together" would be the more accurate term. Progress was moving ahead at such breakneck speed that there was little time (or need) for argument. National power and religious fervor were racing apace.

Then there came upon the scene that quarrelsome Norman archbishop named Becket who brought King Henry II to his knees as an act of public penance. It was a time charged with electric emotions. A tug of war ensued over Church and state properties as well as whether the archbishop owed obedience to the monarch or the monarch owed fealty to the Church. An angry stalemate ensued, which ended with the murder of the future St. Thomas. Public opinion reflected an impatience with the king, but after all he was law, so matters percolated right up to the time of another Henry (# VIII) who, you'll recall, never did anything in half measures. The question of divorce from Katherine of Aragon put the spotlight on the differences between the monarchy and Rome and, in his Act of Supremacy, Henry VIII clearly announced his position.

No more nonsense. He was "the only supreme head on earth of the Church of England." "Bloody" Mary was later to undo the tidy policy package that Henry VIII had bound together. The pope was again in command, but soon Catholicism had to face the Calvinist surge, the rise of Puritanism, and Presbyterianism.

Cromwell was known as the "Protector"—a replacement for the monarchy during the 1650s—and he protected everything but the churches. In fact, many fine buildings and much beautiful art were destroyed in the name of such protective posturing. A woeful time for ecclesiastical architecture. Under Cromwell, the Independent movement gained popularity, but eventually the episcopacy resumed. Puritans, as Thanksgiving legend instructs us, found more expression and freedom in the New World than in the Old. Puritans obtained little tolerance during the Restoration in England. Instead, Presbyterians received greater favor. James II leaned strongly toward the pope, and this alliance was responsible for his downfall.

Throughout the remainder of the Stuart reign, religion provided a sort of welfare state with great attention to and care for the indigent, an urge to spread the gospel to youth, and growing zeal for mission projects. These good works, however, fell into eclipse by the time George I took the throne (1714), and religion generally languished until Anglican Evangelicals took a different course from the Methodists, about half a century down the line. The Oxford Movement in the early 19th century sought to clarify a lot of the variegation in the Christian faith by crystalizing the view that the Church of England was a direct (well, almost) descendant of the Holy Catholic Church. Though the public didn't buy the notion too well, it put into focus the philosophical basis of future English religious activities; you might say it was a theological jockeying for position to capture the minds, hearts, and spirits of the British.

By late in the same century the pot was boiling with controversy again. By now Anglo-Catholicism was defining itself. Modernists asked for more understanding. Debate continued and little was resolved until the Powers Act of 1919, which linked the Church of England to Parliament.

From that time onward the mechanism was established for the British nation to participate through elected officials in the eventual disposition of their own souls. In practical terms, the Church now functions free of any governmental overview, and, naturally, worship by numerous faiths is practiced all over the nation. If there are any major controversies of the moment within the Church of England, the main one centers on the debate over the ordination of women as priests. The church itself has ended almost two decades of ardent (sometimes furious) discourse and decided to approve the measure—an act which resulted in huffy retirement for some male clerics. Parliament may put the final blessing on the issue by formalizing passage in the year of Our Lord 1994.

# A PREFACE TO YOUR TRAVELS

*Gatwick Airport*

## BEFORE YOU GO

### PASSPORTS

Britain doesn't appear to be such a *foreign* country. The British speak English (exceptionally well) and certainly are our cultural cousins. Nevertheless, a passport will still be required to enter the United Kingdom. There are new passports today for U.S. citizens and they are now green instead of blue. Also they incorporate a sneak-proof optical device similar to a hologram, special inks, and graphics to deter counterfeiters. If you have an older blue one it can be used until the expiry date. Your U.S. document will be valid for ten years for persons 18 years or older and costs $65; for those under 18, it's $40 and valid for five years. In addition, $7 is charged to applicants who are required to apply in person. That processing fee is waived, however, for those whose latest passport was issued within the past 12 years, who were 18 or over when it was issued, and who are able to submit that passport with their new application. If you meet these requirements, you are eligible to apply by mail and should obtain Form DSP-82, "Application for Passport by Mail," which may be sent to one of the passport agencies mentioned below. Applicants who can't qualify under the rules above must apply in person.

Have two photos (2" x 2", and snapped within the last 6 months) ready to adorn the document. For your first passport you must present in person a completed Form DSP-11, "Passport Application," at one of the agencies located in Boston, Chicago, Honolulu, Houston, Los Angeles, Miami, New Orleans, New York, Philadelphia, San Francisco, Seattle, Stamford, and Washington, DC, or at one of the several thousand federal or state courts or U.S. post offices that accept passport applications. Be sure you have proof you are a U.S. citizen (birth or naturalization certificate) as well as proof of identity (driver's license). Forms are available from any of those offices.

For those abroad, petitions for new passports may be made by mail in numerous countries; otherwise, you'll have to appear in person at the nearest American Embassy or Consulate. Your old, dog-eared, cancelled friend will be returned as a souvenir when the new one is issued.

## TELEPHONE

Access code to USA: *0101*; USA Direct *(0800) 89-0011* (a special AT&T service). To phone England: 44; time difference (Eastern Daylight) plus 5 hours. When dialing within the UK, the area indication is augmented by a "0" in front of the number. In other words, a "71" number which means you are phoning to central London becomes "071" if you are phoning from your London hotel for a dinner reservation or it is "71" if you are calling from abroad. (London also uses an "81" prefix in some districts.)

## TRAVEL BUDGET

You get a lot for your money in Britain. On top of that, you'll find bargains if you know where to look. To a large degree that is the function of this book. If you are an average vacationer, you can save more than half of the total expenditure of your holiday by joining a tour. Because startlingly lower group rates are charged by most hotels for exactly the same rooms (this also applies in most restaurants and other facilities), because the lump transport of the baggage is a fraction of the same transfers by individuals, and because of a score of similar fiscal benefits built into them, simple economics dictate that they've got to be dramatically less. Along the same lines, if you are willing to buy a "package" that combines ground arrangements with your overseas flight, the relative price will be lower (perhaps 30%) than if you traveled entirely on your own. Air carriers are clued in to their clients' desires for flexibility; therefore, they are making it easier for you to fly cheaply, leave the flock if you wish, and even explore on your own once you've taken advantage of the special transatlantic ticketing. Some are even providing the option of a lowcost car rental during slow months. British Airways is especially enlightened on these points, so be sure to look through the section ahead called "Getting There".

We've included the top restaurants in this volume so that you may take your choice, but below the multistar listings of the stellar-grade chefs are many superb little "sleepers" and numerous pubs where you might prefer to be anyway, because here is where you will find the real hometowners tucking in their napkins.

Another way to economize is to live out of the main centers. It is true that rural living is cheaper, but it is still rural. Since more visitors travel to Britain to sightsee, museum-hop, shop and dine (rather than simply to relax in the country), think twice before embracing this mode of cutting back. Consider your motives for this trip and then decide, but with either program, Great Britain has lots to offer in town *or* country.

## PLAN YOUR HOTEL STOPS

Your fondest (or worst) memories of a city often may be associated with the accommodation you secured (or endured). Alas, travel agents don't always travel—and that's a great disadvantage for you. Not infrequently they are prompted by promoters and, being only human, they respond with recommendations that sound good, look good on paper and may not live up to the hype.

Perhaps it's wiser to go armed with your own suggestions based upon your particular needs, whims, or preferences. In the United Kingdom there are several excellent confederations composed of tasteful hotels, and their approaches to innkeeping differ widely.

Getting acquainted with them can be helpful in providing greater pleasure on your trip. (Read about the ones mentioned here under the appropriate regional chapters so you'll know about their special flavor and appeal.)

As you will discover under "Intimate Corners" in the London section, the "signature" hotel has come to town. These are also called "boutique" establishments and provide a country flavor in the city. The movement is an open endorsement of how successful this concept has been in the shires and away from the big cities. Now every metropolis has several—a naked denial of the values of traditional English innkeeping.

On the other hand you may enjoy those hallowed traditions that gave England such a grand reputation as a host for so many generations. If these are your desires, you should incline toward the great names that band together in **The Leading Hotels of The World**. Their European headquarters is in London at *15 New Bridge St., EC4V 6AU;* ☎ *(71) 583-4211; FAX. (71) 353-1904. You can also reserve in the U.S.A. by* ☎ *(800) 223-6800; FAX: (212) 758-7367.* This mighty association has within its realm such names as **Claridge's**, **Connaught**, **Inn on the Park**, the **Berkeley**, and the **Savoy**, in London, impressive **Cliveden** at Taplow, or the lovely **Chewton Glen** at New Milton in Hampshire. There are numerous others too.

Then there are the hotels that aim more for a cozy mood, generally with fewer rooms and dedicated to personal attention and homelike facilities. **Relais & Chateaux** does an excellent job in this respect. They have a fine brotherhood of hotels in their British chapter, plus a handful of restaurants. Here you will probably chat with the proprietor soon after you check in—and most likely become long-term friends. My wife and I are forever grateful for meeting Peter and Sue Herbert, who own **Gravetye Manor** (East Grinstead) through a Relais & Chateaux booking. You would know the Herbert touch no matter where you went in the world—and so it is with all these proprietors and their respective houses. You'll undoubtedly also enjoy knowing Michael and Patty Harris at the **Bell Inn** at Aston Clinton. These retreats evoke such charm and special identity that you'll soon be referring to them as "the Herberts' place" rather than by name—quite different from checking in at a Hilton or a Sheraton. For a listing of their charm spots phone the public relations office in *London* ☎ *(71) 581-2759) and speak with Erika Schole-Grosso.* She can put you in touch with a wonderful world of leisure and gastronomy. If you have time to write, the address is *Relais & Chateaux, 28 Basil St., London SW3 1AT.* The FAX number is *(71) 584-0439.*

The pleasures of this kind of living can be extended further by a consortium called **Pride of Britain**. There are some marvelous (and proud) hostelries in this group. There are, for example, the **Athenaeum**, **Dorset Square**, and the **Beaufort** in London, or the stately **Caledonian** in Edinburgh. They've also got the atmospheric **Thornbury Castle** near Bristol, inviting **Cromlix House** up at Dunblane in Scotland, stone-clad **Calcot Manor**, a honey-toned beauty in Gloucestershire, and many more. *In the States you can find out about the entire league by* ☎ *(800) 323-7308.*

An organization that recently brought two regional groups together into one is called the **Small Luxury Hotels of the World**. I've long been a fan of their Welsh delight at Llandudno, **Bodysgallen Hall**, **Middlethorpe Hall** in York, the **St. Andrews Old Course Hotel**, and **Hintlesham Hall** near Ipswich. They also have some I'm not quite so enthused about, such as the **Ritz** in London or the **Royal Crescent** in Bath. Overall, it's a fine banquet of choices—about 3-dozen of 'em and each one distinctive. They, as all of them do, produce a tempting brochure, and you can order it by ☎ *(800) 345-3457* in the U.S.

The moderately priced **Romantik** chain now has links in Great Britain. **Roman Camp** is a stout old soldier in Callander up in Scotland, and **Chedington Court** is an enchanting address for your Dorset rovings. *In the U.S. for more information:* ☎ *(800) 826-0015 or the following numbers in Canada:* ☎ *(800) 268-7150 or (800) 387-1433.*

You've no doubt seen the ubiquitous **Best Western** candidates all over North America. Well, they are in Europe too—working on the same plan of independent ownership but with assured quality for a reasonable price. I have stayed at quite a few and in general can say that you get good value for your pound sterling. *If you want a U.S. number,* ☎ *(800) 528-1234 or in the U.K. it's* ☎ *(44) 541-0033.*

The giant **Trusthouse-Forte** chain, with the prancing stag as its symbol, used to provide low-cost, highly reliable accommodations all over Britain—even to including washing powder for your travel-weary undies and a line for drying them. They've gone way, way upmarket nowadays, however, and the prices have soared, but overall I would say it's one of the most favored chains in the nation. *Their U.S. touchstone is* ☎ *(800) 225-5843 and in the U.K. it's* ☎ *0345-500.*

In the London chapter you'll find guidance for youth hostels and budget hotels suggested by the British Tourist Authority. These same sources can provide names and numbers for accommodations all over the United Kindgom.

## CAR, VAN & MINIBUS RENTAL

*Except for the final paragraphs in this section pertaining to Connex and British Car Rentals, we recommend that you wait until you've crossed the Atlantic, instead of setting up advance reservations in North America unless car rental comes as part of your overseas package.* Here is our reasoning:

Every good-size city on the Continent has scads of excellent self-drive rentals. Even many of the big chains make use of a string of independent local operators. What you're riding in isn't an AAA or Hertz or Avis car in all too many cases; it's actually a Schmidt or Du-Pres or Angelotti car, booked by the American company for you under an arrangement between these principals. Business travelers, of course, often don't have time to prepare in advance, so they may be forced to take any vehicle (at top rates) from the airports, stations, or hotels where they are residing. Holidaymakers, therefore, have an advantage in obtaining better prices.

While we have no special quarrel in this setup, we'd personally prefer the privilege of (1) selecting our own local operator, (2) examining what we are paying for before agreeing to take it, and (3) making our own deal.

On the first point, the caliber of local operators selected by these and other U.S. agencies varies considerably. Moreover, once you book with any American company, you get the vehicle they give you, and that's that.

On the second point, no single local outfit can stock every kind of car. Before leaving home, you might think you want a Ford or Rover, but after comparative shopping, that Jaguar might be far closer to your personal taste. Remember, too, that gasoline prices are more than double the back-home tariff, and since this outlay comes from your pocket, you may prefer an economical 4-cylinder job such as a Ford Fiesta or one of the new thirstless little Opels.

On the third point, prices are supposed to be standard—but they aren't. If you do your own talking, particularly in off-season, you can end up with quotations that are substantially under the "official" prices that you must pay in the U.S. Older people also can receive discounts, as can travel agents, certain service personnel, and members of some clubs or groups. Also, do the booking yourself instead of leaving it to your hotel porter; you can save an immediate 20% by doing your own dialing. Very often, weekend rentals are half the price of midweek hiring.

One company offers a fascinating concept. It's called **Connex** and its popularity is burgeoning—with very good reason. You pay for your car rental prior to departure from the U.S. or Canada. And while you may be receiving a Hertz, Budget, or some other well-publicized vehicle to drive, the price you pay to Connex will be far below what the nameplate agency charges for the very same transportation. Their benefits of great volume and early reservation through a wholesaler are passed on to you. Connex also does not have to maintain staff at the more than 1000 rental stations used for its customers abroad, a great saving. You can book your car up to 24 hours before departure, rates are guaranteed on a dollar basis, and you may order almost anything on wheels, including campers and motorhomes. Get in touch with Connex, *983 Main St., Peekskill, N.Y. 10566;* ☎ *(800) 333-3949;* in Canada ☎ *(800) 843-5416;* FAX: *1-914-739-0430.* I've seen the price lists for about 20 European countries and they are dramatically lower than local rates car- for-car.

You can also preorder from **British Car Rental** ☎ *1-800-448-3936* in the U.S. FAX: *(201) 778-0005;* 24-hr. service. This is a subsidiary of a major bank and The Rover Group; the choice of vehicles, including vans and estate cars (station wagons) is ample. Once in England the central reservations number is ☎ *(0203) 633400.*

In general, you may be in for a shock since car hire prices abroad are usually much higher than back-home tariffs. The two choices above, however, may help you to know what's ahead and what you'll get for your money.

## LUGGAGE

Buying quality in luggage really pays off. If you are frail and traveling alone, you might require a suitcase with wheels. Poor ones slither across airport lobbies, crashing into vitrines and fellow passengers. So pick a good one, not the tail-wags-dog model. We find the stand-up type with the wheels on the short end of the rectangle and a guiding handle on top to be the easiest to manage. The vertical position allows you to push it along at about elbow level. A small fold-up cart could also be the answer. Fashion and chic are other considerations. You'll pay plenty for these, but generally the materials are excellent. If you travel by car and handle your own pieces, leather is lovely. If you use airlines, forget it; it will soon be nicked to shreds. Tough, light, and handsome synthetic materials are now readily available. Soft sides usually risk torn or jammed zippers, bottle breakage, and excessive wrinkling, but they are light. Hard-siders are usually heavy. Semi-hard require careful attention to the frames. Anyway you look at it, it's a compromise.

## *MONEY*

Sterling can be exchanged anywhere in Britain, whether you are in Scotland or Wales. Don't worry too much about buying sterling in advance.

Most British airports have 24-hour banks where you can exchange dollars or traveler's checks for local currency. (Even so, you should swap the bulk of your bucks at midcity banks, where the rates are usually better.) Banks usually pay a bit more for traveler's checks than for bills, and whenever you're ready to buy anything in a store, ask first if the merchant will give you a discount for them. Once abroad, always cash your checks at a bank, not in your hotel or in a restaurant or shop. The last three's rakeoffs can be rapacious.

For ordinary needs, you should carry the sterling equivalent of about $300 in cash and the balance in traveler's checks. Internationally recognized credit cards (American Express, MasterCard, Diners Club, Visa, etc.) have become almost "must" items in these days of volatile currency reforms; with these you usually receive the exchange rate of the day your purchase was made.

# THE BRITISH IDIOM

International television broadcasts and your own travels have probably given you ample exposure to certain English words or expressions that differ from the American or the Mid-Atlantic counterparts. Just for fun, here are a few comparisons. (My good friends up in Scotland live in yet another language realm, much of it colorful, poetic, and droll.)

First and possibly most urgently, the British rest room is referred to as "The Gents" or "The Ladies." It can also be called the "Cloakroom." The commonly employed term "loo" probably derives from Britain's seafaring days, when gentlemen thoughtfully retired to the leeward (rather than the windward) side of the ship to relieve themselves.

| CLOTHING | |
|---|---|
| **AMERICAN** | **BRITISH** |
| Under Shorts | Knickers |
| Dress | Frock |
| Socks | Hose |
| Boots | Wellies (for Wellington) |
| Raincoat | Mac (for Macintosh) |
| Parka | Anorak |

| CLOTHING | |
| --- | --- |
| **AMERICAN** | **BRITISH** |
| Windbreaker | Wind-cheater (the American term provokes howls of laughter) |
| Necktie | Cravat |
| Bathrobe | Dressing gown |
| Undershirt | Vest or Slip |
| Vest | Waistcoat |
| Suspenders | Braces |
| Bathing Suit | Bathing Costume |
| Sweater | Jumper |
| Diaper | Nappy |

| FOOD | |
| --- | --- |
| **AMERICAN** | **BRITISH** |
| Grain | Corn |
| Whole Wheat | Whole Grain |
| Corn | Maize |
| Peanuts | Ground nuts or monkey nuts |
| French Fries | Chips |
| Ground Meat | Mince or Minced Beef |
| Belgian endive | Chicory |
| Eggplant | Aubergine |
| Cookie | Biscuit |
| Candy | Sweets |
| Dessert | Pudding or Pud (pronounced "pood") |
| Ice Cream | Ice |
| Jelly roll | Swiss roll |
| Molasses | Black treacle |
| Shrimp | Prawns |
| Zucchini squash | Baby Marrows or Courgettes |
| Rare (for roasting) | Underdone |

| WAYS OF THE ROAD | |
| --- | --- |
| **AMERICAN** | **BRITISH** |
| Traffic Circle | Roundabout |
| Highway | Carriageway (dual for 2 lanes) |

## WAYS OF THE ROAD

| AMERICAN | BRITISH |
| --- | --- |
| Automobile | Motor Car |
| Sedan | Saloon Car |
| Convertible | Drophead |
| Station wagon | Estate car |
| Gasoline | Petrol |
| Trunk | Boot |
| Hood | Bonnet |
| License plate | Number plate |
| Dashboard | Facia |
| Windshield | Windscreen |
| High-Low Beams | Dip-Switch or Dimmer |
| Odometer | Mileometer |
| Pliers or Wrench | Spanner |
| Baby carriage | Pram |

## USEFUL DIFFERENCES

| AMERICAN | BRITISH |
| --- | --- |
| Adhesive tape | Sticking plaster |
| Band-Aid | Elastoplast |
| Scotch tape | Sellotape |
| Apartment (unit) | Flat (in a block of flats) |
| Balcony (at theater) | Gallery |
| Closet | Wardrobe |
| Cotton batting | Cotton wool |
| Cuffs on trousers | Turn-ups |
| Druggist | Chemist |
| Editorial | Leader |
| Information | Directory enquiries |
| Intermission | Interval |
| Lawyer | Solicitor (barrister for courtroom work) |
| Legal Holiday | Bank holiday |
| Line | Queue |
| News dealer | News agent |
| Broadcaster (news) | Reader |
| President (corp.) | Chairman |

| USEFUL DIFFERENCES | |
|---|---|
| **AMERICAN** | **BRITISH** |
| Sideburns | Sideboards |
| Stove | Cooker |
| Time payment | Hire purchase |

A friend might refer to you by your surname rather than your first name—Christian name is your family—or may speak to you over the "blower" instead of over the telephone. TV is seen "on the box" or the "telly" and movies at the cinema or "cine" (pronounce it to rhyme with skinny). If an Englishman wishes to tell someone off or cause chagrin he will "take the mickey" out of that somebody. And while he is likely to tell you his wife is "homely," he is actually complimenting her.

London has a language legacy all its own. A Cockney or true Londoner is said to be anyone born within the sound of the Bow Bells, from a church called Bow (St. Mary-le-Bow) in Cheapside. The speech is historically distinctive and added to the fun-loving luster of this patois, the Cockneys have applied their own code of rhyme. Certain stock words that come up frequently in conversation are given comic equivalents. As examples, "trouble and strife" is the Cockney label for "wife," "tea leaf" equals "thief," "dog-and-bone" is "phone," "apples and pears" mean "stairs." In this exchange, the more complex the rhyme, the more jovial the conversation becomes. But as a first-time experience you may think either you or they have taken cleave of their winces.

# A LONDON CALENDAR

Just for starters, there are certain fixed (or almost fixed) dates for events that recur annually within or near the capital. Knowing about them may help you plann your visit. Clearly this is only a smattering. The London Tourist Board can provide you with material for every minute in the year.

**January:** The New Year's Day parade kicks things off with a blanket invitation from the Lord Mayor of Westminster. It usually runs from Berkeley Square to Hyde Park. The London Boat Show, arguably the most exciting in the world, is at Earls' Court during the first half of the month. The theater, opera, and concert season is in full swing.

**February:** Many art galleries have exhibits this month. Crufts Dog Show is a howling success at this time. Clown Service at Holy Trinity Church (Beechwood Rd., Dalston) is always the first Sunday of this month. Clowns from all over the world attend in costume to celebrate the memory of Grimaldi, the inspiration of today's comic performers.

**March:** The Oxford-Cambridge Boat Race and the Head of the River Race occur late in the month or even into April. Viewing from the banks of the Thames is ideal. My favorite spot for the everyday practice and warm-up training is in the lovely town of Henley. For the race days (the route is the same for both) put a blanket down on  Surrey Bank above Chiswick Bridge. March usually signifies the beginning of the Shakespeare Theatre Season: Performances (check first about the new Globe) are sometimes at the Barbican in London plus the Royal Shakespeare Theatre, Swan Theatre, and The Other Place at Stratford-on-Avon. Ask about special transport to Warwickshire and back. Now is the first phase of the Chelsea Antiques Fair. For racing fans, the Gold Cup is at Cheltenham.

**April:** The London Marathon takes a 26-mile course from Greenwich to Westminster, with some 60,000 feet pounding the pavements for charity. Though not too old, the Contemporary Art Fair is catching world attention. If you feel like traveling up to Merseyside, the fabulous Grand National is held at Aintree. There's nothing like it in sport for excitement.

**May:** Springtime means the fabulous Chelsea Flower Show at the Royal Hospital Ground. It's not only for blossoms; tools, garden furniture, and even advice are offered to broaden the spectrum for visitors with green thumbs and deep pockets. For opera lovers, the Glyndebourne Festival opens its glittering season. Special trains zip over from London to Lewes (East Sussex) and back around midnight. The Royal Windsor Horse Show is at Windsor, and the incredible Badminton Horse Trials occur at this majestic private estate in Gloucestershire.

**June:** Beating Retreat and Trooping the Colour are splendid military shows. The latter celebrates the Queen's official birthday. Both events occur at the Horse Guard's Parade. (If you happen to be up in Scotland, don't miss the Royal Highland Show in Edinburgh.) Derby Day is run at Epson Racecourse, the primary contest for three-year-olds. Ascot, with its famous Gold Cup, is colorful since the Royal Family arrives each day from Windsor in open carriages. It's one of the major society events of the year. The Grosvenor House Antiques Fair draws collectors from all over the globe. The Henley Royal Regatta occurs usually late this month or early in July.

**July:** Wimbledon, with its legendary grass court tennis, usually bridges the time between late June and early July. If you seek tickets, write between October and December to the All England Lawn Tennis & Croquet Club (P.O. Box 98, Church Rd., Wimbledon SW19 5AE and include a self-addressed envelope. Applications, alas, allow for only one person per household. Other major sporting events this month include the "Glorious Goodwood" horse races at Goodwood (Chichester), the British Open golf tournament and, down at Cowes, the Admiral's Cup and related sailing frenzy in the Solent between the mainland and the Isle of Wight. The "Proms" (Promenade Concerts) are held from July to mid-September in the Royal Albert Hall. Some associated ceremonies occur in the open at mansions such as Kenwood House (Hampstead) or Marble Hill (Richmond). Do as the Brits do and take a blanket and picnic for an evening of music.

**August:** A sea of human wildlife comes to Notting Hill for the Caribbean Carnival; steel bands, brass bands, and, occasionally, unruly bands mix in overheated streets. The London Riding Horse Parade for the best turned-out horse and rider is more sedate. Admission is free (at Rotten Row, Hyde Park). If the city is too hot, pop up to Edinburgh for the nonstop Festival doin's and the Military Tattoo. The Scottish capital is always cool in summer.

**September:** A busy time. There's the Covent Garden Festival with street theater, music, and hilarity. Thamesday is a family scene at South Bank. There's the Great River Race from Richmond to the Isle of Dogs. The autumn Chelsea Antiques Fair brings thousands of visitors to town. You might care to see the Druids honoring the Autumn Equinox on Primrose Hill or the dramatic Farnborough Air Show. Art exhibits and fairs are throbbing this month. Down at Southampton there's the highly esteemed Boat Show, and far up in Grampian, Scotland, they are featuring the well-publicized Braemer Royal Highland Gathering with games and plenty of color.

**October:** More flower, art, and antiques shows. Pearly harvest at St. Martin-in-the-fields (Trafalgar Square) is a jovial and colorful Cockney celebration for street traders. This is the time for the Horse of the Year Show at Wembley's indoor arena. The horse gives way to the automobile at the Motor Fair. While this used to be a tradition at London's Earls' Court, it now occurs in Birmingham, so hop on a train for the day (or rent a Jaguar) and see the latest in automotive panache. Trafalgar Day Parade brings out the best in British pomp and circumstance.

**November:** Automotives buffs will thrill at the famous London-Brighton Veteran Car Run. Guy Fawkes is fireworks night. (For details, phone ☎ *(71) 730-3488* and the Tourist Board will tell you where and when.) Phone also for specifics concerning the spectacular Lord Mayor's Show, a tradition dating from the 13th century. In mid-month Parliament begins a new session. Christmas lights go on in the major shopping districts.

**December:** A shoppers' paradise! Great theater and extensive cultural activity. There's a concert almost every night, the Olympia Showjumping Championships are on, holiday exhibits are going full tilt, special dinners are offered at festive dates. The Christmas tree in Trafalgar Square is always a gift from Norway, an expression of gratitude for Britain's help during World War II. Carols are sung around the giant spruce nightly.

## GETTING THERE

### *ENTERING THE U.K.*

No people in my career of traveling have shown more courtesy over the years than the British Customs personnel. If you're lucky, you could sail through the "Nothing to Declare" gates without one bag being checked. The speed of your clearance usually depends upon the traffic or any security measures, which may be strict or lenient at the time you come through the control. Here are some helpful hints:

Be affable and cooperative, but don't be overly conversational. Their sole interest is to get rid of you. If you keep your mouth shut, things will move twice as fast.

Hold your passport casually in hand—don't flaunt it!—so the inspector can identify you. (This might sound absurd, but sometimes it's surprisingly helpful.)

The Common Market nations permit 300 cigarettes, 1-1/2 liters of hard liquor (2 "fifth" bottles should pass), 3 liters (3/4 gallon) of wine, 1-1/3 lbs. of coffee, and 1/4 lb. of tea.

London is arguably the most international metropolis on the globe, so the airlines of the world fly in to Heathrow or Gatwick regularly or on charter. The industrial hubs of the Midlands and the northern terminal in Scotland also are favored if London is not the demand city. Usually it is, however, and most tours of the British Isles begin and end with the English capital.

There is a revolution going on, and it can bring you significant benefits in terms of travel costs. While British Airways has been privatized, competition is regrouping under new structures provoked by deregulation. The ensuing air battles and link-ups with other carriers certainly will encourage fare reductions. The next question is whether existing service standards can be maintained or bettered. In my opinion, it won't be easy to top **British Airways**. This carrier not only runs one of the most modern fleets aloft, but so much attention has been given to pleasing the client that it is simultaneously one of the most efficient and pleasurable rides in the sky to be found over any sea or continent. You can step on board a BA jet at any of 164 cities in 76 countries. Supersonic Concorde zips over the Atlantic with twice-daily flights in each direction between London and New York plus three calls a week to Washington. BA effectively operates from 18 U.S. gateways. Then BA ties in with United Airlines, providing through check-in convenience to almost 400 destinations worldwide. Europe also is BA territory, adding the Continent to its easy, seamless service.

The Greater London gateway is served by 5 airports: London (Heathrow) Airport, ever-expanding Gatwick (mostly for charter but some scheduled carriers fly in, too); a fine North Terminal for long and short BA hauls, using bus or train excellent, speedy connections to town; there's a helicopter dash to Heathrow, Luton (more Charters), the London City Stolport (more for business hops; specialized; see below), and the new Stansted facility (again, see below).

Heathrow itself is divided into Terminal I (British, Irish, and a few North American flights), II (European airlines), III (mainly intercontinental), IV (BA's main hub for long-haul passengers as well as those going to Paris and Amsterdam). Buses to town are frequent and stop at various points in the city. Incidentally, there's a subway link (carry your own luggage) between Heathrow and Piccadilly Circus (under an hour) with trains leaving to and fro every 4 minutes during peak periods. Grocery-style baggage carts are available at Heathrow free of charge; alas, porters have become obsolete.

London City Stolport is chiefly for national and nearby European connections. It's in the City's East End; the name is derived from STOL, aviation parlance that stands for Short Take Off and Landing—planes that need runways of only 2500 feet in length. You may find this handier if you are destined for Paris, Amsterdam, Brussels, Dusseldorf, or Rotterdam.

Stansted is about 30 miles northeast of London at the site of a former U.S. airbase. There's a rapid rail link to the city and many other modern conveniences. Air UK is based here, serving Paris, Amsterdam, Brussels, and the Channel Islands. Other carriers include American Airlines (via Chicago), Air France, and Ryanair (of Ireland).

Incidentally, since BA is such a volume purchaser of bed nights, restaurant reservations, and theater tickets, you can use the airline itself for these services and benefit from discounts.

# AFTER YOU'VE ARRIVED

## *WEATHER FORECAST*

The British did not invent rain, but with their *Macs, Wellies, brollies* (umbrellas), their cashmeres, Shetlands, Burberrys, and so forth, they have learned how to tame what falls from above. They call it an oceanic climate, which means it is neither too hot nor too cold. To be safe, in summer take a medium-to-lightweight raincoat. You can wear light wool for summer nights and cottons by day. If it becomes cloudy, you might need a sweater in the daytime. This is very often the case in the northern counties and in Scotland or along the Atlantic coast. The best shoes are those that can resist damp and are comfortable for most conditions. In winter, snow and ice are experienced from time to time in the border lands of the north and in the high-lands of Scotland. The chill factor is notable, so a muffler and wool cap can be useful. In any case, it may also rain, so proper gear for harsh conditions will be welcome. (Why not buy your tweeds and woolies right on the scene where they were born?) Around London, a well-lined raincoat or an overcoat will serve most purposes. The wind howls along the streets, but the hotels and restaurants are amply warm. Hence, heavy outerwear and medium suits, jackets, and dresses are the best combination. For all seasons, all sexes, and all ages, the blazer is the universal attire. Don't let the warnings above frighten you; there is also plenty of sunlight. In matters of dress, however, it is safer to be prepared for the worst.

## TOURS

Many fine ones exist, and if your time is limited you might find it best to put yourself into the hands of a specialist who knows the sites, the hotels, and the nuances of each district. Of course, this will be more expensive than doing it on your own, but then this is the se-lective way to see Britain and it comes at a luxury price. (Otherwise, U.S. tour packagers put together fairly representative circuits for bulk traffic at moderate cost.) One of the best companies I've found in the top category is **British Tours Ltd.** (6 South Molton St., W1Y-1DH; ☎ *(71) 629-5267*; FAX: *(71) 629-4173).* Contact its personable Managing Director Gerda Doll-Steinberg, who can show you illustrated documentation on 3-14-day adventures. She can also arrange special tours and London sightseeing—all chauffeur-driven, of course.

## MEDICAL ADVICE

Immunization isn't required for travelers to Britain. The nation has good public health officials, fine doctors, and the latest drugs; many of the last appear on British pharmacy shelves years before they are put up for sale in North America—even when they may be produced by U.S. manufacturers. (Europeans often test the new products more quickly than the FDA.)

Though vaccinations are not required in Britain, you may be trav-eling on to other destinations; information on foreign immunization laws for countries farther afield can be obtained from the U.S. Public Health Service. Check your phone book under "U.S. Government Department of Health, Education and Welfare." Also helpful is an organization called International Association for Medical Assistance to Travellers. IAMAT (736 Center St., Lewiston, NY 14092) can provide the names of English-speaking doctors in many foreign nations. I have had occasion to meet and use a few of its colleagues and feel the service is worthwhile.

World traveler and student of travel medicine, Dr. David Corwin offers some tips on staying in shape: Naturally, everyone is cautious about the drinking water in questionable places. The British Isles are probably as safe as anywhere in the civilized world. If the time of year is hot it might be wise to avoid mayonnaise left in the sun. Factory bottled dressings (made with preservatives) are usually safer than fresh ones, which may invite bacteria if they are not properly protected. Many people are staying away from slightly cooked meat, poultry, fish, and eggs (also dressings made of raw egg).

"Turista" is likely to lurk anywhere, so nonprescription Polymagma or Pepto-Bismol are useful health aids in liquid or tablet form. Diarrhea can cause loss of salts and fluids, so Dr. Corwin suggests having sugar in hot tea; it apparently enhances the absorption of salt. Imodium (also in liquid or capsule forms) is fast-acting and seems to be effective in keeping people on the tourist trails and worry-free.

Motion sickness, states Dr. Corwin, has many combatants in tablet form, some of which produce drowsiness, so it may be a trade-off as to whether you would prefer to be alert or queasy. Meclizine (generic), Antivert, Dramamine, and Bonine taken anywhere from a half to one-hour before the motion begins are often effective. At the onset of nausea, lozenges, suppositories, or injections of Phenergan, Compazine, or Tigan are indicated. CIBA's Transderm-V (scopolamine) (yes—the truth serum of espionage novels) is a novel approach to relief. It's a dime-size adhesive patch that can be worn behind the ear or elsewhere on the body; the skin absorbs protective chemicals for up to 3 days and in the amounts demanded by the circumstances— an easy way to wear instead of swallow your medication.

## SPECIAL NEEDS

**Handicapped** • The American Automobile Association (AAA) distributes a guide for handicapped travelers. Another organization, the Society for the Advancement of Travel for the Handicapped, offers further aid; it is located at *26 Court St., Brooklyn, NY 11242;* ☎ *(212) 858-5483.*

**Ambulance Service** • Three companies specialize in airlifting disabled travelers to Stateside medical centers. Since their programs are tailored to specific needs, write to them for details. HOME and NEAR cater more to individuals while SOS works chiefly with corporate accounts. Here's how you reach them: HOME, International Travelers Association, *1100 17th St. NW, Washington, DC 20036,* ☎ *(301) 652-3150;* SOS Assistance, P.O. Box 11568, Philadelphia, PA, ☎ *(215) 244-1500.* If your normal insurance does not include this expensive phase of assistance (and most will pay only for land ambulances), it is worth considering separate coverage.

**Medic Alert Foundation** renders an invaluable nonprofit service to travelers who suffer from any hidden medical problem. It furnishes lifesaving emblems of 10-karat gold-filled, sterling silver, or stainless steel to be worn around the neck or wrist. Should the patient be unable to talk, medical personnel or law-enforcement officials are instantly informed of dangers inherent in standard treatment. The tag carries such warnings as "Diabetic," "Allergic to Penicillin," "Taking Anticoagulants," "Wearing Contact Lenses," "Neck Breather," or whatever difficulty. It also bears the telephone number of the Medic Alert Headquarters in California, to which anyone may call "collect" from anywhere in the world at any hour of the day or night for additional file material about the individual. The organization also features an electric unit worn around the neck that alerts a telephonic standby facility if the wearer suffers a medical crisis. For more information about this splendid organization (donations are tax-deductible), write to Medic Alert Foundation International, *Turlock, CA 95380-1009.*

# GETTING AROUND

## *TAXI TO TOWN AND ABOUT TOWN*

In my view, the London chariot is the finest, most comfortable, best-designed taxi in the world. The classic version, however, is being challenged by the gradual introduction of a sleeker style called the Metrocab, operated chiefly by "*mushers*" (owner-drivers). While it would take almost a decade to fully replace the older cabs, a chorus of harrumphs is being heard across the land. It's a hollow bruit in my opinion because, if anything, the new hacks are better than the traditional FX4 models. An average trip in the center of the city runs around £3. For each additional rider above one person, there's an extra charge.

If you're traveling between the capital and Heathrow Airport and choose not to utilize the bus (about £2.50) or subway shuttle (£1.50), legislation now limits the hop to whatever is shown on the meter (it should average about £20 plus a 10% tip). British law, incidentally, permits sharing a cab with as many as three other occupants. If there's not too much luggage, this can bring the cost down considerably.

## *RIDING THE RAILS*

Early this year, the Eurotunnel linking England with the Continent by rail finally may open after several delays and funding headaches. The "Chunnel" crosses the English Channel (called the Manche by the French) at the narrowest point: at Folkstone (near Dover) to Coquelles (near Calais), a distance of 38 kilometers (roughly 20 miles). Services, however, may not be complete in every respect until 1998, so check on these details with a travel agent before diving in.

The British probably have more railroad stations per capita than other nations in the world. And even though they have closed many of these terminals recently in the name of economic efficiency, it's still easy to reach hundreds of destinations by rail. The speedier **Intercity** rockets roar along at close to 125 mph. Because Great Britain is longer than it is wide, sleeper services exist almost only between the north-south routes. The cars are excellent, seats are comfortable, air conditioning is nearly always available, and the cuisine is predictably poor.

The popular money-saving **BritRail Pass** is available only outside of the United Kingdom. BritRail travel information offices in New York, Los Angeles, Dallas, Vancouver, and Toronto can provide you with all of the details; most travel agents also can provide the ticketing. The Pass is valid for unlimited rail travel on scheduled services in England, Scotland, and Wales, and it applies to both standard and economy class *(Silver card)* or first class *(Gold card)*. Young people, aged from 16-25 inclusive, receive special discounts, as do senior citizens over 60 years of age. Sprogs from up to 4-year-olds travel free, and those from 5-15 years may take advantage of the half-price benefits. Within the plan are three ticket categories: one is for 4 days of travel over a period of 8 days; another is 8 days within a period of 15; and finally, 15 days during a one-month term. These may be used any time of the year. The British have hitched their wagons to the French Rail Service (with the BritFrance Rail Pass), so now Continental coverage can be combined with your U.K. visit.

## BY BUS

The **BritExpress Card** provides a discount of one-third of the adult fare for any number of journeys taken during any month (any consecutive 30-day period). While this is offered to visitors from 16-59 years of age, men and women over the upper limit and children from 5-15 years qualify for the same one-third discount without purchasing the BritExpress Card. Bring along your passport for evidence of age. This program is valid for Britain's National Express, Caledonian Express/Stagecoach, and London Express. These serve approximately 1500 destinations in England, Scotland, and Wales. In London you can purchase the BritExpress Card at the Coach Travel Center, 13 Regent St., S.W.1 or at the Victoria Coach Station. Full-time students also should ask about the availability of special discounts that are valid up to one year. The same bus companies also offer a **Tourist Trail Pass**, with exceptional bargains for dedicated wanderers. The special low prices apply to 5, 8, 15, 22, or 30 consecutive day periods.

## FOR LONDON ONLY

The capital offers a special rate for unlimited travel on the Underground and bus networks, called the **Visitor Travelcard**. This is available the year round on 1-, 3-, 4-, or 7-day blocks.

The BritRail organization can tell you more about these and arrange the purchase.

## BRITAIN'S NATIONAL TRUST

The Brits have found a highly successful way to share their wealth with visitors. It opens doors that would otherwise be closed to a vast, appreciative audience; moreover, since many private owners might not be able to afford the upkeep of such stately homes in this era of high taxes and inflationary costs, it provides a method for preventing decay while enhancing erudition and pleasure. Within the nation are more than 1000 castles, homes, and gardens that have been opened to the public, on payment of a modest fee. The National Trust, a nonofficial, nonprofit body, now owns 260. Of the grand total, 40 are "Great Houses"; the balance consists of stately mansions, country manors, abbeys, and sentimental shrines such as Rudyard Kipling's former residence. Most popular and most outstanding is **Woburn Abbey** and **Zoo Park** (42 miles from London, 54 miles from Stratford-on-Avon), belonging to the Duke of Bedford Trust; 1.5 million guests per year "oh" and "ah" at the 3000 deer, the safariland of African animals, the multimillion-dollar art collection, 3000 acres of enchanting parkland, the model village, the cable car system, the exhibition of 17,000 toy soldiers, the Zoo restaurant, and the splendid antique furnishings. High in popularity is **Chatsworth** (on River Derwent, 33 miles southeast of Manchester), which is renowned for its magnificent gardens with water effects. The duke of Norfolk's **Arundel Castle** (near Brighton), the duke of Marlborough's **Blenheim Palace** (8 miles north of Oxford), where Sir Winston Churchill was born, **Beaulieu Abbey** and **Palace House**, with a fine vintage automobile museum (14 miles from Southampton), and the Marquess of Bath's **Longleat** where 50 African lions roam the ancestral park (24 miles from Bristol) are also favorite tourist targets. Lord Astor's **Cliveden** is now a deluxe hotel that also can be viewed by the public two days per week. The later home of Sir Winston, **Chartwell** (2 miles from Westerham in Kent), is a beloved monument to recent history. It maintains the flavor of the period between the wars—the happiest years of the great statesman's life. Queen Elizabeth joined the peerage by opening her 274-room **Sandringham House** in Norfolk to the public (except from July 21 to Aug. 9, when she is in residence). Be sure to check whether the day of your visit coincides with the variable schedule at the mansion. Buckingham Palace is now open, too, but more about this in the "London" section further along. If you are seriously interested in touring this circuit, the oversize, exhaustively detailed annual *Historic Houses, Castles, Gardens in Great Britain and Ireland* (ABC Historic Publications, London Rd., Dunstable, Bedfordshire, England) is an absolutely invaluable aid. Then, if you intend to visit the great estates and magnificent gardens of this nation, be sure to join the National Trust; subscription is so low in cost that in a couple of days you will begin to realize significant savings over the individual admission charges (which usually range up to about £6 per entry). Its U.S. affiliate is The Royal Oak Foundation (285 W. Broadway, Suite 400, New York, NY 10013), a public charity, which means your membership is tax-deductible. (The National Trust fee is not.) There are other benefits, too, so write Director Damaris Horan for details. Avid sightseers can literally save hundreds of dollars over an extended vacation—and the rewards are spellbinding. Meanwhile, you have the satisfaction of knowing you are contributing toward the preservation of a valued heritage.

## GREAT BRITISH HERITAGE PASS

This is no pass at all. You pay for it ($45 to $70 in 15-30-day versions), but it unlocks the doors to nearly 600 noteworthy places throughout the nation. Look for it at information desks at air-and-sea-ports; some travel agents handle it, as does the British Travel Centre at Piccadilly Circus.

## U.S. CONSULAR SERVICES ABROAD

If you should encounter serious trouble on your trip—anything from a lost passport to an arrest to death of a companion to a spectrum of other deep crises—communicate immediately with the nearest American consular office. They are, however, proscribed from extending loans to travelers in financial distress. Although they will give restricted aid in a dispute that could lead to legal or police action, furnish a list of reputable local lawyers, and try to prevent discrimination under foreign law, regulations prohibit them from participating on the direct level. If a citizen is arrested they will visit him or her in detention, notify relatives and friends, provide a roster of attorneys, and attempt to obtain relief if conditions are inhumane or unhealthy. Here are some of their other duties: (1) assistance in finding appropriate medical services; (2) guidance on how to inform the local police about stolen funds or on how to inform the issuing authorities about missing traveler's checks; (3) the full extension of notary facilities; (4) help in locating missing Americans; (5) protection of U.S. voyagers and residents during civil unrest or in natural disasters.

It may be useful to leave behind at home the following direct Washington telephone numbers of the Office of Special Consular Services:

- To find missing wanderers about whom there is special concern or to transmit emergency messages: ☎ *(202) 647-5225.*

- To transmit funds to foreign soil when commercial banking facilities are unavailable or to arrange medical evacuation: ☎ *(202) 632-9706* or ☎ *(202) 632-3529.*

- For questions about members of your clan who have been arrested and how to get money to them: ☎ *(202) 632-7823.*

- For help when an American dies abroad: ☎ *(202) 632-1423* or ☎ *(202) 632-2172.*

- For civil judicial inquiries and assistance: ☎ *(202) 632-2400.*

- Night and weekend emergency number for all of the above: ☎ *(202) 655-4000.* Ask for the Duty Officer.

The Overseas Citizens Services ☎ *(202) 632-5225)* is a general helpmate for troubled travelers.

Don't ask these officials to do the work of travel agencies, information bureaus, or banks, search for missing luggage, settle disputes with hotel managers or shopkeepers, help get work permits or find jobs.

# HOMEWARD BOUND

## *WHAT YOU BRING BACK*

Today's duty-free allowance is $400 in retail value. (The next $1000 in value is taxable at only 10%.) These goods must accompany you personally on your return. Your free importation of wines or booze is 1 quart per person 21 years or over—a monument to the enormous power of the U.S. liquor lobby in Washington. Most states admit more than a quart if a modest duty is paid on the overage; others, such as California, confiscate all extra spirits.

Regarding other regulations, here are some key facts and suggestions:

(1) Go easy on Coronas and champagne, because 100 cigars and one quart per person are all you may import without fee (foreign-made cigarettes are limited to one carton). With certain limitations, booze may be "shipped to follow."

(2) Foreign fruits, meats, plants, and vegetables might carry pests and could destroy millions of dollars in livestock, food, forests, or ornamentals: virtually all are confiscated. Most foreign-made eatables are banned unless all ingredients are printed on the label.

(3) Your exemptions may include alterations or repairs on anything you originally took abroad. If your car throws a piston or your watch gets a dunking en route, charge off the cost of making them tick again.

(4) Antiques 100 years old (exceptions: rugs and carpets made after 1700) are unrestricted. They include furniture, hardware, brass, bronze, marble, terra cotta, porcelain, chinaware, and "any object considered to have artistic value." Be sure to bring certificates of verification, if available.

(5) Original works of art (not copies)—paintings, drawings, and sculptures of any age—and stamps are duty-free. So are books, prints, lithographs, and maps over 20 years old.

(6) Gifts costing less than $50 may be mailed from abroad on a duty-free basis, with no effect on your exemptions. Alcohol, tobacco, and perfume are ineligible. No one person may receive more than one gift in one day; plainly mark the package "Gift—Value under $50."

(7) Certain trademarked articles—especially watches, perfumes, optical goods, musical instruments—require written permission of the foreign manufacturer or U.S. distributor before they may be cleared intact. (Accordions are especially hairy.) A few well-known manufacturers of cosmetics and beauty products are so stingy that nothing may be imported without documentary consent. Most companies, however, allow bona fide tourists to bring back at least one unit as a souvenir. They way around it? Remove or obliterate the trademark.

(8) If you sell some articles within 3 years after importation on a duty-free basis, you'll be fined double the normal quotation. But you are permitted to sell anything that was initially purchased for your personal or household use. Original intent is the key factor.

(9) Everything in your baggage must be for your personal use or the use of your immediate family, or for gifts; samples and other merchandise will be taxed.

(10) Finally, egret feathers, ammunition, narcotics, and various other commodities are contraband.

Be especially careful of items made from the skins of certain types of crocodile, spotted cat, or other endangered species. The list of God's creatures that are rapidly vanishing from our planet is too lengthy (and stretching day by day) to include here for purposes of up-to-the-minute accuracy. If you're considering this type of purchase, ask U.S. Customs before departure for a summary of those species; critters dispatched in a brutal fashion are also under protection and thus these pelts, too, can be seized by officials. Arrests for violations are not unknown; moreover, ignorance of the law is, as usual, no excuse.

If you have three or four parcels, your inquisitor has been trained to inspect the one wrapped with the greatest care. Likewise, if there is a choice between a bag and an independent package or case, he will usually examine the latter.

If the duty is too high, or if you're carrying a taxable item to a second or third country, Customs will hold it in escrow at the border for your return, without charge—and it's usually safe.

## FOR MORE INFORMATION

**U.S.A.**: *British Tourist Authority, 40 West 57th Street, New York, New York* ☎ *(212) 581-4700;*

**CANADA**: *94 Cumberland Street, Suite 600, Toronto, Ontario M5R,* ☎ *(416) 925-6326.*

# LOOKING AROUND

*Suffolk cottage with thatched roof*

## A PRIMARY GLANCE AT ENGLISH ARCHITECTURE, FOLLIES, AND SQUABBLES

A well-traveled author once opined that "Half of all tourism to anywhere is in search of good food and the other half in the avoidance of good churches." Still, there's a healthy market for both. If you are exploring on your own, you'll know when you are fed up in either area and can turn off at will. Group tours, however, tend to be given a surfeit of the latter. In the smaller towns and villages, the church is generally the only monument of pride to be viewed. In the surrounding countryside there also may be "stately homes" of distinction and magnificent gardens or parks, many of them open for public viewing, as I've already described for the National Trust and Heritage Pass. A vast number of these were designed and executed by the greatest architects of their day. It was the fashion to have a Lutyens house or a garden landscaped by William Robinson or Capability Brown (his first name was Lancelot, but he had a bent toward hyperbole). The same labels keep reappearing in brochure after brochure until you think it must have been illegal to build a mansion that didn't contain an Adam fireplace or a portico that was not born from the inspired seed of the John Wood studio (where father and son got onto the notion of crescents and gave Bath an everlasting identity that no Lord Mayor or town council has ever dared to touch over the generations).

## ENGLISH ARCHITECTURE

Christopher Wren had all the luck. His was an architect's dream come true. First, London was converted into one giant potato chip by the great fire of 1666 and then in flew Wren, who was commissioned to rebuild it. Although Sir Christopher is best known for having completed St. Paul's by the last year of his century, he also constructed about five-dozen other major churches and an endless string of streets and buildings. It is thanks to Wren that the London skyline is chiefly of uniform low height—affording fresh air and sunlight to play nimbly over the graceful parade of midtown buildings and creating a mood that every metropolis should envy. Such factors are overlooked and possibly even scorned in today's race to the top, with skyscrapers squeezing the last farthing out of the real-estate investment and leaving hamlets of disgruntled residents below to live in the shade.

As a coordinated concept, the **Anglo-Saxon** influence, which began sometime in the region of A.D. 500, held sway until the end of the first millennium. And since it was such an early and forthright creation and existed during many martial periods, not a lot of it exists to be seen today. **Lincoln** has some good examples; so do **Lindsey and Sompting**, with lanky slim towers containing windows that are nicely rounded on the tops; these are designated as **Early Romanesque**. This is less ornamental than the **High Romanesque** forms that are noted more frequently and are often copied today. The Celtic elements appear strongly, especially in the numerous stone crosses that centuries of wind and rain have weathered but not erased.

Then, during the Conquest era, the **Normons** came romping onto the British Isles and made an imprint that man can hope will last forever. They were master builders and tasteful ones at that. Moreover, they had an appetite for construction such as had not been experienced since Roman times. (Even in England, the Romans erected Hadrian's Wall, one of the all-time greats in the fortification business.) The most impressive architecture of early France—such as that around Caen—had come to British shores with such éclat that it was immediately embraced and then flourished for two centuries. The Norman zeal for building was so extensive that scores of cities, towns, and hamlets still point with honor to their movements, which, ironically, are celebrations to God for the might of William. **Durham**, **Oxford**, **Peterborough**, **Norwich**, and **Gloucester** all are splendid starting points, but if you admire this style, you must travel to **St. Albans** to see the granddaddy for the finest and oldest Norman ecclesiastical architecture. In the capital, the Tower of London remains as a Norman remnant, and it's doubtful that any Norman contribution is so distinctive and rewarding that it would be worth considering a hop across the Channel to see the bicultural interface at the Museum of Bayeux. This brings together at once—in an entertaining and educational fashion—the events that shaped England's future for the next thousand years. (Let's also tip our hats to Matilde, who, while her husband William was out a-conquering, had the patience and skill to embroider her magnificent graphic frieze.)

After the 12th century began, the fine lines of distinction between periods became a bit clouded. In general, this is the birth of Gothic influence, and it was so developed through the next four centuries that you can hardly believe that its several segments should fall under the one category. Experts would resist calling it derivative, but surely there is a temptation to see it that way. **Early English**, for example, has a decidedly Gallic complexion. And why not? The French regarded parts of England as their own colony for several centuries. The famous **Cinque Ports** (pronounced "Sink Ports" on English turf) were a quintet of very special naval installations facing the French waters. I was amused once—to divert to linguistics—when I was searching, quite unsuccessfully, for a pub described to me as "The Three Chimneys" in Kent. Told where it was, I found no such pub with three smokestacks to define it. Later, a maid of Kent admonished me courteously, "But, sir, that pub where the three roads meet is called "The Three Chimneys" because we hereabouts mostly cannot pronounce it the way the French people do" ("Trois Chemins").

Anyway, back to architecture—and the British way is very similar to the French but with another accent. The Gothic style comes in several versions. The Early English, which ended in the middle of the 13th century, is a cousin of Early Gothic on the Continent. The **Decorated** expression (High Gothic), such as you'll see in the choirs of Westminster Abbey and at Lincoln Cathedral, ran on for another century when the very stately **Perpendicular** form was introduced—corresponding to Late Gothic in Europe—and remained a favorite for two more centuries. The latter is the most ornate, and you are sure to see it at its best at Winchester Cathedral or, if you attend Evensong, at Cambridge in the King's College chapel, an experience you will carry away at least into your next incarnation. Finally, riding on the coattails of these, is the distinctive **Tudor** style, with the mannerism of its noble arch as its finest feature. When you think of the Gothic development, it might help to remember the Greek architectural idioms moving from simple pure Doric to the moderated Ionic to the richly carved Corinthian. The same process occurs in almost every society as stone masons naturally find more to do when citizens or states prosper.

Moving away from Gothic influence, which flattered and glorified God in his high heaven, architecture crossed a threshold, a transition into the **Renaissance**, with all the richness of the continent. The world was the monarchy's oyster, and sovereigns such as Henry VIII had broadened man's vision well beyond the English shores and even farther than the shadow of the tall church steeples of Albion. The new structures of **Elizabethan** and **Jacobean** periods were exciting and more human in dimension. You'll probably go to Hampton Courts, a short drive from London; try also to see Longleat or Hatfield House. Within the same Renaissance bracket were the wonderfully graceful **Palladian** forms—as light as eider and as fresh as zephyrs, compared to earlier styles—and the absurdly showy **Byzantine** features, which advertised appreciation for exotic distant cultures. Could anything be more silly or capricious than Nash's ice-cream sundae at Brighton? Nevertheless, the Royal Pavilion remains one of the most successful public halls in the history of British architecture.

The time from the 16th to the 18th centuries was busy, indeed. The prosperity and might were meant to be noted by any passerby. Wouldn't you hate to share the geegaw-infested dreams of John Vanbrugh (Blenheim), for example? A splendid manifestation of calm and proportion came along with the **Georgian** effect. It marked the resumption of what is often called the neoclassical period. That was in the beginning of the 18th century, and while this movement focused on Greco-Roman simplicity melded with a certain majesty, it seems strange that citizens of the same era were seeking to recall the ghosts of the long-mordant Gothic codes of yore. Charles Barry put his myriad talents to work creating the Houses of Parliment in the middle of the 19th century. England was pretty nearly full-up on churches, so the spotlight turned to secular buildings in the cities, breathtaking gardens, and the rural redoubts of lords and noble gentlemen of field and stream. The ladies concerned themselves with interior decoration; fine textiles, furniture, porcelain, and glass were produced to fill vast homes that were showcases of wealth or political prowess. **Regency**—its name alone speaks volumes—caught hold of the 19th-century imagination. And then that arbiter of almost every walk of life and limb, Queen Victoria, took the stage and single-handedly began an influence that English society admires even now at the doorstep of the 21st century.

A new form of building became possible through the use of iron and steel. Today the British are trying to recover the **Victorian** rail stations that had begun to vanish a few decades ago as marks of shame and outmoded antiquity. Now they are prized and given major dollops of taxpayer funds to keep them alive. The canal networks from the last century are busily being dredged out, and while their commercial contribution is uncertain today, they are certainly part of the English recreational heritage. There was until recently a restaurant in London called Inigo Jones, where the stained glass was a lot better than the cuisine. (New name, as you'll see later, and better food; the glass is still tops, however.) There's another restaurant that was an ironsmith's workshop, now primly restored and without brimstone. The Industrial Revolution is revolting again, but only as a souvenir brought back as an expression of self-mockery.

If you really want to be buffeted by discourses on modern architecture and how it is depriving English society of its inherent good taste, delve into the writings of the courageous (and some say loquacious) Prince Charles, who has made the preservation of Old England and its human dimensions his personal crusade. His status quo stopped about the time modern material made it possible for men to build tall towers for habitation and work. His question is whether those same people choose to live that way or whether society forces them to endure such insults. His book is titled *A Vision of Britain*, and it is published by Doubleday.

## THE FOLLIES OF THE ENGLISH

When a proper English gentleman stoops to folly it's probably merely an architectural caprice. You will see hundreds of "follies" as you adventure into the British countryside—pergolas, gazebos, well houses, solitary pillars on lonely hillsides, artificial lakes—an extra expression of leftover construction zeal after the main house was completed. Most of these whimsical and perhaps boastful fillips are nonfunctional status symbols, almost useless in real terms unless you consider their decorative statements to be significant. Indeed, many of the larger ones at the stately homes became objects of rivalry between a self-aggrandizing landlord and neighboring members of the gentry. Then, after the coveted gazebo was finished, the immodest proprietor often employed the fashionable artist of the moment to dream up an oil painting of pudgy nymphs lounging in that balmy romantic setting in diaphanous attire. Never mind that hardly any English female hide could endure the outdoor climate so skimpily clad. Never mind the Victorian logic. Follies were not meant to be reasonable. There are aristocratic ones, such as at the duke of Marlborough's Blenheim Palace, the birthplace of the ultimate British democrat, Winston Churchill; Waddesdon Manor, a Rothschild retreat, features more filigree and Gallic finesse. At Luton Hoo, where Faberge's art is on display, the gardens are dotted with architectural afterthoughts. Up at Portmeirion, the fanciful Clough Williams-Ellis seems to have created an entire hotel in this winsome mood, a frolic of Mediterranean structures on the chill Gwynedd coast of Wales. Perhaps even the ancient Druids had folly in their blood. Until the real purpose of Stonehenge is proved, there may always be a doubt.

## WHERE SQUABS NO LONGER SQUABBLE

An offshoot of the folly—perhaps a bit more practical—is the dovecote. In Norman times pigeons were raised for food, but as the prolific fowl became too numerous and other flesh became available, the idea itself went foul. Their feathered appetites were responsible for consuming tons of grain daily and they latterly were perceived more as pests than as plump, cooing pets. Hence, husbanding pigeons was abandoned, although many of the buildings (once totaling 26,000) remain, some of them quite handsome. A few are still used to house racing breeds such as those descended from the **Blue Rock**, the Adam and Eve of almost any street pigeon you'll meet anywhere in the world today. My favorite cotes are the tall, stout octagons, usually of stone and brick and often capped by a campanile atop the conical roof. (Don't confuse these with the simple yost houses of Kent, employed in curing and brewing local ales.) There's a fine one of these 18th-century monuments at **Baliffscourt** in West Sussex. **Nymans Garden** is another good choice nearby and close to Haywards Heath. **Snowshill Manor**, just outside of Broadway, is such a classic that it has been categorized as a National Trust. **Roushman House** at Steeple Aston is one of Oxfordshire's finest examples. It is the proud centerpiece of an exquisite walled garden. And, of course, not to be outdone by anyone in any period of time, you'll probably visit **Clivden**, where doves flocked in a luxury such as they've never fluttered over before or since. Their pigeon redoubt resembles an ornate lighthouse ringed with brick and stone and topped by four levels of roof to be surmounted by a polished orb. Rare avis, indeed!

# LONDON

*London and the Thames*

## THE SIGHTS OF LONDON

The British Tourist Authority at airports, rail depots, and many foreign capitals (New York, Los Angeles, Chicago, Dallas, Toronto, etc.) will give you full details on hours and locations of important London sightseeing events, art exhibitions, and theatrical performances. Once you arrive in town, head for the **Tourist Information Centre** (☎ *[71] 731-3488*) at Victoria Station Forecourt. They not only can show you a multitude of options, but they also sell the tickets to start you on your way.

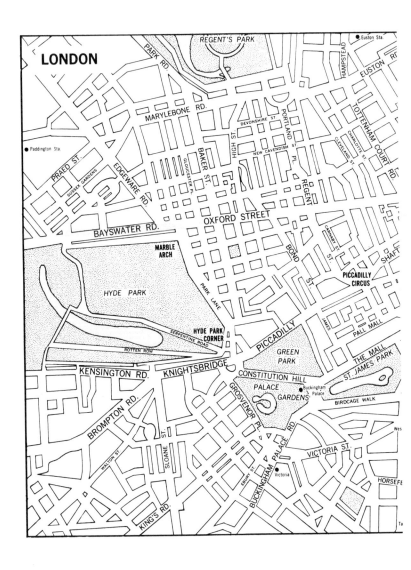

For a basic general survey, the **Original London Transport Sightseeing Tour** offers the most for the least. This 2-hour, 20-mile bus excursion glides past 28 of the capital's most famous landmarks, including Cleopatra's Needle, Trafalgar Square, Marble Arch, Hyde Park, Piccadilly Circus, and Westminster Abbey. High-season departures are made from Marble Arch, Victoria Underground Station, Baker St. Station, and Piccadilly Circus almost hourly from 10 a.m. to 9 p.m.; in winter they cease at 4 p.m.

### Walking Tours

With only a modest expenditure of energy and practically no money, you can see most of the London sightseeing scene through organized walking tours; these cover not only the major targets but the minor ones, the offbeat ones, and the droll. Most take about 90 minutes and cost in the neighborhood of £4 for the expert guide service. A pub tour or something of that sort would not include the price of drinks. Here's a sampler of some of the popular circuits: "In the Footsteps of Sherlock Holmes," "1660s: Great Fire and Great Plague," "Ghosts of the City," "SPQR—Roman Londinium," "1888: East End Murders—Jack the Ripper," "Legal and Illegal London—Inns of Court," "A Journey Through Tudor London." Incidentally, for the pub tour, children under 14 are not admitted to these establishments, those between 14 and 15 must be accompanied by an adult, and no one under 18 may imbibe. You can make your selection from the following companies with confidence: **Streets of London** (☎ *(81) 346-9255*), **London Walks** (☎ *(71) 435-6413*), **City Walks** (☎ *(71) 700-6931*), or **Exciting Walks** (☎ *(71) 624-9981*).

### The River Thames

The river makes its way through the port, 3000 acres of wharves—now becoming rather chic in the "docklands" district. The "City" (Wall Street), Westminster (Capitol Hill), the West End (Times Square and Fifth Avenue), Soho and Chelsea (Greenwich Village), Mayfair (Park Avenue), and many other clusters split the metropolis into its components. Good fun is the 50-minute **Boat Ride** from Westminster Pier, Tower of London, or Charing Cross to lovely, nautical outlying **Greenwich**, to the **Docklands**, or to the **Thames Barrier**. Some even operate at night and serve dinner aboard. You can phone ☎ *(71) 730-4812* for all the details. These operate at 20-minute intervals year-round, and the round-trip prices are about £5 for adults and £3 for children. You can board and inspect the original *Cutty Sark* (in drydock), visit the Gypsy Moth, idle through the charming streets—and if you've packed a picnic, take your lunch beside the viewful Wolfe Statue in Greenwich Park (the plan was designed by Charles II). Or you can straddle the Greenwich Meridian, which bisects the path a few yards north of the gates to the 17th-century Royal Observatory. After lunch (almost everything is within walking distance), take in the National Maritime Museum. At your option, you can return to London on the deck of a riverboat or on a doubledecker bus. A splendid excursion; highest recommendation.

### Mudlarking

The Thames provides other pastimes for those with boots—scavenging for treasure! If you've got Wellingtons, low tide is the time to burrow (especially at inward curves) for coins, battle relics, marine artifacts, and whatnots from the ages. Best locations are on the south bank near London Bridge and downstream of Vauxhall, Black-friars, and Kew Bridges. The Port Authority *(☎ (71) 476-6900)* can tell you the times of ebb and flow.

## A 1994 LONDON SPECIAL

### Shakespeare's Globe Theatre

*Southwark.* The theatre is this year's highly deserving recipient of the Fielding Travel Award. It is the realization of a lifelong dream nurtured by the distinguished thespian Sam Wanamaker. The American actor-director searched out the Thames-side site of the Globe of 1599 and amiably returned the wraith of The Bard to the original boards. The complex is faithfully—and delightfully—Elizabethan. Productions are presented largely as they were during Shakespeare's lifetime, but with the benefit of modern technology in the mounting of the shows. You won't find such theatre anywhere else in the world, and the Wanamaker effort brilliantly adds to the cavalcade of knowledge and appreciation of the brightest hours for the English language.

**Tickets** available at theatrical agencies or directly through Shakespeare's Globe, 1 Bear Gardens, Bankside, Liberty-of-the-Clink, Southwark, London, ☎ *(071) 620-0202*; FAX: *(071) 928-7968*. Handy underground stations are Mansion House or London Bridge.

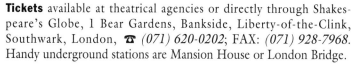

## *CITY OF LONDON*

The city of London, sometimes called "The Square Mile," is a small part of today's greater London that was originally founded by the Romans. The City, as it is commonly known, is now synonymous with London's commercial and financial district. And with its own police force and roughly 6000 permanent residents, it is something of a private town within a big city. Because of the terrorist bombing at the Baltic Exchange, motorized traffic is somewhat restricted and subject to spot checks for the time being.

### Tower of London

*Tower Hill.* William the Conqueror built this world-renowned fortress in the 11th century. Within its sturdy walls are the Crown Jewels, the Chapel of St. Peter's, Sir Walter Raleigh's prison cell for 12 years, the death ground of the tragic Little Princes, and the execution row on which Anne Boleyn, Lady Jane Grey, and numerous other political victims met their fate. While in this district, don't miss a stroll around; **St. Katharine's Docks** with its Thames barges snug at the piers is fun for seafarers.

### Chapels Royal

The sublimity of these little chapels is one of London's best kept secrets. The reason? Unless the tourist dresses conservatively and is mannerly, he or she is not wanted by the vicars and congregations. Also, cameras are banned. Sequestered in many of London's most famous buildings, some of these chapels date back to the 11th and 12th centuries. Should you wish to attend, you will find a listing of the locations and hours in Saturday's better-grade London newspapers.

### St. Paul's Cathedral

*St. Paul's Churchyard.* This magnificent cathedral crowns Ludgate Hill (and London's landscape) as Sir Christopher Wren's finest architectural feat. Most wanderers prefer the brilliant dome to the chilly nave (usually a trend in human relations, too). Wren, Wellington, and Nelson are among the greats who are buried in the crypt. There is an admission charge of about £2 weekdays (1/2 price for children and seniors); no fees on Sundays or for those attending services. Don't miss the "Whispering Gallery"!

### Guildhall

*Off Gresham St.* Near St. Paul's Cathedral, this majestic 15th-century hall has long been used for ceremonial occasions. It now houses a beautiful library and art gallery.

### Barbican Centre for Arts and Conferences

This is London's costly arts complex—a project that ran 10 times over budget and was finally hatched for $285 million! The London Symphony and Royal Shakespeare Theatre now call it home; the latter, however, is suffering from financial problems and its continuation here is moot. There are galleries, exhibition halls, a library, 2 restaurants, conference rooms, 3 cinemas, an artificial lake, and even a rooftop greenhouse aflutter with full—grown trees. The **Museum of London** also was set up here, with its artifacts dating to the time of Roman occupation; its Fountains garden restaurant serves breakfast and lunch, plus afternoon tea.

### Old Bailey

Famed Old Bailey dispenses English criminal justice in open session. It is the basis of much of America's jurisprudence. Worth a visit if you're a barracks lawyer, a veteran juror, or just plain snoopy about other people's malfeasances.

### Dr. Johnson's House

*17 Gough Sq., near Fleet St.* This is where Johnson lived while writing his Dictionary. A small museum now houses his relics, some first editions, and contemporary portraits.

# WEST END

## Covent Garden

For more than three centuries, Covent Garden was London's central market for produce and flowers. Now its delightfully airy structures house 49 quaint shops. You'll also find many cafes and restaurants here. The cheerful malls are often filled with the music of street musicians called "buskers" who, because of the glass covered roofs, are able to play to pedestrians or those seated in the "open" restaurants during any weather conditions.

# ST. JAMES'S

## Buckingham Palace

*Buckingham Palace Rd.* This is the official royal residence of Queen Elizabeth II, and the royal flag flies above the roof when the queen is at home. In August and September (when she's away), the 600-room landmark will admit up to 7000 visitors a day, but not, of course, into the private apartments. While the salons are only somewhat more ornate than the lobbies of some continental hotels, the Picture Gallery is stunning. Tour agents have snatched up their allotments of tickets for years ahead but you can still purchase one (or a maximum of four) at a booth in nearby St. James's Park. The price is £8 per adult with reductions for the young and the elderly. The line (queue, that is) will be forming along The Mall. Other information can be obtained by ☎ (71) 930-4832. Also, don't miss the famed Changing of the Guard that takes place on alternate days at 11:30 a.m. (weather permitting).

## St. James's Palace

*Pall Mall.* Built by Henry VIII, this lavish structure still serves as an official royal residence. The palace itself is closed to the public, but the lovely courtyards are open.

## National Gallery

*Trafalgar Sq.* This distinguished institution displays priceless works by artists of every major European school: El Greco, Gainsborough, Holbein, Da Vinci, Michelangelo, Rubens, and Titian are only a few examples. The house has recently undergone a dusting and a rehanging of many pictures, so it offers a fresh aspect from previous years.

## National Portrait Gallery

*2 St. Martin's Pl.* Portraits of just about every famous English person in history are in this fascinating gallery, which stands just behind the National Gallery.

# WESTMINSTER

## The Houses of Parliament

*Parliament Sq.* The House of Commons and the House of Lords are located here, the seat of English government. Look to the towers to see if they are in session; a flag by day and a light by night (above Big Ben) are the signals. To witness a debate from the Strangers Galleries of either House, wait at St. Stephen's Entrance for admission. When in session: Commons Mon.-Thurs. 2:30-10 p.m. and 9:30 a.m.-3 p.m. on Fri.; Lords Tues. and Wed. and occasionally Mon. from 2:40 p.m., Thursdays from 3 p.m., and some Fridays from 11 a.m.

### Westminster Abbey

*Broad Sanctuary.* This glorious Gothic church is now past the 9th-century mark. Within its marble floors and crypts rest so many historical figures that it is perhaps the English-speaking world's most famous shrine. It is open daily.

### Westminster Cathedral

*Francis St.* This church is a good example of the early Byzantine style.

### Tate Gallery

*Millbank.* It has recently been refurbished and many works were rehung. A new chronology enhances the viewing experience. Its collection of English painters from the 17th to the 20th centuries is supplemented by Continentals (Seurat, van Gogh, Rouault, Picasso, Chagall, Renoir, and Braque), as well as by an assortment of Americans (Pollack and de Kooning, among others). The neighboring **Clore Gallery** has taken over and augmented the Turners—about 300 oils and a feast of 19,000 watercolors and drawings that appear in ever-changing cycles.

### Imperial War Museum

*Lambeth Rd.* Anything that went "boom" from 1914 is represented in British dimensions here. It is a fond and heroic repository of many of England's finest hours.

## *BLOOMSBURY*

A delightful district so often given to song, it contains several pretty squares including Bloomsbury, Russell, and Bedford. The area was the home of many famous literati, most notably Virginia Woolf, D. H. Lawrence, and E. M. Forster. Also within its bounds are the University of London and the British Museum.

### Sir John Soane's Museum

*13 Lincoln's Inn Fields.* Perhaps a bit more for the specialist, Soane's collection includes paintings, drawings, and antiques. Most noteworthy are Hogarth's *Election* and *The Rake's Progress,* as well as original Piranesi drawings.

### British Museum

*Great Russell St.* This extraordinary edifice is so massive that it challenges any first-timer to spend at least three or four days among its fabulous archaeological, historical, and literary wealth. Those in a hurry usually beeline for the Elgin Marbles, the Rosetta Stone, the Magna Carta, and the Egyptian Sphinxes; the reading room that spawned part of Karl Marx's utopian works is also popular for a peek. Open 10 a.m.-5 p.m. on weekdays and 2:30-6 p.m. on Sun.

## Dickens' House

*48 Doughty St.* Dickens lived here only two years (from 1837 to 1839), but many of the great writer's relics flavor this charming terraced house.

## Jewish Museum

*Upper Woburn Pl.* A handsome and impressive collection of Jewish ritual objects and antiques.

# KNIGHTSBRIDGE

## Victoria and Albert Museum

*Cromwell Rd.* Founded (at another site) during the 1851 Exhibition, the museum offers a melange of works from various periods and from many cultures. The English period rooms are perhaps the best feature, but splendid collections of armor, ceramics, paintings, and metalwork are also worthwhile.

## Science Museum

*Exhibition Rd.* A vast and interesting collection illustrating the history of science and its effect on industry.

## Natural History Museum

*Cromwell Rd.* Built in 1881, the vast halls contain spooks from zoology, entomology, paleontology, and botany.

## Hyde Park

You may graze over 363 well-groomed acres that are a constant delight to natives and visitors alike. The renowned Speakers' Corner, near Marble Arch, is a Mad Hatter merry-go-round for debaters, who are permitted to blow off steam on any subject short of obscenity (not unknown). Fanatics from all over the world rant, rave, and spout their philosophies here on Sunday. Bring a lunch or stop for a bite at the nearby park food kiosk.

# KENSINGTON

## Kensington Palace

*Kensington Gardens.* William III converted this charming building into a palace in 1689. Its exterior was designed by Wren.

## Kensington Palace Gardens

A street lined with some of the fanciest mansions of the 19th century. Many were designed in the grand Italianate style by the famous architects of that era.

# AROUND TOWN

## Tea at the Ritz—and elsewhere

Posh? Indeed. But since so many tourists in jogging shoes (read "Americans") have been popping in for a cuppa and destroying the proper English atmosphere, it is usually restricted to hotel guests only—or so they say. If you are in conservative attire you might try it anyway. For a glimpse of the stately London of yore, I suggest you book in advance (for 3:30 and 4:45 p.m.) and then go to the spacious, gracious, changeless ground-floor lounge of this oldfashioned landmark. Its assorted finger sandwiches are excellent. Men should wear jackets and ties. On Sundays there's tea dancing to turn back a page of nostalgia. If this one is blocked, the Chinoiserie of the **Carlton Tower** is always pouring in a most democratic fashion. The **Savoy** is also a traditional choice, in the mirrored Thames Foyer. The best teatime nibbles are at **Claridge's**, and the service can't be topped. The clotted cream is abundant enough to keep a team of cardiac specialists in business well into the next century. The Palm Court of the **Waldorf** is something special for Edwardian atmosphere. I like **Brown's** for its easygoing fireside teas in its homey lounges; and while the patrician **Connaught** tries to obtain the same mood, I find it stiff. Hyde park vistas are available at the **Royal Garden**; it has lower prices, too, and since most of the above charge £10-12 per service, a little economizing might be in order.

### Markets

For antique hunters, the outdoor stalls on **Portobello Road** are a Saturday walk. That's also the best time to visit **Camden Passage** in the suburb of **Islington**. Friday mornings are the most rewarding time to browse through the **New Caledonian Market**. **Fulham** and **King's Road**, Chelsea, are for those who can afford sentimentality in the more expensive bracket; **Beauchamp Place**, just off Knightsbridge and now mainly for clothing and jewels, is for zillionaires; **Kensington Church Street** and **Notting Hill**, Gate, remain popularly priced playgrounds.

### Boat Tours

"Jason's Trip" is a fine midtown canal cruise from **Argonaut Gallery** *(60 Blomfield Rd., ☎ 71-730-4812)* to the Camden Town locks. You will glide through Regent's Park, its world-famous **Zoological Gardens**, and other points, in a 90-minute loop. Book well in advance, get a confirmation that your boat will sail, and hope for good weather. As an alternate, you can sail from Westminster Pier upstream to Kew, Richmond, and Hampton Court in almost 4 hours (each way; summer only). If the ride up covers more water than you care for, your tickets also will enable you to ride the train home. The same company (Thames Launches and Thames Motor Boat Co.) operates evening cruises with launchings at 7:30 p.m.; there's a regular daily trip to Tower Bridge and Greenwich. The Regent's Canal Zoo Water Bus departs hourly between 10 a.m. and 5 p.m. in summer from Little Venice; the combined fare and entry to the Zoo is about £6. The *Jennie Wren* plys between Camden Town and Little Venice; similar low rates and good value.

### Thames Flood Barrier

Today's newest tours actually cruise right through the colossal barricades, providing you with an eye-to-eye encounter with the engineering forces that may one day save London from seaborne extinction.

Departures at 11:15 a.m. and 1:30 p.m. for Westminster Pier; duration about 3 hours; an engaging bit of guidance as to the haunts of Dickens, Nelson, and other habitues of England's primary waterway. One of the world's modern wonders—and you can almost touch it!

### A Week on a Barge

*The Captain Webb*, a hotel barge, offers London and Thames cruising featuring six-day jaunts with full sightseeing programs. The vessel is shoulder-high in fun, frolic, and gastronomy. Prices are not at all painful when you consider the novel means of covering the ground, water, and skyscape of England. Phone **Another Britain** (☎ *0836-202408)* and ask for Gaynor Waterman—and how's that for an apt handle?

### Theater

London has 50-plus theaters. Nurtured by Shakespeare and Jonson, needled by Wilde and Shaw, and up-ended by Osborne and Pinter, they display the greatest talent and variety in the world. Tickets £6 to perhaps £25 and a bit more for musicals; seats usually (not always) plentiful; box offices usually open at 10 a.m. Should you purchase ducats through an agent, you'll pay about 20% more per booking, so if you are buying for a family of five you can thus save on the overall bill by going directly to the theater. For half-price tickets, **TKTS Booth** (*Leicester Sq., W.C.2*), is the place. Same day's sales for West End matinees from noon-2 p.m. and from 2:30 p.m.-6 p.m. for evening shows. Fee of £1 tacked on to your reduced tariff. The **National Theatre** (*South Bank*) is a sensation. It contains the 900-seat **Lyttelton**, the 1150-seat **Olivier**, and the small, experimental **Cottesloe** theaters beneath one roof. The least expensive seats go on sale at the box office at 8:30 a.m. on the day of any performance

Don't forget that this year the **International Shakespeare Globe Centre** is due to open at 1 Bear Gardens, Bankside SE1 9EB. It's a reconstruction of the original Globe at its home site plus a 1500-seat theater and a permanent exhibition devoted to the Bard and Elizabethan trappings.

### Madame Tussaud's

*Marylebone Rd.* With its Grand Hall, Madame Tussaud's displays dummies (some lifelike, some not), of nearly every major headliner in this century, as well as scores of earlier notables. Its eerie Chamber of Horrors, in the tomb style cellar, is tailor-made to bring years of nightmares. Admission about £6; children under 16, £4; Royal Ticket (combined) pegged at another £1 or so adds a visit to the London Planetarium too (£8 for adults, £5 for children, Family Ticket available for 2 adults and 2 youngsters); operative 10 a.m. to 5:30 p.m. on weekdays, to 6:30 p.m. on weekends.

### Concerts

The **Royal Festival Hall**, (*South Bank, S.E.1*) is the most noteworthy. It provides a dramatic, handsome backdrop for the orchestra—a tableau dominated by copper, silver, and gilded organ pipes. If you feel like dining, there is an adjoining restaurant midstream in the Thames with candle illumination and vast plate–glass windows overlooking the sparkling riverscape. For lower-cost refreshment, there is a cafeteria downstairs plus snack bars off the lobby. The acoustically splendid **Royal Albert Hall** (*Kensington, S.W.7*) should also be in your notebook. The **Barbican Centre** (*Silk St. EC2*) is one of the most ambitious civic undertakings the city has assumed. Something is always going on here. The underground stop is Moorgate-Barbican. In addition, a lot has been happening lately at the **Queen Elizabeth II Hall** (South Bank), which accommodates smaller groups. The **Royal Opera House** is in Covent Garden; **Sadlers Wells** produces lighter works as well as ballet, plus Gilbert & Sullivan productions through the D'Oyly Carte Opera Co.; **English National Opera** performs at the Coliseum (St. Martin's Lane, W.C.2); **Holland Park** is the place for alfresco chords when the Kensington skies are at their kindest.

### Parks

The **Kew Gardens** botanical display would thrill Luther Burbank himself. The capital is full of scenic parks, the most famous of which are **Hyde, Regents, Kensington, St. James's**, and a little further out, **Hampstead Heath**. All of them are infinitely safer for strollers than New York's Central Park.

### Publications

Pick up the weekly magazine *What's On In London*. We think it's infinitely useful and the best. *Time Out* is also a sound bet. *Rolling Stone* offers clues to the pop music scene.

## LONDON TRANSPORT

**AUTHOR'S OBSERVATION**

*The most frequently used numbered buses will begin disappearing toward midnight. For night owls, London Transport lays on a few late-late runs that have their own sets of numerals and distinctive routes. Grab a cab if you can afford it (you can legally share a taxi with another fare); if not, a lengthy conversation with the conductor may be necessary to determine if his vehicle might pass somewhere not too far from your destination. Both bus and underground (subway) are linked in a money-saving travel card scheme for visitors. Passes are available for varying lengths of stay and at corresponding price discounts. Inquire about these at any underground Kiosk.*

The big red doubledecker buses are legendary. William Gladstone said "The best way to see London is from the top of a bus." It's still true. London Transport has also begun experimental runs with 16-passenger minibuses, but they're nowhere near the fun of their big brothers. When the conductor arrives, pay according to your destination. If you're not sure where you're going to step off you can usually arrange with him to remit the difference after leaving your seat.

There's a new breed of smaller vehicle called the **Hop-a-Bus** specifically created for sightseers and shoppers; just hop aboard for 70 pence and go anywhere on the circuit. The C-1, C-2, and C-3 routes go to the most popular attractions.

When waiting at a bus stop, fair-minded Britons form a line so that everyone will board in turn (unlike on the underground, where it's every man for himself).

**Underground routes** on the London "tubes" are wonderful—almost always clean, and always much, much faster than taxis or buses over any appreciable distance. Tickets are by zones you cover; outside of the morning and afternoon rush peaks, seats are nearly always available. A map is indispensable. They are available free at the **Transport Enquiry Offices** at Piccadilly Circus, or any station ticket office.

For **Buckingham Palace**, the tube stations are St. James's Park or Green Park; for **Westminster Abbey** and **Parliament**, it's Westminster; the **Tate Gallery** is Pimlico; the **National Gallery** is Charing Cross; the **British Museum** is Tottenham Court Road; **St. Paul's Cathedral** and **Old Bailey** are St. Paul's; **Tower of London** is Tower Hill; **Madame Tussaud's** is Baker Street; **Speakers' Corner** in Hyde Park is Marble Arch; the **Stock Exchange** is Bank; **Dickens' House** is Russell Square; **Johnson's House** is Blackfriars. It's almost impossible to get lost in this well-marked network.

Don't count on a late tube-train home, because all routes shut down between about midnight and 5 a.m. If you're a late-night rider (this is when the rare muggings are beginning to occur), sit in either the front car or the rear car, where guards are posted. Should you be stuck with no trains running, check the Yellow Pages of the phone directory for all-night taxi services. Hotel porters will phone one for you if you offer a modest tip.

A self-drive rental van (with hydraulic lifts) service for wheelchair travelers is available at Heathrow and Gatwick airports. Rates aren't bad. For details: **Wheelchair Travel**, 1 Johnston Green, Guildford, Surrey GU2 6XS; ☎ *(0483)39661.*

For other transportation tips check under "A Preface To Your Travels."

## WHERE TO STAY

### TRADITIONAL MOODS

**Dorchester** ☆☆☆☆☆
*Park Lane W1A-2HJ;* ☎ *(71) 629-8888; FAX: 409-0114.* Freshly revamped but maintaining its traditional tastes, here is one of London's best classic hotels. Every room different; 4 excellent restaurants (the classic Grill, the gorgeous Penthouse Suite, the Terrace and the audacious but delightful Oriental (Cantonese) Salon); The Bar (one

of the most distinctive in London with its ingratiating Delft panels); a health spa; large proportion of suites, most overlooking Hyde Park. You can expect the service to be up to the same old Dorchester standards. Superb.

### Claridge's ☆☆☆☆☆

*Brook St. W1A 2JQ;* ☎ *(71) 629-8860; FAX: 499-2210.* Time has been taught to stand still here; even renewals carefully maintain a dated character. General Manager Ronald Jones is mixing in spice and vitality without altering its mandate on age-old values. Entrance in the style of 1932 with dazzling Art Deco fillips; restaurant given its original grace and nobility; soft-spoken piano or string ensemble music at times in the lounge; numerous rooms renewed and air-conditioned; staff on full alert all the time. Within London circles, this house and the Connaught probably have the greatest social standing or, said another way, snob appeal. The two related hotels do not cultivate this purposely. It just builds over the decades out of loyalty to everlasting British quality.

### Berkeley ☆☆☆☆☆

*Wilton Pl. SW1X;* ☎ *(71) 235-6000; FAX: 235-4330.* Though contemporary in comfort, this fine house has a legacy of many generations. The address is Belgravia, a sterling residential district within walking distance of the top shops. At hand are such features as the wood-paneled restaurant in brown hues with chintz-shaded lamps on tables and soft intimate tones; the historic Buttery, linked to Le Peroquet bar, with buffet lunch and Mediterranean (fish/pasta) dishes at night; the gorgeous penthouse pool with sliding roof, refreshment facilities, and sauna. There are 27 suites and 160 doubles; the flawless demisuites among the latter group are favorites in the house. A beautiful oasis ably managed by Director Stefano Sebastiani.

### Connaught ☆☆☆☆☆

*Carlos Pl. W1Y 6AL;* ☎ *(71) 499-7070; FAX: 495-3262.* This soft-spoken old-timer couldn't be a more felicitous choice for the traveler in search of comfort and tranquility in the homespun way. If you desire a spacious room, flawless service, a superior restaurant and grill, a faintly English-Manor-House atmosphere, and gentility that is nearly Edwardian in tone, here is surely the place for you. It's for the quiet man and quiet woman—quiet children are accepted, too—not the blatant or boisterous. Incidentally, if you enjoy game, here is one of the best kitchens in Britain for these specialties.

### Savoy ★★★★

*The Strand WC2R OEU;* ☎ *(71) 836-4343; FAX: 240-6040.* This is often the choice of theater and literary personalities. It's good, big, and impressive. Minibar in every accommodation but personal service always available; color cable TV throughout; vast majority of abodes exceptionally spacious. You may enjoy the Thames Foyer with its atmospheric period mirrors and teas and pre-theater light bites at very reasonable prices; a mezzanine snackery over the front entry. These are augmented by the River Restaurant for lunch and dinner. Savoy Grill (harp music; 6 p.m. service for theatergoers) with traditional food reinterpreted for modern tastes. The public rooms are grand.

### May Fair Intercontinental ★★★★
*Stratton St. W1A 2AN;* ☎ *(71) 629-7777; FAX: 629-1459.* It's traditional but bright as a Beefeater's buttons. The entire house has been given sparkle. Beginning with its white marble-clad entrance, it moves to a stunning wood and polished-stone reception, then to the handsome Chateaubriand restaurant and the off-lobby bar. All bedchambers have been sedately styled in English and French motifs; throwaway card keys are employed for security; there's color TV plus free in-house movies; baths in pink Portuguese marble; hairdryers; large beds; many fine suites. The approach is clever and successful.

### Hyde Park ★★★★
*Knightsbridge SW1Y 7LA;* ☎ *(71) 235-2000; FAX: 235-4552.* You'll see how it got its name when you sit in the Park Room overlooking the greenery (with live piano music). The hotel is now more than a century old and very well maintained. General Manager Paolo Biscioni is a thoughtful and able host. Two big pluses are the spaciousness and its splendid location in the epicenter of the Knightsbridge shopping bonanza.

### Park Lane ☆☆☆
*Piccadilly W1Y 8BX;* ☎ *(71) 499-6321; FAX: 499-1965.* Here's a great dowager with youthful vigor. Immediately you are struck by the polished refinement and the faithfully maintained antiquity. I'm especially fond of the elegant, wood-lined, and mirrored Bracewells restaurant; a gleaming silver bell reveals a staple of the house; roast beef and Yorkshire pudding; the dressed crab also was superb. A few steps below Bracewells you'll find an inviting palm-dotted bar with more foliage in the Garden Room restaurant. Air-conditioned suites, many facing the park and some with Jacuzzi-fed baths; harmonious colors in bedrooms, all with double-glaze windows, color TV, and frigobar. A pleasant experience.

### Ritz ★★★
*Piccadilly W1V 9DG;* ☎ *(71) 493-8181; FAX: 493-2687.* The spaces are high and mighty with pillared corridors, a glittering chandeliered lobby, palm-court lounge for tea-timing, and huge rotunda dining salon displaying gilded garlands of laurel; many upstairs rooms sumptuous and spacious; a few routine singles have been joined to form deluxe twins featuring Louis XVI marble fireplaces. Below the ground level, an independently run casino in formal attire gambols along. The situation is excellent for shoppers, sightseers, and theatergoers. You'd better stay here if you plan to enjoy the ritual of "Tea at the Ritz." Friends who were living elsewhere in London said that as "outsiders" they would have to wait 3 weeks for a confirmed reservation!

### Brown's                                                                ☆☆

*Albemarle & Dover St. W1A 4SW;* ☎ *(71) 493-6020; FAX: 493-9381.*
Since 1837 this has been one of the most famous hostelries in the British Empire, a staunch guardian of traditionalism. Lounges (at tea
time) are filled with adoring patrons—and politely admiring Yanks.
Mazelike corridors, a result of linking 11 townhouses together to create this composite; older units beautified; 142 rooms and 5 suites;
Dover St. chambers quieter during the early morning hours than are
those facing Albemarle St.; an overall feeling of slow motion activity
among antebellum furnishings. Incidentally, tea time here is better, in
my view, than in the sacred precincts of the Ritz.

### Grosvenor House                                                        ☆☆

*Park Lane W1A 3AA;* ☎ *(71) 499-6363; FAX: 493-3341.* It's vast, busy-
busy-busy, commercial, group-conscious, and, as one might expect,
lacking in personal attention. It does, however, feature the lovely and
tranquil Nico At Ninety Park Lane dining salon with entrance lounge,
homelike appointments, and firelit hearth; excellent food, too, by
Nico Ladenis, one of London's legendary and most controversial
chefs. (Personally I like the guy and his cooking.) Breakfast Pavilion
for light meals; poorly done Pasta Shop with routine Italian cookery;
a magnificent swimming pool; Crown Club executive floor. Many
groups settle down here.

## CONTEMPORARY STYLES

### Inn on the Park                                                  ☆☆☆☆☆

*Hamilton Pl. W1A 1AZ;* ☎ *(71) 499-0888; FAX: 493-1895.* It's hardly
an "Inn" and though it is modern and large, the interior manages to
exude a particular personality. The lobby has wood paneling, crystal
illumination, sandy-beige marble flooring, and a table where guests
sit, rather than stand, to register. Secluded enclave of shops; mezzanine dining complex composed of the window-lined Four Seasons
Restaurant with its own lounge plus the Queen Anne-style Lanes for
lunch and theatergoers, also with a bar; cuisine in both of international prominence. Cleverly engineered "Conservatory Rooms" on
second floor; tasteful furnishings; TVs set into stately highboys; marblesque baths. Its 27 suites vary in motif and mood, while their prices
are universally stratospheric.

### Hyatt Carlton Tower                                              ☆☆☆☆☆

*2 Cadogan Pl. SW1X 9PY;* ☎ *(71) 235-5411; FAX: 235-9129.* It rises to
a proud 18 stories—hence, a Tower by London's measure. On the
upper reaches (visible without a telescope) you'll see the
glass-and-steel structure containing the health club and gymnasium.
An ultramodern business center has been plugged in. The famous Rib
Room on the ground floor is rich with wood paneling and fine paintings; more attractive food displays; an Oyster Bar is another pearl. The
Chelsea Room (one of my favorites in the capital) remains sedate and
in the finest tradition of international haute cuisine. Bedroom themes

employ muted colors in a sundae of beige, peach, blue, pistachio, and other flattering hues. With all this massive revamping, the dignity and Chippendale mood have not been diminished.

## Capital ☆☆☆☆
*Basil St., Knightsbridge SW3 1AT;* ☎ *(71) 589-5171; FAX: 225-0011.* There's a chic here that has been noted on five continents. A lot of it has to do with the feeling of friendship and the exceptionally convenient location. On top of that, the elegant French-styled restaurant has generated a mighty following of culinary loyalists. No real lobby to speak of—merely a hall porter's desk and reception counter; cozy-corner bar; not the most spacious rooms, but cleverly engineered; compact baths. If you are staying a week or longer, ask about savings to be had in the apartment wing. There are no historic or sylvan vistas from any of its 60 windows; proprietor David Levin devotes every erg to his discerning clientele—the key to his enormous success.

## London Marriott ☆☆☆☆
*Grosvenor Sq. W1A 4AW;* ☎ *(71) 493-1232; FAX: 491-3201.* This American import resides (appropriately) opposite the U.S. Embassy and within walking distance of major shopping tenderloins. The Diplomat restaurant (in 2 tiers) is attractively clad with palewood paneling. There's the chipper and classy Regent Lounge with 24-hour service—one of the most elegant round-the-clock operations I have seen anywhere. As for accommodation, the King rooms are best for size because most normal doubles appear somewhat restricted in their dimensions. Manager Henry Davies is an earnest host who is determined to enhance even the abundant luxury to be found under his London roof.

## Montcalm ★★★★
*Great Cumberland Pl. W1A 2LF;* ☎ *(71) 402-4288; FAX: 724-9180.* There's a muted mood of earth-tones here—no hues that cry. Sand, beige, sable, fawn, sorrel, umber, cocoa, chestnut—you'll find them all. Most of the ground-floor walls are upholstered in suede; furnishings are in leather; even the elevator has kidding around it; baths are carpeted. Suites feature spiral staircases and attractive 1-1/2-story windows; ordinary twins are not spacious, but they are passable if your stay isn't a long one. The cuisine is artfully conceived in a primarily occidental fashion even though the hotel is owned by the Nikko interests and Japan Air Lines.

## Intercontinental ☆☆☆
*1 Hamilton Pl. W1V OQY;* ☎ *(71) 409-3131; FAX: 493-3476.* This one resides in the same hotel cluster as the Hilton, the Inn on the Park, and other top-line contemporary stalwarts, but not near the May Fair Intercontinental, a sister operation. The chilly first impression belies the rich colorations and the luxurious comfort provided by its bedchambers. Softly elegant Le Souffle restaurant; coffee house for uninspired yet costly snacks and buffet breakfast; viewful 7th-floor

discotheque in art retro for sipping and dancing; sauna and cool-off pool; select boutiques with price tags that may send you reeling; underground parking. The better, costlier units face Hyde Park (with the dual-glaze windows shut, they are quiet); extra-light sleepers may opt for a vistaless courtside address.

### Sheraton Park Tower                                   ☆☆☆
*101 Knightsbridge Rd. SW1X 7RN;* ☎ *(71) 235-8050; FAX: 235-8231.* A very well-situated 18-story-tall cylinder in Knightsbridge. Viewful suites; wide bay windows; impressive travertine lobby enriched with wood, modern tapestries, orange textiled furniture, metal sculpture, and cunning illumination; inviting bar adjoining; casino; spring-daubed Le Cafe Jardin coffee shop in dustry rose and grass green; underground garage. The architecture is decidedly not Typical London, but inside it is suggestive of a solid North American hostelry.

### Hilton on Park Lane                                   ☆☆
*22 Park Lane W1A 2HH;* ☎ *(71) 493-8000; FAX: 493-4957.* This one is near the Intercontinental and Inn on the Park, not to be confused with its lower-cost Kensington cousin. Impressive mahogany and marble lobby; English-toned restaurant plus Trader Vic's Polynesian patch in the basement; several bars, plus the sip-and-dance nightclub; health center; underground parking; every unit with radio and TV plus full-length movies via videocassette; one Y-shape wing houses studio-style accommodations only. There are 6 viewful executive floors with private lounge for complimentary breakfast and cocktails —at an overall premium cost, of course.

### Westbury                                              ☆☆
*Conduit St. W1A 4UH;* ☎ *(71) 629-7755; FAX: 495-1163.* This well-known and well-situated house is better in its public sectors than it is in its limited-size bedchambers. Cheerful color schemes lend an eye-expanding illusion; the baths remain bruisingly narrow-sided. It is convenient for shopping and theater going.

### Londonderry                                           ☆☆
*Park Lane W1Y 8AP;* ☎ *(71) 493-7292; FAX: 495-1395.* In the same high-rent cluster as the Hilton, this smaller house shines with luster. There is so much polish and starch—receptionists wear tailcoats and boutonnieres—that they crinkle when they walk. Gleaming marble lounges; delightful intime cocktail bar; dignified Ile de France restaurant; smallish bedrooms; fully air conditioned. Recommended for its location and its snap, crackle, and English pop.

### Halkin
*4 Halkin St. SW1;* ☎ *(71) 333-1000; FAX: 333-1100.* This is a cool-ish newcomer in the up-market Belgravia district; that means it's quiet but probably requiring a taxi ride to reach the major shopping precincts. Its sedate 6-story exterior follows the fashion of this residential neighborhood. Nearly $50-million has been awarded to its 40 rooms

and restaurant by its petro-proprietor, Christina Ong, a well-known figure in Singapore. The mood is not my choice for a cozy stay, but some might enjoy the straightforward, fresh approach. Each bedroom differs; fully outfitted from FAX to VCR and even to dual phone lines. The chef is also not one of my favorites. Prices unload at £200 per twin.

### Holiday Inn Mayfair ☆☆
*3 Berkeley St. W1X 6NE;* ☎ *(71) 493-8282; FAX: 629-2827.* Set only a block from Piccadilly Circus. Clean-lined marble-and-wood reception and foyer; costly and suave white-and-gold Louis XV restaurant; adjoining cocktail area; convenient underground parking. Most bedrooms are expansively proportioned (ask for a large unit).

### Cavendish ★
*Jermyn St. SW1Y 6JF;* ☎ *(71) 930-2111; FAX: 839-2125.* This one also has an exceptionally handy location for shoppers, but in a more up-market part of town. Attractive public rooms including the 24-hour Ribblesdale Restaurant, dark-tone Sub Rosa Bar (named after the original Cavendish's famed Rosa Lewis), and mezzanine lounge-bar. All bedchambers with tiny baths; limited luggage space; building-wide fresh-air ventilation; only continental breakfast or snacks served in the rooms. Ask for units ending in "21".

### St. James Court
*Buckingham Gate SW1E 6AF;* ☎ *(71) 834-6655; FAX: 630-7587.* This is an expensive renovation in exclusive Buckingham Gate. Public rooms and restaurants (beautiful Auberge de Provence, Mediterranee, and the Szechúan Inn of Happiness) very appealing, but bedchambers cool and zestless. Ownership by the Taj Group of India attracts many upper-echelon Asiatics as clientele.

### St. George's
*Langham Pl. W1N 8QS;* ☎ *(71) 580-0111; FAX: 836-7244.* For the dedicated shopper, this one would appear to suffer from its remote situation, but it is easily (and economically) within reach of the visceral midsections of the city; split-personality building shared with B.B.C. headquarters; ground-floor entrance; 14-story lobby; adjoining panoramic Octave Restaurant; bar-lounge combination; all units with truly spectacular townscape vistas through huge full-wall windows.

### Hilton International Kensington
*179-199 Holland Park Ave. W11 4UL;* ☎ *(71) 603-3355; FAX: 602-9397.* This place, way out on Holland Park Ave., near Shepherd's Bush, is offered to Hiltonians at nearly 1/3 off the deluxe rates of the Park Lane entry. While it is handsomely decorated in richly textured materials, the location is unfortunate because today's taxi fares can push daily expenditures up to top-line levels. If, however, you don't mind using public transport, the subway (tube) and bus stops are practically at your doorstep. Buff brick facade; Nipponese restaurant;

periodic medieval feasts in the Tudor Tavern; individually adjustable thermostats in all units; likewise refrigerator/bar and color TV. Very well presented; here's a concept that we laud.

### Howard ★

*Temple Pl. WC2R 2PR, The Strand,* ☎ *(71) 836-3555; FAX: 379-4547.* From its perch on the strand, this deluxe rehash of an older hostelry overlooks the Thames. Elegant 18th-century decor; 150 bedrooms; penthouse suites; Quai d'Or French restaurant with Temple Bar adjoining; terraced apron of gardens.

### Royal Garden

*Kensington High St. W8 4PT;* ☎ *(71) 937-8000; FAX: 938-4532.* Here's a T-shape giant staring into Kensington Gardens and Hyde Park. Much of its physical plant is designed for efficiency, comfortable and reasonably appealing to the eye. During all of my various visits, tour groups have been rolling in by coachloads. Personally, I have always had adequate-to-good service here—and I've always booked in incognito—but travelers sometimes complain of staff indifference. The rates are reasonable.

### Portman Intercontinental ☆

*22 Portman Sq. W1H 9FL;* ☎ *(71) 486-5844; FAX: 935-0537.* Sunday Brunch in a New Orleans jazzy mood at the Truffles restaurant is part of this dynamic milieu. Otherwise the cuisine is in the modern French style. There are also a pub and a cleverly cooked-up bakery, which add to the gustation and fun hereabouts. British Airways maintains an office too; theater tickets desk; jeweler; news kiosk; car park. Accommodations in 2 towers.

### Selfridge ☆

*Orchard St. W1, West End;* ☎ *(71) 408-2080; FAX: 629-8849.* If shopping is your bag, then here you are—and here you may stay. This one is tucked right into the middle of Selfridge's, the famous department store. Handsome wood, glass, and burnished-metal entry and foyer; paneled lounge; cobble-paved Fletcher's Restaurant with a vendor's barrow of garden produce to tempt incomers; charming oaken Stoves Bar recalling the days of Dickens; chipper Victorian Picnic Basket coffee shop open from 7 a.m. to 1 a.m. Its 330 units feature room-wide windows that provide an impression of space when, in fact, little exists. Fitted Empire furniture enhances the clever maximizing of minimum dimensions.

### Churchill

*Portman Sq. W1A 4ZX;* ☎ *(71) 486-5800; FAX: 935-0431.* Its gigantic lobby is an immediate indicator of this era in mass-minded hotellerie; you'll be instantly struck by the fact that as many as 1000 souls can live here at the same time. Here's a Winnie that went Pooh, as far as I'm concerned.

**Forum**
*97-109 Cromwell Rd. SW7;* ☎ *(71) 370-5757; FAX: 373-1448.* This jumbo is zooming toward success not only because of the jet thrust from its airline sponsors, but because it is a model of what keen administration, smart budgeting, and shrewd architecture can do. While the bedrooms are cramped (the brochure is a triumphant illustration of what the wide angle lens can do for a microscopic subject), the prices are at bedrock level for these cheerful surroundings.

**Kennedy**
*Cardington St. NW1 2LP;* ☎ *(71) 387-4400; FAX: 387-5122.* It is convenient to Euston Station, but huddled neglectedly in a metropolitan backwater that I doubt many travelers will like. Okay for its moderate tabs, however.

**Royal Lancaster**
*Lancaster Ter. W2 2TY;* ☎ *(71) 262-6737; FAX: 724-3191.* This is another one plying its trade chiefly with tour groups. The handsome Beefeater Restaurant has spring–like tones to complement the branch-top vistas from its wide windows; the Mediterranean Cafe features a lovely centerpiece ceramic tree; the Pub glows with burgundy undertones. The premium bedrooms offer wonderfully restful views.

**Gloucester**
*4-18 Harrington Gardens SW7 4LH;* ☎ *(71) 373-6030; FAX: 373-0409.* It's vast but it doesn't evoke that sensation. There's an airy lobby arcade rising to a mezzanine level; clubby grill; Hunter's Lodge restaurant; sumptuous lounge; Le Chateau wine bar (upstairs portion with tables; cellar section with counter libations), a very popular fad in present-day London; sauna; hairdressing facilities for men and women. The accommodations, though extremely well equipped, seemed rather spare in dimensions.

**Holiday Inn Marble Arch**
*134 George St. W1;* ☎ *(71) 723-1277; FAX: 402-0666.* Since this house is more conveniently sited than its crosstown counterpart (see below), its designers opted for fewer frills as inducement to register; the accent is therefore on functional simplicity.

**Holiday Inn Swiss Cottage**
*128 King Henry's Rd. NW3;* ☎ *(71) 722-7711; FAX: 586-5822.* Named for the neighborhood, it's a 10-minute subway ride from Piccadilly. Architecture and decor? Arabesque, with persistent use of arches, vaulting, tiles, and carpets. Henry VIII Restaurant overlooking a garden; King Henry Bar studded with director's chairs and potted palmery; indoor pool; soft-drink and free-ice machines stationed like stoic sentinels on each floor. All 300 chambers duel with the din on two main arteries; all sport goatee-sized balconettes. The slightly lower tabs here versus those of its downtown cousin can be nullified with the flick of a taxi flag.

### President

*61 Russell Sq. WC1N 5BB;* ☎ *(71) 837-8844; FAX: 837-4653.* This 7-story candidate is on the tour circuit, or so it seems. Gold and brown carpeting, fresh wallpaper, and cheerful curtains; dining room with saw-toothed counter available. The service kills it, however.

### Bedford

*83 Southampton Row WC1B 4HD;* ☎ *(71) 636-7822.* Here's what might be dubbed a 180-room vice president. Similarly conceived lounge and dining room, but pleasant garden adjoins; minuscule bathrooms with separate toilet; closets much too small. Routine.

### Washington

*Curzon St. W1Y 8DT;* ☎ *(71) 499-7000; FAX: 495-6172.* As an example of mass-production hotel technique, this was 60% enlarged by a streamlined wing. It still doesn't come off for me. Neither does the staff, who seemed to prefer being elsewhere.

### Bloomsbury Crest

*Coram St. WC1N 1HT;* ☎ *(71) 837-1200; FAX: 837-5374.* Here's a lackluster commercial pod that occupies part of an office building near Russell Square. In my judgment, this dreary number wouldn't be fun for holidaymakers. Its sister operation, the **Regent Crest** near Regent's Park, peeps from its garden with 350 rooms—each cross-pollinated to resemble the original plant.

### Novotel

*1 Shortlands W6;* ☎ *(81) 741-1555; FAX: 741-2120.* This hotel has bunk space for 1300 far out on Talgarth Road. You might hope you are not one of the inmates.

### Tower

*St. Katharine's Way E1 9LD;* ☎ *(71) 481-2575; FAX: 488-4106.* The 826-bedchamber Tower reflects all the charm of the World Trade Center it was meant to complement.

### Royal National

*Bedford Way WC1H ODG;* ☎ *(71) 637-2488; FAX: 837-4653.* This place has 556 units, functions chiefly for tours. Reasonable prices; reasonable rewards.

### Imperial

*Russell Sq. WC1B 5BB;* ☎ *(71) 837-3655; FAX: 837-4653.* The fountain entrance is nice; then comes a prairie-size lobby pointing clients to cubicles in 3 wings; mass-production dining room; achingly tiny bedchambers and unbelievably cramped baths. No thanks.

### London Metropole

*Edgware Rd. W2 1JU;* ☎ *(71) 402-4141; FAX: 724-8866.* Near Marble Arch, this hotel counts a mere 555 accommodations. The entrance is so awkward for motorists that they would find it much easier to drive only to the back portals. I like the efforts made here to stoke up decorative warmth in the public rooms. The sleepers, however, remain little more than body-size cubicles.

## INTIMATE CORNERS

Not all the hotel choices need be big and brassy or overwhelming in the facilities they provide. A new wave of personalized conversions has come to London following the burgeoning success of numerous English country houses that appropriately became cozy hideaways for weekenders. In London, among these so-called "boutique hotels," this same homespun mood prevails, albeit smartly clad in absolute professionalism. Since service is their pride (and your joy), staff-to-client ratios are usually higher than in the tower hotels where cool-handed efficiency is the main thrust. Consequently, prices will not be at household levels; often they are right up there with the big boys. Here are some of the politely whispered choices of the moment:

**Dukes** ☆☆☆☆
*35 St. James' Pl. SW1A 1NY;* ☎ *(71) 491-4840; FAX: 493-1264.* Dukes is the granddaddy of the swanky "insider" hostelries in the capital and (with the next entry) is considerably larger than the 10-15-room tykes to follow; it's a 1908 model fitted out to recapture the gaslight era. (Those are horseless carriages outside its cobblestone court.) Wrought-iron entrance; clubby brown-and-green lobby; tiny bar; St. James's restaurant. Total of 52 tiny fiefs (29 named for illustrious duchies), some of which are in a separate enclave; soft, earth-tone carpeting; bath, telephone, TV, 3-channel radio; suites with fireplaces and fully equipped kitchens. The staff not only will try to address you by name, milord, but will stock your castle with fresh flowers, a salver of fruit, and a warmed copy of the *Times.*

**Stafford** ☆☆☆☆
*16 St. James' Pl. SW1A 1NJ;* ☎ *(71) 493-0111.* This hotel is a bewitching manse tucked away in a little mews. It sparkles with a distinctive personality that evokes the flavor of Jolly Old England. Handy location that is quiet, though the house is merely 100 yards from Piccadilly; private-home-like lounge; bustling dining salon; graceful bar (from which, it is vowed, the first martini was exported to the Colonies); classical decor; 75 ample-size units, all with bath; not for bargain hunters. A newer wing fronting the courtyard contains luxury suites that are among the best in the city, and utterly private. Definitely for the discriminating.

**Beaufort** ☆☆☆☆
*33 Beaufort Gardens SW3;* ☎ *(71) 584-5252; FAX: 589-2834.* Beaufort is nearly in the shadow of Harrods. This appeal to shoppers is irresistible. Light, springlike tones in decor; warmhearted hospitality by Ms. Diana Wallis, a TV-producer-turned-hotelier—and with feeling; some nice surprises such as Walkmans and a no-tipping policy; membership

in a health club for guests. Bar libations are part of the overall tariff (W.C. Fields, obviously, never slept here). A lovely, handy haven.

### Fenja ☆☆☆☆
*69 Cadogan Gardens SW3 2RB;* ☎ *(71) 589-7333; FAX: 581-4958.* Here is a gleaming gem beautifully given to fine antiques, oils, and sumptuously rich textiles. The rooms (named for artists or literati of the realm) are filled with thoughtful touches that pamper a traveler's whims. Dining is in the salon, but while meals are excellent they are not designed to satisfy your he-man hunger for a big night out. Indeed, they are tasteful, light, and thoughtfully composed; room service is also available. It's the atmosphere that is so appealing.

### Draycott ★★★
*24-26 Cadogan Gardens SW3;* ☎ *(71) 730-6466.* Draycott is a neighbor and caters to a similar clientele. It has two dozen accommodations, plush appointments, and a tranquil residential location that is a nice (but not so short) walk to the central shopping districts. Still, taxis are always available on this street.

### 11 Cadogan Gardens
☎ *730-3426.* This is both its name and address. It was probably one of the earliest hotels of this ilk and had a lot to offer when its rates were low. Prices recently have gone up stunningly, however, and I'm not convinced the value has kept pace. Sedate, a bit sleepy, no restaurant, no bar, no central heating, but it does have homely electric heaters.

### Blakes ★★★★
*33 Roland Gardens SW7 3PE;* ☎ *(71) 370-6701; FAX: 373-0442.* Here is a small intime Victorian hideaway (but only in structure) on two sides of a residential street that caters chiefly to the With-It crowd, fashionable communications executives, stunning top-line models, and youthful upmarket travelers who shun the conventional. The novel approach features a Pacific-island lobby covered by a colossal garden parasol and dotted with wicker furnishings that are more decorative than comfortable. There's a dismal retro-deco downstairs restaurant-cum-bar, a spotlit lounge, a sauna, and a host of smiling staff members, often in jeans; across the lane are the "Bosies" and "Benzies" annexes with additional accretions now linked in. No two nests are alike. Its tiny baths are often whacky in layout but charming in presentation. Sometimes adequate space is at a premium, but overall there is such an air of fetching, luxurious Bohemianism at every turn that most adventurous wanderers will forgive the occasional bruised elbow or overflowing closet.

### Halcyon ★★★★★
*81 Holland Park W11 3RZ;* ☎ *(71) 727-7288; FAX: 229-8516.* This house is out at Holland Park (one of the capital's fashionable residential neighborhoods), but excellent subway connections put you within

15 minutes of the shopping and theater districts. The decor is stunning, all of it assembled by the talented American Barbara Thornhill. The lounge overlooks a tree-lined street; in the salon there's a hearth, a grandfather clock, fine paintings, and rich, brocaded chairs. Rooms reflect the splendor of the Belle Epoque with flowers on every surface and an abundance of riches throughout its 44 rooms and suites, many with four-posters, all air conditioned and some with Jacuzzis. The six categories of accommodation begin at close to £100 and range up to the £350 Halcyon Suite, with its own conservatory and view onto the park and tennis ground. Downstairs the lounge and adjoining Kingfisher restaurant are the "in" hideaways for the most distinguished members of the theatrical community.

### L'Hotel ★

*28 Basil St. SW3;* ☎ *(71) 225-0011.* L'Hotel nudges shoulders with its posher brother, the Capital (see earlier), sharing the same expert management of proprietor David Levin. Prices, however, are significantly below Capitalist levels while taste and space considerations in bedrooms are nearly the same. Furnishings lean to American Colonial: fabric-sheathed walls; 4 units with gas-burning fireplaces; direct-dial phones; TV-clock consoles; every amenity is here. There's also Le Metro, a splendid wine bar downstairs with snacks available.

### Portobello ★

*22 Stanley Gardens W11 2NG;* ☎ *(71) 727-2777; FAX: 792-9641.* This 20-room, 5-suite sweetie is just plain fun. A handsome pair of Victorian homes have been joined in harmonious wedlock by Tim and Cathy Herring, an affable, young, and talented couple about whom you might say the same thing. Palms abound, cheer pervades, and good taste is in evidence down to the smallest detail. Its main drawback is in the miniature baths.

### Pelham ☆

*115 Sloane St. SW1X 9PJ;* ☎ *(71) 589-8288; FAX: 259-6977.* Pelham is in a noisy area, but inside it is as silent as a blink. Rich textiles mix with fine Victorian furnishings, antiques, and oils. A useful variety of room sizes for singles, pairs, or families; recommendable cookery; very attentive staff and caring management.

### Hazlitt's

*6 Frith St. W1V;* ☎ *(71) 434-1771; FAX: 439-1524.* This place is in the theater district and very useful for midtowners. Though the area is not too appealing, this trio of houses melded together creates a private escape from the hurly-burly. Prices are moderate, comfort assured. Fun and a bit creaky.

### Abbey Court

*20 Pembridge Gardens W24 DU;* ☎ *(71) 221-7518; FAX: 792-0858.* Abbey Court comes on with explosive showers of flowers, truly lovely. Some units with four-posters; light touches in color and concept. Very fresh—something you won't feel if you happen to get one of the fifth-floor walk-up bedchambers. Be sure to book on the lower levels.

### Dorset Square

*39-40 Dorset Sq. NW1 6ON;* ☎ *(71) 723-7874; FAX: 724-3328.* This complex is composed of a pair of Georgian houses near Regent's Park; the location and the hotel share the same name. Polished antiques, half-tester beds, and blossoms everywhere bespeak the distinctive personality of this dozy 30-room retreat. Enthusiastic new management.

### Cadogan

*Sloane St., SW1X 9SG;* ☎ *(71) 235-7141; FAX: 245-0994.* Here's a well-situated address in Knightsbridge where Oscar Wilde courted Lillie Langtry and where the management had the notorious playwright arrested and turfed into Reading Gaol. An air of pristine traditionalism pervades this stately house, harking to Edwardian allures and lore, yet boasting an abundance of 20th-century comforts. A fireside ambience, at once intimate, appealing, and, well, arresting.

### Lowndes

*Lowndes St., Knightsbridge SW1X 9ES;* ☎ *(71) 235-6020.* Structurally and decoratively here is one of the more attractive small hotels in London—with the added advantage of having one of the best addresses in the embassy neighborhood of Belgravia. The traditional Adam style predominates, a signature of its elegant heritage, which is now trending toward popular mass appeal. Good value for £s.

### Chesterfield

*35 Charles St., Mayfair W1X 8LX;* ☎ *(71) 491-2622; FAX: 491-4793.* This comprises the union of two old houses, incorporating charm, varilevel stair climbing, nice rooms, a Buttery spread with reasonable food buys, and a restaurant that glows with a Regency tradition. Very central. The location is wonderful for shoppers, sightseers and theatergoers. And to have a comfy apartmentlike accommodation in this central zone can be a blessing. No restaurant, and one is not necessary since you'll be surrounded by dining choices in the neighborhood. Snacks are available, however.

### Dolphin Square

*Grosvenor Rd. SW1;* ☎ *(71) 834-3800; FAX: 798-8735.* And speaking of apartments, here is an exceptional value. A total of 1050 privately leased units are contained in a quadrangle of houses, each named after a British naval personage. Rodney House is the operative nexus and the site for 150 transient accommodations, available by the day, week, or month. Quiet, convenient location; hall porter, reception, key and cashier counters; extraordinarily well planned and executed all-purpose shopping arcade; overlooking the heated indoor pool is a pleasant, popular-price restaurant open from 7:30 a.m. to midnight; 2 bars; 8 squash courts; Finnish log saunas; 350-car underground garage; attractive gardens; 26 automatic elevators. One-, 2-, 3-room apartments; 30 so-called Guest Rooms for economizing voyagers (public toilets and tubs). Tabs very low for the market; discounts usually given for stays of a week or more; most accommodations with fully equipped kitchenettes; TV installed upon request for a small additional charge; free maid service 6 days per week.

For additional apartment choices contact specialist Harry Barclay of the **Barclay International Group**, who can open many doors to London for you. Some of the runners in his stable include **Flemings, Grosvenor House, Huntingdon House**, and **Lambs**, all very well located. Address: 767 Third Ave. New York, NY 10017; ☎ *(212) 872-8357* or *(800) 223-1912*; FAX: *(212) 753-1139*.

## ASSORTED HOTELS

These come in all sizes and shapes, some old and some new, some distinctive, others routine. No attempt is made to rank them within the general category because of the vast differences in style. Let's hope the descriptions give you an idea of their virtues or deficits.

### Lanesborough

*1 Lanesborough Pl. SW 1;* ☎ *(71) 259-5599; in the U.S.* ☎ *800-323-8500.* Here's an expensive luxury candidate in the fast lane of Hyde Park Corner. Fresh open-style conservatory and cozy library-style bar (now almost a cliché in hotel decoration); rose-toned dining salon to flatter m'lady's complexion; butler on every corridor. The accommodations are predictably sumptuous (at £230 for starters), ranging up to a Royal Suite that is provided with a chauffeur-driven Roller for just a shade under $5000. My first impression of the see-me peacock walk around the lounges was one of suffocating pretense, but that is surely unfair to both clientele and establishment. The cuisine, mainly British, was pleasing. Undoubtedly this house will mellow and mature with dignity.

### Le Meridien Piccadilly

*21 Piccadilly W1V 0BH;* ☎ *(71) 734-8000; FAX: 734-8000.* As the name suggests, this dilly comes from France. The worldwide chain swept across La Manche to create an opulent Gallic version of English fin de siecle. Well, it almost works. Above the entrance, on a pillowed terrace, you will discover a conservatory with a brasserie. The Oak Room features the Burgundian masterwork of chef Michel Lorain as well as English cookery. There's a music room, a night club, a glittering array of architectural trinkets from the Age of Elegance and—oh, yes—even some bedrooms. The last combine traditional English stylizations with up-to-date accoutrements. There's a health club, too, plus golfing opportunities at Richmond Park (1/2-hour drive—by limo, not One Wood).

### The Chelsea

*17 Sloane St. SW1X 9NU;* ☎ *(71) 235-4377; FAX: 235-3705.* This 220-unit midtowner features a swimming pool in its courtyard overlooked by the Bohemian Bar and the romantic Papillon Restaurant. All public sectors are attractive. Very convenient.

### Wilbraham

*1 Wilbraham Pl., Sloane St. SW1X 9AE;* ☎ *(71) 730-8296.* There's a worthwhile assortment of 62 rooms, most with bath; substantial and nice as a London townhouse. Prices are surprisingly low for the reward but reception staff are sometimes brusque, possibly a result of too much success.

### Langham Hilton

*1 Portland Pl. W1V 3AA;* ☎ *(71) 636-1000; FAX: 323-2340.* First a hotel in 1865, reopened after several changes of career over the past century. Restoration of the noble Edwardian structure cost about £85 million, but the revision has maintained the space and grace concepts of its era chiefly in the public rooms. The bedchambers (410 units including 50 suites) are largely contemporary and hardly inspired.

### White House

*Regents Park NW1 3UP;* ☎ *(71) 387-1200; FAX: 388-0091.* This former apartment style abode overlooking Regents Park was transformed into a medium-budget hotel. Circular lobby marblesque and carpeted; dining salon with a growing reputation; the Wine Press in auberge style for sipping as well as for club breakfasts.

### Elizabetta

*162 Cromwell Rd. SW5 0TT;* ☎ *(71) 370-4282; FAX: 244-7764.* Here again there's a relatively far-out location. Listless, 7-tiered exterior; silver slipper-sized bar-lounge; miniaturized restaurant with Middle Eastern cuisine. A grave disappointment to us.

### Kensington Palace

*De Vere Gardens W8 5AF;* ☎ *(71) 937-8121; FAX: 937-2816.* Though many tours pause here, it maintains a personalized attitude. The lobby is tasteful and air-conditioned; coffee shop bubbling from 7 a.m. to 12:30 a.m.; good maintenance. Only a few of its accommodations in dismal studio motif; conventional twins much better by comparison.

### Ramada

*10 Berners St. W1A 3BE;* ☎ *(71) 636-1629; FAX: 580-3972.* Here's an American import with Edwardian touches, molded ceilings, and Italian marble. The Carvers' Table is a cut above average for hotel dining. Rooms well outfitted but not too spacious; convenient for those in the fashion and textile trades since Oxford St. is only 50 yards away.

### Royal Trafalgar

*Whitcomb St. WC2H 7HL;* ☎ *(71) 930-4477; FAX: 925-2149.* This 110-box bastion is excellently positioned for addicted sightseers—but that's about that, as far as I'm concerned. Tiny lobby; a steak-house for dining plus Battle of Trafalgar pub. All rooms seem to have been thoughtfully proportioned so that guests can reach almost anything from dead center; all come with bath, radio, TV, and round-the-clock service.

## Leinster Towers

*7-11 Leinster Sq. W2;* ☎ *(71) 229-9641.* This place is a community of several former houses, offers 165 accommodations under one roof. Hodge/podge interior; all units with weensie private baths and more than half with cooking facilities; possibly the narrowest beds this side of Fort Bragg.

## Strand Palace, Regent Palace

*WC2R 0JJ;* ☎ *(71) 836-8080; FAX: 836-2077, and Piccadilly Circus W1A 4BZ;* ☎ *(71) 734-7000; FAX: 734-6435.* These two hotels are in a chrome-steel, imitation-leather motif. Chillingly sterile a few moons back, but their Trusthouse Forte masters are successfully pumping color and life into this pair. The basic mood at both, however, is cool and commercial.

## Norfolk

*2-10 Harrington Rd. SW7 2JN;* ☎ *(71) 589-8191; FAX: 581-1874.* Norfolk retains its splendid 19th-century mien; cheery brasserie and darkly handsome winery plus a rich atmosphere in its English Tavern; well-appointed bedrooms.

## Basil Street

*8 Basil St. SW3 1AH;* ☎ *(71) 581-3311; FAX: 581-3693.* In London's prized shopping district, Basil Street is an enchanting meld of Edwardian and Georgian motifs; a lovely period piece of innkeeping with many fine antiques.

## Cumberland

*Marble Arch W1A 4RF;* ☎ *(71) 262-1234; FAX: 724-4621.* This place is a frenetic colony that's undergone extensive revamping; commercial, but very good value; coffee shop excellent, as are the Dukes Bar and the Japanese restaurant.

## Swallow International

*Cromwell Rd. SW5 0TH;* ☎ *(71) 973-1000; FAX: 244-8194.* A hotel with a cavernous marble lobby; Cavalier Room and Cromwell Coffee Shop for pack'em-stack-em feedings; Stuart Bar, a dim watering hole. No thanks.

## Embassy

*31 Queens Gt., S. Kensington SW7 5JA;* ☎ *(71) 584-7222; FAX: 589-8193.* Embassy blends modernism with period themes in a happy meld of two distinct ideas. The medium tariffs and the all-out effort of the staff are big pluses.

## Mt. Royal

*Bryanston St. W1A 4UR;* ☎ *(71) 629-8040; FAX: 499-7792.* Mt. Royal is a commercial colossus offering excellent amenities but not an over-abundance of flair; groupy but reasonable in price.

### The Londoner

*Welbeck St. W1M 8HS;* ☎ *(71) 935-4442; FAX: 487-3782.* Less frenetic but just as mercantile. It seemed very expensive for the value.

### Belgravia Sheraton

*20 Chesham Pl. SW1X 8HQ;* ☎ *(71) 235-6040; FAX: 259-6243.* Provides shophounds with excellent fields for the chase. Sit-down check-in plus a special welcome to ease you into the hospitality; thoughtful touches for women guests; expanded atrium lounges; glass also covering the restaurant and lightened with mirrors and painted wallpaper; 9 studio suites; refashioned doubles, all with in-house video and color TV. A warm, clublike reformation.

### Hyde Park Towers

*Inverness Terrace W2;* ☎ *(71) 221-8484; FAX: 221-2286.* This hotel gave its 114 rooms a face-lifting. Restaurant with dancing; coffee shop; commercial but sound.

### Plaza

*Lancaster Gate W2 3NA;* ☎ *(71) 262-5022; FAX: 724-8666.* Opposite Hyde Park Plaza, is an amiable bet for families, provided the children are carefully watched whenever they cross traffic-clogged Bayswater Road.

## MONEY SAVERS

### Bailey's Hotel

*Gloucester Rd. SW7 4QH, near Gloucester Rd. tube station;* ☎ *(71) 373-6000; FAX: 370-3760.* An ancient landmark in Kensington with 143 old-world spacious bedrooms; about 60% have a bath or shower. A special type of ambience.

### Goring

*15 Beeston Pl. SW1W 0JW, near Buckingham Palace, Victoria Station, and the Air Terminal;* ☎ *(71) 834-8211; FAX: 834-4393.* Resembles Bailey's in feeling. All chambers centrally heated; modern plumbing, radios, and phones. Again, very good.

### Fielding

*4 Broad Ct., Bow St. WC2, very near Covent Garden Opera House;* ☎ *(71) 836-8305; FAX: 497-0064.* Each of the 26 units in this 300-year-old house is different. As an example, try #24, a duplex with cozy sitting room one flight down. Not in any way related to this guidebook.

### Coburg

*129 Bayswater Rd. W2 4RJ;* ☎ *(71) 221-2217.* Warm and inviting 120-room inn. Good connections to West End via the Queensway and Bayswater station. Units with bath have TVs. Some traffic noise, so light sleepers should book in the back.

### Royal Scot

*100 King's Cross Rd. WC1;* ☎ *(71) 278-2434.* Large; caters to tours. Borders Islington, so ideal for antiquaries.Mini apartments with tea- and coffee-making equipment, bath, and shower; 3 bars; restaurant. Single rate: £40; twins at £65; suites (some with canopy bed and color TV): £70, plus taxes. Superb value.

### Royal National

*Bedford Way WC1H 0DG;* ☎ *(71) 637-2488; FAX: 837-4653.* Similar in size and personality. Near theater district. All units with bed consoles for TV and radio; phones. Also a good buy.

## BUDGET CHOICES

Due to this season's tourism crisis, several budget hotels in London have gone bust or are about to close, according to very recent input from my London sources. The following candidates are the strongest.

### Driscoll House

*172 New Kent Rd. SE1;* ☎ *(71) 703-4175.* Wonderful hospitality by Mr. Driscoll himself. Multinational following in convivial age mixture from 18 to 70. Expect to pay £140 per week with partial board. Many happy reports from travelers.

### Hansel & Gretel

*68-76 Belgrave Rd. SW1;* ☎ *(71) 828-1806.* 100 rooms in 7 houses. Good breakfasts; always busy.

### College House

*13 Cromwell Rd. SW7;* ☎ *(71) 589-1275.* A Royal College of Art collage open from July 17 to Sept. 26; no meals.

### Stanley House

*19-21 Belgrave Rd. SN1V 1RB;* ☎ *(71) 834-5042.* Fair for the low prices; a 30-room, well-sited sleep-in.

### Cranley House

*8 Cranley Gardens SW7;* ☎ *(71) 373-3232.* Well-regarded by readers for many years. Solid value.

### Alison House

*82 Ebury St. SN1N 9QD;* ☎ *(71) 730-9529.* Ditto for this one. Extensive updatings make it better than ever.

### Linden House

*4 Sussex Pl. N2 2TP;* ☎ *(71) 723-9853.* Fresh and well managed; 30 beds; singles a hefty £30; twins at £10 more.

## HOSTEL ACCOMMODATION

Plenty. Ring up the **Youth Hostel Association** *14 Southampton St. WC2;* ☎ *(71) 240-3158*

## AUTHOR'S OBSERVATION

*The* **British Tourist Authority** *now offers a brochure listing 4-score-or-more hotels in four conveniently central areas at tariffs ranging from £9 to £17 per person per night, including continental breakfast, service, and tax. Write BTA (40 W. 57th St., New York, NY 10019) requesting London Value Hotels.*

## HEATHROW AND GATWICK AIRPORTS

### Sheraton Skyline

*Bath Rd., Hayes;* ☎ *(81) 759-2535; FAX: 750-9150.* Suavely luxurious. Large, tropical-lush, central Carib Patio featuring a fine pool, and a popular, b-i-g Sunday buffet-brunch from 11 a.m.-2 p.m.; Diamond Lil's reincarnated Gold Rush Saloon with honky-tonk ivories and bouncing banjos; Colony Room, an Edwardian dine-and-dancer; Cafe Jardin; excellent maintenance throughout; expensive.

### Heathrow Penta

*Bath Rd., Hounslow TW6 2AQ;* ☎ *(81) 897- 6363; FAX: 897-1113.* This place is a sprawling, 4-level structure. Sweeping lobby-lounge; expansive polar-frosted Rib Room; the Flying Machine and Sir Francis Drake bars with respective aero/nautical gimmickry; coffee shop; discotheque; indoor pool, bar, and sauna bordered by flowers and fountains. All of its soundproofed chambers provide vivid hues, TV, and air-conditioning.

### Holiday Inn

*Stockley Rd., West Drayton;* ☎ *(81) 895-4455; FAX: 0895-445122.* Architecturally splayed like a 3-bladed prop; its sister ship is 10 miles away at Slough. Blue Ribbon feedery revving till 2 a.m.; hearty Beefeater Bar; Satellite Coffee Shop; health center embracing pool, sauna, massagery, gym, and tennis courts; golf links. All 300 units sport smallish but practical baths and showers, the standard entertainment package, floor-to-ceiling panes, and annoying open wardrobes; kids under 12 ride on their parents' ticket.

### Sheraton-Heathrow

*West Drayton;* ☎ *(81) 759-2424; FAX: 759-2091.* Resides on a mile-distant pasture that overlooks an unsightly factory. Low-profile concrete building; cockpit-size lobby in Star Wars Gothic; raised bar; Cranford Restaurant for seafood and grills. The Nightclub, staged as a Victorian pub, also offers vittles. Pool plus steam room; poolside snacks; frequent bus connection to Knightsbridge.

### Excelsior

*Bath Rd., West Drayton;* ☎ *(81) 759-6611; FAX: 759-3421.* Still superior for its purpose and still richly priced for its league. Its coffee shop, pub-style Tavern Bar, brick-bound sunken Rotisserie, and posh Draitone Manor restaurant are further pluses on its manifest. Adjoining this, there's the 8-table "Library" with crystal glasses, superb cookery, and genuine bookery.

### Radisson Edwardian International Plaza

*Bath Rd., Hayes;* ☎ *(81) 759-6311; FAX: 759-4559.* This place (formerly Skyway), has 460 rooms, including 9 suites, all with bath, telephone, and TV; most facilities nearly always open, with restaurant on 24-hour and snack bar on 20-hour basis; intentional orientation toward business travelers; heated, floodlit, open-air pool; shopping arcade; flight transportation provided to terminus. The efficient, amiable service standards are a blessing.

### Ariel

*Bath Rd. Hayes;* ☎ *(81) 759-2552; FAX: 564-9265.* 184-room, doughnut-shape structure. Soundproofed, air-conditioned bedrooms; showers in each bath; TV and radio; free transportation to and from the airport; a specialty restaurant functioning night and day.

### Post House

*Sipson Rd., West Drayton;* ☎ *(81) 759-2323; FAX: 897-8659.* Practically a self-service sanctuary. Imposing 10-tier house posted on 15 acres; vast lobby bordering on the brash; supermarket carts for transporting your own baggage. Great Britain Grill, Buttery, and Bar all in tribute to I. K. Brunel, the 19th-century marine wizard; pool, bank, boutiques, and news kiosk rounding out the public precincts. All units are routinely furnished and are available in 8 color schemes; a continental breakfast will be left outside your door; offspring under 16 slumber gratis if they share the parental billet.

### Ibis

*112-114 Bath Rd., Hayes UB3 5AL;* ☎ *(81) 759-4888; FAX. 564-7894.* A link in a European economy chain. Nearly 250 rooms with doubles about £40 and singles in the £35 range.

### Gatwick Airport

Choose either of two **Copthornes** (*Effington Park,* ☎ *0342-714994; Gatwick,* ☎ *0342-714971*) at this base. Both are adequate to pleasant. Both are expensive.

### Hilton (☎ *293-518080; FAX: 28980*)

Offering 586 rooms, this hotel is up to the usual solid Hilton International standards; it's only a 5-minute walk from the terminal. This luxury entry offers a pool, squash courts, and sauna.

### Crest

☎ *0293-29991.* A good value at low cost. Simple reception; Globetrotter Bar only 800 feet from a runway; lusterless Silver Table restaurant. Look-alike sleepers with radios, phones, adjustable air cooling and, reportedly, the only triple-glaze panes in or around London.

If you're ever stuck for a place to stay, bookings can be made at the Victoria Station Tourist Information Centre (forecourt) or the Heathrow Tourist Information Centre.

# WHERE TO EAT

The opportunities are limitless. Strangely, top prices do not always mean top quality. In fact, this city is currently in an eccentric period. As billings continue to skyrocket in the smart establishments, a reaction among yuppies is evolving that sends them to some of the ugliest "in" spots to be seen this side of a cafe by the steel factory. Decor is not only minimal, it is purposely hideous. The worse it becomes, the more rapturous become the Hoo-rah Henrys (clad in pinstripe suit jackets over jeans and their blow-dried Sloane Rangers). Moreover, this ardent audience of inexperienced "Foodies" is now paying only marginally less for indifferent bistro cooking than they would for top-grade gastronomy in a beautifully decorated and comfortable salon.

While English nutrients are both inventive (historically) and very, very pleasing, chefs, in my opinion, have not sufficiently exploited their own British treasury of recipes. Instead, they are cribbing more and more from French themes. As you read this section you may be startled to see how many of the capital's shrines of gastronomy have French names and Gallic-based preparations. Good it is, but a pity, too, because the British larder is bursting with unnoticed opportunity. The blame (or credit) for this might rest on the shoulders of the famous Roux family (Gavroche and a host of other restaurants) who have trained cooks in their French heritage and generously set up many promising young talents in their own establishments. While this influence now has almost reached cult proportions, I, personally, regret observing the suppression of purely British culinary efforts.

Mayfair is chichi and costly; Soho and Chelsea are more theatrical and bohemian in flavor, although the tabs can run plenty high here too. Most major independent restaurants and hotel grill rooms (not hotel dining rooms) are shut tight on Sundays. It is always wise to make advance reservations in London, regardless of the place or hour.

## FASHIONABLE DINING

### Tante Claire                                                            ☆☆☆☆☆

*68 Royal Hospital Rd. SW3 4HP.* Long a leader, it seems to get even better as the seasons pass. Proprietor-chef Koffmann prefers to play to a small and discerning audience. Indeed, his style of gastronomy is so thoughtfully planned and individually composed that he is necessarily restricted in his offerings. Perhaps more than any other cuisiner functioning in London today, his preparations represent an "instantaneous" selection of what is best on the morning market and the cultivation of a full meal around those selected items. A modern, soft-spoken mood prevails. (Open Mon.-Fri.; ☎ *(71) 352-6045.)*

## Nico Central ☆☆☆☆

*35 Great Portland St. W.1.* Named for Nico Ladenis, who left his original digs and after an airing in Berkshire, which he sold, he opened this one. Nick is a genius who sometimes can cast himself as a brat when the customer doesn't suit his fancy. Nevertheless, temperament can produce fine victuallers, and here's a case in point. (Open Mon.-Fri.; ☎ *(71) 630-8061.*) He has another patch— and a lovely one it is—in the Grosvenor House (see "Hotels"). It refers to its address, not the patron's age and it's called Nico At Ninety • 90 Park Lane, W1; ☎ *(71) 409-1290.*

## Walton's of Walton Street ☆☆☆☆

*121 Walton St. SW3 2HP.* Continues to be the choice of the Rolls-Ferrari set and foreign high society. The cuisine is judiciously innovative. Georgian windows overlook the quiet street; a dark inner nook is available for more intimacy (better after-theater). On recent visits, I've sampled such inventive creations as a lightly whipped camembert mousse, roasted lobster with coriander and ginger, sauteed Scotch beef with marrow and pine kernels, a salad of yogurt, mushroom, and celeriac, and a white-and-dark chocolate slice with coconut flavoring. The wines disclose their patrician bearing—and are priced accordingly. Some of its additional attributes include Sunday opening as well as special fixed-priced options for after-theater supper and a very reasonable meal at midday. (Closed Easter and Christmas; ☎ *(71) 584-0204.*)

## Le Gavroche ☆☆☆☆

*43 Upper Brook St. W1Y 1PF.* In the past this entry had failed to garner my personal enthusiasm, but it seems to have shifted gears and now approaches gastronomy with less ornament and with dedicated honesty. However good the food, I still find it difficult to swallow the absurd prices. A few bistro dishes are exceptions, but these are not why you came. The atmosphere is sophisticated and sedate. (Open Mon.-Fri., closed Dec. 23-Jan. 2; ☎ *(71) 408-0881.*)

## Rue St. Jacques ☆☆☆☆

*5 Charlotte St. W1P 1HD.* Another in the modish all-Gaul tradition, even though talented chef Gunther Schlender has Teutonic roots. Try his armagnac-scented lobster mousse—a masterpiece of modern gastronomy; juniper-flavored guinea hen is also a favorite of mine here. The mirrors, posh decor, and intimacy evoke the sensation of grand richesse though an evening here will cost about half of one at Le Gavroche. (Open Mon.-Fri. and Sat. p.m., closed Christmas, Easter, bank holidays; ☎ *(71) 637-0222.*)

## Olivo

*21 Eccleston St. SW1 9LX.* Formerly the Ciboure. There's a cheery greeting from the flowered window boxes at its entrance. The hospitality is carried inside with a foyer bar and 3 tables, plus more further in; pale yellow walls; black-and-white contrasts; fresh gray or white tops over striped undercloths on well-dressed tables. If you've failed to reserve and can't get in, **Ken Lo's Memories of China** is just across the lane and is an excellent Oriental choice. (The master chef from China has a similar but wonderfully viewful branch at Chelsea Harbour, the latest redoubt of the "in" set.) (Open Mon.-Fri. and Sat. p.m., closed one week Aug.; ☎ *(71) 730-2505.*)

### L'Arlequin                                                        ☆☆
*123 Queenstown Rd. SW8 3RH.* The food is superb. The people—Chef Delteil and his wife—are warmhearted. And now that it has stretched out into the adjoining masonry, it is marginally more comfortable. When you taste the thinly sliced duck and other preparations, however, you may be able to forgive any space limitations. Try also the chubby scallop-fed ravioli should any doubts linger. Luscious! (Open Mon.-Fri., closed 1 week winter, 3 weeks Aug.; ☎ *(71) 622-0555.*)

### Clarke's
*124 Kensington Church St. W8 4BH.* Everybody is talking about this eccentric. It features home cooking for people who hate to eat at home—and this extends to pseudo-California notions that are big hits under the grey skies of London. The £30 menu is not only set, it is hammered in stone: one choice of first course only; the same for the main dish and sweet. In my case, the "choices" for two of the plates were simply not items I cared for and, hence, I felt like a spoilsport for leaving so much on my platter. The quality and presentation, however, were exceptional, and Hostess Sally Clarke is an everlasting dear. Plain room with blanched wooden floor and modern paintings. On this same street (which is becoming a gastronomic district) there are two restaurants I much prefer: **Kensington Place** *just up the lane at #201;* ☎ *(71) 727-3814* where the decor is awful but the cookery is splendid, and **Boyd's** *across the street at #135;* ☎ *(71) 727-5452* where the conservatory atmosphere is pleasant, the people are cheerful, and the dishes are delightful, especially the offal preparations, the sweets, and the ambitious cellarman who provides a fine cave. (Open Mon.-Fri., closed 2 weeks Aug., 1 week Christmas, 4 days Easter, bank holidays; ☎ *(71) 221-9225.*)

### Bibendum
*81 Fulham Rd. SW3 6RD.* Breathlessly sought after by the young and fashionable, taking perhaps two weeks to secure an evening table (lunch is easier). While the bistro cookery (hardly cuisine) is flavorful, I feel foolish paying almost $60 for fish-and-chips (fried plaice and french fries), which costs $2 at street stands (admittedly not as refined). Very chic, rather wan decoratively, and oh-so-de-rigueur. (Open Mon.-Fri. plus Sat. lunch only; ☎ *(71) 581-5817.*)

### Alastair Little
*49 Frith St. W1V 5TE.* This place is even more of a not-so-beau-geste and it, too, is dazzling to those Little-known disciples for whom fad is fonder than fact. The ugly, hideous, almost frightening illumination

has to be seen to be truly believed; then come cheap, chipped plastic tables, paper napkins, bus station cutlery and tableware, a gloomy downstairs bar (where the snacks are excellent) crudely presented food by ill-kempt and sloppily groomed minions, and flavors that kitchen trainees might revere but experienced diners can live without. Ah, where's the finesse of yesterday, Alastair? (Open Mon.-Fri.; ☎ *(71) 734-5183.*)

## Sutherlands ☆☆

*45 Lexington St. W1R 3LG.* Less minimal in its bid for otiose style; hence, a touch of grace to greet the eye and smart personnel to offer a decent reception. The long salon has a spacious air so that business types (or better yet, romancers) can speak privately. Chef Hollihead manifests a legacy of careful tutorage under master cuisiners. His combinations of ingredients are vivid in flavor and not silly simply to be innovative. There's a sense of intelligence and responsibility. Moreover, it just tastes good. (Open Mon.-Sat. except Sat. lunch; ☎ *(71) 434-3401.*)

## Le Caprice ★★★

*Arlington St. SW1A 1RT.* Here is a reincarnation of what was once London's most fashionable establishment. Models, design leaders, and theater personalities are always propped at the counter or at its lively tables. Cuisine is chiefly brasserie style, unpretentious and damned good. Main courses run from £4 to £8; not bad for being on the cutting edge of the city's sophistocategory. The Sunday brunch is a wow! If you like this mood, you'll also enjoy lunch (only) at **L'Express** *16 Sloane St.*, below a boutique Bagel and lox for (gulp) £10; chicken tika at £8. Ample food but ample prices too. Very, very noisy with happy sounds. **Joe's Cafe** *126 Draycott Ave.* is a brother operation that functions at night as well as at noontime. (Open all week; ☎ (71) 629-2239.)

## Quaglino's ★★★

*16 Bury St. SW 1.* An extravagant brasserie for 300 people-watchers. If you don't wish a full repast (and the food is good if you order shellfish) you can munch on antipasto at the mezzanine bar and view the noisy cavalcade at ground zero. Best eats at the Crustacean Altar; not wildly expensive; ☎ *(71) 930-6767.*

## Hilaire ☆☆☆

*68 Old Brompton Rd. SW7 3LQ.* Still attracts South Kensington's disciples of the newest of nouvelle-isms from the hardworking kitchen. At £50 or so for two, the value certainly is here when it comes to such labor-intensive comestibles. The set lunch is a good buy, but wines are lofty in price. (Open Mon.-Fri. plus Sat. p.m.; ☎ *(71) 584-8993.*)

## Cecconi's ☆

*5A Burlington Gardens W1Y 5DT.* The address is one of London's best. Trellis-back chairs with French- blue cushions; fresh-cut flowers; filmy curtained windows along 2 entire lengths of the salon. Elegant simplicity is the keynote, sung to the tune of very small portions of fine Italian cuisine. If the seemingly limitless prices don't disturb you here, then certainly nothing else should.

### Santini

*29 Ebury St.* Seeks this same up-market Italian following but its cold mood and frigid staff can't bring it off, in my opinion. Food's okay but spare. (☎ *(71) 434-1500.*)

### Eleven Park Walk

*SW10.* Purloined its straightforward moniker from its swanky address —and a very chichi spot it is. The house is abubble with charming young things in the latest fashions, all escorted by a bedizened host of admiring suitors. It is clearly the haunt for second-magnitude stars, dressed-to-the-nines models, and denizens of the couture cult. It glitters with mirrors on 2 sides, broadening the outlook and providing the perfect backdrop for such overt narcissism. Cookery leans toward North Italian preparations. (Open Mon.-Sat., closed Sun. and bank holidays; ☎ *(71) 352-3449.*)

### Orso

*27 Wellington St. WC2E 7DA.* Straightforward, telling you like it is for Italian cookery. Journalists, editors, and publishers are usually at this Covent Garden site at lunch while theater personalities dominate at night. (Closed Dec. 24-25; ☎ *(71) 240-5269.*)

### 192

*192 Kensington Park Rd. W11 2JF.* The spiritual cousin of Groucho's, the most with-it private club on tonight's London scene. The same faces to see-and-be-seen at G's also appear here with frequency. Many gifted media personalities, artists, and well-endowed smoothies comprise the gentry. Cookery leans toward Continental-Italian, i.e. more cream than tomato; some wine-bar snacks too. Anyway, the food's less important than the inhabitants. Both, however, are recommended. (☎ *(71) 229-0482.*)

### L'Incontro

*87 Pimlico Rd. SW1W 8PH.* The rage for chic ladies at noontime. Chiefly seafood of Venetian style and very light. The black-and-white decor is spare but fresh. (☎ *(71) 730-6327.*)

### Lindsay House

*21 Romilly St.* In the nucleus of the theater district, with both pre- and after-performance sittings. The talented Malcolm Livingston (see below) put it all together—and a beauty it is. Ground floor reception and lounge in salon style. Upstairs dining room with antique mirror over the stately hearth; pleated wall textiles and curtains; fine oil paintings. My traditional Southdown duck in spices was superb; veal and watercress also is excellent, but do leave room for the ambrosial summer pudding.

### The Greenhouse ★★

*27a Hays Mews W1X 7BJ.* Situated a half-story below ground; white walls plus lazy ceiling fans, candles, and fresh flowers on the tables. Friendly, professional reception with no haughty pretense; great variety in the menu. As with so many appealing places, it's the full experience that counts—and this one rates mighty high by that measure. (Closed Sat. lunch, Sun., 1 week over Christmas-New Year; ☎ *(71) 499-3331.*)

### The English House ★★

*3 Milner St. SW32QA.* This one is a cousin of the above Lindsay House and is similarly appealing. Emphasis is on ornate presentation. Indeed the house itself is a Victorian masterpiece. Ground-floor dining; a tier above for drinks and conversation; wonderful private salon above that. To some the decor may be stifling, but it is a carefully groomed monument to a rich, bygone era. (Closed Dec. 25-26; ☎ *(71) 584-3002.*)

### English Garden ★★

*10 Lincoln St. SW3 2TS, near Sloane Sq.* Sprouted from the Milner St. concept and is directed by Malcolm Livingston, the genius who started **Walton's**. This one reveals a bit less frill and finesse, but its atmosphere is more animated. Main restaurant in light restful tones enhanced by lots of glass. Upper salon for more private gatherings. A fashionable spot and not terribly expensive. (Closed Dec. 25-26; ☎ *(71) 584-7272.*)

### Eatons ☆☆

*49 Elizabeth St. SW1W 9PP, off Ebury St.* A mere 12 tables in 2 cozy adjoining rooms; beige Hessian walls; attractive art; white timber beams. Its modest menu and wine list (the house red is quite nice and reasonably priced) belie the splendid quality produced in the kitchen. Some selections to try: the melon with shrimp and avocado, the salmon blinis, the curry chicken pancakes, the veal scallop, and the pork with red cabbage in a pastry shell. For such reliable quality, tariffs are surprisingly reasonable. (Closed Sat.-Sun. and bank holidays; ☎ *(71) 730-0074.*)

### Frederick's ★★

*N18EG, in Camden Passage.* Two unusually attractive dining levels, with the upper one displaying a variety of wines; lower segment, down a few steps, fronted by tall, wide windows overlooking a garden patio. Popular and worthy. (Closed Sun., Dec. 26, Jan. 1; ☎ *(71) 359-2888.*)

### Boulestin ☆☆☆☆

*1A Henrietta St. WC2E 8PS.* Offers an elegant salon with gleaming old chandeliers and cunning illumination; a constant parade of inventive dishes from imaginative chef Kevin Kennedy; meticulous attention from staffers; very well regarded—and with good reason. (Closed Sat. lunch, Sun., 3 weeks Aug., 1 week Christmas; ☎ *(71) 836-7061.*)

### Turner's

*87 Walton St. SW3 2HP.* Turner's is in the city's prime restaurant district, and Brian Turner has one of the top names in gastronomy. Then why weren't several tries at the tables very rewarding? The frontage of blue-enameled cottage windows is appealing; the interior is fresh; Mr. Turner is hospitable, but the pudding was not proof of his exalted reputation. (Closed Sat. lunch; ☎ *(71) 584-6711.*)

### La Croisette

*168 Ifield Rd. SW10 9AE.* Recalls a Riviera mood, contrived as it is with service personnel in oystermen's sweatshirts, iced seafood displays, and artwork of the Cote d'Azur. I thought the entrance tatty; it led down a chipped and scruffy spiral staircase to a miserably ventilated arched cellar. Extremely cordial reception; immediate offer of an aperitif, gratis; abundant and superior set meal, plus rather expensive wines. (Closed all day Mon. and Tues. lunch; ☎ *(71) 373- 3694.*)

### Le Suquet

*Around the corner from Walton's at 104 Draycott Ave. SW3 3AE.* This one, operated by the La Croisette people, is done with open beams, stucco walls, bottle glass windows, tiny flower bouquets, and candlesticks on dark blue cloths; the floors are tiled, the chairs small, the atmosphere Provencal. Waiters in blue sweaters serve better wares, in my opinion, than their colleagues at the alma mater. (☎ *(71) 581-1785* and *225-0838.*)

### Quai St. Pierre

*Stratford Rd. W8 6RF.* Another member of the La Croisette sisterhood. More Old World in style; busy and upbeat; brightly illuminated. Different and deserving of attention. (Closed Sun., Mon. lunch, 2 weeks Christmas; ☎ *(71) 937-6388.*)

### L'Estaminet

*14 Garrick St. WC2E 9BJ.* Tucked away in a former mission house in the heart of the theatrical district. It had been a stained glass works associated with Inigo Jones in the past but has now become a pleasant bistro.

### Tartine

Wine cellar in association with L'Estaminet. Exposed brick and simple carpentry; gothic windows; romantic illumination. Lamb and salmon were excellent. (☎ *071-379-1432.*)

## MEDIUM-PRICED DINING

### Harvey's                                    ☆☆☆

*2 Bellevue Rd. SW17 7EG.* In a grim area south of the river, but chef Marco White is changing the local ecology. Fresh, lighthearted, vernal decor with clever use of mirrors; highly inventive dishes from jewel-like terrines to a novel and (gulp) Old English pig's head with spices; set menus from £20 to £33 at lunch and maybe twice as much at dinner. Mr. White reveals a distinct talent over his skillets, a venue better suited to his success rather than at his client's elbows where he is sometimes a nuisance. (Closed Sat. lunch, Sun.; ☎ *(81) 672-0114-15.*)

### L'Etoile ☆☆☆

*30 Charlotte St. W1P 1HJ.* L'Etoile started off nobly when this century was in diapers. How it continues to get better, I'll never understand—but it does. Now other London restaurateurs are copying its evident style. The French-based cuisine is, in fact, more delicate than that of some of the biggest names in Paris. The wines are exquisite and treated with grace and solemnity. Highly skilled waiters in swallowtail coats; yellow walls ending at a ruby border; red-figured carpet. The same clientele keeps coming back delightful year after delightful decade. (Closed Sat., Sun., bank holidays; ☎ *(71) 636-7189.*)

### Green's ★★

*Opposite the Cavendish Hotel at 36 Duke St., St. James's SW1Y 6BR.* Evokes the atmosphere of a private club without any of the stuffy associations common to this English institution. Old World mood in a fresh setting; splendid reception and service; cheerful cocktail bar and champagne lounge; polished darkwood counter and banquettes; numerous Spy prints for decor; handsome paintings. The menu is extensive and praiseworthy for its dedication to British selections. Especially appealing are the dressed crab, grouse, and pheasant (in season). Both the toping and the dining segments are highly recommended. (Closed Sun. p.m.; ☎ *(71) 930-4566.*)

### Luigi's

*Tavistock St. WC2E7PA.* Recommended especially as an after-the-final-curtain entry. Reservations a must; bid for more ingratiating upstairs perches. (Closed Sun., bank holidays; ☎ *(71) 240-1795.*)

### Borgo San Frediano

*62 Fulham Rd. SW3 6HH.* Honest, fun, and good. Wonderful antipasto table at entrance; house wines excellent; palsy greeting and smiling, rushed service. A spot to enjoy—at about £16 per maw.

### Sale e Pepe

*9 Pavilion Rd.* and **Montpeliano** *13 Montpelier St.* Boisterous, and the latter is so snobby, that I can easily make it through this life and the next without 'em. (Closed Sun., bank holidays; ☎ *(71) 584-8375.*)

## ENGLISH TRADITIONAL DINING

### Simpson's-in-the-Strand ☆☆

*100 Strand WC2R 0EW.* Around the corner from the Savoy, still lives up to its long and distinguished reputation. Men's Bar in cellar and venerable, paneled, groundfloor restaurant (ladies admitted to latter only on Sat.); rich, decorous, comfortable main restaurant up one flight (ladies always welcome). The splendid Chandelier Room features a new lunchtime menu aimed at fish and vegetarian choices. Closed Sun.; mandatory to reserve in advance for lunch. It's the custom to tip your carver. Two oddities: (1) gentlemen are requested not to smoke their pipes in the dining room, and (2) tea is available but politely discouraged here. (Simpson's avows it's for teatime only—an hour when its portals are shut.) (Closed Sun., Easter, Dec 25-26, bank holidays; ☎ *(71) 836-9112.*)

### Rules ☆☆

*35 Maiden Lane.* A short hike from the Savoy Hotel, presents a charming Edwardian impression of seediness. Creaky, rippled floors; dimensions cramped; friendly welcome. Game, pies, mutton chops, the hearty fare (and feel!) of Old England. (Closed Sun.; ☎ *(71) 836-5314*)

### Wilton's

*55 Jermyn St. SW1Y 6LX.* A turn-of-the-century period piece, appeals to well-heeled Edwardian traditionalists who use it almost as a private club. Although roast beef is not the main attraction, it is always available and nearly always excellent. For decades this busy bistro has been famed for its piscatorial splendors, which retain the highest quality. The Oyster Bar is a pleasant voyage into the past; then sail home with savouries (such as welsh rarebit) or Old English puds (sample a syllabub). (Closed Sat. lunch, Sun.; ☎ *(71) 629-9955.*)

### George and Vulture

*3 Castle Court EC3V.* A 2-story, open-grill rough-and-ready chophouse, with ancient, friendly waiters and a near-medieval setting; it claims title as the oldest tavern in existence, founded in 1175. Open for lunch only, Mon. through Fri.; go before 1 p.m. or after 1:45 p.m., because its regular stockbroker clientele keeps it jammed. Medium prices for no-nonsense cookery; more British than the British; you may have to share a table. Not spectacular, but veddy, veddy Plantagenet. (Closed Sat.-Sun.; ☎ *(71) 626-9710.*)

## SEAFOOD

### Poissonnerie de l'Avenue ☆☆☆☆

*82 Sloane Ave. SW3 3DZ.* Generally the first choice for maritime wares. It's not fancy; it's simply good. A clublike nookery that grew over two oak-paneled floors; chummy counter service plus numerous tables; specialties chalked onto a blackboard; big, varied menu; beautiful presentation; outstanding quality. Top recommendation, but getting a seat will be a problem. Lunchtime is easier than evening. (Closed Sun., Easter 1 week, Christmas 2 weeks, bank holidays; ☎ *(71) 589-2457.*)

### Scott's

*20 Mount St. W1Y 5RB.* Decked out with raspberry-damask wall coverings, marble columns, Spy prints on white brick, bas-relief panels, and crystal chandeliers. The posh surroundings come with greatly improved service and lofty prices. (Closed Sun. lunch, Christmas, Easter, bank holidays; ☎ *(71) 629-5248.*)

### Sheeky's ★★

*28-32 St. Martin's Court WC2N 4AL.* For the broad-minded. Steamed or grilled seafood only (an oddball lease prohibits frying the fish). Old creaky atmosphere that I love; worn wooden floors; chummy service by waitresses in dental-assistant gowns. The steamed turbot is sinfully delicious; so is the grilled sole. Smack in the theatrical district, so very useful to pre-show diners; also serving until 10:45 p.m. A 10-strike for no-frills sea fare. (Closed Sun., Easter, Christmas, bank holidays; ☎ *(71) 240-2565.*)

### Wheeler's

*19 Old Compton St.* The original link in the chain that includes **Vendome** and numerous others. While both registered high for ambience in the traditional British mood, the quality of the cooking at each was mediocre-to-poor, in my view.

### The Ivy

*1 West St.* The Ivy which left Wheeler's and was refashioned by the Caprice interests (except for its lovely stained glass windows) is now regaining the glory it enjoyed back in the early decades of this century. Author Kingsley Amis says "The furniture has lost weight." He refers to the streamlining undergone here since days of yore. As it still plays to a theatergoing public (around Covent Garden), a mighty plus is its early opening (5:30 p.m.) and its late service (last orders at midnight). Main Courses ample in size and of classical background; Amis has a good word for "the afters" (puddings). Still fun. (Open all week; ☎ *(71) 836-4751.*)

### Manzi's

*1-2 Leicester St. WC2H 7BL.* The oldest maritime den in London; reasonable tabs; grilled sole the specialty; unusually rewarding and money-saving. (Closed Sun. lunch; ☎ *(71) 734-0024.*)

### Bentley's

*11 Swallow St. W1R 7HD.* Swims in as a firmly fleshed midtown wiggler. Busy ground-floor bar and oyster counter; one-room upstairs restaurant with azalea-red walls hung with paintings; unwatchful disattention by frumpy waitresses; rush-rush atmosphere. Cookery that is almost too simple (some would say "bland"); reasonable-to-rich prices. (Closed Sun., bank holidays; ☎ *(71) 734-4756.*)

## HOTEL DINING

### Capital ☆☆☆☆☆

Capitalizes on a well-deserved reputation for distinguished continental fare. The styling is another fillip of gracious swank and Louis XIV comforts. Few tables, so reserve ahead; small adjoining lounge for studying the tempting menu over an aperitif; trainees sometimes muddle your drink orders.

### Halcyon ☆☆☆
Offers its very springlike Kingfishers restaurant and inviting bar, opening onto a patio. It has quickly caught on with theatrical luminaries. Dishes are inventive, pique your imagination, and seldom let you down; wines are costly. A different experience.

### Connaught Grill ☆☆
A fixture on the London scene for decades. It is traditional and reliable, but not exciting gastronomically. Sunday lunch in the dining room is an institution.

### Savoy Grill ☆☆
A London staple, but the decor is cold.

### The Upstairs
Overlooking the hotel entrance. One of the fun snack spots in town. Chef Anton Edelmann is one of London's best.

### The Buttery ★★
*The Berkeley.* The nexus for an excellent buffet at midday with the accent on pasta and Mediterranean fish preparations at night. (More properly, these relate to the Adriatic, since so many recipes are Venetian.) This is an historic room that was taken almost intact years ago from the older hotel in another part of London.

### Claridge's ☆☆☆
Claridge's has been given a shot of adrenaline, plus better lighting, and the chipper little cosmos known as the **Causerie** for buffet choices. The latter is not only excellent, it is one of the most entertaining corners of London for the Smart Set.

### Hyatt Carlton Tower's Rib Room
Retains its mandate on beefeaters but now is far more attractive than it was during the height of its popularity in the seventies.

### Chelsea Room ☆☆☆
This place is also in the Carlton. Personally, I have always found it worlds better than its more famous companion. The staff attention is perfect; the crystal wall panels glisten, as does the glassware on the tables; wide windows overlook the lovely park. Distinguished, but relatively unsung for such outstanding culinary performance.

### Inn on the Park ☆☆☆☆
Its parking places are mentioned under "Hotels"; chic and top quality, especially at **Four Seasons**.

### Hilton
Conventional dining is available, but most people know it for the **Trader Vic's** Polynesian hutch.

### Intercontinental's Le Souffle ☆☆

Offers a soignee effect evoked by an interior room (no windows) in rouge and black. Prices are as stunning as the surroundings. And the souffles live up to the promise.

### Meridien ★★★

Its **Oak Room** offers French as well as (praise be!) English cooking. Chef Michel Lorain is a great talent, and his handsome lair is one of the most beguiling dining redoubts in town.

### Ritz

Boasts one of the most gorgeous rotundas in Europe; the gastronomy has been noteworthy at times, but on a recent trial it varied between ho and hum. Director Terry Holmes undoubtedly will be giving this aspect full attention.

## DINING ADVENTURES

### River Cafe ★★★

*Rainville Rd.* A moody, romantic spot on Thames Wharf in the unchic Hammersmith district. It's the reverse-snobbism syndrome that is responsible for it catching on, so catch it while you can. The gastronomy tends to Piedmontese selections and other North Italian fixin's. Some continental choices too. Frolicsome. (  *(71) 385-3344.*)

### New Serpentine ★

*Hyde Park.* This waterside creation of Prue Leith—she's famous with London's foodies—brings the country to the city. Prue has a delicate touch and an inventive mind, all of which conspire to produce contented tummies on the south side of the Park. On a sunny day, Hyde and seek. (May-Sept. 10:30 a.m.-10:30 p.m.; 5:30 p.m. in winter; ☎ *(71) 402-1142.*)

### Justin de Blank

*54 Duke St. W1M 5DS.* A sort of do-it-yourself delicatessen for the celebrity set. This is the scene for take-it-home Londoners, tourists who are closet snackers back at their hotel rooms, and drop-ins. Cute and costly. (Closed Sat. p.m., Sun.; ☎ *(71) 629-3174.*) You can also lunch on this master's recipes at **The General Trading Company** *144 Sloane St., Sloane Sq.* in between shopping.

### Planet Hollywood

*Trocadero Centre, near Leicester Square.* The address is the only thing even remotely square about this all-new Piccadilly hangout. The loud music decimates the decibel system. "Smile police" in baseball caps keep asking you if you are happy, zealous service minions slaver over you with unctuous concern, washroom attendants are at the ready to hose you down with cologne or towel you off with a paper doily, and movie snippets are projected onto the silver screens overhead. The line to get in is equally stage-managed and the inner din is seismic. If you can enjoy a $10 hamburger for his price, you're welcome to it.

# KOSHER COOKERY

### Bloom's

*90 Whitechapel High St. E17 RA.* A no-nonsense ethnic candidate. Takeout order section and standup counters near the entrance where legions of ravenous lunchtime landslcit celebrate the glories of pastrami, corned beef, roast beef, chopped liver, tongue, and other inspired deli-cacies; table area with napery as white as a bar mitzvah boy's collar also jammed with midday mavens munching blintzes, gefilte fish, kreplach, and other traditional tempters. (Closed Fri. p.m., Sat.; ☎ *(71) 247-6001.*)

### The Widow Applebaum's

*46 S. Molton St. W1.* A snack and sandwich noshery on a midtown pedestrian mall. (Remember that "corned beef" becomes "salt beef" in the land of the Picts.)

# EAST INDIAN CURRIES

### Red Fort                                                                ☆☆☆

*77 Dean St. W1V 5HA.* Cool but still exotic, with dishes not often experienced in the west and from remote regions of India; Goa-style fish is one example. (☎ *(71) 437-2525.*)

### Last Days of the Raj                                                    ☆☆☆

*22 Drury Lane WC2.* Can you imagine Indian nouvelle cuisine? Here it is—light and lovely. (Closed Sun. lunch, bank holidays; ☎ *(71) 836-1628.*)

### Bombay Brasserie

*140 Gloucester Rd. SW7 4QH.* Weaves a spell of elegance while producing many delicious specialties. Try the vegetarian highlights. (☎ *(71) 370-4040.*)

### Veeraswamy's

*99-101 Regent St. W1R, with entrance on Swallow St.* Larger than Jamshid and more famous; residents often are cynical about this colorfully decorative old-timer, but year after year I find it provides top value. An Indian friend opined to us, "It suffers from having been the first of its kind in London." (☎ *(71) 734-1401.*)

### Gaylord

*79-81 Mortimer St. W1N 7TB.* Possibly the plushiest exponent of tandoori cookery. This is an overnight marinade of chicken and kebabs baked in a special Indian oven (the "tandoori") and followed by the curry course. (☎ *(71) 636-0808.*)

# ITALIAN

Quite a few have been noted in the foregoing sections, but you might wish to add **La Lupa** *23 Connaught St. W2* and **Trattoria Dei Pescatori** *55-57 Charlotte St. W1P 1LA;* ☎ *580-3289* to your list.

**Portofino**

*Camden Passage N1, the antique district.* A favorite. Excellent cuisine, reasonable prices, fun atmosphere. Remote-from–midcity location but fine if you are antique hunting.

**Pasta Prego**

*La Beauchamp Pl. SW3.* Creates marvelous, light, fresh farinaceous platters for about £2 per serving. About a dozen choices. The Beauchamp Place mats are more inviting than Kew-pads.

## POLISH

**Daquise**

*20 Thurloe St. SW7.* There's a warmhearted tribal feeling at this ancient magnet of Middle Europeanism. If you can avoid the wonders of borscht and piroshki, perhaps you have room for the delicious duck, roasts, or the tempting sweets. Reasonable prices. (☎ *(71) 589-6117.*)

## VEGETARIAN

**Crank's**

*9 Tottenham St. W1P.* This was one of the first major vegetarian restaurants in Europe. Now several more have opened in this excellent chain. Here you can enjoy one of the most savory repasts that botany can provide. Juice bar; cafeteria; health-food kiosk; delicious cookery in nice simple surroundings. A welcome change of viands. (Closed Sun.; ☎ *(71) 631-3912.*)

**Oodles**

*Edgware Rd. W2.* Oodles tries to do similar things, but they come off poorly, in my opinion.

## CHINESE AND ASIAN FOOD

**Tiger Lee**

*251 Old Brompton Rd. SW5 9HP.* Tiger Lee has been, from time to time, one of the most talked about Chinese kitchens in Europe. I still find it distasteful in many respects—from pushy, hard-sell waiters to boring modernistic decor to undistinguished platters at head-thumping tabs (only the host receives the menu with the prices) to myriad mistakes in ordering and billing—which may or may not be intentional. Who needs it? (Closed Dec. 25; ☎ *(71) 370-2323.*)

**Zen**

*Chelsea Cloisters on Sloane Ave. SW3 3DN;* ☎ *(71) 589- 1781,* **Zen Central** *20-22 Queen St. W1X 7PJ;* ☎ *(71) 629-8103,* and **Zen W3** *83 Hampstead High St. NW3 1RE;* ☎ *(71) 794-7863* have developed a following at these three locations. I've tried only the first and that was splendid. Quite fashionable too. How about **Now and Zen**? That's a 3-story tale at *4a Upper St. Martin's Lane, WC2.* Water tumbles through each level down a series of glass plates. Good food but kooky-looky. (☎ *(71) 497-0376.*)

### Ken Lo's Memories of China

*67-69 Ebury St. SW1W 0N3, plus the scenic new one at Chelsea Harbour* and **Poons** *41 King St., in Covent Garden WC2E 8JS* and not the hole-in-the-Chinese-Wall in Soho that also is called Poon's, are recommendable chopstick stops; both are for the up-market trade. Decor smart and refined—like the clientele. (Ken Lo's closed Sun., bank holidays; ☎ *(71) 730-7734*; Poons closed Sun., Dec. 25-26; ☎ *(71) 240-1743.*)

### Lee Ho Fook

*15-16 Gerrard St. W1;* ☎ *(71) 734-9578.* Has a split personality; it is divided into two segments. Though the fancy address wins most of the attention, I've always much preferred the modest and cheaper family nookery just around the corner at 41-43 Wardour St. W1. Look into both, and take your choice.

### Good Friends

*139 Salmon Lane E14 7PG.* An old-timer in Soho. Cantonese dishes at reasonable tariffs. Dull, no-nonsense ambience. On Sunday, popular with Chinese Embassy personnel. (☎ *(71) 987-5541.*)

### Mandarin

*197C Kensington High St. W8.* Authentic Malaysian-Chinese cooking, generally more piquant than Cantonese fare. Marvelous Laksa soup, practically a meal in itself, in £2.50 and £3.50 portions. (☎ *(71) 937-5854.*)

### Poons & Co.

*27 Lisle St. WC2.* Forthright and simple in Soho's China row. Generally superb; wonton soup tasted as if meat filling had been smoked. House delicacies: tangy wind-dried duck, sausage, and beef. The place itself is a dump, but the people are kind, the selection is vast, the prices are low, and the quality is high. (☎ *(71) 437-1528.*)

### Gallery Rendezvous

*55 Beak St. W1;* ☎ *(71) 734-0445.* Despite its unlikely name, specializes in northern fare; it is one of my favorites, as is the same-ownership **Dumpling Inn** *15A Gerrard St. W1;* ☎ *(71) 437-2567* although the staff in the latter seemed to think it was bestowing a favor by serving mere mortals. (**Soho Rendezvous** and **Ley on's** are other members of this tong.)

### Mr. Chow

*151 Knightsbridge SW1X 7PA.* Remains a pacesetter for London's trendy set. I'm not a part of this trend and while I have enjoyed the cookery both here and at its Manhattan precincts, the service in both places has been as low as the prices were high. (Closed bank holidays; ☎ *(71) 589-7347.*)

# JAPANESE

**Saga**

*43 S. Molton St. W1.* Offers a tavern atmosphere with open beams and booths; tables up front and cooking counter farther back; attractively costumed waitresses. The raw fish (very expensive) platter and tempura were excellent. (Closed Sun., bank holidays; ☎ *(71) 408-2236.*)

**Suntory**

*72 St. James's St.* Often considered the most expensive ethnic representative in London (approaching $300). The Imperial Tepanyaki is a feast in a special room. The Kaiseki is superb. Set lunches at £25 and £35, depending on where you sit. Expense-accounters love it.

**Masako**

*6-8 St. Christopher's Place W1M 5HB.* Set in a charming mews amid antique shops and boutiques. Cork walls divided by black enamel beams; red carpets; small stage surrounded by bamboo; excellent sukiyaki, tempura, and many more Nipponese creations. Others in this group include **Sushi-Masa, Nanten, Ginnan, Nankin,** and **Hiroko** of the Kensington Hilton. (Closed Sun., Easter, Christmas, bank holidays; ☎ *(71) 935-1579.*)

# TEA DANCING

**The Waldorf Hotel**

*Aldwych, WC2 B4DD.* Takes a step backward in time each Friday, Saturday, and Sunday from 3:30 to 6:30 p.m. in the Palm Court. It takes some doing to distinguish the performers from the clients. The price is £16.75; other days of the week, tea and snacks here cost £10.50. A more down-market version of the dansant occurs daily at **Cafe De Paris** *3 Coventry St. W1* beginning at 3 p.m. Both can be fun in their manneristic manners, but the tea and nibbles are better at the Waldorf.

**Chelsea Harbour**

The hottest spot in the burgeoning docklands. The central building is in Sing Sing architecture, containing several eateries: The Canteen (very à-la-mode for quality food at low-ish prices; chipper, light-hearted atmosphere, eg., playing cards theme woven into the banquettes), the previously noted **Ken Lo's, Deals** (a noisy tavern with California-style cookery), **Chantegrill** (steakhouse with a salad table and heaps of flowers), and the **Waterfront** (oyster bar plus many Italian choices). Take a stroll in the marina afterward. (*Harbour Yard SW10*; closed Sun. p.m.; ☎ *(71) 376-3232.*)

## AUTHOR'S OBSERVATION

*Covent Garden, the central London complex that features its renowned Opera House, today blossoms with scores of restaurants and shops. The fun here is plucking just the flower that suits your mood.*

## SNACKS

### Deals West
*14-16 Foubert's Pl., W1.* A mock-Tex rancho for yuppy-yi-yis. It looks like the set of Wagon's West, but the grub is good and the Hi-ho Sloane Rangers love it. (☎ *(71) 287-1001.*)

### Pasta Mania
*1 Cranbourne St. WC2.* It's all-you-can-eat pasta for £3—if you're voracious for something farinaceous.

### Wimpy
Though not a favorite, this is the most mammoth restaurateur in the U.K.; 306 shops in London and as many nationwide. Routine in every way, as the American counterparts in this global bunfest.

### Upstairs/Downstairs
*Basil St. SW3 (just a few paces from Harrods).* Downstairs counter and wine bar; make your selection, pay, get a chit, retrieve your food. Delicious dish of the day about £2; other good selections at £1; wine by bottle or glass. Upstairs more airy; huge all you-can-eat salad board (your choice for £2); cafeteria-style service; £3 for full lunch. Both open noon-3 p.m. and 5:30-11 p.m.; closed Sun.

### Granary
*39 Albemarle St., W1.* Serve-yourself counter-style. At least a half dozen types of quiches. Wonderful midday stop. Open till 7 p.m.; closes Sat. 2:30 p.m. and all day Sun.

### Rowley's
*113 Jermyn St. W1;* ☎ *(71) 930-2707 Branch: 38 Beauchamp Pl. SW3;* ☎ *(71) 589-4856.* Great, provided you enjoy its lone specialty— grilled entrecote in Cafe de Paris sauce, served with French fries, salad, a rich dessert, and wine poured from magnums (charge depends on how much you drink). Feast for 2 will absorb £18.

### Gatsby's
*South Molton St. W1.* Just across from the Widow Applebaums. Not so kosher but conventional light meals substantial, prices low, and atmosphere subtle. In the same house where William Blake resided (he often noshed with Applebaum).

### Creperie
*Down the mall and in an alley on the same side as The Widow A's.* Enormous selection of buckwheat crepes. Apple-and-calvados was a petit package of pure culinary bliss. Other items available, but stick to low-cost house specialties.

### The Museum Tavern
*49 Great Russell St. WC1, opposite the British Museum.* Collects sandwich-hungry culture-vultures. Cut-price lunches in an animated atmosphere. Good beer.

### Hard Rock Cafe

*150 Old Park Lane W1Y 3LN.* A smash-hit for the young but hardly for the impoverished. Loud taped music; burgers; American beers; grilled steaks; chili; hot fudge sundaes; apple pie a la mode. Dinner for two with house wine about £25, which makes it—perhaps with the newer Planet Hollywood—one of the world's more expensive hamburger joints. The built-in chic bumps up the price tags. Open noon till after midnight daily. ( ☎ *(71) 629-0382.*)

## FISH-AND-CHIPS

This is one of the best budget meals going. Chips, as you probably know, is the anglicism for lightly fried potatoes, sometimes in the form of French fries and occasionally appearing as hash browns. Hundreds of counters dot the townscape, chiefly in working districts where the clients often walk away from the stalls bearing cones of wax paper filled with these ingredients and topped with tartar sauce or ketchup. The better kiosks feature haddock, plaice, cod, and the poor cousins of sole. Cheaper dens often utilize dogfish, skate, and shavings of ray. Here are a few choices.

### The Rock and Sole Plaice

*47 Endell St. WC2.* Obviously puts its menu into its title. If you are in the Covent Garden area, it is handy and agreeable.

### Sweetings

*39 Queen Victoria St. EC4.* Realizes that even habitues of the banking district must economize occasionally. It is amusing to see sartorially perfect executives with copies of the *Financial Times* daintily digesting their chippies with absolute aplomb. Evidently, this "joint" is a bit more upmarket than most.

### Upper Street Fish Shop

*324 Upper St. N1.* Handy to the antique grazing lands of Islington and Camden Passage. An ideal excursion. Browse among the whatnot stalls on Saturday morning and take lunch here.

### Sea Shell

*49-51 Lisson Grove NW1 6UH.* Offers top-quality sole from the Dover coast as well as more modest wigglers. The variety is in full flood at every meal. Don't miss the fish cakes. (Closed Sun.-Mon; ☎ *(71) 723-8703.*)

## CHAINS

### Strand Hotels Group

*Regent Palace, Strand Palace,* and *Cumberland hotels.* Offers "Carveries"; all you can eat for perhaps £12. After the appetizer tuck into at least six choices of hot or cold roasts. Appetizing presentation; coffee included. Excellent value.

## DRINKS

The celebrated **Public House**—"pub," for short—traditionally has been the heartbeat of England. On one side you'll find the **Public Bar**—plain, utilitarian, for drinkers who want no nonsense. On the other side, with a separate entrance, is the **Saloon Bar**—better decorated, more comfortable, the one you'll probably head for. Prices are usually a trifle higher in the latter. Then, of course, there are three styles of classic pubs: **City Tavern** (spirits and wine featured above draught beers), **Gin Palace** (typically Victorian if authentic), and **Alehouse** (plain, ancient, and historic).

As for what to order, there are three major British brews: **mild ale** ("mild"), a medium-sweet, medium-brown, inexpensive choice that is becoming more rare in central London; **bitter beer** ("bitter"), a pale brown, heavier variety; and **Burton** ("old"), which is deep brown, quite sweet, and richest of all. Burton is available September and June only. Incidentally, if you happen to hear that a British friend "has gone for a Burton" it will not be to satisfy a thirst. It means the poor chap has gone to his Maker.

English beer had been getting devoted tipplers into a froth because the size of the head was never officially controlled (costing drinkers an estimated £225 million per year in suds). Now publicans must use a government-approved glass with a line to indicate a full pint of liquid. Naturally, the fair shake will cost money; so figure on paying a splash more for your pint than the usual sum of about £1.60 in the London area. Brewers generally are lowering the alcohol content of their products in order to hold the line on rising costs.

**Beer**, **gin**, **rum**, and liqueurs are plentiful and good; **Scotch** is costly (and it's weaker than that which reaches the U.S.). You'll pay £1.30 for a "small" (understatement of the year) and perhaps £2.20 for a "large" (junior-size) portion in today's London.

**English wine**. Local viticulture gradually is coming to harvest—a very slow process if you consider that the Romans, the Normans, and the British of the Middle Ages had vines growing all over London. Today, Harrods carries a sampling of the 140 products from England's commercial vineyards. Some of the more notable names include *Beaulieu, Felsted, Pilton Manor, Hambledon, Kelsale, Hascombe, Cavendish Manor, Lamberhurst,* and *Chilsdown.* I doubt that you'll become addicted.

**AUTHOR'S OBSERVATION**

*Don't drive a car if you have consumed even as little as two pints of beer! Under the mercilessly stringent provisions of the Road Safety Act, the vehicle operator doesn't have to be drunk to face huge fines, four months in the pokey (or both), and loss of his or her license for one year. Suspects are required to take a roadside "Breathalyser" test. There is no recourse for either resident or visitor. The police are tough, too.*

# CHARACTERISTIC PUBS

### Cockney Pride

*Jermyn St. SW1.* Large cellar room festooned with cornball Victorianism; old-fashioned horseshoe bar offering such Olde England standards as faggots (mincemeat-and-peas pudding), toad-in-the-hole (sausages in batter pudding), shepherd's pie, and many more historic tidbits—all priced at a pittance. Waiters in fancy vests and bowlers; waitresses in long Gay Nineties gowns; player piano tinkling in the background.

### Red Lion

*48 Parliament St. SW1.* A favorite with students from Guys Hospital. The Public Bar is on Parliament Street, the Saloon Bar on Derby Gate. Downstairs is best; no darts; ladies welcome.

### Antelope

*Eaton Terrace.* A gem—not too moldy, not too chichi, a gentle introduction to the science of pubbery. Prices higher than average but still low; excellent for a plain, cheerful dinner.

### Prospect of Whitby

*57 Wapping Wall E1.* Like the **Cheshire Cheese** (where you should be sure to sit at Samuel Johnson's table) and the **George and Vulture,** is a tavern drawing huge numbers of tourists rather than a true pub. It once installed a Hawaiian band and a singer—to me, the ultimate abomination in these ancient English surroundings. Hangout of students who are sometimes rowdy. Dock area; rambling, helter-skelter building raised in 1520; Pepys Room for dining; stuffed alligator, human skull, and other oddities suspended over bar. Closed Sun. (**Dirty Dick's** and **The George** also attract droves of rubberneckers.)

### Sherlock Holmes Tavern

*Northumberland St. WC2.* A so-called museum tavern. On the ground floor, you'll find the main bar, a scattering of tables, and, as wall decorations, a fascinating collection of "memorabilia" from his most famous "cases" (a plaster mold of a "paw print" of the hound of the Baskervilles, Detective Lestrade's "handcuffs," the "code" used in the story of the dancing men, etc.); to the side there's a painfully plain little nook for the earnest toper. Upstairs is the grill, with tapestried wall coverings and white banquettes; to the rear of this section is a glassed-off montage of the famous fictional sitting room shared by the great sleuth and Dr. Watson at "221B Baker St." Food adequate for pub (not restaurant) level.

### Dickens Inn

*St. Katherine's Docks E1, near the Tower of London.* The quay area stirs merrily with life aboard several Thames barges and scores of recreation boats. The restaurant is located upstairs in an ancient warehouse that was moved on wheels to this colorful site. The neighboring **Beefeater** is chiefly for dining and a touristic type of cabaret evening.

### The Buccaneer

*Leicester Sq. WC2.* An imposing example of its namesake. There's a galleon theme floating on a Polynesian undercurrent.

Not enough? Then try these: For visual appeal, the **Admiral Codrington** *Mossop St. SW3*; for filmmakers, the **Intrepid Fox** *Wardour St. W1*; for doctors, the **Crown** *in Chelsea*; for rowing enthusiasts, **The Dove** *19 Upper Mall W6*; for oldtime smugglers, **Anchor** *1 Bankside, Southwark SE1*; for world travelers, the **Fitzroy** *Charlotte St.*; for cinema types, **The Victoria** *10a Strathearn Pl.W2*; for experimental theater, **The King's Head** *the back room at 115 Upper St. N1 in the antique district of Islington*; for Egyptologists, the **Museum Tavern** *49 Great Russell St. WC1*; for members of Parliament, the **St. Stephen's Tavern** *just a skip from Westminster SW1* (listen for the bell—a signal that a vote is about to be taken in the Commons).

## WINE BARS

Doubtless these are beginning to supplant the pubs. These colorful oases serve quiches, goulash, cold meats, pates, and cheeses, generally in the range of £3 per platter. An overwhelming variety of fair-quality wine is on hand for prices that vary with the quantity you order (pitcher or individual glass); fortified pressings are also on tap. In most cases they function from 11:30 a.m. till 3 p.m. and 5:30 till 11 p.m.; some remain open later and on Sun.; the hours are extremely variable. Although tipping is not expected in pubs, it is definitely required in wine bars, especially when food is consumed; 10% is considered reasonable.

### Le Metro

*28 Basil St. SW3.* The most talked about conversation pit in London, is downstairs in L'Hotel. A wine bar with super food that is supervised by the Capital chef. Top-grade vintages are available by the glass.

### Ebury

*139 Ebury St. SW1.* Occupies the ground floor of a converted early Victorian house with walls of dark green wash and cream paint. The salads are excellent. One nice feature: tables can be reserved.

### Cork & Bottle

*44-46 Cranbourn St. WC2.* Reached through a garden gate and composed of two adjoining cellars. Its owner strives to add adventure to the cookery. A good candidate for a pre-theater nip.

### Penguin

*7 Cheval Pl. SW7.* Popular with young people who don't seem to be bothered by unloosened purse strings. Costly.

### Fino's Wine Cellar

*123 Mount St. W1.* Approached by a steep staircase beneath its stained-glass and wooden canopy. The bar is long and narrow, with small recesses for those who may collapse in obscurity. Very "in" with the advertising world.

# COUNTRY DINING NEAR LONDON

All the following are easy excursions on a sunny day.

### L'Ortolan           ☆☆☆☆☆

*On Church Lane in the village of Shinfield (near Reading)* is my choice for the top British restaurant in this category; certainly it stands proudly against any offerings on the Continent too. Elegant country house and garden; bar lounge just off entrance; lawn tables for sunny days; inner salons plus an airy, charming conservatory. John Burton-Race is a young genius whose gifts are revealed in the composition, the exquisite presentation, and the harmonious yet complex evocations of his kitchen. As he is continually experimenting, the dishes change with frequency. His amiable French wife Christine can help you decide on a cascade of jewel-like combinations from his modern masterworks. Cold stoves Sunday evenings and all Mondays; best to phone for a table: ☎ *(0734) 883783.* Watch this one for stellar recognition.

### Gravetye Manor         ★★★★★

*Refer to "East Grinstead," (West Sussex) where it is not, but where it is near.* To get there, take A-22 (the Eastbourne Road); about 7 miles past Godstone, at the crossroads, turn right on B-2028 to Turner's Hill. Advance reservations advised; if you get lost, ☎ *(0342) 810567* and a St. Bernard with a packed hamper will be promptly dispatched.

### The Compleat Angler

*At Marlow, Buckinghamshire (31 miles)* with riverside or garden-front bedrooms and private baths. This inn—with its famous but not terribly inspired Valaison restaurant and cheerful bar—which sits beside a peaceful view on the Thames, reaches a pinnacle of pastoral beauty. It had hit a dry spell for some years, but now that Trust House Forte is the gillie, you are possibly going to see better results soon. My latest try at the tables was dismal, however.

## BERKSHIRE

### Ye Olde Bell            ★

*Hurley (32 miles; about 30 minutes beyond Northold on M-4).* Dates from A.D. 1135; for overnighters, 25 rooms and Trust House Forte supervision. It's oozing with lazy charm; sound but not top-London-class fare yet it is charging top London-class prices; limited selections. (☎ *(0628)82 4244.*)

### Waterside Inn          ☆☆☆☆

*Bray (31 miles).* An evergreen veteran, a training ground for great young chefs and a frequent shrine for gourmets. A recent sampling proved to be superb, but there have been less glorious moments. The experience of going is enchanting—and the food can be, too. Reserve ahead. (☎ *(0628) 20691*; FAX: *784-710.*)

### The Great House

*In Sonning-on-Thames (36 miles), a captivating rural village.* Enjoy country roast beef while watching the boats skim past. Reserve ahead of time. (☎ *(0734) 692277)*

### French Horn

*In Sonning-on-Thamex (36 miles), a captivating rural village.* Across the bridge from Great House, (more costy) with a better river view, but the specialities are more continental. Reserve ahead at both.

### King's Head

*At Church Rd. in Little Marlow (5 miles from Maidenhead).* Still another worthy destination on a clear day. (☎ *(0628) 484408.*)

### Little Angel

*In Remenham (36 miles).* A cozy and genial retreat across the bridge from Henley; solid, unelaborate cookery; nice clientele. (Closed Sun. p.m. and Mon.; ☎ *(0491) 574165.*)

### Skindles Hotel

*Maidenhead (27 miles).* Once the pick of the area, has skidded in my view. No longer recommended.

### Bel and the Dragon ★★★

☎ *(06285) 21263.* Has resided in Cookham Village since the reign of Henry V, early in the 15th century. It is constructed of wattle and daub, with plenty of open beams, signets of age, and cozy warmth. Easygoing atmosphere; fair cuisine; medium prices. "Bel" incidentally, is derived from the name of a Babylonian idol. Even if you don't dine here, do stop for a drink in the bar and look around.

## BEDFORDSHIRE

### Paris House ★★★

*42 miles.* Located beautifully inside famous Woburn Park. Distinguished cuisine in a stately setting. (Closed Mon.; also Sun. eves in winter, all Feb.; ☎ *(0525) 290692.*)

## SURREY

**Mayflower Hotel** *Cobham (19 miles)* is a plush oasis for the Hungry Man; also nice here is the **Talbot**, which boasts ownership of Nelson's chair. **Whyte Harte** *Bletchingley (22 miles)* is a 14th-century inn with old beams, open fireplaces, and better-than-routine vittles. The **Old Bell** *Oxted (22 miles)* is another inn of the same vintage without quite the flavor of the Whyte Harte, but very pleasant all the same. **Onslow Arms** *West Clandon near Guildford (about 30 miles)* is a 1623 roadside hostelry thick with atmosphere, and mellow with its Free House varieties of beer, ale, and porter. (Closed Sun. p.m., Mon., Dec. 26; ☎ *(0483) 222447.*) **Great Fosters** *Egham (18 miles)* features a unique four-centuries-old garden and 23 guest rooms for lovers of antiquities and service. (☎ *(0784) 33822.*)

## SUSSEX

**The Maltravers** *Arundel (58 miles)* is in the forefront with its gastronomic delights, its furnishings of rare antiques and fine paintings, and its unusual policy, for rural establishments, of staying open until 11 p.m. or after; closed Mon.; as good as ever.

# NIGHT LIFE

London's nightscape—as in Paris, New York, Hamburg, and a host of other cities where the moon is better known than the sun—is one of the fastest-changing in the world. Entertainment establishments rise and fall so swiftly that even the most up-to-tonight tip sheets have difficulty keeping au courant. If you are looking for something special, ask the night hall porter at your hotel.

The expensive **Royal Roof** of the Royal Garden Hotel gracefully combines sophistication and well-trained staffers with a fine flair for theatrics. Beautiful presentation of the Royal Strings, a harmonic blend of seven violins, a guitar, and an accordion that plays en masse for several numbers, then the musicians individually stroll among the diners while maintaining perfect melodic unison; 20-minute performances at 11 p.m. and midnight.

### Tiberio

*22 Queen St. W1X 7PJ.* Offers most of its glitter in the celebs who attend. Piano tunes during dinner; live quartet for dancing. Kitchen work chiefly Italian. (Closed Sat. lunch, Sun.; ☎ *(71) 629-3561.*)

### Elysee

*13 Percy St.* A haven that effuses a Hellenic charm all its own. The decor is routine, but when the crowd is right it's delightfully lively. Big Greek patronage—and what people are merrier? Ground Floor with 15 tables, a small bar and dance floor, three to four musicians (bouzouki and accordion). Summer roof garden for nearly 100 midday or evening munchers, some of whom spontaneously leap up to provide impromptu entertainment; hours noon to 3 p.m. and 6:30 p.m. to 3 a.m. (☎ *636-4804.*)

Among the hotels, the **Savoy**, the **Inn on the Park** (Vintage Room only), the **Hilton**, and **Grosvenor House** all offer the Light Fantastic in their restaurants (separate from their grills); **Claridge's** doesn't believe in all that jazz.

## PRIVATE AND CHIC

Ask friends to squeeze you in to **Groucho's, Ormond's, Regine's** (only a stagger from veteran **Annabel's**), **Stringfellows**, or **Tramps**. More for dining than for nighting are **Brooks's, Boodle's**, and **Whites; Kit-Cat** is the society leader for women only. All of these are in the forefront of the London scene. You'll need local sponsorship and perhaps $400 if you wish to join. (Temporary membership is less if they permit it.)

# GAMBLING

Almost everything goes except pitch-and-toss—a game played by miners that all too quickly can involve staggering sums. The British casino doesn't have much truck with slot machines (fruit machines, in local parlance); the fancier clubs scorn them. Horses, dogs, football, the gender of an expected royal heir—just name it, and somebody will snap up your wager, but usually in one of England's 2000 licensed betting offices. Better bring cash or traveler's checks, not personal checks, if you plan to play. Some houses are stricter than others about this. Stringent laws now require visitors to register in advance at the clubs where they wish to gamble.

## AUTHOR'S OBSERVATION

*Pick your place carefully, especially if you roll 'em high!*

*Meal and spirits services follow the rules governing pubs (now much more liberal than in former years); no alcohol is libated at the gaming tables; hours also can vary with the neighborhood, so it would be wise to check first if you wish to imbibe at gaming tables.*

### Victoria

*150-162 Edgware Rd. W2.* Possibly the largest contender in the British Isles or Europe, might be termed a "gambling factory" production-belt operation that woos "mass" (vs. "class") patronage; first floor featuring blackjack, roulette (London's wheels have only one zero, not two), and chemin de fer; second level offering gin rummy and kaluki (13-card rummy); slot machines; restaurant service from lunch to breakfast. Only this house and the **Sportsman** *Tottenham Court Rd.* offer craps in London (with slightly more favorable odds than in the U.S.).

### Clermont Club

*44 Berkeley Sq. W1.* With 85% of its 5000 disciples from overseas, known to be chic. The stakes are high and the membership is ultra-exclusive.

### Rendezvous

*The Hilton.* Lures many Middle Easterners.

Historic and famous **Crockford's**, *30 Curzon St. W1*, is operated by Curzon House. It's a staple.

Other choices in this group include the **Charlie Chester Casino**, *12 Archer St.*, functioning noon to you-name-it, with roulette, blackjack, and Las Vegas dice and the **Golden Nugget**, *22 Shaftesbury Ave.*, six types of play. None of these measures up to the establishments listed above. Still other boxcar candidates include a casino in the **Sheraton Park Tower**; one operates in the cellar of the **Ritz** (refer back to "Hotels"), where the French Salon features blackjack, American roulette, and punto blanco.

## DISCOTHEQUES

These, of course, are among the most perishable of all institutions in the entertainment field. They pop up quickly (generally with insufficient investment capital), stay "in" for a short lifetime, and fold up when the "chic" crowd takes its fickle fancies elsewhere.

**Groucho's** is, as ever, the talk of the town but, as I've just mentioned, it is private, exclusive, and occasionally by invitation of the management.

**Shaftesbury's** seems to be the focal point tonight. A modest fee is charged to enter (higher on weekends), but whatever the fee, it will be long remembered back in Duluth. Food and beverages stretch the imagination for exotica. **Gullivers**, *15 Garton St. W1*, is more upbeat than its address might suggest. **Studio Valbonne**, *62 Kingly St. W1*, with excellent music for dancers, is averred to stage topless waitresses around a swimming pool. **Miranda**, across the street, is popular at lunchtime with well-groomed gents from the financial district. **Hippodrome, Le Palais**, and **Curzon** also seem to hang in there as stalwarts.

## TOP SHOPS

### HOURS FOR SHOPS

In general, 9 a.m.-6 p.m. with some Sat. closings at 1 p.m. and others at 5:30 p.m. Large department stores, as well as other shops, open one specific weeknight (Thurs. on Oxford St., Regent St., Bond St., Kensington High St.; Wed. at Harrods in Knightsbridge and on King's Road and Sloane Sq.); smaller shops in Chelsea, Soho, and similar districts close at 1 p.m. on Thur., but are usually open all day Sat.; shops at Covent Garden open 10 a.m.-8 p.m. Mon. through Sat.; although everything used to be shuttered on Sun.; except for a few delicatessens, a scattering of food shops (mornings only), and a handful of all-night drugstores ("chemists"), an increasing number of small merchants are keeping their doors open then. If in doubt, it is advisable to check before setting out.

### SPECIAL SALES

A bonanza twice a year: after Christmas and late June, extending into July. Planeloads of bargain hunters fly into London for these three-ring circuses, and their purchases save enough to pay their plane fare. At Harrods you'll even find eager shoppers camping on the doorstep overnight waiting for the morning stampede.

### PUBLIC HOLIDAYS

Jan. 1, (Good Friday), (Easter Monday), May Day (May 3), Spring Holiday (May 30), Late Summer Holiday (Aug. 29), Dec. 25-26.

### A GUIDE TO SIZES

British women's clothes are one size larger than North American. Women's shoes: 1-1/2 sizes smaller. Men's trousers: one size larger. Men's shoes: 1-1/2 sizes smaller. Hats: one-eighth smaller. The following items are equal in size: men's suits, shirts, pajamas, collars, and

any measurements given in inches such as bust sizes. Now that Britain
has partially gone over to the metric system, clothing size tags show
centimeters as well as inches.

## DUTY-FREE PURCHASES

Upon presenting their passports, overseas visitors may buy clothes and
most other goods free of the 17.5% Purchase Tax. Retailers make
over-the-counter sales on this basis, provided the buyers carry all of these
items and the accompanying documents in their hand luggage, produce
them for inspection by the Departure Customs (whose officials will sign
the forms, which then must be mailed back to the stores, which will later
send a refund of the tax), and export them within a three month period.
V.A.T. (Value-Added Tax) is also returned on purchases shipped overseas
but often, in this case, the price quoted is the export price on which the tax
is already deducted—saving on the paperwork. Merchants are under no ob-
ligation whatsoever to offer this service. If they do, legally they may deduct
a modest sum from the refund to cover their costs. Since a large number of
the leading establishments do subscribe, however, be sure to inquire when
your purchases are substantial. (The minimum amount you must buy to be
eligible for these rebates has been see-sawing, so check locally at the time
of your visit.)

Now, an alternative V.A.T. refund system is operational. Tourist Tax
Free Shopping (with its red, white, and blue stickers) is one service. Participating stores will display the emblem to show they are associated with it.

Vouchers have been simplified and can be issued for as little as £40.
Once stamped by Customs, all the forms can be returned in one envelope
to the company, and the refund is made quickly by one check to the purchaser's home address in his own currency or to a credit card account. The
rebate is minus a small administrative handling charge.

Europe Tax Free Shopping has made it very easy for airline passengers to
claim their refunds. If you are departing from any of Heathrow Airport's
four terminals, look for their booths, always located near Customs. They
are open 6 a.m.-midnight and return the tax to you right away upon presentation of your receipts. This goes for purchases made in countries other
than Britain, so it's really a useful service.

## ORDERING BY MAIL

Large-scale mail-order traffic was in full bloom here at least a century
before it became big business in North America. Over the long span when
the Sun Never Set on the Empire, it provided a vital lifeline to English,
Scottish, and Welsh purveyors for colonists from Borneo to Honduras to
Hudson Bay to Somaliland to hundreds of other far-flung outposts.
Hence, however odd the request, a proper English merchant will wrap it
and send it to you.

**Chinacraft's** nearly 100-page color catalog shows off their merchandise
to perfection. Write to them at Parke House, 130 Barlby Rd., London
W10 6BW to obtain it, or for even speedier attention you can phone in England ☎ *(81) 960-1100*; Telex: *923550* or FAX: *(81) 960-9232*. This firm

provides outstanding service to the customer, and I think you could not do better.

The 264-year-old **House of Floris**, Perfumers to Her Majesty and Manufacturers of Toilet Preparations to His Royal Highness the Prince of Wales, would be pleased to post to you a fully illustrated catalog of their extensive range of glorious English flower perfumes, toilet waters, bath essences, soaps, and much more.

**Halcyon Days** issues free color catalogs displaying their antiques and contemporary collectors' items, and they take great care to expedite orders efficiently. **The Irish Shop** has brochures available that they'll send at no cost to you upon request. The famous **House of Burberry** and the charming-to-its-roots **General Trading Company (Mayfair) Ltd.** both guarantee safe arrival at your doorstep of everything processed through their seasoned Export Departments. The latter will mail you their tempting general and Christmas catalog for the equivalent of £2 plus handling charges.

**Dunhill** for smokes and **Foyle's** for books both have active mail departments. **Gidden** can outfit both horse and rider with their handcrafted tack by (what else?) posting. **Frank Smythson Ltd.** is one of the world's prestige names in stationery, pads, and fine leather desk equipment; ask for the documentation. **Eximious** offers a galaxy of giftware—and, even better than ordering through the U.K., it features a Stateside facility for greater convenience (with dollar quotations too!). Write P.O. Box 8455, Winnetka, IL 60093 or ☎ *(312) 446-8171.*

## WHERE TO BUY

London can be divided roughly into seven main precincts: (1) **Oxford St.** (big department stores, chain operations, and boutiques), (2) **Regent St.** (more department stores and specialty shops), (3) **Bond St.** (high fashion, jewelry, and exclusive luxury items), (4) **Kensington High St.** (boutiques, chain stores, antiques), (5) **King's Rd., Sloane Sq.,** and **Fulham Rd.** (youthful fashions, oddments, and "in" articles), (6) **Knightsbridge** (Harrods and Harvey Nichols, the two most exclusive department stores, other top-name shops and fashionable boutiques), and (7) **Covent Garden** (a potpourri).

When the Conran interests rehabilitated the Michelin Building, an architectural landmark of an earlier era, **Brompton Cross** was born. It's where Brompton Road meets **Fulham Road**; suddenly this junction has taken on star quality. A rather different restoration program is underway in the Docklands district as part of an entire urban renewal scheme. Merchants both large and small have set up at **St. Katharine Docks**, near Tower Hill, and most recently at **Tobacco Dock**, close to Tower Bridge, and the **Hays** Galleria, a complex in the shadow of London Bridge. All are realities, but there is more to come. Riverbus service, the Docklands Light Railway, and extensions to the London Underground system will create easy access to these rather out-of-the-way zones. Right at the center of things, a far cry from Thames River activity, is the **London Pavilion** building at Piccadilly Circus. This rejuvenated old edifice now contains three floors of shopping possibilities.

## *HELPFUL PREPARATION*

Early in your visit, you may wish to make a reconnaissance to either or all of the exhibits at the **Design Center** (*28 Haymarket*), **Contemporary Applied Arts** (*43 Earlham St., Covent Garden*) and the **Crafts Council Gallery** (*12 Waterloo Pl., Regent St.*). Each dispenses information on where you can obtain their products. The first is a showcase especially assembled for goods intended to interest the import-export trades. It is run by the Design Council, which in turn receives much of its support from the Department of Trade and Industry. Admission is free; there are three floors of items all of which are for sale plus a register of thousands of British goods—many samples, too. The second shows textiles, pottery, furniture, glass, lighting, and pieces of jewelry by artists and designers who usually work for themselves. Slides are on file and the information center augments their new Commissioning Service. The last offers another index craftsmen, a slide library, research facilities, and an education department. It sells cards, posters, brochures, craft books, magazines, and catalogs.

**Antique Fairs** form another aspect of the art market scene. Four of the most widely known and well respected include: (1) **Arms Fair** (*Royal Lancaster Hotel, Bayswater Rd. W 1; May and Sept.; an armory of military paraphernalia*), (2) **Chelsea Antiques Fair** (*Chelsea Old Town Hall, King's Rd. S.W.3; Mar. and Sept.; all categories of goods*), (3) **Fine Art and Antique Fair of Great Britain** (*National Hall, Olympia, Hammersmith Rd. W.6; June; merchandise of varying caliber and wide-ranging prices*), (4) **Grosvenor House Antiques Fair** (*Grosvenor House Hotel, Park Lane; from second Wednesday in June; top-grade specimens with equivalent prices*).

The greatest variety of antique markets at decent prices is found in the permanent indoor installations. Here, the dealers know their business and the competition is keen. The two oldest are the **Chelsea Antique Market** (*253 King's Rd.*) and the **Antique Supermarket** (*3 Barrett St.*)—neither of which, in my view, is nearly as good as **Alfie's** on Church St., Marylebone. Each contains at least 100 stalls. Many articles cost less than £50. **Gray's Antique Market** (*58 Davies St. and the adjoining 1-7 Davies Mews*) is a maze of stalls with a stream running through the hall. Anything from jewelry to lace to books to oogah horns will be on display. Great fun for browsers. **Antiquarias** (*135 King's Rd.*) is more trendy and generally more expensive.

The open-air street markets are greater fun. The **Portobello Road Market** (*Notting Hill Gate tube station start at the Westbourne Grove end*) famous for its Collectors' Corner, **Islington's Angel Market** (both Sat. only), and **Islington's Camden Passage** (Wed. and Sat. mornings) are currently the hottest bets among hunters in the know; the last, founded when 12 friends got together, has blossomed into importance. Historic **Petticoat Lane** (*Liverpool St., Aldgate, Aldgate East tube Stations*), around Middlesex St. (Sun. morning only until 2 p.m.) is often characterized as the old clothes exchange of London. Finally, the **Bermondsey Market** (*Bermondsey Sq., just south of Tower Bridge, Friday mornings*) is a lodestone for dealers rather than for visitors, and often dazzling fresh shipments from the country are put on sale here at ridiculously low tariffs. The catch is that to be successful you must be on the scene around 5 a.m. At **Camden Lock** (*Camden High St., and Chalk Farm Rd.; Sat. and Sun. 9:30 a.m.-5:30 p.m.*) crafts, clothes and antiques appear.

The **London Architectural Salvage and Supply Company Ltd.** (*Lasco Mark St., off Paul St.*) is for homebuilders as well as homemakers. Need old doors, banisters, grills, knockers, knobs, hinges, or moldings? Hire a container and fill 'er up.

For items related to the performing arts—books, pictures, and paraphernalia—the stage is **Cecil Court**, an alley behind St. Martin's Lane fringing the theater district. The boutiques are minuscule.

**Fulham Road** and **King's Road**, Chelsea, are for those who can afford sentimentality in the more costly bracket; **Beauchamp Place** (pronounced "Beecham"), just off Knightsbridge, is another choice. **Westbourne Grove, Kensington Church St.**, and **Notting Hill Gate** are other targets. At 19 Marylebone Lane, the **Button Queen** (antique buttons) is amusing.

Where should you bargain? In all markets and in all holes-in-the-wall that carry second-line merchandise—but never in the top-notch places, so haggle your hardest and stand your ground most resolutely there.

**The London and Provincial Antique Dealers' Association, Ltd.**, known as LAPADA, can supply you with lists of all their members and their specialties arranged by areas. Write to Heather Collingwood at *535 King's Rd., London SW 10* or ☎ *(71) 823-3511* or *FAX (71) 823-3522* them.

## FURNITURE, LINENS, KITCHENWARE AND GIFTS

The General Trading Company (*144 Sloane St., Sloane Sq., London, 10 Argyle St., Bath, and 2-4 Dyer St., Cirencester*) lives up to its name perfectly. And it's a joy. Occupying four elegant Victorian terraced houses, GTC evokes a unique and urbane atmosphere. Established in 1920 and owned by the Part family, this shop has a deserved reputation for well-chosen and carefully selected merchandise to suit the eclectic. Its English period pieces, prints, pewter, accessories, china, and *objets d'art* are displayed in softspoken, traditional surroundings while the modern furnishings are shown in a more contemporary setting. There is a comprehensive collection of bone china and porcelain tableware from Royal Worcester, Spode, Wedgwood, Herend, and many others, as well as fine glassware both collectible and functional. For the keen gardener, there's a Burbank of choices as well as the Garden Cafe, run by Justin de Blank. As a quintessentially English establishment, GTC proudly displays its four Royal Warrants. Export packing and shipping can be arranged to anywhere in the world; mail-order catalog available.

If General Trading doesn't have what you're hunting for, try famous, two-century-old **Asprey** (*165-169 New Bond St.*) for anything from an Adam fireplace to a gold swizzle stick to Ringo Starr-designed chess and backgammon sets to historical figures in porcelain. **Algernon** (*27 Bruton Pl.*) comes up with an interesting span from antiquities to contemporary pieces. In the very top leagues there is **Bernheimer Fine Arts Ltd.** (*32 St.*

*George St.*) of Munich fame. Here is a treasure house of antique furniture, sculpture, Chinese art, carpets, tapestries and textiles.

**Nina Campbell** (*9 Walton St.*) and **Colefax and Fowler** (*39 Brook St.*) are rightfully well regarded. **Eldridge of London** (*99-101 Farringdon Rd.*) has been a well-kept secret for years—as specialists in original 18th- and 19th-century furniture. Schedule time at **Thomas Goode Co.** (*19 S. Audley St.*) for traditional china, or **Peter Jones** (*Sloane Sq.*), **John Lewis** (*Oxford St.*), or **Heal's** (*Tottenham Court Rd.*) for modern china or glass. The area around Kensington Church St. is an especially good hunting ground for antique porcelain and pottery. **Wedgwood** and **Worcester** have showrooms, respectively at *34 Wigmore St.* and *30 Curzon St.*; arrangements may be made in both to visit their factories.

## ART PRINTS AND PAINTINGS

**Stephanie Hoppen** (*17 Walton St.*) is both the person (charming, too) and the legend behind this name. The works (collected usually from great private estates) can be seen in a homelike salon setting, framed and often hung with a motif in mind. Many subjects are available, and you may even order a theme that Stephanie can possibly find for you somewhere across the face of Europe. Locales also at *Suite 1000, 305 E. 61st, New York, NY* and at *9 Sultan St.* in Toronto.

## AUCTIONS AND ART GALLERIES

**Sotheby's** (*34-35 New Bond St.*) and **Christie's** (*8 King St., St. James's*) are the world's greatest auction rooms, as everybody knows. The latter is more than 200 years old. Consult their listings in the London newspapers for what is being sold during your visit. As a rule, the most important sales occur in July and December. **Phillips** (*7 Blenheim St., off Bond St.*) reliable and good, vends less expensive things than those of the Big Two; they specialize in antique furniture; its sales days are Mon. and Fri. **Bonham & Sons, Montpelier Galleries** (*Montpelier St.*) is also crowding the peacemakers. For more than 75 years, **Glendining & Co.** (*7 Blenheim St.*) has specialized in placing on the block small objects such as military medals, decorations, coins, commemorative medals, and the like. Although the by-laws of these houses prohibit them from issuing certificates of authenticity, their staffs are totally honest in their advice to their clients. Please never hesitate to seek this; it is entirely expected of bidders, regardless of the sum involved. Then set your limit, and stick by it.

As for straight galleries, try **Arthur Tooth Co.** (*Bruton St.*) and **Leger Galleries** (*13 Old Bond St.*) as two of the choicest for paintings only; **Ackerman** (*33 New Bond St.*) for fine equine oils, prints, and sculptures; **Harra Gallery** (next to the Hotel Connaught) for Impressionists onward: **Colnaghi** (*14 Bond St.*) for Old Masters to the present; and **Michael Parkin** (*11 Motcomb St.*) for English works from 1850-1950.

## BOOKS

**Foyle** (*133-119 Charing Cross Rd.*) is probably the world's biggest bookstore, with an inventory of four million volumes, but **Hatchard** is coming up fast. **Waterstones** (*121-125 Charing Cross Rd.*) is part of an excellent chain. At the other end of the scale, **Bondy** (*16 Little Russell St. W.C.1*), with an apt address, sells miniature books chiefly as well as tomes for antiquarians. **Bloomsbury Rare Books** (*29 Museum St. W.C.1*) does what it says, but upstairs **Arthur Page** (another appropriate monicker) proffers parchments from medieval manuscripts. **J.A. Allen** (*1 Lower Grosvenor*), a trot from the Royal Mews, is devoted singularly to horses while **The Book Dump** (*19 Great Ormond St. W.C.1*) purveys its bargains in bulk and by weight. For the bibliophile, London is ecstasy under the covers.

## BOUTIQUES AND YOUNG DESIGNERS

A wave of fresh, provocative new talent has rapidly and totally changed London's fashion lookscape. The punk-rock music cult has found expression in threads as well as chords. Designers such as Dexter Wong, Helen Robinson, Wendy Dagworthy, Joseph Ettedgui, Katharine Hamnett, Vivienne Westwood, John Galliano, Alistair Blair, Arabella Pollen, Betty Jackson, Rifat Ozbek, Janice Wainright, Sheridan Barnett, Anthony Kwok, Joe Casely-Hayford, and Stevie Stewart and David Holah of Body Map are influential. Look, too, for evocations by groups such as English Eccentrics, Workers for Freedom, Artwork, Arkitekt, and Design Studio. For Sloane Rangers more into the establishment mode, names such as Caroline Charles, David and Elizabeth Emanuel, Paul Costelloe, Jasper Conran, and Anthony Price are staples of the moment. Jean Muir and Zandra Rhodes are living legends who continue to excite the fashion world, and the late Laura Ashley created an empire in home furnishings as well as clothing that continues. Names in the news—designers who dress "Royals"—include Victor Edelstein, Belville Sassoon, and the Houses of Hardy Amies and Hartnell. Literally hundreds of small, chic shops have sprung up, particularly on Bond St., in Knightsbridge, and in Chelsea. Now the capital is a-brim with talent that produces everything from classic to elegantly casual to fun-filled or horridly kooky models.

**Miss Selfridge** (*Selfridges Department Store as well as Regent St. and Knightsbridge*), in my opinion, has merchandise that is simultaneously inexpensive, and sometimes junky but fashionable. **Next** is all over town (for women: *160 Regent St., 728 King's Rd.*; for men: *53 Brompton Rd., 137 Kensington High St.*) Their formula for success: classic styles at reasonable prices. **Brown's** (*27 S. Molton St.*) mixes the lines of Armani, Missoni, Chloe, Norma Kamali, and Sonja Rykiel with its own design label. **Linda Cierach** (*54 Hartismere Rd.*) made headlines as the designer of Fergie's wedding gown. **Bruce Oldfield** (*27 Beauchamp Pl.*) dresses her, too, as does boy wonder **Jasper Conran** (*37 Beauchamp Pl.*). **Monsoon** (*67 South Molton St. and 35 Beauchamp Pl.*) takes its inspiration from the East. **Franka** (*11 Dover St.*) cut her first swath in couture but now has added her own boutique. A smart flair in basic conservatism. **Anouska Hempl**, owner of ultrachic Blakes Hotel, carries her talents to yet another dimension. At 2 Pond Pl. (this area is really "in" right now) she has a design studio where she'll dress you from tip to toe. To make an appointment, Blakes Hotel ☎ (*370-6701*) and they'll put you through.

The name **Hartnell** (*26 Bruton St. and 3 Stanhope Mews West*) is back in the news. The house has been revived. **Ian Thomas** (*14 Motcomb St.*) stitches for the Queen herself. **Karl Lagerfeld** (*173 New Bond St.*) features the maestro's beautiful handmade creations as well as perfumes, shoes, and accessories. **Lucienne Phillips** (*89 Knightsbridge*) is a treasure trove of the high-styles of Britain's best. **James Drew** (*3 Burlington Arcade*) draws legions of sophisticated ladies for his dashingly created shirts in ombre- and moire-look jacquard silks, satin, crepe de chine, and fine cotton woven specially for the house; separates are also accented, as are Outlander knits. **Margaret Howell** (*29 Beauchamp Pl.*) caters to a similar clientele, who like her skillful tailoring of country fabrics. **Caroline Charles** (*11 Beauchamp Pl.*) is another name to be reckoned with for sophisticated elegance. **Nicole Farhi** (*193 Sloane St.*), who designed for "French Connection," is off and running on her own, and what a success. (She leans toward the relaxed sophistication of American and Italian stylings, and this is most appreciated by her loyal following.) **Kenzo** (*17 Sloane St.*) serves both sexes; all ready-to-wear garments for Her originate on the drawing board of the illustrious designer himself. **Katharine Hamnett** (*Sloane St., next to the Chelsea Hotel*) still sticks to the basics. Remember her T-shirts some seasons ago? **Joseph** (*13 South Molton St., Brompton Rd., across from the newly restored Michelin Building, and 6 Sloane St.*) has sharp, bright styles. The shop at the latter address is now called **Esprit Piero de Monzi** (*68 Fulham Rd.*) and is also currently popular among the bigger spenders; his specialties are cunningly conceived day and evening garb, casuals from France and Italy, chunky belts and bags, plus footwear.

Another current standout is **Kanga** (*8 Beauchamp Pl.*). The pure silk dresses are knockouts. **Palmer** (*4a Montcomb St.*) is a serene oasis that features up-to-the-minute selections by top-drawer English and Continental designers. Since style is the watchword here, the range of tariffs is broad. **Letetia** (*18-20 Grosvenor St.*) is a cheerful entry where you will find entrancingly classic Italian and French models by Cerutti, Michael Goma, and other glamorous fabricators.

Now for two specializing in "street fashion"; **Kensington Market** and **Hyper Hyper** vis-a-vis on *Kensington High St.* More up-market but also young is **Whistles** (*St. Christopher St.*). For the young and innocent there's the previously mentioned **Laura Ashley** (*9 Harriet St., 256-258 Regent St. and Fulham Rd.*).

## BRASS

**J. D. Beardmore and Co.** (*3 Percy St.*) has larger pieces as well as a mighty array of doorknobs, letter slots, locks, drawer pulls, hooks, latches, door numerals, lighting fixtures, fireplace hardware, and the like in this versatile metal. In the Notting Hill Gate area, **Jack Casimir** (*23 Pembridge Rd.*) is the brassiest gent for miles around; he has a whole floor of it.

## BURBERRYS RAINWEAR AND APPAREL

Since Thomas Burberry invented his celebrated weatherproof cloth around 1856, **Burberry** has become a familiar name to literally millions of shoppers from Tampa to Tokyo (you'll even find the name in Webster's). Now its twin homes at 18 Haymarket (near American Express) and at 165 Regent St. house what is probably the world's finest collection of weather-proofs and other wearables under the sun (and clouds!). Because the Burberry Look has developed from a practical necessity into high fashion, the stores are shrewdly designed to cater for this ever-increasing demand. There's an extensive collection of ladies' topcoats as well as a distinguished choice of casuals and knitwear including a Burberry logo lambswool series in a dozen flattering colors. You'll find forests of tweeds, indescribably soft cashmeres and camelhairs, superbly chic Burberrys luggage, a wide range of golfing gear, as well as a splendid Burberry fragrance for men. But the crowning glories are those definitive trenchcoats (and overcoats) lined either in the instantly identifiable traditional Burberry check, or in a subtle alternative based on this pattern. (Personalized monogrammed labels together with six months' free insurance on rainwear are standard if your purchase is made from one of Burberry's own stores.) These evoke a sporting mood that can be augmented by additional matching Burberry accessories—from a jaunty peaked cap to a smart-looking scarf to a neatly rolled 'brolly—a full ensemble that is both uplifting and timeless. And timeless they are, a durability as prevailing as the British Empire itself. Burberrys has recently added sunglasses, wristwatches, food and toweling to their collection. All major credit cards are accepted. At both Haymarket and Regent St. they understand North American tastes and will go all out to be helpful. If you're heading for Scotland, there are branches in Glasgow, Aberdeen, and Edinburgh.

## CASHMERES, TARTANS AND MATERIALS

**The Scotch House** (*flagship store at corner of Knightsbridge and Brompton Rd., two others at 84/86 and 191 Regent St.*) has been a titan in this field for more than a century and a half. Go to the circular Tartan Room at the Knightsbridge home and see more than 300 patterns, plus the guides to the clans. Fabulous Highland accessories, sweaters, tweeds, cashmeres, Shetlands, lambswool, and exciting wardrobes and combinations of ready-to-wear items for men, women, and children. Also for cashmeres, you might like a peek in the Burlington Arcade, where **N. Peal** and **Berk** are reputable purveyors.

## CHILDREN'S CLOTHES

No V.A.T. is applied on items for kids under 14, but this could change. **Anthea Moore Ede** (*16 Victoria Grove*) is where the Establishment goes to dress its progeny. **Please Mum** (*69 New Bond St.*) is a mecca for half-pint nabobs; it's very expensive, as is **La Cicogna** (*6A Sloane St.*), an Italian connection. **Benetton-012** (*S. Molton St. and King's Rd.*) is sprightly and colorful. **NBG** (*S. Molton St.*), part of the Next chain, caters for kids in an easy-going, moderately priced way. **Buckle My Shoe** (*19 St. Christopher's Pl.*) has as many eyecatching models for youngsters as its amusing name implies.

## CHEESE

**Paxton & Whitfield** (*93 Jermyn St.*), founded in 1797, sells over 100 different types and will mail anywhere in the world.

## CHINA

**Chinacraft** leads the parade with such brilliant style that you'll not want to miss this trend-setter. And because it has been a front-running purveyor for nearly half a century it enjoys an intimate association with the prestige manufacturers themselves. Diversity and luxury it provides all around the calendar, but if you are seeking bargains, try to arrange a visit during the sale periods of January and July. Brides, of course, are grateful for the flexible and comprehensive Wedding List Service detailed in a special brochure. Furthermore, companies can order Christmas gifts or conference novelty items under the promotional gift plan. Here are a few addresses of Chinacraft outlets: Inn On The Park and Grosvenor House hotels, *198 Regent St., 556 Oxford St., 7/11 Burlington Arcade, 130 New Bond St., 50 Brompton Road.*

## CHOCOLATES

**Bendicks** (*55 Wigmore St., 107 Long Acre, and 20 Royal Exchange*) is world-renowned for its Bittermints. **Prestat** (*24 South Molton*) defies diets with handmade truffles and brandy cherries. **Charbonnel & Walker** (*28 Old Bond St.*) offers number charts indicating fillings, tongs to pick up the soft-hearted masterpieces, and lettered chocolates to spell out a message as a sweet treat. You'll be pleasantly surprised how sparkling fresh the after-dinner mints from **Marks & Spencer's** food departments can be.

## COINS

**Spink** (*5-7 King St.*), **B.A. Seaby** (*11 Margaret St.*), and **Coins and Antiquities** (*20-22 Maddox St.*) offer the most interesting coinage in this realm.

## COVENT GARDEN "VILLAGE"

Don't miss the general-purpose Jubilee Market surrounding the central area, restaurants, wine bars, a constellation of engaging stores, trendy boutiques, and other facilities. Among the unique merchants who have settled here are **Suttons Seeds** (*Catherine St.*), which offers 13,000 different species, the **Kite Shop** (*69 Neal St.*), which claims to stock the biggest range of kites and flying disks on earth, and **Glasshouse** (*65 Long Acre*), which is a cooperative of artisans who produce their wares on the premises and sell them in their front showroom. This is the capital's first permanent late-night shopping center, open until 8 p.m. six nights a week—and it is booming.

## CUFF LINKS

**Paul Longmire** (*12 Bury St., St. James's*) is top drawer. Aside from the enormous variety on hand, personalized orders are welcome.

## DECOYS

**Robert Coyle** (*10 Holland St. W. 8*) is the ducky choice for collectors of such carved decorator items.

## DEPARTMENT STORES

**Harrods, Harvey Nichols, Selfridges, Marks & Spencer** (goodness, how "Marks & Sparks" is climbing!) and **Peter Jones** are the pacesetters; **John Lewis Partnership, Peter Robinson,** a pair called **House of Fraser** (Oxford St. and Kensington), and **Dickens & Jones** are also worthy.

**Liberty** (*Regent St.*), with outstanding antiques, furniture, luggage, notions, and a number of other categories, regards itself as an upper-bracket department store. Notwithstanding, I believe the main emphasis here is on its internationally famous printed fabrics, silks, and sublime carpets. It has opened an Oriental Bazaar to bring back the flavor of an old-time trading company. A British monument.

## DOLLHOUSES

**The Singing Tree** (*69 New King's Rd.*) is the world in miniature—both modern and antique. All the little items that go into this microculture are here too; write for the catalog (about £4).

## DUTY-FREE AIRPORT SHOPS

Our suggestion is to skip these marts in the Final Departure Lounges of Terminal 2 at Heathrow and Gatwick. Reasons? First, except for perfumes, cigarettes, and spirits, the prices are no cheaper than they are in the city. Second, in these three discounted categories they are among the costliest airport installations in all of western Europe. Third, the variety is downright poor, the stylings of clothing are often passe, and the camera, optics, and electronic counters do not compete with the best products on the shelves elsewhere. When you buy in town for export, your purchases will truly be duty free—and their quality should be higher.

## ENAMELS, PORCELAIN, AND ANTIQUES

**Halcyon Days** (*14 Brook St., Mayfair W.1 and 4 Royal Exchange, Cornhill E.C.3*) is just about as fetching as any one of its splendid small collectors' pieces, which are inspired by the finest *objets d'art* of 18th-century England. The house is famed for its enamels—boxes, clocks, picture frames, and all manner of decorative items. Fired on a copper base with superb luster and finish, they are exquisite creations in a tradition of perfect Georgian refinement. The artistic themes cover a multitude of subjects: family pets, flowers, genre scenes, heraldry, and famous people and events. The new Halcyon Days Porcelain was recently introduced in the form of irresistible tiny scent bottles and desk seals, influenced by the Chelsea miniatures that are among the most sought-after of all 18th-century English porcelain. Each hand-painted piece is mounted in gold or vermeil, and some are set with precious stones. The antiques selection at Halcyon Days is vast: 18th-century English enamels, Chelsea porcelain miniatures, rare shagreen, Staffordshire pottery, papier-mache, japanned ware—there is an incredible variety spanning from less than £50 to thousands of pounds. Susan Benjamin is the genius responsible for these beautiful collections. Speak to her or any of her expert assistants and ask for the tantalizing catalog for back-home orders.

## ENGLISH LIFESTYLE

**Mulberry**, the Mulberry House (*11/12 Gees Court, St. Christopher's Pl., plus boutiques in Harrods, Harvey Nichols, and Liberty's*). There is a lovable eccentricity that pertains to British tradition, and many of its trademarks are reflected in the clothing and accessories that become cherished classics. Founder and designer Roger Saul is able to translate his awareness of these subtleties into wardrobe and study, pocket and purse, hatwear and footwear, and many items betwixt and between, including a new "At Home" collection, devoted to enhancing your surroundings.

## EXOTIC HANDICRAFTS

**Inca** (*45 Elizabeth St.*) recalls the moods and fashions of Peru.

## FISHING GEAR

**House of Hardy** (*61 Pall Mall*) and **Farlow's** (*5 Pall Mall*) are the hooks to any angler's hearts. Clothing, equipment, and solace are offered in taste and abundance.

## FLOWERS

**Moyses Stevens** (*6 Bruton St. W1*), **Constance Spry** (*64 S. Audley St.*), or **Pullbrook & Gould** (*127 Sloane St.*) will possibly make the biggest impression on Her or on your hostess. **Kenneth Turner** (*8 Avery Row*) decorates London's most illustrious tables, and he's in demand worldwide too. His dried flowers are gorgeous and now he's added scented candles and potpourris. He has boutiques at Bergdorf Goodman in New York and Marshall Field in Chicago, but there is nothing like seeing the original.

## FOOTWEAR FOR GENTLEMEN

**Alan McAfee** (*5 Cork St.*) has had smartly shod feet beating a path to its various doors since this century turned its corner. While its world-wide reputation was made in custom (bespoke) footwear, modern methods now allow the same expertise to apply also to an extensive range of all-fitting stock shoes. **Church & Co.** (*58 Burlington Arcade*) has represented a stout foundation in this field, too, for a century. As quality goes, there's none finer. Several outlets in town, but this is the matrix. **John Lobb** (*9 St. James's St.*) fit boots for royalty since Queen Victoria's day. The cobblers only work from your own personal last, so expect to wait six months before you make a Lobb footprint anywhere.

## GENEALOGY AND HERALDRY

The **College of Arms** (*Queen Victoria St.*) is a venerable institution where all the official records of all the coats of arms granted are housed. They will pursue your lineage for you, as will the **Society of Genealogists** (*37 Har-*

*rington Gardens*). The latter contains a library open for self-service of your very own self.

## GIFT BOUTIQUES

**Rally** (*11 Grosvenor St.*) rallies an interesting collection of glossy imports in belts, costume jewelry, gold-plated goodies for the bathroom, and other specialized items; although worthy, t'aint cheap. **Eximious** (*10 West Halkin St., Belgravia*) devises highly personalized surprises such as custom mono-grammed playing cards, soaps, trays, tablemats, paperweights, or even ice buckets reproduced from your color photographs. Travel items are a big thing too. **Zarach Ltd.** (*48 South Audley St.*), also costly, is even more un-usual. **Presents of Sloane St.** (*No. 129*), for the Man Who Has Everything, stocks just about every conceivably amusing gadget that moves, jumps, crawls, shines, creeps, glistens, hobbles, squeaks, or bubbles. **Saville-Edells** (*25 Walton St.*) has those embroidered cushions you've seen in other peo-ple's houses with cutsie messages such as "Age Does Not Matter Unless You Are Wine." Their mail-order catalog (available by writing to *41 Queen Victoria St.*) is loaded with ideas for the home and fashion accessories. **Hab-itat** (*206 Kings Rd. and 156 Tottenham Court Rd.*) has a large patronage of young marrieds who are decorating their homes in the modern mood. **Mu-seum Store** (*37 The Market, The Piazza, Covent Garden*) is bursting with collectibles that are uniquely British. The atmosphere of Chelsea Green is like a country village. Around its perimeter are two delightful finds. **Chris-tine Schell** (*15 Cale St.*) deals in antique silver frames and objects of tor-toiseshell. Brian King can advise you as to the do's and don't's of importing the latter into the States. **Felicity Wigan** (*8 Elystan*) has a wee house with a burgundy painted door. It's chockablock with delights obvi-ously chosen by someone with a discerning eye and eminent good taste.

## GLASS

**W.G.T. Burne** (*11 Elystan St.*) is a specialist in antique English and Irish crystal.

**Delmosne & Son** (*4 Campden Hill Rd.*) is highly esteemed too.

## GOURMET PROVISIONS, DE LUXE GENERALIA

**Fortnum & Mason** (*Piccadilly*) used to be one of the greatest centers for gourmet delicacies in existence. The food products may be in a temporary slump of sorts, but there is still nothing like it as a period piece of a genteel era that's otherwise bygone. The famous haughty attendants in striped trousers and cutaway coats still flit among the rows of canned goods and will discourse with you for hours on the virtues of a certain brand of lichee nuts or what to look for in your cock-a-leekie soup. Its ground-floor res-taurant is still good for light lunches. **Wearables** and another restaurant are upstairs. The splendid **Food Halls** in Harrods and in Selfridge's win our local blue ribbon for versatility.

## GREEK GOLD JEWELRY

**Ilias Lalaounis** (*174 New Bond St. and Harrods, ground floor*). This is the greatest name in the field since the days of Pericles! You've seen his work worn by chic women everywhere—a hot-looking gold with a flushed pink glow, heavy bold ancient patterns, and delicate touches of Byzantium. There's a modern collection, too, with its focus on the cosmic elements of our universe. This makes it both timeless and eternal. Since the Brits are almost all dipped in silver at birth, Lalaounis has created a Silver Department at the New Bond St. address containing his inspired revelations of pieces from Cycladic ancient Greek and classical epochs. His jewelry includes creations (or interpretations) from twelve other ancient civilizations. At Harrods the boutique features Lalaounis along with a half-dozen other "greats" of the jewelry world who exhibit in an inspired neoclassical hall built especially for them. To own a Lalaounis piece is to start a collection. You just can't stop.

## HAIRBRUSHES

The Mason & Pearson brand is one of the best. Widely stocked in London stores.

## HALLMARKS

For the novice silver collector, a reliable and concise booklet entitled *British and Irish Silver Assay Office Marks 1544-1963* has been compiled by Fredrick Bradbury, FSA, and published by J.W. Northend Ltd., Sheffield 1 U.K. From its illustrations and detailed descriptions, the reader can instantly identify all registered marks on silver, gold, imported plate, and Old Sheffield Plate; assay offices and relevant dates are also listed. It costs a trifle.

## HANDKNITS

**Beatrice Bellini** (*74 Pimlico Rd., Belgravia*) specializes in handsome hand-knitted coats, suits, day dresses, evening dresses, and other feminine fancies that are crafted by highly qualified women who operate on a piecework basis. Because the ready-made inventory is limited, be prepared to allow from 8 to 10 weeks for your order to be completed. Although the price tags are high, the workmanship is so fine that both the investment and the wait seem well worth it to me. The homely arts of tapestry and other thread magic come into their own as well.

## HANDPAINTED CHILDREN'S FURNITURE

**Dragons** (*23 Walton St.*) is masterful; it even has a lock on Winnie the Pooh and other A. A. Milne characters for decorative purposes. Your own child's name can be applied as well; ask for a catalog.

## HATS (LADIES')

Most English women wouldn't be caught bareheaded at most social occasions. This is really big business and the Royals lead the fashion parade.

**John Boyd's** (*91 Walton St.*) creations can always be seen in the best places—society weddings, Ascot, garden parties, luncheons, and charity affairs.

## HATS (MEN'S)

Continuously since 1759, there has existed only one top-ranking center in the Western world—**James Lock Co., Ltd.** (*6 St. James's St.*) The lid on this prize package is the hat—every conceivable male headgear for formal or leisure wear.

## IRISH SPECIALTIES

**The Irish Shop** (*11 Duke St.*) is the answer if you want to avoid the humdrum atmosphere of department store shopping. Go to this intimate London establishment for its out-of-the-ordinary selection of tweeds, traditional Irish linens, Belleek china, Claddagh rings—symbols of friendship and love—Celtic jewelry, handicrafts, and that classic of classics, Waterford crystal. There are rich Aran hand-knitted sweaters, ladies' jackets and capes by Avoca, plus that stunning Royal Tara china from Galway. You can even find books and Irish music. (☎ *(71) 935-1366.*)

## JEWELRY (ANTIQUE)

**Cameo Corner** (*in Liberty, Regent St.*) stocks a particularly lovely collection.

## JEWELRY (COSTUME)

**Butler & Wilson** (*S. Molton St.*) has fakes galore. Their knock-off of the highly-publicized flamingo pin of the Duchess of Windsor caused a furor.

**Arabesk** (*156 Walton St.*) uses beads for its one-off sophisticated necklaces, bracelets, and belts. Wrapped in one of their 36 strand jobs where the colors melt into each other, you'll feel like an African princess, at least. Magically, these can be worn in three different startling ways. Special orders for their dazzling accessories are always welcome.

## JEWELRY

**Garrard** (*112 Regent St.*) has been a synonym for the finest British jewelry almost since the day it opened in 1735. There are gifts for every occasion, many at very reasonable prices. With a heritage of more than two-and-a-half centuries to preserve, you can well expect the legendary service for which Garrard is known.

**Alex** (*41A Burlington Arcade;* ☎ *(71) 493-2453*) is a talented designer of masterful fresh creations. He is more than willing to refashion pieces you own, producing startling results for you from old stones. A bit difficult to sniff out the correct doorway, but once you've got it, ring the bell and go upstairs. These digs are temporary so phone (the number remains constant) just to be sure. His prices are quite reasonable in today's market. **Annabel Jones** (*52 Beauchamp Pl.*) is a treasure trove of antique and contemporary pieces, and they have carefully selected silverware plus Old Sheffield Plate. **Tiffany** (*Bond St.*), known to Americans far and wide, put down roots a few years ago and has blossomed. Enlarged premises; all the exquisite merchandise found Stateside now available for our British cousins to ooh and aah over.

## LACE

**Lunn Antiques** (*86 New King's Rd., Parsons Green*) will pamper you with bed and table linen edged in gorgeous lace. Everything is white, fresh, and romantic in a 19th-century mood.

## LEFT-HANDED TRAVELERS

Bill Gruby's **Anything Left-Handed Limited** (*65 Beak St.*) comes as a salvation to the worldwide fraternity and sorority of benighted southpaws. Pens, saucepans, scissors (33 models), irons, can openers, corkscrews, playing cards, garden tools, artists' palettes—even special kitchen sinks—have been designed to mitigate the constant irritations encountered by these souls in our 88% right-handed civilization. More than 40 utensils or gadgets have been tailor-made for easier and more comfortable manual dexterity. It's about time Mr. Gruby came along!

## LINEN SPECIALISTS

**The White House** (*51/52 New Bond St.*) goes beyond its linen genre to glamorous silken nightwear to Victorian organdy cradles to quilted coverlets to table sets and personal attire for ladies, gentlemen, and youngsters. Accessories, too, with quite a lot of the merchandise chosen from the finest of France and Italy. The store itself is one of London's handsomest keepsakes. At the **Monogrammed Linen Shop** (*168 Walton St.*) you'll be able to fill your cupboards with luxurious sheets and towels. Loads of bed and bath extras and gift ideas galore. Specialist embroiderers who'll stitch a coronet as easily as an initial. The **Irish Linen Company** (*35 Burlington Arcade*) is tucked away at the Burlington Gardens end of this elegant covered walk. Have a look at the handkerchiefs and panoply of household chic.

## MAPS

**Edward Stanford** (*12-14 Long Acre W.C.2*) is one of the oldest in the business, having begun in 1852. The collection is vast and global. **The Map House** (*54 Beauchamp Pl.*), encompassing five galleries, concentrates on old England. **Jonathan Potter** (*1 Grafton St.*) is a well-regarded expert. His catalog may be obtained for a fee. **Weinreb & Douwma** (*93 Great Russell St.*) stretch round the globe.

## MEDITERRANEAN MOODS

**Casa Pupo** (*56 Pimlico Rd.*) Do you want to create the ambience of the Mare Nostrum right in your own home? Have the Middle Seaside as a companion on your summer terrace? Catch the colors of the Levant in the celebration of that special sense for living colorfully that Casa Pupo can provide? The cascades of ceramic fruit, bright fixtures, lovely utensils, cane furnishings, and unique household selections from Europe's sun-kist lands are the stock and trade of this fun-spot. Additionally, there are wicker accessories for boudoir or bath, dining salons or conservatories, or just the piece to brighten the sullen effects of ordinary corridors. Deliveries of headboards, sofas, and the full range of interior design can be managed easily. If you wish to hand-carry or mail back smaller packages, the friendly staff here will help you in these routine favors. Go in and feel the sun around you.

## NAUTICAL GEAR

**Capt. Watts** (*45 Albemarle St.*) offers just about everything imaginable for anyone who ever puts out to sea—clothing, safety items, chandlery products, books, charts, and much, much more.

## NEEDLEWORK

For unusual designs, try **Luxury Needlepoint** (*325 Kings St. W6*). **Tapisserie** (*54 Walton St.*) is a labor of love—the owner is an art connoisseur, and her taste is reflected in the exquisite designs that are available. **Woman's Home Industries** (*85 Pimlico Rd.*) is an institution in the same passionate pastime. If you're really into this eyeful craft, you'll want to visit **Ehrman** (*14-16 Lancer Square*), which has a loyal following. Incidentally, the **Royal School of Needlework** (*5 King St., Covent Garden*) will give lessons in any needlework technique, depending on ability. The actual workshop, where restoration and the like is done, is to be found in Apartment 38 of Hampton Court Palace. The **Contemporary Textile Gallery** (*6A Vigo St. W1*) has continually changing exhibits of yarn and textiles turned into art objects. They are all for sale and very desirable.

## PAPER

**Falkiner Fine Papers** (*76 Southampton Row WC1B 4AR*) is England's leading center. It continuously scouts the globe to supply bookbinders, calligraphers, picture framers, printers, artists, and others. Among its clients are the restoration departments of a number of museums.

## PERFUMES AND TOILETRIES

**J. Floris** (*89 Jermyn St.*) founded in 1730 by Juan Famenias Floris, quickly established itself as the leading perfumer in London, and remains so today. In its eighth generation of family management and in the same charming but extended premises in which it was begun, Floris offers an exquisite range of flower perfumes, toilet waters, bath essences, soaps, bath and shower gels, body milks, and talcum powders. Among the 15 classics, Florissa, Lily of the Valley, Stephanotis, Malmaison, and Rose Geranium remain firm favorites, joined by Zinnia—an enchanting bouquet of summer flowers enhanced with Rose, Violet, and Iris accords. The well-established "traditional" range of Lavender, Moss Rose, and Wild Hyacinth in soaps, bath oils, and toilet waters remains enormously popular, as do the luxury toiletries for men in fragrances—No. 89 and Elite. These have recently been joined by J.F. for Gentlemen, a signature fragrance in the best traditions of quality for which the House of Floris is known—a fresh citrus fragrance with a slight herbal aroma, on a woody and musky amber base. For the home: room sprays, potpourris, and perfumed vaporizers. To complete the picture there is an extensive choice of bathroom and other luxury accessories from natural sponges and goosedown puffs to a new range of handmade ivory-effect shaving and hair brushes. You'll receive a 10% discount on all mail orders and a free comprehensive catalog on application.

And now, right next door at #88, you'll find **James Bodenham & Company**, a Floris off-shoot. They are specialists in skin care products whose milks, creams, and oils (perfumed or unscented) will pamper you from tip to toenail. In addition, there is a small line of luxury food items (without preservatives and artificial colorings), china and glassware, plus other gifts.

## PEWTER

**The Pewter Shop** (*16 Burlington Arcade*) has mugs that range from £50 to £75, and napkin rings go from £10 up. On my most recent visit the premises were being shared with a souvenir stall. It's possible they've given up entirely now, but please check this out if you are especially interested.

## PIPES AND TOBACCO

**Dunhill** (*30 Duke St., St. James's S.W. 1*) should need no introduction to anyone, because no other establishment anywhere has ever offered more consistently fine quality in its smoking products; it also stocks gifts, clothing, ladies' accessories, and mens' toiletries.

## POSTCARDS

**Post Card Shop** (*24 Carnaby St. W1*) or **London Pavilion** (*Piccadilly W1*) combine nostalgia and contemporary messages.

## REJECT CHINA, CRYSTAL AND AFFORDABLE GIFTS

**The Reject China Shops** (*Beauchamp Pl. S.W.3, 134 Regent St. W.1, and in Windsor at 1 Castle Hill*). Don't be fooled by the name. Sure enough, you'll find odd-lot items and "seconds." But now "Reject" has grown so muscular that it dominates the field and puts on its shelves highly prized "firsts" at prices well below those of fancy competitors. It's a policy of the house to pass along the benefits of their vast buying power to you—and not just for obscure brands, but for the legendary products that always made London a favorite hunting ground of serious shoppers. Since so many of the top brands are already known to you, you can probably find exactly the styles and pieces you desire for surprisingly low sums.

## RENTAL CLOTHING

Its advertising slogan, "Practically Every Well-Known Man in the Country Has Used the **Moss Bros. Hire Service** at One Time or Another!" is the flat truth. This remarkable British institution, with headquarters at Covent Garden, 38 branches throughout the country, and two branches in Paris, would be pleased to doll you up in a jiffy, in a well-fitting, absolutely correct garment for any required occasion.

**One Night Stand** (*44 Pimlico Rd. S.W.1 and 148 Regent's Park Rd., N.W.1*) hits the nail on the resident headliner as well as the unsung visiting female who vitally needs some glad rags but who doesn't feel like spending £600 for a one-use ballgown, a slinky cocktail dress, or any mode for any mood that pops up. Inventory of 400 stylish lovelies plus accessories; £50 to £75 rentals for three or four days. (If you *must* have it, you can also buy it, and there are especially good bargains at their clearance sales in Aug. and Feb.) Dressmaker on hand for minor hitches and stitches. Phone Joanna Doninger for an appointment (☎ *(71) 730-8708*). Recommended for taste, hygiene, and strategic planning.

## SADDLER

**W. H. Gidden Limited** (*15d Clifford St., New Bond St.*), established in 1806, is Seventh Heaven for the equestrian, with a seemingly limitless galaxy of beautifully made saddles, bridles, bits, harnesses, horse clothing, horse boots, other accessories, and chic riding outfits for both genders. Ask for Michael Gidden.

## SHIRTMAKERS

**Hilditch & Key** (*with three addresses on Jermyn St.: #s 73, 87, and 37, plus at Harrods and 42 Beauchamp Pl.*) represents a partnership that was cemented just before this century was born. Their world-renowned talents now extend to women as well as to men. **James Drew** (3 Burlington Arcade) does his numbers in silks and cottons just for ladies. Stocks, ruffles, bows, full-cuts, and built-in elegance.

## SHOES

**T. Elliot & Sons** (*76 New Bond St.*), the **Chelsea Cobbler** (*165 Draycott Ave. and 33 Sackville St.*), **Rayne** (*15 Old Bond St. and 57 Brompton Rd.*), and **Manolo Blahnik** (*49/51 Old Church St.*) cater to a variety of happy feet for ladies.

## SHOTGUNS

**Purdey** (*57-58 S. Audley St.*) goes back to the early days of fine hunting guns. **Holland & Holland** (*13 Bruton St.*), also remarkable, is almost as expensive. Both are side-by-side in quality. Both can personalize your gun or sell one off the rack.

## SILVER

**Mappin & Webb** (*170 Regent St.*) has long been one of the pillars of an industry that has made English silver so respected throughout the world for the past two centuries. The sterling, of course, is the measure by which most other silver is compared. But simultaneously, many of these prestigious designs also have become available in Mappin & Webb's silver plate (officially designated as Mappin Plate and considered the best in the world); it carries a lifetime guarantee and costs approximately one-fifth of the sterling price.

The **Silver Vaults** in Chancery House (*53/63 Chancery Lane*) offers new and second-hand collections and a vast underground shopping area comprising about two dozen shops.

## SNUFF

**G. Smith and Sons—The Snuff Centre** (*74 Charing Cross Rd.*) boasts 22 of their own blends. Their brightly colored handkerchiefs are a novel expression of the lore.

## SOUVENIR ITEMS

**The Old Curiosity Shop** (*13/14 Portsmouth St.*) couldn't be more touristy. Loaded to the scuppers with "antique" china, pottery, silver, glass, pewter, plaques, playing cards, silhouettes—you ask for it and they'll find it, because the gent who owns the place isn't about to lose a single customer. Open seven days a week(!). You might try some of the wacky holes-in-the-wall around Trafalgar Square for canned London fog, tins of country air, pieces of the White Cliffs of Dover, and similar tomfooleries.

## SPORTING EQUIPMENT AND SPORTSWEAR

The glittering six-floor jungle of **Lillywhites** (*Piccadilly Circus*) is a paradise for outdoor types.

## STATIONER

**Frank Smythson Limited** (*54 New Bond St.*), which holds the Royal Warrant of Stationers to Her Majesty the Queen, is a delight in its atmosphere, its tastes, and its friendly welcome. They are famous for their Bond Street Blue paper—it is quite unique. Suddenly, you'll become a prolific correspondent because **Stokes** (*Elizabeth St.*) and **The Walton Street Stationery Co.** (*13 Walton St.*) have such desirable papers, unusual pens, and unforgettable ink colors and desk accessories.

## SWEATERS

**Edina Ronay** (*141 King's Rd. and Burlington Arcade*) is not merely to keep warm. Here is the leading edge in smart sweater fashion—from cashmere, cotton, silk, ribbon, Fair Isle (with lace) to ensembles that produce a "total look." Tweeds, too, and even styles for men. Don't miss this one. She is now stocked by Harvey Nichols if you don't make it to her own shop. **Moussie** (*109 Walton St. and 28 St. Christopher's Pl.*) has hand-knitted sweaters that you'll warm up to immediately. A calendar, the alphabet, naif images, a ski motif, flowers and animals—these are all highly amusing. There are dressy, beaded cashmeres for evening and bobbly stitch casuals. Coordinating skirts, culottes, waistcoats, and embroidered blouses complete the picture. Both shops are charming enclaves with painted wood floors. It's just right for the country-club set.

## TEA

**The Tea Centre** (*Regent St., near Lillywhite's*) is an aromatic delight to tempt any tea lover. **The Tea House** (*15a Neal St.*) is another cuppa. It also sells all of the items that should suit you to a "tea": pots, caddies, strainers, infusers, and other tack for tea–timing.

# TOYS

**Hamleys** (*188-196 Regent St.*) will gladden your young or old heart. Infinite variety; prices refreshingly lower than many in the States. **Pollock's Toy Museum** (*1 Scala St. W1*), resembling a three-story Victorian expo of playthings, carries a large line and specializes in miniature theaters.

## TOY SOLDIERS

**Under Two Flags** (*4 St. Christopher's Pl.*) is the leader, with the highest standards and finest quality. The owner turned his lifelong hobby into this business more than a decade ago. New, unpainted types are also stocked. Its quotations are commensurate with its superiority. At **Tradition, Ltd.** (*Shepherd's Market*) and **Stall 410** in the Antique Supermarket, the conditions of their ample offerings vary from excellent to poor, with the prices adjusted accordingly. The best source for information on this commodity is John Ruddle, Secretary, The British Soldier Society, 22 Priory Gardens, Hampton, Middlesex, ☎ *(81) 979-7137.*

## WALKING STICKS

**Swaine Adeney Brigg & Sons Ltd.** (*185 Piccadilly*) has stomped down the gales of all its competition since 1836. All types of canes, seat sticks, hunting and shooting paraphernalia, umbrellas, dog collars, whips, picnic baskets, small gifts—and everything in high quality. A landmark.

# THAMES AND THE CHILTERNS— ENGLAND'S "HOME COUNTIES"

*Oxford*

The River Thames could be considered the lifeline of the nation; so much of English history is written on its surface. It rises modestly enough from a trickle in the folds of Cotswold landscape, a source appropriately named Thames Head. From here in Coates parish it builds and rushes along for a little more than 200 miles before losing its identity; Tower Bridge crosses it about two-thirds of the way down. In its course it narrows to as little as 150 feet at Oxford and widens majestically between Sheerness and Shoeburyness to a spread of almost six miles. Whatever its dimensions, every inch or fluid ounce of the Thames has been packed with drama. The beautiful soft-spoken Windrush and the support network of rivulets surrounding Oxford create the so-called "backwaters," a slow-moving inland sea that is also a nature preserve. Not far from Goring and Pangbourne, the Thames creates an interface between the Chiltern Hills and the upper reaches of Berkshire. This skirts the southern fringe of Coombe Hill and the famous, well-trod Icknield Way. The curve brings it past that delightful sporting settlement of Henley-on-Thames, a redoubt of British landed gentry and genteel aristocracy.

As you can imagine, along this watercourse—about 200 miles of associated streams and canals—are some of the most frequently visited historic sites, splendid gardens, parks, and stately homes, so budget your time accordingly. Most of the declared Area of Outstanding Natural Beauty falls within Oxfordshire (covered in Shakespeare Country) and Buckinghamshire. Hertfordshire runs toward the easterly flank, and then there is Bedfordshire. Heading west it holds hands with the North Wessex Downs, forming a handsomely rumpled landscape. If you wish, you can cross the most historic real estate in Albion by foot by taking the 85-mile Ridgeway Path. This, the oldest trail in the nation, links Dorset with The Wash; more exactly, it connects Ivinghoe Beacon with Avebury. Beechwoods and bluebells, chalk slopes and downland scarps are among the scenic glories of the Chilterns. In the autumn the beech leaves vary widely in color due to the variations in altitude and moisture. Then you have the additional delights of the Upper Thames from Marlow to Henley, Pangbourne, Goring, and Wallingford, where boats may be hired to explore the idyllic "windin-the-willows" riverscapes.

Places of interest for a day's outing include **Whipsnade Zoo** near **Dunstable** and **Hughenden Manor** near **High Wycombe**, Disraeli's former home. Then there's the simplicity of a changeless hamlet like **Ewelme**, with its black barn, almshouse, and undisturbed ancient church.

**Dunstable Downs** is an open stretch of terrain on the northeastern fringes of the Chilterns; it takes its name from the rather dismal urban sprawl sited at the junction of Roman Watling Street and the older Icknield Way. The town of Dunstable—now rapidly merging with the air-center and city of **Luton**—was the site of an imposing 12th-century priory (you can still see the nave and west front). The most compelling aspect of the Downs is the 200 acres devoted to some 2000 animals of **Whipsnade Zoo**.

**Ivinghoe Beacon** is reached by a narrow road just outside the village. From its summit, nearly 800 feet high, you can absorb a sizeable portion

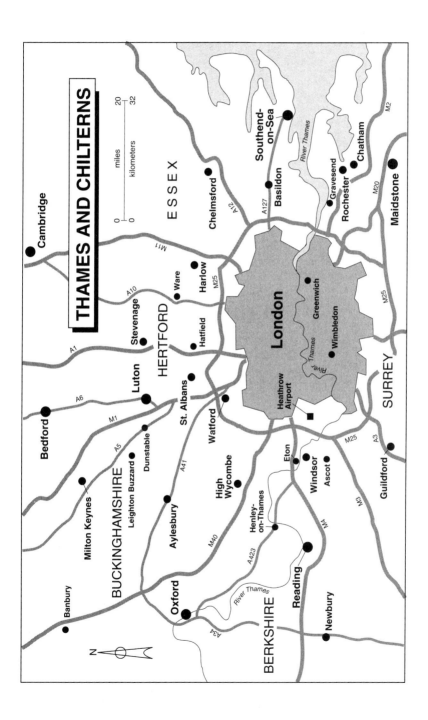

THAMES AND CHILTERNS

of the Chilterns and the Downs. **The Coombe** (dry valley) typifies the arid terrain hereabouts. You'll find these fissures in many counties.

## WINDSOR

As a home county, **Berkshire's** most notable resident is the Queen, who keeps a cozy suburban retreat in Windsor. The county is etched across its northern boundary by the Thames. It is handy to London and an easy excursion destination if you wish to remain in the capital. The Royal Family often occupy **Windsor Castle**, a site that must be seen by any first-time visitor to the United Kingdom and which is now recovering from the recent fire which gutted several tenderloins and threatened a marvelous art collection. **Windsor** itself grew out of its services to the mighty fortress that is the largest inhabited castle in the world. The grounds within this stately, massive, royal compound occupy 13 acres and the perimeter is more than a mile in length. The mighty round tower in its center is eye-catching from far over the rolling land. The **State Apartments** include St. George's Hall, the Audience and Presence Chambers, the Grand Reception Room, and Guards Quarters. All these salons contain numerous priceless objects of art and fascinating nuances of life in the castle. Most notable in this connection are the Picture Gallery (engaging if you have a historical bent), the Rubens Room, and the magnificent Van Dyck Room. Three of the salons retain their original ceilings by Antonio Verrio, and there are some beautiful carvings by Grinling Gibbons, the top whittler of his day. Any time you come across his name it's an automatic badge of distinction for the estate that contains his carvings. In the Royal Library you may study the collection of drawings by old masters, including important works by Leonardo da Vinci, Michelangelo, and Raphael. There is also a fascinating series of Holbein portraits, often considered the finest assemblage in the world. These drawings focus revealingly on the chief personages of the court of Henry VIII.

The State Apartments are not open to the public while the Queen is in residence, but next to these chambers is the fantastic **Queen Mary's Doll House**. It was designed by the esteemed architect Sir Edwin Lutyens and presented to Her Majesty in 1924, a masterpiece of craftsmanship, a perfect and complete reproduction of a 1920s royal mansion.

**St. George's Chapel**, beloved by Hollywood for costume films, was designed to be the grandest of halls for the Order of the Garter, begun by Edward IV. It is one of the finest examples of Perpendicular architecture in England and certainly one of the world's most impressive rooms. Above its dark oaken stalls are the honored insignia of the individual knights, their swords, helmets, and banners. The last fall in colorful drapery the length of the room. The Chapel ranks next to Westminster Abbey as a royal mausoleum. In all, ten monarchs are at rest. Edward IV is buried here, his tomb enclosed by the most remarkable piece of ironwork of its type in England, dating from the late 15th century. A vault in the middle of the choir floor contains the bodies of Henry VIII; his third wife, Jane Seymour, and that of Charles I. *(Menage a trois des roi?)* Other royalty buried here are Edward VII and Queen Alexandra (on the right hand side of the high altar). Effigies of George V and Queen Mary are to be seen in the nave. George VI, always a bit standoffish, is tucked securely between the westernmost pillars on the south flank of the nave. The Albert Memorial Chapel, to the east of St. George's, was created by Henry VII as a royal tomb. It was restored by Queen Victoria in memory of Prince Albert, whose cenotaph stands before the altar.

South of the castle, beside the **Home Park** or Great Park, as it is also called, is the Royal Mews and within the park is **Frogmore**. The house was first renovated by Queen Charlotte in 1790, who sought refuge among its colonnades during George III's lapses into dementia. An overall refreshening was recently completed. Usually it is open in August and September, but closed Monday and Tuesday. Its gardens contain the mausoleum of Queen Victoria and Prince Albert. An oak tree marks the supposed site of **Herne's Oak**, said to be haunted by the ghost of Herne, the hunter who figures in Shakespeare's *Merry Wives of Windsor*. The Long Walk leading into the park was planted by Charles II in 1685, consisting of 1650 giant elms. However, because of the obvious hazards, these were cut down and replaced by smaller trees earlier in this century. Among various buildings within the Great Park is **Royal Lodge**, once a favorite residence of George IV. At the southern boundary is a beautiful artificial lake called Virginia Water.

Windsor's (the town) architecture is a product of the castle's residents, the most influential being derived from Victorian and Georgian drawing boards. Sir Christopher Wren designed the **Town Hall**, which made its debut late in the 17th century. Be sure to go inside to see the displays of local monarchial history and the splendid portraits of Windsor sovereigns on its walls. At the **Royalty and Empire Exhibition** at the Central Station the waxwork of Madame Tussaud recreates the resplendent Diamond Jubilee of Queen Victoria in 1897, including 70 Coldstream Guards! Even though the town of Windsor clings to the skirts of the castle walls—it, too, is not original from Norman times—the support settlement has just a few remaining ancient houses. One often visited is that of a Miss Eleanor Gwyn, better known in history (and to Charles II) as Nell. She made the gossip columns of her day as a celebrated actress and, not incidentally, royal mistress. Her house had to be near as she was often on call. Also at hand is the parish church of St. John the Baptist. Though it was rebuilt in the 19th century, go in to see the fine examples of Grinling Gibbons' earlier wood-carving.

The name Windsor is opined to be a variant of "winding shore." Among others, this was probably the site of a Roman settlement. Roman tombs—a pair of them—were discovered at **Tyleplace Farm**. In the last century or so, Roman antiquities were unearthed at **St. Leonard's Hill**. Saxons also occupied Old Windsor, and perhaps Edward the Confessor had a fortress here. In 1922, *New Windsor* became a royal borough; only four other English towns were so honored.

Another attractive and interesting target to visit is **Eton**, home of **Eton College**, the intellectual proving ground of the nation since Henry VI opened its portals in 1440. He was on to a good thing because since the 15th century some of the country's greatest thinkers and leaders (20 prime ministers) have been graduated from here. The attractive little town is on the Thames not far at all from Windsor and can easily be included in the same excursion. The town's chapel is noted for wall paintings and brasses, if you have extra time.

On the south side of Windsor Great Park you'll find **Ascot**, with its famous racecourse. It was Queen Anne who inaugurated the Royal Ascot race meeting in 1711. It remains a landmark social event every year in June, being presided over still by the Royal Family, who present the legendary "Gold Cup" as one of the great trophies of equine prowess. The royals arrive in brilliant carriages (commoners only in "Rollers," Royces, that is); the landaus make a ceremonial turn of the course before the starting signal.

## EXPLORING BERKSHIRE

**Henley-on-Thames** is pure postcard country, having some of the finest homes in Britain lining the course for the famous Royal Regatta, held in the first week of July. It is indeed one of the great social events of the season, and most of the viewing is done from marquees put up on the lawns bordering the towpath. Incidentally, watching the practice sessions each morning or late afternoon can be just as interesting as the race. The flow of water is controlled to prevent too much resistance, coaches ride bikes and bark their commands to the crews with loud-hailers, oarsmen ashore give constant vigil to stop-watches, and residents urge favorite teams to pull harder. At regatta time the beverage of choice is a Pimm's Cup, but at other times try the local bitter known as Brakspear. The urban area is couched in wooded hills; a picturesque 18th-century bridge spans the wide curve of the Thames. Somehow there is the ambience of a college town about Henley that is pleasant at any season but enchanting in spring.

**Sonning**. An interesting 11 arches create the 200-year-old bridge across the Thames. The scenery itself is sylvan and inviting. Three miles southeast of Henley is the meadow of **Runnymede,** where King John signed the *Magna Carta* in 1215. A memorial marks the spot, which, of course, attracts many visitors. You can probably live without it.

**Reading,** 38 miles west of London, the county town and an important rail center, resides on the Kennet River near its confluence with the Thames. Though much of the town is modern, all of the ancient and important churches here have been restored: **Greyfriars** was completed early in the 14th century; **St. Mary's** was rebuilt in 1551 from the remains of a nunnery founded by Aelfthryth (remember him?).

**St. Laurence's** is a Perpendicular building with Norman and Early English features; **St. Giles's** was damaged during the English Civil War and now, after a delay of a few centuries, is almost wholly rebuilt. The **Municipal Museum,** containing an art gallery and other exhibits, includes Roman relics from Silchester and pertinent finds from the Thames. Ancient **Abbey**

**Gate** still guards Forbury Street; Jane Austen and her sister went to a school within its walls. The rascal Oscar Wilde was imprisoned here; paying dividends to literature while serving time, he wrote his *Ballard of Reading Gaol.* Each summer afternoon at about 2 p.m. there's a boat that chugs from **Caversham Bridge** to the splendid shore of **Mapledurham House,** with its waterside gardens (see below). Just south of Reading is **Wellington Country Park** and nearby is **Stratfield Saye House,** a 1630 estate filled with a unique collection of paintings, prints, furniture, and personal belongings of the first Duke of Wellington; also on display are Napoleon's tricolor, elegant books in leather bindings, and a memorial statue of Copenhagen, the Duke's cavalry charger at Waterloo (subsequently buried on the grounds). The structure was rebuilt during the reign of Charles I and has been the home of the Wellingtons since 1817. The Wellington Exhibition is an intimate look into the life of the British hero and reviews the Battle of Waterloo. You will also see the Duke's funeral carriage.

If you're looking for an expensive meal that you'll never forget, look back to "Country Dining near London." The splendid 5-star **l'Ortolan** is at nearby **Shinfield**.

**Newbury** is an old market town that is more known today for its steeplechase. The beautiful Tudor **Church of St. Nicholas** was financed by John Smalwoode, a well-suited clothier with deep pockets. A brass dating from 1519 commemorates him in the church. The town museum occupies the 17th-century Jacobean **Cloth Hall** on the wharf and tells the story of the Civil War battles in which **Donnington Castle** played a prominent part in 1643 and 1644. Alas, today the latter is nothing but a handsome ruin.

**Littlecote,** located just four miles south of the M4 (junction 14) near Hungerford, is one of the great Elizabethan residences of the nation, begun late in the 15th century. Visitors can see history brought to life here, with exhibitions of falcony and jousting, plus an extraordinary collection of Cromwellian armor. Imagine yourself as a guest in the Great Hall, the tapers gleaming along a table that is 30 feet long. All in all, it's an enriching experience.

**Highclere Castle** (1838), south of Newbury is renowned mainly for its priceless Egyptian treasures.

**Boxford** is an enchanting Berkshire village with a huddle of cottages, a gabled windmill, huge shade trees, the Lambourn River bathing the verdant banks, and an easy country pace. If you just wish to soak up a fine suburban English atmosphere, here's a lovely weekend choice.

**East Garston**, just off the A338, features many of the ancient timbered cottages with individual bridges from their doorsteps. Driving through the Lambourn Downs toward the Vale of the White Horse you reach **Wantage**, the birthplace of the Saxon King Alfred in 849. A statue notes this royal occasion. Soon you'll arrive at **Basildon Park,** which is just seven miles northwest of Reading between Pangbourne and Streatley on the A329. This classical 18th-century edifice in mellow Bath stone was built by John Carr. The house is positioned with a commanding view over the Thames

Valley. It has an unusual Octagon room, fine plasterwork, important paintings, and rare furniture. During both World Wars it was occupied and used extensively by the military. It was finally purchased by Lord and Lady Ilifle and after having restored it with great taste they donated it to the National Trust in 1977.

**Child Beale Wildlife Trust** is worth a visit with its vast collection of exotic birds and animals, all set out with pleasant walks and areas for the children.

**Pangbourne** is where Kenneth Graham, the author of *The Wind in the Willows,* lived and died. Literary fans can find many of the sources for his inspiration in the district. The **Nautical College** founded in 1917 by Sir Thomas Devitt is also at Pangbourne.

Finally, and still in pursuit of literary links, you come to tree-laced hills enclosing the hamlet of **Mapledurham. Mapledurham House** is a late 16th-century Elizabethan estate belonging to the Blount family. The brick is punctuated with flint lozenges; it has original molded ceilings, a great oak staircase, a fine collection of paintings, and even a little chapel, all this uniquely set in grounds that tumble down to the Thames. John Galsworthy set part of *The Forsyte Saga* here. An earlier author, Alexander Pope, wrote and dedicated love poems to the two Blount sisters. The windmill on the grounds of Mapledurham House dates from the 15th century; you still may watch the flour being ground in a traditional manner.

## BUCKINGHAMSHIRE—"THE QUEEN"

The "Queen of the Home Counties" is formed of two geographically contrasting areas: The Chilterns, running across the south of the county and, to the north, the rich agricultural region of the Vale of Aylesbury. The county town of **Aylesbury** is a handy center from which to explore the Chiltern Hills. So why not start with luxury? Head north about 20 minutes in the direction of **Waddesdon Manor**.

The estate was conceived for Baron Ferdinand de Rothschild and contains a magnificent collection of French art and furniture. You can see very well that the man who made loans to regents lived in higher style than the monarchs. The tall trees in the park as well as the gardens are wonderful for contemplative walks. Just 8 miles northwest is **Claydon House**, dating from 1752. The stone-faced West front contains a series of impressive and unique rococo state rooms, including Florence Nightingale's bedroom and salon.

**Wendover** is just 5 miles southeast of Aylesbury, the well-known site of **Chequers,** a 16th-century house that has been the country home of the Prime Minister in office since 1917. Even though the house is not open to the public, you may (and should) use the footpath that crosses part of the estate on a nine-mile circular walk through the surrounding woods and hills. From Wendover you can also ascend **Bacombe Hill** and **Coombe Hill,** with spectacular views from the chalk escarpment.

**High Wycombe**, another useful bivouac for roaming the Chilterns is on the A40. The Romans established a base here, and its citizens have prospered enormously over the centuries. Textiles made most of the money, first wool and later lace. **Castle Hill House** provides a museum dedicated to chair making, its current mainstream industry. Furniture is derived from the abundance of beechwood in the Chilterns. The **Guildhall** and **Little Market House** are other points of interest from antiquity. As you cross to **West Wycombe,** itself a National Trust protectorate, you'll find some impressive architecture extending over several centuries. Particularly hand some and impressive because of its position is the **Church of St. Lawrence,** with its golden ball that sits in solitary glory to the Lord on a dominant hill. There is nearby a Palladian house set in an 18th-century landscape park with classical temples. **Dashwood Mausoleum** reminds the world of the firebrand Sir Francis Dashwood, a dasher, indeed, and an 18th-century eccentric who ignited the infamous Hell Fire Club, which met in the nearby man-made chalk caves—which would certainly frighten a holy man. Here is where Dashwood and his elite chums held many orgies. On a more intellectual pursuit—and why most visitors come this way—you can next take the A4128 across the River Wye and about 2 miles further on you'll see **Hughenden Manor,** which was the home of Prime Minister Disraeli during the reign of Queen Victoria. Disraeli took a plain white farm dwelling and gave it a rich brick Jacobean jacket over a gothic core; the intense colorings, textiles, and furniture are also impressive. The house—visited by the queen as a compliment to her minister—was remodelled in 1862 and is today a museum. Disraeli is buried in the local churchyard, preferring that to a state ceremony in London. West of the town is **Bladlow Ridge,** which is well worth climbing for the inspiring view.

**Penn** is one of the most enchanting corners of the Chiltern range. Here the taste is for Georgian houses. View the church and surroundings; inside the church are monuments dedicated to the Penn and Curzon families. William Penn is buried about ten minutes away in **Jordans,** an early Quaker center, which would be of great interest to Pennsylvanians.

**Bekonscot Model Village** is not far away on the Warwick Road (Beaconsfield). The kids will love the reproductions in this the world's first miniature settlement. There's a flying club and a seven-station train network plus a thriving little town with 1200 hand-carved citizens doing their little things. Then you can pause at **Denham** to see an attractive collection of fine real-life homes, especially 17th-century **Denham Place.** The church, of about a century later, contains some valuable wall paintings related to the Day of Judgment, obviously not studied carefully by that neighbor, Francis Dashwood.

**Chalfont St. Peter**. By driving via secondary roads (ask locally) toward the highly attractive **Chalfont St. Giles,** you'll reach **Milton's Cottage,** just west of town. It was in this dwelling that the aged and solitary John Milton lived. Outside, the horrors of the plague were raging. Closeted within, Milton wrote his manuscript for *Paradise Lost.* It was completed here in 1665 and, going blind, he also began *Paradise Regained* as his poetic postscript.

**Amersham** is a smart residential town at the foot of the Chilterns in the Misbourne Valley. **Market Hall** (1682), the **Drake Almshouses** (1657), and the **Town Hall** (built by Sir William Drake in 1682), all are of sightseeing interest. Then, on the A413 between Aylesbury and Buckingham you'll come to **Winslow Hall.** It was built between 1698 and 1702, but what gives it the greatest distinction is that it was certainly a creation of the great Sir Christopher Wren. It is also—thank goodness—in the same state as when Wren finished it. That much is known, so preservation has been strict. Chinese art and exceptionally fine furniture are housed within. Also in this rarefied category is **Ascott House,** on the outskirts of **Wing.** Originally a hunting lodge, Ascott eventually became a prize Rothschild property. Try to see the collection of paintings, which arc exceptional, as are the French and Chippendale furnishings. The garden with its circular pool is in Victorian style and covers 12 acres, somewhat out of keeping with the half-timbered pattern of the house itself.

If your timing is right, you've got a pleasure in store. Four miles north of **Buckingham** town is **Stowe House**. This 18th-century estate, the handiwork of numerous architects, was built for the Duke of Buckingham. For most of this century it has been a school, and during the Easter and summer holidays you can walk the grounds. The gardens are among the wonders of Europe. There's a mystical feeling in the mood coupled with the obvious willingness to impress the visitor with the grand architecture. Capability Brown and William Kent were responsible for the semi-formal style; they later tucked in lakes, secret glades, temples, statues, a Palladian bridge, and an assortment of attractive surprises.

# BUCOLIC BEDFORDSHIRE

It's old, it's small, and it's choice. Very often tourists simply drive out from London for the day. The children of many Londoners are educated in this beautiful shire, so in some ways it is a living campus in the Great Ouse Vale. The 4000-year-old Watling Street and Icknield Way cross it. And probably the most revered pedestrian to live and work within its frontiers was John Bunyan, author of *The Pilgrim's Progress.* Catherine of Aragon, who passed her empty days (and nights) at Ampthill Castle while waiting for her divorce from Henry VIII, is said to have introduced the pillow-lace-making that is one of the cottage industries that this county was famed for in early times. Rail and road communications are excellent from London. It is served by the M1 and the A1. It also has an international airport at Luton specializing in charters.

**Bedford,** the county hub, lies 50 miles from London and, while built-up, it still benefits from the fertile valley conditions. The **Church of St. Paul**, mainly Decorated and Perpendicular styles, contains the tomb of Sir William Harpur, who rose in stature to become Lord Mayor of London and thereafter became a loyal benefactor of this, his native town. The Congregational Chapel, called "Bunyan's" or the "Old Meeting," stands on the site of the building in which the non-conformist John Bunyan preached—illegally. (He was jailed several times for this and spent more than 12 years in the lockup.) In the panels of a fine pair of bronze doors in the chapel are scenes illustrative of Bunyan's *The Pilgrim's Progress.* Portions of the tower of **St. Peter's Church** predate the Norman invasion in the 11th century.

**St. Mary's** is in part Norman and **St. John's** is the much later Decorated style. The town offers miles of riverside walks, gardens, and water meadows. Two miles south of Bedford is **Elstow,** Bunyan's advertised birthplace. (Actually he was born in **Harrowden** in 1628, but Elstow continues to steal the thunder.) Other Bunyan memorabilia are at **Houghton House** (said to be his "House Beautiful") and at a rise on the A418 (thought to be his "Hill of Difficulty"). Southwest of the county seat is **The Swiss Garden,** which was developed in the early 1800s and recently restored. It presents a wealth of unusual trees, shrubs, ornaments and buildings in an unusual setting.

Nearby is the air-worthy **Shuttleworth Collection** at **Old Warden**. Flying displays are held on the last Sunday of each month from April to October. At **Cardington**, incidentally, those two colossal hangars are for airships. The doomed R-101 was based here before its Indian adventure. At the nearby **Locks** you can watch and engage in canoe slalom racing. The course is man-made—and so are the dunkings.

**Woburn Abbey**, is the most important focal and/or entertainment point in Bedfordshire without a doubt. This, of course, is where the Earls and Dukes of Bedford resided and ruled for more than 300 years. It became a trend-setter as one of the first country mansions to be tagged a stately home. That meant the public could come in and the winnings would go to pay off the staggering inheritance taxes. Well, "stately" becomes a moot matter when tour buses pull up and disgorge throngs looking to be rewarded with anything from camels and yaks to Van Dycks and Rembrandts. Cruel cynicism apart, the house and grounds are marvelous for their beauty and the great sense of history that is imparted through seeing at close hand the estates of the mighty—or, perhaps, "the high and the mighty," if you are interested in "The Flying Duchess of Bedford" who vanished at 72 in a solo flight the same year that Amelia Earhart disappeared, 1937. Better to concentrate on the Canalettos, the 3000 acres of tigers and deer, and the Grotto of Shells.

**Luton Hoo**, a stately home of (south of **Luton**) is visited by most pilgrims for its unique collection of Russian imperial family treasures, the costumes of the tsars, and Fabergé jewels. Its setting is almost gemlike, too—in a park landscaped by Capability Brown in the 1770s. Masterpiece paintings, tapestries, medieval ivory, and furnishings are also on view. There are two lakes, a rose garden, and some majestic cedars. All this is situated just 30 miles north of London off the M1 at Junction 10. The great mansion, with its six massive columns and perfect symmetry, was conceived by Robert Adam. Probably the diamond tsar of the time, proprietor Julius Wernher also participated in creating such a grand concept as a showcase for his riches.

**Dunstable**, a town itself is worth seeing. It has been inhabited for thousands of years. **Five Knolls** lies just outside the town—quints of round barrows or burial mounds from the Bronze Age. Hospitable coaching inns still survive and carry on Bedfordshire traditions. High above this is the previously mentioned Whipsnade Park Zoo.

**Leighton Buzzard**, despite its gloomy name, features the **Wilkes almshouses,** which are delightful and are the setting for one of the more strange socioreligious practices in Britain where, every May, a choirboy stands on his head while parts of the Founders Will are read to the amused audience. A more conventional sightseeing target is the Market Cross. You can take a steam-train ride through enchanting Bedfordshire from **Pages Park Station.** The vehicle is the incomparable **Leighton Buzzard Light Railway** and the distance is the grand total of four miles!

**Eaton Bray** is proud of its deceptive little **Church of St. Mary the Virgin.** The simple chalk exterior from the local quarries provides not the slightest hint of the delights within. The portal introduces it with magnificent, intricate, foliated ironwork. That crafting alone is more than 700 years old! Go next to the north arcade of the nave; the capitals here are exceptional Early English design. For a village church it certainly is noteworthy; some say it's a rival to Wells Cathedral in Tom Thumb proportions. The village is 4 miles southeast (via A4146) of Leighton Buzzard.

**The Thames** nibbles its route through pure chalk at **Goring**. Then down it plunges into an enchanting wooded vale. Glimpses of the **Goring Gap** can be seen from the A329 and B4009 between Wallingford and Pangbourne, but it is seen more dramatically from viewpoints such as **Streatley Hill,** a prominent spur of chalk that stands 500 feet above the meanders. The 15-mile drive between Wallingford and Pangbourne offer recreation for most tastes: attractive villages, riverside walks, fishing, a wild-life park, the castle ruins of Wallingford, and Basildon Park with its Georgian manse set in beautiful grounds. (Boating is available at the last.)

**Lambourne**, dotted with Georgian houses and fine stables, is best known for racehorse training. The prehistoric Ridgeway Path, fun to walk in the summer or when the weather is favorable, but awful in the rain, passes four miles to the north, an area that contains the impressive **Lambourn Seven Barrows,** a group of tumuli or mounds. The **Uffington White Horse Hills** also are not far away.

## HERTFORDSHIRE—A ROMAN HERITAGE

This fertile county is a bedroom community of Greater London, but on its own it contributes much to both industry and agriculture. Lovely gardens are also a part of its makeup; interspersed amid the four busy new towns are quiet rural areas, the raw material of convenient suburban residency. Access is excellent via the M1 and the M25 orbital motorways. Most visitors take a day trip from London, usually to Hatfield House or St. Albans.

The county is to the northwest of London, sprawling over a chalk spine that is really a geological cousin of the Chilterns. Thus, the beech-clad hills prevail, and numerous rivers have gnawed through the rock to create gorges that have now filled up with woodlands. Being so close to London, it was in the thick of political disputes—the War of the Roses being one of them. St. Albans, founded in the 1st century B.C. and occupied by Romans in 43 A.D., was a battleground twice, and the village of Barnet was the scene of an important conflict as well. These areas are so built up today that you could probably wager safely that only a few who live here even know of those long-ago battles. St. Albans and Bengeo are sites of important religious establishments from Norman times, the former for its Abbey and the latter for its apsidal church and interesting wall paintings. Hemel Hempstead, Weston, and Abbot's Landley reveal Norman forebears. The churches of Ware and Hitchin and several other villages have fine examples of Perpendicular church architecture. Buntingford's Carolean brick, Offley's Georgian Gothic chancel, and Ayot's classical St. Lawrence's are expressions not often seen in Hertfordshire. Brasses are often the showpieces of these churches, and Hertfordshire has many of them. Being prosperous for so long, parishioners were generous in their endowments.

Jacobean and Georgian secular buildings abound; these are fine contributions across the county. Rye House marked the beginning of a new fashion in 1445. Brick suddenly was the thing. It was seen in such important buildings as Hatfield Old Palace, Little Hadham Hall, Hatfield House, and Knebworth House, all landmark structures.

**Hertford**, occupied by Saxons and Romans, has long been a hub. It is now a market town some 22 miles from London where the rivers Mimram, Beane, and Lee meet and flow through. The Lee is navigable this far up too. The midcity **Castle** has been occupied for more than 1000 years; it is now used as municipal offices, still retaining the wall and part of a tower of the Norman period. (If you look in, ask to see the Mayor's Parlour and Robing Room.) At its fringes are many old and colorful timber houses. Two miles southeast of the town is **Haileybury** and the **Imperial Services Colleges,** an interesting amalgam from the time of the East India Company (1492). To the north is **Knebworth** and just east in the direction of St. Albans is **Hatfield**.

**Hatfield**, 45 minutes north from Hyde Park Corner on the Great North Road, is to a satellite community that is usually on the tourist circuit because of a singular building. **Hatfield House** has vivid associations with Henry VIII, Mary Tudor, and Elizabeth I (who grew up here). It stands close to the site of the 15th-century palace of the bishops of Ely. Today the main edifice is Jacobean and made of mellow ocher stone. Of the red brick structure, built around a large quadrangle, just a lone facade is intact. It contains the Banqueting Hall with a minstrel gallery, now employed as a reception zone and for festive meals. After the Dissolution, Henry VIII still retained a fondness for the homestead; its most lasting memory is probably of the child Elizabeth, who spent so many years here and came to the throne from her time at Hatfield.

James I exchanged the house for Theobalds, an estate that belonged to the Earl of Salisbury. That was early in the 17th century. The Earl was in a mood for change so he destroyed much of the old place and built the present building (except for the original segment mentioned above). Following a custom of letters that was a holdover from medieval fortress construction, this impressive showcase was planned in the shape of an "E." All around are mulberry bushes. James I was the royal gardener who ordered the initial plantings, but the patterns were altered during the occupancy of the Cecil family down the centuries.

The treasures are plainly overwhelming: exceptional paintings, fine furniture, and rare antique tapestries. The items of armor are a peculiar counterpoint to the fine silk stockings being shown as part of Elizabeth's wardrobe. Many of Her Majesty's frivolities are also on display, providing an insight into court life. In addition to these there's a knot garden from Elizabeth's time, herbs, scented plants, a maze, model soldiers, vehicles, and the royal stables. There's the usual touristic hype associated with the banquet operation, but for simply looking in on the monarchial style, this exhibit is one of the finest in the nation.

**Old Hatfield** has been a market center for eons. Walk around and absorb the town the Cecils built. The local church is a good place to start. Then look in on the palace of Cardinal Moreton. For refreshment there's always the everlasting **Eight Bells Pub**. Dickens wrote about it in *Oliver Twist*.

**Knebworth**, on the B197 and following the Great North Road, is home to **Knebworth House**, another trove of outstanding paintings, household items, and signets of power. The reigning tribe here has been the Lyttons, in residence since the 15th century. It was transformed with spectacular high Gothic decoration employed by the erudite Sir Edward Bulwer Lytton, who was as well known in his day as a historian (*The Last Days of Pompeii*) as he was as a Victorian novelist. Interesting combination: the period intellectual and man of letters as a graphic artist. The furniture and the Tudor Hall, with excellent Jacobean craftsmanship, are often reasons for visiting the house. It offers wooded parkland with bridle paths, an adventure playground, deer herds, and a narrow-gauge railway (often a passion of those Brits who refuse to grow up). The Norman **Church of St. Mary** is noteworthy for its selection of tomb monuments, not the most joyful of subjects but historical nonetheless.

**Ayot St. Lawrence**, a tiny village not far away, is the home of George Bernard Shaw, who lived there most of his creative life. **Shaw's Corner**—not up to his usual level of imagination—was the name of his home. It is still preserved (in four of the rooms) as they were until his death in 1950.

**St. Albans**, the primary town of Roman Britain, is named for a soldier of the Latin legions. He embraced Christianity and as a result of giving protection to the cleric who brought him into the church, became a martyr, his remains being unearthed when King Offa of Mercia created a Benedictine abbey at this spot late in the 8th century. The abbey was the most important in Britain from the 12th to the early 15th centuries; it became a **cathedral** in 1872, and it's one of the largest in the U.K. The painted vaulting in the nave and choir are lovely antiques in perfect preserve. Today's town resides on a rise over the River Ver, where there was the Roman town of Verulamium. Between 1403 and 1412, a **Curfew** or **Clock Tower** was wound up in the middle of the village; you can see it as it was then as well as some of the oldest dwellings in the nation, which huddle in this district.

Just outside modern St. Albans you can visit the original **Roman amphitheatre,** which served the thriving Latin community. The lifestyle must have been luxurious judging from the mosaic floor that was uncovered. Exhibits of all these findings can be seen at the **Verulamium Museum**.

Nicolas Breakspear, the sole English Pope, was born in St. Albans; after his election in the middle of the 12th century he adopted the name Adrian IV. You might offer him a toast at the **Fighting Cocks Inn** (claimed to be the oldest in England—but don't put your faith in that since I've tippled in quite a few that made a similar pledge to antiquity).

For a change of pace, how about some English roses? You'll find them in overwhelming glory south of town at the **Royal National Rose Society** headquarters. Thousands are on display in this spectacular flower patch. Breeds are tested over a period of three years and established flowers are displayed in a welldesigned showcase. The high point of the year is July. There are also collections of shrub roses, a variety of species and those of historic and botanical interest, as well as several model rose gardens. This complex is situated in Chiswell Green Lane.

**Gorhambury House**, west of St. Albans, is where Sir Francis Bacon, the Elizabethan gentleman of letters who later became Lord Chancellor under James I, was born. The existing 18th-century structure contains interesting possessions that are part of the Bacon heritage. Visitors also are drawn to the enameled glass exhibit. About 1 mile southeast of **Rickmansworth** is the stately **Moor Park Mansion,** a three-story Palladian building reconstructed in 1720. It has magnificent interior decorations consisting of ceiling paintings and murals. Many accord it the highest accolades. The park is also enchanting.

**Ashwell** is a bewitching little village with Elizabethan undertones. William the Conqueror lived in the area. So did Saxons, Romans, and many other peoples, most of whom came for gain and settled for peace. Certainly the tranquility today is alluring. Be sure to visit the timber- framed Early Tudor **Town House,** where there is a museum of village life. The time span goes back to pre-history. Ashwell is 4 miles northeast of Baldock between the A1 and the A505.

## WHERE TO STAY AND EAT

As these form a fair share of England's "Home Counties" you will probably visit the areas on excursions out of the capital. Nevertheless, a few highlights are provided for your convenience. Other points are covered under "Country Dining Near London."

# AMERSHAM

**Crown**
A comfy midtown hotel of two dozen rooms. (☎ *0494-721541.*)

**Kings Arms**
Attractive at mealtimes.

# ASTON CLINTON

**Bell**                                    ☆☆☆☆
Chimes on both sides of the A-41 London- Oxford trunk road in Buckinghamshire. Restaurant-cum-inn, complete with courtyard on one flank; captivating, seasonally toned dining salon with separate bar; ambitious cuisine that shuns nouvelle intrusions. Many doubles have been beautified and expanded into junior suites—the taste exquisite and the maintenance perfect. Energetic Michael Harris, whose courage and skills everyone admires, has a mind-set for hospitality. I must confess my hopeless prejudice for the Harris clan and their wonderful house. (☎ *0296-630252;* FAX: *631250.*)

# AYLESBURY

**Hartwell House**                           ☆☆☆
This hotel has links to the exiled French monarch, Louis XVIII, who lived here for 5 years. Jacobean in style; extensive gardens; noble English tastes in decor and cuisine. (☎ *0296-747-444.*)

# BEDFORD

**Barns**
A hotel with personality, and that's welcome in Bedford. Some very old parts, and well restored. (☎ *0234-270044;* FAX: *273102.*)

# COLD CHRISTMAS

**Fabdens Park**                               ★
A sweetie with a quartet of artful suites, a trio of lounges with open fires, and a good little restaurant. This stucco-and-brick charmer is near Ware, off the A10 en route to Cambridge. (☎ *0920-463484.*)

# HENLEY-ON-THAMES

**Regency House**
A few rooms on the River Terrace. (☎ *0491-571133.*)

**Stonor Arms**                              ☆☆
Wonderful for dinners or for midday mealtiming on Sundays. (☎ *049-163345.*)

# HIGH WYCOMBE

**Crest**
A reasonable shelter if you are visiting Hughenden Manor. (☎ *0494-442100.*)

## LEIGHTON BUZZARD

**Swan** is adequate but not much more. (☎ *0525-372148*; FAX: *370444.*)

## READING

**Caversham** has a pleasant river frontage. (☎ *0734-391818*; FAX: *391665.*)

### Cliveden

An ultra-posh hotel near Reading with rates dancing from £150 per night to £350 for the grandest Nancy Astor suite. Clearly, for such tariffs one would expect imperial treatment —or probably shares in the estate. (When the Sun. and Tues. bus tours roll in, guests are separated from gawkers by only a velvet rope.) Alas, one has to ask, is this game worth the candle? Its broad windows in the exquisite dining room and library overlook expansive, well-tended gardens and Berkshire landscape. If space permits (and that could be frequent at such rates) non-residents may dine here at close to £50 per setting. Service standards have improved now that it has mellowed somewhat. And, certainly, the site is majestic. Should you be tempted to such extravagance, look for Taplow on the map or phone ☎ *(06286) 68661*—after you've consulted your accountant!

### Swan Diplomat

Far more reasonable (about $165 per duo) and the riverside perch is ever so romantic. You'll soon get over the shocking yellow exterior. (☎ *0491-873737.*)

## ST. ALBANS

### Sopwell House

A bit out of the center but worthwhile. (☎ *0727-64477*; FAX: *44741.*)

## SHINFIELD

### l'Ortolan

My choice for one of the top restaurants in Britain, is covered under "Country Dining Near London"; it's close to Reading.

## SONNING

### The Great House

Famous for its roses by the Thames. Pleasant rooms at varying rates. (☎ *0734-692277.*)

### French Horn                                                ★★

Offers accommodations, but it is primarily known for its fine traditional gastronomy and waterside dreams. (☎ *0734-692204.*)

## STANSTEAD ABBOTTS

### Briggens House

A reformed stately home in 45 acres of park near Ware. The gardens and arboretum are nicely maintained. Very English and maybe a bit fussy. (☎ *0279-792416*; FAX: *3685.*)

# WARE

### Hanbury Manor

This new golf and leisure center near Thundridge will surely steal the thunder of other local luxury complexes. There are about 90 rooms in an extended mansion, a large and well-designed pool area, three restaurants, and an inviting snack service in the conservatory. It's just off the A-10, so ask about it, because this one sounds like it will be one of the proudest buttons in Hertfordshire.

# WINDSOR

### Oakley Court

A lovely riverside setting and park. The central part of the hotel was once used to film horror films (Hammer Production Studio headquarters), so a few of the spooks still haunt the precincts. The new wing is spiritless, however. A pleasant curiosity, and an expensive one. (☎ *0628-74141*; FAX: *37011.*)

### Sir Christopher Wren's House

A most relaxing stop. (☎ *0753-861354*; FAX: *860172.*)

# ENGLISH
# SOUTHLANDS

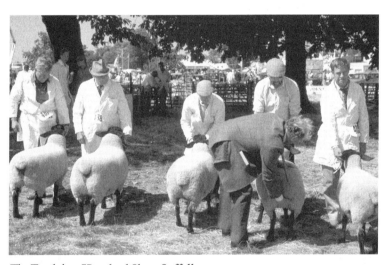

*The Tendring Hundred Show, Suffolk*

## HISTORIC HAMPSHIRE

Whether you are a Briton living in northern Aberdeen or hail from the lower reaches of Southampton, you will probably say at some point that you are traveling "up to London." It doesn't matter what compass direction you take, London is *always* "up." It could, of course, suggest that London is the capital and therefore is of higher station than any other city, but more likely the expression derived from those residents—perhaps the original Jane Austen "gentry"—who occupied these suburban southern counties and continued to utilize London as their cultural home base. Hampshire—decidedly Austen country—is one such example. It has always been a historical shire since it runs directly from the major ports merrily up to London.

Hampshire was forever a desired spot and often the scene of disaster and recovery. The Romans desired it and added their stamp in the middle of the first century. Traces of their invasion and control are featured in the town walls of Silchester and Portchester Castle. These were most likely the western flank of the Saxon shore. About seven centuries later, the county appeared in the Anglo-Saxon Chronicle, not a local newspaper but a careful recording of administrative jurisdiction in which Wessex was noted as the heart of the English kingdom. Winchester, a marvelous city today, was its capital. At Christchurch, Odiham, Portchester, and Winchester there are substantial remnants of that militant epoch. At Southhampton—as at Winchester—town walls and evidence of advanced fortification still survive. Later coastal defenses of the 16th century are to be witnessed at the dramatic and stalwart Calshot and Hurst castles. As with many cities of sinew, World War II struck Portsmouth and Southampton; both were severely damaged by air raids. These old soldiers, however, have a durability that has seen them through worse. They are fine, thriving cities today with scarcely a trace of the travails of the past.

Geologically, Hampshire is of four minds. A significant belt of chalk sweeps across its girth. The north and south axis are composed of clay, sand, and gravel, and these bases are cloaked in rich heath and woodland. The oldest rocks sprout in the Wealden area, now one of the most romantic segments of this ancient county. The Tertiarys up north around Aldershort and Farnborough are the same foundations that run over to Reading and even create the well-known clay upon which the British capital sits. Some strata (such as Barton and Headon) are virtually fossil mines. The body of water known as The Solent—home of Britain's prestige regattas—is the decorative interface between the Isle of Wight and the mainland. Prehistoric habitation is probable, according to finds of specialists. Tools appear from Paleolithic and Mesolithic periods; these were unearthed from the chalk and heath near Petersfield. Neolithic long barrows are also etched onto the Hampshire map. Coming much later, the bastions of Danebury, Hengistbury, Ladle, Old Winchester, Quarley, and St. Catherine's are testimony to the Age of Iron and the man of might.

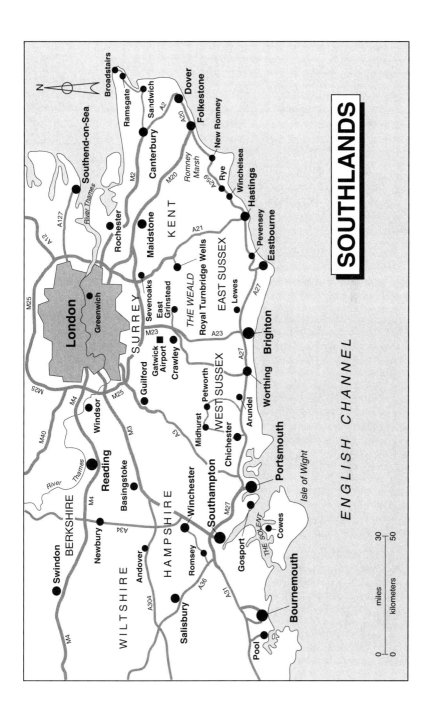

## PORTSMOUTH

**Portsmouth** retains worldwide maritime fame originating from its valiant service as a naval base. From the visitor's point of view the city is always enhancing its numerous benefits. You must, for example, see the majestic wraith of the British flagship *Mary Rose*. She belonged to the fleet of Henry VIII, and her bitter end came before the very eyes of its royal reviewing party in the River Solent in 1545. She lay on the muddy dark bottom for a chilly four centuries, but her status—like that of the glorious *Wasa* in Stockholm—was one of benign preservation. Sprays, chemicals, and a modest facelift brought the dowager vessel a youthful visage once more. The nation is duly proud of her resurrection and establishment as a major attraction. Priceless archaeological treasures have been retrieved; most are on view in the **Mary Rose Exhibition**.

Another must is the even more famous HMS *Victory*, introduced to battle in 1778. Her glorious moment was Oct. 21, 1805, at the Battle of Trafalgar. Lord Horatio Nelson overpowered the Spanish and French fleets with *Victory* as the command ship. Go aboard and see how life was below decks in the British Navy. At the **Royal Naval Museum** you can observe a scale panorama of the Battle of Trafalgar with formidable sound effects.

On a quieter note, Portsmouth produced perhaps the greatest of English novelists—Charles Dickens (1812-70). The house in which he was born has become a memorial to the author; this museum is located at 393 Commercial Road. (His tomb is in Poet's Corner of Westminster Abbey in London.)

**Portchester Castle** is probably one of the most authentic Roman fortifications to be found north of Italy, and yet there also are Norman traces as well as Romanesque legacies. The castle has had a varied career. Agincourt's fate was outlined here by Henry V. Its **D-Day Museum** exhibits embroidery showing the complete story of Operation Overlord. This graphic history in textile of the invasion extends a full 272 feet in length and is 3 feet high. It took five years and 200 nimble fingers to complete the masterpiece, a work inspired by the Mathilde Frieze at Bayeux in Normandy.

Between Portsmouth and Southampton is the home of Lord Mountbatten, **Broadlands**, which exhibits many relics of the earl's life in statecraft. The grounds slope beautifully to the edge of the River Test and create a wondrous setting for the Palladian estate that was created by Henry Holland and Capability Brown. Lord Romsey is the name on the doorbell now (he's the earl's grandson), and many of the faces you see daily on the front page of your newspaper ring it to find solace from the world outside. It has been the honeymoon hideaway for two generations of English royals and a celebrity circle for eons. There's a mood of escape to a gentler realm that pervades the soft air. The drive from London takes about two hours.

## ON THE COAST

The indomitable Henry VIII saw the defense potential of **Southsea**, and what today serves as a **Naval Museum** was formerly a fortress created by that warrior monarch. From its promontory you will immediately see how

it controls both Portsmouth and Langstone harbors, with a view to the
entry to Chichester Harbor as well. While at Southsea you may wish to visit
the **Royal Marines Museum,** the nearby **Beam-Engine House,** and **Cumberland House.** An 11-mile drive from Portsmouth brings you to **Havant.** This
brief circuit includes **Waterlooville,** the **Forest of Bere,** plus a good look at
**Hayling Island**, with its Abbey of Jumieges which was gobbled up by the
sea in 1325. A Roman villa was found at **Langstone**; **Havehunte** was listed
for taxes in the Doomesday Book. Havant is an 18th-century town, but the
12th-century **church** is noteworthy. Most important old-world documents
were quilled onto Havant parchment, famous for a thousand years until
fabrication regretfully was terminated in this century. Also in the area are
**Sir George Staunton Country Park** and **Leigh Park,** with gardens and a lake.
Further north you can visit the **Queen Elizabeth Country Park,** with a craft
center, a reconstruction of an Iron Age settlement, and numerous trails for
walking.

**Fishbourne** (over into Sussex) is close enough to visit on the main pike
to **Chichester**. A **Roman palace** of the first century was excavated here, and
scholars have opened many areas to the public; you can also observe the
continuing digs at one of England's largest and richest Roman sites. The
most famous mosaic, *Boy on the Dolphin,* is available for you to study and
admire. There is even a Roman bath, probably first stoked up as the syba-
ritic Latin empire was starting its decline.

**Southampton**, the mighty port of Atlantic travelers of yore, stands near
the head of Southampton Water, an inlet of the English Channel on a peninsula formed by the rivers Test and Itchen. The Romans began its maritime career, and today Southampton is the third largest among English
ports and still the first in regard to passenger traffic. (That's not saying
much.) The Normans immediately recognized an opportunity to follow
their most ardent passion: fortress construction. They started with ramparts and a moat, then created a navy to decorate The Solent at its fortstep.
Henry IV designated Southampton as a county unto itself in 1447. It was
from here that the *Mayflower* set sail with the Pilgrims to open the New
World. Norman walls strengthened by towers and having six main gates
stand in fragments even today. An 800-year-old house known as **King
John's Palace** is one of the earliest dwellings intact in the nation.

The south and west portals of the city date from the early 14th century;
the northern entry is later. The **Mayflower Memorial** is at the West Gate.
The Puritan ship weighed anchor in 1620 with the intention of speculating
in Virginia; navigation must have been abysmal as they landed, of course,
at what is now Plymouth, Mass., signing the Mayflower Compact on board
before debarking.

**St. Michael's Church** comes equipped with an 11th-century tower to
wow the sightseer. The spire, built in 1745, was later raised a further nine
feet to serve as a mark for mariners. Look inside at the font of Tournai marble and the arches. The 13th-century **Netley Abbey,** on most tour circuits,
is three miles southeast of town; it was created by Henry III and peopled
at first by monks from Beaulieu. The **Guildhall,** now used as a courthouse,

is situated over the archway of the Bar Gate. **Tudor House,** a merchant's residence in medieval times, is a museum.

The prosperity of Southampton was assured with the opening of the railway link with London in 1840. The harbor, of course, remains one of the finest natural ports in Britain; moreover, it has the advantage of a double tide. A great many all-time VIPs have sailed away on that Southampton tide. Richard-the-Lionheart began his Third Crusade from here in 1189; Edward III (in 1345) and Henry V (in 1415) commenced their sea-borne assaults against France from these docksides. And, in 1912, the *Titanic* began her doomed voyage from here.

Today Southampton is a bustling city. An excellent art gallery is open to the public; it contains modern English works plus the famous Burne-Jones *Perseus Cycle.* It's a reasonable base for excursions to the New Forest, Winchester, or day-tripping to the Isle of Wight.

### FARTHER AFIELD

**Romsey** is less than a half-hour's drive northwest of Southampton and is known for the landmark **Abbey,** which has Saxon roots and Norman limbs, revealing the changes of fortune here over the last thousand years. There is little remaining of its Saxon heritage, but the church is a fine example of the later Normans, who were probably second only to the Romans in their zeal for construction. There is a Saxon crucifix in the south choir and some traces of the 10th-century birth of this Benedictine convent. There are interesting elements that follow the living progress of this much esteemed institution, so reads the guide legend near the entry to the East or West wings.

**King John's House,** a museum today, is not far away, and in this same district—if you are a motoring buff—you can head for **Beaulieu Abbey,** which John constructed in the beginning of the 13th century. The huge gatehouse—well, huge for a gatehouse—later became the swanky address of the rich and famous Lord Montagu of Beaulieu (pronounced Byou-Lee). The area is usually swarming with rubbernecks who tumble out of  the buses each morning to help pay for the upkeep of Beaulieu Park. Its best feature by far is the riveting **National Motor Museum,** containing vintage marques, racing cars, cycles, and breathtaking prototypes. Most of these are rare models, but all of them are in stunning condition. In some cases they reveal exceptional design or engineering developments in man's sequel to the horse. The displays are excellent and the tour is rewarding both educationally and aesthetically. The other pastimes and amusements on the estate are *pur sang* honky-tonk, meant for coach groups and mass entertainment. What a pity to spoil the otherwise selective exhibit! Ten miles southeast of Southampton are the wondrous and ever-so-peaceful **Exbury Gardens,** nurtured by the Rothschild family. This is a tranquil contrast to the hoopla of Beaulieu.

## WINCHESTER

**Winchester** hastily deems itself one of the chief fabricators of English history—part truth, part fiction. As England's capital for so many years, it has certain privileges. In any case, as a market town on the Itchen River and only about two hours' drive from London, it is an interesting excursion destination. Even though there is no physical evidence to prove it, Winchester is inevitably associated with Arthur and his faithful vassals. King Alfred also may have become liege of England here. Historic buildings are in abundance, disclosing a variety of architecture spanning eight centuries. The city was known to the Romans as *Venta Belgarum,* and during the Saxon period, around 519, it had already become the capital of Wessex and was called *Wintanceaster.* In fact, Egbert of Wessex celebrated his coronation as Sovereign of the Realm here, becoming England's monarch in 827. So, of pomp and circumstance, Winchester has assumed a king-size portion in its time.

Its time began winding down in 1645 when Cromwell marched in. The core has not grown much physically since then so it is interesting today to see the size of what used to be London's equal.

The city's chief house of worship is certainly appropriate for witnessing such rituals. **Winchester Cathedral** measures in as the longest in England and indeed exceeds that of any other church of its character: 526 feet. The temporal longevity, however, of the original Saxon building was very slight and, as usual, its place was taken by a Norman one erected by an ambitious bishop intent on saving Hampshire souls. The **Church of St. Swithun**— known through the connection with his feast day every 15th of July—is considered to have enlarged the cathedral since it is a neighboring structure. St. Swithun, not incidentally, served as bishop of this city in the 9th century. Ethelwold and Alphege contributed to the overall architecture in a similar fashion. St. Swithun's lies in the lower part of the city in a wide and handsome walled close. While the main arched window and twin spires are beautifully proportioned, the cathedral is not very conspicuous from a distance. A frequent criticism is that the central tower barely can be seen above the general level of the roof. It was obviously of Norman origin. The Lady Chapel, which forms the eastward segment, was commissioned by Bishop de Lucy and reveals a font that is French. The finish of the exterior is noble, clean-lined, and severely plain; the interior is intricate and lovingly detailed. The perpendicular nave is the estimable contribution of Bishop Edington and the celebrated William of Sykeham. Norman traces from the original building can be studied by following both transepts while the choir sings its praise to Bishop Edington. The arches in the nave pay homage to some of the illustrious princes of the church, including its founder. The door of ornamental iron at the north nave is distinctive both for its elaborate work as well as for its antiquity—probably from the 11th or 12th century. Near this point you will find the oft-visited tomb of Jane Austen (8 College Street is where the writer died).

While on the subject of letters, Winchester Cathedral's **Library** contains a Latin edition of the Bible that goes back to the 12th century. The definitive architect of his time (the 17th century), Christopher Wren, is associated with two houses in this district. The one at **26 St. Swithun's Street**

was built for James II, while the one in **Kingsgate** was created for the Duke of Buckingham.

Formal education clearly was becoming a fashionable concept. **Winchester College,** founded in 1382 by the city's bishop and the oldest public school in England, is also known as the College of St. Mary; it is still one of Britain's best. Bishop Wykeham was so interested in education that he participated to a major degree in establishing New College in Oxford a few years earlier. Henry VI fudged a copy by creating Eton College. Many other knock-offs followed. **Wolvesey Castle,** now a ruin but part of which has become the Bishop's Palace, was built by Henri de Blois in the 12th century.

At the appropriate end of High Street is the historically important 13th-century **Westgate,** which shares a lot of its tourists with neighboring **Castle Hall.** The big draw at the latter is the **Round Table of King Arthur,** but there are several more adequately documented elements within the building. It was probably built by William the Conqueror, destroyed in the 17th century, and was rebuilt to become one of the most eventful institutions in the land—and throughout almost every epoch of British development. Nevertheless, the magnet remains that doubtful piece of furniture that may or may not have hosted a noble circle of two dozen knights loyal to a mythic regent perhaps named Arthur. Legend? Fact? Who will ever know this side of Camelot?

## *COUNTRYSIDE, SMALL TOWNS, AND VILLAGES*

Northern Hampshire's patchwork of shimmering ponds, tumbling streams, and forested hills has been described for many armchair travelers and animal lovers by Richard Adams in *Watership Down.* The **Test Valley** is a hospitable replica of just such scenery. Then you have the heartwarming thatched hamlets and engaging history of ancient Hampshire towns. **Selborne** and Selborne Hill offer more than natural backdrops for distinctive architecture; here you'll find the inspiring **Gilbert White Museum**, where you can experience the sensitivity and spirit of one of the first men to really go eye-to-eye with wildlife. If you wish to follow in White's footsteps, you may wander among the beeches where he recorded so many tender and meticulous elements of nature. Then scramble up the serpentine trail for the view from Selborne Hill. Over at **Fleet** (not to be confused with the one over in Lincolnshire) there is yet another **nature preserve**; it is near **Addershot**.

As if the name were purloined from a comic book, **Middle Wallop's** claim to fame is a **military museum** (devoted to flying). Then you can rusticate in an Iron Age exhibit that is also here. A few miles away is **Alton**, today only a simple market town but once widely regarded for its brewing and fabrication of woolen textiles. It was also a stop on the pilgrimage path. There are tall, trim Georgian buildings and an Elizabethan cottage where Edmund Spenser lived and wrote much of his classic verse. On a more earthy (or earthly) note, the **Curtis Museum** contains exhibitions of antique tools.

There are also furnishings, glass, ceramics, and a doll collection. **Chawton** is just down the road a piece. Stop by and visit the unassuming—well, even ugly—18th-century, two-story, red-brick cottage where the nation's esteemed Jane Austen lived from 1809 until her closing chapter. The author penned most of her later novels in this dwelling, *Emma* and *Persuasion* the most noteworthy.

## THE NEW FOREST

Well, not exactly "new." William the Conqueror made it an official preserve in 1079. Prior to that the West Saxon kings used it as a favorite hunting ground. Its leaves fall mainly on southwestern Hampshire between Southampton Water, The Solent, and the Avon rivers. This tidy region of 130 square miles is of unique scenic beauty and serves many of the recreational purposes of a national park. At many turns you might find yourself muzzle-to-muzzle with wild, free-roaming ponies, mules, cows, and horses, part of the resident community throughout the grounds. They may sample your picnic and often wander onto restaurant patios to nod hello. The deer are a bit more timid. Naturally, driving everywhere is done slowly and with a cautious respect for these four-legged friends.

**Lyndhurst** is the hub, and generally is considered to be the tourist center. Its **parish church** is Victorian with some lovely stained-glass by Burne-Jones, as well as other masters of this art. Alice Liddel, *Alice in Wonderland*'s namesake, is buried in the town's churchyard. You can have a meal here, buy your postcards, film, and stamps, or just browse in a hospitable town-and-country atmosphere. Continue along the A35 until you reach the Swan Inn, where you turn right; about half a mile further you'll see the New Forest Inn, where you turn left; your drive then will take you along one of the most attractive stretches in New Forest.

Three miles further you'll come to **Island Viewpoint**, where you turn sharply left, and 2 miles more takes you to **Knightswood Oak.** This old-timer has a mighty girth—a diameter of more than 21 feet! The tree is believed to have survived more than 600 years. An alternative drive would be to take the A337 to Cadnam toward **Minstead**, where Sir Arthur Conan Doyle is at eternal rest. On this route you will pass through the area of **Furzey Gardens,** one of the beauty spots of botanical Hampshire. Going northwest for  another 30 miles or so you come to the **Rufus Stone,** established in 1745. Though this may sound like the beginning of a vaudeville wheezer, legend says that it was placed here to mark the spot where King William Rufus was struck dead by a stray hunter's arrow in 1100. (Old Rufus must have been a monarch of questionable efficiency if it took six-and-a-half centuries to commemorate his demise.)

**Brockenhurst** is a handsome spot for a pause. Of course, like every other inhabited place in this part of the world, there is a Norman association—and, as usual, it is to the church where you look first. While you are at prayer, you might contemplate the gigantic yew outside, believed to be older than the Knightswood Oak by perhaps 400 years. Yep, that pushes it over the millennial mark.

**Burley** can provide some excellent photographic opportunities from the 300-foot crest of **Castle Hill.** While enjoying a pint at the Queen's Head, you can study the unlikely collection of souvenirs, trophies, and weapons, all heaped together in utter disregard for chronology.

A drive across the flat carries on south to **Barton-On-Sea,** a lackluster resort but one that affords good views from its cliff-tops of the distant **Needles** and the **Isle of Wight.** The Needles has always been a landmark for mariners, just as important today as it was to Nelson or his Viking predecessors.

Drive to the end of the Promenade and follow the wiggles in the route that lead to the coast road going east to **Milford-On-Sea.** The purpose of this is for the continuing panorama of a historic and impressive morsel of English maritime lore. On a promontory about 2 miles southeast is **Hurst Castle;** Henry VIII created it as a coastal defense, and a mighty one it was. Its greatest fame, however, derives from its use as a prison for Charles I in 1648, about a century after it was built. Locals claim that there are only three ways to reach Hurst Castle: by foot, by boat, or by commitment of the crown.

If you start pointing north you'll soon arrive at delightfully salty **Lymington,** a busy and bustling resort and one of England's great yachting playgrounds. From here a ferry will chug you over to the Isle of Wight, a brief pleasant crossing made all the better from the open top deck on a fine sunny day. This body of water is almost an aquarian shrine for sailors. It's called **The Solent** and it serves **Cowes,** capital of the greatest British regattas.

Landlubbers, or those with decidedly green thumbs, may prefer a half-hour's drive southwest of Southampton to visit the previously mentioned, glorious **Exbury Gardens,** an Eden packed beautifully into 200 acres by Lionel de Rothschild. That gentleman gardener tamed the forest and created a unique park early in this century that has become renowned for its rhododendrons, azaleas, magnolias, and camellias.

## ISLE OF WIGHT

The Isle of Wight lies off the south coast of England, a small but tasty morsel of Hampshire. It is separated from the mainland by The Solent, probably the most celebrated sport sailing territory in the Northern Hemisphere—well, maybe both hemispheres. If you are driving, the middle section is almost devoid of building or traffic. The climate is mild and (to an Englishman) salubrious. Wight has been in fashion, out of fashion, and is now starting to revive its upper-crusted image again. Its high point was during its Victorian "discovery" epoch. The principal communications with the mainland are between Ryde and Portsmouth, Cowes and Southampton, and Yarmouth and Lymington.

Its composition is an everlasting invitation to geologists—all within a tight, easy-to-see zone. To the ordinary visitor the variety simply looks appealing. **Culver Cliff** is in the east and the **Needles** are in the west. In between is all chalk. It isn't only white but changes color as you move. Alum used to come in vast quantities from **Alum Bay**, now more of a tourist attraction for its multicolored sandstone cliffs. Along the south coast the incisive work of lovely streams has clawed and picked out dramatic gullies called chines, the most visited being at **Shanklin** and **Blackgang**.

The Isle's pedigree goes back to Paleolithic times; however, the Early Bronze Age was more popular with prehistoric trippers who seemed to popularize the island (once attached to the shore). The Romans called the terrain *Vectis*, and of their presence scholars are sure. Not quite a thousand years later, Wight became the southern stronghold of the Danes, and from the 14th to the 16th century—like all settlements on these waters—the island constantly feared invasion by those much-too-close French. In 1404 all those anxieties were realized and there began a long series of tiffs on the cliffs—the reason for English forts being built at Cowes, Sandown, Freshwater, and Yarmouth. Sights you probably will stumble over in your rovings include about 170 mounds mostly from the Bronze Age, the Long Stone at Mottiston, which is a 13-foot-high monolith, Roman villas (a good one at **Brading**), an earthwork on Chillerton Down called the Five Barrows; a ruined 14th-century **lighthouse** on St. Catherine's Down, and the decaying medieval Cistercian **abbey** at **Quarr** near Ryde.

**Newport** is the chief town and capital lying at the inner terminus of the Medway estuary. About a mile out of town is **Carisbrooke Castle,** set in 7 acres of land, with interesting earthworks to explore. Even though its original purpose was as a fort against the pesterings of the French and the Spanish, it (like Hurst) is better known for having served as a prison for Charles I as well as for his children.

The A3020 going north from Newport will bring you to **Cowes**, the world's epicenter of yachting competitions. It is here during the first week in August that the greatest international regattas take place, the home of the Admiral's Cup races. **Cowes Castle** was built by Henry VIII in 1540 and now houses the Royal Yacht Squadron. Even as a non-member you can view the races from the fringes of its terrace overlooking the start line. The society atmosphere and excitement are pulsating.

**Osborne House,** a mile away, was Queen Victoria's seaside residence during the happiest years of her life. It was built in 1845, and she and Prince Albert spent a blissful time here until his death, which almost drove her to reclusiveness within the estate. The house and gardens are as they were during her occupation. It was the place of her death in 1901; King Edward VII presented it to the nation.

**Swiss Cottage** located in the compound was specially imported from Switzerland as a playhouse for the queen's children. To enjoy the visit properly will take a full morning or afternoon.

**Freshwater's** *Farringford* has been converted into a hotel; it was originally the home of Alfred Lord Tennyson. His monument can be seen along the trail between Freshwater and Alum Bay on the High Down. For three decades the poet experienced the same inspirational vistas here that you can enjoy today. If the sea is calm, you probably can arrange for a boat excursion under these great cliffs, which lead from Freshwater out to the Needles. As you approach Alum Bay you'll see the colors of the rock changing, a gift of nature wrapped gaily in shades of green and moving to the hotter tones of orange, red, and yellow. And as the sun sets these hues undergo dramatic mutations before your eyes.

**Yarmouth** is one of the busiest little ports on the island, a popular sailing center for yachting fans. The streets are alive with shoppers, sailors, and visitors. There are fun pubs and cozy corners galore. **Yarmouth Castle** was part of the coastal defenses of Henry VIII. Completed in 1547, it was the very latest fashion in military engineering of its day.

**Parkhurst Forest** lies south of Cowes, and you'll pass it if you are motoring to Newport on the A 3020 out of Northwood. It is the only major patch of green on this rather bare and windblown island. The Red Squirrel is a joyous native of its foliage, a fact that attracts naturalists to view this rare critter. It is also a lovely retreat for a picnic by two-legged visitors.

**Appuldurcombe House**—pronounced Applercombe and a monument to one man's vanity—is situated about a half mile from the village of **Wroxham**. This is a sort of pseudo-mansion that seems to have represented an intended status symbol rather than a home. Sir Robert Worsley commenced his folly in 1701 but did not get very far due to a lack of funds. The east facade is an exquisite example of English baroque. Completion of the house was effected toward the end of the 18th century; today only a shell remains. The surrounding park was designed by the legendary Capability Brown.

Additional island targets? Well, try the 18th-century **Old Town Hall** in **Newtown** (a contradiction in terms?). Then study the Norman features in the **church** at **Shalfleet**. Down on the South Shore, **Brook House** in **Brook** is engaging, and have a look at the geological phenomenon called **Brook Chine,** a rock fissure big enough to embrace a pasture; you'll also discover a magnificent beach here. **Chale Abbey** and the smuggler's cove of **Blackgang Chine** are at the southern tip of the island's ring road. Up above the latter (before **Niton**) you can climb **St. Catherine's Hill,** from which you can have an overall look at the island as well as a browse through **St. Catherine's Oratory.** This point is almost 800 feet above sea level—and the sea's level is right down there in front of you.

**St. Lawrence** blew its chances for international recognition. Once the proud possessor of "the smallest church in Britain," it thoughtlessly tacked on a porch and bell tower in 1842 only to lose its singular claim to fame. *Sic transit gloria.* Now the coastal road takes a swing to the north and soon you are in **Bonchurch**, which, throughout the Romantic period and later, attracted some of England's most noteworthy men of letters. Perhaps they sought inspiration at the island's most lofty (and most anomalous) point, **Boniface Down** (down means up, geologically speaking), peaking at 785 feet (St. Catherine's Hill —in case you are a statistician—is 12 feet shorter).

**Shanklin** holds the island's record for receiving the most sunshine during the year. Obviously its PR chief is not from St. Lawrence. Once upon a time it was a sleepy fishing village consisting of a group of thatched buildings, the Crab Inn, and St. Blasius's church. The sunlight hype and the excellent beaches have made it into a powerhouse of tourism. Such is the force of public relations on an island only 23 miles long and 13 miles wide!

## SURREY, THE LONDON SUBURB

Here's a tiny county in size but a densely populated one. It, too, serves as an extended bedroom community of London since transport to the capital is abundant, fast, and usually reliable. (At rush hour on a wet day all bets are off.) There's a lot of history packed into Surrey. Its proximity to the doin's in London over the centuries has had a major spill-off effect in leaving behind important ruins, estates, some churches, and important archaeological foci.

First, let's take a look at the lay of the attractive land. The northern portion is low. The western shelf is what geologists call the Bagshot Beds—not a reference to the opening comment about Surrey's dormitorial proclivities. London Clay is in the east. You'll see plenty of it when the Thames is low. It also has a few moderate size ridges and a chalk base along the North Downs, one of its best features.

In terms of antiquity, both Farnham and Abinger attest to very early (Mesolithic) settlement. In the Iron Age, communities already were busy with this first phase of man's mini-industrial revolution while Celtic peoples had dug in at Dorking. Kings of West Saxony used Kingston-on-Thames as their "king's-town," a site to crown their regents. At the Town Hall you can have your picture taken beside the Coronation Stone. After the Romans arrived, the inevitable road-building began—out to Portslade and Lewes; the Stane Street pike also was a product of enterprising Latin civil engineers. Pilgrims to Canterbury may have taken a trail that had been known since Neolithic times. This skirts the edge of the North Downs, one of the county's most attractive areas. The region was abuzz with social life and cultural pursuits. At Southwark, Elizabethan theater was thriving. Archaeologists and Sam Wanamaker (see the 1994 Fielding Travel Award) now believe they have discovered the original Globe Theatre, which burned down in 1613 after a 14-year run. (There was a brief reprise but it vanished again in 1644.) The new Globe is due to raise the curtain on a born-again career this season, so be sure to check the schedules or ☎ *(71)620-0202* for further details. Convenient tube stations are London Bridge or Mansion House.

Early religious fervor is manifest in stone near Woking, where the Augustinians constructed Neward Priory; Waverley Abbey dates as far back as 1128. Albury, Compton, and Chaldon, as well as Stoke d'Abernon and Leigh are additional destinations for ecclesiastical architecture. But Surrey is really an outer district of London, so many major projects were reserved for capital expenditure, so to speak.

## RICHMOND

This town—now an area that seems to be within the purview of London's suburban sprawl—has majestic associations with various monarchs. One look from the top of **Richmond Hill** and the riverscape flashing in the sunlight below will help you understand why the tastemakers of the past chose to live here. If you have plenty of time, arrive the way the regents of ancient times transported themselves: by boat from the center of London. Alternatively, a drive along the Thames is also pleasant. A great deer park existed; lakes and waterways were teeming with fish and fowl. It was here that Henry VIII created a majestic palace as only the flamboyant sovereign of all time could decree. It was here that Elizabeth I chose to expire. It was from here that William Byrd felt inspired to carry the memory of such scenery back to his home on the James River and to give the Virginia settlement the name of Richmond in the mid-18th century. In the Victorian era the enjoyment of Richmond and its surroundings became somewhat more democratic.

Recreational facilities abound. There are golf courses open to the general public, cricket can be watched on the local pitch, you can take a rowboat or a power vessel up and down the Thames, observe some of the finest tennis in the world at nearby **Wimbledon**, ride horses through sun-dappled ancient forests, or ice skate on a rink where some of the world's greatest champions were trained.

Within easy reach you can (and must) visit **Hampton Court**, the royal redoubt in **Twickenham**, which is an easy excursion point from either Richmond or London. This overwhelming palace was dreamed up by the crafty Cardinal Wolsey who—ever the consummate politician—made a gift of it to Henry VIII. From 1526 and for some years following, it was Henry's residence of preference. That canny old Wolsey opined that if he hadn't presented it to the headstrong monarch, Henry probably would have "obtained" it by some other means. Hampton Court enjoyed a blue-bloodline right through the reign of George II, and it was through the generosity of Queen Victoria that the grounds and some of the more important chambers were revealed for public inspection and enjoyment. Today approximately 1000 units exist as "grace and favor" quarters, provided by the crown for families related to heroes who distinguished themselves through service to the nation.

The great Gate House is a fine place to start your tour. Henry VIII added wings to either side of this, leading to the Base Court through Anne Boleyn's passage and finally to the Clock Court. Here you'll find the Great Hall (hardly an understatement), the Royal Staircase, and columns in a corridor created by Christopher Wren. Here, George II ordered a portal that leads to the beautiful Fountain Court and ultimately to the Great Fountain Garden. You're probably familiar with the Chapels Royal of England, which were specially commissioned precincts of worship designed specifically for the sovereigns of the land. The one at Hampton Court created by Cardinal Wolsey was redesigned by Henry VIII in one of his more reverent moments. The famous wood carver of the epoch, Grinling Gibbons, provided embellishment to the scene. Early in this century a bridge commissioned by Henry was discovered under a moat that had been filled in by Charles II. In an effort to return the building to its previous state the moat was re-created—a very successful gesture by modern archaeologists. Any avid tennis player ought to visit the Royal Tennis Court. You may have seen paintings of Henry VIII involved in this pastime, which was the original version of the game we play today. Royal Tennis (or Real Tennis) is followed in only a few places in the world, and apart from the presence of a racket and a ball, you'll probably see very few similarities to what you witness when Becker and Lendl are on court.

Hampton Court Gardens reflect the Dutch influence associated with the period of William III. Apart from the orangeries and the flowers when they are in blossom, the most noteworthy aspect of Hampton Court is its maze. The living puzzle, composed of tall shrubs, has attracted the attention of the world ever since it was created. The key to the maze—that is, for arriving at the center—is to turn left on entering. Then, on the first two occasions when there is an option, make a right and thereafter keep going left. Got that? Now try to find your way out.

Beyond Richmond itself and Hampton Court, there are several other engaging day-excursion points that can enhance your Greater London roving.

**Kew Gardens** is a mile from Richmond on the southern side of the Thames. There are something like 40,000 species of plants on view within the Royal Botanic enclave. These are spread over 9 acres (down from 300 acres before urbanization moved in) and within vast greenhouses that you can visit. Ferns, orchids, and plants from Australia are especially well shown. Many splendid trees—woefully numerous ancient oaks —were knocked down in recent hurricanes, but if you had not seen Kew before the destruction it will look marvelous to you anyway.

**Ham House** is across the river from **Twickenham**, about five minutes south of **Richmond**. It is under the care of the National Trust but because of the fine arts revealed within its walls, the curating is entrusted to the Victoria and Albert Museum of London. It represents a peek into the lifestyle of 17th-century privilege. There is a portrait gallery and furniture from the time of the Georgians as well as of Charles II, a Stuart.

**Greenwich** is another fascinating target and, like Richmond, it can be visited on a boat ride from London. The first **Royal Observatory** is the main reason for going, of course, and its feet are planted firmly on the **Greenwich Meridian.** (See Herstmonceux Castle under Sussex for the newer observatory.) For salty types, here is the site of the **Royal Naval College** and, on the same frontage and near the main pier, you will see the proud shape of the beautiful *Cutty Sark,* a not-fully-retired tea clipper that was one of the swiftest vessels on the British trade routes of the last century. Today this gorgeous relic serves as a training base for merchant sailors—and what an exotic school she be! Though still in use and serving her country, you may visit—and surely admire—her. Another lady—this one more modern in line and shape—resides in the same neighborhood. She is the *Gypsy Moth,* the incredible one-man sloop that handily circumnavigated the globe. The "one man" was the ailing and elderly Sir Francis Chichester, her crotchety master, who fretted and coaxed her svelte figure around the planet to give her everlasting status in the chronicles of sail.

Not to abandon the nautical aspects of Greenwich just yet, if you are not sufficiently bedizzened, follow the charts out of King William Walk toward Romney Road and on to the **National Maritime Museum.** It is divided into three areas: the earliest segment is represented in the Queen's House; the colorful period from the 17th century until the early 19th century is contained in the West Wing; more recent naval history is displayed in the East Wing. (You won't need a compass.) There are other showcases, too, so plan to give yourself enough time for browsing.

**Guildford**, which became a borough as early as 1131, is a satellite community of London containing some 63,000 souls who find life better high on the Hog's Back than with their feet in the London Clay. The **Hog's Back** is a moderately lofty ridge west of town that provides some of the most captivating countryside scenery to be found near any megalopolis in the world. It's a delight to run out here on a London weekend just to get away from the city fumes. The town itself harks back to medieval times and was once the wool-rich county hub. Its High Street (universally employed in Britain for the U.S. equivalent of "Main Street") is not only high at one end, but is steep all along its way. At one of its lower points you'll see the **Town Hall (Guild),** with a weather vane above its arched cupola and a resplendent gilded clock on a beam extended over the heedless traffic. At this end you'll find a couple of wonderful old churches, while at the top end you'll discover another house of prayer from a later period and the town's pride, the **Grammar School,** sponsored by Edward VI in the mid-16th century. (The chained books inside are an indication of the naughty library habits of those early readers.)

Other interesting sightseeing targets include **Abbott's Hospital** and a house called **The Chestnuts,** where Rev. Charles Lutwidge Dodgson expired in 1898. What? Never heard of him? Perhaps you remember him by his *nom de plume,* Lewis Carroll, a handle he employed when he was not teaching mathematics and was writing *Alice in Wonderland.* Dickens also had associations with this town and wrote its praises with unstinting fervor.

Within the environs of Guildford you can visit the engaging Tudor mansion called **Loseley House,** in the direction of Compton, or continue to the wondrous waterlily ponds at Frensham; spring and early summer are best for the flowers, of course. In the other direction (northeast) you have the generously endowed **Clandon Park,** a Palladian house and garden. The latter was designed by the evergreen and ever-ready Capability Brown; the interior features unusual collections of needlepoint and porcelain. You can forget the red-brick exterior, which evinces an Italian pedigree. **Sutton Place** (not the one in Manhattan) was begun in 1525. Among its residents was J. Paul Getty.

## A YARN

Somewhat to the south (only a few minutes away) is perhaps the world's most forlorn tribute to voyeurism. It's a tranquil pond called, appropriately, **Silent Pool**, thickly surrounded by foliage and overshrouded by trees. A maiden fair of yore thought she might have found privacy enough for a bath in the buff, but lurking in the shadows was that dirty old Plantagenet, King John. The shy damsel spied the monarch in the bush and was shocked. So to cover herself and hide her parts as well as her unbearable chagrin, the modest miss disappeared beneath the surface—and drowned. Hugh Hefner doesn't believe one word of it.

Within about 15 minutes' drive from Guildford, **Albury Park** is a curious site. An architect named Pugin must have suffered from a chimney fetish, or the proprietary Duchess of Northumberland must have been cool-natured from long family ties to England's colder climes. There are 64 mantels within the manor and no two are the same—amazing versatility for hearthside inspiration. Displayed within this fine house are numerous clocks—obviously bought for such fireplaces—and an important art collection. Speaking of clocks, there's a hamlet within easy (excuse the pun) striking distance called **Abinger Hammer**, which takes its name from a rather strange timepiece. The clock features a muscular blacksmith who hammers away at his trade, seemingly oblivious of the hours he's putting in. If the skies are clear, drive through the Downs to 1000-foot-high **Leith Hill**, take a picnic, and enjoy a magnificent view of that tiny little settlement on the horizon called London.

**Horley** is just north of Gatwick and a pleasant stop if you're killing time prior to your airport appointment. The Six Bells Inn will help you wile away a few bells at least, and the church has roots that began growing in the 14th century.

**Tinsley Green** is where the top-rank international marble shoots are held, close to Horley. The story goes that on these grounds a couple of swains challenged each other to a mighty game of marbles. The prize was to be a charming lass who both chaps admired and wished to wed. Never mind who won, but ever since that fateful fudge, the global marble contest has been held here. Such is the course of true love and sportsmanship. Hef probably wouldn't swallow that one either.

If you have a fondness for shrubs and trees, follow the Mole River north via Leigh and Betchworth toward the North Downs. The growth is varied and the trees have been allowed to grow for eons.

At **Box Hill** the slope of the Downs is a carpet of box and beech trees and at neighboring **Mickelham** you'll find **Norbury Park**, with a forest of yews. You might enjoy combining this loop with a visit to **Epsom Downs**, the colorful flat-racing course where the ponies have been competing since the 18th century. Here is where the annual Derby—pronounced Dar-bee by the English—is held. Every newspaper and sports broadcast on television can tell you what is going on at any time at the oval.

A short detour to the west brings you to **Stoke d'Abernon** (no, you have not crossed **La Manche**). The name relates to the brass in the town church associated with Sir John d'Abernon and harks back to the 13th century. The children might prefer a visit to nearby **Chessington Zoo.** Historians and visitors from the Tar Heel State will probably have an interest in the hollow where Sir Walter Raleigh lies at rest. You'll find him in the wonderful Norman church at **West Horsley,** which must be one of the oldest in England. The church of East Horsley is also very ancient, but ardent citizens have changed it considerably throughout the Christian era.

Another scenic way back to **Guildford** and on into London is via **Crawley** and **Haslemere**. Alfred Lord Tennyson lived near the latter; his home, **Aldworth**, is on the Black Down south of the city. Unless you have come for the summer music festival there's not much reason for pausing here, so cut north to **Hindhead**, with its high point, **Gibbet Hill**, overlooking the marvelous, lush Witley Forest below you, Waggoner Wells to the southeast, and the Devil's Punch Bowl in the west. The hamlets, the foliage, and the geological phenomena conspire to form an unforgettable panorama. A quick return route to London is on the A-3.

Surrey is full of eccentricities, engaging oddities, collections of rare this-and-thats, breathtaking gardens, stately homes, and cozy corners. Its only fault is that it has been lived in so intensely for eons as an adjunct of London. But as you get to know it, you may appreciate the trees despite the presence of the forest.

# KENT'S GARDENS AND MIGHT

In a sense Kent has long been England's gateway to the Continent or, at other times, the nation's bulwark against it. It's tranquil now and even enjoys the title "The Garden of England" because of its blossoming orchards and hopfields. (Those peculiar round buildings with conical lids are oast houses to treat the hops for ale and beer fabrication.) Quiet though it is today, in early times Kent attracted invasions and settlements from adventurous and/or hostile explorers. Neolithic flint tools testify to an agricultural largess that was thriving eons before the brewers discovered it. This was a tempting plum for outsiders. If you require proof of such early occupation, have a look at the well-known Kits Coty megaliths (chambered tombs) of the Medway Valley or the long barrow (mound) at Chilham in east Kent. From neighboring countries there is ample evidence of exchange via the distribution of Beaker pottery plus some of the Bronze Age finds in Kentish soil and elsewhere. Belgic invad-

ers dropped an assertive calling card at Oldbury when they left behind one of their hill forts.

This is the region of the five **Cinque Ports** ("Sink," to the British),
which was a confederation of defense stations. It originally contained
Hastings, Dover, Hythe, Romney, and Sandwich, and later added
Rye and Winchelsea as Head Ports. As there was no Royal Navy,
these confederates operated under contract with the king: 57 ships
and crews at 15 days a year. For this they received many royal perks
and favors. They also grew rich from unabated smuggling and some
choice pickin's in piracy. Even today remnants of their importance to
the crown in the 13th and 14th centuries appear in British pag-
eantry.

Due to its proximity with the land mass to the east and as a cultural
spillway *par excellence,* Kent possesses a seemingly endless supply of
monastic ruins—enough to keep your pilgrimage on fire for weeks.
Front-runners include the priory of **Christ's Church** in Canterbury
and the nearby **Abbey of St. Peter and Paul (St. Augustine's)**. Then,
at **Folkstone**, there's a 7th century nunnery. This was a time of feverish ecclesiastical building. Within a few decades more nunneries
popped up in Reculver, Minster-in-Thanet, Minster-in-Sheppey,
Lyminge, and that great priory of St. Martin at Dover. All were
begun within thirty or forty years of each other. Time and war wore
away some, but many soldiered on into the present century. **Dover**,
**Folkstone**, and **Rochester** are the places to look, as well as at **Faver-
sham**, **Malling**, **Dartford**, **Aylesford**, and **Boxley**. This Phase Two of
religious fervor for stone and mortar occurred chiefly from late in
the 11th century, peaking in the 12th and 13th centuries, and trick-
ling into more modern times—well, modern by Christian standards,
anyway. While religion commanded so much time, money, and attention in the Middle Ages, your church-to-church rovings can include more temporal targets. **Leeds Castle**, for example, is one of
the "musts" on any itinerary. **Knole** is a splendid choice, as are
**Penshurst** and **Ightham Mote**, the last moated manor with features
harking back to the 14th century.

As you drive through Kent you'll see vineyards near **Chart Sutton**
and **Leeds**. Great dairies produce fine cheese from **Milton**. Cherries,
first brought from Flanders, took root in Kent under the command
of Henry VIII. He may not have been as fruitful in some ways as he
would have wished, but since the introduction of the cherry, England went full tilt into the orchard biz and never looked back.

## CANTERBURY

**Canterbury**, of storied and saucy Chaucerian recall, is only 55 miles from London (and a mere 16 miles from Dover, if you are on your way to France). It lies by the Kentish Stour, which funnels the tumbling waters into tranquil open passages and onto the broadening marshy plain. Eons ago the creek ran from the channel that separated the Isle of Thanet from the mainland. Canterbury seems to have been a settlement at the head of this arroyo. Excavations indicate that as early as 200 B.C. there was a heavily stockaded and ditch-rimmed stronghold. There was at least one complex gateway in what is now the southeastern quadrant of the city walls. St. Augustine founded a **Benedictine monastery** and as this appeared to be a smash hit, his next act was the **Cathedral**. Not bad, because it became the prime "See of England", a status maintained ever since. With his left hand, he also converted King Ethelbert of Kent to Christianity.

On December 29, 1170, four knights, believing they were carrying out the wishes of their king, Henry II, crept into the sanctum and stabbed to death Archbishop Thomas Becket—"that troublesome meddling priest"—and forevermore sacrificed his loss of life to the enrichment of the arts, Many of the major struggles and political events of medieval English history were enacted at Canterbury. The Peasant's Revolt, also known as the War of the Roses, had its roots in local soil. The 14th century provided Canterbury with an early tourist trade based, of course, on the pilgrimage to the shrine of St. Thomas. The most appalling human barbecue of Protestant martyrs (apart from London) took place in this supposedly "holy city" under Mary I between 1553 and 1558, when 41 people found their destiny at the stake.

The original cathedral—and today it remains the base of the English primate—has been reconstructed more than once. In the 12th century, for example, the Choir was demolished, extended, and unctuously introduced with bruited ceremony as the new Glorious Choir. Unfortunately—but not unusual for buildings of that era—this was destroyed by fire only 44 years later. Another decade and it was revamped yet again, etcetera, etcetera, etcetera, until 1495 when Prior Goldstone provided a rather complete and final version. Imagine your first sight, in times gone by, of this magnificent building with a golden angel gleaming in the sunlight almost 25 stories above the groundlings beneath. The angel has vanished but the Bell Harry Tower remains a powerful image. Inside there is a feeling of awe and grandeur transmitted from the midpoint of the double cross aisles; the Choir is flanked by chapels and terminates in the east with a circular tower commonly known as Becket's Crown.

Please pardon the statistics, but on the outside chance that someone might want them, the principal dimensions of the cathedral are 522 feet in length, the nave is 178 feet, and the choir is 180 feet. In subjective terms that's almost twice the size of a rugby pitch. You will probably sense something of a split personality about the interior, especially if you are a student of medieval architecture. It was built over many decades, even centuries, so the styles did not remain consistent from Day One onward. Look, for example, at the area where the nave and choir join; then in the choir there is a plethora of decorative carving and intricate masonry; visitors flock in to be told about the arches here and the contrasting colors of the stonework. The English and Norman architects are shaking hands in the House of God. Close to Becket's shrine is the tomb of Edward, the Black Prince; nearby are those of Henry IV and Queen Joan of Navarra. The priory was the infamous scene of the murder of Thomas Becket. In time he was rewarded by canonization; there are constant pilgrimages to his tomb. (Becket was credited with a vast number of "miraculous" cures.) Henry II offered a reverent penance in 1174 by walking barefoot to Canterbury and being flogged at the side of the tomb. Had he arrived by horse he probably would have put his mount into a "canter," a word which has come into the language because the pilgrims employed such a comfortable gait en route to Canterbury. (The Anglo-Saxon name for the town, incidentally, was Cantwarabyrig.) In 1538 the petulant Henry VIII decreed that the shrine be destroyed. Don't leave the cathedral without seeing the marvelous cloister that is about half the girth of a football field and displays within the vaulting more than 800 shields. (You can't tell the players without a score-card.) The Chapter House is another impressive stop; it is covered by a vast oak roof.

Many of the local churches contain architectural features of interest: The nave arcades of **St. Alphege** and **St. Dunstan** are good examples. It was in the latter that the head of Sir Thomas More was interred.

Canterbury was severely burned and fractured in World War II during a massive air raid in June of 1942. The cathedral, however, was only superficially damaged. The Chapter library was leveled, but the Chapter House itself was rebuilt in 1954. Canterbury is the home of the ancient King's School—the sovereign being Henry VIII, who founded it. William Harvey, who discovered the circulation of blood, was a student here, as was Somerset Maugham, who related his life at Canterbury in *Of Human Bondage*.

**St. Martin's** is fondly known as the "Mother Church of England." Dates are not certain, but by any measure it is one of the nation's oldest houses of worship. Very likely the Romans had a structure here, too, and there is also evidence of Norman stonework.

In the **Poor Priest's House** you can kick the wheels of the *Invicta*, a steam locomotive puffed-up by R. L. Stevenson in the early 1800s. This pioneer ran on one of the earliest routes in Europe: from Canterbury to Whitstable.

A legacy of the city's Roman past can be seen at the **Roman Mosaic House**, which has a magnificent, intricate floor and underground heating as revealed in excavations in the 1940s.

## INTO THE COUNTRYSIDE AND DOWN TO THE SEA

These drives will take you into surrounding orchards and hops fields. Two miles northeast is **Fordwich**, which has a tiny **Town Hall** (c. 1400) from which the views of Canterbury are marvelous. But the big talking point here is the "ducking stool," which was once used to "dip" nagging wives into the River Stour. Traveling two miles southwest of Canterbury you'll come to **Chilham**, a lovely medieval village with a castle built for Henry II in 1174. It is enclosed within 300 acres of grounds with lakeside walks, woods, and an exquisite rose garden. The heroic and ever-so-moving **Museum of the Battle of Britain** is here.

**Sandwich** is the granddaddy of the Cinque Ports, which alone is quite a distinction. This means there is a lot of meat to digest here as a sightseer; the Cinques were prosperous and active for numerous decades. **Old House** is Tudor, and many of the town buildings were begun in the 15th or 16th centuries. Here also is the site of the **Royal St. George Golf Course**, one of the legendary clubs of Great Britain. See also **Fishgate** for atmosphere and the **Barbican** for antiquity. You probably already know of this city's link to the world's first fast-food addict. The Earl of Sandwich was such an avid gambler that he never had time to eat a proper meal at the gaming tables. He is said to have told the pitboss of the day to slap some meat between two pieces of bread and that would keep him going. Hence, the Sandwich.

Traveling toward the coast are many coffee-stop (er, tea-stop) villages and towns, all with a distinctive character. **Deal**, as one example, has a long-standing maritime history even though it has no harbor. The treacherous **Goodwin Sands** (now well marked), lying seven miles offshore, have caused many a ship to come to grief. Deal today is a popular seaside resort despite its shingle beach. The **castle** was built by Henry VIII; he decreed it to be in the form of a six-petalled flower (rose) and it now houses a museum. At neighboring **Walmer** you can visit **Henrian Castle** and the beauty that surrounds, which probably soothed the fevered brow of the duke of Wellington, who passed away here in 1852. Among his many personal possessions on view are the waterproof boots that gave his name to the footwear of today. A short drive away is **Ringwould**. The "ring" probably refers to the ancient earthworks near **Free Down;** you can also visit the **12th-century church**, which reflects the riches of the ages and the privilege of residing in one of these several important coastal towns.

**Dover**, another one of the Cinque Ports, is immediately and forever associated with Vera Lynn's "White Cliffs of Dover." It was already a rollicking seaside resort in Queen Victoria's day. Hovering nearly 400 feet above its port is **Dover Castle**, one of the oldest of a concentrically planned and well-known type in England. The keep of the castle was built at the command of Becket's fair-weather friend, Henry II, in the 12th century. As a dry indication of its might and importance for coastal defense, two statistics tell it all: The walls are 8 yards thick and 10 stories high! The unique and compelling "Pharos" within the castle precincts was originally a Roman lighthouse. It is fascinating to see in this century. The everlasting significance of Dover is its strategic and close link to Calais, France, across the English Channel.

**Folkestone** is another holiday destination—and jammed to distraction in summer. The "Leas," a windy open lawn at the rim of the dominant cliffs, is marvelous as an escape from the crowding of the shore. (In summer there are just too many Folkes in Folkestone.) On a clear day you can see

Calais. Five miles north is **Acrise Place**, an Elizabethan and Georgian manor house containing an admirable costume collection. **Spade House**, now a museum, used to be the home of H. G. Wells, the novelist.

From **Hythe** onward the coast is fairly flat. This is where **Romney Marsh** begins, an open, windswept area largely devoted to flower cultivation and sheep. It once was the playground of smugglers. Hythe is another one of the Cinque Ports that began a high-profile defense career in the 12th century, keeping it up until the 19th century, when the Royal Military Channel was cut to hold back Napoleon. Today it's as peaceful as morning in a tea parlor. Stroll over to **St. Leonard's Church** for a lovely overview.

In 1606, Lord North is credited with the discovery of the mineral springs that made **Royal Tunbridge Wells** a much-frequented spa. Its principal feature is the **Pantiles** a colonnaded, raised promenade where visitors drank the waters. Queen Victoria resided at Calverey House for a spell, or a cure. Due to the resort's appeal to monarchs, Edward VII named it Royal Tunbridge Wells in 1919. The novelist William Makepeace Thackeray once lived here; his house can be seen. Among other personalities, Lt. Col. John By of the Royal Engineers, the founder of Ottawa, died at **Shernfold Park** in Frant, East Sussex, near Tunbridge Wells; he rests in the local churchyard and is awarded homage by numerous visiting Canadians each year.

## COUNTRY HOUSES AND CASTLES

**Chartwell** is only one-and-a-half miles south of **Westerham**, a village that will always be cherished for its links with Sir Winston Churchill. This was Winnie's private redoubt and escape from the winds of war until his death in 1965. The estate has been preserved just as he left it, many fascinating documents, photographs, and paintings of his and other personal mementos remaining for you to see. In two of the rooms you'll find the numerous gifts he received from grateful and admiring people all over the world. A terraced garden leads down to the lake with its celebrated black swans.

**Squerryes Court**, also in Westerham, is a William and Mary manor house built in 1681 and owned by the Warde family for over 250 years. A fantastic collection of paintings, tapestries, and furniture adorn its interiors; in the Wolfe Room are pictures and relics relating to General James Wolfe, hero of the Battle of Quebec, who received his military commission on the grounds of the house; the spot is marked in his honor.

At **Sevenoaks**, a mid-15th-century edifice, **Knole**, is considered to be one of the largest private houses in England and a masterpiece of pure Tudor architecture. Confiscated by a covetous Henry VIII in 1537, it was later granted to Thomas Sackville by Elizabeth I. Sackville's descendents reside here to this hour. It is said that the house has a room for every day of the year, a courtyard for every day of the week, and a staircase for every week of the year. Virginia Woolf, a frequent guest, used Knole as the location for her novel *Orlando*. The furnishings, as you would expect, are sumptuous and elaborate. Knole is about five miles north of Tunbridge Wells and 25 miles from central London.

**Ightham Mote** is a wonderful medieval moated house in Ivy Hatch, Sevenoaks. A stone bridge crosses the watery division into the spacious courtyard. From the Great Hall, a Jacobean staircase leads to the Old Chapel and through to the solarium (with an oriel window) to the Tudor chapel. This is a gem that's now under the protection of the National Trust. Try to see it.

Though Gothic since early in the last century, **Hever Castle** is a noble holdover from the 1200s. Anne Boleyn contributed to that exalted heritage, having lived and danced through the flowers here in her youth. As she grew, her simple country life became more political. Anne rewarded Henry VIII with a daughter who was later to become Elizabeth I. Through the years and the decline of the Boleyns, Hever served in later epochs as merely a farmhouse. Through the benediction of the American tycoon William Astor, Hever was brought back to greatness and grace. Astor also constructed the spectacular Italian gardens and the enormous lake (35 acres in size!) through which the River Eden flows. Of all the "living" castles I have seen in Great Britain, this, to my taste, is the most intimate and engaging.

**Penshurst Place** is a grandiose Gothic-style mansion, one of the most outstanding country houses in Albion. King Edward VI presented the estate to Sir William Sidney, and the family has not seen fit to change its address for more than 400 years. It was the birthplace (in the 16th century) of Sir Philip Sidney, well-known in his day as a man for all seasons. The able and astute Sidneys took the title of earls of Leicester. You can now see (here) the *original* **Leicester Square**, which gave its name in later years to the prime real estate of London Town. You'll also want to visit the splendid State Dining Room and Queen Elizabeth Room; the Stable Wing offers an interesting Toy Museum.

**Chiddingstone** greets you with a meticulously tidy appearance. The **Castle** contains a variety of collections including Stuart relics. The actual **Chiding Stone**—hence, the name of the town—is where noisome wives were taken to be chided by the rabble in much the way earlier peoples stoned their fellow citizens for their sins. (Neither Chiddingstone nor the previously described Fordwich were very big on women's rights in those dark days.) The town itself, however, is a charmer in its trim 16th-century attire, houses with leaded windows, and many-gabled roofs. **Edenbridge** is also blessed with handsome ancient buildings including a 13th-century house of prayer. At **Fordcombe** the half-timbered cluster of dwellings is arranged around the village common, a captivating scene that shouldn't be missed if you are in the area.

## DICKENS—A KENTISH MAN

**Rochester**, 30 miles from London, is a riverside resident of the Medway. This is an engaging old town—and old it truly is. St. Augustine founded his church headquarters here early in the seventh century, and it is on this same spot that the historic Rochester Cathedral stands today. Rochester has often been referred to as "Dickens Country," as it was here that the novelist spent most of his life. **Dickens Chalet**, in Eastgate House, was built in 1590. The area seems to unite the historic architecture of maritime Chatham and the countryside of rural Strood. A stroll along the High Street, now restored to Victorian splendor, will introduce you to the **Charles Dickens Center**, the **cathedral**, the impressive neighboring **Castle**, and a host of other sightseeing rewards.

The Cathedral is the centerpiece of the city, of course. It is very similar in character to that of Canterbury, strongly Norman as most ecclesiastical construction was during the many centuries of their reign. The nave is typically Norman, but there are other elements that vary from the purist style. Look, for example, at the fascinating raised choir (which has a fragment of a 13th-century wall painting of the Wheel of Fortune), and the stalls that also were erected in this period. In its nether reaches—*not* nearer my God to Thee—the crypt is colossal in size and concept. Kent, in a sense, is twice-blessed, being able to boast of two great cathedrals in one county.

**Rochester Castle** is one of the toughest examples of Norman military architecture to be found. Now only the keep and curtain walls remain, but when it was a building from the 11th to the 12th century it had a tower that was claimed to be the tallest in England. The exact height is unknown.

In Maidstone Road you'll find Dickensian lore at **Restoration House,** a scene out of *Great Expectations*. Both Miss Havisham, a character in the novel, and Charles II (in real life) spent time here. For more curiosities, you can shop the lanes for Dickens. Many dwellings and buildings have notations on them concerning their associations in literature. The neighboring town of Chatham is where he spent his youth, but **Gad's Hill** was his home during his mature period.

**Cobham** is depicted in *Pickwick Papers*. Its **Leather Bottle Inn** is a local repository for items pertaining to the author. While here **St. Mary Magdalene Church** is of historic importance for the numerous brasses in the chancel. Have a look—whether you are a scholar or not. **Cobham Hall** was extended from its 16th-century measure by James Wyatt as well as other later admirers; now it's a girls' school. On a more outdoorsy note, **Cobham Park** is famed for its massive clusters of rhododendrons. May-June is blossom time.

From Rochester, hop along to **Maidstone**, the county town. It resides just 12 miles to the south. You'll pass **Aylesford Friary**, a Carmelite institution that has existed for almost 800 years. The cloister is the essence of peace and reflection, so pervading, in fact, that the settlement itself takes on a shrinelike personality.

**Maidstone** is literally in the core of the "Garden of England," with exceptionally bewitching countryside, fragmented into hopfields and orchards, resplendent in spring with every hue and cry of flowering Britain. The town and surroundings offer a variety of things to do and see. **The Archbishop's Stables** contain a unique collection of antique carriages as well as a museum and an art gallery housed in a 16th-century manor house.

Then drive out to the overwhelming **Leeds Castle,** a vast, almost fairy-tale dream built upon two small islands in a lake. The romantic fortress dates from the ninth century, serving as a favorite home of the medieval queens of England. Henry VIII converted it from a stronghold to a royal palace. It was in the 1920s that the present collection of art, furniture, and tapestries was assembled. The surrounding parkland is adorned with gardens, aviaries, a grotto, and even a small vineyard. There's a delightfully eccentric collection at the **Dog Collar Museum** in the castle's Gatehouse. In neighboring **Otham** there's a small and attractive half-timbered manor house—mainly late 15th century—with a Great Hall, crownpost, and an ambitious exhibit of painstakingly intricate embroidery work.

**Broadstairs**, 20 miles more-or-less east of Canterbury, is a seaside town on the **Isle of Thanet**. From 1837 to 1851, **Broadstairs** was the choice hideaway of Charles Dickens, who actually lived in **Bleak House**, where he conjured up *David Copperfield*. In his sketch, *Our English Watering Place*, Dickens described the community as "left high and dry by the ride of years." High indeed. The chalk cliffs above the sands are a major spectator draw today. A concert pavilion has been tootling along since 1933. The small pier for fishing boats was built by Henry VIII—and so it goes bumpity-bump through the casual centuries without much spectacular attention from the world but often the pick of distinguished tastemakers, authors, and sovereigns. Even as late as 1949, the valiant Viking ship *Hugin* arrived with 32 courageous Danes to commemorate the landing in 449 of Hengist and Horsa! Remember them?

## SUSSEX—EAST AND WEST

Sussex has witnessed a mighty portion of English history. Schoolchildren, in fact, often grow up believing there was no history before 1066. It was in that landmark year, of course, that Harold set the English crown upon his royal head and William landed at Pevensey with every intention of knocking it off. The intrepid Conqueror marched to Hastings to join battle. There had been extensive to-ing and fro-ing across the Channel, but on October 14 fate sealed the outcome forevermore. On this site, William built his votive Abbey of Battle. As mentioned, Hastings was one of a quintet of powerful seaports, a key player in the confederation of Cinque Ports. (The French and English idioms exchange easily in the neighborhood.) You can see later versions of first-line defense, too, from the time Napoleon threatened invasion; the same coast became dotted with a network of Martello Towers, squat and stumpy round structures as part of an early warning chain for alarming the troops.

Brighton, meanwhile, ignored the fuss, later to cater to the vanities of the emerging rich. It became the chic place to be seen. To give it added verve, Britain's Prince Regent undertook to create his gaudy and fanciful Royal Pavilion here. Sea bathing became smart, people took holidays on the coast, resorts blossomed, urbanization flourished. London moved to the south for the summer.

The area of Sussex is not extensive so travel is fairly direct. In midsummer road traffic can be a nuisance. The most noteworthy monastic remains are those of Battle Abbey (with its splendid gatehouse), Bayham Abbey, and Lewes Priory—all pretty close together. Then come the tatters of Robertsbridge Abbey, Michelham and Shulbrede Abbeys (both Augustinian), as well as Wilmington Priory. These all dovetail with newer architecture that integrate as well as preserve the valued antiquities that otherwise would have vanished. The impressive friary chapels of Chichester, Winchelsea, and Rye are also compelling for their history as well as their aesthetics. Sussex grew  through a deeply religious period, so the countryside is thick with arches, spires, fonts, and chapels—mainly from the epoch around the Norman Conquest. Such names as Bosham, Sompting, and Worth come immediately to mind. Pevensey Castle—existing within the already impressive walls of a Roman fortress—features an early Norman keep that was constructed around 1250. At Lewes the original keep and later barbican are top attractions. Amberley came on the scene in 1377, and the enchanting moated fortress of Bodiam, is its contemporary. Herstmonceux Castle, today occupied by the Royal Conservatory, was built almost a century later and of brick; it begins to reveal a manifestation of the change in attitudes, a new sense of security and, consequently, a conversion in architectural needs. Thus, here you'll see a defensible great house rather than a true castle. Later great houses such as Parnham, Petworth, Up Park, and others turn to lavish boast instead of genuine muscle and might.

Sussex has always been blessed with cool forest quilts such as Ashdown and St. Leonard's, but it also is involved in agriculture, especially hops for brewing. From these eastern tiers with tall screens, poles, and funny shaped buildings for curing the important cash crops, the terrain goes rolling west in a series of chalk hills. Then, of course, the southern flank becomes sandy as it approaches the beaches and playgrounds of the coast.

That historic littoral has changed radically within the space of a few centuries. Look, for example, at Selsey, where the site of the Saxon Cathedral is now approximately a mile out among the fishies. On the other side of the geological coin, a major chunk of Pagham Harbor was reclaimed but later returned to Davy Jones. There's a huge apron of gravel and silt where salt water once edged the powerful seaports of Winchelsea and Pevensey.

Early man lived through many of these alterations of topography, so say the paleontologists. Well, maybe he did and maybe he didn't. The noisily bruited Piltdown rage turned out to be a fraud, according to findings four decades ago, but now support for the claim is growing again. Other evidence? There are sites on the Sussex Downs where prehistoric occupation probably became fairly sophisticated. Have a look at Whitehawk and Trundle. Ancient Worthing whispers of mining while Cissbury and Harrow Hill suggest flintstones from those primitive digs hit the utensil market with grand *éclat.* And what of those bell barrows at Bow Hill and Monkton Down? Or the great fort that undoubtedly existed at Andcrida? Here walls still stand as high as two-story buildings. Moreover, these people were traders with contacts well beyond the narrow borders we usually apply to them. In other words, you don't have to look far or even very deeply into the Sussex grass roots to find a rich groundwork of antiquity. Here you'll see signs of the valor of the sailor and the soldier and the enterprise of the tinker and the tailor intermingling over the centuries to spin out dramatic yarns of imagined success or unexpected defeat.

## *CONQUERING EAST SUSSEX*

**Battle**, after its hour of glory in the 11th century, is today a tranquil market town nine miles northwest of Hastings. It took its name, naturally, after the landmark military conflict in 1066. The winner was William (the Conqueror), duke of Normandy. The prize was England. Before the historic clash took place on high ground overlooking today's town of Battle, William vowed to erect an abbey as an act of gratitude if he won the day. True to his word, in 1094 the **abbey** was unveiled, the votive altar being placed exactly where Harold fell. The impressive gateway survives from 1338. The abbey, with its wonderful vaulted ceilings, had become a school and was reformed again to become a private estate following the Reformation. The parish church is from the 12th century, its deanery being created much later when bricks were developed in Tudor times.

As mentioned earlier, French is often used in this district. Senlac was the French name for the battlefield given by Orderic Vitalis. Despite the excess of Gallic chauvinism—actually Orderic's label sounds more appropriate for a soft drink—even in the *Doomsday Book* this is referred to as the "Battle of Hastings." So be it. No Franglais here.

**Lewes** is on the Ouse. It stands above the river vale, a proud fortification eight miles northeast of Brighton and 51 miles from London. From prehistoric times it has been of strategic importance. Stone and bronze tools and defensive earthworks tell the story. You can see this evidence in a museum called **Barbican House**, parts of the building dating back more than 500 years. After the Battle of Lewes in 1264—a tussle between Henry III and Simon de Montfort's rebels—the town was walled; it still contains many fine dwellings dating from the 16th century. One was given to Anne of Cleves as a divorce settlement by Henry VIII. Today her abode is a **folk museum**.

Try also to see **Southover Grange** and the later **School Hill House**. William de Warenne (the son-in-law of William the Conqueror) ordered a fort to protect the pass through the Ouse Valley. The remains of two shell keeps are on this site today and can be inspected. There's a great sense of very essential British history on these twin mounds. De Warenne and the high-born Gundrada (William's daughter) sponsored a religious project in 1077, a priory to honor the deeds of St. Pancras. This generous offering contained a church 450 feet long, considerably bigger than Chichester Cathedral. The testy Thomas Cromwell had the **priory** destroyed during the Dissolution; however, some fragments were not "dissolved" and can be seen.

Lewes achieved great prosperity from its wool production in the 13th century. You'll notice many houses and buildings produced as a result of such wealth. Today television cameras whir for its flamboyant Guy Fawkes festivities every November 5. Then the town's bonfire societies celebrate in the light of massive nonstop pyrotechnics. This occurs in many towns in England, and efforts are underway to reduce the dangers inherent in shooting off the rockets and explosives.

**Glyndebourne**, is the ticket if you're in the mood to dress up and take a picnic hamper to the sodden turf. The **Opera House** has been expanded, special trains run from London, and if you can get a ticket to a performance, it will be one of the memorable artistic moments of a lifetime. The problem will be in obtaining seats. The season is May to August.

**Hastings** is something of an historical misnomer. It is routinely remembered because of the "Battle of Hastings" even though this dustup took place some nine miles away in the town of Battle. Hastings is linked to St. Leonard's by a three-mile promenade along the sea; both have been popular resorts ever since Queen Victoria smiled favorably upon them. Here is the site of the first Norman castle in Britain. Although in ruins now, it was originally built on a hill overlooking Hastings in 1067. King John razed it in a fit of pique, so to speak, in 1216. Later it served as a church and monastery until—again the victim of royal indisposition—it suffered the rude blows of Henry VIII. From the latter part of the 16th century it was owned by the more pacific Penham dynasty.

In modern times Hastings itself has become its custodian. Hastings—not to miss out on the Mathilde Frieze craze going on at Bayeux on the French side—is courting tourists with its own embroidery, first exhibited in 1966. It is a remarkable achievement tracing in intricate needlework 900 years of English history. The Battle of Hastings, the Coronation of William the Conqueror, Robin Hood, and many others tell the story in 27 panels, 243 feet in length, depicting 81 scenes. This can be seen in the **Town Hall,** but if you are truly interested in these events, there can be no comparison here with the comprehensive program put on by the French at Bayeux.

Other places of interest are **St. Clement's Caves,** a unique **Shipwreck Heritage Center,** and the **Doomsday Exhibition.** A host of other choices are also within easy reach. The **Fisherman's Museum** is a reasonable catch. **Hastings Model Village,** with its exhibit of a miniature Tudor settlement in landscaped gardens, makes an afternoon quite pleasant. The **Hastings Museum and Art Gallery** offer displays of Sussex pottery, Wealden ironwork, and European ceramics; its adjoining **Dumbar Hall** contains collections from Asia and Oceania. How about a visit to the **Carr Taylor Vineyard** to taste English wine? You can see the 21-acre culture, winery, and winemaking machinery. It was here that England's first *methode champenoise* for producing sparkling wine was employed. A *votre* very good health! (Frankly, Mumm is not a bit worried.)

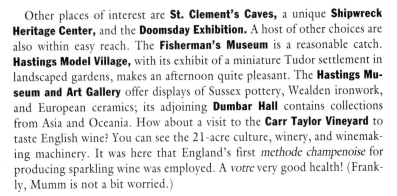

Among the many historic estates and castles that are open for visitors, all relatively close, an exceptional choice is **Great Dixter House and Gardens** near **Rye.** This is a stalwart example of a large 15th-century timber-framed manor. Its Great Hall was restored by the brilliantly inventive Sir Edwin Lutyens, for whom I confess a strongly favorable prejudice. The beautiful gardens feature flower borders, a topiary, yew hedges, and meadow gardens. Inside, the furniture and needlework are noteworthy.

**Bodiam Castle**, near **Robertsbridge**, was built in 1385 as a bulwark against the French invasion that never occurred. From the 17th century onward it has remained uninhabited. The walls and towers, which are reflected in the surrounding moat, are in perfect condition.

The name "Rye" means *island,* although it is decidedly part of the mainland today. In ancient times, **Rye** was a favorite with smugglers and flourished as such. The sea receded, leaving behind a high and dry Rye. It is laced with narrow, cobbled streets that twist and turn, buildings huddled alongside with sagging roofs and crooked chimneys. Mermaid Street, with the **old Mermaid Inn**, is a must whether you stay or not. Have a look up the spacious chimney. It used to be stashed full with contraband. Officials would come to the pub looking for bootleggers and have their pints shoulder to shoulder with the felons, the lolly tucked only a few feet away inside the smoky air shaft.

**Land's Gate** was the entrance to the old town; only a single line of traffic passes between the massive 40-foot towers. Though Rye suffered attacks from the French fleet, it was able to survive and regroup in plucky Elizabethan style. When Elizabeth I visited the town in 1573 she gave it the distinction of royal recognition. Notable buildings in the town with architectural or historic interest include the 13th-century **Ypres Tower**, sheltering the **Rye Museum**, and 15th-century **St.Mary's Church**, which sports a curious clock with two cherubs on either side. These angels are known as the "Quarter Boys" because they loyally strike the quarter hour, rather incessantly. (For only a mere 700 years!) The huffing and puffing from climbing the wooden stairs and ladders that take you up to the bell tower will reward you with a sweaty brow, a puce visage, and an impressive view of **Romney Marsh,** the town, and the sea. Rye Museum offers a collection of military objects, toys, Cinque Port relics, and pottery. **Lamb House** was the address of Henry James from 1899 to 1916.

**Winchelsea**, proudly (and now safely) situated on a hill, was founded by Edward I in the 13th century after the previous lower town had been covered and destroyed by floods. You'll recall that it, like Rye, was honored as a Head Port following the confederation of Cinque Ports. It thereby prospered enormously. Its lovely old church, which is in Early Decorated style, dates from about 1300. The interior—albeit without a nave—is dappled with light through fine modern glass and graced with the tombs of the Alard family, prominent patrons who occupied its pews for generations.

On the outskirts to the north of Rye is **Smallhythe Place**, former home of one of the most applauded Shakespearean actresses, Dame Ellen Terry. She died here in 1928. The half-timbered yeoman's house—appropriate to the Bard's time—was built in the first half of the 16th century. Within are mementos of the actress in her prime, a collection of personal and theatrical biblots, costumes, and assorted items of hers and other famous strutters on the boards. The neighboring 15th century **Priest House** is also engaging.

**Eastbourne** has remained for generations one of England's evergreen seaside resorts. There's a promenade that's three miles long, a pier with a theater, a pulsing range of entertainment, and holiday diversions that are nonstop in season. The creaky old **Mint House**, where coins were forged as long ago as 1076, is now used as an antiques showcase, with access to the Haunted Chamber, Edward VI's boudoir, and the Priest's Secret Room. It contains some exceptional 14th-century carvings and frescoes.

**Pevensey Castle** is massive; it's at the site where William the Conqueror landed to finally defeat Harold at Battle. You won't see a harbor, however. It has long ago silted up, leaving this town almost two miles from the waves. The castle's perimeter is Roman, built as a Saxon fort; within this the Normans created another oval-shaped castle, now in ruins. The towers, dungeon, keep, and chapel can be seen today. (Those Elizabethan cannon and catapult balls are from comparatively "modern" times.)

The **Redoubt Fortress** is a partially restored Napoleonic structure with battlements and gun emplacements. It juxtaposes a militant collection of the Royal Sussex Regiment and Sussex Combined Services Museum with a peaceful open-air concert series in summer. The **Towner Art Gallery** and **Local History Museum** are probably worth a mention for the collections of 19th- and 20th-century paintings and prints. Finally, for all the family, a visit to the **Butterfly Center** could be a colorful end to an Eastbourne-again experience. There's an indoor exhibition of live, free-flying indigenous, tropical, and semi-tropical butterflies, all set out in landscaped gardens with waterfalls, fountains, and pools.

**Beachy Head** (three miles west of Eastbourne) is where you can pick up the chalky beginning of the **South Downs Way,** a trail that pushes west. Walk or drive past the **Belle Tout Lighthouse** and you will come to **Birling Gap,** well-known in the past by the best of the bootlegging community.

From here you can see the white, gleaming spires of chalk called the **Seven Sisters.** There were more sisters, but the family was worn away by the sea. The cliffs and public park are within a zone known as the "Heritage Coast."

## WITHIN A DAY'S DRIVE

Moving north, you will pass through downland hamlets snuggling in the cups of the hills with sturdy Anglo-Saxon towers and quaint old churches, village greens, and awfully nice people. A gentle climb brings you to **Windover Hill,** a viewful rise where you can see the prehistoric **Long Man of Wilmington,** a colossal figure cut out in the turf, the chalk outline showing through. Its meaning remains a mystery.

**Hailsham**, the largest market town in Sussex; it maintains a mood and tradition that date back to Norman times. About half a mile farther along is **Michelham Priory;** only the remains of this Augustinian building survive. Founded in the 13th century, it also includes an Elizabethan dwelling that is handsome today, a 14th-century gatehouse, and an old bridge that spans the moat. Postcard country, if you ever saw it.

Keeping on the B 2108, you will come to **The Weald**, a place of charming towns and villages on hillsides between the North and South Downs; this region was once part of the prehistoric Forest of Anderida. Nearly all the settlements in this area are attractions for their character and special charm. One example is **Cross-in-Hand**, which has an ancient windmill standing 500 feet over the Weald. Part of the priory has been converted into a retirement home.

Travel through high wooded country to **Eridge Green**, with its comely assemblage of "urbanized" cottages as a backdrop for the Victorian church. Nearby is the sandstone outcrop called **Bowles Rocks,** where beginning mountaineers gain their nerve. A bit farther is perhaps the largest of these geological phenomena, named **High Rocks;** it has to be for graduate-level cliffhangers.

**Bayham Abbey,** "dissolved" by Cardinal Wolsey, is generally considered the most important monastic ruin in Sussex. Its various parts were begun in the 13th century. Wolsey's rash act gave it additional status in history. **Owl House** is a worthy sightseeing choice, standing in 13 acres of parkland surrounding the 16th-century wool-smuggler's cottage. There are romantic walks through the woodlands, a sunken water garden, and a breathtaking variety of flowers.

**Scotney Castle Gardens** is another dream spot for green thumbs. It was created by the Hussey family in the 1840s around the attractive shell of a 14th-century moated castle.

Cross over the River Rother and you arrive at **Burwash**, where—if your morbid interest is piqued—in the churchyard you can view an iron grave slab that spooks avow is the oldest in the land. Otherwise the town is pretty and inviting, with a few hospitable pubs on its singular main street.

## *KIPLING'S REDOUBT*

Half a mile along stands **Bateman's**, a 17th-century ironmaster's house built in the undulating Wealden valley. It achieved importance when it became the home of Rudyard Kipling in 1902. He fell utterly in love with it and remained here until 1936. It was here that he wrote *Puck of Pook's Hill* and many other tales. The impression of the house on approach, with its reflection in the pond, is quite a stunning and charming view. The house itself is constructed of richly colored local sandstone. The Kiplings took one look in their search for a house and bought Bateman's on sight. The furniture, carpets, and furnishings chosen by Kipling and his spirited spouse add tasteful vitality to every corner. Over the porch a carved date suggests it was constructed in 1634. Kipling did a lot to it, too, and got involved in the power generation from a local water source. The cable, incidentally, came from the original transatlantic telephone line. Inside are trinkets, books, art, and souvenirs of Kipling's travels in Asia. His wife was more prone to art of a European nature, but Rudyard's personality dominates, as you might expect. His desk and even some of his writings are available and on view. More importantly, there is a surviving air of success, happiness, folly, and entertainment in everything that touched the author's rich and busy life at the zenith of his career. The window-and book-lined study at the top of the staircase is today as it was when Kipling took pen to paper. The nearby Mill had been brought back to working condition by Kipling himself. From his racing around the world to his racing around the Sussex hills in expensive fast cars—he sat in the back seat cheering while his chauffeur maneuvered the curves—Kipling comes alive through a tour of Bateman's.

After a climb that takes you over the River Dudwell and through **Dallingron Forest,** you will reach **Woods Corner** and the **Swan Inn,** and still farther along come to **Boreham Street**, which is not a street at all but an enchanting village with a most appealing character. Half a mile away and with its feet sunk into water is **Herstmonceux Castle,** a great brick fortress that serves today as the **Royal Greenwich Observatory.** The castle was first built in 1441; two of its rooms contain an exhibition of modern astronomy and castle history. Nearby is **Wartling**, which is quite proud of its distinctive 18th-century pulpit in a church with box pews. If you enjoy Georgian architecture, the area is rich with it.

**Brighton** first made a splash around 1750 when Richard Russell, a supposed health guru, broadcasted the miraculous virtues of sea water. He settled in Brighton to put his pseudo-medical theories into practice. This finally provoked a wildly successful era of sea-bathing. In 1783 the Prince of Wales, soon to enjoy promotion as Prince Regent and finally King George IV, supported it with princely verve. His capricious palace, the **Royal Pavilion**, is Indian in concept, with white domes and minarets as well as gilded latticework fit for a sultan. Inside it is more Oriental. His whim cost 376,000 pounds sterling—a monarchial extravagance even in those profligate days. Henry Holland did the first version in 1787 and John Nash followed with the current rendering, starting his overture in 1812 and completing the opus over eight long years. Later it was offered to the town by Queen Victoria and is now a public building devoted chiefly to conventions. The investment was a sound one because it's one of the most frequently booked halls in Britain. Now, after its latest refit, it is launched upon yet another surge of public service. The furnishings in the State and Private apartments are from the 18th and 19th centuries and can be seen on tours of the fantasy world. The Dome in its center had been a royal stable, a quite different site in its heyday than the congress hall of today.

The London-Brighton railway line brought holidaymakers to this coast in the middle of the 19th century. Another product of that engineering epoch was the splendid Chain Pier in the form of four long suspension bridges. Regrettably, its future was not to be as durable as that of the Iron Horse. Motorists in this area may pass through the **Devil's Dyke.** It's not a dyke at all but a natural pass through the chalky cockscomb at the top of the South Downs. This is indicative of the forces of nature and of time at this interface where England had been joined to the continental landmass.

## OVER TO WEST SUSSEX

Let's begin at **Poynings**, a lovely hamlet northeast of Brighton via the previously mentioned Devil's Dyke. The road is not a major one but the trip is worthwhile across the down. There's an adequately antique church endowed by who else but Michael de Poynings. The rectory is from a later period.

If you take the A 283 you will find yourself among dainty little towns such as **Edburton**, known for its ceramics ateliers, and **Castle Rings**, both of which have attracted attention on Edburton Hill since before man learned to write. **Bramber**—a bit like Edburton, which smokes salmon for commerce—has gained attention from smoking, too, but this time with its **House of Pipes,** a museum for followers of this pastime. Within are 25,000 examples on display. There are some Norman ruins; the town had been a port of some importance, but continuous silting isolated it. Both **Steyning** and **Wiston** have interesting houses of the 14th and 15th centuries. They are ideal for a pause and a browse.

**Chanctonbury Ring**, off the A 283 but not far, is a high spot for a picnic. When you come back to the main road (about a mile) the route carries on to **Storrington** with its **Kithurst Hill**, another birdseye venue for avid photographers. Close to the village is a nature reserve called **Sullington Warren**. One mile away is **Parham House**, a delightful Elizabethan dwelling with a wonderful collection of art. It displays throughout every foot of its unusual length Elizabethan, Stuart, and Georgian portraits, furniture, china, and rare needlework. Parham is further enhanced by a deer park and braced by splendid mature gardens.

Do budget your time to include a fine establishment in this area called **Petworth House**, situated in **Petworth** itself. The town is an everlasting joy for antique shoppers, especially on weekends when it is alive with browsers. The hillside estate edging the town is an imposing late 17th-century creation standing in yet another vast, undulating deer park designed by Capability Brown—follies and all! It boasts a fine trove of oils by Van Dyck, Gainsborough, and Reynolds, and carvings by the master whittler of his time, Grinling Gibbons.

Now, crossing back over to East Sussex, you come to **West Firle**, which even today retains a medieval mood. **Firle Place,** with an Elizabethan soul and Georgian accessories, is a long, three-story mansion surrounded by ancient trees. It is noted for its treasury of Continental and English paintings as well as masterful Sevres porcelain; the Louis XV furniture is also an important feature of the museum. This has been the home of the Gage family for over 500 years. General Gage commanded British troops in the War of Independence; his wife was American. Early connections with "The Colonies" are documented for visitors to see. A short walk will bring you to **Firle Beacon,** a place of solitude and haunting beauty.

If you have children, you might opt for a stop at **Drusillas Zoo Park** (still farther east) and then drive a bit south to **Alfriston**, graced with fine old timber-and-stucco houses. This is a charmer, fit for a movie set, with a polychrome ship carving on the front of one of its inns (The Star). The **George** is also attractive. While here, see the **Market Cross, Clergy House,** and the town's proud and meticulously carved **Church.**

If you make the loop going south and then west again, you return to **West Sussex**, and after **Brighton**, **Hove**, and **Worthing** on the lower coastal swing, you can visit mighty **Arundel Castle,** standing guard over the Arun and home of the Dukes of Norfolk for more than seven centuries. Try to catch it with the sun setting behind it; here's an epiphany not to be forgotten. Within the huge park is Swanbourne Lake; there's a drawbridge from the time of Edward the Confessor—and that goes back to early in the 11th century. Later, that destructive Oliver Cromwell knocked down most of the castle and the one of today was built in the 19th century. Inside are splendid 16th-century furnishings and paintings by Gainsborough, Reynolds, Van Dyck, and numerous others. Like Windsor, it has a fine collection of Holbeins. In fact, the overall form reminds me of Windsor, maybe even nicer in its proportions. The town offers a few interesting churches.

## *CHICHESTER AND SURROUNDINGS*

**Chichester**, at the lower slope of the South Downs, is lined with handsome Georgian houses and has an attractive urban center. The suffix "Chester," incidentally, means "market" in the old idiom. The first part comes from "Cissa," who was a Saxon of note locally. It was founded by the Romans and certainly reveals the Latin logic of being divided in quadrants by North, South, East, and West streets, all converging at the sturdy central **market cross**; the last was not from pagan origins, of course. It was placed on the Roman square by none less than the famous Bishop Story. The town is a convivial place earning deserved acclaim for the **Chichester Festival Theatre**, established in 1962 when its first director was the late Lord Laurence Olivier. Try to catch a performance. Prices are low and the quality is superb.

The **cathedral**, too, meant Chichester had a significance in early times, its roots going back to the Norman conquest. It was destroyed several times by fire, but important aspects have been salvaged. Parts of the nave are original, so look for a guide within the building in order to see these segments. The impressive cloister comes from a much later period, as do some of the fancier decorations, the windows, and the main tower. The spire, incidentally, is a very friendly point of reference for navigators passing this stretch of coast. It is distinctive because the belfry is not attached to the main structure; this seems to be unique in British church architecture. To bring in a more contemporary note, have a look at the Graham Sutherland painting, as well as the tapestry by John Piper. These will convince you that **Regnum** (Chichester's Roman name) has come a long way since its foundation as a crossroads, then its youth as a Norman fortification and later as a wool port, and then as a controversial center during Puritan times. On the outskirts is the harbor linked to natural flats, waterways, and marshes alive with bird life. Of course, it is ideal for ornithologists, and you are invited to be one.

Farther west you will come to **Bosham**, with a Saxon church. That's nothing too new, but this one is included stitch-for-stitch on the historic Bayeux Tapestry. Bosham was the port that Harold used in 1064 to launch an assault on the Norman armies. (He failed.) In this same district you can visit the first-century **Palace of Fishbourne**, perhaps England's first Early Stately Home. It was Roman, of course. The mosaic flooring in some of its 100 rooms are in fine condition and gardens have been rebuilt to their original plan. The story of the Palace (actually a villa) is related at the museum with audio-visual techniques.

**Goodwood House**, a product of the late 18th century and clearly revealing its Jacobean bloodline, lies north of Chichester. This magnificent creation is the home of the dukes of Richmond and Gordon. It contains fine furniture, outstanding paintings, and innumerable other treasures too vast to list. Important equestrian events take place at the **International Dressage Center** in the park. Within these same grounds is the "Glorious Goodwood" racecourse, where the main event is held every year at the end of July.

When you are touring this countryside you might care to visit the **Weald and Downland Open Air Museum**, which capsulizes all types of buildings commonly seen in the Old South of England. You can enter a reasonably "authentic" farmhouse or a charcoal burner's hut; see how the blacksmith worked; watch a ceramics exhibit or just generally browse, absorbing the mood of folkloric Albion.

About 20 minutes north of Chichester by car is **Midhurst**, hunkering primly in the valley of the River Rother. It's an appealing place to pause, with antique houses, markets, and inns just waiting to be explored. Look in at the **Spread Eagle**, one of the oldest inns in the county. Nearby is **Cowdray Ruins**, reflecting at least three different periods from 1520 to 1708. Unfortunately, much of it was consumed by fire in 1793, nearly all its contents being lost. In one of its wings, however, is a museum with recovered engravings, paintings, photographs, furniture, and numerous other exhibits. The grounds—vast open spreads—become electric with the pounding of pony hooves during the polo matches that often occur here. Perhaps you'll be lucky enough to catch a chukker or two as you pass.

# WHERE TO STAY AND EAT

## *HAMPSHIRE*

### ALTON

**Swan**

A 38-room house with a reasonably good restaurant; in the center, on High St. (☎ *0420-83777*; FAX: *84046.*)

**The Grange**

Half the size of the Swan and also quite recommendable. It's at Holybourne on the London Rd. (☎ *0420-86565*; FAX: *541346.*)

### BROCKENHURST

**Balmer Lawn**

A Hilton hotel with lots of amenities and sporting facilities such as indoor-outdoor pools and squash. Space for about 100. (☎ *0590-23116*; FAX: *23864.*)

**Rhinefield House**

A quieter redoubt in Victorian mansion style. It's out of town on Rhinefield Rd., almost bordering the New Forest.

### BURLEY

**Burley Manor**

Already inside the New Forest and surrounded by parkland. Cuisine is substantial and the setting is heavenly. Look for it on Ringwood Rd. (☎ *04253-3522.*)

**Moorhill House**

A fair choice off the A-31. (☎ *04253-3285.*)

### LYMINGTON

**Passford House**

A country-type reformation on Mount Pleasant Lane. (☎ *0590-682398.*)

**Stanwell**

Situated on High St. and very agreeable. (☎ *0590-677123*; FAX: *677756.*) Both are seasonal only.

**Provence**

Silver Street at nearby **Hordle**. This restaurant can produce some enviable Gallic dishes, often running to richness in content but not in price. Don't look in Tues. or Sun. nights. Open for both meals otherwise. (☎ *0590-682-219.*)

# LYNDHURST

## Park Hill
On the Beaulieu Rd., a pleasant 20-room country house. (☎ *042128-2944*; FAX: *3268*.)

## Crown
On High St. at the edge of the New Forest. (☎ *042128-2922*.)

## Lyndhurst Park
In the National Park (*78 High St*.) and quite good for a short stay. (☎ *042128-2834*.)

# MIDDLE WALLOP

## Fifehead Manor
An ancient cutie with only 16 rooms and not too much of a wallop for your wallet. (☎ *0264-781565*.)

# MILFORD-ON-SEA

## Westover Hall
Offers a glorious view of The Needles and the racing grounds of the world's top regatta boats. A pleasant Victorian cozy corner. (☎ *0590-43044*; FAX: *44490*.)

## South Lawn
On Lymington Rd., this hotel is fairly well known for its restaurant; good, solid accommodation. (☎ *0509-43911*.)

# NEW MILTON

## Chewton Glen ☆☆☆☆☆
A stately Georgian mansion growing within a sea of flowers in the New Forest, has long been one of the most glorious inns in England. Now it has outgrown its "inn" status and while still offering super-luxury in every respect, the intimacy of yore has dwindled to up-market efficiency—or possibly the coefficiency of continued success. Red brick edifice sprinkled with green shutters; convenient and attractive parking entry; homey lobby; thickly carpeted, book-lined Sun Lounge; Marryat Restaurant with justifiably renowned fare; Golden Room dinery, cocktail bar, tennis; indoor-outdoor swimming pool; small golf facility. Main house expanded gracefully on garden side; independent wing reached by a covered walkway just the ticket for romantic types. There are color TVs throughout the house and many additional sparklers that heighten the luster of this gem. Proprietors Martin and Brigitte Skan are working wonders here—virtual perfection at expensive tariffs that merit every single pence.

# ROMSEY

## White Horse
33 attractive accommodations on the Market Place. It's a useful alter-

native to overnighting in Southampton. (☎ *0794-512431*; FAX: *517485.*)

### Old Manor House
A handsome spot for dining.

# ROTHERWICK

### Tylney Hall
Near Hook, displays 66 acres of park and gardens by Gertrude Jekyll. A very expensive and fine country home with very ordinary cuisine. (☎ *025672-4881.*)

# SOUTHAMPTON

### Polygon                                                        ★☆
One of the larger and better hotels; it's on *Cumberland Place.* (☎ *0703-330055*; FAX: *332435.*)

### Dolphin
Another in the Trust House Forte chain; fair but nothing special. (☎ *0703-229955*; FAX: *333650.*)

### Northlands
A pleasant smaller hotel on *Northlands Rd.* (☎ *0703-333871.*) The hotels have fair dining rooms. Otherwise, try **La Brasserie** on Oxford St.

# SOUTHSEA

### Pendragon
Faces the Common and is adequate shelter. (☎ *0705-823201.*)

# WINCHESTER

### Wessex                                                         ★☆
Built over a Roman well, and the pacesetter. Situated across the lawn from the world-famous cathedral; 20th-century architecture that does not clash, odd as it might seem, with the moss-raked edifice; sound restaurant overlooking the hallowed resting places of some of Albion's greatest personages.

### Buttery
A cozy stop for late-hour snacks; well-appointed rooms. (☎ *0962-61611*; FAX: *841503.*)

### Lainston House                                                 ★★
Outstanding for accommodations and stately mansionhood, but management has an amateurish cast to it. When and if it mellows this could be one of the truly prestige addresses of Britain. The services in both dining salon and reception seemed to be of callow but well-meaning trainees. But lovely it is.

# ISLE OF WIGHT
## BONCHURCH

**Bonchurch Manor**
Small and cozy; shuttered Jan.-Feb. (☎ *0983-852868.*)

## COWES

**Fountain**
A squirt of 20 rooms, some with water. (☎ *0983-292397.*)

## NEWPORT

**Bugle**
Blows the best. Lots of innlike atmosphere and a fun spot to dine. (☎ *0983-522800.*)

## SHANKLIN

**Cliff Tops**
The tops here. (☎ *0983-863262.*)

## ST. LAWRENCE

**Lawyers Rest**
Allows the punishment to fit the crime. Actually, it's fair reward for the outlay. (☎ *0983-852610.*)

## VENTNOR

**Peacock Vane**
One I tried to find but somehow missed. Friends, however, like its casual ambience and handful of Victorian chambers. They also enjoyed the food. (☎ *0983-85-2019.*)

# SURREY
## BAGSHOT

**Pennyhill Park**
Set in 112 acres of rolling country with trout fishing available, clay-pigeon shoots, and tennis. Attractive three-story brick manor house with ivied walls, sumptuous lounges, and superb cuisine. (☎ *0276-71774;* FAX: *73217.*)

## FARNHAM

**Bush**
A pleasant stop with 68 rooms; some for non-smokers. (☎ *0252-715237;* FAX: *733530.*)

**Trevene House**                                                                  ★
More resortlike, offering lovely scenery, tennis, and a pool. It's out on the Alton Rd. (☎ *0252-716908.*)

**Hog's Back**
With 50 units, about 15 minutes from town at Seale. Quite attractive. (☎ *02518-2345.*)

# GUILDFORD

**Post House**
On Egerto Rd., is probably the best of the larger in-town hotels. (☎ *0483-574444*; FAX: *302960.*)

**Inn on the Lake**
At Godaliming offers more modest accommodations but at a lower price and with appealing waterfront views. (☎ *04868-5575.*)

# HASLEMERE

**Lythe Hill**
A handy overnight stop if you are delayed visiting Petworth House and the town. (It's on the road to it.) Ample comfort and good cookery in its Auberge. (☎ *0428-51251*; FAX: *4131.*)

# HINDHEAD

**Devil's Punchbowl**
Provides fair shelter at reasonable rates. It's on the highway to London. (☎ *042873-6565*; FAX: *5713.*)

# HORLEY

**Chequers**
On the Brighton pike serving a lot of Gatwick traffic. Still, it's a useful address. (☎ *02934-786992*; FAX: *820625.*)

# KINGSTON-ON-THAMES

**Kingston Lodge**
The best stop in this ancient coronation town. Its 65 units are satisfactory. (☎ *081-5414481.*)

# RICHMOND

**Kings Head**
In the town center with the market at your doorstep. (☎ *0748-2311.*)

**Howe Villa**
Only 4 rooms, but they are lovely, and the site at Whitcliff Mill is blissfully tranquil. (☎ *0748-850055.*)

**Shoulder of Mutton**
Another tyke of an inn for just a few lucky souls. (☎ *0748-2772.*)

## *KENT*

# BROADSTAIRS

**Castle Keep**
On Cliff Top with a marvelous sea view. (☎ *0843-65222.*)

**Castlemere**
Faces the water but from the Western Esplanade. (☎ *0843-61566.*)

**Royal Albion**

A worthy alternative on Albion St. (☎ *0284-760884*; FAX: *755476.*)

# CANTERBURY

**Chaucer** ☆☆

On Ivy Lane in midcity, would be my choice of the bigger hotels. (☎ *0227-464427*; FAX: *450397.*)

**Slaters** ★

An old standby in the cathedral zone. (☎ *0227-463271.*)

**County**

On High St. and also close to the cathedral, highly recommended. For dining, there's not much that a beefeater would enjoy since the upstairs **George's Brasserie** is Gallic in nature and **Tuo e Mio**, in a petite house, favors Italian dishes and fish. **Michael's** and **Sully's** are other possibilities.

# COBHAM

**Ye Old Leather Bottle** ★

Long the talk of High St. Moderate prices; don't confuse this town with the one in Surrey. (☎ *0474- 814327.*)

# DEAL

**Royal**

Offers about 30 rooms on the sea, along Beach St. (☎ *0304- 375555.*)

# DOVER

**Moat House**

Part of a large chain and here's a reliable link. (☎ *0304-203270*; FAX: *213230.*)

**Crest**

Adequate but hardly exciting. (☎ *0304-821222.*)

**Cliffe Court**

Continues to please because of its good location. (☎ *0304-211001.*)

**Midmay**

It will do if all others are booked solid. (☎ *0304-204278.*)

**Wallet's Court**

Try for dinners only. Very old and handsome.

# EASTWELL

**Eastwell Manor** ☆☆☆

This hotel has been a dwelling of some sort since 1069 and today is a grand greystone estate surrounded by beautifully tended formal gardens. Both food and comfort are at luxury level. Look for it near Broughton Aluph, between the M-2 and the A-20 on a spur designated A-251. (☎ *0233-966281.*)

# FOLKESTONE

### Clifton
Located *on The Leas*, offering numerous bedchambers. (☎ *0303-51231*; FAX: *851231*.)

### Burlington
Reliable, too. (☎ *0303-55301*.)

### Banque
Small—only a dozen rooms—and without a restaurant. The hospitality is its big reward (☎ *0303-53797*.)

# MAIDSTONE

### Embassy Great Danes ☆
120 units, convenient to Leeds Castle, being on a 20-acre park that is nearby. (☎ *0622-30022*; FAX: *35290*.)

### Larkfield
Less than half as many rooms, also fairly expensive. (☎ *0732-846858*; FAX: *846786*.)

### Grangemoor
Intimate and moderately priced. (☎ *0622-677623*.)

# ROCHESTER

### Crest
*On the Maidstone Rd.*, about the only show in town—and it's a fairly costly one for the rewards. (☎ *0634-678111*; FAX: *684512*.)

### Bridgewood Manor
(Same road) a little less expensive. (☎ *0634-201333*; FAX: *201330*.)

# TUNBRIDGE WELLS

### The Spa ★
Resides in 15 acres of nature and offers a bloodline going back to 1766. Its 76 units are well outfitted. (☎ *0892-20331*; FAX: *510575*.)

### Calverley
*On Crescent Rd.* and only a leaf's fall from Calverley Park, also offers tranquility, but for about 30% less than The Spa. (☎ *0892-26455*.)

### Thackeray's House
This inn probably never fed William Makepeace as brilliantly as it can reward today's literati. The cookery is contemporary in style and presentation. Refined and comfortable.

### Sankeys
In a nearby zone, more casual and straightforward in its approach. The sea fare is noteworthy. Both of these establishments are in former dwellings.

## SUSSEX—EAST AND WEST

### ALFRISTON

**The Star**

A solid conventional choice with 35 inviting bedchambers. (☎ *0323-870495*; FAX: *870922.*)

### AMBERLEY

**Amberley Castle**

Just below the historic South Downs Way, near famous Arundel. It's a marvelous storybook setting that harks back some nine centuries. Ideal for tranquil living and as a base for touring. (☎ *0798-831992*; FAX: *831998.*)

### BATTLE

**Netherfield**

Guarantees peace and quiet with a beautiful buffer zone of garden and park.Only 13 rooms and very nicely outfitted. (☎ *04246-4455*; FAX: *4024.*)

**George Inn**

*Right in High St.* with 21 units. Fair but not inspiring. (☎ *04246-4466.*)

### BRIGHTON

**Grand**

A sprawl of 160 rooms *on King's Rd.*; prices seem lofty for the rewards, but at tea time you will more than receive your money's worth if only in atmosphere. (☎ *0273-21188*; FAX: *202694.*)

**Dudley House**

A 6-unit cozy corner *on Madeira Pl.*, not to be confused with an 80-room whopper called the Dudley on Landsdowne Pl. (☎ *0273-676794.*)

**English's**

*On East St.*, For dining, the mood of Early Brighton is brightest at (☎ *0273-25661*), midday.

**Browns**

*On Duke St.*, hardy, medium-priced, and reliable.

**Noblesse**

*At the Hospitality Inn*, thumpingly expensive.

### CHICHESTER

**Dolphin and Anchor**

A fine mooring *on West St.* with 54 bedrooms and a so-so restaurant. (☎ *0243-785121*; FAX: *533408.*)

### Goodwood Park

Out at Goodwood with a manager named Goodall. In spite of all that, it's still pretty good. (☎ *0243-775537*; FAX: *533802*.)

### Crouchers Bottom

Worth visiting if only for that arresting title. It's on Birdham Rd. at **Apuldram**, a delightful, intimate country hotel where the people, the comfort, and the cookery are pleasantly straightforward. The breakfast is a happy start to any day. A friendly Bottomland with ample appeal. (☎ *0243-784995*.)

## EASTBOURNE

### Grand

A sister operation of the same-name institution in Brighton. Similar in most ways except that the **Mirabelle** restaurant here is elegant and very pleasing if you are looking for a distinguished atmosphere. (☎ *0323-412345*; FAX: *412233*.)

### Landsdowne

On the same row; a Best Western participant, and a reasonable buy. (☎ *0323-25174*; FAX: *39721*.)

### Croft

Offers only seven rooms, a pool, and tennis. Nice people too. (☎ *0323-642291*.)

## EAST GRINSTEAD

### Gravetye Manor ★★★★★

An authentic Elizabethan stone mansion from 1598, surrounded by an enchanted realm conceived and created by England's pioneer landscape gardener, William Robinson. It has the advantage of being in a thousand acres of forestry commission land—as well as enjoying the blessing of Peter and Sue Herbert as hosting proprietors, two radiant and genteel professionals who tend to their guests, their splendid gastronomy, their exceptional wines and their clients' comforts as ardently as they tend their immaculate grounds. It is a marvelous place to linger, but if time is too short at least try to schedule a meal stop for a repast that certainly will be memorable. Four new rooms add a bit more space, but getting a reservation is not easy since so many world travelers go out of their way to spend a few nights here and enjoy the magic of the Sussex countryside—with sights aplenty to see by day. (☎ *0342-810567*; FAX: *810080*.)

## HASTINGS

### Beauport Park

Offers two-dozen bedchambers just *on Battle Rd.*; quiet they are, however. The gardens are attractive too. (☎ *0424-851222*; FAX: *52465*.)

# LEWES

### Shelleys
Seems to be the usual choice, possibly because it is handily sited *on High St.* (☎ 0273-472361.)

### Millers
Also *on High St.* but has only three rooms and is a little charmer. There's no dining salon but you can hop over to **Kenwards** on the same row and have an excellent meal in a 12-table room that looks like a loft. (☎ *0273-475631.*)

# LOWER BEEDING

### South Lodge
In 90 acres of Downsland and close to Gatwick (10 miles), Glyndebourne, and Goodwood. Very homey and amply luxurious. (☎ *040376-711*; FAX: *766.*)

# MIDHURST

### Spread Eagle
This spot goes back almost 600 years, but it seems as youthful as the day it opened. Very attractive appointments in 40 bedrooms. (☎ *073081-5668.*)

# PEVENSEY

### Priory Court
A coastal location with nine adequate rooms and plenty of hospitality. (☎ *0323-763150.*)

# RYE

### Mermaid
Feudalism fused with modern provincial comfort. Long stucco and timber ivy-clad building topped with chimney pots; oaken dining den; Dr. Syn's Chamber paneled and lettered with aphorisms from the Bard of Avon; Giant's Fireplace Bar (look up the flue, which was once used by smugglers); tranquil courtyard. Eighteen of the 29 accommodations come fully plumbed; all tend toward the diminutive but are jam-packed with Elizabethan emollients such as four-poster beds and brassy lamps. Somewhat groupy. (☎ 0797-223065).

### George
Nice in a more predictable mode. Good solid comfort. (☎ *0797-222114.*)

### Jeake's
Serves no food but it does offer a handful of pleasant rooms.

### Flushing Inn
Up *on Market St.,* good for sea fare. (☎ *0797-222828.*)

## STORRINGTON

**Little Thakeham**                                    ☆☆☆

A product of the genius-architect Edwin Lutyens. It resides on six acres of garden designed by Gertrude Jekyll. What a heavenly combination. The proportions, comfort, and cuisine are soul-soothing. Prices are suitably high. (☎ *09066-744416.*)

## UCKFIELD

**Horsted Place**                                      ☆☆☆☆

A Victorian redoubt for many visitors to the nearby Glyndebourne opera season. Elaborate interior that is authentic but overpowering in its zeal. The sumptuous suites are shockingly expensive. Gastronomy excellent, but similarly costly. (☎ *0825-75581*; FAX: *75459.*)

**Hooke Hall**

A cozy choice and much cheaper. It offers authentic Queen Anne elegance but is still homelike; friendly restaurant—and the owner (the kindhearted Alister Percy) will pack a picnic for your opera evening. (☎ *0825-761578*; FAX: *768025.*)

# SHAKESPEARE COUNTRY VIA OXFORD AND THE COTSWOLDS

*Castle Combe, The Cotswolds*

London is the undisputed champ of international gateways, probably your landing point and most likely your departure city for returning home. It's a natural springboard, therefore, for your explorations of Great Britain. If you set out by car from Nelson's Column in Trafalgar Square, for example, before you feel the first gnawings for a midmorning snack you will be into the heart of England. Since most of the earliest driving will be through bedroom communities and satellite villages of London, you might as well take the M-40 directly northwest to Oxford, which resides at the confluence of the mighty Thames (local parlance dubs it the Isis), the sleepy River Cherwell, and the legendary Oxford Canal.

## OXFORD—TOWN VS. GOWN

Caparisoned in their respective attire, the "town" and the "gown" of Oxford form an uneasy union. The first goes about its business in an agitated state of chaos appropriate to a modern city. And just to make sure you recognize this city's character, the traffic congestion at peak hours is nearly perfect—a bit different from when it was simply *Osca's ford*, or the "ford for the oxen." But with all that activity going on, the **University** still lives in an insular, scholastic world and has molded brilliant minds for the benefit of humanity since at least two centuries before Columbus set sail for the New World. In the pre-Columbian era, there were already four colleges in operation, and today there are ten times as many sancta, or halls, which are open for public viewing. To check the visiting times, stop by the **Tourist Information Center** in Saint Aldate's. This should be complemented with an overview of the old town.

If you are strong of leg and equally stout in constitution, climb the **Carfax Tower**, which is all that remains of the 14th-century St. Martin Church. What you see below is almost a compendium of important English structuring. The splendor of the college architecture lends a striking dignity to the more mercantile town of Oxford. Since you probably won't have time to visit all or even a fraction of the colleges, some noteworthy candidates, which have been famous for centuries, include **Merton** and **Balliol**, both with 13th-century foundations; the former is particularly esteemed for its ancient library. If there is time, take in **Christ Church**, **Magdalen** (pronounced Maudlin), which stands at the end of High St. (traditionally called The High), and **New College**. From Magdalen, enjoy a stroll along Addison's Walk through the water meadows. Christ Church—a name inspired by its conception as a cathedral—is exceptional because of the 15th-century choir vaulting and the Norman pillars; a little closer to the Carfax Tower, **St. Edmund Hall** is compelling since it is the only relic of the medieval structures founded here in 1220 and predating the colleges.

Oxford's stellar attractions, of course, are the edifices associated with the university. The **Bodleain Library**'s collection of rare manuscripts is a gem—it vies with that of the Vatican—as is the **Ashmolean**, brimming with treasures from Europe and the Orient, as well as a richly endowed art gallery containing drawings by Michelangelo and Raphael. If you want later publications, go to **Blackwells**, probably the most famous bookshop in the world since it turned its first leaf in 1664.

For a second bird's-eye view of the university complex, you may wish to ascend to the graceful cupola at the **Sheldonian Theatre**; it was designed by Christopher Wren the year Blackwells opened for business. That 14th-cen-

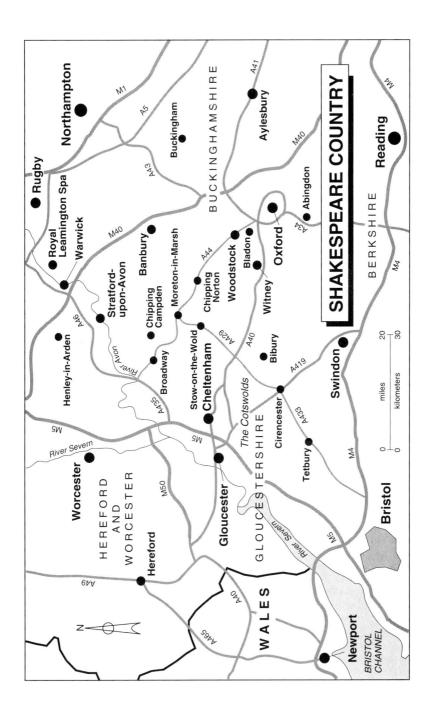

tury spire you see stands majestically over the **Church of St. Mary the Virgin**, which is often considered the centerpiece of the High. At its skirts you will find pubs, restaurants, and antiques and curios shops for browsing away the afternoon. Visitors with a green thumb might also like to view the gardens of Pembroke, Magdalen, and Christ Church, not to mention the **Oxford Botanic Garden**, which achieves prestige as the oldest "teaching garden" in England.

As mentioned earlier, the traffic congestion within Oxford is so catastrophic at peak hours that my suggestion is that you leave your car in the major parking zones skirting the city. One is on the Woodstock Rd., near the Peartree Roundabout (English nomenclature for traffic circle). Another is on Botley Rd. near Faringdon, and the third is on the Abingdon pike, which flows southeast of Oxford. From any of these you can take public transportation into town. If you want to risk it, there are several parking patches in the center, but usually these are filled, and it's hard on the nerves to arrive within the ever-circling traffic pattern only to discover there is no place to shuck your vehicle. Once you have separated yourself from the miracles of modern transportation, you will find that everything within Oxford is readily accessible by foot.

Doubtless you will wish to include the Cotswolds in your visit to Britain, but should time grow short, you can have an excellent exposure to rural England on an abbreviated tour into the surroundings of Oxford—huddling little villages, stately homes, green meadows, and blue skies (yes, often blue) punctuated by church spires.

## SOUTHWEST AND EAST OF OXFORD

**Stanton Harcourt**, 9 miles to the west, features a number of thatched-roof cottages and a medieval tower with a kitchen that stands within the grounds of a modern house. Alexander Pope once lived and wrote in this settlement. Nearby there is a 17th-century parsonage and the handsome man-made ponds that have been the residence of assorted fish since the early Middle Ages. Blessing the entire scene is a remarkable Norman church.

**Abingdon** offers a small but absorbing mixture of houses and structures dating from the 13th century and later. The **County Hall**, which came along about four centuries afterwards, is now a local museum; try also to see the **Guildhall** here. You can pass through the Abbey gatehouse and walk the boards of a reconstructed Elizabethan theater. **St. Helen's Church** is possibly the centerpiece because of its elegant spire that dominates the countryside.

South of Abingdon, where the Thames meanders lazily through the fertile vale, a tree-crowned chalk knoll sometimes called the **Wittenham Clumps** provides a spectacular, isolated viewpoint and a breezy escape from the still and occasionally sultry river valley. An easy passage eastward across **Day's Lock** and the shimmering river meadows brings you to the Roman town of Dorchester with its massive Norman abbey and ancient earthworks.

**Clifton Hampden** is less than three miles north, past the attractive thatched hamlets of **Little** and **Long Wittenham**. If you cross the Thames here via the distinctive narrow bridge, you'll find the inviting **Berley Mow Inn**. Readers of Jerome K. Jerome will recognize it from his book titled *Three Men In A Boat*. Afterwards—just off the A-40 2 miles south of Witney—you come to **Cogges Manor**, a 13th-century dwelling and an Edwardian homestead standing on 11 acres. Here many traditional farm skills such as hurdle-making and sheep-shearing can be witnessed. The interesting tools, wagons, and horse-drawn vehicles illustrate how yesterday's farmers worked and raised their livestock. Follow along a historic trail marking the moated manor, the deserted village earthworks, and field systems of medieval times.

**Uffington** is a small town in the valley beneath the hill fort known as **Uffington Castle** and the prehistoric outline of the **Uffington White Horse**. The latter is an extraordinary legacy from the Iron Age. It can be appreciated best in the vale below along the B-4508 road or from the town itself, where the church tower is an excellent vantage point.

**Sutton Courtenay** is one of those dreamy Thames-side villages that so often tempts the photographers of picture postcards. A broad green wood hugs the sprawling 17th-century **Milton Manor** somewhat outside of town; its library (apparently not such a big draw for its books) contains an excellent collection of porcelain. The lanes of the hamlet are lined with half-timbered houses. The author George Orwell and Britain's prime minister in 1914, Lord Asquith, have found their final resting places in this bucolic Chiltern setting.

**Little Wittenham** would be your next stop for a brief airing on the top of the ridge that affords such spectacular views of the Chilterns. The old fortress is a reminder that times were not always peaceful.

**Long Wittenham** can offer you a pint of refreshment at its old inn on the l-o-o-o-o-n-g main street. A number of villages in this area are built on this pattern, with half-timbered houses lining the two sides of a single lane. Both the church, quite old, and the museum are worth a brief pause if you have the time.

**Dorchester** lies just at the northern fringes of the Chilterns, a town that appears frequently in English literature. As you stroll down the captivating cobbled High Street, you will see a variety of antique buildings, the **church** being the jewel in the crown with its magnificent sculpture and dramatic stained glass windows. While in the area and especially if you have children in tow, you will probably want to see the **Aston Rowant Nature Reserve**; it's on one of the loftier razorbacks in the Chiltern hills. Typical villages with medieval architecture include **Ewelme**, **Thame**, and **Long Crendon**. The pews and benches at Tycote **Chapel** exemplify the great skill, craftsmanship, and love that the people here built into their houses of worship.

## NORTH OF OXFORD

**Headington**, with a splendid 12th-century village church just to prove its heritage, was a center for stonework in ancient times. Many of the colleges of Oxford were created out of cuttings from local quarries.

**Stanton St. John**, not far away, will be interesting as a pilgrimage for Bay Staters; John White, one of the architects of Massachusetts, was born here in the late 16th century. There are plenty of photographs for back-home New Englanders: stone cottages snuggling into the landscape, thatched roofs, a wonderful manor house, and, of course, a **church** that has inspired many in our own Up-Eastern states.

**Brill** offers as its main talking point a 17th-century windmill that catches the breeze above the sleepy Vale of Aylesbury. The ancient clapboard house containing the gearing system stands above the brick millroom, which can be visited by the public. Though the village has all the trademarks of antiquity, with cottages, an almshouse, a Tudor manor, and plenty of color, I must confess that I have never seen the famous Aylesbury ducks anywhere in this region. Perhaps they will be more visible to you.

**Lower Heyford** is best known for its 13th-century church, which commanded the souls of residents in this most attractive valley of the River Cherwell. You might check the sundial on the patio to see if the time is correct. It was originally set by 15th-century astronomers. And now you can cross the river and the Oxford Canal to visit **Rousham House**, designed by Sir Robert Dormer of window fame. While the dwelling contains some interesting features—shooting holes in the doors from the time when it was a royalist garrison—its greater appeal lies in the gardens, which were laid out by William Kent. The outdoor portion is open from 10 a.m. to 4:30 p.m., while the house receives visitors on Wednesdays, Sundays, and holidays; during the warmer months only from 2 to 4:30 p.m.

**Deddington**, now mellowed after centuries of history and weathering of the local stone works, was once an active crossroads during the Civil War. The Cherwell also became an important feature at this north–south span of the river.

**Great Tew** is a wee hamlet of stone and thatching plus a holy ground in its center with ancient stocks for the viewing. The mood bespeaks antiquity to this day (but the stocks are seldom employed).

**Charlbury** is not too interesting except for **Ditchley Park**, esteemed for its splendid interior decorations. It is one of the larger 18th-century buildings in Oxfordshire. For 350 years it has been occupied by the Lee family. (Confederate General Robert E. Lee is on the family tree.) Ditchley was also the frequent weekend haven of Sir Winston Churchill during World War II. Today the building houses an Anglo-American Conference Center.

**Witney**, with links to the American family of the same name (and with variations in spelling), began its prosperous career in the wool trade, and just to make sure everyone in the district appreciated the ostensible wealth of its residents, it created a spire on its church tall enough to refute any doubt of modest means in this village. Another interesting feature of Witney is the **Butter Cross**, which is supported by stone pillars. About 10 minutes to the northwest you can also visit the **Minster Lovell Hall** (see later under "Burford, The Cotswolds") and **Dovecote**, which began hosting English gentlemen and ladies (and fowl) in the 15th century. About 300 years later the Yorkist remains of what is thought to have been Lord Lovell were discovered in the basement of this edifice. His grave had been missing since 1485, when he fought on the losing side at the Battle of Bosworth.

**North Leigh** is nearby, and while it is picturesque for its windmill and the Saxon tower of its church, its greater fame is derived from the **Roman villa** that dates back to the 4th century. It was a farming center serving the Roman settlement of St. Albans and Cirencester. The original villa probably had as many as 60 rooms surrounding its courtyard, but over the centuries many of the artifacts have disappeared to "collectors."

**Bladon** is well known because of the grave sites of Sir Winston Churchill and other members of his family. His birthplace, however, is considerably more interesting: **Blenheim Palace** resides in a park of its own containing 2500 acres and an enormous lake. The name derives from the English victory over the French at Blenheim in 1704. The reward to the duke of Marlborough was this palatial gift from Queen Anne. Parliament also provided a generous sum for the building of the palace, which today is better known for the debut of the infant Winston Churchill. The legendary Christopher Wren was originally commissioned to design the monument to glory, but his plan was replaced by the architecture of John Vanbrugh, who, in my estimation, created one of England's more hideous shrines of conquest. At least the gardens, partially cultivated by the talented Capability Brown, are a compensating factor that may draw your eyes away from the comedy of  stonework produced by Sir John. Inside the palace are corridors and halls full of paintings—and excellent ones—that relate to the flamboyant family history. You will also see the rather modest room (possibly the only "modest" one in the structure) to which Winnie's mother adjourned to give issue to England's most illustrious prime minister. As time passes, you'll discover, a garden restaurant, a snack center, a motor launch for rides on the lake, and a train. The palace and grounds are open daily from 11 a.m. to 6 p.m. from mid-March to late October.

**Woodstock**, previously a royal manor, is one of the more charming villages in the region and by far my first choice for dining or pausing as a substitute for the facilities at Blenheim Palace. A small hotel on the main street called **The Feathers** is ideal for refined gastronomy and comfort. Tourists, however, are often drawn to the famous **Bear Inn**, which has been doing business as usual for more than 750 years, obviously a local attraction. It still serves a reasonable meal in the traditional pattern. For lighter refreshment you might consider the **Star**, across the street. It offers modestly priced buffet selections at midday. The bar is decorated with chamber pots; apart from this questionable expression of taste, the food is quite acceptable.

**Banbury** boasts Saxon roots, though few remnants exist from that early period. And the famous Banbury Cross alluded to in the nursery rhyme?

That's just a copy erected in the 19th century. Banbury's first cross was razed in anger by the Puritans before they departed for America. More myth? "The lady on a white horse" is a figure oft viewed in Oxfordshire because she is represented on Banbury's coat of arms. Yet, who she is nobody seems to know. Today, Banbury has little time for rhyme and reverie, being more involved in commerce and cattle.

**Broughton Castle** is 2 miles southwest of Banbury. This moated Elizabethan mansion has an early 14th-century nucleus, 16th- and 18th-century plaster ceilings, and handsome 16th-century chimney pieces. The china exhibit appeals to specialists as many of the pieces are quite rare.

## THOSE INSPIRING COTSWOLDS

*Wolds*, in the language of the ancient residents, refers to the tranquilizing rolling terrain that is immediately visible. The prefix—not unlike our modern word for cottage—applies to the dwellings that dot the undulating countryside, laced by streams and shaded by lovely trees in tidy gardens. The names are enchanting: **Chipping Norton**, **Stow-on-the-Wold**, **Upper Swell**, **Chipton-under-Witchwood**, the **Upper** and **Lower Slaughters**, and even a magical river called the **Windrush**. These names alone hint at how sensitive the early occupants of this weald were to the effects of nature and the beauty that surrounded them.

As a touring area, the Cotswolds is not large or daunting. From the east—let's say you are approaching from Oxford—the soft dales and leafy hills of the wolds spread from the Upper Thames Valley until, in the west, you can experience the overall panoramas across the Severn Valley from the north-south axis, which rises to a ridge. When you have driven even a few minutes into this enclave, you will note a distinctive character in part created by the use of local stone for the cottages, the walls, the borders, the streams, and even the benches for strollers. In the sunlight it is a golden straw tone, mellowing to honey, and finally darkening with patches of lichen and spotted antiquity.

To some degree the hewn stone was a merit badge and status symbol of the prosperity developed in this region as a result of the wool trade. The ample riches of its citizens resulted in the endowment of lovely churches—well-proportioned relative to the size of the villages. You'll find a sturdy, forthright personality to the homes, which is aided by storybook settings in the green patchwork of hills. Moreover, in these hamlets you will also experience the double vision of attractive dwellings that are reflected in ponds and streams that run before the houses and along the main streets.

Ancient man was drawn to these scrub-covered uplands. He cleared the woodland, cultivated the soil, and fed his animals on the rough pastures. These early efforts at agriculture and animal husbandry left permanent memorials called barrows or mounds. There are more than 100 of these distinctive formations in the Severn Valley and Cotswold region.

The Romans marched onto the scene around A.D. 47 and they did some clearing of their own—mostly of local tribes, which they subjugated. As road builders, the Romans are legendary. Look, for instance, at the Fosse Way and Ermine Street at Cirencester as examples of their civil engineering. Latin muscle and might are manifest in the forts at Gloucester and Cirencester. Opulent villas and even entire towns were created under the *pax romana*. Not to miss a trick, the Romans also recognized the value of the primitive wool trade. Exportation became important, followed by the weaving of finished cloth. This continued to grow until it dominated the English economy in the Middle Ages.

The sleepy Cotswolds of today, if you can believe it, once contributed more than half the total of wool textiles produced in the world. Nearly everybody who lived in the area participated in some way in this industry. The merchants, of course, were the biggest shots of all, at the very pinnacle of the commercial success ladder. Alas, by 1600 the great days were over and the center of wool work moved first to the southwest and then to the north, finally to be challenged by the cotton industry in the 18th and 19th centuries. Strangely, the decline helped preserve much that had been created in the more prosperous days, since little development took place during the descending period. This situation is not unlike the droughts of India, which are credited with preserving many monuments and even entire regions because they were hastily abandoned, not attacked and, hence, never experienced the changes of continuous habitation. There's something to be said for benign decay.

If you have the time—or try to make it—this is walking country such as you'll find nowhere else. The many lanes lead to open commons, fields, woodlands, to knolls with breathtaking panoramas. Stately homes, gardens, and manor houses abound. The Cotswold Way stretches almost 100 miles along a dramatic upland trail that invites endless photography. Happily, there are many attractive hostels and inns that can provide several bedrooms and, while not inspiring, at least nourishing regional cooking. More formalized sightseeing would include the cathedral cities and spas such as Gloucester, with fascinating glimpses of its Roman origins, and Cheltenham, one of England's most engaging Regency towns.

## CHELTENHAM AND THE NORTH COTSWOLDS

Cheltenham became a "destination" in the 18th century following the discovery of waters with supposed medicinal attributes. It was the heyday of spas. Then during the next century, as its popularity increased, the town was reconstructed in the lavish Regency mode that seemed appropriate for its upper-crust clientele. The **Pittville Pump Room**, which stands on a beautiful green common, is typical of the architecture employed hereabouts. The columns—and there are many—are Ionic, and their aspect is indeed stately. The museum within delineates the history of the spa; moreover, there is a Gallery of Fashion. If you stroll over to the **Promenade**, opposite the Imperial Gardens and along London Road, you will see some of the best examples of period iron work; this has often been compared in delicacy to fine lace. White stucco is generally the outer garment of Regency buildings. Along this same London Road, on Lansdown Road, and in Suffolk Square, you can note examples of meticulously cut stone facades, and to really reach for neoclassical status, visit **Montpellier Walk**, which is also known as the "Street of Statues." Spaced glamorously between the shops are mock Caryatids, copies of Greek female figures used as support elements—those ladies usually associated with Bijou theaters and palaces of entertainment.

**Cheltenham**, for obvious reasons, remains an attraction today. Culturally, the annual **International Music Festival** is a glorious and rewarding event. Gustav Holst, the composer, was born here, and there is a **museum** commemorating his most noteworthy notes. Children from two important private schools in the area, along with many tours, are trouped through the excellent art gallery (superb Dutch painting) and museum (English ceramics, Chinese porcelain, and archaeological findings). Chiefly it's the setting that continues to draw people back century after century. The view from **Cleeve Hill** reveals a natural nesting place between the Cotswold and the Severn Vale. The oval below is **Prestbury Race Course**, scene of the well-known Gold Cup challenge. Off in the distance, that weathered rock promontory is the **Devil's Chimney**. Then, if you drive south of town to **Crickley Hill**, you can scramble through a fascinating fort from the period of the Iron Age; it is surrounded by acres of parkland.

**Burford**, today an unspoilt medieval town on the A-40 from Oxford, was prominent in the 18th century as a popular coaching stop. The Windrush hardly rushes by and neither should you. Visit the old bridge and you'll see the products of ancient wool prosperity. Many of its former inns in Elizabethan and Georgian style still line its dramatically steep High Street—well, High only at one end. **The Priory** and **The Tolsey** are the sites of ancient marketplaces where tolls were collected. The Normans left behind a church of splendid and distinctive architecture. Antiques dealers thrive here; so will you if your passions are thus inclined. Going south you'll come to a **wildlife preserve**, where nature's creatures (yourself included) may roam around 120 acres of gardens and parkland. Its Gothic-style manor house also can be visited.

**Minster Lovell Hall**, a stark, ruined edifice in a tranquil aquarian setting with tall trees whispering of its grisly past, is rumored to be haunted by the shades of its namesake, Lord Francis Lovell, who may have trapped himself inside a secret room while hiding from his enemies. (Henry VII never forgave him for his friendship with Richard III.) The only confidant to know of his hiding place apparently passed away, leaving no information as to his Lordship's whereabouts. The Clandestine Cache (and *possibly* Lord Lovell) were unearthed in the early 18th century. A similar fate was met by a young lady about to be wed in the moated tower. Go into the town over the 15th-century bridge where the **Old Swan**, a charming inn, offers far more hospitable surroundings and memories.

**Northleach**, on the Leach River, adds to the spooky heritage with its **Prison Block Museum**. The alms houses, however, and the honey-toned, stone-built cottages are appealing.

Driving northeast from Cheltenham you can have yourself photographed on **Belas Knap**, a man-made creation dating back to about the time of the pyramids. This is a lateral long barrow—one of the mounds associated with this region.

**Winchcombe** about 2 miles to the north is the ancient capital of the Saxon kingdom of Mercia. Its **abbey**, presently being worked on by earnest archaeologists, harks back to the 8th century. And an inn, called **The George**, was erected in the 13th century and was known to some of the pilgrims in later times who left England for the New World. Henry VIII, one of England's more vigorous monarchs, romped all through these parts. **Sudeley Castle**, open to the public, was the residence of Catherine Parr, the last of Henry's daisy chain of wives. Sudeley also was the headquarters of Charles I during the Civil War. While the building itself contains a noteworthy collection of arts and treasures, the exhibitions in falconry are riveting. Catherine may have pondered her fate at **Hailes Abbey**, a short trip as the falcon flies; now in ruins, it once served as a 13th-century Cistercian retreat.

If you are at all inclined to landscape painting, search no farther. Unpack your easel and roam through the magnificent wooded area to the town of **Stanway**. The **Tithe Barn** is highly paintable, as is **Stanway House**, which lies beyond a still proud 17th-century entranceway.

**Stanton** is another delight, with its Elizabethan courtyard and **Warren House**, both handsome manor-isms that are enhanced for your canvas by thatched-roof barns.

**Broadway** is often thought of as the capital of the Cotswolds. It is really an extended village along a main street with suppressed aspirations for becoming a town. If I am attending any of the plays at the Royal Shakespeare Theatre in Stratford-on-Avon, this is usually where I reside. It is quieter, and the drive over to Stratford is less than half an hour. Except on the weekends it is relatively uncrowded, the shopping is good, and the restaurants are amusing. The **Lygon Arms**, famous all over the world as a hotel today, offers a well-preserved segment that harks back to its 18th century origin as a coaching inn. **Prior's Manse** goes back three centuries before that and is probably one of the more antique houses in the county. Nature lovers can find rewarding pastimes on the trail from **Fish Hill**, in the views from **Broadway Beacon**, or on a tour of the folly called **Broadway Tower**, erected in the 18th century by Lady Coventry.

**Chipping Campden** owes much of its attraction to the wealth of the wool trade. There are several "Chippings" in the region, the word referring to market. This one's **Market Hall**, constructed in 1627, with arches facing lovely gabled stone and half-timbered houses. It's a fine display of Jacobean architecture. An even earlier example of the good times is **Woolstaplers Hall**, vintage 1340. Though the neighboring country **church** is original, **Campden Manor** was resurrected after a fire destroyed it during the Civil War. As a side trip you might like a tour of **Hidcote Manor**, 3 miles to the north, which offers formal gardens, rare trees, hedges, shrubs, flowers, and bulbs.

There is a pulchritudinous triangle of towns that lie within the area vaguely known as the **Vale of the Red Horse**. Probably the best-known center is **Moreton–in-Marsh**, which is situated on the Fosse Way and boasts an elegant **market house** (recently restored) along with a row of other fine buildings. Charles I signed the registry at the **White Hart Hotel** here in the middle of the 17th century. The monarch's name is further honored in **Chastleton House**, a proud Jacobean manor built in 1603. We have another "market" at **Chipping Norton**, once a thriving linchpin of the wool trade. The signs of its early success are abundant and bewitching. The area obviously had been settled many centuries before; evidence of this occupation is provided a few miles to the north, where you will find the **Rollright Stones**, not a rock group but Bronze Age circles exquisitely designed to confound archaeologists of the present era. You might ponder three of these mysterious and crude works: The **King's Men**, **King's Stone**, and **Whispering Knights**. Probably you'll aver theories about their purpose, but certainly there are ample legends nurtured by local residents as to their function and historical significance.

Take the route B-4450 from Chipping Norton to **Churchill** (Warren Hastings, first governor general of India, was born here) to the hilltop perch of **Stow-on-the-Wold**, with its spacious market square, stocks, and a dramatic 14th-century cross. If you have time, peep into the church, which houses an excellent crucifixion by Gasper de Craeyer, a contemporary and friend of Rubens and Van Dyck.

**Bourton-on-the-Water** is to the south—the water being the captivating Windrush River. If you're in a hurry you can see the entire town in miniature in the garden of the **Old New Inn**, where each stone building, shop, house, church, and bridge has been reproduced with care. Ornithologists can find ample pastimes at **Birdland**, where our feathered friends number more than 600 different fowl. There is also an engaging **Village Life Exhibition**, a **motor museum**, a **model railway**, and the **Cotswold Perfumery**.

## *CIRENCESTER AND SOUTH COTSWOLDS*

After your march through the urban sprawl of London, it is hard to imagine that Cirencester could once have been England's second city in terms of size and importance. Nevertheless, that is just what it was in the second century, when the Romans called it **Corinium**. Latin occupation put it on the map and, of course, the road building proclivities of those early people brought many visitors to its doorstep as well as much prosperity. Coins, mosaics, and other artifacts of the Latins can be viewed at the **Corinium Museum**, while the remains of an **amphitheater** occupy some prime real estate on Queen's Hill. Solons of this outpost dispensed wisdom along with their administrative talents in the restored **Town Hall** in the abbey grounds. Its prestige dwindled after the Romans returned to their peninsula, but it recovered again during the successful period of the wool trade. Ionic and Corinthian columns were replaced by ecclesiastical art, as manifest in the parish **Church of St. John the Baptist**. Approaching cathedral standards, it boasts an imposing tower added around the year 1400; inside are many treasures, including a silver cup made for Anne Boleyn in 1535. Located in an old brewery, there is an earnest and bustling art center called the **Cirencester Workshops**. And, if the children are being particularly obstreperous, how about a trip to a restored two-cell **gaol** (jail) in Trinity Road?

To the northeast of Cirencester in the village of **Chedworth**, you may visit a **museum** as well as the best-preserved **Roman villa** in England. Having survived since the second century, the mosaic pavements as well as its 32 rooms are in excellent preserve.

From windows on the past to windows on the gently flowing River Coln at **Bibury**. Many of its stone houses proudly display gardens that tilt gently to the river's edge. Especially attractive are the homes along **Arlington Row**. Some of the 17th-century weavers' cottages are held by the National Trust. **Arlington Mill**, another product of the 17th century, is a farm museum today. Water not only contributes to the aesthetic beauty of Bibury, but is important economically since many tiers of ponds in the town or in its suburbs are devoted to trout ranching, something which is well worth seeing while you are in the area. If it is mealtime when you are passing through, **The Swan**, a former coaching inn, does an excellent job with several trout recipes. You can also pause at the **Bibury Court Hotel**, a Jacobean creation, for similar vittles.

**Ablington** is noteworthy for one of the aforementioned barrows as well as for a handsome 16th-century **manor house** with its vast barn. Tributary stops worth discovering along the River Coln include **Barnsley**, for its church of Norman origins, and **Winson**, for its stately mansion house.

To the southwest is the market town of **Tetbury**, with a special house at its core serving as the center of trading activity since 1655. The good citizens still worship in the shadow of the tall and graceful steeple of **St. Mary's Church**, but if for any reason they do not seek a virtuous course in life, there is a reminder of crime and punishment at the **Police Museum** in the Court House. Perhaps you remember war stories based on Tetbury's **Malt House**; this was the secret headquarters of the American Army in this sector prior to the Normandy Landings. If the weather is benign during your visit, be sure to stroll through the **arboretum**, which contains more than 100 acres of trees, plants, and flowers.

Turning north, you can take the byway to **Berkeley Castle**, where Edward II was murdered in 1327. The same Berkeley family has resided here for more than eight centuries. Then on to the textile center of **Stroud** and the walled town of **Painswick**. You can return to **Cirencester** through the rolling and fertile **Golden Valley**, which was formed by the River Frome. The vale is sprinkled with ancient hamlets. Sapperton's **Daneway House** dates back in parts to 1250. Joining the waterway system here are the Thames and the Severn Canal Tunnel, the latter being one of England's busiest barging channels in times past. While the vessels themselves have vanished, many of the old inns continue to serve today's wheelborne traveler.

Driving eastwards from Cirencester brings you to the upper reaches of the Thames, an historic and beautiful confluence of river valleys created by the **Coln**, **Churn**, and **Leach**. The **Golden Valley** of the Dore River is aptly named, especially if you are passing through during the autumn—or perhaps if you are buying property in this much prized and expensive district. Autumn is also a good time to visit the **Cotswold Water Park**, formed out of abandoned gravel pits.

At **Lechlade** an extensive garden runs along the banks of the Thames; hence the park offers additional nature scenes with a classical 18th-century **mansion** as its centerpiece. The period paintings contained within it are certainly worth a pause. If the season is right, save some of your film for **Filkins**, where wisteria and clematis blossom on vines covering the pale stone houses along lanes shaded by chestnut trees. Despite its obvious touristic appeal, the **Cotswold Wildlife Park** is well presented and puts on show an ample variety of game.

Moving on to **Eastleach's** the scenery is no less compelling for the avid photographer. This is really a village of twin hamlets joined by an old stone bridge. Of course, the **churches** are the chief elements of the local architecture, and one is noteworthy because of its five sundials.

**Quenington** also boasts a handsome assemblage of 17th-century houses, but of particular note are the beautifully carved Norman doorways on the 12th-century **church** in the village.

**Fairford** is justifiably proud of the stained glass windows in its house of worship. Standing beside the River Coln with four spires rising high above its parish realm, the **church** overlooks the square where the pattern of dwellings is today very much as it was two centuries ago. Don't miss an opportunity to pause beside the watermill at the edge of town.

## GLOUCESTER

On their western edge, the Cotswolds are flanked by the River Severn, and here stands historic Gloucester, inhabited since the earliest times of European mankind. Established by the ancient Britains (who called it *Caer Glou*), it became important under the Romans (*Glevum* in Latin) who used it as a fortification for the routes to Wales. The **City Museum** offers excellent exhibits of Roman and medieval occupation; the **Roman Wall**, in fact, runs through the underground portions of this edifice. Over at **Eastgage**, the defenses are visible aboveground, and at **Coopers Hill** there is a Roman villa dating from the first century A.D.

After the Norman conquest the town metamorphosed gradually from a fortification into a place of distinction. William the Conqueror held court here; Henry III enjoyed a coronation here; Edward II's remains still lie in the soil here. **Gloucester Cathedral** is one of the finest examples of a Norman abbey church you can find within the U.K. Its tower soars as high as a modern skyscraper; the east window is one of the largest to be found in church architecture; the roof tracery is exceptional; the painted organ case is of everlasting beauty and is the largest one in Britain. If you wish to take home a self-made souvenir, the brass rubbing on these premises is extremely productive. Further highlights of interest in the area are the **Blackfriars** and **Greyfriars monasteries** as well as **Elmore Court**, (an Elizabethan estate), which dates from the 13th century. The town itself (**Elmore**) is worth a look for its **church**.

Gloucester underwent quite a severe drubbing at the hands of Charles II following the Civil War because of the vengeful vendetta by the monarch for the city's opposition to his father. The good news is that the rebuilding program paved the way for Gloucester to become a thriving commercial center. The first ships steamed through the Gloucester and Berkeley ship canal in 1827. The colorful **docks** provide vivid evidence of its success. Many of the enormous warehouses of that time have been retained. Among these antique entrepots, there are today many facilities for leisure and entertainment. Shoppers will surely want to browse through the **Antiques Center**, which is located in one of these gigantic buildings. It is cleverly executed, with three different tiers of Victorian streets lined with individual shops. Other options include the **Robert Opie Collection**, the **Gloucester Folk Museum**, and a pedestrian way known as **Via Sacra** that has been created roughly along the line of the old Roman Wall.

## *TEWKESBURY*

This could be considered the northern gateway to the Cotswolds, a charming town that was spared the fever of the industrial revolution and thus retains its old-world ambience. **King John's Bridge**, in fact, was not renovated until a few decades ago—and that was first built in the early 13th century! It resides at the watery junction of the Severn and the Avon and is dominated by one of the largest **abbeys** in Britain; this was begun in 1092, with roots into the eighth century. Among its panoply of fine Norman masonry are tombs and memorials to some of England's greatest families, many of whom perished just south of the city, where in 1471 one of the bloodiest battles of the War of the Roses took place. In fact, the site where Edward IV collided with (and defeated) the Prince of Wales is today called **Bloody Meadow**. See the **Bell Inn** and the **Hop Pole**, the latter for its association with Mr. Pickwick.

# RAISING THE CURTAIN ON SHAKESPEARE COUNTRY

**Stratford-upon-Avon**, to employ the Bard's own phrase, seems to answer "the huge army of the world's desires" when it comes to pilgrimages to a one-man shrine. As the birthplace of Britain's landmark playwright, it has become the most visited hub in England. It is in the true center of the county. The gentle Avon, England's most historic river after the Thames, flows under the main street and through Warwickshire, nourishing, as it goes, numerous fetching Elizabethan villages, vast farms, and tiny, tidy gardens, noble and stately homes, and active gentrified suburbs. Much of this was the ore and substance of Shakespearean writing.

Historic and colorful Warwick with its mighty castle and blissful Kenilworth live and breathe, even today, the magical moments created by Shakespeare, while Stratford is now a toddling town, hustling and bustling with a superfluity of tourism. Some might remember it as a market center with a lively, cosmopolitan atmosphere. It does provide a focal point for absorbing the local lore, reasonable comfort, and a few adequate restaurants. It is, alas, no longer a tranquil place although there are numerous peaceful hamlets nearby.

There is, of course, more to Warwickshire than Shakespeare and Elizabethan heritage. A delightful contrast is provided by **Royal Leamington Spa**, an elegant 18th-century Regency redoubt. To the north, **Nunneaton** offers fascinating literary associations with George Eliot, one of England's pre-eminent novelists. Rugby, home of the well-respected school that introduced its version of football, is close by. The rich and fertile **Vale of Evesham** lies to the west. Magnificent in blossom time, it later harvests much of the country's fruit and vegetables. South from Stratford brings you into the marvelous **Stour Valley**, where some of England's important rivers and canals interconnect. This region is better known through the paintings of its landscapes than the poetry of its occupants. Whichever way it is known to you, it is worth seeing and enjoying anew.

## THE BARD HIMSELF

Shakespeare is reckoned to have arrived on this planet on St. George's Day, April 23, 1564, in downtown Stratford. He was the eldest son of John Shakespeare, a glover and curer of skins, and Mary Arden of Wilmcote, a prosperous farmer's daughter. The house where he was born is, of course, open to visitors and is guaranteed to be on every tour that enters or leaves Warwickshire; it is located on Henley Street. William was christened in the parish church on April 26. Remember these dates.

Stratford was in those days a bouncy, progressive commercial center with its own corporation and numerous ambitious craftsmen; at that time the chief labors were linked with agriculture. Its population of about 1500 meant it was a town of consequence. William's father was a man of money and position, but destiny was to work against him, and his fortunes dwindled into debts. This development however, came late enough to provide William with a comparatively wealthy and comfortable youth. He was probably educated at the King's New Grammar School. Below his classroom was the Guildhall, where touring players would perform from time to time. Scholars opine that Will's initial exposure to the boards occurred here. He must have learned quickly because at 18 he married 26-year-old Anne Hathaway, a charming maid of Shottery. Three children eventually came of the union, but just a few years after the nuptials, around 1585, Shakespeare saw the bright lights of London. Leaving his family behind, he prospered in the big city as both an actor and as a playwright. It is noted somewhere that he performed before Elizabeth I. He became the groom of the Chamber to James I, but, apparently tired of grooming, the now legendary figure retired to Stratford in 1611. He then lived in the New Place, the largest house in town, which he had bought during his ascendancy more than a dozen years earlier. He died on April 23, 1616, and was buried in the Chancel of Holy Trinity Church. While the date of his demise is certain, the coincidence of his birthday similarly being on April 23 (remember the christening?) gives rise to some doubt as to when he started life. Shakespeare could have made fine mystery from the matter.

## SHAKESPEARE'S STRATFORD

Quite apart from Shakespeare memorabilia, Stratford is an active hive of humanity. There is a wealth of domestic architecture; there are many attractive and unusual shops, reasonable pubs, and so-so restaurants; on the Avon you can go rowing, touring, and fishing. But Shakespeare remains the be-all and end-all of almost every activity. And the mecca for thousands of visitors is still to be found in Henley Street, Shakespeare's birthplace. True to the form of the day, the style of the house is half-timbered, from the early 16th century. Furnished in Elizabethan style, it contains some fascinating books, manuscripts, and art objects, giving an impression of the poet's life and times. You may walk through the oak-beamed salon, the bedroom where Shakespeare was born, the fully equipped kitchen, and the museum. The garden behind is also pleasant. The adjoining **Shakespeare Center** is a library and study room.

If you'd like a stroll, follow the attractive mile-long footpath to Shottery to the comely little thatched-roof **Anne Hathaway Cottage**, with its old-fashioned garden. A passionate William ran this route many times when he was bedizzened by the allure of his future wife. Much original Tudor furniture has been retained.

**Mary Arden's House** is at Wilmcote, 3 miles out. The home of Shakespeare's mother—who was obviously pretty comfortable as a girl—was an outstanding farmstead built of oak and stone. Now it's a museum. A sturdy structure, a dovecote, a dairy, and a cider mill contribute to the rural scene, but be sure to go into one of the barns to study the bicycles, traps, crossbows, cradles, and whatnots of the era.

**New Place** is on Chapel Street in Stratford. It's not so new and not too authentic, but it's still a big attraction. Unfortunately, the original house was torn down around 1760. Only a few foundations, a part of the cellars, and two walls remain. The entrance is via **Nash's House**, which once belonged to the husband of Shakespeare's granddaughter. It now contains an exhibit of local history. The garden is lovely and a local trust keeps it up. (And well it should, since it is one of the biggest moneymakers of any patch hereabouts.)

**Hall's Croft** was the abode of Shakespeare's daughter Susannah and Dr. John Hall. It's a proud Elizabethan townhouse, one room devoted to an illustration of the practice of medicine at the time. Diverting, especially for sawbones.

**Holy Trinity Church** is where Shakespeare was baptized and interred. His wife and daughter also are entombed within. The church itself is quite handsome. The tower is early English (around 1210), and the spire was added in 1763. The rest developed without heed to any particular period or continuum of style.

**Quiney's House**, where the Tourist Information Centre is situated, was once the home of Judith, Shakespeare's youngest daughter. Here staff can point you to the **Old Grammar School** and the **Shakespeare Monument** in Bancroft Garden. While at the Tourist Centre, you will be very close to **Harvard House**, built by the grandparents of John Harvard, who left the grand sum of almost £800 to start a university in America. Walk over the Clopton Bridge and also visit the **Almshouses** (both 15th century) to wrap up your monument tour.

If you are an automotives buff, the town has a small but excellent **Motor Museum**. (One super-posh English vehicle was created only for tiger-hunting in India!) Then there's an **Arms and Armour Museum**, a **Brass Rubbing Center**, and a **Butterfly Farm** (Tramway Walk) for added color.

**The Royal Shakespeare Theatre** was constructed in 1932, and it is certainly a must for admirers of drama. The classics (sometimes in modern or other-period dress) are produced regularly by the Royal Shakespeare Company almost nonstop throughout the year. The main season of plays runs from mid-March to late January. There's a short season in February. Tickets are very reasonable in price.

**The Stratford Festival** is held the first two weeks of July. It consists of plays, concerts, and jazz and folk evenings. There are two additional theaters. The **Other Place** offers contemporary drama and new plays in a simple setting. **The Swan**, on the site of the original Memorial Theatre, is reminiscent of an Elizabethan house; it specializes in works by other dramatists of the Shakespearean era.

## THE COUNTRYSIDE THAT INFLUENCED SHAKESPEARE

His works are steeped in love for his native soil, and this love rolls through page after page of poetry and drama. Do you recall the passages in *The Taming of the Shrew* that pictured a great mansion? That was **Clapton House**, and he also had some words for **Barton-on-the-Heath**. The **Forest of Arden** spread its limbs into *As You Like It*. (He often was a guest at **Billesley Manor**.) **Southorn** appears in *Henry IV* and **Babington** in *Richard III*. *Venus and Adonis* uses pure elements of local terrain when he describes the chase of the hare. Mr. Justice Shallo in Henry IV chides the Squire from Charlecote who caught young Will poaching deer. Poaching humor appeared frequently in his writings. If you are a serious Shakespeare fan, take some of his volumes with you and have a quiet read while on location. Alive as his words always are, the experience can be even more enriching.

Within a short drive there are many reasonable destinations: **Charlecote Park** is where Shakespeare may have poached for deer. The Elizabethan mansion is lovely and impressive; it is also open to the public. The Avon is at its doorstep.

**Warwick Castle** is reflected in the Avon, a vast and mighty fortress, faithful on the exterior to its Norman origin. The interior is of a later period, containing splendid staterooms, gloomy torture chambers, a silver vault, and several towers. Another castle can be reviewed at **Kenilworth**, farther north. It was immortalized by Sir Walter Scott and, while now it is only a beautiful ruin, it was formerly one of the best addresses in Jolly Old England, a place exalted enough for the entertainment of Elizabeth I by the grand and powerful Earl of Leicester.

**Warwick** bristles with scores of ancient buildings. The **Church of St. Mary**, originally from the 12th century, was reformed in 1694 after a fire. Its lofty Tower (Perpendicular) contains ten sonorous bells, and Beauchamp Chapel is proudest of its original glass and marble. The glass was by royal commission. There's also a ducking stool in the Norman crypt. **Lord Leycester's Hospital** began life in the late 14th century as a guild, later to serve the needy. The **Court House** has a Georgian ballroom in an Italian shell. **Elizabeth Oken's House** offers the sparkle and whimsy of numerous dolls and toys. Also impressive is the lovingly preserved 18th-century **Shire Hall**. **St. John's House** has a focus on crafts along with the valiant trophy of the Royal Warwickshire Regiment. Some of the town walls, including the East and West Gate, have been very well maintained over the centuries.

**Leamington Spa** provides a lovely contrast. As the "in" spot for its mineral springs in the 18th century, it has many well–copied and expensive Georgian, Victorian, and Regency examples of architecture—trademarks of the town's prosperity. Farnborough Hall is a National Trust property with a legacy of three colorful centuries. The enjoyment of the terrain is repeated in the interior, which is full of nature scenes replicated in the plaster carving and decor.

**Upton** has **Upton House**, with its awe-inspiring views over the countryside. The furnishings here are among the finest in the region.

**Church Hill** (not related to Sir Winston this time) is an unusual beacon station above **Burton Dassett**. A pause at the settlement, as well as above it, can be rewarding.

**Kineton**. Looking east, you can walk among the ruins of a walled fortress; that's a windmill tower you see in the distance.

**Edgehill**. There's a battleground here where a major engagement of the Civil War (1642) took place. The pub in Edgehill is fun. Climb the crenelated tower for a commander's overview of the battleground.

**Upper Tysoe** is often visited for its excellent 16th-century manor house. The name of the town has nordic origins. Nearby is **Rising Hill**, which is supposed to have an equine figure etched into its surface, thus providing the name Vale of the Red Horse to the district. The horse, like the story, is a bit obscure today. **Compton Wynyates** is an enormous, imposing brick mansion with a splendid topiary garden. You may view the latter, but the Comptons have not opened the house to visitors since they moved in around 800 years ago.

**Ebrington** is a picturebook Cotswold scene right down to its snug stone dwellings with banks of thatch and its fine little church.

**Ilmington** is attractive for the same reason; the attractions include the **tithe barn**, the **rectory**, and the **manor house**. If you'll pardon the anomaly of language, you can scramble up to the top of Ilmington Down (the highest point in Warwickshire) for excellent photos.

From the church which gave its name to **Alderminster** in the 1200s, the romantic **Stour** can be seen etching its tranquil path to the Avon. No wonder so many artists have set up their easels in this valley.

A second day's drive takes you northwest of Stratford. Here the highlights are:

**Bidford**. Falcon Inn is where Shakespeare used to tipple in high spirits. Sorry, the pub is now a private abode so, ods bodkins, don't bid for a bitter.

**Abbots Morton** offers the best of Britain's black-and-white architecture. Try to overlook the corny postbox with thatching on the common. The enchantment is provided by half-timber cottages and the slightly raised 14th-century stone church in midvillage.

**Ragley Hall** is a Jacobean creation, longitudinal in concept and surrounded by formal gardens. There is the awesome Great Hall with tall windows, superb plaster, and finesse in every detail. Exceptional oil paintings and porcelain complement the rich brocade.

**Alcester** offers tilting 16th-century cottages leaning over the narrow lanes. **Butter Street** is sure to charm you good and proper. The proudest antique is probably the **Old Malt House**, where the first yeast rose nearly 500 years ago. **Coughton Court** was where the courageous Throckmorton tribe held court. They were known to be Catholic, and, during a delicate period in English religious conflict, they were associated with the Gunpowder Rebellion. The gate house and the secret chamber are interesting, but be sure to see the family coat, which was made from fleece that was on the sheep in the morning and became a completed garment by evening.

**Henely-in-Arden** was on an old coaching route, and the present-day allure of the place derives from the pubs and boardinghouses that developed out of this enterprise. It still retains a lived-in feeling.

**Wootton Wawen** holds a capsule history of England in mortar, brick, timber, stucco, thatching, and glass. Most of the important expressions in architecture from the remote Nordic influence to the present-day chemist shop (drugstore) are represented.

**Aston Cantlow** has a long history, associated since early times with the Church of England. The village, with both black-and-white timbered and red-brick houses is rather unique for this combination. Shakespeare's parents probably quoth "I do" to each other in the local church in 1557, preparing the way for more eloquence in the English language during the next generations.

# WHERE TO STAY AND EAT

## *OXFORD AND ENVIRONS*

### ABINGDON

**Crown & Thistle**
A bit basic but comfort is adequate and it has personality.
(☎ *0235-22556.*)

**Abingdon Lodge**
More hotelish (despite the "Lodge" in its name). (☎ *0235-22556.*)

### CHARLBURY

**The Bell**
A reasonable "little" stop (14 rooms) near Blenheim Palace.
(☎ *0608-810278.*)

### DEDDINGTON

**Holcombe**
About a dozen pleasant bedchambers and good solid country cooking
are offered; less than an hour from Oxford in a town of about 1500
souls. (☎ *0869-38274.*)

### DORCHESTER

**White Hart**
A charming, intimate, and ancient coaching inn. The cuisine is as
tasteful as the surroundings. (☎ *0865-340074.*)

**The George**
500 years old, about the same size as White Hart and also agreeable
for food and shelter. (☎ *0865-340404.*)

### GREAT MILTON

**Le Manoir Aux Quat' Saisons**                    ☆☆☆
A 3-story red-roofed edifice of yellow stone, is attracting ample attention to its 27 acres, 10 bedrooms, and stellar gastronomy. There's tennis and an outdoor pool. Best of all, there's the peace and refinement
of an English country lifestyle in tiptop form. Though it has a great
fame for its cuisine, I am shocked by the prices and not that impressed
by the well-regarded imagination and presentation. The accommodations, however, are among the finest in the U.K. in my opinion.
Closed Jan. (☎ *08446-8881.*) In Oxford, the same enterprising proprietor, Raymond Blanc, has his **Le Petit Blanc** at *61a Banbury Rd.*
Light and all-Gaul in concept.

### MOULSFORD

**The Wedge & Beetle**
Offers waterside allure in its main dining salon, its "boathouse," and
an outdoor spread for sunny days. The Sunday roasts are gaining fame
locally, but everyday sweets fans are pleased by the puddings. The

scenery is good reason for going to this lovely tie-up on the Thames between Oxford and Pangbourne. (☎ *0491-651381.*)

# OXFORD

### Linton Lodge
On Linton Rd. and a jovial choice. (☎ *0865-53461.*)

### Randolph
An old standby with numerous updatings and a few Gothic touches. The Buttery is fun for light dining. (☎ *0865-247481.*)

### Welcome Lodge
Good for motorists; it's out at the Peartree Roundabout. (☎ *0865-54301.*)

### Brown's
*5-11 Woodstock Rd.*, seems like a private club, with comfortable chairs, soft music, and moderate prices for adequate no-flair vittles. A good dining choice for families. (☎ *0865-511995.*)

### Old Parsonage
Oozes personality from its stone walls and leaded windows. (☎ *0865-54843.*)

### Elizabeth
Just below Tom Tower at *84 St. Aldate's.* It's not too usual to find wild duck in restaurants, so here is a fine seasonal opportunity for this and other fowl. Very good prices, too, and an old-shoe comfy atmosphere. (☎ *0865-242290.*)

### The Bear
(*Alfred St.*), for color and tavern fare. The **Oxford Brewhouse** (*Gloucester St.*), and **Turf Tavern** (*Bath Pl.*) are also worth a visit.

### The Perch
(On *A-420*) A thatched hideaway near the waterside. Inexpensive but no great shakes.

### Le Petit Blanc
Preferable (in my mind and to my taste buds) to the ultra-costly Le Manoir Aux Quat' Saisons. (☎ *0865-53540.*)

### Gees Brasserie
(Also *61a Banbury Rd.*) is on the same property as Le Petit Blanc and produces casual fodder that is a bit twee for the Tweedy Set. Very popular and not too costly.

### 15 North Parade                                    ☆☆
(address the same) Offers a suave modern concept of cooking; there's a chummy room lined with antique photos providing a politely eccentric atmosphere. The talented Georgina Wood applies similarly curious touches to her dishes—often lovely reflections of her imagination. Superb value even though the tabs are highish. (☎ *0865-513773.*)

# WOODSTOCK

### The Feathers ☆☆☆
15 smallish rooms and a grand following for its excellent gastronomy. Decidedly the talk of the town. Tiny lounges; garden-side bar; clean, fresh atmosphere and willing personalized service at upper-tier prices. Many of the main dishes are classics but with modern fillips. (☎ *0993-812291.*)

### Bear ★★
The fourth-oldest inn in Albionis is 750 years old. Its three structures face the town market, the most ancient comprising a thickly beamed and happily hearthed lounge-bar, a taper-lit dining room further brightened by flowers and mellowed by pewter and brass, and a tally-ho cocktail nook with loads of tourists. (☎ *0993-811511.*)

### King's Arms
A fine wee stop with plenty of color. (☎ *0993-811412.*)

## *COTSWOLDS*

## BIBURY

### Swan ★★
For sleeping or for trout specialties, a great catch. It is right by the ponds where the rainbows, browns, and other wigglers breed. (☎ *028574-204.*)

### Bibury Court
Also recommendable with slightly lower tariffs. (☎ *028574-337.*)

## BOURTON-ON-WATER

### Old New Inn ★
On the main *High St.* at Bourton model village. About 2-dozen adequate rooms. (☎ *0451-20467.*)

## BROADWAY

### Buckland Manor ☆☆☆☆☆
A mile from Broadway (*on A-46*), this hotel is set on a hillside where horses graze and tall beeches are silhouetted against some of Britain's loveliest skies. The mounts are available to guests; there's tennis, a pool, croquet, a putting green, and gracious gardens on the estate; golf is nearby. While the manor dates to the 13th century, its 11 bedchambers and public rooms offer every contemporary comfort in traditional tones: polished oak furnishings, deep-pile carpets, candles, flowers on almost every surface, leaded windows, rich textiles, open fires, and wide-open, nonstop smiles from the staff. Dining is as masterful for its flavor as it is for its presentation. (☎ *0386-852626.*)

### Lygon Arms

Standing directly in the center of Broadway for more than six centuries, this is an inn with strong commercial tendencies since it has expanded well beyond its original structure. This ancient-and-modern hostelry (now under the London Savoy aegis) is usually a pleasure. In its way, the 20th-century wing is every bit as appealing as is the very room where Cromwell courted the sandman. (☎ *0386-852255*; FAX: *858611.*)

### Broadway

Half timbered and stone, across the main pike, and more modest. Lower rates; amiable family atmosphere; handsome 2-story lounge and adjoining gardens. (☎ *0386-852401.*)

### Dormy House

On the forested escarpment above Evesham Vale, 5 minutes by car from Broadway. There's a cozy blend of Cotswold stone, fires in hearths, tall trees, good cuisine, and ample comfort in its 50 bedchambers. (☎ *0386-852711.*)

### Collin House

Recommended by world travelers who certainly know the inns-and-outs of country life. It's a 16th-century home with inglenook, log fires, mullioned windows, eight acres of park and gardens, plus the hospitality of Judith and John Mills. (☎ *0386-858354.*)

### Hunter's Lodge

Substantial for dining.

**Buckland Manor** and **Dormy House** set nice tables among the hotels. Shoppers should not miss a visit to **Keil** for antiques (some say he has a better collection than the Victoria and Albert Museum in London) or **Heyworth**, where the stylish woollens and cashmeres dramatically undercut U.S. prices for top quality. Both are on the main (and only) street.

## BURFORD

### Lamb Inn

Only 14 rooms, and a little, fleece-lined charmer. It is, of course, on *Sheep St.* (☎ *099382-3155.*)

### The Angel

Formerly Masons Arms *in Witney St.*, this inn is right in the fever of the antiques whirl. Two ancient bars, home-cooked vittles in its snug, homey restaurant; bar meals offered and a willingness to serve at every turning. Mrs. Jean Thaxter is the thoughtful inspiration here. (☎ *0993-822438.*)

### Inn for All Seasons

The place to be cozy. (☎ *04514-324.*)

## CHELTENHAM

**De La Bere**
A Tudor redoubt in its own park and with country-club aspirations; about 50 rooms. (☎ *0242-237771*; FAX: *236016*.)

**The Greenway**     ☆☆☆
Southwest of Cheltenham near Shurdington off the A-46. Large country-style lounges with log fires, leaded windows, cheerful decor, conservatory for dining, formal and sunken gardens. In every way, an English charmer for tranquil types. (☎ *0242-862352*.)

**Lords of the Manor**
The choice at neighboring **Upper Slaughter**. (☎ *0451-20243*.)

**Lower Slaughter Manor**
Also small. My pick in **Lower Slaughter**. (☎ *0451-20456*.)

**Queens**
Reigns supreme on the Promenade. (☎ *0242-514724*.)

**Redmond's**
(*12 Suffolk Rd.*) My choice for serious dining but now **Number Twelve** (*12 Suffolk Parade*) has come to the fore as a contender. Both are excellent, but farther along on Suffolk Rd. (at #24) there's **Le Champignon Sauvage**. In any case, you won't suffer from starvation in the Suffolk zone.

## CHIPPING CAMPDEN

**Charingworth Manor**     ★★★★
A delightful Cotswold-stone mansion about 3 miles from town (off the B-4035). It was mentioned in the *Doomsday Book* and it's been onwards and upwards ever since. Most of the present building is 14th century and it still maintains an estate and gardens comprised of 54 acres. Handsome beamed ceilings; crackling open fires in lounges; fine antiques; excellent English taste in a warmhearted homespun mood. The cuisine is masterful too. A delight for a pause of several days to several weeks. Highly recommended. (☎ *038678-555*; FAX: *353*.)

**Cotswold House**
Situated on the Square, it's easy to find even in a town of 2000 population. (☎ *0386-840330*.)

**King's Arms**
More well known as a pub.

## CHIPPING NORTON

**Crown & Cushion**
As the name implies, this hotel offers royal comfort at modest prices. (☎ *0608-2533*.)

**White Hart**
Resides on the lovely Market Sq. (☎ *0608-2572*.)

# CIRENCESTER

### King's Head
Faces the Parish Church *on Market Pl.* Rather large (70 rooms) but good. (☎ *0285-3322.*)

### Fleece
On the same square, smaller in size and in price.

### Slug & Lettuce
*On West Market Pl.*, the place to go for pub food.

# GLOUCESTER

### Crest
The big, routine hotel choice *on Crest Way*, 2 miles from the center. (☎ *0452-613311*; FAX: *371036.*)

### Clearwell Castle
In the Forest of Dean, off the M-4. Only 15 rooms, most with four-poster beds. (☎ *0594-32320*; FAX: *35523.*)

# MORETON-IN-MARSH

### White Hart
An 18-room coaching inn *on the High St.* (☎ *0608-50731.*)

### Manor House
On the same row, but double the size and more expensive. (☎ *0608-50501.*)

# TETBURY

### Calcot Manor                                        ☆☆☆
A colony of stone farm buildings; the dining is superb and so are the hospitable Balls who graciously run the estate. (☎ *066689-355.*)

### The Close
Well outfitted, and the cuisine is noteworthy. (☎ *0666-52272.*)

# WINCHCOMBE

### The George
Very old and atmospheric, offering a dozen rooms *on High St.* (☎ *0242-602331.*)

# *SHAKESPEARE COUNTRY*

# ALCESTER

### Arrow Mill
Both a hotel and a restaurant, the latter being the better part. Romantic setting beside the mill pond; solid fare; run-of-the-mill (ouch) service by nice people who mean well more than they render. (☎ *0789-765170.*)

# BIDFORD-ON-AVON

### White Lion

About 2-dozen cozy dens on the main street of this town of 3000. The bar lunch is attractive; dinner is more formal. (☎ *0789-773309*.)

# (ROYAL) LEAMINGTON SPA

### Manor House

In midtown, this is a reliable 53-room hostelry. (☎ *0926-423251*; FAX: *425933*.)

### Angel

Less costly and very agreeable. (☎ *0926-881296*.)

# STRATFORD-UPON-AVON

### Moat House

This hotel hunkers discordantly upon four acres of carefully Tudored riverside garden. Long, low structure of 260 rooms; Warwick Grill of no special distinction; octagonal Actor's Bar; ballroom; parking area. Rooms reasonably proportioned; each offers an individually controlled thermostat; a radio, taped melodies, and a direct-dial phone. (☎ *0789-67511*.)

### Welcombe

A venerable presence *on Warwick Rd.*, an inconvenient 3 miles outside town but soothingly quiet, the best-known luxury house in the region. Sprawling park surroundings with 18-hole golf course; originally constructed so there would be a window for every day of the year. There may be as many chimneys too. (☎ *0789-295252*; FAX: *414666*.)

### Shakespeare

Charming Tudor architecture replete with gables, open timbers, leaded windows, and hanging flowerpots; gimmicky names for the bar ("Measure For Measure"), the dining room ("As You Like It"), and the bedchambers—all of which bear the title of a play, a poem, or one of the Bard's characters (we can't tell if the bridal suite is "Romeo and Juliet," "A Lover's Complaint," "Much Ado About Nothing," or "Love's Labor's Lost".) (☎ *0789-294771*; FAX: *415411*.)

### Swan's Nest

Generally modern; comfort in abundance; above-average kitchen. (☎ *0789-66761*.)

### Alveston Manor

Unfortunately this hotel has been slipping. Fine old main building that contains only the smallest fraction of the complement (and which often is chilly in winter); 100 rooms in Charlecote and Warrick wings with simple, almost raw, billets. (☎ *0789-204581*.)

### The Falcon

A timber-and-stucco house that reflects the general antiquity of the town; basically sound; reputedly superior cuisine. (☎ *0789-205777.*)

### Stratford House

A Georgian establishment about 100 paces from the Royal Shakespeare Theatre and near the Avon. Bed and breakfast at reasonable tariffs. (☎ *0789-68288.*)

### White Swan

A Tudor-style inn with 60 pleasant rooms and few private baths. (☎ *0789-297022.*)

### Ettington Park

In 42 acres of woodland near Alderminster (south of town), is a somewhat spooky Victorian Gothic holdover from the mid-19th century. Grand in concept, but the lovely mood sometimes is eroded when groups move in. (☎ *0789-740740.*)

### Billesley Manor

On 11 acres of parkland 3 miles from Stratford (*on a spur off the A-422*). Gracious lawns and architecture. A fine reputation but I've never overnighted here. (☎ *0789-763737.*)

### The Elms

A little farther west toward Worcester at Abberley. It is another stately country house for luxury living, lazing before log fires, and dining by candlelight. (☎ *029921-666.*)

### Grafton Manor

Built in 1567 but probably was occupied in another form six centuries earlier. Stratford is about a half hour's drive away. Very refined decor; fishing; golf nearby. Quite expensive but excellent. Near Bromsgrove. (☎ *0527-31525.*)

Dining possibilities are extensive in Stratford, but the outlying luxury hotels offer the best gastronomy. Here's how I rate the ones I sampled in the town itself:

### Giovanni's

A refined continental tone; bar with stools and leather Chesterfield chairs; restaurant with cassis-hue walls and sconces; good quality for average prices.

### Marlowe's

Can be reached via a narrow midtown alley and up a flight of steps; private house of timber and stucco; entry bar; two richly antiquated dining salons; brass chandeliers, plus candles and an open hearth.

### The Dirty Duck

A spoof—so named by the proprietor of this outstanding drop-in spot as a parody on the neighboring White Swan. A favorite haunt of thespians.

**The Beefeater** comes next, and then **Mayflower**. (This Chinese restaurant overlooks Harvard House through wide windows; simple, large room, poor service, but very digestible cookery—if you're not from Yale, that is.) The upstairs restaurant of the **Shakespeare Theatre** offers a steak dinner for about £11. Be sure to book your table in advance.

## UPTON-UPON-SEVERN

### White Lion
10 intimate accommodations *on the High St.* (☎ *06846-2551.*)

## WARWICK

### Mallory Court                                        ★★★★★
An elegant hotel sitting placidly in 10 charming acres of rolling countryside on Harbury Lane, at Tachbrook Mallory (Leamington Spa) about 2 miles from Warwick. Allan Holland masterminds the French cuisine (some of it nouvelle) that appears in the oaken dining salon; bedrooms are spacious and individually distinctive; service is Mallory Courtly. (☎ *0452-30214.*)

### Lord Leycester
An in-town alternative with about 50 rooms; solid comfort. (☎ *0926-491481*; FAX: *0202-299182.*)

### Hilton
*Out on the A-46* to Stratford and boasts 150 units of Hiltonian quality. (☎ *0926-499555*; FAX: *410020.*)

### Westgate Arms
Attractive, small, and tasteful; the gastronomy is exceptional. (☎ *0926-492362.*)

# CAMBRIDGE AND EAST ANGLIA

*Cambridge*

The melding of Essex, Suffolk, Norfolk, and Cambridgeshire makes up what today is labeled East Anglia, a busy corner where the sun rises earliest over English turf. This country derives its name from the arrival of the "Angles" who, like many others, were eventually dominated by the Danes. The last king of East Anglia ruled from Bury St. Edmund in the ninth century. By the 12th century great prosperity blessed the citizenry as a result of the region's prowess in textiles. This wealth transferred north as King Coal came along to fuel the British economy.

In this union of counties, the quiet villages are often gladdened with thatched, pink-washed cottages. Exposed timbers stretch out over the streets and roofs and even walls lean in at impossible angles. It's a pleasant setting to explore the winding lanes, fascinating shops, fine museums, and jovial pubs. Pargeting—an eye-catching architectural fillip—can be seen to best advantage in a good part of East Anglia. It is defined as "patterned plasterwork," but this description hardly does justice to this ancient expression of the builders' craft. The 17th century was the golden age for the richly decorated designs of the master pargeter, even though this feature has been traced back as far as 1237. Here, too, is Constable country. England's best-loved landscapist was born in the wondrous Dedham Vale and faithfully and lovingly captured his surroundings on hundreds of major canvases.

East Anglia is blessed with remote and secret places such as the impressive solitude of Minsmere Bird Sanctuary, an Otter Trust at Earsham, the mystic forest of Tunstall, and the wild marsh creeks of Iken. There's a village pub at Burnham Thorpe where Horatio Nelson waited for the call to serve his country. Here in East Anglia, nearly 4000 American servicemen gave their lives in World War II and now rest in graves at the American Military Cemetery at Madingley near Cambridge. Many New Englanders probably know that John Winthrop, founder of Boston and First Governor of the Massachusetts Bay Colony, was squire of Groton Hall in Suffolk.

The countryside is an open, rolling patchwork of farms. You'll be listening to the skylarks, spotting a hovering kestrel, hearing the cackle of wild geese, or seeing the acres of brilliant yellow rapeseed and the carpet of lavender that undulates over the land. The composer Benjamin Britten launched the now famous Aldenburgh Festival, which occupies two enriching weeks in June. Folklore declares that Anne Boleyn was so happy as a child here that she requested her heart be buried in the local church in Erwarton. Workmen uncovered a heart-shaped casket a few years ago sealed in a wall. When it was opened, only dust—plus a modicum of lingering curiosity remained.

The heritage of farm and sea continue today as the rural life predominates, although each county has important market towns or cities. The pastoral tapestry is cross-hatched by several enchanting rivers: the Waveney, Yare, Orwell, Wensum, Deben and Stour. West of Cambridge stretch vast orchards and grazing plains down to low fenland. Northeast and southwest of Ipswich is a landscape of rural beauty you see repeated many times in art galleries and museums.

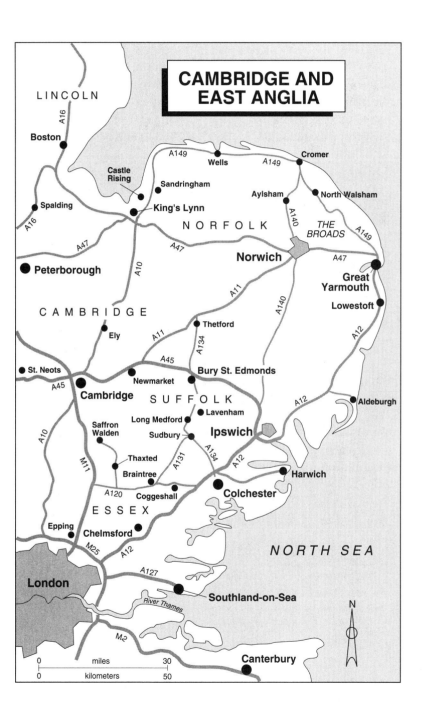

# CAMBRIDGE AND EAST ANGLIA

LINCOLN

Boston

A16

A149
Wells

A149
Cromer

Castle
Rising

Sandringham

Aylsham

North Walsham

Spalding

A16

King's Lynn

NORFOLK

A140

THE
BROADS

A149

Peterborough

A47

A10

A47

Norwich

A47

Great
Yarmouth

CAMBRIDGE

A11

A140

Lowestoft

Ely

A11

Thetford

St. Neots

A45

A134

A12

Newmarket

Bury St. Edmonds

Cambridge

A45

SUFFOLK

A12

Aldeburgh

A10

Long Medford

Lavenham

Saffron
Walden

Sudbury

Ipswich

M11

Thaxted

A131

A134

A12

Braintree

A120

Coggeshall

Harwich

ESSEX

Colchester

Epping

Chelmsford

NORTH SEA

M25

A12

N

A127

London

River Thames

Southland-on-Sea

M2

| 0 | miles | 30 |
| 0 | kilometers | 50 |

Canterbury

The rolling meadows and rustic villages are only part of the Constable palette. The estuaries of the Stour and Orwell break up the coastline into a plethora of small bays, shingle beaches, and reedy marshes.

In cities like Peterborough and Ely the star attractions continue to be their cathedrals. Colchester is the oldest recorded town in Britain while Cambridge jealously prides itself as home to one of the oldest university communities in England. The numerous overcrowded seaside resorts have obvious appeal to holiday makers, and during the fringe seasons even the outlander may find them appealing. Stanstead, a legendary wartime airbase, is on its way to becoming an important international airport. Euro-executives use it for hops to Belgium, Holland, and other destinations that are now almost within commuting time of their London offices. It links to town via rail too. In 1943 it was the headquarters of America's 344th Medium Bombardment Group. Several of these springboards for the air war against the Luftwaffe survive today and are visited frequently by the heroes of a bygone era. Glen Miller sipped his last drink at the Swan Hotel in Lavenham. James Stewart drawled through a command at Tibenham. Some of these bases now house important and interesting museums.

From 1620 onward, Protestant dissenters set off with stern jaws to cross the Atlantic in their determination to obtain religious freedom. They landed at Boston, put down temporary roots, and later moved on to the warmer climes of Virginia. Others followed in their wake to begin homesteading in Massachusetts and Connecticut, where they christened their settlements with names like Braintree, Colchester, Coggerhal, and numerous other signets of their nostalgia. East Anglians forged a special link with the New World they were discovering and the New England they were developing.

## CULTURE AND FENS OF CAMBRIDGESHIRE

All but the southernmost rim lies within the Fen district, fens being the reedy marshlands that blanket the flats. In a county of wide skies and broad horizons, even such minor chalk hills as the wonderfully named Gogmagogs, southeast of Cambridge, or the hillock upon which stand the cathedral and the city of Ely, assume an importance far beyond ordinary stature. The scenery of the rolling southern parcel of the county is more varied, with color-patch villages and farms among scattered woodlands. The dry chalk uplands around Cambridge with clumps of beech are seen at their best in the area around Newmarket heath. Geologically, the oldest member of the series of rocks is Jurassic Oxford Clay; this oozes northwest from Cambridge toward Peterborough, where the landscape cowers below the prickly clusters of chimneys of its extensive brickworks. The county is rich architecturally—from Norman buildings such as Stourbridge Chapel near Cambridge to the parish church of Thorney to a fascinating abbey founded by the Benedictines in 972, to mention only a few. The magnificent Cathedral of Ely and the colleges and chapels of Cambridge are outstanding treasures. Among the many Early English examples, the church of Cherry Hinton, also near Cambridge, should be mentioned, and those of Trumpington and Bottisham are fine specimens of the Decorated style.

The East Anglian Fenland evokes a special character with its mists, its dramatic stormy skies, and its spectacular sunsets. It is mainly farmland with an abundance of wildlife; you'll very likely meet the Whooper, Bewick's Swan, the Blacktailed Godwit, or the Ruff. Here also the amateur naturalist will discover Milk Parsely, the foodplant of the Swallowtail Butterfly. The Ouse Washes move sluggishly across the Cambridgeshire fens where hundreds of thousands of ducks, swans, and marshbirds gather. It is poetry on the wing to observe this inspiring exhibit of wildfowl.

## *CAMBRIDGE*

Cambridge, with its legendary university complex, is only 56 miles northeast of London in the southern part of the Fen country. Slight hills rise gently on the south and west. Most of the city is built on the east bank of the Cam, a tributary of the Ouse. The modern name of Cambridge probably is derived from a corruption of the original *Grantebrycge* or Grantbridge (*Granta* was the name of the Cam). Early earthworks can still be seen at Castle Hill and Market Hill. Stourbridge Fair was one of the greatest of English gatherings held at riverside Barnwell from about 1200, but by the beginning of the 18th century its importance diminished and was finally extinguished in 1934. However, there still exists the three-day Midsummer Fair carried on since 1505.

**Cambridge University:** Many will declare categorically that this *alma mater* is the "only true university town in England"—the wealth and beauty of the colleges providing nearly all the outstanding features of the architectural scene. The history of the educational center began in 1209 following disturbances at Oxford between the scholars and the townspeople. The fussing resulted in a mortarboard migration to Cambridge.

**Peterhouse** was the first college to welcome scholars; they enrolled in the year 1284 and through the seven centuries of its existence Peterhouse has grown very slightly in size but enormously in respect and dignity. Thomas Gray was one of its many noted pupils; its most impressive physical feature is the Laudian Chapel (1628).

In 1441 Henry VI founded the splendid houses of St. Mary and St. Nicholas, today known as **King's College**. The chapel, where you should try to time your visit to coincide with evensong (vespers), has mellowed in color from the original limestone. The soft tones enhance the reverent mood. The fan vaulting, the choir stalls, the glorious stained glass, and the delicate organ screen are masterful features.

**Clare College** was born in 1326 out of a nunnery and born again in 1338, aided by the generous midwifery of Lady Elizabeth de Clare. The most noteworthy feature here is the "Clare Bridge" leading over the Cam to the Fellows' Garden. (Indeed, Your Ladyship!)

Trumpington Street is the venue of **Pembroke College**, founded about the same time by another noblewoman, the Countess of Pembroke. The chapel has the distinction of being the initial major architectural creation of the legendary Christopher Wren, which in itself is a reason for going to see it.

**Gonville & Caius College** (pronounced "keys") on Trinity Street was begun in 1348 by Edward Gonville. Two centuries later John Caius made extensive changes and expanded it. The Three Gates symbolize the student's academic career (well, *some* students): the Gate of Humility, the Gate of Virtue, and the Gate of Honor. Dr. John Caius's humble, virtuous, and honorable tomb is in the chapel.

**Trinity Hall** began life in 1350 by the grace of the then Bishop of Norwich (religion and philosophy were major academic themes); it contains a splendid library and the setting is charming.

**Corpus Christi,** also on Trumpington Street, came along two years after Trinity, and its Old Court has much that is original. Two guilds started this one through donations.

**Queen's College,** in Silver Street, came into being about a century later and is frequently considered the most attractive for structure alone. Try to visit the First Court of red brick, which contains the Hall, the Library, and the Old Chapel. Then, for Elizabethan touches, look at the Cloister Court, which now serves as the President's Lodge, a beautiful early 16th-century half-timbered building.

From the Cloister Court, cross the Cam over the wooden **Mathematical Bridge,** so named because it was built (before computers, mind you) on scientific theory to determine and test the stresses. From here you will step into the glorious **College Gardens**.

**Jesus College,** logically, is on Jesus Lane. John Alcock, the Bishop of Ely, was the guiding spirit back in 1496. Malthus and Coleridge were two of many noted registrants here. Its chapel is early English, and the stained glass windows are of particular interest since they were composed by the leading specialists of this art.

In St. Andrew's Street is **Christ's College,** begun in 1505 by Lady Margaret Beaufort, mother of Henry VII. She also created the adjoining **St. John's College,** which now appears to be more modern since the reformations over the past five centuries. Still, try to see the wonderful old passage under the Gatehouse, an everlasting addition to the finest works in the college community. From the Library, the Bridge of Sighs spans the river—a blissful scene in springtime—leading to the College Grounds. Students at St. John's included Ben Jonson and Wordsworth, as only a few of the greats on the roll.

**Magdalene College** is where Samuel Pepys attended and finally left his important library to his beloved school. The foundations of "Maudlen"—that's how it is pronounced locally—had formerly been the building of a religious order, and some aspects have been retained.

**Emmanuel College** has many links to the search for religious expression in America. Some of its scholars looked west and helped build a new God-fearing nation through the Pilgrim Movement. The Chapel and Cloister were designed by Christopher Wren. If you enter the chapel you'll see a window that was dedicated to John Harvard, the founder of another College in another Cambridge.

**Sidney Sussex College** began class in 1596, and **Downing College** was a latecomer from 1800. The women's institutions are **Girton,** the first college to be founded for women (1869), and **Newham,** which came along two years later. All these are the architectural legacy of seven centuries. The gardens of seven colleges slope gently to the edge of the Cam and form an extended park and promenade known to the students and romantics as the "Backs." The university library contains some 2 million volumes, and since 1662 it claims to have a copy of every book published in the kingdom.

**Fitzwilliam Museum** provides a splendid collection of antiquities, including Egyptian items, ceramics, glass, coins, manuscripts, and much more.

**Sedgwick Museum of Geology** displays fossils from all over the world, both vertebrate and invertebrate. Kids are usually awed by the mounted skeletons of dinosaurs, reptiles, and mammals.

**Cambridge and County Folk Museum** takes you back to yesteryear on the banks of the Cam, while the **Scot Polar Research Institute** focuses on current exploration in the Arctic and Antarctic together with earlier expedition relics and polar art.

**Kettles Yard** contains a permanent collection of paintings and sculptures from the 20th century.

## SIDE TRIPS

About 15 minutes north by car you'll arrive at **Impington Hall** in Impington, former home of the Pepys family. (Remember, Samuel was a Cambridge student.) Going on to the northwest, you'll come to **Huntingdon,** where Oliver Cromwell was born on April 25, 1599. He and Samuel Pepys attended the lower school here. Have a look at **St. Mary's** and **All Saints** churches; the latter can boast of having a record of Oliver Cromwell's birth and baptism. Of its once famous castle there are now only ruins, but also in the region is **Hinchingbrooke House,** a nunnery in its earliest years. When Cromwell came to power such buildings were usually turned to private use as a policy of the Dissolution. This particular one "dissolved" right into the Cromwell estate.

**Saffron Walden,** set in colorful surroundings, is about a half–hour from here. Try to see it in early spring since it takes its unusual name from the yellow crocus that flowered in such abundance. Saffron manufacture was a major business from the time of Edward II until the 1800s. The Saxon cemetery provides it with ample credentials for longevity. There are earth fortifications of this period and traces of Roman occupation, when it was called *Waledana.* The well-preserved houses offer graphic examples of pargeting; the finest of these is the **Sun Inn.** A very interesting **museum** on Castle Hill boasts a large and mysterious turf-cut maze near its doorstep. Speculation surrounds the maze and its bastions, but experts are still puzzled as to why it was built. The castle, incidentally, was of Norman inspiration, but now it's a ruin. While you are out and driving you can have a tilt with the old windmill at **Finchingfield**, a lovely hamlet, or pause at the Tudor-styled **Spain's Hall**. The latter is considered one of the county's best examples of this period in architecture. Both of the latter are candidates for your "short list" of things to see from the 15th and 16th centuries.

**Madingley** receives numerous visitors within its intimate limits. They come to the attractive village for two objectives. One is to view the **Postmill,** a stately windmill that pivots on a central pylon, its sails driven by the eternal winds of this region. The other is **Madingley Hall,** an Elizabethan manse that has been given over to university students. Among its bunkmates were Edward VII and George VI. The glen where it resides is lovely.

**Brampton** was where Samuel Pepys went "so to bed"—a lovely gabled cottage first owned by his parents and later by himself. If your inclination is for picnics, one of the most inviting spots is **Grafham Water,** a huge reservoir that has become a public parkland and leisure facility. It offers amenities plus hiking paths along the banks, boating, fishing, and mealtime sites all laid out.

**Grantchester** was spotlighted by Rupert Brooke in his poetry, and he also lived there. One visit, and you can well understand his inspiration.

**Trumpington**, the local church, offers for your viewing brass dating from 1289—highly revered in Britain.

South of Cambridge is the commanding **Imperial War Museum,** and then if you drive cross-country you'll arrive at **Wimpole Hall** just off the A-603. The latter is a spectacular mansion open for public viewing.

## CHURCHES AND CATHEDRALS

Almost as prevalent as evil in the Old World are the churches that combatted it. Cambridgeshire has **Barnack**, which covers almost every period of Christianity—starting with the second-century tower and spire (one of the oldest in England). **Cottenham Church** is interesting because of its queer tower with sturdy stepped buttresses and oriental fruit pinnacles. In **Ickleton** there is an exceptionally complete early Norman parish church. **Great St. Mary's, St. Benet's,** and many others could keep you on a crusade for the next decade.

Henry I granted **St. Ives** the right to hold a fair that became one of the largest in England in the 12th century and for many years afterward. Oliver Cromwell (statue) stands watch over the marketplace today, possibly showing concern for his former holdings at **Hinchingbrooke**. The bridge crossing the Ouse here has wonderful Tudor arches plus a funny little church at midstream. (Could crossing have been so risky?)

Half a mile away is **Hemingford Grey**. Now, there are a lot of ancient houses in Albion, but locals declare that this moated retreat is the oldest one that has been lived in continuously. That would mean from way back in the 1100s. Anyone care to dispute it? Its lovely little **church** sits cozily on a verdant loop in the river. **Woodwalton Fen** was endowed as a nature reserve in 1919. Thousands visit this area each year to enjoy the special flora. The large copper butterfly was reintroduced into England from the Netherlands about 10 years after the fen received official status, and today these beautiful creatures have become a major attraction.

**St. Neots** has a certain power to charm. The jumble of doll-house dwellings are tucked away this way and that way. Have a look at **St. Mary's church** from five centuries ago and possibly a meal at **Chequers Inn**. Northwest of St. Neots on the A-45 you'll find **Kimbolton House,** a Tudor specimen remodeled by Vanbrugh (who happens to be no favorite of mine). It contains Pellegrini murals and a splendid Adam gatehouse.

An absolute must during your Cambridgeshire rovings is a trip to **Ely** to see its famous **cathedral**. It was founded in A.D. 673 by Ethelreda, wife of a Northumbrian king. (She was later sainted.) The present building dates from 1083 and, unfortunately, it needs another modern-day Ethelreda to give it a woman's touch. This giant of architectural achievement dominates the fenland skyline, being the third-largest religious building in England. The Octagon, which seems more appropriate in Rome than here, is an engineering masterpiece, and the lantern above it is a fine example of 14th-century carpentry. If you appreciate stained glass, there is a wonderful exhibit of it in the cloister. The nave is long, beautiful, lofty, and inspiring. While here, walk over to the Lady Chapel, which is regarded highly for its purity of style. By the way, there's an exceptional photograph to be taken of the cathedral from a place called Stuntney, where the Cromwell family resided. They also lived in the vicarage of a nearby church. Ely, by the way, obtained its name not from a person but because it had been called the "eel island" and stood in the marshes, almost impossible to reach unless you had a savvy guide. There's a story of a hapless commander who was trapped here by William the Conqueror. The cunning fellow was well and truly cornered, but by making bales of brushwood he swiftly created an escape route to cross the swamps and lived to fight another day.

## COLCHESTER

It is said to be the oldest city in England. It's birth certificate is at least 3000 years old. The Celts settled here, the Romans attacked, the Saxons named it, and the Normans refined it. Its history goes back to the Iron Age, and successive generations have contrived to embellish this medieval town. Shakespeare's Cymbeline decided this would be an important capital; in actual history that personage was Cunobelin. It wears a Latin jacket, a thick one because the walls are often three strides across. Only the Keep, the largest in Europe, remains today of the original castle; it is utilized as a museum of Roman and other antiquities. (Appropriate, since the fort was constructed on the base of a Claudian shrine.) **Balkerne Gate** is another imposing feature to be relished; it dates from about A.D. 140. Other notable ruins are the 14th-century **St. Martin's Church** in West Stockwell; **Holly Trees**, a Georgian mansion; **St. Botolph's Priory** founded by Augustinian monks; **Trinity** Church with its Saxon tower, and **Siege House**, which held out against prolonged attack in the 17th century. During the Middle Ages textile fabrication was the major industry in Colchester, so there are even some tattered remnants of that enterprise to be seen.

This northeast corner of Essex has long been a major gateway to and from the Continent. Its attractive countryside mixed with historic towns and a beautiful coastline is strongly associated with the oils of the matchless John Constable. The fields of roses and the excellent oysters are other reasons for going. The latter have been drawing bivalve fans to its annual October festival ever since 1667.

Colchester also has lasting connections with America. During World War II American servicemen served at several local airfields, the most famous being Buxted, which was the home to the 56th Fighter Group, valiantly known as "The Wolf Pack." These fliers had to their credit the destruction of more enemy aircraft than any other assault team.

Standstead Airport is directly connected with Colchester via the A-120/A-12 or, if you are driving up from London, the A-12 takes you there directly; there's also a rail connection.

## RAMBLING IN ESSEX

Leaving London in the direction of Colchester on the M–11 you soon come to **Epping Forest**, created and maintained as a royal hunting preserve with a lodge for Queen Elizabeth. As that career ended, the handsome timber and stucco building became the **Museum** for the Epping history. In 1882, Victoria converted the whole forest into a public area. Within close range are many inviting villages and towns, some of which follow.

**Thaxted** is 43 miles north of London and an architectural gem. It is a venue for a successful **Music Festival,** held for 14 days at the end of June. Thaxted also is noted for the **Morris Ring** held on the first weekend after Spring Bank Holiday, attracting more than 300 dancers from all over the country. The timbered **Guildhall** dates from the 16th century, and the church is about a century older.

On the way to Braintree, be sure to pause at the previously mentioned **Finchingfield,** which could qualify as a regulation tourist attraction. It is quite open, with a feeling of space. And then across the footbridge and over the Common in the distance you'll see a **windmill.** If it has any faults at all, it could be that at times too many other admirers halt to share the same fine scenery. Neighboring **Great Bardfield**, also with a stately **windmill,** contains a mixture of snug homes, shops, and a fine little 14th-century **church.** There's ample lacework of pargeting adorning the townscape.

**Braintree**, just 15 miles west of Colchester, owes its development to the wool trade, which was skyrocketing during the 15th century. **Bradford Street** was Status Lane, and 500 years later there is still the evidence of the sweet smell of success hereabouts. As the need for wool was becoming satisfied, the citizens used their brains and found that silk could be woven as well and would answer the desires of the emerging rich. Their silk appeared at very special occasions such as royal weddings and coronations. Unfortunately, the factory was closed in 1971.

**Braintree Company,** with headquarters in the adjoining community of **Bocking**, was a group wishing to pursue religious beliefs more fully; they sailed for America in 1632 on the *Lyon* and finally settled in Massachusetts. John Bridge, who became the first supervisor of Harvard, was among its passengers. Anyone with a curiosity about American ancestry and settlement will find rich pickin's in the registries of the churches in this district.

For the antique hunter, **Coggershall** is lined with fascinating shops. The historic buildings include **Paycockes House,** a richly ornamented merchant home dating from 1500 (with a most beautiful display of local lace) and **Grange Barn** (a 12th-century relic), one of the oldest and largest timber-framed buildings in Europe.

If you are looking for sea, sand, and interesting coastline, turn your steering wheel toward **Clacton**, **Frinton**, and **Harwich**, typical English seaside resorts that have genuine character and personality.

**Brightlingsea** is a good choice, too, and it's only 10 miles southeast of Colchester on a creek feeding the Colne. Even before 1442 it was a significant fraction of the Cinque Port of Sandwich. The entire sweep from the Colne to the Stour estuary is renowned for its bird and wildlife; nature lovers are almost as numerous as the fowl here. Oyster harvesting is the main industry, and yachting is the main pastime. The parish church is situated on the highest point, with the town snuggled around it. Visitors come to admire some magnificent ceramic tiles or to dine at **Jacob's Hall,** a 14th-century relic converted into a restaurant.

**Colne Valley** hosts a myriad of villages known collectively as The Colnes. The De Vere family prevailed for eons here. You'll see a **Benedictine priory** that was supported by one of the De Veres at **Earls Colne** in the 12th century. The De Vere name remains prominent in England to this day. **White Colne** yet again displays that impressive expression of pargeting that is common to this part of the country. **Colneford House,** a fine example, dates from 1688.

**Dedham** is a charmer of a village smack in the heart of Constable Country. It is nestled on the exquisitely romantic River Stour, which gave its name to the American waterway in New England. Enthusiasts of Constable will immediately recognize the landmarks in his great painting *Vale of Dedham.* **Flatford Mill,** which is nearby, was faithfully re-created by Constable in his famous work of the same name. You will see outstanding natural beauty and the Tudor, Georgian, and Regency houses reflecting the variable moods of the ages. **Castle House**—partly Tudor, partly Georgian—was the home of Sir Alfred Munnings, the extraordinary painter of race horses and animals.

**East Bergholt** is the birthplace of John Constable, the son of a wealthy miller. He was born on June 11, 1776, and attended the local grammar school. The **Church of St. Mary** is filled with paintings by its most celebrated citizen. Not far away is **Stour**, home of the late Randolph Churchill. As you can see from the gardens, which he designed and created, his talents and passion follow the attributes of many a proper English gentleman.

## EASTWARD TO SUFFOLK

This easternmost county of England still seems to attract artists just as it did in the times of Constable and Gainsborough. Their works doubtless have created an awareness of its compelling beauty. Suffolk is an area of rolling meadows and rustic hamlets where the inhabitants would appear to live in the peaceful past. The appeal today lies in its fishing villages, flint churches, historic homes, and national monuments that strangely enough, are rarely visited by tourists from abroad. The major towns are Bury St. Edmunds, its capital in the west, and Ipswich in the east.

**Newmarket**, 62 miles from London, is famous for its racecourse and the top-of-the-breed meetings held here throughout the year. The horses have competed on this turf since the time of King James I. Even if you don't place a bet, go to visit the unique **National Horse-Racing Museum.** The exhibits cover more than three centuries of the sport. The area is steeped in equestrian lore, stud farms, training centers, stables, and ranches.

**Bury St. Edmunds** is the capital of West Suffolk, a market town situated 26 miles northwest of Ipswich. Beodricsworth, as the town was originally called, was important from the ninth century because of its position on the Lark. Sigebert, King of the East Angles, founded a monastery where the remains of the slain King Edmund were deposited around 903. In 1010 the fame and wonder over supposed miracles at this shrine spread. Logically, they called this spot St. Edmunds Bury, but man being an incurably contrary creature, changed the name to Bury St. Edmunds in the 15th century. After the monastery was destroyed by the Danes—they never seemed to leave poor Edmund at rest—a **Benedictine abbey** was established and consecrated in 1032. About two centuries later this became the focal point of all England. Lords of the realm took an oath here that would lead to the signing of the Magna Carta by King John.

To the south is **St. James's Cathedral,** at prayer since 1914, a Norman tower at its side. The parish church of St. Mary dates from 1121, a richly carved Perpendicular building where lie the mortal remains of Mary Tudor. (The tower clock is an awful, modern touch.) Though there are many timber-framed houses and old inns in Bury, the town is essentially Georgian. **Moyses Hall** dates from the 12th century, a Norman house that became a museum in 1899. **Angel Corner,** a Queen Anne structure, contains the John Gershom-Parkington memorial collection of clocks, which any fancier of timepieces should try to see. The **Guildhall** has an early Tudor porch, while the **Athenaeum,** with an Adam-style ballroom, and the **Town Hall** are 18th-century buildings. In the Traverse stands what is probably the tiniest pub in England, with a very appropriate name: **The Nutshell**.

**Sudbury** perches daintily on the River Stour, a thriving market town playing mother to the smaller villages and communities that surround it. The artist Thomas Gainsborough was born in 1727 at what is now addressed as 46 Gainsborough Street and serves as a museum to his honor. A bronze statue on Market Hill also pays homage to a favorite son. Dickens referred to Sudbury as "Eatanswill." Like many others in this region, the town's prosperity came from fleece; the local weaving industry even goes back to the 13th century, and today you can still find fine silk that is produced here. The wedding dress of Princess Diana was woven in Sudbury, as are other garments for royals. Take a look at the rows of weavers' cottages. **Sudbury Hall,** a 17th-century brick house, contains exquisite plasterwork ceilings, Laguerre murals, and a staircase carved by Pierce.

The **Corn Exchange Chantry** and **Salter's Hall** are also notable buildings. **St. Peter's Church** is a 15th-century building containing some fine paintings by a local artist named Robert Cardinall. **St. Gregory's** is gorier. It was commissioned by the Archbishop of Canterbury, who was murdered in the late 14th century; his head, however, remains in the house of worship. **Hedingham Castle** is southwest of Sudbury in the direction of Halstead. This is the seat of the De Veres family, which wielded such power in the Middle Ages. It was besieged by King John and visited by Henry VII and Elizabeth I. The Garrison Chamber and the Banqueting Hall with Minstrel's gallery are beautiful. Outside is a lovely Tudor bridge built in 1496.

**Long Melford**, 61 miles north of London and to the south of Sudbury, is the destination of almost every serious antiques collector or shopper whoever came to Britain. It is just as it sounds—a "long" main street simply lined with antiques shops. Its fame—due to the early cloth makers here—grew in prestige and importance in the Middle Ages. Among the many old structures is the *Glory of the Shire* of the 15th century. **Lady Chapel** is interesting because it contains a multiplication table that dates from 1496. The tower was added in 1903. **Bull Inn** is a 15th-century timber-framed building. **Trinity Hospital** was founded by Sir William Cordell and restored in the 19th century.

Dominating the village is **Melford Hall,** built between 1554 and 1578, also the work of Cordell. This strange but stately building features the most straightforward windows but almost Byzantine towers; within are exhibits of pictures, furniture, and Chinese porcelain. **Kentwell Hall**, nearby, is a stately E-plan Tudor estate in red brick; it also has a moat and certainly is worth a visit. The weekends are busy here when antique hounds from all over the countryside romp in for a browse.

**Lavenham** is one of England's model villages, situated 7 miles from Sudbury and 11 miles from Bury St. Edmunds. With its pink-wash cottages and half-timbered Tudor houses, this once important wool town during the 14th and 15th centuries still remains unspoiled. It, too, was one of the great weaving centers in the Middle Ages. The highspired church of **St. Peter & Paul,** in Perpendicular style, is considered to be one of the nation's proudest "Wool Churches." The clerestory and windows of the side chapels are impressive. The marketplace is dominated by the attractive timbered **Guildhall of Corpus Christi,** now a museum. Have a pause at **the Swan**, a notable specimen of timbered pack-horse-inn architecture dating from the 14th century; it has been carefully converted into a hotel.

Among Lavenham's mementos of its wealthy and vital past are the **Wool Hall, De Vere House,** the old **Town Cross, Shilling Old Grange,** and an ancient hand-operated fire engine that is immaculately preserved.

**Hadleigh** resides 10 miles west of Ipswich on the River Brent. It was known to the Saxons as *Heapde-leag.* At one time it was a Viking royal town, and again the importance of wool brought money to its coffers. The buildings are mainly Georgian and Victorian. Despite this, however, you'll see the typical pargeting so common in this part of England; it blends harmoniously with other expressions of architecture. The **Church of St. Mary the Virgin** is Perpendicular, with an Early English tower and a beautiful Decorated spire. The **Deanery Tower,** a turreted gatehouse that is a remnant of the palace of Archdeacon Pykenham, is of brick and dates back to 1495.

**Woodbridge** offers an attractive display of dwellings in a curious arrangement. This little port town has its houses clustered together at **Shire Hall,** an interesting centerpiece exhibiting numerous period influences. Woodbridge Church is also a product of such changes in taste throughout the passage of time. If you've ever been interested in a substitute for fossil fuels, have a look at the white wooden mill down by the river. This stalwart old-timer functions on the "new concept" of tidal power. Many regattas are watched from the beautiful banks of **Kyson Hill.** The town's best-known resident was Edward Fitzgerald, the Victorian poet and translator of the *Rubaiyat of Omar Khayyam.*

**Butley** can be reached after driving through cool, leafy forest. An extraordinary 14th-century **Gatehouse** here hardly reveals the wear and tear of time. You may see busy groups of art students and historical scholars intent on the carvings hewn into stone left over from an earlier religious edifice.If you carry on to the coast, the scenery turns to flat marshland that also served as part of an ancient defense network.

**Orford** is one of the most spectacular and oldest of these, having a fort dating back to the 12th century. The sands flow out to protected nature reserves and haunting Suffolk coastal washes. If you turn north from the Butley intersection, the road leads to an attractive culture center at **Snape** that has gained great respect for its annual **Aldeburgh Music Festival**. (Snape is on the Alde River.) This event takes place in the unique **Maltings Concert Hall**.

**Aldeburgh** contemplates the North Sea. It is a favorite retreat for many travelers. British composer Benjamin Britten used to live in this area. He founded the **Music Festival** in Snape back in 1948. If you are in the district in June, inquire about tickets to this outstanding seasonal concert series. The town's attractive **Moot Hall** is in a moot position, you might say. It has stood tall since the 16th century but now the sea is slowly creeping up on it. It has been a reliable landmark, however, since early times.

**Thorpeness** within a few miles' drive of Aldeburgh is a contemporary community on Lake Meare. The town's most talked-about structure is the **House in the Clouds**, which is a Tudor dwelling standing on a slender base about five stories high. It really houses a water tank for the community. The nearby **windmill**, another anachronism, adds to the curious scene.

**Leiston**, is home of **Summerhill**, a well-known center for progressive education. Only a mile away is the "portable" **Leiston Abbey.** Minsmere Marshes was the site of its 12th-century cornerstone, but about two centuries later it was moved to where you find it now. It has had several facelifts since, so you may recognize some Tudor touches among its older wens and wrinkles.

**Stratford St. Andrew**, an endearing hamlet is three miles from **Snape**. Nearby is the Elizabethan **Glemham Hall,** with a fine walled garden. All of this is surrounded by 350 acres of pure nature. Exceptional Queen Anne furniture, paintings, and porcelain may be viewed in its paneled rooms. The main staircase is also noteworthy.

**Parnham**, a short drive due west, features stocks at its town church to remind sinners to behave. Drive out to see **Moat Hall**, a 16th-century building with its own (guess what?) moat. Instead of being for defense, today it is purely for beauty, since the purpose of the estate is agricultural.

**Framlingham**, on the B-116, is the site of the impressive 13th-century Norman **fort.** There's quite a lot to wander through in the almshouses of a later period, the shopping lanes, and just for soaking up the tranquility. Very near is **Saxtead Green**, which attracts visitors to observe its ancient **postmill.** All the machinery is still in perfect condition, so you may see it spinning as you wind your way. Then if you move along toward dusk to **Helmingham Hall**—the area was a favorite of Constables—you may witness a drawbridge being lifted at the entry to the estate, an elegant redoubt, indeed. This nightly ceremony is performed not out of fear of a tourist invasion but to keep the visitors (outside) happy. The affably recondite Tollemache tribe has resided behind its gates for almost five centuries, peaceful enough today to host a friendly population of deer that roam unceremoniously around the vast compound. En route to Ipswich stop off at **Ashbocking**, **Witnesham**, and **Westerfield**, all with exceptional medieval churches.

**Ipswich** is one of the nation's oldest towns. It boasts no less than 12 medieval churches, a Tudor mansion, a host of colorful merchants' houses, and the country's finest example of pargeting (displayed in the **Ancient House**). It can also take the title of "Floral Town" with its 700 acres of parks and recreational grounds. **Christchurch Mansion** is like an enclave in midtown—an extensive park developed by a rich merchant and kept intact through the centuries. The powerful Cardinal Wolsey was the inspiring spirit of the 16th-century **Cardinal College of St. Mary**. The great churchman was a native of Ipswich and remained loyal to it though his duties took him elsewhere. Just a short stroll from Buttermarket (site of Ancient House) is the **White Horse Hotel;** you might remember it from *The Pickwick Papers.* Of the various churches, try to see **St. Mary-le-tower.** The pulpit was carved by Grinling Gibbons, one of the greatest artists of his day, whose works are considered priceless.

## NORFOLK AND ITS BROADS

Norfolk, bounded by the North Sea, is the biggest of the East Anglian counties. With marshes, bogs, and heaths, you might think you've crossed over to the Netherlands. Even the windmills and dykes conspire to give this impression. The Norfolk Broads is an ideal place to drive, walk, birdwatch, sail, or just loaf. The marshes and waterways are fed by almost a dozen rivers and their tributaries. The Yarmouth is probably the best known. To travel in the area, a car or bicycle will do admirably, but by boat is best. That way you come in closer contact with the marsh birds, fish, and flora that abound. From **Potter Heigham** you can rent a skiff or powerboat. The attendant will point out the best routes through **Hickling Broad**, a circuit that certainly will be rewarding. Prices for such rentals are surprisingly low. The flats around **Wrexham** might be considered the heartland for such excursions. By automobile your tour will be much more fleeting, but if time is short, it is convenient. The villages within this area have many delightful, interesting, and absorbing huts, houses, shops, and churches.

**Norwich** is known as a cathedral city that signifies its importance through the ages. It grew from the banks of the River Wensum and looks west across the Norfolk Broads or northeast to the Wash. The prayerful city praises the divine with almost three-dozen medieval churches and scores more that developed during the intervening centuries. The dominant **Cathedral** has a slender central spire surrounded by a quartet of lesser ones that are meant to be seen over the flats by mortals for miles around. It certainly achieves that purpose; from almost any direction you are drawn to the imposing Norman house of worship. As you come nearer its mass becomes awesome. The seed was planted in the eleventh century and the building grew for nearly two centuries more. Alas, its spire toppled in 1362 to be reshaped in the present Decorated form, soaring to a majestic height that is well over thirty stories tall, the second highest in England.

The Bishop's Throne is almost certainly the prizewinner for antiquities within the cathedral. Some have dated this as early as the sixth century. Look for it behind the main altar. The nave seems huge, but the Cloister claims title as the biggest in Britain. When you walk around it you can begin to imagine the number of clerics who must have been associated with this vast institution. The intricacy of the carving throughout is a positive indication of the time consumed by so many hundreds of masons and artisans over the endless decades. Even with modern techniques it is difficult to keep ahead of the simple wear and tear that time itself imposes. **Norwich Castle** was begun a short while after the cathedral. **The Keep** (aptly named) had been a prison until the late 19th century, then was converted to an exhibit hall for a fine collection of art. Try to see it.

Historic buildings—and there are many—include the 15th-century **Cow Tower, St. Giles Church,** the **Guildhall, Stranger's Hall,** and **Bridwell.** The last two have engaging displays of everyday life in Norwich during ancient times. **St. George Colegate** of 1459 is perhaps the most interesting of the smaller medieval churches in Norwich. **Dragon Hall,** its contemporary, is a timber-framed commercial enterprise that was thriving in its day. If you are heading north, bid farewell to this town via the **Bishop Bridge,** one of the oldest in Britain.

**Aylsham**, grew more or less in parallel with Norwich but which was far less ambitious. It is a small market town that shows a long history of prosperity. On its outskirts is **Blickling Hall**, a large brick mansion (1616) of Jacobean disposition. The Peter the Great Room proudly displays a splendid Russian tapestry; you may also like to visit the textile center for conserving old works through new techniques. The garden is of the 18th century.

**Blofield** is abundantly quaint. It is on the southern flank of The Broads. The church here serves almost as a beacon to those out on the flats.

**Acle** is a little farther seaward and in countryside that becomes increasingly like those lands beyond the North Sea. The skies are vast and always moving. Here is a handy spot for a meal, a drink, or a longer pause. The church even sports a thatched roof if you are in a picture-taking mood.

## A ROMP THROUGH
## THE NORFOLK BROADS

**Great Yarmouth** is a sparkling holiday resort as well as being an important port. The former is served by a 6-mile-long sandy strand and the latter grew from its history as a fishermen's haven, situated chiefly along South Quay. Though many of the narrow byways here, called Rows, were damaged in World War II—there were more than a hundred—have a stroll down the minilane known as **Kitty Witches Row**. Then see the 300-year-old **Merchant's House**. (It's the place that has counted three centuries, not the tradesman.)

In the same neighborhood you'll find the 14th-century **Greyfriar's Cloister** and in the **Elizabethan House Museum** there's a child's delight—a happy-land of toys from the Victorian period. At the end of this "row" there's the 19th-century **Town Hall**, and on Marine Parade there is greater fantasy in the ship's models at the **Marine Museum**. There is also a **Wax Museum** with the usual personages to remind you of English history. Youngsters all seem to enjoy **Merrivale Model Village**. The Promenade, piers, and beach are certainly attractions, but mainly the city is in contemporary style so once you've seen the sights, you can move on without missing too much.

From **Acle** you will pass through many slightly known settlements—some historical, like **Caister-on-Sea**, where you can browse around the **Museum of Veteran and Vintage Cars;** some rustic and serene, like **West Somerton**, edging the marsh meadow of Marthan Broad; or perhaps **Mundesley**, with its sea-sand-and-cliff setting where you can cast out a fishing line and forget your troubles. This stretch forms the extremity at the North Sea end of the Norfolk Broads.

**Cromer** is active in summer with the tourist trade. Otherwise it concentrates its attention on crab fishing. The nearby 17th-century **Felbrigg Hall** is often visited for its marvelous library, orangery, and wooded park with lovely lakeside walks. The distinguished interior is Georgian. The **Felbrigg Church** is noteworthy for its brasses.

**North Walsham**, with its romantic suburban layout, is suggestive of a campus with a funny old church and some inviting shops, tea parlors, and pubs. In this area, **Trunch** and **Paston** offer additional church architecture.

**King's Lynn** is an admirable base for exploring the surrounding coastline of The Wash and North Norfolk, including some of the out-of-the-way villages and towns. This variegated and handsome center was exerting its vitality and importance even before the Norman conquest, but through the zealous organization of these talented builders and traders it became one of the most successful hubs of Northern Europe. In fact, the physical townscape reflects the numerous alliances and marketing influence through the ages. As one example, the **Hanseatic Warehouse** was built in 1428 to accommodate the adventurous and valiant ships of this pioneering maritime League, a sisterhood of the sea that prevailed almost until the beginning of this century.

A pair of fine esplanades, where the twin **Guildhalls** of the 15th century are situated, graphically underscore this same socio-economic picture. The **Greenland Fishery House** remains a tribute to its harvest of the vast seas during the 1600s (now a fishery museum). Formerly called only by its last name (Lynn), **King's Lynn's Customs House** was ordered by the town's mayor more than two centuries later, and has a decidedly continental flavor as a result of English exchanges and commerce with the Lowlands; Henry VIII issued the kingly affixation in honor of his royal grant to permit it both a Saturday Market and a Tuesday Market, still held each week. **Thoresby College** is similar. **Red Mount Chapel** and **Clifton House** are other stirring revelations of reverence and richness in the heyday of Norfolk supremacy. **Hampton Court** covers nearly 400 years of continuing change and appreciation of outside influence. The parish church **(St. Margaret's)** displays a pair of Flemish memorial brasses that are claimed to be the champs (for size alone) in all of England. **Holy Trinity Guild** (just opposite) houses the sword and cup of King John (said to have been lost with the crown jewels). The building bears the flint-chequered markings so distinctive of the period.

## HISTORIC HOUSES

Most visitors to this district block off a day or at least a morning to devote to these historic houses.

**Sandringham** is the royal property of Queen Elizabeth II. It occupies 7000 acres that are 8 miles northeast of King's Lynn. The house is a 19th-century mock-Tudor structure of some 200 rooms. The park of 300 acres is open to the public, as is the house. The church, too, should not be missed for its splendid oak-roofed nave, the walls covered with signets of power, the organ, the silver altar, and the many emblems of pomp pertaining to those such as George V, Queen Alexandra, and George VI, who had spent time here and died at this grand estate. As it is still used by the living British monarch, the house is off limits only when the Royal Family is in residence. The park is open at all times, however, so try to visit the grounds at least.

**Holkham Hall,** at Holkham, is a stately 18th-century palladian structure that will certainly pop your eyes with its magnificence. Apart from the art and overall grandeur, there's exquisite plasterwork on the walls, ceiling, and surrounding the doorways. The furnishings and especially the breathtaking Marble Hall exemplify the ornamental splendor employed by William Kent, one of the English masters of all time.

**Houghton Hall** (near King's Lynn) was born and bred for Sir Robert Walpole, the first prime minister of England. Here, again, you can experience the decorative genius of William Kent. Have a close look at the radiance of the State Rooms. Young and old soldiers may prefer the displays of model military antics—more than 20,000 troops! Never mind, they are quiet and won't destroy the priceless porcelain collection on display by the Marquess and Marchioness of Cholmondeley, Houghton's present owners. There's a tea room and picnic area for lingering.

**Beeston Hall,** near Wroxham, is a country house in flint-faced Gothic style that also incorporates Georgian elements. The classic interior is typical of English great houses—oodles of portraits of the Preston family, who have slept in these beds every night since October 12, 1640. Sir Ronald and Lady Preston offer tea in the orangery regularly.

**Castle Rising** lives up to its name, which was, indeed, a Norman stronghold with great defenses designed to protect the harbor. Today, however, the water has receded so far as to leave doubts that it ever was an important port. In the Keep you can roam through numerous chambers and adjoining facilities all linked together by a cleverly crafted staircase. The late Norman **Church of St. Lawrence** is usually visited because of the west facade and some of the fine carving inside and on its portals. A few paces away from this parish church you'll see a veteran of many seasons called both **Trinity Hospital** and **Bede House,** which dates from the 1600s. It is an almshouse with chapel constructed for elderly ladies who sometimes don ceremonial costume of the period; it is still occupied by them—although the present crop are not holdovers from the 17th century.

Still on the fortress route, you might like to head southwest a few miles to see **Castle Acre,** which is embraced by the bailey of an 11th-century fortification. Basically the foundations remain, but there is a trace of a 13th-century portal and minor elements of early military construction. Then up to the north near Brancaster Bay there are earthworks that go back to the early first century. These are at the village of **Thornham**—a peaceful place some 2000 years later, where the golfers, bathers, and anglers never give a thought to marauders, pirates, or vandals.

# WHERE TO STAY AND EAT

## ALDEBURGH

### Brudenell
Enjoys a sea view from the southern flank of The Parade. Nice rooms and good value. (☎ *072-452071.*)

### Upland
A useful choice *on Victoria Rd.*; prices are a bit lower. (☎ *072-8852420.*)

## BRAINTREE

### White Hart
Provides bedchambers and reasonable tariffs right in the center of the sightseeing zone. (☎ *0376-21401.*)

## BRAMPTON

### Farlam Hall
About 10 minutes from midtown and amply peaceful. (☎ *06976-234.*)

### Brampton
Located *at the A-1 Roundabout* via the Great North Rd. (☎ *0480-810434.*)

## BURY ST. EDMUNDS

### Suffolk
A smooth contender in the center facing The Buttermarket. (☎ *0284-753995;* FAX: *750973.*)

### Angel
Perched *on Angel Hill* and also in the middle of the tourist zone. (☎ *0284-753926.*)

## CAMBRIDGE

### Post House
At **Impington** *on the Bridge Rd.* and probably the most professional operation around. (☎ *0223-237000;* FAX: *233426.*)

**University Arms**

This hotel sits upon stilts (parking beneath) overlooking the green. It's fair but nothing great. (☎ *0223-3512441.*)

**Garden House**

Trades heavily with groups. (☎ *0223-63421.*)

**Moat House**

*At Bar Hill*; adequate but rather costly accommodation. (☎ *0954-80555;* FAX: *0954-80010.*)

**Midsummer House**

On the Common of the same name has a sophisticated air and continental fare for dining. Atmosphere and solid pub values are to be found at the well-regarded **Free Press** (Prospect Row) and **Cambridge Blue** (85 Gwydir St.).

## COLCHESTER

**King's Ford Park**

Offers a handful of tasteful rooms *on Layer Rd.* (☎ *0206-34301.*)

**Red Lion**

Small, and located *on High St.* (☎ *0206-577986.*)

**Stour Bay Cafe**

(*39-41 High St., Manningtree*). A full-blown restaurant that serves lunch and dinner through the week except for Sun. evening and all of Mon. The style is Californian in taste and mood; management is American. Ever had Essex Gumbo? (☎ *0206 396687.*)

## DEDHAM

**Maison Talbooth**  ☆☆☆☆

On a verdant slope among rolling Essex hillsides, in the Colchester region, this small hotel *on the Stratford Rd.* has 10 sumptuous Victorian suites that look out onto 3 acres of beautifully maintained garden.

**Le Talbooth**

Under the same care as Maison Talbooth, this hotel is a half mile away from its sister. An ingratiating half-timber house, this converted mansion dates back to 1500. Two of its rustic dining rooms peep through leaded windows onto the romantically reflecting Stour River. While art followers will recognize the house from Constable's painting *Dedham Vale*, New Englanders will probably be fascinated with this site and the church in Dedham itself, which has Colonial connections. The same team operates an amusing restaurant down the road called **The Pier** at nearby **Harwich**. Decoratively, it was copied from an American counterpart in Boston, a sprawling maritime edifice that overlooks the salty pilotboat harbor of one of England's major ports.

**Dedham Vale Hotel**

I am not very fond of this hotel or its fussy Terrace Restaurant.

# FRINTON

**Maplan**
> Cozy, with a scenic position *on the Esplanade.* (☎ *02556-73832.*)

# HARWICH

**Tower**
> A fair stop *on Main Rd.* (☎ *0255-504952.*) Refer back to Dedham for a restaurant choice.

# HUNTINGDON

**The George**
> The traditional standby here; it's *on George St.*, of course. (☎ *0480-432444.*)

**Old Bridge**
> Another colorful choice. (☎ *0480-52681.*)

# IPSWICH

**Hintlesham Hall**                                                ☆☆☆☆
> A fabulous country house providing magnificent views of East Anglian countryside, and (if you are so inclined) excellent bird shooting in season. The obverse of the estate is in stately Georgian while the reverse-side architecture is in ingratiating Queen Anne style. Some units majestic and vast; others more intimate and with open-beam ceilings; still others (the least expensive) in more conventional decor. Cuisine derived chiefly from the estate and commendable for presentation and flavor. There is much to see in the region so 3 or 4 days would not be overdoing it. (☎ *047387-268.*)

**Post House**
> *On the London Rd.* this is more of a conventional address. (☎ *0473-690313;* FAX: *680412.*)

# LAVENHAM

**The Swan**
> The pride of *High St.* An appealing Tudor feathernest. (☎ *0787-247477.*)

# LONG MELFORD

**The Bull**
> A friendly inn *on Hall St.* The dining here is casual and fun. (☎ *0787-78494.*)

**Chimneys**
> Also *on Hall St.*, is an amusing mealtime stop, easygoing in nature.

# NEWMARKET

**White Hart**
> Possibly the best of a fairly weak field. (☎ *0638-663051.*)

**Moat House**
> Another contender to consider. (☎ *0638-667171.*)

**Swynford Paddocks** ★★
> A handsome country house of 15 rooms and excellent food. (☎ *0638-234*; FAX: *283.*)

## NORWICH

**Nelson**
> Well situated in town and on the banks of the river *on Prince of Wales Rd.* (☎ *0603-760260.*)

**Maid's Head**
> In a similar category, is at Tombland. (☎ *0603-761111*; FAX: *613688.*)

## SAFFRON WALDEN

**Saffron**
> Tiny, but like its name, colorful. It's in mid-village. (☎ *0799-22676.*)

## ST. IVES

**Dolphin**
> A handy choice at a reasonable price. (☎ *0480-66966.*)

## WOODBRIDGE

**The Crown**
> Not far from the Felixstone ferry point; small, nice, and reliable. (☎ *03943-4242.*)

**Sackford Hall**
> Offers more of a country homelike mood. (☎ *0394-385678*; FAX: *380610.*)

## *NORFOLK BROADS*

### GREAT YARMOUTH

**Carlton**
> The big boy with space for about 200 souls. It's situated along the Marine Parade. (☎ *0493-855234*; FAX: *852220.*)

**Two Bears**
> More intimate (only a dozen rooms) and much more modestly priced. (☎ *0493-603198.*)

**Seafood Restaurant**
> *On N. Quay* is splendid for lobster and other marine harvests. (☎ *0493-856009.*)

### CROMER

**Birch House**
> No dining facility, but that's even better because you should not miss

the boiled crab at the salty little taverns that dot the area. This is the capital of crustacea and great for golfing too. (☎ *0263-572521.*)

# KING'S LYNN

### Duke's Head
A conventional and reliable hotel *at the Tuesday Market*. (☎ *0553-774996;* FAX: *763556.*)

### Globe
On the same square, is more modest but quite adequate. (☎ *0553-772617.*)

### Congham Hall
Wonderfully resort-like in the country at **Grimston**. (☎ *0485-600250.*)

### Congham Hall
Try the heavenly duck here or at **Swinton House** at **Stow Bridge**. (☎ *0366-38315.*)

# THE WEST COUNTRY

*Land's End, Cornwall*

Enveloped within this variegated and historic region is a mighty six-pack: Wiltshire, Avon, Dorset, Somerset, Devon, and Cornwall. Just pop off the cap on any one of those counties and you can pour out antiquity in great drafts. The heady heritage brew contains abbeys and gardens, castles and cathedrals, pubs and panoramas—certainly enough to keep the tourist industry thriving and lucrative. History comes alive when you actually touch the old stones, walk into the great halls, and see the way various classes of Englishmen lived through the ages—some in stately homes, some in humble cottages, some in bastions. The sea has had a strong influence on West

Country history. Defenses were thrown up against foreign invaders and often torn down by them. Sir Francis Drake, Sir Walter Raleigh, the Pilgrims, and many of their followers rode the outgoing tides from these ports. The stories of their adventures are myriad. And for stories and literature the West Country has been a rich lode to be mined for the printed word. Titans such as Hardy, Tennyson, Shelley, Austen, and Du Maurier are only a few of those inspired writers who left a legacy of their presence for us to enjoy today.

If you can spare the time, there are more than monuments to see. There are fine zoos, water meadows, and gardens created centuries ago by some of the world's greatest landscape architects. You'll also find wildlife preserves, farms, marine parks, husbandry exhibits, bird sanctuaries, and even butterfly camps.

Sometimes this mythic terrain is referred to as the "Land of a Living Legend." King Arthur is the heavyweight champ in this department, of course, with lesser titles going to witches, colonies of pixies, dragons, continents that sank beneath the sea, gallant knights, magic broadswords, and a Holy Grail or two. The fun will be to pick out the nubs of truth from the myth—or, possibly, the reverse. Either way, the West Country lives its legends convincingly.

With great frequency, city dwellers in England are looking west. There is a peace to be enjoyed around this patchwork of countryside and coastline. If this northerly nation can have a "sun belt," then this area would boast of a few notches. The backdrop is certainly there—splendid wide beaches, great fishing, appealing terrain, an amplitude of facilities, long piers and jetties into the ocean, boats for charter, horses for rent (bicycles, too) and every kindness that could befall a determined holidaymaker. Some ports are being rediscovered by the retirement population and the second-home weekender. Sleepy estuaries are becoming banks for up-market gentrification. The waterfront is changing from ticky-tacky to tickertape, and architects are smoking fat cigars down on this coast. It was not always so rosy. In the 16th century, in fact, all appeared to be lost. But then, during that period's darkest hour, a valiant admiral named Drake nonchalantly completed a game of bowls, buckled on his saber, excused himself from his companions, and sailed off to defeat the "invincible" Spanish Armada. A legend? Well, hardly—but a firm part of legendary naval history in Britain.

Try to plan your trip for the spring—perhaps to dance around the Maypole—or for the summer months. If you are coming by automobile, the superhighways M4 and M5, streaking west of London, will

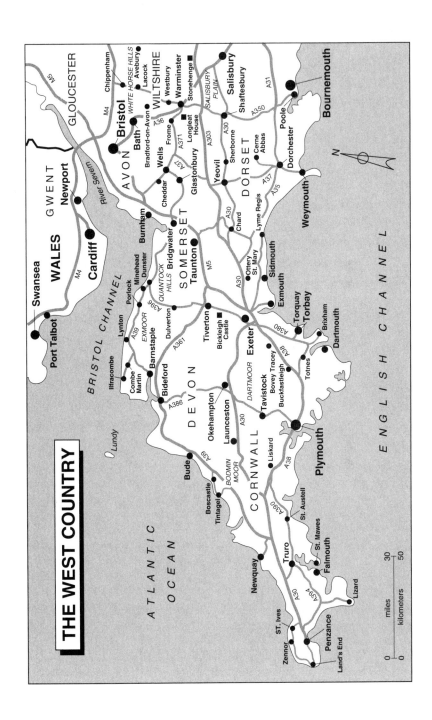

THE WEST COUNTRY

zip you right over to Exeter, a fine central springboard for the West Country. High-speed trains will whisk you way down to the pirate shores of peaceful Penzance—the Far West of Albion. Or, if you'd like to leave the driving to someone else, ease back in reclining seats aboard the Luxury Rapide Coach services from London. You'll be waited on by hostesses—and if, heaven forbid, sightseeing brings on a yawn, you can tip your chair back and watch a film while rolling on. None of these suit you? Then travel by air on a full program of scheduled services that connect with the major towns; while you are about it, you might like to chopper off to the Scilly Isles for an off-the-beaten-airlane excursion that is quick, easy, fun, and, of course, expensive.

The magical redoubts of the British upper (and often ruling) class, country houses, were for centuries not merely elegant homes but also symbols of landed power. They remain treasured showcases of architecture and art. And best of all, the finest examples are open to public viewing. (See my comments on the National Trust membership plan.)

Each of the following half-dozen counties has its own distinctive charm and attraction, and each is unique with respect to coast, countryside, and history.

## THE DRUIDS OF WILTSHIRE— ENGLAND'S OLDEST STONES

Here you'll ramble over rolling terrain cloaked in the mists of Arthurian legend. It is ridged by Gloucestershire at the top and Berkshire and Hampshire on the eastern flank, Dorset and Hampshire on the bottom, with Somerset to the west. Two-thirds of Wiltshire has its feet in chalk and grassy uplands that roll colorfully to distant horizons; its workaday pursuits focus on dairy farming and plain old hoedowning. Consequently, you will experience the outdoor cheer and community life so unique to English market towns. And what about prehistory? Well, here the plains are still haunted by Druids, clouds of ancient mystery, witchcraft, and, of course, they are closely related to Camelot.

On the Wiltshire Downs you'll discover some of the nation's definitive stately homes, the furrowed, abundant valleys and leafy, inviting slopes that reveal storybook villages. When you climb or drive to the inspiring fresh air crests of these ridges you'll overlook unforgettable panoramas of the downlands. English architect Christopher Wren, the designer of St. Paul's Cathedral in London and scores of other grand landmarks, was born at *East Knoyle* in 1632. Within his 90-plus years, Wren literally changed the face of the nation, its values, its reverence, and its innermost passion for pomp and elegance. His dubious modesty was interred with his bones at

St. Paul's, where his epitaph reads "Si Monumentum Requiris, Circumspice" ("If you seek a monument, look around you"). Sir Christopher, say no more.

## SALISBURY

Salisbury lies in a chuckling river junction, the valley formed by the Avon, where its aquarian sisters the Naddar and Bourne also unite. Artists have always drawn word or graphic pictures from its historic buildings, surrounding fields, Tudor inns, and stately homes. Constable painted the truth of it. In fiction it became Melchester for Hardy and Barchester for Trollope. The most historic landmark, and the one you'll see first as you drive across the plain—is without doubt its Cathedral. Early in the 13th century Salisbury was 2 miles from its present address, at Old Sarum. That hyperactive Norman, William the Conqueror, hustled up a fortress on this strategic site together with a great house of Christian worship. They were not to last too long, alas. Due to a ruction between the Holy Fathers and the then military-industrial complex, it was decided to erect a new prayer hall in a more commodious location. In the name of harmony, the original cathedral was abandoned and the town moved down the pike to **New Salisbury**. That move was in 1220, when both the dwellings and the great church were reformed from the building blocks of the previous structures. What was left behind of the foundations of the first church can still be walked over at **Old Sarum.** Salisbury achieved great riches during the textile boom brought on by the wool exchange. Market Place serves in that same role today as it did in medieval times. If you are touring the town you'll soon realize that one gentleman enjoyed almost flagrant prosperity; he was John Halle, a wool merchant residing on **New Canal Street** and whose house you can visit. The **Guildhall** is another reflection of the largess that came to this city because of the abundance of fine British fleece. Many of the buildings in this area are noteworthy for the same cause. Have a look at **New Inn** in New Street, **Joiner's Hall,** and the Avonside's wonderfully antique pub out at East Harnham called **The Rose & Crown**.

Today the multisided, conical peak of the **Salisbury Cathedral** still draws thousands of admirers; the 404-foot stone spire can be seen for many miles by pilgrims—just as Hardy stated. In this period of feverish stone masonry, the tower and the upper finial were completed in less than four decades—jig-time by ancient standards. This, the tallest spire in England, was the masterpiece of Robert Farleigh, but the numerous masterpieces in oil by John Constable of this cathedral probably afford it an even greater immortality in graphics history. The building is rendered mainly in Early English style, its beauty accentuated by a forest of slim Purbeck marble pillars. The piers in a similar material support a great weight but still give the impression of slenderness due to their height. **Chapter House** dates from 1364. The nave also features black Purbeck marble; the clock in the north transept must be seen—well, heard anyway—since it features no dial. Considered the oldest of its type in the world, this timepiece has been striking the hours dutifully since 1386, when it was constructed. The **Lady Chapel** is about a century and a half older; look at the glass here; it is original—and that is really saying something for durability (almost 8 centuries!). The **Cloisters** and **Chapter House**—if they seem familiar to you—are replicas of those at Westminster Abbey. In the **Library** you will find a rather important first edition of English history, the original *Magna Carta.*

Don't leave town without seeing the decorative glories at **Mompesson House**, possibly England's most glorious vicarage. And to really appreciate the view of the cathedral and relive what inspired John Constable, drive out to look at it from the other side of the Avon beyond West Walk. This is where Constable frequently set his easel (he painted it numerous times) and where it seems to emerge from behind the surrounding foliage in its most romantic aspect.

## THE OUTSKIRTS

**Stonehenge**, possibly man's first calendar, is on **Salisbury Plain**, 10 miles north of the city. Mornings and evenings are best, when the tourist crushes are lightest and when you can ponder the druidic message of the ages in relative solitude. Not long ago you could walk among the stones, but to avoid damage to them the area has been fenced. Many locally obtainable guidebooks speculate on their meaning; you may have your own opinion as to the riddle. A tourist reception center has been inaugurated, local Englishmen are still scratching their heads and wondering why it took an enterprising group of Japanese to put up this center when the English had prehistoric domain over Salisbury Plain.

Stonehenge is formed of two (megalithic) concentric rings of upright stones guarding an inner core shaped as a horseshoe. The diameter of the outer circle is roughly the length of a football field; stones are not uniform but are of several types: sarsen, sandstone, and bluestone, adding to the mystery. Bluestone comes from Wales; the others are from sites about 25 miles away. Look for the "Friar's Heel," "Slaughter," "Station Stones," "The Altar," and "Aubrey Holes" (discovered by John Aubrey). There is frequent public transportation from nearby towns. You might consider renting a bicycle and picnicking in the area if the day is pleasant. On Midsummer Night, when the long dead Celtic priests are supposed to "return," the surrounding fields are dotted with sleeping bags.

Five miles northwest of central Salisbury is **Wilton House**, ancestral home of the Earl of Pembroke and formerly the site of an ancient abbey. The main hall is generally lauded as one of the nation's proudest emblems. Wilton was constructed in 1647, a product of John Webb and the esteemed Inigo Jones. One's initial impression of simplicity turns into admiration mixed with awe upon entering. The seven salons are elegant to the point of being magnificent. The roll call of visitors is impressive too: from Shakespearean troupers to that venerable old trooper, Ike Eisenhower, who with his advisers plotted the D-Day landings at Normandy. Oils by Van Dyke, Rembrandt, Rubens, and Reynolds adorn the walls. The Double Cube and Cube Room are actually galleries for artistic masterpieces. Stroll into the gardens near the Holbein Porch; then walk over the romantic Palladian bridge to the riverside Eden. In today's commercial world, **Wilton** town is the loom and womb of the famous Royal Carpet Factory.

**Avebury** is a village 6 miles west of Marlborough on the Kennet and at the foot of the Marlborough Downs. Some of it lies within one of the largest prehistoric ceremonial sites in Europe—probably the world—an area of approximately 28 acres! Avebury is spooked to this day by shreds of ancient spiritual life suggested in the strange surrounding circular earth banks of the Stone Age known as barrows. Other circular forms are in stone, one being vast indeed. These—for size alone—outstrip even those of Stonehenge; however, as you realize, they are not as famous. They date back to the neolithic period and are made of sarsen and sandstone, pieces of which were carted away, hacked up, and used for building houses. Attempts have been made to reestablish the whole. Imagine these 700 colossal stones set in three circles.

The so-called **"Kennet Avenue"** comprises about 200 stones. These appear two-by-two from Avebury itself to the **Sanctuary** on Overton Hill, a mile away. (Naturally, locals could not resist naming one pair "Adam and Eve.") To the south you may climb around on the full six acres of **Silbury Hill**. At five stories in height, here is what is claimed to be the most ambitious prehistoric man-made effort discovered in Europe. Its purpose? No one is sure, although guesswork is rife. Add yours to the collection. Obviously the **West Kennet Long Barrow** is part of the early regional culture. Take time to explore what is believed to be a giant tomb that contained bones and artifacts of the Early Stone Age. This had to have been a busy center of human activity at one time, but specifics are still left only to speculation.

**Lacock**, 7 miles west of Avebury, is Wiltshire's best preserved time capsule, a National Trust Village of the Middle Ages entirely built of local stone, lichened brick, mossy rooftiles, and ancient timbers. The snug cottages tilt with perilous amity toward each other over flowered lanes. Chimneys and gables punctuate the skyline. **The Abbey** is supplied with instruction "fans" that describe in detail far more than you'll ever remember; you carry them and read as you walk; there's even a copy of the *Magna Carta* for close study. Most important, of course, is the fact that the Abbey is also the former home of William Henry Fox Talbot, a pioneer of film development and photography; his story is told in this living museum.

**Malmesbury** is quaintness itself, a tiny town with crooked houses and a medieval cross from the 1500s. The **abbey**—providing a long history here—offers six of the original nine bays of the nave; the style is Norman and Early English; its interior is fascinating.

**Westbury**, northwest of Salisbury by about 25 miles (in the direction of Longleat), draws visitors chiefly to see its fine Norman **All Saint's Church**. Scholars are attracted by the *Paraphrase* of the New Testament effected by Erasmus. **Edington Priory**, once the home of Catherine Parr, is in private hands today.

**Uffington**, an Iron Age fort, has become one of Britain's major tourist targets. The reason is the spectacular blanched **"White Horse"** cut out of the chalk hillside, which draws your eyes inevitably to **Westbury Hill**. This impressive 374-foot-tall equine tribute is etched onto the green backdrop between Westbury and Bratton. There are other such etchings in this district—the reason the area is called the "Vale of The White Horse"—but this one is considered the original. It is possible that it dates back to the time of England's first acknowledged king, Alfred The Great. If true, that long-lived stallion is close to 11 centuries old.

## VILLAGES—HOUSES—GARDENS AND PARKS

**Castle Combe** is one of Britain's preeminent beauty spots, having won many awards for preserving its Old World flavor. This is noted immediately when you see the covered **Market Cross** from the 1200s. There are no overhead power lines, no antennas. It's entirely built of honeycolored Cotswold stone; there are neat lawns, low dry-rock walls, and lovely little footbridges. It was a textile, wool, and weaving settlement that perhaps you remember as the setting for the *Dr. Doolittle* film. A jovial clutch of old buildings, not tainted by aluminum, fake shingles, or other modern construction techniques, huddles at its core. There are a few pubs and inns that faithfully carry the antiquity into the interiors, so a pause is recommended.

**Bradford-on-Avon** attracts many artists who first come to sketch its narrow lanes and terraces winding attractively to the banks of the river. Later they come to live forever in the lovely colony. The **bridge** is distinctive; it features nine graceful arches; two of these are more than 700 years old! Moreover, in the middle is a small chapel-cum-jail that has met saints and sinners over the passage of the centuries. **St. Lawrence Church** is of Anglo-Saxon origin and in excellent condition for its age. It's a fine example of its straightforward epoch in ecclesiastical building.

Also interesting is the beautifully constructed **Tithe Barn,** with its massive open-beam vaulting and its exhibit of early farm implements. You'll find it on **Barton Farm**. Roughly 20 minutes from Bradford-on-Avon is **Longleat House,** one of the first of the stately homes that "went public" and invited tours in to enjoy the grounds, the marvelous 16th-century estate, and the ghastly East African hype. Capability Brown did the first garden. Lord knows who made the Safari Park—unique in Europe for its time. The lord of the manor ordered this successful zoological attraction to make money to keep up the goods works. Kids love it; aesthetes abhor it; the Marquess of Bath keeps the till. Not far away is **Ilford Manor,** a delightful Elizabethan structure with an 18th-century facelift. It overlooks the Frome, which is spanned almost at its front door by a muscular old arched bridge from the Middle Ages. Once the home of Harold Peto, a landscape architect, Harold did his thing with pools, statues, a colonnade, and a plethora of plants from his botanical notebook.

**Chippenham's** Sheldon Manor is a Plantagenet address occupied as a family nest for a mere 700 years. If you have a passion for English oak furniture, this has some of the oldest and finest in the land. Its porch is 13th century, and it incorporates a detached chapel from the 15th century. Get there on the A-420 from Bath. **Westwood Manor,** near Bradford-on-Avon, originally was a 15th-century stone structure; it was re-manored, so-to-speak, toward the end of the 16th century. Westwood is rich with exceptional art (in the King's Room) and fine furniture.

Plan time, too, for the gardens and the yew-phemistic park, which is outstanding. **Stourhead** is a National Trust keepsake of the mid-18th century, a grand house designed by the talented Henry Hoare. The gardens are breathtaking, too, with Palladian temples and grottoes around a tranquil lake; flowers, shrubs, and beeches are in abundance. The house contains a fortune in Chippendale furniture. **Woodland Park** is near Westbury and the White Horse district. Take your best walking shoes and enjoy an alluring 80 acres of field and stream. Mother Nature, take a bow.

**Amesbury** occupies one of the Avon's most romantic vales. It rests on the chalk downs 8 miles north of Salisbury and is often used as a base for visiting the Stonehenge attractions. The **Church of St. Mary**—note the decorated windows—is worth a visit. So is **Amesbury Abbey**, inspired by the great Inigo Jones for the Dukes of Queensbury. The **park** will be a curiosity for historians and war buffs. The foliage marks the tactical plan of Nelson as he brought his ships up to fight the Battle of Trafalgar. Pipe clay once was taken from the soil here; it became an important hub for this particular commerce in the 17th century.

# ROMAN AND MARITIME AVON

The county's name, of course, speaks of its history. The Avon River nourishes the land and finally contributes to the great Severn watercourse that is the natural ally of the Bristol Channel—looking west and thereby to the maritime glory that became England's heritage from the Age of Discovery. Bristol, Bath, and Weston-super-Mare are its major centers.

## *BRISTOL*

Bristol is the largest city in the West Country, having a busy-busy population of nearly half a million. Only 10 miles from patrician Bath, it contains a morsel of the Cotswolds and is a neighbor of Stonehenge, so it's a good base for excursions. John Cabot must have thought so. Five years after Columbus discovered the southern shores, Cabot landed on the northern coast of what was then being called the New World. If you go up to the top of **Brandon Hill** you'll see **Cabot Tower**, Bristol's homage to one of its greatest navigators. His son Sebastian followed in his father's footsteps and wake to explore the lands from Newfoundland to Florida only a year later. On the dark side of its history, much of the city's early prosperity was derived from the commerce in human souls during the decades of the slave trade. Bondage followed a western course while the New World sent back tobacco, rum, and sugar to Bristol. The *Great Western*, one of the first steamships to cross the Atlantic, sailed from the port. It was designed by Brunel, England's legendary engineering genius. Mr. Isambard Kingdom Brunel also created the big black SS *Great Britain*, and in 1843 it was considered the most modern ship afloat—and the largest. It was entirely made of iron and moved by force of a screw-type propeller. Strangely, it still carried a bowsprit. She was salvaged from the Falkland Islands and again resides in her Bristol birthplace for public viewing.

As money accumulated, Bristol gradually added a patina of grace to its mercantile persona. In the 18th century it had also assumed the role of a spa, a vaporous fame resulting from the exploitation of **Hotwells**, where the water gurgled out of Mother Earth at a temperature of 70°—hot stuff in a cold, damp climate! The uppercrust immediately began householding and the exclusive suburb of **Clifton** emerged. (Brunel's famous **Clifton Suspension Bridge** is further out in the **Avon Gorge**.) As a comforting footnote to Bristol's history of enterprise, keeping warm has long been a preoccupation of the Avonsiders. A canny 14th-century textile specialist in the town thought it might not be a bad idea to sleep under wool instead of in your clothes. He made such a cover and immediately gained what was to be everlasting acclaim for his clever idea. His name? Mr. Thomas Blanket.

Bristol, due to its fine port, traded in everything. The ruthless slave economy gave way to all manner of exotica—silks, wines (Bristol sherry), spices, tobacco, and art. The city challenged London for top billing, but never quite made it. World War II gave the port a drubbing. There was widespread destruction of industrial facilities as well as historic buildings. It recovered, but the cool-natured structures that replaced the atmospheric waterfront are contemporary and zestless. Moreover, roads, flyovers, and traffic add a 20th-century dimension that can only detract from its more historic properties. The city, on the other hand, has always made generous contributions to the cultural tapestry of England. One of the earliest free libraries in Europe turned its first page here early in the 17th century. Bristol began its own newspaper in 1704, declaring its independence from London's editors. That was quite an important step, for while some areas of the globe enjoyed freedom of expression, it had been generally considered until then to be a privilege only of editorial writers from the capitals, to put their thoughts before the public. The first savings bank in England began serving Bristol depositors in 1812. Literature was served well too. Thomas Chatterton and Robert Southey were poets born of Bristol parentage. Coleridge had associations with the city, and Sir Thomas Lawrence was an illustrious son of the Avon.

The city's main house of worship (founded by Robert FitzHarding as early as 1140) was ultimately awarded the status of a "cathedral" by that most sanctimonious of monarchs, Henry VIII. That was in 1542. Over the centuries many clerics, noblemen, and citizens have altered the various segments, but almost all visitors agree nowadays that the most compelling area for beauty and grace is the **Choir**. The **Chapter House** and **Gate House** are of Norman influence and reflect the assurance of line and durability of that era. The **Berkeley Chapel** must be seen because of the brass chandelier.

**St. Mary Redcliffe** is also highly esteemed and sometimes more cherished than the cathedral by local parishioners. The name is straightforward, deriving from the scarlet hue of the oxide in the rocks upon which it was constructed some seven centuries ago. The massive spire soars almost as high as a 30-story building, and inside, the feeling of great height is enhanced by the finesse of the masonry, which seems so spare considering the weight it is bearing. In a certain light it evokes thoughts of webs by busy spiders. (One tends to thank Heaven that this is not a land bothered by earthquakes.) As with many English churches there are certain colonial connections. St. Mary Redcliffe is the burial site of a British admiral named Sir William Penn; his son, of course, contributed the prefix of Pennsylvania, and to further this hands-across-the-sea relationship, one chapel carries the shields of the various individual states on the kneeling blocks. (This decoration appears in several English churches, where many townsfolk went to sea and headed west.) The overall impression within the church is one of richness, and that is due to the donations of the many wealthy congregants who prayed here and showed abundant gratitude for their immense fortunes. Fortunes, incidentally, rode with the ships on the risky nature of commodities. Debts were satisfied with dispatch. To pay "on the nail head" meant to put your money on one of a quartet of tables called Nails that stood before the Corn Exchange, the headquarters of the grain market. (That's one way to coin an expression.)

If you walk from here toward Queen Square, on King Street you will see the nation's oldest living theater (**The Royal)** and across from it is the **Llandoger Trow,** a wonderful 17th-century tavern. The yarns that came out of this seaman's haunt are supposed to pertain to both *Robinson Crusoe* and *Treasure Island*, as both Defoe and Stevenson tippled here. On a more religious note, the long-lived John Wesley passed most of the 18th century in an evangelical calling not far away. His **New Room** was the matrix of Methodism, and his faith went out from here—probably straight down Christmas Street. George Whitfield was a spiritual sidekick who supported the revival.

There was a need for guidance. The city was a warren of blatant success and discontent. Corruption seeped in; the poignantly grim trade in slaves was having a moral effect; fights and violence were common place. As Wesley's light was failing, so too was Bristol's golden age coming to a close. Around Christmas Street you can still get a feeling for the Old Town. Houses were elbow-to-elbow as you might imagine from reading the opening scenes of *Treasure Island.*

**Red Lodge** is a splendid example of 16th to 17th-century building. The carving is exceptional. The **City Museum** contains china, pictures, and other works of art brought back by Bristol seafarers who traveled the globe. Bristol is full of things to see, but because of war, economic decline, and commercial rebirth several times in its long and turbulent history, the city itself seems contemporary in mood. Many first-time visitors are looking for an old and rather homogeneous atmosphere in a town. If that too is your goal, then you could hardly do better than giving extra time to Avon's smaller but ever-so-enchanting Bath, a near neighbor of Bristol.

## BATH

Bath, in terms of tourism, is England's second city, a dignified and ageless health resort in the Avon Valley. Because it's only 100 miles from London, many see it as an excursion destination, but I recommend it as a place to spend several days. It is certainly the most visually gratifying town in Britain today. There are some good hotels in the city and many 5-star country house manors in the surrounding hills. The name naturally is derived from the millions of gallons of mineral water gushing from its hot springs at a constant temperature of 120° F, almost twice as hot as at the Bristol springs. The Celts were the first to dip in their toes; then came the Romans, who had long had a love affair with hot water and steam. Being uncontrollable builders given any cause whatsoever, the Romans constructed a fine temple and bathhouse. Popularity diminished after the classic period, only to make a bigger splash in its second era of prosperity following a visit by Queen Anne in 1701. The **Roman Baths Museum** documents very well its importance in the ancient world of leisure and luxury, not to mention salubrious living. They called it *Aquae Sulis*, and its healing waters have been sought after for more than 2000 years. During the 18th century Bath bubbled up for the nascent aquarian jet-set.

 It is from this yuppiehood that its distinguished shape, tone, and elegant proportions were established. The mellow ocher stone—golden in the sunlight—was quarried from the Cotswold hills. It attracted architects such as the inspired John Wood & Son to create graceful crescents of primarily Georgian motif. The Woods employed a logical plan that resulted in enduring beauty and harmony, a masterful concept that has been manifest in few other places in the world. From any high point around the town you can enjoy the terraces, tiers of structures, rings, and integrated movement with the landscape. The citizens of today revere this asset and strive to preserve it. The city, naturally, would appear frequently in English literature. Beau Nash gave it panache. Dickens and Thackeray wrote fondly of it (you can visit the Card Room that appears in *The Pickwick Papers*). Nelson, Pitt, and General Wolfe praised its restful mood. Gainsborough loved it. Henry Fielding enjoyed the gossip and the frolicsome mood. (Temple Fielding found peace, comfort, and abundant luxury here.) Every personality or politician of note over the Georgian years seemed to develop a familiarity with the town.

**Bath International Music Festival** tootles along in late May and early June. It is regarded as one of the summer's heavyweight cultural events. Also popular is the **Contemporary Art Fair.** At any time, theater is a big attraction. Many of the shows that will later appear in London go on the boards first here. You will automatically be drawn to the **Roman Baths,** of course, plus **Cross Baths** and the **Pump Room.**

**Bath Abbey,** just across from the Roman Baths is one of the most significant religious buildings of the Christian era, harking back to the 16th cen-

tury. When you see the multitude of windows you'll understand why the
ancients gave it the nickname "Lantern of the West." Vast, lanky arches
stand colorfully between the buttresses. The tower carries slim spires at
four corners. Basically in Perpendicular style, the well-lit interior is admired for its extraordinary fan vaulting. Rather than fans, you have the
feeling when beneath it that you are Tom Thumb on the floor of a mushroom forest.

The **Assembly Rooms,** close to the Circus, were from the studio of John
Wood. He did the design in the middle of the 18th century. They suffered
in the war years, but the Bath citizenry put everything right again. The included **Costume Museum** displays four centuries of mode and fashion.

**Elizabethan House,** among residences (rather than public buildings), is
the oldest dwelling you'll find in the city. It was constructed over a ruined
monastery, but even before that some Roman probably had an address
here.

Stroll through Bath's neoclassical district. **(Queen Square** and **Gay Street**
are two straightforward examples.) Probably the town's most photographed row is **Royal Crescent**. At No. 1 you can see the interior of such a
line of fine residences. This same concept in design has been copied from
Wood's drawing board numerous times throughout the nation. The classical **Theatre Royal** is one of Britain's oldest and most respected; it is right
in mid-city. Since the 1805 curtain raiser, some of the greatest thespians in
England have played here. Children of any age are fascinated by the **Bur-
rows Toy Museum,** which covers a period going back over nearly two centuries. Also fun is the **Carriage Museum.** Carrying coals to Newcastle, so to
speak, Yanks are always amazed to visit the excellent **American Museum** in
**Claverton**, near Bath. The numerous rooms cover certain periods exclusively, and the span covers two centuries, ending at around the time of Lincoln. A very authentic mood is created in the 18 showcase units. This was
the first American museum to be established outside the U.S. and, in my
opinion, is better than most found in the New World.

The southern shank of the captivating Cotswolds is near Bath, an ideal
excursion area if you choose to base in the old Roman spa.
Bradford-on-Avon is also nearby and into Wiltshire; it, too, is lovely. Then
there's the man-made lakeland of **Chew Valley** and **Blagdon**, with splendid
opportunities for fishing, sailing, and picnics. Or take a day trip to
**Weston-super-Mare**, south of Clevedon on the Bristol Channel. It has
looooong sandy beaches, frigid water, a little zoo for little people, an inland seawater marsh and lake, an aquarium, and a model village. This part
of the coast is popular with birdwatchers. If the sea is calm, there is a pleasant ferry link between here and Bristol Harbor at Avonmouth.

# TO LAND'S END IN CORNWALL

Land's End says it all. This is the far Far West of England, but it was
once an independent land with an independent language. Unless you are
standing in a hole or are fogbound you should be able to see—perhaps

even smell—the ocean from any rise in the country. There's a Celtic mood and a mystic sense about the place. Smugglers peopled this rugged cliff-shore. There are fishing villages and some mining settlements (mostly abandoned). There's farming and grazing in the interior—not much of that however, since anywhere in Cornwall you'll be within 10 miles of salt water. This union with the sea ensures waves of tourists in high season. The best time to visit Cornwall for the scenery and tranquility will be spring or fall. In winter Cornwall is the receptionist for all that the Atlantic can dish out. Euphemism was invented at a piece of coastline on the southern rim called "The Cornish Riviera." It's a good place to find out about chillblains. Nevertheless, it is warmer and more genteel than the upper cut running from **St. Ives** to **Tintagel Head**. It just happens I prefer the colder, more savage sea-and-wind-tortured north to those advertised tropical climes 20 miles away. Please be advised that whether you choose the English Tropic of Cancer or the Cornish Arctic Circle, woolly clothing will be comforting. (The actual difference in temperature is only a few degrees.)

Added to the myths about the weather are the legends surrounding Cornwall's early residents. There are numerous megalithic totems, colonies, or circles suggesting religious or settlement interests. The "Hurlers" near **Liskeard** is an evocative prehistoric wonder. Evangelists from the north passed this way. Many believe Arthur established his Camelot in the region. All of this can be pondered while visiting marvelous villages such as **St. Ives**, **Looe**, **Polperro**, **St. Mawes**, **Mousehole**, **Fowey**, and many more.

For more than 600 years the English king's oldest male heir has been the Duke of Cornwall. Of the many duchies in the land, this is the oldest and therefore carries the greatest prestige. Still, the people are hospitable and simple, proud of a heritage that predates even the crown and recalls a nationhood and bond that penetrates the mists of time as it does the mists of its ancient shores.

**St. Ives**, 7 miles north of Penzance, stands out in the sea, a tiny chapel above the town and a sandy beach at its feet. With its cozy cottages and cobbled streets, this port has been a favorite of artists over many years. In a sense it is artsy-craftsy, but basically it is more honest than that. Turner was deeply fond of the mood of this fishing village. Sickert and Nicholson also committed the great cliffs to canvas. Recently London's Tate Gallery did something to formally recognize this love affair of England's graphic varsity for St. Ives; it opened a branch here to honor the 20th century works inspired by the region. Barbara Hepworth made her home and did her sculpting in St. Ives throughout most of her great career. **Trewyn Studio,** a short stroll from the Tate, contains a bit of her work as well as a collection of photographs and other documents on her highly creative life, which ended in 1975. The 15th-century church with its definitive 12-story granite spire looms over a cluster of snug houses. The town spreads casually out from here.

**Lelant**, a little farther inland beyond Carbis Bay, nestles on the handsome banks of the **Hayle**. Its Norman church and a 17th-century sundial are the cause for many photographs and paintings by the St. Ives Set. In summer, campers swarm in, but if you get there first or afterwards, the area can be very attractive.

**Marazion**, along the southern flank, is a fishing hamlet that also attracts squadrons of serious ornithologists, a British passion. The swampy flats that surround it provide cover and food for the fowl. For an overall sweep of the coast, take your binoculars and camera up to **St. Michael's Mount,** a rock dot that stands half-a-mile offshore in Mount's Bay. It can be visited by walking out to it when the tide is low or, at other times, there is a boat from Marazion.

On the summit is a Benedictine **priory** and **fortification** ordered by Edward the Confessor. He ruled until the Norman invasion of 1066, so here is one of the nation's oldest royal buildings. (The castle is now a house.) Before beating the tide back to the mainland, look in at the **chapel,** which was built three centuries later. It features a great collection of armor as well as furniture (for more pacific types). Once out here the island is bigger than it appears at first. Allow time to browse, and it's best to ask about opening times before leaving from Marazion.

**Penzance** is a town blessed with a sea-kind (for Britain) temperament, which is why it is such a popular holiday resort. You have to be determined to get here since it is 280 miles from London, the last stop on the Cornish Riviera Express and England's most westward city. The previously mentioned Mount's Bay is below, and because of the moderating effect of the Gulf Stream, a surprising number of sub-tropical plants enjoy their thoroughly scornful attitude about the northern latitude. *Pensans* may have been the original name for St. Anthony's place of worship and contemplation along the headland south of the harbor. St. John the Baptist is also associated with the port, yet despite its sainted background it will undoubtedly always be more remembered for a less holy pair named Gilbert and Sullivan. Their "pirates" are not merely myth. Many smugglers and shady types occupied this shoreline. Among the curiosities is the **Egyptian House,** which resembles a tomb, the fabulous **Trengwaintan Gardens** (2 miles inland), **Morab Gardens,** and a **Museum of Natural History** at **Penlee**.

From Penzance it's an easy hop, sail or chopper ride over to the **Scilly Isles**, which are very near.

In the Penzance neighborhood there are quite a few sightseeing targets. **Chysauster Ancient Village** presents an intriguing assemblage of colossal stone shelters from prehistoric times. **Lanyon Quoit** is only one tomb of the many neolithic and Iron Age remains in this vicinity. A gigantic rock table stands on enormous stumps, but the crude form has the essential grace of a Corbusier creation. The boulevard of stones called **The Nine Maidens** is another curiosity from pre-history. Almost any drive from Penzance will reveal charming coves and hamlets.

**Mousehole** is a good choice, and it is just a few minutes south of Penzance. This selection, however, might make you feel as if you had been transported backward in a time machine. It's like a movie set of what you'd expect from a fisherman's port built more for photographic reasons than for residence. The peculiar name, incidentally, is not what you probably think; linguistic sleuths suppose that it came from some Mediterranean culture, perhaps of Phoenician derivation at the dawn of this millennium. Some of the stone monuments in this region bear a resemblance to prehistoric building in the Balearics and Sardinia. The village is pronounced Moo-zell and probably meant "watering spot" or "safe haven."

**Lamorna Cove** is a delightful little corner for sailors, lovers, or strollers. You'll notice from the granite surroundings that here was a natural and handy port for the neighboring stone quarries. The scenery is, indeed, dramatic, as many artists from all over have discovered. Many oils, water colors, and sketches are on sale in summer.

**Treen** a village on the coast boasts the gigantic **Logan Rock.** Stop by the local pub, have a pint, and listen to the legend of how, in 1824, the nephew of Oliver Goldsmith overturned this 60-ton boulder. Then came the really bad news: He had to put it back just as he had found it! (He did, too.)

**Porthcurno** is the site of the original transatlantic cable terminus. It is a contemporary village with—this time, not golden—but snow-white sands on its beach. Just a few feet short of the Atlantic Ocean you will find the astonishing **Minack Theatre,** an open-air playhouse specializing in Shakespearean drama. It was hewn out of solid cliffside with seats among the protrusions. This improbable and fascinating theater became a reality thanks to the steel temperament and determination of the remarkably imaginative Rowena Cade. She started her gigantic project in 1931; it took half a century to complete. Perched so precipitously that the Atlantic pounds into a chasm beneath its irregular stage, its backdrop is the open and sometimes angry sea. There is a cliff-top exhibition explaining how Miss Cade conceived and realized what is probably the most unusual theater in the world.

**Land's End** is the "End" only if you happen to be looking west—as many people did during the Age of Discovery. It is also the beginning of England and Europe, if you are looking east. The 900-mile hike from this English springboard to *John O'Groats* in Scotland is a jaunt undertaken by many fund-raising zealots every year. You'll read about these in the newspapers. This kind of publicity and the fact that Land's End by definition is an "ultimate sightseeing target" brings tourists in droves to absorb the savage but nevertheless haunting beauty. If you can catch it (or the sunset) at a tranquil moment—one lone beacon off the shore—you will have a lifelong

memory. The **Heritage Museum,** the **Man And the Sea Exhibition,** the **Worzel Gummidge Collection,** and the **First and Last Craft Workshop** are all worthwhile indoor pursuits.

**Sennen** is slightly northeast and a natural landing point for invaders. At one time they were Nordic raiders and now they are frequently Scandinavian sun worshipers. The adjoining Whitesand Bay is motive enough. If the weather turns bad or if you wish to send a message to the welkin from Europe's last religious outpost, hasten into the 15th-century **Church of St. Mary**. Then comes palm-fringed **St. Just**, just a bit farther north, with possibly an even older house of prayer. It's an interesting stop for wandering souls. Still moving northward along this wild, sparsely populated rock shelf you'll come to *Pendeen*—and here the local church is somewhat different and not so antique. It is an approximate duplicate of Scotland's Iona Cathedral, not a cathedral at all but something more on the order of a chapel. Iona is a tiny island in the Hebrides from which the navigator-monk Brenden set off to Christianize Europe. You may remember the replica of the leather sailing ship that crossed the Atlantic as an homage to the courageous cleric.

**Morvah's** few citizens were miners—as most of this coast was once involved in tin and copper extraction. Neighboring **Chun Castle,** far out on the moors, was built during the Iron Age. **Chun Quoit** goes back even further on the Penwith clock—a mysterious early structure, probably a burial site. A bleak pair of rather forlorn targets.

**Zennor** owes its touristic winnings to a fleeting time when boisterous Virginia Woolf resided and frolicked at the **Eagle's Nest** (still there today). The more solemn D. H. Lawrence penned his works in an isolated house in the same neighborhood. The **Folk Museum** and some mermaid lore (manifest in carvings in the town **church)** have been more enduring attractions than the playground of these authors. Even older is **Zennor Quoit,** not a game of the ancients but a chambered tomb of about 5000 years in age. It's on the moor above the village.

## ACROSS THE MOOR TO BOTH NORTH AND SOUTH COASTS

Perhaps you never realized there is a Fal River and that the port developed at its mouth. In fact, several waterways converge at **Falmouth** and out of this locality vessels that gained fame all over the world for speed and reliability—the Falmouth Packet Boat—set off to deliver the post. There are many nostalgic corners here as reminders of those days when several dozen ships skipped across the seas. Yachtsmen still use Falmouth as a field of battle and some ships carry on the packet boat design in smaller versions. Falmouth's pair of mighty castles, **Pendennis** on one side and **St. Mawes** on the other, were built by Henry VIII to safeguard the King's Highway. As with most high-ground forts, the views are splendid from both. Pendennis Castle was later enlarged by Elizabeth I; the fortress endured a harrowing tiff with Cromwell but finally surrendered to the Protector, possibly the most valiant of the sovereign's holdouts. The **Maritime Museum** contains much colorful background about Cornwall's links to the sea. The steam tug *St. Denys* is an engineer's delight—ideal for salty types.

**Lizard Peninsula**—usually just called "The Lizzard" by sailors—is simultaneously one of the most scenic and treacherous landfalls of Cornwall; it is also the most southerly point of England. The jagged cliffs take the fury of the merciless sea, and it is a welcome sight on a stormy night to catch a flicker from the lighthouse. By day the paths along the same dangerous crags can be inspirational. It's lonely country, but have a look anyway. This is the area where the "serpentine stone" can be found. Shot mainly with exotic green but also with gray, scarlet, and other rich veins, it is frequently used for regional jewelry and souvenirs. When you've passed through a vale farther north called **Helford Passage** (a few miles south of Falmouth), you will arrive at the stunning **Glendurgan Gardens,** known for wonderfully tropical and rare trees, flowers, shrubs, an intricate laurel maze, and a Giant's Stride. They were first nurtured and pruned in 1833 and have been fluffed up for admirers ever since by loyal brigades of gardeners.

**Helston** in early May is where you might happen upon the annual festival of the "Furry" or "Floral Dance," when the antics of the citizens celebrate the occasion when an angry dragon hurled a boulder onto the town. No one knows why the monster's ire was up, but when the stone came down there was no damage. Consequently, thanks have been expressed since the very day the beastie left. Among the stone clutch of dragon-proof houses stands the **Old Butter Market,** a **museum of local history,** and an ancient **cider mill. Flambards Victorian Village** is an award-winning re-creation of earlier times—right down to the shops, carriages, and fashions.

Southwest of here between Gunwalloe and Porthleven is **Loe Pool,** Cornwall's largest natural lake, with a jogging path around it of about 6 miles. This is the body of water into which King Arthur's legendary sword Excalibur was said to have vanished. The scenery here is suggestive of heavy-duty myth. Along the way you will come to villages such as **Constantine**, the seal sanctuary of *Gweek*, and **Portreath**; make a point not to miss the sightseeing opportunities at **Reskajeage Downs** near the last hamlet. From the bay frontage to the clifftops, the ingredients are 100% Cornwall.

Another interesting pause might be at **Breage**, with its unusual 15th-century church hewn entirely in granite. The churchyard features a wheel cross with Saxon tracery, one of the oldest heritage stones in the West Country.

**Godolphin House** is the name given by a Cornish dynasty to this remarkable mansion and village; this was once the home of the Earls who bore this name and also the birthplace of Queen Anne's celebrated Lord Treasurer, Sidney Godolphin. Of course, the front is not pure Elizabethan, but a colonnaded afterthought from the middle of the 17th century. The King's Room has sheltered Charles II (Prince of Wales at the time) prior to his escape from Pendennis Castle to the Scilly Isles. Godolphin interests also obtained and bred one of the trio of valuable—nay, priceless—Arab stallions from which the most important British Thoroughbred horses claim a bloodline. Breeders globally, therefore, consider this a shrine.

**St. Keverne**, with its grand esplanade, is well known to mariners. The 15th-century **church** with its highly distinctive octagonal spire saved many a sailor on sighting it. They knew that nearby were the life-threatening **Manacle Rocks,** an enduring menace to navigators. Salvage is a way of life here as death is the calling of the sea. More than 400 souls caught in the Manacle grip rest in the churchyard.

**Goonhilly Downs,** with its open expanse of blasted moor, is dramatic country inland from St. Keverne. A gigantic satellite tracking station with

10 steerable parabolic dish aerials gaze out over the flats of heather. It will certainly catch your eye as it catches signals from above.

**Kynance Cove,** on the western side of Lizzard, is where you can see the previously mentioned serpentine stone as it pierces the softer surface materials. The colors and shapes will intrigue even the most passive geologist.

**Mullion Cove** is similar to Kynance geologically and aesthetically, but here your mallet may produce sparks from the flintlike greenstone. The town of **Mullion** is on the inland road, a stop for a cup of coffee but not much else. At the more northerly **Poldhu Cove** you will see the **Marconi Memorial,** a bit more modest than Goonhilly Downs. This spot was where Marconi's initial transoceanic radio beam was born. The entire technology from the first weak signal to satellite-based relays and space communication has occupied less than a century.

## SOUTHEASTERN CORNWALL

A one-time resident of this coast, D. H. Lawrence, might have been thinking of the gloomy mood of **Looe** when he wrote "houses that were dark and grisly under the blank, cold sky." It's got its share of gruesome lore—a pillory and stocks at the **Town Hall**, a lockup for townsfolk, and a pen for punishing unruly wives (sanctimoniously located in the church tower), pirate dens, and probably the best locale of all for filming *Son of Jaws.* Here is the home of the Shark Angling Club of Great Britain. Official records of catches are maintained here, and significant brutes are hauled up on hooks almost daily. A major shark festival and competition is an annual feature each fall—so don't fall in the water! And if you feel like praying, the local house of worship is a by-product of local shipwrecks. Until late last century East and West Looe were known as twin towns. They are now united by a stone bridge that spans the River Looe with seven arches. Hikers are often challenged with scaling the clifftops or taking the scenic walk to Polperro (about 1-1/2 hours), sandy coves invite saltwater fishing and sailing, but I wouldn't set a toe into this daunting water. Beyond the terraced town there are more cliff paths for exploring Cornish land-and-seascapes. Frankenstein, Wolf Man, and the Addams family vacation here regularly.

**Wooly Monkey Sanctuary** offers a displaced home to South American Wooly Monkeys. You get to it by driving toward **Murreyton**. You'll also find Chinese geese, nice rabbits, and other amiable critters—all docile—who have complete freedom. There are no pens or barricades, so you may stroll among them and chat in Spanish, Cantonese, or whatever tongue suits the occasion.

**Cawsand** and **Kingsand** are twin communities with representative houses and pubs from the 18th century. Here you'll discover the hospitable **Ship Inn**, about which Lord Nelson and Lady Hamilton kept gossips busy with minor slanders. The famous pair effected numerous trysts here. You are invited to do the same.

A visit to historic houses is routine while touring in this district. **Antony House**, therefore, certainly is worth a stop. The Carew family, still living in it, were much involved in local statecraft. About 2 miles south of Liskeard at St. Keyne you can probably already hear the **Paul Corin** musical collection. Local talents (you, too?) may enter the millhouse and have a romp with a keyboard, a wind-up organ, or a whistle. Fun as a change of pace, or beat.

Not far away is **Dobwalls** with still more toys—this time model trains. Does it look like America? That's the idea. The park copies the U.S. railroad scene. It's very detailed. This is coupled with the **Thorburn Gallery** with the Archibald Thorburn collection, a treasury of paintings and studies of birds. Your next stop could be the **Carnglaze Slate Caves;** one of them could contain a 30-story building; further in is an awesome teal-colored underground lake where the lighting by man as well as by nature is masterful.

**Lanreath** has is an engaging agricultural exhibit with early tractors, crude combines, inventive machinery, farm fixin's, husbandry tools, and realistic displays of how it was to live in Cornish country circumstances.

**Liskeard** and **Lostwithiel**, about 15 miles apart, are two of Cornwall's famed quartet of tin-mining towns. Tin was once a vital source of income in Cornwall, with many shafts running from the land out under the sea floor. The industry is still alive but not particularly well. In the former is **Stuart House,** where Charles I paused for a while in his travels, and on the outskirts of the latter you will find what's left of monumental **Restormel Castle,** where Edmund, the Earl of Cornwall, established his seat of power.

**Polperro** is a cozy pilchard fishing village snug among the rocks with steep descents through tiny streets down to the harbor and beach. Tourists "discovered" Polperro after the invention of the automobile—they still call them "motor cars" here—so in high season the town cannot handle its traffic. An outlying car park takes buses and other vehicles, so exploration must be done by shank's mare, which makes it much more agreeable for all. You'll be pleasantly transported to the 17th century in a jiffy. The dainty cottages, the little stream called the Pol that wends its way through and the prettiness of the whole combination is pure Cornwall. The **Land of Legend** and the **Model Village** give you an insight into the lives of the Cornish people. Down in the harbor the sea laps at the doorsteps, the seagulls argue incessantly, and fishing vessels tug at their lines. Smugglers chose this spot for their base with good reason.

## *INLAND AND THE NORTHERN COAST*

**Truro** and the river on which it resides share the same name. There are numerous waterways that provide a romantic setting for this rolling hillside community of principally Georgian houses. Once very rich from tin and world trade, Truro is the only cathedral city in Cornwall, a clue as to its importance. **St. Mary's** came along, however, rather late, but was given the features of Early English architecture, a proud church for a proud and independent people. The **Cornish County Museum** is especially known for its mineral collection (you'll also find ceramics, drawings, and oils). Since Truro was a stannary town—there were only three others in the entirety of Cornwall and these evaluated the mine products—minerals became the lifeblood of local economy. To comprehend the significance, this museum is certainly worth a visit.

South of Truro by the watershed called Carrick Roads (sic), you'll see **Trelissick Gardens,** ablaze with rhododendrons and hydrangeas in summer; there are extensive pathways weaving through the blossoms and forests. Apart from the aesthetics, there are also botanical exhibits of a more scientific nature.

**Bolventor**, is the site of Jamaica Inn, which is the stage setting in Daphne du Maurier's novel of the same name. Its lonely status continues, and even today local citizens are fighting the Electricity Board in a quest for household illumination. Close by is **Dozmary Pool,** where once again there is yet another—possibly started by armourers—legend that King Arthur's sword was hurled into the deep. (As you will come to discover, there are probably more lakes than swords in England—and the tourist industry thrives on myth.)

A few miles farther down the moor at **Minions** you will see three very ancient stone circles. This early sculpture garden is now called the "Hurlers." The tale is yours to conjure, because it derives from myths of men who were turned into the rock formations for their sins. As you will note at every corner of the map, legend is still woven thickly into the Cornwall tapestry of daily life.

**Newquay** attracts more holidaymakers than bees to a pollen festival. Its sandy beaches, backed by dunes and low ridges with fine houses, are superb; if you like surfing, here's the spot to do it. In the attractive antique port area, some impeccably maintained pilot boats bobble on the waters and fishing smacks still work out of the harbor. To the north of the town, beyond a relic called Huer's Hut, lies **Trenance Park,** a sizable zoo; because of the mild climate, arctic penguins and tropical parrots are the unlikely feathers that flock together. There are many other animal anomalies here.

About a mile up the gentle coast you'll come to the savage **Bedruthan Steps**, golden sandy beaches interrupted by spires of dark granite rocks. (Bedruthan is the resident giant—naturally, another Cornish morsel of mythology.) These glorious strands, unfortunately, are rather isolated; the only way to get to them is down a precarious path and a wiggle through the fissures. If you ask first at Trenance or at Mawgan Porth, the local folk can provide directions. Along the next 5 or 6 miles going north to Harlyn Bay you will encounter off-the-beaten-track villages that the pirates and smugglers of yore loved. Don't rush, but pause along the trail at Porthcothan, St. Mervyn, and ageless Padstow.

**Tintagel**, not a medication but a very, very ancient settlement, is closely related to Arthurian legend; indeed, some say the wise monarch was born in **Tintagel Castle,** in ruins now on the jagged clifftops. If your eyebrows are rising, you are right; the castle was built around the 1100s and Arthur may have lived in the sixth century. Oh, well. The scenery is bewitching on the rocky butte. From here you can see the massive slate caverns on the opposite flank of the turbulent Tintagel Cove and the majestic cascade that hurtles down the frothy stone face. In the town, the slate houselike **Post Office** with Victorian decor seems to be the best rainy-day sightseeing target.

**Boscastle** is where you can see the Cornwall coast in its finest and most potent maritime attire—especially when the tide is rising. It seems to be two hamlets—one on the high road and the port on the low road. Many visitors plan to go during the full moon when the drama is enhanced and more spooks come out to play. Here the Cornish night is at its mystic best—romping and snorting in the gloom where two rivers collide heavily with the sea. As if that were not enough, near the harbor is the **Witches' Museum,** with dark relics related to the occult. Just the thing to witness if your blood pressure is too low. The wild scenes here are quite a contrast to the more recreational and regulated wave action up at Bude, where the open shore, long shallow shelf, and constant winds propel surfers to exciting sport.

**Lauceston**, the former capital of the county and once-upon-a-time a walled city, is rich in historic buildings. Given the British adoration of rail and steam, the **Lauceston Steam Railway** toots proudly about the locomotives built over 100 years ago, stationary steam engines, as well as the car and motorcycle exhibits. In the town itself there are scores of fine dwellings. **Lawrence House** is a splendid example; this one, now a museum, is in the National Trust, so you can visit it. The **White Hart** inn might be more fun as a living manifestation of Cornish pastimes. The 18th-century houses on Castle Hill are clustered around a ruined Norman fort of which only the keep remains. Even before that, however, the Saxons and the Celts found reasons enough to fight over the dominant high ground.

Now for some bridges: Just below Lauceston is **Greystone Bridge,** where pilgrims of yore purchased indulgences, ancient traveler's insurance for the journey ahead. The next span is **Horse Bridge,** which gallops back to 1437. There are lovely walks to Gunnislake, where a **granite bridge** of the 16th century crosses the river. Nearby you'll discover **Cotehele House,** a lovely 15th-17th-century manor that overlooks the Tamar River. It was designed and created slowly as a self-sufficient community; the gardens are beautifully laid out and the interior is a marvelous preservation of life in the Middle Ages. Down by the ponds is a watermill and some ateliers that are enlightening as to early crafts.

At the point where the Tamar leaps into the sea is Brunel's spectacular historic railway bridge called the **Royal Albert,** which links Saltash to Plymouth, the vivid hallmark of Britain's Industrial Revolution.

## DEVON, GARDEN OF THE WEST COUNTRY

Nature was generous to Devon and man has enhanced her work. There are grazing lands, tidy farms, pollution-free rivers, undisturbed estuaries, the cobalt sea, and majestic mountains dominant over flower-strewn valleys and primrose dales. The pace of life is pastoral and ever so kind for human inhabitance. Though a bit smaller than industrious Yorkshire and busy Lincolnshire, Devon real estate totals up sufficiently to be reckoned as the third largest county in England.

It offers the boldest topography, its outline ridged with soaring russet cliffs and deep winding gorges in the north and sailors' havens and quiet bays down south. The Devon Plain is noteworthy for its undulating high grounds: **Dartmoor** in the south and **Exmoor** to the northeast. The sea-tempered climate produces a great variety of vegetation, some of it as warm-blooded as Cornwall's.

As for personalities, Francis Drake, Walter Raleigh, and slave trader and sea captain John Hawkins sailed to great adventure as children of Devon. The poetry of Coleridge and Wordsworth were influenced by its natural moods and rich Devonian textures. William Cookworthy had a name that only fate could have devined. He was a potter who gained fame in the 18th century for almost single-handedly creating the English porcelain industry. It was based upon his Devonshire and Cornish explorations for the proper white china clay. You can visit his early digs in St. Austell in neighboring Cornwall, but much of the burgeoning art, craft, and industry spread quickly and extensively into Devon. John Endecott, who was born in Devon late in the 16th century, became the governor of Massachusetts Bay Colony in the New World. The dairy trades of today owe much to the North and South Devon breeds. Other industries over the years were shipbuilding, gloving, and carpet weaving. Indeed, much of the inspiration for the world's art and industry came from the 2500 square miles of territory called Devon.

**Plymouth**, less than 200 miles southwest of London, links the legacy of the seas to England forever. In 1501 Catherine of Aragon brought prominence to the port when she disembarked here. Later an Armada of 130 ships was to call in the name of Spain. Sir Francis Drake began his circumnavigation of the world from Plymouth in 1577. Captain Cook dropped his lines from the same docks. It was, of course, from this port that the *Mayflower* sailed on its voyage in 1620 with 102 pilgrims who formed the only aristocracy America ever claimed.

**Hoe**, hallowed ground associated with Drake for the last four centuries, is today a public promenade. The courageous and blasé commander calmly played his famous game of bowls here immediately before defeating the supposed invincible Spanish Armada in Plymouth Sound in 1588. Sir Walter Raleigh also slipped out of the port of Plymouth to sail for the Carolinas in 1584. In 1630 the *Mary & John* took another cargo of souls to a more northerly destination. They became the first citizens of Dorchester, Massachusetts. Explore the old part of town called the **Barbican**—now with many too new buildings. Here you'll find the **Mayflower Steps**, where a plaque bears a list of the passengers who boarded that famous vessel. In more recent times Plymouth's port continued the traditions of trade and might. The U.S. Navy made this its European nerve center during World War II. Hence, it was bombed ruthlessly and rebuilt in contemporary style. The Royal Navy has also maintained extensive facilities here since well before the time William III created the **Royal Dockyard** late in the 17th century.

Other places of interest include **Smeaton Tower** (fronting the Hoe), a **lighthouse** (Gotham sailors will be amused that it is called the Eddystone Light), and the **Citadel** that stands east of the Hoe, a fortress constructed during the reign of Charles II and now containing the **Marine Laboratory Aquarium.** The purpose in building the latter was more to show off to the locals the power that Charles had rather than as a defense project. Among the older public buildings in town are the **Guild** (Town Hall) as well as **Plymouth** and **Cottonlan Library.** For religious architecture, **St. Andrew** in Gothic style, **Charles Church** with its fine slim spire, and the **Cathedral** are additional worthy visiting sites.

The **City Museum** and **Art Gallery** is a proper showcase for the great Plymouth porcelain, locally crafted silver, and antiquities pertaining to the city's past. Relive the prosperous era of this trading city at **Merchant's House Museum,** a fascinating peek into the affluent life of the past. Engineers will be delighted to browse through the **Plym Valley Railway Steam Centre.** One of the largest steam engines in the world is on show; it's called the Beyer Garratt No. 4112 "Springbok"; other huffers and chuffers, a very purposeful shunter, and cranes are further examples of this period of English industrial development. Plymouth from the water is also fun; you can board a 60-minute boat trip from **Phoenix Wharf** all through the day. **Drake's Island,** a fortress that stands just offshore, is a pleasant excursion on a sunny day—more for the views of Plymouth than for the island.

Near **Drake's Island**, you'll find the stately Tudor-style **Mount Edgcumbe House and Park,** constructed and composed in the 16th century, affording wonderful photos of Plymouth Sound. In the other direction (east), is **Saltram House,** with its 18th-century facade and Adam features. **Cotehele House,** a medieval estate up the Tamar, is preserved almost completely in its original form. **Buckland Abbey,** a 13th-century monastery bought and made comfy by Sir Richard Grenville three centuries later, finally became a safe harbor and home of Sir Francis Drake a year after his greatest voyage. It has now been converted into a Naval and Folk Museum containing Drake's drum and models of valiant ships of the line. Drake lived here in 1581, and a less glorious element of the commander's past was that he was briefly a politician and served as Plymouth's Lord Mayor.

**Exeter** takes its name from its comfortable address on the River Exe. Romans founded a fortification here in the first century A.D., but long before that it had been occupied. Two centuries after the Latins arrived it was further protected by a massive stone wall. During its long and illustrious history William the Conqueror and many lesser commanders had a bash at it. Sadly for mankind, the Germans bombed away most of ancient Exeter and destroyed many of its revered architectural treasures. Like Plymouth, however, it shoveled out the rubble and began anew.

**St. Mary & St. Peter's**, Exeter's great gothic cathedral founded in 932, stands today as a truly magnificent medieval survivor. It is a study of patience and adoration in stone. Moreover, its history goes back to the Saxon peoples. The Normans, too, had a hand in it, so several different characteristics stand out. The Decorated style and the 300-foot- long nave are immediately impressive for respective exterior and interior appreciation. Soon the subtleties begin to mount and the general effect is overwhelming. The palmlike fan vaulting, incidentally, is the longest extended example of this type of work existing in today's world. The nave features a pair of lengthy cushions on stone seats, a petit-point masterpiece that is often compared with the Bayeux Tapestry. It was stitched by volunteers of the district.

**Exeter Maritime Museum** is a fabulous entertainment center—educational, too, with more than 100 boats from all over the world. Brunel's steam dredger, a tug, a Chinese junk, an Arab dhow, and even rowboats comprise the fleet. The **Guildhall** is the oldest municipal building in the country, with a birth certificate going back to the 1100s. Many sections have been updated; there's a medieval hall and a Tudor facade, and paintings and silver on display inside.

Apart from the numerous Elizabethan, Jacobean, and other period houses, you might also like to visit Drake's favorite pub, called the **Ship Inn. Tucker's Hall** has a mighty timbered roof and fine oak paneling; it was built in the 15th century. Roman mosaics can be admired on Waterbeer Street. **Rougemount Castle** is, alas, only a tattered, time-worn remnant, but some traces of Norman greatness remain.

A short drive (20 minutes) from Exeter brings you to **Powderham Castle**, which was built in 1390. It was restored in the 18th century as well as in other epochs. The Georgian interior is an elegant showcase for lovely furnishings and paintings. It is still lived in by the Earl of Devon, who is descended from the original builder. The fortified bastion is now totally at peace, sitting in a leafy deer park divided by lanes of gracious cedars and holm oaks. A diverting feature is its musical timepiece that plays antique melodies at regular intervals. The interior decor, detailed carpentry and plastering, textiles, porcelain, and abundance of art are all reasons for going. Open in the afternoons from late May until early September.

**Torbay** is the greater region containing Torquay and some smaller communities. To the first-time visitor it is cliff, beach, and sea. No wonder, then, it is such a popular resort for the English. And popular it is—which may be good enough reason for passing it by in High Season. Torquay is one of the fractional portions. It has an attractive frontage and recreational port, but the stalks of apartment blocks are enough to discourage a pause to refresh even the most fatigued of spirits. It is not everyone's cuppa. Man-made attractions include an Aqualand, dance halls, and cotton-candy and taffy stands. Most of the buildings from Napoleonic times are gone. **Babbacombe** is a cutsie-weensie village set in four mini-acres of gardens. Above Anstey's Cove, there's a true-life cave dwelling called **Kent's Cavern,** with the houseware of the Flintstones. **Torre Abbey,** with its tithe barn and gatehouse, is a 12th-century monastery that was desanctified after religious buildings were "dissolved" by political act in the 16th century. Then there's always **Silvers Model World,** articulated figures that provide the magic of "Silvers Circus." Big stuff in Torquay, but a bit of a yawn for the international traveler.

**Paignton**, like the next town, is part of the Torbay network and again developed out of the 20th-century fever for seasiding. Going back a bit, let's say to the 15th century, **St. John's Church** (aka "Bible Tower") is a remnant of a palace for the bishops of Exeter, which is about an hour north of here. The association with the Bible harks back to a supposition—later proved false—that Miles Coverdale translated the Good Book under its roof. A more truthful sightseeing pause might be **Oldway Mansion.** Built in 1873, it changed its old way early and got a "new look" by the turn of the century when the scion of the Singer sewing machine fortune decided to stitch up a smaller version of the Palace of Versailles. You can admire the outstanding marble staircase, fine glass, and a grand salon exhibiting the item that paid for all of it: the Singer Sewing Machine of 1850. Ask to see the souvenir of Isadora Duncan, Singer's mistress. **Berry Head Nature Trail** offers a plenitude of fresh air combined with wide-angle views of Torbay.

**Brixham**, just a few minutes farther south along the same red-cliff row, rambles in a cartographer's squiggle beside the warmish sea. The harbor is small and shared by both crab fishers and summertime sailors. This beach is more pebble than sand. Mainly it is an extension of the Torbay-Torquay-Paignton recreational resort concept, so take your cue from that. As for cultural sites, the parish **Church of St. Mary**, in red sandstone, offers an elaborate 14th-century font and some interesting relics that William of Orange probably saw when he visited here during his reign. **Brixham Cave,** also called Windmill Hill Cave, is geologically similar to the previously mentioned Kent's Cavern or Hole near Torquay. (The ossified fauna seem to be kissin' cousins.) Other fossil caves are in the neighborhood such as **Bench Cave, Berry Head Cave,** and (yup!) **Ask Hole.**

## VILLAGES—THE HEART OF DEVON

**Bickleigh**, north of Exeter and south of Tiverton, is a charming rural niche with thatched-roof cottages all settled around a mill pond and running along a river spanned by the quaintest of quaintly arched bridges. The idea is to reproduce a Devon farm community of about a century ago. And, of course, there's an 11th-century chapel, the oldest complete building in the county. Absolutely camera county!

**Ottery St. Mary** is east of Exeter in the direction of Lyme Bay. It must inspire the muses of literature because Samuel Coleridge was born on its banks and William Thackeray used the town as a backdrop for one of his novels. Be sure to visit the church, which recalls the beauty of Exeter Cathedral. There's a calm pervading the Devonshire townscape disturbed only by the soft-spoken River Otter.

**Cockington** is roughly in the Torquay-Torbay zone, settled cozily in a wooded valley of yesteryear. In the thatched-roof village transport still relies on the horse to a significant degree. It is blessed by a 12th-century **church,** an old **mill,** a **forge**—and, of course, lots and lots and lots of tourists (in season).

**Totnes**, a bit inland, resides as a former fortified town on the west bank of the River Dart, about 24 miles south and to the west of Exeter. It is connected by (what else?) the bridge to Bridgetown. Formerly Totnes was enclosed by a wall; ruination set in but two of the four original gates (North and East) remain. Many colorful old houses have been lovingly preserved within this precinct, and in High Street their overhanging upper floors form a covered mall for pedestrians walking or shopping below. (In some communities this architectural fillip—as a protection against inclement weather—was required by law.) **The Norman castle** that once commanded a place of honor here fell to the whims of Henry VIII, but the keep and upper walls still exist. Close by are the tatters and stones of **St. Mary's Priory**, which today contains merely the gatehouse, refectory, periphery wall, abbot's gate, and stillhouse. The **Town Hall** of Totnes is a portion of the old Priory. The mood here is totally different from that experienced a few miles away at Torbay. There's a scenic boat trip from Dartmouth that is rewarding if you have the time. The town itself is marvelous; it's home of the Royal Naval College (the British Annapolis). Trout and salmon anglers find ample distraction on the banks. The Dart is just one of the many rivers that incise their routes through the great moor that lies northwest of Totnes. Try to see **Dartington Hall** in this district, a wonderful arts-and-crafts community.

**Dartmoor**, to readers of British mysteries, conjures up the gloomy scene of the vast Dartmoor Prison; however, the penitentiary is only a very small dot in this vastness that was chosen to discourage easy escapes. The moor is at the heart of Devon, composed of the easily remembered total of 365 square miles. Ghosts are not uncommon here—well, at least, reports of them are not uncommon. The wind and fog play among the granite crags called tors. These "towers" (from an ancient language) have been shaped by the force of nature as much as by the willingness of man's imagination to see spirit worlds in the granite. Stone circles and clapper bridges derive from prehistoric occupation in this region—a breeding ground shrouded in vapor and legend. But give Dartmoor a little time and your kind indulgence. There are also heathered undulations crested with gleaming rock harmonizing with myriad rivulets rushing out to the sea. In the vales away from the wind-blasted heights, the terrain magically evolves into something quite different, soft and appealing. But one word of warning: return immediately to a known location when the light fades or when fog starts rolling across the moor. For walkers this can be a serious hazard.

If you are exploring Dartmoor, there is a wide variety of nearby places to visit. You might take a picnic to the **River Dart Country Park**, where there is an adventure playground for the children, nature trails, beautiful meadows, and fly-fishing facilities.

**Ashburton Museum** features interesting items of local, historical, and geological finds. The Yeo, Dartmoor's vital river, once fed the textile and tin industries that brought the area considerable prosperity. The streets are cobbled, and it is just what a Devonshire village should be, even to the town church and the barking dog.

**Bovey Tracey**, on the eastern edge of the moor, is where you will find a historic and pleasant settlement. Artisans work in their shops along the main street. The parish church was rebuilt by Sir Thomas de Tracey. (This was an act to seek pardon for his participation in the murder of Thomas Becket at Canterbury.) Walking over the 200 acres of parkland in the wooded valley of the River Bovey, sometimes called Yarner Wood is a pleasure. Is it true that the prettiest girls in Devon come from here? See for yourself.

**Chagford**, with a cordial mid-village of pubs and shops, once was involved in the tin fever of the Upper Teign valley. The families here are house-proud and maintain a lovely ambience in the village. Surrounding them are the famous tors.

**Drewsteignton** is not far off with its stately **Castle Drogo,** built on a hilltop.

**Moretonhamstead**, a pleasant market town on the fringe of Dartmoor, is often photographed for its 15th-century granite **church** and the row of **almshouses.** At the **Mearsdon Manor Gallery** there is a building dating from the 13th century, with a collection of paintings, jade, jewelry, copper, and bronze.

**Widecombe**, situated in a high grove of trees and surrounded by open grazing land, reaches even higher into the Devon skies with its four greystone church spires that can be seen for miles. Perhaps the church architects got their inspiration from **Haytor, Hound, Bowerman's Nose** (a funny one), and the other "tors" in the vicinity. The town has gained acclaim for the annual **Widecombe Fair of Songs,** held in mid-September.

**Buckland-in-the-Moor** is a village tike close to other Bucks such as Buckfastleigh, Buckfast Abbey, and Buckland Beacon. It is at the northern fringe of Holne Chase. The town clock in its church draws many tourists. They come to look at the face on which the usual numbers have been replaced by the reverent message *"My Dear Mother."*

**Haytor Rocks**, stone spires that climbers adore, form an assemblage of dramatic outcrops in the center of the National Park. Some of these in this region were mentioned above with "Widecombe." The views from the top are worth the scramble, but a road serves the more faint-hearted. **Moorlands Crafts Center** exhibits cottage industries with audience participation if desired. Just south of here is *Saddle Tor.*

**Buckland Beacon** rises to a height of 1300 feet, from where you may think you've reached heaven. To confirm this you will find the "Ten Commandments" hewn into Devonshire stone forever. (Buckland Mosaics perhaps?)

**Buckfast Abbey**, south of **Ashburton**, was first baptized in the 10th century, born again after 200 years of life, and given yet another rebirth early in this century. The Benedictines are rightly proud of the building's tile flooring. Otherwise in the area try to see the **House of Shells Museum,** which is provided with much of its riches from the Devon coast.

Not far away and within walking distance, you can reach the origin of the Avon, at this point within the Dart network, at **Holne**. The ancient **church** in town exhibits an hour glass (well used over so many centuries, as you can imagine), which is a curiosity drawing many passersby to its pulpit.

**Budleigh's** claim to fame goes back to 1522, when Walter Raleigh (not yet a Sir) was born on local turf. As every North Carolinian recalls, he was, for a time, the fair-haired adviser, flatterer, and diplomat for Elizabeth I. As author of *History of the World*, he has shown generations of other Budleigh lads that vision has no bounds despite its modest origins.

**Okehampton**, a market town today, traces its origin to the Norman fortification created by Baldwin de Bryonis at the time that William the Conqueror was romping through the area. The influential Courtenay family occupied the castle until Henry VIII took a fitful dislike to one of its members, ordered his head removed from his shoulders (achieved in the year of Our Lord 1538), and angrily dismantled the poor soul's domicile. So much for fealty.

**Lydford**, in the west of Dartmoor, has a sorrowful past. Brooding over the handsome village is its grim-looking **Lydford Castle**, once the prison for those who flouted the mining laws.

**Buckfastleigh** is only a 7-mile ride away aboard a steam train chuffing up the superb Dart Valley, a pleasant alternative, mainly for the journey rather than the destination. Getting there, in other words, is more than half the fun.

**Postbridge**, about 8 miles from Moretonhamstead, is worth the detour to see one of the best-known "clapper bridges" in the county. The town, naturally, was on the post road and was used because of its span over the East River Dart. The clapper bridge, incidentally, looks rather primitive, and well it should since it was constructed with massive stone slabs sometime during the 13th century.

**Two Bridges** is 7 miles southwest of Postbridge, perched strategically to receive the only two roads that traverse the length of Dartmoor. From here there is a pleasant walk to **Wistman's Wood,** a nature preserve extending half a mile along the River Dart. It's at its best in summer, when countless daffodils preen on the fertile banks.

**Yarner Wood** is a nature preserve; there's a walking trail through vast forest, but pick up an entry pass first since the protection and control are understandably strict. **Becka Falls** roars onto the scene with cascades plunging precipitously over a ten-story rush-and-tumble path to a rocky bottom.

**Grimspound**, a long time ago in the Bronze Age, was a place for many sheep and few men; there's a trace of periphery wall and the enclosures for animals plus some primitive dwellings. Sir Arthur Conan Doyle gave it an enduring identity in *The Hound of the Baskervilles*. Any follower of Holmes will recognize it.

## NORTH DEVON AND
## THE DOONE VALLEY

The littoral on the Bristol Channel fairly trembles up here. Ceaseless waves pound ashore onto a shadowy coast of crags and niches that once were the havens of smugglers. The rolling heather provides a mantle of gray-rose and purple—the home of pheasants that sometimes are flushed as you drive by. Deer dart over the uplands at magical moments. This lonely run of sea and shore that sweeps off Exmoor and joins the Devon midriff combines to create a zone called the Doone Valley. Robert D. Blackmore focused on **Hoccombe Combe** as the setting for his stirring novel *Lorna Doone*. Many manuscript pages were written, in fact, under the thatched roof of the **Royal Oak** at **Winsford**. Blackmore built his tale out of misty ancient Doone yarns. **Oare Church** is where Lorna was married as well as shot. The reality of the scenes provide added texture for the fiction.

**Lanke Combe** is a part of the myth as well as the real geography. Here you'll come upon the brilliant cascades that appear in *Lorna Doone*—Forlorna Doone might be more appropriate, since the area is bleak, spacious, and haunted. No wonder the tale took seed in such an atmosphere.

**Barnstaple** lies on the River Taw, the latter being spanned by an 800-year-old bridge—which gives you an idea how long it has been a crossroads. It is the largest market town in Devon and officially the oldest town in all England. A true and fine example of the Georgian concept is the attractive colonnade that was built in 1708 as a trading post. The statue is of Queen Anne and the row is hence referred to as Queen Anne's Walk. This exchange had great commercial significance when the Taw was utilized by shippers and the wood industry was thriving locally. Among the popular sightseeing targets are **Horwood's Almshouses**, the **Guildhall,** and **Salem Almshouses.** The richly endowed church of **Sts. Peter and Paul** is often visited because of its antiquity. Despite updatings through the centuries it still features an impishly irregular spire from the 13th century. If not too faithful artistically, at least it reveals a certain durability.

**Ilfracombe** is probably the oldest resort as such in North Devon, with a resident population of about 12,000 today. It was not until 1874 when the railway came through that it was "discovered," however, and it has been a major target ever since. The town is structurally and topographically unique inasmuch as it was built within the cup of Devonshire hills; to hop off to the beaches is not along the usual promenade, but here you walk through the surrounding mounts via a system of tunnels. The lighthouse high on a butte overlooking the harbor was once the **Church of St. Nicholas.** This probably could be seen farther out in the Bristol Channel than the port light on a rock formation called **Lantern Hill.** Visitors usually call in on the haunted **Chambercombe Manor. Ilfracombe Museum** has little focus, choosing instead to floodlight an overall view of natural history, fossils, Victorian costumes, rare books, and ample minutia of local interest.

**Clovelly**, small as it is, dominates Bideford Bay—and a large portion of the tourist package in summertime. The town of Bideford is less than a half-hour away. An altogether charming and unusual village, it starts at its uppermost tier and tumbles merrily down the mountainside through narrow cobblestone streets to the toy harbor below. Nice? Quaint? Picturesque? (Ugh, not *that* word again!) It is all of these (even picturesque), but every tour conductor also agrees—and there's the rub. No private cars are allowed to circulate. The slippery ascent back to the top by foot can be avoided (if—a big if—you are prepared to wait); just board the handy village vehicle, which chugs effortlessly back to the *up*-town reaches every few minutes. (They used to use pack animals.) A good view of this setting can be had from the pier—as well as a good catch of fish. On the fringe is **Yellary Gate;** from here you enter **Clovelly Court,** where many visitors go for strolling. See if you can discover how local cliff dwellers have their supplies delivered.

Let's start with Martin de Turribus. Little did he realize that as the founder of **Combe Martin** it would be his last name rather than his first that would describe his land grant best. Now every tour bus in the realm seems to have found its way into Martin's little old coombe. A gallant sidekick of William the Conqueror, he was rewarded with this very attractive patch of real estate for his loyalty. It runs through a former mining valley flanked by long-abandoned shafts. Now, instead of producing tin, silver, or lead, it has become known for its strawberry fields. The **Pack of Cards** is an oddity. The inn was built in 1752 by an ambitious card shark, and it actually looks like a player's deck set up to resemble a house of cards. Following the deal of ridiculous to the sublime, the next attraction in Combe Martin usually is the Perpendicular-style English church. Hidden and almost unapproachable are some of Britain's most enchanting beaches, reached only on skiffs run by the local boatmen.

**Hele Mill**, a 16th-century grinder once wound down to ruin, has been renewed and put into service again. The great wheel provides the muscle to grind flour for the locals. You may visit it and watch the production if you wish.

**Chambercombe Manor** is set in a leafy vale between Ilfracombe and Combe Martin. *Combe*, you'll remember, means "dry valley," but this sprawl of buildings reveals extensive use of water for decoration and for gardening. The Norman-style house is 15th century with 17th-century furniture. Encased within is a tiny chapel big enough for only the smallest sins. Haunted? Of course it is. A body that is said to be walled up in a secret chamber sometimes sends its ghostly messenger to whisper in the ear of certain foreign visitors.

**Arlington Court** is a "must" for householders who appreciate fine collections of silver, porcelain, and furniture. The trove includes items from all over the world and though it might sound stuffy, the level of taste is so striking that no viewer can help being awed by this National Trust exhibit (given by Rosalie Chichester, whose family had the estate since the 14th century).

**Lynton**, a Victorian redoubt, is still visited by holidaymakers. It offers a clifftop setting and a curious hydraulic **mountainside elevator** built in 1890. It still functions. The **Catholic church** is admired for its fine marble. It's worth a pause if only for the impressive long-distance panoramas.

**Lynmouth**, a tourist-choked fishing village below Lynton, sits beneath the towering rocks at the junction of sometimes angry rivers. Not long ago its pier was almost swept away by a flood. A strange building called the **Rhenish Tower** (not strange along the Rhine, where its design is common) was originally constructed to contain salt water for "the cures"; it, too, took a bath and was washed away in the deluge, later to be rebuilt. The town is composed of cottages struggling to be appreciated amid the thunder of organized touring. In fall or early spring the better side of its personality shows through.

The waters do, indeed, effect a union at **Watersmeet**: the East Lyn and the Hoaroak. The latter provides dramatic falls, too. Nearby is **Brendon**, situated on the East Lyn. The antique **packhorse bridge** is ideal for photos. If you continue along this waterway you'll come to **Malmsmead,** where you can get your own packhorse and go for a trot. They are rented by the hour or fractions of a day.

## DORSET OF HARDY FAME

"Small but great" could sum up the appeal of this variegated and enchanting county. It is small enough to cover easily and quickly. Its greatness comes in several forms. The magnificent countryside, from the rolling sweep of Blackmoor Vale and the forested mystery of Cranborne Chase, is captivating by any scenic standards. The coastline combines rugged white limestone cliffs, mellow weathered sandstone crags, and golden beaches. While there are many obvious coastal resorts, inland Dorset is generously possessed of dainty thatched cottages, hillocks veined with gently flowing rivers, their banks colored by wildflowers, and inviting hamlets peopled by some of the most hospitable folk of the West Country. The name Dorset refers to "the settlers by Dorchester" or the "Dorchester Set," in modern lingo.

The northern sector remains one of the most peaceful and genuinely unspoiled parts of England. The countryside is devoted chiefly to farming. Scattered through the district is abundant evidence of ancient habitation—grassy burial mounds, earthworks, and remains from Roman times. Dorset is also an exhilarating adventure for hikers or cycle riders. Nature provides the greatest diversion. There are some 120,000 miles of recorded footpaths to ramble across while admiring its unbeatable surroundings. Industry definitely takes a back seat in this pastoral setting.

Dorset, of course, is appropriately labeled "Hardy Country." Nearly every village corresponds to a fictitious Hardian name. The author portrayed this part of England faithfully and in detail in his novels—only changing the names of the towns and characters. You will have no trouble recognizing the scenes. *Far From the Madding Crowd, Tess of the D'Urber-*

*villes,* and many other works derive directly from this pastoral county. Even though Thomas Hardy is buried in Poet's Corner in London's Westminster Abbey (with 3000 other immortals), his heart was removed and returned to Wessex, the name the author substituted for Dorset in his literature.

**Bournemouth** is often referred to as a "garden city," but less flatteringly it also is accused of a honky-tonk atmosphere during high season. The latter is unfair because with all the hype of summer tourism, there are many cultural attractions. The town functions in Victorian garb, having come to full bloom during that queen's reign. In spring Bournemouth literally blossoms in a big way. This is also when visitors walk into the surrounding ravines (called "chines") to admire the wild flora. These lead to a splendid wide beach. In 1840 the resort came off the drawing boards and into reality, soon to become Britain's favorite sun-and-saltwater playground, and it has never looked back. Sea-bathing had become simultaneously salubrious and chic. Far from tranquil today, it has all the drawbacks of any entertainment complex in the organized world. **Bournemouth Symphony Orchestra** is a major contribution to the other side of its split personality. The **Russel-Cotes Art Gallery,** in a Victorian house with Italian decoration, ranges from the 17th to the 20th centuries in its collection. Japanese art can be admired in three of the salons, while the Irving Room offers theatrical relics. The **British Typewriter Museum** and the **Big Four Railway Museum** may be too specialized for most tastes. **Compton Acres Gardens,** 4 miles west of town, is proud of its seven separate showcases: Japanese, Italian, Roman, English, Rock, Heather, plus a Palm Court. But if you do not stray from the town center, the rock garden at the Pavilion should be amply rewarding.

**Christchurch** is 5 miles east of Bournemouth. Locals say that Christ—obviously with no regard for chronology—gave it this name. He seems to have been involved somehow in the creation of a Norman priory. But that took place in the 12th century. And that's A.D.! "Twynham," which means twin rivers, was its B.C. name, obviously thought up by heretics or heathens. Have a look at the ancient fort by the rivulet. Finally, **Red House** (not from rust) **Museum** contains scraps of the Iron Age.

**Poole** has a tasteful, sedate mien—the coming spot for upper-level retirement executives, sun-seekers, and yachting types. It happily looks back through 2000 years of maritime heritage. As the second largest natural harbor in the world, it also incorporates miles of uncluttered golden beaches. These fine sands extend appropriately from the Sandbanks Peninsula to Canford Cliffs. At **Branksome Park** you'll find the dramatic chines or fissures cut into the cliff face that fill with flowers and blossoming shrubs in springtime. In 1964 a dug-out canoe dating back to 295 B.C. was recovered from the harbor, thus establishing the town's credentials in the ancient world. There is reason to believe that the Phoenicians may have sailed in 500 years before that! The Romans used the port in the first century A.D.; it was at this time that the black-burnished pottery of Poole was being traded throughout Britain; examples can be seen in **Scalpen's Court**, a merchant's house of the 16th century that is now a museum.

Take a boat trip out to **Brownsea Island**. If you are male, you probably remember the name from boyhood. Baden-Powell created his first Boy Scout camp here in 1907. The marshland remains a haven for many forms of wildlife. Along the quayside is an **aquarium, craft** and **geological centers**, a **model museum**, and an **amusement complex**. The **Guildhall** dominates the entrance to Market Street; it is used today as an exhibit of local history. And when you tire of sightseeing, pop in for a tankard of ale at the **King Charles Inn**, the oldest pub in Poole, where many a scout has quenched a raging thirst.

**Wimborne Minster** is only a short distance from Poole; here the countryside provides an idyll of peace and seclusion waiting to be explored. It has fertile meadows, heathland, marshes rising to the chalk downs, and the remains of a forest that makes up **Cranborne Chase**. It was once a royal hunting (chase) place, and from its higher ground affords a marvelous panorama of New Forest and the Isle of Wight. Scattered through the area is evidence of people from earliest times. Wimborne Minster takes its name from Minster Church, standing since A.D. 713, where Queen Cuthburga founded her nunnery. Each generation left its imprint: Norman architecture generally, a colorful Saxon chest made from one solid piece of oak, and numerous more fleeting periods represented over more than 1000 years. **Minster Church** has two towers, one Norman in rich reddish-brown sandstone, the other in soft greens and grays. High in the western tower is the town's beloved **Quarter Jack,** a curious wooden figure dressed as a Grenadier of the Napoleonic wars, with a hammer in each hand; these— and thus his name—strike the quarter hours on his bells. Have a look at the peculiar chained **Library,** where the books are literally chained together, a gesture that assures they won't be borrowed and not returned. **Orrery Clock** began ticking in 1320; it sends the sun around the dial each day and the moon once a month. **John Constable's House** is a must for admirers of the artist's nature-inspired paintings. No one—pardon me, if I pontificate shamelessly—ever captured the mood of English pastoral life as well as Constable.

Close to Wimborne Minster is **Chalbury**, which is no more than a hamlet, but it is aptly proud of its unique whitewashed **church**; inside are 18th-century box pews with doors, a wooden gallery, and a three- tiered pulpit. The views from the hilltop where it stands are glorious. The **Merley Bird Gardens** will delight children and adults with its fascinating combination of exotic feathered creatures, impressive landscaping, and sleepy water gardens, all arranged in one of the largest and most historic keeps in the country. At the south end of Long Beech Avenue is **Kingston Lacy House,** a large classical domain built in 1663; paintings by such titans as Rubens, Velazquez, and Van Dyke adorn the walls. The estate experienced extensive alterations in 1830 to accommodate one of the finest private art collections in Britain.

Farther north of Beech Avenue—please count 'em; there are 365 trees on one side and 366 on the other—you will come to the great Iron-Age structure that stands on the grassy summit commanding wondrous terrain.

This windswept soldier is **Badbury Rings,** mysterious and ancient earthworks that is one of the oldest prehistoric forts in Britain. The three concentric circles rise one above the other, covering an area of 18 acres. Farther north the chalk downlands of Cranborne Chase reveal rural Dorset.

**Cranborne** is charming, too, if you want an excursion up north. Citizens still pray at its spacious stone-and-flint 13th-century **church** with its fine tower and engaging wall paintings. The green (or common) also is lovely.

**Cranborne Manor** was the home of the Cecils, a powerful family in the district; the gardens are open for public pleasure. Here, again, you'll find the literary brushstrokes of Thomas Hardy; Cranborne became "Chaseborough" in *Tess of the D'Urbervilles*. Hardy also lived at Cranborne Manor for some time.

Across the harbor from Poole is the **Isle of Purbeck**, with superb vistas over this exceptionally beautiful peninsula, all the way over to Lulworth Cove. Though an island, Purbeck now can be visited by road, car ferry, or any number of other vessels. It is here that the famous Purbeck "marble" (not real marble) is quarried; it has been used in churches all over England, and the stone-cutting that occupied so much of the Hardy novels was of this material. To the west are the scenic Purbeck Hills. Many island-hoppers visit the attractive stone village of **Corfe**, once protected by a now ruined fortress that stands magnificently at a high point in the pass. The steeply vertical fortification with its unique position in the hilly landscape was begun by the Normans in the 12th century. Outer walls and the building's basic form and strength can be fully appreciated today even though it was destroyed by Cromwell in the Civil War in 1645.

**Swanage** is 5 miles southeast of Corfe Castle, a busy resort situated on a sandy bay and backed by gently rolling country. The outstanding feature is a stone terrestrial globe weighing some 40 tons, hardly likely to be "pinched" by local rubberneckers. For extraordinary scenery, make your way to **Durlston Country Park,** over 260 acres of unspoiled countryside atwitter with wild bird populations, butterflies, and smiling flowers. A little bit to the northwest is the rather somber ironstone rock known as the **Agglestone,** hewn to resemble our planet.

See the **Tithe Barn** and then ramble along to **Worth Matravers**, which is a charming hamlet of stone-edged dwellings clinging to a hillside. All through here the country is rich with antiquity and splendid little corners. At **Kingston** have another Hardy exposure at the 19th-century church; it was composed of local stone and talented masonry. Hardy's characters revered stone cutting, and this is a reflection of that inbred pride. **Kimmeridge** is a nice bayside settlement with quite a few thatch-roofed cottages. Quite near is **Smedmore House,** which is open to the public. If you enter you'll discover a compelling collection of dolls from various periods of history.

**Blue Pool** is to the northwest, a short drive. Here's a living monument to the persuasive powers of public relations. Due to the removal of clay, it became an environmental disaster. Nevertheless, it shows how good can come out of bad. The attraction for visitors here derives from the pool itself, made by the excavation, which reveals dazzling shades of blue when light values alter—from deep cobalt to aquamarine to green. The village is built mainly of red brick; its 2-mile sandy beach is sheltered by dunes.

**Weymouth**, back on the mainland and situated in a wide bay, pays homage to its past with a statue of George III, who first came here in 1789 and which is why it later became Everyman's holiday resort. There are several handsome houses (Georgian, naturally) in the town; in Trinity Street the Tudor period sneaks in effectively.

A worthwhile trip from Weymouth is to the **Isle of Portland**, a peninsula linked with the mainland by Chesil Bank. Here this long spit of land features a remarkable beach where the pebbles decrease regularly in size from east to west. Portland, needless to say, is also famous for its quarries; stone from here was used to build St. Paul's Cathedral in London. The island's **castle** was built by Henry VIII. At the southern tip is **Portland Bill,** with a lighthouse and bird-watching station.

**Abbotsbury** is 9 miles west of Weymouth; here you'll find the ruins of a **Benedictine abbey.** The oft-photographed **swannery** belonged to Lord Lichester and appears in records as early as 1393; today it is home to a snobbery of swans that knows no equal in the feathery peerage.

**Lyme Regis** is proudly and historically established at the mouth of the River Lyme, which runs briskly through the town. It has a longstanding function as a port, but this has only enhanced its attractiveness—a resort, to be sure, but one with stair-step terraces rambling to the harbor and numerous cozy hideaways. In the late 16th century its fleet combined forces with those of Drake against the Spanish Armada in a wide bay shouldered in stone and crested by **Golden Cap**. When the sunlight burnishes the surface you'll appreciate its name. You might like to visit **Philpot Museum**, see the fossils and lace exhibits, and trickle in to the **Marine Aquarium**. It was in Lyme Regis in the early part of the 19th century that Mary Anning at the age of 11 uncovered one of the landmark finds in fossils. This led to a brilliant career in an altogether new science. Now thousands of hobbyists and scholars take to these same hills each year in search of natural treasure. Jane Austen was warmly associated with the area. Possibly you may recall the beautiful scenes from the film *The French Lieutenant's Woman*, which was on location here for months. Stroll into **Langmoor Gardens** to refresh your memory. A stiffer challenge is the scramble through **Downland Chasm**, one of the most demanding hikes along the south coast.

Toward the east in the direction of Bridport you'll come to **Chideock**. It is a photographer's ready-made setting with thatched cottages, a couple of pubs, and pure pastoral scenery at the click of every shutter. **Charmouth**, on Lyme Bay, mixes its household thatchery with a smattering of Georgian flavors. Its history includes a few regents who paused here either in pursuit or for relaxation. If you go to the **Queen's Arms** you can learn all about these restless personalities. The views should be enough to lure you to stay at least for a night.

## CENTRAL AND NORTH DORSET— HARDY COUNTRY

Let's step away from the coast for a while. Here in the interior the county could be considered a capsule version of grassroots England. In the south and east lie the Downs with its chalky topography—very different from neighboring Devon, which is noted for its red soil and cliffs; Cranborne Chase is blessed with ancient forests. Take a trip to Bulbarrow Hill for sweeping vistas over much of the county. Then drive across Blackmore Vale, which is an open, lonely vastness with visible limits. Thomas Hardy described how the haunting scenery could grip you.

If you want to appreciate Thomas Hardy more deeply, plan to visit **Dorchester**, a city that dominates the River Frome. In 1886 *The Mayor of Casterbridge* (Hardy's name for Dorchester) provided the town with a distinct literary identity. (The original work is on view at the wonderful **County Museum.**) *Far From the Madding Crowd* also brings into focus the scenes and customs of this section of Dorset. Hardy saw the people and their yearnings through many dimensions. As the area seems to be a portrait of England itself, it also set the scene for the broad brush strokes of life that appear on the Hardy canvas. The author was born at **Higher Bockhampton** only two miles from Dorchester. In his works this spot was called Upper Mellstock, and the house is a handsome two-story dwelling with a thatch roof and flowering shrubs before it. He wrote *Under The Greenwood Tree* here, as well as *Far From the Madding Crowd*. **Max Gate,** on Wareham Road, was where he died.

Many of the town sights of Dorchester that you'll want to see today appeared in Hardy's works. The **Maumbury Rings,** for example, is a carefully maintained Roman amphitheater and would be a significant attraction in any community. **St. Peter's,** with its elegant spire, appears in *The Mayor of Casterbridge* as do the **White Hart** and the **King's Arms** inns. **Maiden Castle,** perched on a hill, is a vast prehistoric earthwork encircled by formidable walls and entrenchments covering 120 acres. The **Old Crown Court** is where the "Tolpuddle Martyrs" were sentenced to death. High Street offers the house of the heartless Judge Jeffreys, who presided over the so-called Bloody Assize in 1685. The oldest building is the early 17th-century **Napier's Mite**.

About 8 miles north you'll encounter something quite earthy—in more than one literal sense. The uninhibited **Cerne Giant,** a 180-foot figure who is part of the landscape, is almost certainly a pre-Roman fertility symbol. His frank, if not rude, outline is etched into the chalk hillside and can be witnessed from miles away, causing embarrassment, giggles, or inspiration—whatever is in the mind of the beholder—to all passersby. **Cerne Abbas**, more sedate, is a hamlet that is proud of its **Benedictine Abbey,** begun in 987. It's basically a ruin now, but it does contain a 15th-century **Gate House** and a **tithe barn** that are worth seeing.

Half a mile east of watery **Puddletown** (on the A-35) you might care to pause at **Athelhampton House,** surrounded by 10 acres of landscaped water gardens (or, possibly, by waterscaped land gardens). The 15th-century manse with Saxon origins is one of the gems of England, and it can be visited by the general public. This was called Weatherbury by Hardy, and the farm of the same name is actually **Waterston Manor.** Egdon Heath is another creation by the author, who used this landscape in his works.

To the northeast is **Milton Abbas**, often mentioned as the nation's first studiously planned town. It suffers not a bit from this accusation. (In fact, the "plan" came about because a cantankerous Lord Milton did not like commoners living so near him at Milton Abbey. He shooed them away into these finer 18th-century digs.) Be sure to see the **Brewery Farm** here, and then push on to **Blandford** which is a holdover of the late 17th century. The several dozen dwellings are wonderful to see for the mood alone. The land around Blandford is a rural paradise kept lush by the romantic River Stour. The Stour, you'll remember, gave its name to the river in New England which pilgrim settlers honored in their nostalgia.

**Shaftesbury** faces the green sweep of Blackmoor from a lofty perch that stair-steps down the hillside. It was already a market town when King Alfred founded the **abbey** in 880. This is where Edward the Martyr was buried. Main street here is called Gold Hill, and it is more vertical than horizontal, so the side-slipping thatch-and-daub dwellings seem to hug at the edge of the cobbled way as they stair-step down, down, down toward Blackmoor Vale. Shaftesbury (on the A-30) is handy to your valley explorations, to Cranborne Chase, Stourhead with its English garden, Montacute House of Tudor origin, and many Hardy revelations. You'll soon find out from every citizen in the town that Shafton (different spellings) was the name of this spot when it appeared in literature. It also happens to be an authentic ancient name for its modern successor.

Within easy reach are **Compton Abbas** and **Sturminster Newton** in the south, **Gillingham** in the northeast, and **Longleat** also to the north, all pleasant sidetrips for snooping, shopping, or browsing.

**Sherborne**, a proud cathedral city, is similar in size, aspect, and origin to Shaftesbury. It prospered for a while and at its finest hour was the hub of the ancient kingdom of Wessex. It had a matched pair of fine castles and a great Benedictine Abbey. Later many period homes were built. Sir Walter Raleigh was one of its more illustrious residents, living for a while in **Sherborne Castle,** which was a gift from his queen. Politics, however, earned him a choice cell in the Tower of London, and he lost this beautiful property as well as a **Lodge** that he added soon after the grant was levied. Since it was passed on to others, the character has changed considerably. If you go into the **Abbey,** head straight for the choir and look upward into the thin light of the Middle Ages. The roof here is one of the best examples of such celestial work in all England. And that fellow standing uneasily between two ladies is a statue of the Earl of Bristol—flanked by his two wives.

A second **castle** in the area is also a tourist target. It was inspired by Bishop Roger way back in the 12th century and was brought down like so many others during the Civil War by the ill-tempered Cromwell.

All through this region Hardy keeps popping up. At **Bere Regis** you will find the actual grave sites of the Tubervilles who appeared in fiction in the settlement of Kingsbere. A few miles away is **Lulworth Cove**, which became Lulstead Cove in *Far From the Madding Crowd*. Tess knew Wool's **Woolbridge Manor** as Wellbridge Manor. And finally—although there are numerous other fact-to-fiction comparisons— **Stinsford** (Mellstock, to Hardy) is where the author's heart lies interred with the body of his wife.

# SOMERSET'S MENDIPS TO "SCRUMPY"

**Somerset**, too, is a varied county not only because of its historical towns and sites but also because of its scenic grandeur—both pastoral and gentle as well as wild and haunting. The northern hills are the Mendips, and they seem to roll forever into the horizon, reminiscent of Virginia hunting country and the Shenandoah Valley at the foot of the Blue Ridge Range. It builds to a tableland that gradually slopes toward the south. Thereafter the fall-away occurs more abruptly in dramatic phenomena called "Combes." As you may recall, these appear in other counties and are often incorporated into the names of places. A prominent combe in Somerset is the **Gorge of Cheddar**. A vast natural savanna is bisected by the Polden Hills, producing the Parrett and Brue. Just north and east of Cheddar begin the lovely Mendips, and to the southwest are the captivating and oft-visited Quantocks. These hills scrape the southern part of heaven respectively at Will's Neck, Dunkery Beacon, and Lype Hill, with heights ranging from 1200 to 1700 feet. Exmoor Forest, a national park, blankets the upper western flank of the county.

Mixed in the natural tapestry is a wealth of architecture; especially noteworthy are the tall, lean parish churches that grew out of early prosperity in wool. **Taunton**, **Glastonbury**, **Huish Episcopi**, **Leigh-on-Mendip**, and **Kingsbury** are wonderful targets for this, so circle them on your map. Lytes Cary, Meare, Martock, Montacute, Barrington, and Brympton are engaging for village architecture and development chiefly during the Middle Ages and in the great Elizabethan epoch. King Arthur and Guinevere could have been citizens of mystic Glastonbury, and very near is the cathedral city of **Wells**, one of the high points of your county rovings. Within a small area are heath, mountain, plain, farm, orchard, vale, and forest. Wooded byways, neat and tranquil villages, unpopulated countryside—except by cows—and graceful spires are the signets of the land. Have some "scrumpy" and a pint of local cider to further enhance the satisfying mood of Somerset.

## *WEST SOMERSET*

**Taunton**, a colorful and thriving market town shares its name with settlers in Massachusetts. It is 48 miles southwest of Bath. That's not far, but it certainly is totally different from the mood of Avon. It was already a Wext Saxon stronghold against the Celts way back in the dawn of the eighth century. The Tone River in the Vale of Taunton Deane runs through, and within sight are the Quantock, Black Down, and Brendon

Hills. Its imposing **Taunton Castle** in midtown dates from the 11th century, and you can park right at its skirts; of the original fort the only remaining segments are the gatehouse and the Great Hall, now one of the luxury hotels of Somerset, with some of the finest cuisine in the nation. There are numerous references here to rompin' Judge Jeffreys' Bloody Assize, a merciless trial that took place after the failure of a rebellion at the battle of Sedgemore (1685). The Duke of Monmouth wore a crown briefly here, hoping to become more than just a Protestant pretender. More than 500 of his luckless rebels were condemned to death by this stern jurist.

The town, more reverently, is proud of its early 16th-century **Church of St. Mary Magdalene**, a fine example of the Perpendicular style, which the English sometimes refer to as Early Gothic. (Many houses of worship in this county are of a similar graceful stature.) Taunton is a comfortable town, excellent as a base for your Somerset rambles and research into the lifestyle of the highwaymen who terrorized the region.

**Cheddon Fitzpaine**, is worth a visit for **Hestercombe House and Gardens**. While the dwelling (1870s) is noted for a splendid hall and staircase, the terraced garden is the focal point, especially in the flowering months. It is cunningly laid out with stone work, enhanced by a Pergola and further cheered by an Orangery on the east side. As you would expect, the best time to see it is June through August. From here you have vistas across Taunton Deane.

Three miles south of Taunton, **Poundisford Park** provides a 16th-century manor, having a rich interior with collections of china, glass, costumes, and needlework. And not too far away is **Hatch Court**, a Palladian-style Georgian house constructed with Bath stone. To the northwest of town, in **Tolland**, you'll find **Gaulden Manor**, an historic 12th-century structure in red sandstone set in intimate gardens. It is a bewitching domestic scene and no doubt why Thomas Hardy used it for a role in *Tess of the D'Urbervilles.* Tea is offered in the Garden Room.

If you turn toward the Quantocks, the road trails on to the tiny settlement called **Nether Stowey**, about 8 miles west of Bridgwater, where Samuel Coleridge lived. The house, which you can visit, is called **Coleridge Cottage.** (Do you suppose he named it?) *The Ancient Mariner* was composed at this inland venue, and over the years Coleridge and his close friend, Wordsworth, shared poetic thoughts while walking these hills. Ask anyone in town to point you to the house (only two rooms are available). Just above I mentioned **Bridgwater**. This is where the Duke of Monmouth enjoyed his self-styled coronation in 1685.

A bit farther on you can visit **Sedgemoor**, where he lost that crown, and see the relics of his historic battle. Out of this came the aforementioned trials before Judge Jeffreys and the swift revenge of the law. Bridgwater had another famous son. Robert Blake answered an aquarian calling; he was given command of Cromwell's navy. Today his birthplace is a museum to his career and an homage to the Battle of Sedgemoor.

You would think from its name that **Minehead** must have an inland location but, in fact, it has been a seaport since the early 17th century. North Hill, which is where it is advertised to be, overlooks the generous protected bay and the important transportation routes of the Bristol Channel. A handsome little parish church gave illumination not only to local souls but also served as a beacon for wanderers on the moor as well as to navigators at sea. Other points of interest: the daub dwellings in **Higher Town, Quirk's almshouses** (1630), the **Old Manor House,** the 17th-century cottages at the **Quay,** and **Church Steps.** Visit the impressively grand **Blenheim Gardens,** especially at night when a miniature town is the showpiece.

Take the steam railway to Bishops Lydeard and stop off at **Crowcombe** to see **Church House,** a 15th-century stone building with a graceful timber roof. A bit south of Minehead (below Watchet, on B-3188) is the home of Sir Francis Drake's wife, Elizabeth Sydenham. The house is called **Combe Sydenham**— and by it hangs a tale. On view is an ominous cannon ball which, when it suddenly arrived one day in 1585, is believed to have shattered the marriage plans of another swain who also sought the hand of this maiden. If not too subtle, at least the missile conveyed an effective message, and she later married the bombastic Drake. There's a deer park, monastic ponds, Elizabethan gardens, and a trout farm to stop you in your tracks today.

**Dunster**, a couple of miles southeast of Minehead, appears to be a fully intact medieval village. This was because one family (the Luttrells) seemed to control things here for six continuous centuries. They obviously liked it the way it was, so they preserved it with tender loving care. And thank goodness they did. The **castle,** with its oak paneling and elaborate ceilings, is possibly the finest single target if time is short. Its storybook turrets and towers can be seen on a rise from every direction. The **Yarn Market** reflects the town's successful period in the textile field. **Luttrell Arms** is just one of the charming huddle of dwellings to be seen, most cloaked in a mellow-toned sandstone.

**Exmoor National Park:** If you turn back to the west now you'll see some of Somerset's beloved wild ponies and red deer dashing through the great preserve as you travel. Now you are in "Lorna Doone Country" again, which was more extensively covered under "Devon," its western neighbor. Then, if you are feeling—are you ready?—hardy (ouch), hike up **Badgworth Water,** which trickles right into the Doone Valley. The trail, which runs parallel to the river, is the heartland of this literary supplement to nature. One good place to begin is at **Webber's Post.** This is on a 3-mile loop incorporating open moor and shaded woodland. Just back from the coast and the fine little port of **Porlock Weir** you'll find England's smallest church—all of 10 strides long and four across. It's called **Culbone,** and the tiny stone Norman building is set amid forested hills, with an ancient graveyard at its doorstep. Another curiosity of the region are the so-called **Tarr Steps,** north of Dulverton. The "steps" are really stepping stones that have been maintained across the Barle River for nearly 1000 years. Of a similar antiquity is the nearby **Caratacus Stone** (puzzling but not very interesting, even if you solve the puzzle) and the great prehistoric earth-works called tumuli, which are really standing stones and barrows observed in many parts of Somerset. Try, if convenient, to see the stone circles near **Porlock Hill,** or drive over to **Selworthy** or **Allerford**, which are the raw material of many English postcards. Both are lovely little settlements with old houses, bridges, tumbling vines, and ducks on the water.

## MYSTIC AND ANCIENT NORTHEAST AND CENTRAL SOMERSET

The terrain in this sector is low and boggy. Few people live here now, but up on the Mendips early man maintained a thriving civilization in the caves and hills that provided protective cover and food. Good examples of this community are found at Cheddar and at Wookey Hole. Farther east, there was greater habitation and later habitation, resulting in more advanced enterprise especially among the active wool communities, which occupy the banks of the River Frome. The most frequently chosen centers from which to tour the area are Wells and Glastonbury.

## WELLS

Wells, 21 miles from Bath, its one-time rival, resides quietly at the southern shoulder of the Mendip Hills and, like the neighboring spa, fished its name out of the local waters. Pilgrims as well as sybarites have long believed in curative and soothing powers from the "wells." The town's historic **cathedral**, a beautiful architectural paegn to St. Andrews, was begun in 1174 by the ambitious and devoted Bishop Reginald Fitz-Jocelin. The original one, however, was created King Ine almost 500 years before that! It remains the focal point of any visit—an amazing presence in a place of fewer than 10,000 souls. Nearly every solid item in the town has some relationship to this awesome structure. The transepts (transitional style) are the oldest standing segments, but the honey-tone western face with its 400 statues on 6 tiers is probably one of the most impressive church frontages you'll ever see anywhere. The statues, incidentally, were once painted (as were early Greek statuary), so try to imagine the facade in polychrome.

As with so many church buildings, the architects were extremely confident in showing off the full structure. Hence, there is no buffer zone of foliage or shrubs, but the greensward comes directly to the edge of the outer walls. Behind these you see the icicle-thin spires atop the stout 14th-century central tower. Inside, the exotic fan-style vaults were created later. The Chapter House and Lady Chapel (this one with exquisite star-pattern vaults) belong to the Decorated period (1300-40), while the Cloisters depends on the more classical Perpendicular mood.

Obviously there is no shortage of variety in this extended "religious village." The builders were inventive too. They had to be, when they believed that the central tower was sinking with woeful rapidity. The clever and graceful answer was to apply a unique but untested double-pointed arch. The tower has stood firm for more than six-and-a-half centuries. The north transept contains an astronomical clock at the top of an arch that was wound up for the first time long, long ago. Ever since 1392 the figures of mounted knights have been leaping into action at the strike of the hour. Thomas Beckington, another well-endowed, ardent bishop, built Penniless Porch (where handouts were collected), Browne's Gate, Chain Gate, and Bishop's Eye in the middle of the next century. The "Eye" peeps in on the Bishop's Palace, which is otherwise enclosed by a wall and moat; a lamentation of obedient and punctual swans jingle a bell at two specific feeding times. Now, after the snack with the swans (11 a.m. and 4 p.m.) continue across Chain Gate to see Vicar's Close, an altogether enchanting assemblage of several dozen 14th-century dwellings. The mood created by this street is a fair portrait of Europe itself during this epoch. Try not to overlook it since it conveys a message of how far society has progressed out of the Dark Ages.

Indeed, this region of England was still haunted at that time by hangovers of mysticism. Glastonbury (see below) might have been the capital of eerie and baffling spirits. Possibly the neighboring caves—Wookey Hole, Cheddar Gorge, and Gough's and Cox's Caverns—evoked a spell even on the generations who came later. Some avow to this day the effects are still alive. Why not visit them and see for yourself? Or, if you don't believe what you see, just ask the Witch of Wookey.

## AUTHOR'S OBSERVATION

*This is the precise district to sample Cheddar cheese as you may never before have had it. Stilton, for example, is the only British dairy product that is protected by an official trademark. They learned from Cheddar that a good thing is often copied—and the imitation frequently pales beside the original. Hence, the Cheddar you taste in this region is the original and has far more tang and zest than the knock-off versions that flood the world market.*

## GLASTONBURY

Glastonbury's hallowed ground could be the foyer of the Otherworld. Scientists know it was once an island. Could that have been Avalon, the final home of the Holy Grail? And the two bodies that Edward I had exhumed in 1191—were they the mortal coils of Arthur and Guinevere? Medieval pilgrims were drawn in thousands to Glastonbury Abbey, which is linked to many ancient mystic rites. The **Abbey Church** could possibly be the oldest one in England. Certainly the fact that three of the nation's earliest regents were interred here gives it ample credentials for antiquity. Physically, a few walls and arches are all that remain. What has stuck are the legends surrounding the abbey—such as the one involving St. Joseph of Arimathea, who forced a wooden pike into the ground that took root and now (or so the story goes) a twig sprouts anew each Noel. **Glastonbury Tor** is the barren, broad-based hill within the town. At its foot is **Blood Spring,** where the chalice that held Christ's blood is supposed to be buried. From here to the top could occupy a half hour of easy, casual climbing, and along the simple unadorned trail you may find dozens of visitors at prayer or in varying states of meditation, depending upon the faith or fashion of the religion or occult following.

Natural or supernatural, whatever your calling, the view from the summit's ruined chapel tower is inspiring. **Glastonbury Tribunal** depicts the history and the tall tales pertaining to this mysterious site, and artifacts of the prehistoric lake cultures nearby. As mentioned, hardly anything is left of the massive ancient abbey that was as long as six football fields. Nevertheless, you should try to see the **Lady Chapel** with its intricate arcades and the substantial morsels of corner construction that probably formed twin towers embracing the portal. Also interesting is the **Abbot's Kitchen,** with four fireplaces where you could still roast an ox for a rich pilgrim. (The abbot's hospitality was boundless if the supplicant indicated affluence. More humble faithfuls were given a crust of bread in the forecourt.) The **George Inn** is where you'd hang your wimple if you paused for the night. (There are better hotels in the district today, however.) You wouldn't ordinarily think that the **Somerset Rural Life Museum** would be a whiz of a tourist attraction, but it is because of the striking, well-preserved 14th-century **Abbey Barn** and a quaintly maintained farmhouse and yard. It looks into the life of an ordinary farm worker during Victorian times and focuses on Somerset cider-making and similar trades, which demanded so much personal involvement. Just a short drive away, southwest of town, is **Sharpham Manor,** where the frolicsome Henry Fielding gave his first cry of life. The 18th-century novelist was an ancestor of the founder of this guidebook series, so says the family chronicle.

## OTHER OPTIONS

Turning south, after having visited Bridgwater and Sedgemoor, you'll come to **Burrow Bridge** and **Burrow Mump**, where you will enjoy a wonderful view of the historic battleground, if you climb the latter hump or mump (so much for early English spelling). Then comes **Muchelney**, with a very, very old (7th-century) Saxon **chapel**, a handsome Benedictine **abbey**, and a thatched dwelling known as the **Priest's House**. Then, just a bit to the north, is **Huish Episcopi**, proud of its **church** with noteworthy glass, a Norman portal, and a much-revered 15th-century tower. **Long Sutton** and **Somerton** are eye-blink hamlets, but try to see them. The latter was a West Saxon seat of government eons ago. The ancient structures testify to that. Go first to the **Church** and the **Town Hall**. The colorful **Hext Almshouses** and the squat **Market Cross** can be incidental fillers for your day.

The next landing spot is **Yeovilton**, which retired carrier-pilots should relish. The Fleet Air Arm Museum is devoted to the exploits of brave Navy fliers and the aircraft they maneuvered. Not far from here is **Cadbury Castle,** with the usual connection to that evergreen monarch, King Arthur. Further along you may wish to stop at **Pilton**, one of the beauty spots of Somerset, which draws many to see its **tithe barn** and a 15th-century **church**. From here continue along A-371, which will take you back to Wells.

An alternative route for a day's outing could begin at **Croscombe**, which has an old **church** (nothing new), this one blessed with outstanding carvings in the oaken interior—wood so hard after seasoning for four centuries that you probably could not drive a nail into it. (Please don't try.) Continuing east, **Shepton Mallet** is a little market town today that in former times made it big in the fleece trade. The wooly prosperity was responsible for the many attractive buildings in its legacy.

On the way to Frome, **Nunney** offers **Nunney Castle**, a gaunt 14th-century structure that stands out hauntingly with its quartet of thick towers, its moat, and a low surround of trees and huddled cottages. **Frome** itself is a lovely town and a nice place to pause for tea during your rovings. Again, its obvious richesse came from the burgeoning epoch of woolen textiles, and the shops and dwellings reflect this wealth at every turning, even today. Most visitors see only Cheap Street, but there is much more to enjoy if you take the time to wander away from the center.

**Rode Tropical Bird Gardens** are close to Frome too. It's a wonderland for rare and exotic feathered friends. It's a wonder, too, that such southern inhabitants can exist at all up here—quite a compliment to the Somerset climate.

From this point, it is as easy to head north to Bath as it is to point southward to Wells.

# WHERE TO STAY AND EAT

## *WILTSHIRE*

### AMESBURY

**Antrobus Arms**

A pleasant haven if you are doing the Stonehenge loop. It is also near Salisbury. Small, cozy, and not terribly expensive. (☎ *0980-23163.*)

### BEANACRE

**Beechfield House**                                                           ☆☆

Offers a couple of dozen rooms in a Victorian manse that is almost on the outskirts of Bath. Tennis, outdoor pool, and croquet. Noteworthy cuisine in both French and English style. (☎ *0225-703700*; FAX: *790118.*)

### BOX

**Clos du Roy**

About 20 minutes north of Bath in the Box House, a Georgian redoubt that is very appealing at mealtimes. Be sure to reserve for lunch or dinner. (☎ *0225-744447*; FAX: *743971.*)

### BRADFORD-ON-AVON

**Woolley Grange**                                                             ☆☆

An intimate 17th-century country house with a heated pool and tennis facilities. Expect to pay a lot, but the taste— both at the table and in the surroundings—is superb. (☎ *02216-4705*; FAX: *4059.*)

### Priory Steps

A modest Newtown shelter with about a half-dozen units built into ancient cottages once used by local weavers. Prices are well below those of Woolley Grange, and the people are hospitable. (☎ *02216-2230.*)

### Burghhope Manor

Situated in a lovely Avon vale; only 7 rooms but very appealing. (☎ *022122-3557.*)

### Leigh Park

A bit out of town, with 20 bedchambers, tennis, and a rural setting. (☎ *02216-4885.*)

## CASTLE COOMBE

### Manor House         

One of the oldest inns in Britain. Portions of this one date back some 600 years. Wonderful English dining room with magnificently polished oak tables, candlelit at night. Tennis and pool. A good headquarters for touring the area. (☎ *0249-782206*; FAX: *782159.*)

## CHIPPENHAM

### Angel

Handy to Sheldon Manor if your day's tour ends there. Adequate but not too inspired. (☎ *0249-652615*; FAX: *443210.*)

### Bell House          ☆

At Sutton Benger, which is not far away. It is a cozy little charmer and set on comfort and coddling. Book away from the roadside if you are a light sleeper. No special view but very nice in every other way. (☎ *0249-720401.*)

## LACOCK

### The Sign of the Angel         

The heart of the matter if you are searching for antiquity; only a few bedchambers but a marvelously intimate hearthside pub of 5 tables and a promising wine cradle above the mantel. Honest English fare with one grill available per mealtime. The potted crab, salmon mousse, and roast pork were splendid. Rates run about £80 per night per couple, the most expensive in the hamlet. Indeed, its name came not from heaven but from an "angel" or gold coin of the era. (☎ *024-973230.*)

### King John's Hunting Lodge          ★

Boasts a mere 2 rooms, one of them with a four-poster.

### Carpenter's Arms         

In Wiltshire stone, and twice as large.

**Red Lion**

Proud of its accommodation with a half-tester (not a member of the staff, but a bed with 2 posts instead of 4).

**Old Rectory**

The final choice except for the private houses, which rent twin units for about £30. You can inquire about the latter at the National Trust House on the main street, where you can also find excellent souvenirs and gift items of regional flavor.

## MALMESBURY

**Old Bell** ★★

Chimes with antiquity along Abbey Row, just where you will want to be for sightseeing. Prices are a bit steep, but so are the rewards. (☎ *0666-822344*; FAX: *825145.*)

**Whatley Manor** ☆☆

Three miles west of town in a park with tennis, fishing, and swimming facilities. The house with its 2-dozen rooms is in the 18th-century mood. (☎ *0666-822888*; FAX: *826120.*)

**Crudwell Court**

Formerly the home of the local vicar. I've never stayed in this 15-room retreat, but friends who have say no vicar (nor bishop) could have greater comfort. Prices, however, are at papal levels. (☎ *0666-7194*; FAX: *7853.*)

## MARLBOROUGH

**Castle & Ball**

Handy to Avebury and the prehistoric finds along "Kennett Avenue." A good solid Trust House Forte address. (☎ *0672-55201*; FAX: *55895.*)

**Ivy House**

A pleasant, less costly, historic inn on the trail toward Bath. A very good alternative. (☎ *0672-55333.*)

## SALISBURY

**Rose & Crown**

The most historic address. It's at Harnham on the Avon River. Only 28 units, but oozing with atmosphere. (☎ *0722-27476*; FAX: *412761.*)

**Kings Arms**

On the same St. John's St., but only offers 15 bedchambers. These antique ones are agreeable, however, and about half the price of those at the White Hart. (☎ *0722-27629.*)

**Rose & Crown**

For dining this is a classic of Olde England. Don't miss it. **Langley**

**Wood** and **Silver Plough** are other attractive choices on the outskirts of town.

# WARMINSTER

### Bishopstrow House

Stands in its own glorious parkland with almost as many flowers inside the handsome Georgian mansion as outside, the soft-spoken Wylye whirling gently below its grassy slope. The Wessex conviction for melding home and garden unites antiques, a conservatory, fireplaces, and sumptuous furnishings with views of the rolling Wiltshire panorama. Bedrooms with individual decor, color TV, books, fine carpets, and artwork. The palladian indoor pool and tennis court are elegant indeed for sport. (☎ *0985-212312*; FAX: *216769.*)

# *AVON*

# BATH

### Hunstrete House

One of the most tastefully outfitted and purely beautiful mansions to be found anywhere in the British Isles. Only a few minutes out of town, surrounded by meadows with free-ranging deer, the estate has roots dating to the 10th century. Nowhere, however, are there signs of age or neglect. The exquisite antique furnishings, the artwork, the textiles, the cheerful mien enhanced by flowers are captivating. A tennis court and pool are in their own sector to ensure peacefulness. The gastronomy is both honest and luxurious; it's served in a graceful, window-lined salon facing a fountained patio. What a marvelous and enchanting place to relax! (☎ *07618-490490*; FAX: *490732.*)

### The Priory

Stands at the edge of the town inside its own walled Eden. Rooms are not always the largest (ask for one facing the blossoms); dining is in the manorly restaurant or in the cheery Orangery. Its 21 rooms are pleasantly outfitted and the size overall is conducive to a clublike atmosphere. There's a pool in the garden. (☎ *0225-331922*; FAX: *448276.*)

### Royal Crescent                                      ★ ★ ★

In the town of Bath, is located within the famous 18th-century crescent of buildings that overlooks the vale. Historically it is unique, one of the few public hotels to occupy such important premises. Elegant public rooms, but disappointing dining facilities; expanded accommodations; majority of the units with fireplaces; maintenance standards lower than what I would have expected for such a patrician establishment. Very expensive. (☎ *0225-319090*; FAX: *339401.*)

### Bishopstrow House ☆☆☆☆

Southwest of Bath, lies in the captivating Wessex Downs, but well within the realm of activities that define this area and its attractions. (See "Warminster" in Wiltshire.) (☎ *0985-212312.*)

### Francis ☆

Features a washed facade and busy lounges, offers 94 rooms, all with private plumbing; clean and pleasant; friendly staff; spectacularly accoutred restaurant with cuisine that pales by comparison. Since the front faces a lovely park, but also borders a noisy street, light sleepers should bid for the back of the house. (☎ *0225-24257*; FAX: *319715.*)

### Homewood Park ★ ★

Overlooks the vale of Limpley Stoke. It is 5 miles south of Bath adjoining 13th-century Hinton Priory, an attractive ruin. One of the best Victorian-style addresses in Britain. (☎ *0225-723731*; FAX: *723820.*)

### Lansdown Grove ☆

High in the city, tranquil; it sets a fair table, too, especially for the midday buffet. (☎ *0225-315891*; FAX: *448092.*)

### Hilton

Relatively large with space for about 300 guests on Waleot St. (☎ *0225-463411*; FAX: *464393.*)

### Queensberry

Offers 2-dozen units on Russel St., an attractive part of town. No major dining facility, but very appealing in mood. (☎ *0225-447928*; FAX: *446065.*)

### Oldfields

Again without a restaurant, a good moderately priced house with a dozen rooms on the Wells Rd. (☎ *0225-317984.*)

### Fountain House

Specializes in luxury apartments in central Bath; 1-3 bedroom options with lounge; fully equipped kitchens. Nice idea for long stays or big families. (☎ *0225-338622*; FAX: *445855.*)

### Bath Spa

Devoted to unkinking your knots, muscular or psychological. You receive tea, tests, stress counseling, facials, aroma therapy, and everything a health club and a squad of fitness technicians can throw at you. The cuisine and accommodation are tiptop for luxury, and you are guaranteed not to twitch—at least until you're presented with the bill. An all-inclusive inspection and tune-up at this lavish body shop can total $350 per night, and at least two full days are advised for most human foibles. Verrrry relaxing. (☎ *0225-444424.*)

For dining in an independent restaurant, try **Le Clos de Roy** at the nearby town of **Box**. For dining among the independent restaurants, the famous old **Hole-in-the-Wall** now is chiefly Italian in scope. **Popjoys**, where Beau Nash once lived, is still quite good and pleasant for atmosphere. The **Moon and Sixpence** also weaves an alluring spell.

# BLAGDON

### Butcombe Farm
Goes back 500 years as a pastoral establishment. Now it has a heated pool, 8 nice rooms, and an ingratiating character. Not expensive, but very good value. (☎ *0761-62380.*)

# BRISTOL

### St. Vincent Rocks
Offers about 50 rooms on Sion Hill. (☎ *0272-739257;* FAX: *238139.*)

### Grand
In midtown and much larger but okay. (☎ *0272-291645.*)

### Hilton
Typical accommodations and services for this chain. (☎ *0272-260041;* FAX: *230089.*)

### Holiday Inn
In midcity beside a motorway. (☎ *0272-294281.*)

### Thornbury Castle
Outside of town in a 16th-century Tudor compound of its own. It's a dream in period costume—from fourposters and open hearths to tapers and flowered tables. Gastronomy has always been one of its strong suits and now deep-down palatial comfort has been added to the assets. The grounds are also magnificently maintained. (☎ *0454-418511;* FAX: *416188.*)

# WESTON-SUPER-MARE

### Royal Pier
Offers a grand view of the waves. It's the Best Western in Weston-Super-Mare. (☎ *0934-626644.*)

### Grand Atlantic
Bigger and somewhat more commercial. (☎ *0934-626543;* FAX: *415048.*)

# *CORNWALL*
## BUDE

### Strand (☎ *0288-3222*)
Larger but the little canal-side **Falcon** (☎ *0288-2005*) is also pleasant in a modest way. **Hartland** is more luxurious (☎ *0288-55661*).

## CAWSAND

### Criterion
An amusing hutch of eight fisherfolk shelters overlooking Plymouth Sound. (☎ *0752-822244.*)

# FALMOUTH

**Idle Rocks**
Also could be considered under St. Mawes because of its harbor position. (☎ *0326-270771.*)

**St. Michael's**
Located at Gyllnygvase Beach, which is usually tranquil.

**Greenbank**
Just at the colorful port, with space for about 100 guests. (☎ *0326-312440.*)

# FOWEY

**Marina**
Offers a dozen rooms overlooking the waterway from the Esplanade. (☎ *072683-833315.*) Try to dine at the delightful **Food For Thought**.

# HELSTON

**Nansloe Manor**
The essence of tranquility. Tiny, hospitable, and with substantial offerings from the kitchen. (☎ *0326-574691.*)

# LAMORNA COVE

**Lamorna Cove** ☆☆
An 18-room luxury address in this lonely part of Cornwall near to Land's End. The sea-toned cuisine is excellent. (☎ *0736-731411.*)

# LISKEARD

**Well House** ★
Known best for its table, but it also has a handful of very pleasant accommodations. (☎ *0579-42001.*)

**Country Castle**
Also small but blissfully peaceful. (☎ *0579-42694.*)

# LIZARD

**Housel Bay**
In the cove of the same name, offering about 20 rooms with lovely views from most. Look along Penmenner Road for other choices, boarding houses and inns. (☎ *0326-290417.*)

# LOOE

**Klymiarven**
A wondrous view, and a handy stop if you are visiting the nearby monkey preserve. (☎ *05036-2333.*)

# LOSTWITHIEL

**Restormel Lodge**
Moderately priced tuck-inn if you are exploring the castle digs. (☎ *0208-872223.*)

# MARAZION

**Mount Haven**
Provides a fine view of St. Michael's Mount. Small and inviting.
(☎ *0736-710249*.)

# NEWQUAY

**Atlantic**
Probably best because it is somewhat remote from the town and therefore quieter. (☎ *06373-2244*.)

**Bristol**
Located on Harrowcliff facing the bay. (☎ *06373-875181*.)

# PENZANCE

**Abbey**
A charming antique from the 17th century with only 6 rooms and a cozy hearthside lounge. It also sets one of the best tables in the shire. (☎ *0736-66906*.)

**Mount Prospect**
Two-dozen accommodations and good solid amenities.
(☎ *0736-63117*; FAX: *50970*.)

**Queen's**
Occupies a waterfront address on the Promenade. It's a reasonable base for exploring. (☎ *0736-62371*.)

**Tarbert**
In midtown and a cheaper alternative. (☎ *0736-63758*.)

# ST. IVES

**Tregenna Castle**
A huge walled fort on a hillside. Within the turreted keep are 73 accommodations. A unique setting. (☎ *0736-795254*.)

**Garrack**
Offers only 20 rooms, but the coastal views are splendid.
(☎ *0736-796199*.)

**Porthminster**
A 50-unit Best Western entry on the Terrace. (☎ *0736-795221*; FAX: *797043*.)

# ST. MAWES

**Tresanton**
Breathtaking sea views, luxury accoutrements, excellent cuisine, and lofty prices. (☎ *0326-270544*.)

## TRURO

**Alverton Manor**

A former convent, provides comfort at rather lofty rates. (☎ *0872-76633*; FAX: *222989.*)

## WEST LOOE

**Hannafore Point**

Offers reasonable comfort close to the fishing fleet. (☎ *05036-3273.*)

## *DEVON*

## ASHBURTON

**Holne Chase**

A peaceful retreat beautifully sited on the route to Two Bridges. (☎ *0364-3471.*)

**Dartmoor Motel**

On the edge of the moor at Peartree Cross. (☎ *0364-52232.*) At Two Bridges itself, the tiny **Cherrybrook** is fair. (☎ *0822-88260.*)

## BARNSTAPLE

**Imperial**

Attractively located by a Taw estuary. (☎ *0271-45861.*)

**Lynwood House** ☆

Just a handful of attractive rooms, but its main focus is on cuisine —which happens to be delicious. (☎ *0271-43695*; FAX: *79340.*)

## BICKLEIGH

**Bickleigh Cottage** ★

Actually a cottage, with thatched roof and poised on the bank of the river; only a few rooms, some from the 17th century—but with 20th-century amenities. (☎ *08845-230.*)

## BOVEY TRACEY

**Coombe Cross**

Offers a couple of dozen rooms at moderate rates. Reasonably good pub food and an attractive bar buffet at midday. (☎ *0626-832476.*)

**Willmead Farm**

Tiny—only 3 rooms—but the setting is all peace and tranquility in a 600-year-old family house. (☎ *064-77.*)

**Bel Alp**

Not a Swiss transplant but a hospitable, 9-unit Devonshire country house slightly out of town at Haytor. (☎ *03646-217.*)

## BRIXHAM

**Quayside**

Lives up to its portside name. A total of 30 adequate rooms. (☎ *08045-55751.*)

**Northcliff**
More modest; on a cliff looming over the waves. (☎ *08045-2751.*)

# CHAGFORD

**Gidleigh Park**                                                    ☆☆☆
A long linear country house, American managed but wonderfully Devonshire in every way. Very remote in a stream-fed forest with flowered gardens; spacious accommodations; some balconies; excellent food and exceptional wines, many from California. (☎ *06473-2367;* FAX: *2574.*)

**Teignworthy**
Another country house and not quite as expensive as Gidleigh. Only 9 rooms; substantial cuisine. (☎ *06473-3355;* FAX: *3359.*)

**Easton Court**
Similarly small and viewful. (☎ *06473-3469.*)

If these are full try the modest **Mill End**, **Torr House**, **Three Crowns**, or **The Globe**. All are tiny.

# COMBE MARTIN

**Coulsworthy**
A worthy stop in a quiet setting with about only a dozen rooms. Enjoyable food that's country style, like the house. (☎ *027188-882463.*)

# EXETER

**White Hart**
Goes back almost 3 centuries; once a coaching inn, now it offers all the old-world hospitality with 21st-century comfort. The restaurant and wine garden are very appealing. (☎ *0392-79897.*)

**Royal Clarence**
In the Cathedral Yard; all 50 units very well maintained offering good comfort at upper-moderate prices. (☎ *0392-58464;* FAX: *439423.*)

**Gypsy Hill Country Hotel**
A nicely run suburban choice. (☎ *0392-65252;* FAX: *0392-64302.*)

**Nobody Inn**
A cheerful 7-room old-timer at Christow (Doddiscombsleigh). Inn-expensive, too, if we must answer their own pun. (☎ *0647-52394.*)

# GITTISHAM

**Combe House**
(Near Honiton) goes back to Saxon times: wonderful park setting; handsome stone building; excellent comfort; French-based cuisine. (☎ *0404-42756.*)

# ILFRACOMBE

**Lee Bay**
In the same cove of the hotel's name. Moderate size and prices. (☎ *0271-63503.*)

**Lee Manor**
Smaller and quite pleasant. (☎ *0271-63920.*)

# LYDFORD

**Castle Inn** ★
Offers 8 modest accommodations and a registry that goes back four centuries. A cozy little place. (☎ *082-282242.*)

# LYNMOUTH

**Tors**
Quite all right for an overnight. (☎ *0598-53236.*)

**Lynton Cottage**
An expensive choice over at Lynton, overlooking the waterfront. (☎ *0598-52342.*)

# MORTONHAMSTEAD

**Manor House** ★★
A splendid Jacobean mansion in gray stone on the Exeter fringes; excellent golf club; tennis; elegantly sporty. (☎ *0647-40355.*)

**White Hart** ★★
This inn was a posting house; now it's a cozy nest with 20 units and great warmth. (☎ *0647-40406.*)

# OTTERY ST. MARY

**Salston**
Recommended by friends, but I don't know it personally. (☎ *040481-2310.*) They also recommend the **Lodge** for dining.

# PAIGNTON

**Palace**
Offers solid comfort at relatively high cost on the Esplanade Rd. (☎ *0803-55512;* FAX: *527974.*)

# PLYMOUTH

**Mayflower Post House**
Celebrates one of the more famous voyages west from Cliff Rd. About 100 rooms and reasonable quality. (☎ *0752-662828;* FAX: *660974.*)

**Moat House**
Another big-chain operation and also adequate. (☎ *0752-662866.*)

**Duke of Cornwall**
Smaller and with more atmosphere, especially because of its salty location.

### Holiday Inn
A large hotel on Armada Way and as commercial as you might expect. (☎ *0752-662866*; FAX: *673816.*)

## TORQUAY

### Imperial
Vintage 1866—a reliable, vaguely elegant Trusthouse Forte candidate in this very busy resort. The **Regatta** restaurant is exceptional. (☎ *0803-294301*; FAX: *298293.*)

### Manor House ★
More intimate with sea views and some four-poster beds; moderate prices. (☎ *0843-605164*; FAX: *606841.*)

## TOTNES

### Old Forge
Antiquity itself; just a handful of bedchambers and no dining facilities. (☎ *0803-862174.*) A nice excursion would be to the **Carved Angel** at Dartmouth for fine English cookery. (☎ *08043-2465.*)

## WIDECOMBE

### Wooder Manor
With 10 rooms, located on the moor and okay for a brief pause if you need shelter. (☎ *03642-240.*)

## *DORSET*

## BOURNEMOUTH

### Norfolk Royale
Offers about 100 rooms on Richmond Hill. (☎ *0202-21521*; FAX: *299729.*)

### Royal Bath ☆☆
On Bath Rd. and somewhat larger; in the resort mode with excellent cuisine and atmosphere is **Oscar's Restaurant**. (☎ *0202-25555.*) **Tralee** and **Wessex** are other worthy choices.

## CHRISTCHURCH

### Waterford Lodge
Cozy, small, and reasonable. (☎ *04252-72948.*)

## DORCHESTER

### Kings Arms
Seems okay as a midtown choice. (☎ *0305-65353.*)

### Wotton House
Ask about this newcomer on Abinger Common.

### White Hart ★
An attractive 17th-century haven with only 15 rooms. (☎ *0865-340074*; FAX: *341082.*)

# LYME REGIS

### Alexandra
A sea view hotel and my first choice. (☎ *02974-2010.*)

### Mariners
A bit smaller, but equally comfortable. (☎ *02974-2753*; FAX: *2431.*)

# POOLE

### Mansion House                                                         ☆☆
Small and rather costly. Pleasant antique personality with one casual restaurant and another more formal. Service is a bit slow. (☎ *0202-685666.*)

### Hospitality Inn
Larger, routine, and nicely situated on the Quay. (☎ *0202-666800.*)

### Haven                                                                       ☆
On Banks Rd., about 15 minutes out. Refined, but also a bit large for my taste. (☎ *0202-707333.*)

### The Warehouse
For seafood this restaurant comes recommended by Davy Jones himself. Excellent and fun.

# SHAFTESBURY

### Grosvenor
A pleasant stop beside the town common. (☎ *0747-52282*; FAX: *51552.*)

# SHERBORNE

### Post House
Offers a safe tie-up for your Devon wanderings. Prices are upper-moderate. (☎ *0935-813191.*)

# STURMINSTER NEWTON

### Plumer Manor                                                    ★★★
A fine 17th-century house in the Hardy heart of Dorset. The cuisine and hospitality are tops. (☎ *0258-72507.*)

# SWANAGE

### Grand
Features 30 units that are substantial. It's a Best Western link. (☎ *0929-423353.*)

### Suncliffe
Also on the Burlington Rd., modest in price and worthwhile. (☎ *0929-423299.*)

# WAREHAM

### The Priory
On Church Green, a garden setting on the edge of the Frome. I prefer

the Abbotts Cellar—it was a 16th-century priory—to the restaurant called Greenwood. Both provide a fine meal, and the hotel is the last whisper for intimacy. (☎ *0929-552772.*)

## WEYMOUTH

**Prince Regent**
Faces the water from the esplanade. Adequate. (☎ *0305-771313.*)

**Rex**
Also on the esplanade; about the same. (☎ *0305-760400.*)

## WIMBORNE MINSTER

**King's Head**
A small hotel in the middle of the touristic zone. A reasonable choice. (☎ *0202-880101.*)

## *SOMERSET*

## DUNSTER

**Luttrell Arms**
A mine of antiquity not far from the castle itself. (☎ *0643-821555.*)

**Osborne House**
A relative youngster with only 7 rooms bordering Exmoor. (☎ *064382-475.*)

## FROME

**Mendip Lodge**
Just out of town, a pleasant base for dipping into the Mendip Hills. (☎ *0373-63223.*)

## GLASTONBURY

**George & Pilgrims**
Small and a bit costly for its modest offerings, but useful for visiting the Tor and local sites. (☎ *0458-31146;* FAX: *210081.*)

## MINEHEAD

**Periton Park**
Only 7 rooms, and set in a peaceful pocket of nature. Very nice. (☎ *0643-6885.*)

## SHEPTON MALLET

**Bowlish House**
Out on the Wells pike, greeting its few guests from an 18th-century Palladian perch. The place fairly oozes contentment and welcome, from flowered tables to illuminated tapers. The only complaints seem to come from the timber floors that squeak underfoot. A charming, inexpensive spot to pause, dine, and relax. (☎ *0749-342022.*)

# STONEASTON

**Ston Easton Park**                              ☆☆☆☆

A Palladian mansion of majestic proportions on a 200-acre expanse of Somerset terrain—the house itself being far more imposing than the surrounding countryside. It is one of the exceptional manifestations of West Country architecture with high ceilings, broad windows, gorgeous moldings, and the trappings of elegance that can never be recaptured in the present era. It is purely a period piece of the highest caliber. The kitchen work is a meld of English traditional country fare and French delicacy. An indication of its clientele is suggested by the glittering assemblage of Rolls-Royces in front and the occasional private helicopter on the nearby landing pad. (☎ *076121-631.*)

# TAUNTON

**The Castle**                                   ★★★★

Famous for its refined antiquity and superior kitchen. It's just in the heart of things here. (☎ *0823-272671*; FAX: *336066.*)

**Mount Somerset**                               ☆☆

A more costly rural retreat with only about a dozen rooms or suites. (☎ *0823-442500*; FAX: *442900.*)

# WELLS

**Swan**

A comfortable nest on Saddler St. (☎ *0749-78877.*)

**Ancient Gate House**

More modest in price and on the same street. (☎ *0749-72029.*)

# THE ROMANCE OF THE LAKE DISTRICT

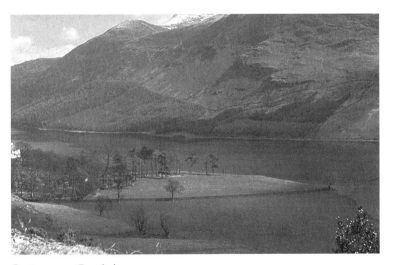

*Buttermere, Cumbria*

It's a small area—only about 30 miles in diameter—but an impressive one. Cumberland, Lancashire, and Westmoreland all lay claim to parts of it. Their pride and jealousy are well understood. Windermere is the largest lake (10.5 miles long) and the highest English mountain in the district is Scarfell Pike. The bracelet of cobalt shimmering waters and green flower fringed hills combine to produce pure magic. The midpoint of the Lake District is more or less at a spot called Easedale Tarn near Grasmere; numerous ridges and dales radiate out of the mountain skein, making it fairly convoluted for point-to-point travel. Nevertheless, it is best to pick a starting site such as Grasmere or perhaps the largest town, Keswick—just a junction with a scattering of hotels. It's in the north sector, but the road network southward heading to Windermere and Kendal is good and fairly swift. The area is a sleepy place even in season, but once cool weather begins, nothing stirs except the current in the electric lines. Many of the lakes can be seen by boat and can be spectacular, especially in spring and autumn. Ask anywhere about these services, which are easy, cheap, and tremendously rewarding. Otherwise, driving and wandering by foot across the ridges is deeply rewarding since distances are relatively short. Day-long walks carry you over wonderous country and waterside, to return to hotel lounges at tea time in the company of other outdoor buffs who have shed their shoes for biscuits and conversation. More serious hikers can huff-and-puff up all the larger hills, with stout shoes, rainwear, and some precaution for bad weather and mist. Still greater challenges await rock climbers, particularly around Wasdale Head and neighboring cliffs.

As in most northern hill regions the rainfall is heavy, averaging more than 100 inches every year in many of the places you will want to visit. Lakes, therefore, become a by-product of the mountains that feed them. Within this microcosm—which looks vast as you walk over it—the geological shape is more like a cupcake with the upper lava crust resembling irregular dollops of icing. In this central zone you'll find Scell Pike, Scafell, Great Gable, and Helvellyn, all at close to 3,000 feet in height, as well as the Langdale spires, which are not so high but certainly are bewitching for their beauty. A bit to the north the well-known Skiddaw and the slightly lower Saddleback are composed of sedimentary elements.

The southern lakes (Windermere, Esthwaite, and Coniston) have an abundant wardrobe of greenery. Their richly fertile vales or tree-clad banks contrast dramatically with the mountains through which the streams pass to fill them; these also have a totally different personality from the more savage landscape that appears to the west. Wastwater and Ennerdale are good examples of this wilder but equally satisfying topography. From a historical point of view, much of the earth movement is a modern drama that ended only around 10,000 years ago. Glaciers performed the basic masonry. They provided the escape routes for the ice and created pools where the melting caps could settle. And nice that they did, too, since the streams often transform into brilliant waterfalls. Lodore, Dungeon Gill, and Piers Gill are glorious examples of such cascades and are best appre-

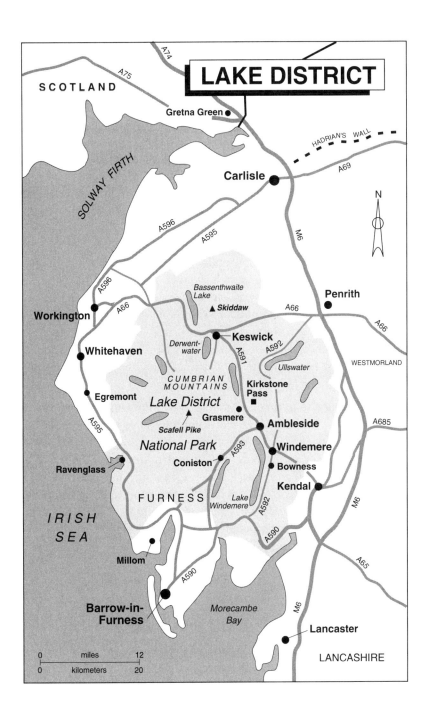

ciated following hard rainfalls, when the show is best and the soundtrack is thunderous.

The Lake District began to be a tourist attraction during the time of the Elizabethans, but only since 1951 has it been protected as a federal preserve. Indeed, there's a unique quality to this small but enchanting park. Some have referred to it as a Switzerland in miniature. Artists by the score have put it to canvas, and countless poets have put it to verse.

An admiring Wordsworth—usually given to fusillades of purple praise—seemed stunned into monumental understatement when he merely called his beloved natural shrine "the loveliest spot that man has ever known"—as forthright and true as from the typewriter of Mr. Ernest Miller Hemingway. Writers, painters, and lovers have all succumbed to its subtle beauty. The countryside and waterside are unrivalled in England. No wonder then that traffic snarls develop on remote mountain lanes in high summer. Never mind; take the next bend to where there are no cars or people in sight; absorb the panoramas across Morecambe Bay, climb one of the isolated fells, or if you are feeling ambitious, the crags; trek in solitude through the Arnside Peninsula, with its multiplicity of smaller streams, ponds, and meres. Then you will know why these hills and mirrored waters became the birthplace of English Romanticism.

For quite a long time city folk accorded the Lake District a rather mediocre press. Daniel Defoe—always sensitive to the forces of nature—did a lot to improve its image. Up to then the outdoors was considered for rustics only. Then Thomas Gray and William Gilpin put the spotlight on the lakes as a new adventure in mankind's awareness program. Wordsworth whomped up excitement for the area as one of England's most important centers of creative writing. After he saw the light he attracted Samuel Coleridge to become a follower and Coleridge in turn lured Robert Southey to its shores. In the 19th century Thomas de Quincey took up residence at Grasmere. John Wilson set up shop—and home—at Windermere. The idea had caught fire. By the next century Hugh Walpole and Constance Holme were in the swim. Ruskin, Shelley, Tennyson, Keats, Faber, the Brontes, Beatrix Potter, and numerous others developed an identity with the region, often incorporating it into their works. Its press had improved. Its future secured.

The Lake District is provided with good connections from major cities for motorists. You can come off the M6 at the eastern flank. Then you can decide to start from a central position such as Grasmere or Ambleside or work your way across the dales on attractive two-lane roads. Once here, however, you should buy a detailed map for the bylanes and trails. Then you also have an extensive network of footpaths. Picnic points and refreshment possibilities exist on many trails. As indicated, climbers usually head for spots such as Wasdale, Great Gable, and Scell Pike. These uplands for summitry also can be attained without the vertical approaches taken by athletic types, but as mentioned, proper shoes and clothing are essential. The best places to buy boots and rainwear would be around Keswick or Windermere. For boating, the bigger lakes (Windermere, Derwentwater) have steamers in summer. These and the smaller lakes often provide launches and a few have windsurf boards. (But don't fall off. The water is freeeezing!)

# IN THE SOUTH
# (OF POETS, STEAMBOATS AND CRITICS)

**Kendal,** on the River Kent, about 3 miles southeast of the National Park, is the largest market town in Westmoreland. Four road bridges cross the river to "Auld Gray Town," as it is known historically. The **parish church,** the oldest part dating from 1200, is unusually large; it features five aisles and a square tower suggesting it has been more important in the past than it would seem today. In the clock tower of the **Town Hall** is a carillon, and if you are invited to the mayor's quarters you will see paintings by George Romney, who died in Kendal; relics of a greater past include the book of devotions that belonged to Catherine Parr—who needed it after her wedding to Henry VIII. The outline of a **Roman fort** can be walked at Watercock; **Castle How** is now only a pre-Norman hump in the Cumbrian turf. The town itself was royally recognized by William I and ceded to Ivo de Taillebois; one part of the castle was passed on to Sir William Parr, an ancestor of Catherine; it was here that the fated damsel was born. Through the passage of time, it finally came to the daughter of Catherine's headstrong husband, Elizabeth I. Alas, all that remains of such glories is the ancient ruins east of town.

In the 14th century, Kendal, like many other English market towns with sheep around, prospered from an abundance of fleece and a global hunger for wool. The regional credo was "Pannus Mihi Panis;" translated, it means "Wool Is My Bread." The rough textile appears in Shakespeare as Kendal Green, not unlike denim is the serge of Nimes in France (*de Nimes*). Oddly, in the 16th century there was a thriving tobacco exchange; textiles (then cotton) were traded for tobacco from the New World. The **Kendal Mint Cake,** frequently a choice of mountaineers, sailors, and explorers on their voyages or expeditions, has been baked and shipped from here since 1869. In the neighborhood, **Elizabeth Levens Hall** offers exotic topiary gardens five miles to the south. In the same area you'll find **Sizergh Castle,** with a 14th-century tower and a Hall dating back to Elizabeth's day.

The biggest drawing card of the district undoubtedly is **Lake Windermere,** the largest lake in England. It hosts the unfathomable total of 20,000 vessels registered here! The town of the same name is settled on the east end of the lake, the chosen spot for boating and sailing for more than a century. Fourteen tiny islets nestle within Lake Windermere; **Belle Island,** a beautiful afterthought, can be visited by boat. And speaking of boats, the **Steamboat Museum** contains a splendid collection of Victorian and Edwardian freshwater vessels. *Dolly,* who first said hello in 1850, is the oldest mechanically powered boat in the world! A pause here can occupy a full morning—or much more if you are a steam freak. Hopping aboard the museum steamer—it can be done from the museum pier—is one of the most sedately pleasurable ways to absorb the beauty of such surroundings. (If the day is cool, the First Mate may make you a cup of tea from the ship's boiler. Delicious too!)

On the western littoral of Windermere stands the 19th-century **Wray Castle** (with lovely grounds), **Graythwaite Hall Gardens** in its Tudor splendor, and a handful of inviting hamlets. **Far Saurey** is one. Then, if you travel on to **Hawkshead,** here is where Wordsworth received his primary education and close to **Sawrey,** the 17th-century **Hill Top Farm** was the happy warren of Beatrix Potter, author of the Peter Rabbit bookshelf. If you are a follower of Peter, Jemima Puddle-Duck, Mrs. Tiggy-Winkle and the Potter family, pop over to **Bowness** where there's a theatre devoted to her Lakeland Tales. Then over at **Hawkshead,** the office of her lawyer husband has been turned into the **Beatrix Potter Gallery.**

**Coniston,** in the midst of enchanting walking country, occupies a magnificent position beneath the savage Yewdale Crags. That early tastemaker, John Ruskin, is buried in the churchyard; an interesting collection of his works can be studied in the **Ruskin Museum** not far from the church. Just north of Coniston is **Tarn Hows,** one of the most captivating forest parks to be found in any wilds; the hills and lightly covered rounded mountains reflect dramatically in the dark waters of deep ponds and wider lakes.

**Coniston Water** could be described as a pint-size Windermere. It was on these still surfaces that sportsman Donald Campbell fearfully sought to break the water speed record in 1967 and, true to his anxieties, met his death with dramatic suddenness. The "Old Man of Coniston" soars high above the lake and valley offering glorious views from its summit; this 2,631-foot mountain is well worth the two-hour scramble if you are stout of limb and willing to climb.

**Ambleside,** five miles from Windermere, is at the heart of the **Lake District National Park.** It is beautifully tucked among the bare hills surrounding the forested valley of Rothay. And for ambles beside the water, well, it was properly named for such pastimes. **Wansfell Pike** is on the east, **Oughridge Fell** on the west, **Rydal Fell** and the ridge below **Snarker Pike** to the north.

Just a bit farther and you can visit **Rydal Mount,** the home of William Wordsworth. This quiet little village provided endless inspiration for him from 1813 until his death in 1850. There were other neighborhood poets such as Coleridge and Southey, but none was linked in print or emotions more closely to the Lake District than Wordsworth. Three of the houses he occupied at various stages of his career are available to visitors; the one at Cockermouth is where he was born; **Dove Cottage**—perhaps the most famous—is located at Grasmere, where he wrote avidly from 1799 to 1808; about 10 minutes away is **Rydal Mount,** where he spent his twilight years. The last two residences contain some of the poet's books, pictures, and effects and are, therefore, more compelling.

The village and lake of **Grasmere** share the same name, both being popular holiday targets. The settlement lies near the head of the lake into which the Rothay River flows. Tourists also pour in during the summer months, when the tranquility at some moments seems to be ebbing away forever. But simply drive or walk a few minutes toward the surrounding woodlands of **Rydal Fell, Fairfield, Loughrigg Fell,** or **Silver How** and you will regain the peace of the valley. The above mentioned **Dove Cottage** was the home of William and Dorothy Wordsworth during intervals of the author's most productive years. The Dove cote, incidentally, also had homing instincts for fellow author Thomas de Quincey. Today it is a Wordsworth museum; his tomb, along with that of Coleridge, is in the ancient churchyard of **St. Oswald.** Grasmere's only fault is that it is simply too beautiful, and the penalty is its loss of composure at certain times of the year. During the fringe months when only a few residents are on hand, it can be blissful.

## IN THE EAST

Leaving Windermere on the A-592, you'll arrive at **Troutbeck,** which is dominated to the north by the Kirkstone Pass and the peaks shouldering either side of it. A **Yeoman's House** of the 17th century can be seen at the outskirts of the village; the roof, chimney, steps, and windows are typical of the cottage architecture of the time. At the other end you can refresh body and soul at **The Mortal Man,** a 17th-century inn often cheered by the yeomen and lasses of today.

Driving over the pass you come to **Patterdale** and **Glenridding** on the southern end of Ullswater, both being excellent centers for walkers. To the southwest is **Hellvellyn,** the third highest peak in the Lake District. The scramble by foot to the top takes a full 3-1/2 hours, but the views are magnificent. **Ullswater,** incidentally, is my own favorite lake of the region. It is more remote than Windermere and Grasmere, so far less traffic troops to its shores. At the foot of Hellvellyn is **Thirlmere,** a reservoir that also contains Ullswater within its system. This is the second largest of the lakes, with ideal conditions for sailing and fishing. On its shores is **Gowbarrow Park,** Wordsworth's inspiration field for "Daffodils."

From **Pooley Bridge** (at the entry end) you can rent a private vessel, or tour boats putt-putt around the shore to explore the sights. Not too far away is the fantastic **Aira Force** waterfall, and just above Pooley Bridge is **Martindale** with its great forest abundantly populated by red deer. Ullswater—to orientate you once again—is the southern watershed of the Lake District only 9 miles northeast of Barrow-in-Furness.

The **Church of St. Mary's,** founded way back in 1111, is worth a look-see even if you're in the district more for nature than for architecture. (Church-going for the tourist is akin to herrings to the Finn or apples for the American: At least one a day keeps the doctor away.) This one retains the original (Transitional) south door but is mainly Perpendicular in concept; the altar tomb of 1588 is noteworthy too. **Swarthmoor Hall,** former home of George Fox and an important landmark for the Quaker movement, is in the care of the Society of Friends. The **Lighthouse Monument** on Hoad Hill is to the memory of Sir John Barrow, the explorer, who was born in the parish.

A short drive brings you to **Penrith,** which was the capital town more than 1000 years ago. The 14th-century **castle** is, alas, but a ruin today. Don't despair, however. **The Gloucester Arms,** dating from 1477, is still alive and thriving. It is one of the oldest inns in England, having given shelter to Richard III in its heyday. The **Town Hall** offers only an 18th-century pedigree, but the **church** goes way back and features two rather peculiar creations in stone. **Giant's Grave** and **Giant's Thumb.** Legend tells us that they honor His Royal Highness Owen, the Liege of Cumbria in 920. His tomb is readily understood but his prehensile disposition is still a mystery.

A medieval span leads to the little hamlet of **Eamont Bridge** residing, of course, on the Eamont River. Here there is a prehistoric earthwork about the size of a football field that is inaccurately known as **King Arthur's Round Table.** The neighboring 100-acre **park** is open for viewing deer, rare breeds of sheep and cattle, European mammals, and a host of other animals.

If you are planning to return to Kendal, stop at **Shap,** one of the loftiest points in this range. Those mountains you see around you belong to the comically named **High Street** family. Within the vale are the ruins of **Shap Abbey,** created by canons around 1191.

## THE NORTH LAKELANDS

**Keswick** is one of the most popular tourist magnets. The town was formed on the River Greta close to Derwentwater and is embraced by an almost alpine range of hills. **Moot Hall** and **Greta Hall** (once the home of Coleridge and later of Southey) are the in-town attractions, while outside the village a collection of 48 enormous stones in two configurations make up the megalithic monument known as **Castlerigg Circle,** always a drawing card. Locals have debated their significance for thousands of years and, of course, the mystery has bred no end of speculation and legend to keep visitors entertained over the centuries. The many poets who admired Keswick in print or in private are remembered in the **Fitz Park Museum.** For outdoor souvenirs, **Friar's Crag** and **Castle Head** are excellent spots for photography.

**Derwentwater,** not far away, is within a chalice of tall mountain peaks. The broad lake features pods of trees to break the uniformity; it is outlined by a 2-mile nature trail along the shoreline. On the western bank are **Lingholm Gardens,** the house serving as the home of Lord Rochdale. Daffodils dominate in spring, yielding to explosions of rhododendron and azaleas in the later summer months. **Lodore Cascade** is an extraordinary show too. The glittering waterfalls are at the southern rim of Derwentwater. Southey referred to the Falls of Lodore in his verse.

The magnificent birches of **Grange-in-Borrowdale** and **Rosthwaite** deserve a place in literature too—or at least a place in your itinerary. They are spectacular in the sunlight. Then drive toward **Buttermere** via Honister Pass. This cozy little village lies between the lakes of Buttermere and Crummock. **Scale Force,** diving more than 15 stories into a glade, is often called the most beautiful waterfall in the Lake District. (Well, the Tourist Office thinks so.) It is accessible via a footpath. Indeed, many walkers and climbers pursue their sport in this region.

Moving north alongside Crummock Water brings you to **High Lorton**. Here you turn east onto the B-5292 and begin the easy ascent to **Whinlatter Pass.** You'll soon find the shaded canopy of **Thornthwaite Forest** and start descending to **Braithwaite.** It is from this point that the sporty types lace up their boots to conquer **Grizedale Pike,** not exactly Everest but still a respectable 2,593-feet high. When you join the A-66 to **Bassenthwaite Lake** you'll drive along the peaceful, flat waterside road, which then opens to face some of the highest mountains in the area; this is the Skiddaw group.

Where the rivers Cocker and Derwent join there's the wonderfully ancient and still thriving town of **Cockermouth.** The Normans constructed a great fort here, but time has left only a remnant—and part of that came from an earlier Roman fortification. Georgian buildings enhance its broad main street. Wordsworth was born here, and much of the house, which was built in 1745, remains unchanged from its original form.

# GOING WEST

## *(TO CLIMBING COUNTRY AND MAN-MADE BEAUTY)*

From Ambleside you can follow the natural upward contours west over a pass that brings you to **Eskdale**. Alternatively, if driving from **Keswick** or **Cockermouth,** you can head for **Larton** and **Loweswater.** En route you'll come to **Ennerdale Water,** the loneliest lake in the region. That is quite a favorable statement now that so many areas of the Lake District are jammed with hikers, buses, and roving cars. This is inspirational walking country—across the fells and over to **Ennerdale Forest.** Between Larton and Loweswater are **Wasdale** and **Wastwater.** The latter is the deepest of the English lakes. To the east you'll see the misty tops of rugged Scafell and Scafell Pike rising majestically.

**Scafell Pike** from any direction is serious business for a climber. Its many faces along with those of its neighbor, are demanding; the cliffs before the approach to the summit are among the most challenging in Britain. In fog or mist there can be increased danger; even the beginner's trail is only safe in good weather. Wasdale Head offers the easiest ascent from the camp site at the head of Wastwater. If you opt for the southern route, Hard Knott and Wrynose passes are quite steep.

A well-marked spur leads over to **Duddon Valley.** This is one of the least known in the system—lacking in lakes but abounding in quiet wooded tracts, flowing streams, and breathtaking views of the high fells. From **Duddon Bridge** there are narrow and twisting lanes providing many picnic spots; take the path to the stepping stones of the Low Cragg Gorge heading west. This valley has two almost secret beauties; lakes that can only be approached on foot: **Seathwaite Tarn** and **Devoke Water.**

**Hard Knott Pass** is nearly 1,300 feet above sea level; near the top you'll find a stone wall and the ancient outline of a Roman fortification that commands the scenery all about you. Obviously, this was ideal as a military post. Down below is **Eskdale,** a dale with a dual character—soothing and gentle at its nadir and brutal and spectacular at its upper reaches. Here the river plunges between the Scafell and Bow Fell. The **Stanley Ghull Nature Trail** will lead you into the verdant lowlands and beside a 60-foot waterfall called **Stanley Force.** From Eskdale Green, a short drive brings you to Wastwater, set in some of the most dramatic scenery in the Lake District.

If you tire of motoring, you can hop aboard a train from **Dalegarth Station** and relax through beautiful countryside to arrive at **Ravenglass**. Its coastal position at the mouth of three rivers once made it a port; tourism is now its main industry. Access to the **Ravenglass Nature Reserve,** the largest breeding colony of black-headed gulls in Europe, is by permit only—unless, of course, you happen to have feathers and a black head.

There are both a Nature Trail and a "tree trail" within the grounds of **Muncaster**; also you'll see a 13th-century fortress with a 14th-century peel tower built on the site of the Roman fort of **Glannavenia**—obviously conceived because of its commanding position over the Esk estuary. Now it overlooks a relentless attack of rhododendron. The castle, with its plethora of oils, furniture, stonework, and textiles, will keep your eyes busy for hours.

**Furness Abbey** is a frequent choice of visitors to the Lake District. You'll find it—possibly with trepidation—by entering the "Vale of Deadly Nightshade" 20 minutes from the old town of **Ulverstone.** It used to be one of the most generously endowed religious institutions in the land, its roots having been planted by King Steven in the early 12th century. Some parts are intact today, but the nave and several other features have collapsed. The Cloister is especially attractive. It is easy to imagine the busy atmosphere it enjoyed under its Benedictine administration. Even as a ruin, the tall rose-tinted stones evoke an air of taste, nobility, and achievement.

**Birdoswald** is one of the best locations along the 73 miles of Hadrian's Wall to view the energetic Roman construction. On the entire stretch there were 27 major fortifications, and here you can observe a pair of portals and an early watchtower. Ask locally for directions.

Early man seemed to have a passion for stone circles in this nation. Stonehenge is only the most famous ring, but many places had them. **Castlerigg** is about 35 strides across and features 39 monoliths called the **Keswick Carles.** You come upon them almost as a surprise—which adds to the wonder.

**Haweswater** is one of the most enchanting lakes in the entire watershed. Just try to ignore the fact that every drop is artificially held by a man-made dam. Since it is a reservoir, the water authorities have put in some roads that afford spectacular panoramas. Try the one from Brampton to Haweswater Beck. You'll probably find a ranger who can show you some of the best walking trails up to the ridge. Again, do this only in good weather and with proper footwear.

**Johnny's Wood.** I never found out who Johnny is (or was), but his terrain is breathtaking and the forest floor is alive with flora and hospitable fauna. The shade provides an unusual carpet of ferns, and the rills and cascades are bordered by jackets of moss.

**Lanercost Priory** was borrowed from the Romans. They had built a wall somewhat to the north, and this provided the building blocks for this centuries-old institution. (Could this then be Borrow-dale stone? Ouch!) In any case, a parish church has been composed of pink and gray—all of it lovingly carved by non-pagan hands. Take the trouble to go inside to enjoy this early Christian inspiration.

**Langdale Pikes.** Pikes, traditionally were a British weapon, but these geographical pikes produced axes. You might find one if you poke through the rocks of Stickle Pike, where prehistoric man fashioned his first axes and even developed a sort of European commerce in trading them for other products. From Great Langdale Beck a small feeder road leads up to the rockslide, but you'd better ask for directions to Langdale and Stickle to be sure.

**Longsleddale** is another secret patch of wondrous English real estate that should be seen but often isn't. It's not difficult to find either since it is a cul-de-sac on a spur off the busy road (A-6) between Keswick and Windermere. (Watch out for the Watchgate turnoff.)

The **Northern Fells**—the Highlands of the Lake District, is seldom visited by the bus tours. The Romantic English poets usually disported themselves in the south. Only John Peel—a bit dour for coach lectures—is associated with **Caldbeck**, where he was born and where he rests today. If you are not in a hurry, go up to **Uldale, Mosedale,** or **Hesket** to begin your explorations. These fells are not markedly different from the lower ones, but the absence of human activity imparts a special mood and beauty that is rarely experienced in the hustle of the modern touristic whirl.

**St. Bees Head**. Have you ever seen a puffin in the wild? Here they populate the rocky outcrops and chatter away with other feathered cliffhangers. It is a joy to watch them in flight and in residence among the crags. Most are surprisingly tame and tolerate humans nearby. Both the St. Bees Head lighthouse and the beach are ideal and inspirational spots for a picnic. If you are a serious walker, here is one of the starting blocks for a trail that links the Irish seacoast at Solway Firth with the North Seacoast—quite a hike. A moderately vigorous stroll along the seawall can occupy most of one day. From here it is not far by the inner road (Cockermouth) or the coastal road (Workington) to Carlisle in the north.

## *CARLISLE—THE FRONTIER CITY*

Carlisle is 300 miles north of London and 9 miles south of Scottish turf, more or less along the line of Hadrian's Wall. The River Eden bathes its doorstep, and both roads and rails pass through it on the important north-south route. The Romans maintained a fortified camp at Petriana (now in the suburb of Stanwix); this cavalry squadron of 1,000 mounts was the advance patrol at the time of the Wall. In later generations **Carlisle Castle** was created out of stone brought from Petriana. William Rufus announced that the city would be English henceforth from 1092, then hastened to give meaning to his words with a great fortress and his own set of defense walls. Five centuries later Henry VIII put his own military imprimatur onto the masonry due to the growing use of artillery. The citadel was constructed as a subsidiary fortification. Later on Elizabeth I fluffed it up a bit to accommodate Mary Queen of Scots, who fled from Scotland. She walked into Carlisle Castle as a guest and was carried out as an enemy of the state—to await execution elsewhere.

Only the castle keep is of any interest now. The longest siege endured was that of General Alexander Leslie, Earl of Levens, in 1644. It was then that almost two thirds of the cathedral nave and much of the cloisters were pulled down to repair damage done to the castle and walls. A century later the city fell again, this time to Bonnie Prince Charlie, the Young Pretender. Toward the end of the 18th century the prosperity of the town burgeoned with the development of the railway. The **Newcastle-Carlisle Railway** (1835) was the first east-to-west line in England, and it opened an explosive period of trade and travel.

**Carlisle Cathedral,** one of the smallest in England, was born from the faith and enterprise of William II. Much of the building was razed twice by fire: in 1292 and 1392. Today merely the bays of the Norman nave remain, its arches still warped by the effects of the ages. This serves as a memorial chapel to the valiant soldiers of the Border Regiment. The choir reveals unusually delicate 15th-century woodwork. It has some particularly well wrought misericords and a small head (carving, that is) of Henry IV at about the time of his death. The colossal East Window is replete with tracery of the Decorated period, a masterpiece of craftsmanship still containing some of the glass installed late in the 14th century. Sir Walter Scott had the good taste (as usual) to be married here in 1797.

The city can take up a lot of your time usefully if you visit the **Town Hall** of 1717, the **Courthouses,** the 14th-century **Guildhall,** and **Tullie House** (1682), a fabulous collection of items from the Roman occupation and a zipless counterpoint in its museum of contemporary art. Fragments of the city wall remain, and there is a market cross, vintage 1682. The town's corporation plate is curious; it features a pair of 16th-century racing bells, the original trophy awarded for horse racing in this realm of everlasting equine pride.

A day's drive can take you into Scotland, Northumberland, or the Lake District, but if you are only going to be here briefly, drive out to **Hadrian's Wall,** which extends from Wallsend in the east to Bowness on the Solway Firth in the west. Aulus Platorius Nepos was dispatched to this frontier by Hadrian in A.D. 122 and commenced the 73-mile wall, which he completed a decade later. The purpose, of course, was defense against the northern raiders. With fire beacons at strategic points, it served as an early warning system, and troops could be sent along the wall to trap the marauders. Originally it was 10 feet thick and 20 feet high; today, the highest existing structure reaches only close to head height. The most interesting construction is between **Chollerford** and **Greenhead,** within the Northumberland National Park. Chollerford also offers a well-preserved fort known as **Chesters,** designed for a cavalry unit of some 500 men. Overall, the defense incorporated 5500 cavalry and 13,000 infantry. It once bristled with as many as 27 major forts along its length as well as a series of milecastles (a fort every Roman mile, 1620 yards), turrets, and signal towers. Another section of the wall that's worth a visit is between **Lanercost** and **Gilsland**. As if to ignore the pagan influence, the **Church at Chollerton,** just 3 miles east, has monolithic Roman columns on the south arcade and a Roman altar used as a font.

**Gretna Green** was formerly the lusty target for overheated romancers who scooted up here to marry. (Close to the Scottish border, it's a neighbor of Carlisle.) The local blacksmith performed the nuptials. Scottish law required no witnesses. The town has ceased to be of use in the marriage game, but it still carries a comic impact in British vaudeville and music hall antics.

Just to provide a quick review of the surrounding sites if your excursions only commence from Carlisle, at **Birdoswald** there is one of the major **Roman forts**. Near **Banks** there are several important sites, including a milecastle, and apart from the wall there are fine houses, castles, and churches of interest. **Carby Castle** is a splendid mansion set in beautiful grounds. Another is **Featherstone Castle**, built around a courtyard, dating from the 13th century. **Bellister Castle** is a 17th-century house, but most impressive is the richly endowed **Naworth Castle,** dating from the 14th century. It has a great hall, oratory, and exceptional ancient tapestries. It can be visited by arrangement. There is a superb Norman church at **Warwick Bridge,** a lovely little one at **Talkin,** and a particularly fine one at **Haltwhistle** for quick prayer stops along your way. **Lanercost,** remember, has the remains of a priory that was built with stones from Hadrian's Wall.

# WHERE TO STAY AND EAT

## AMBLESIDE

### Langdale Chase Hotel

Only a skip from Windermere, and one of the most panoramic vantage points in the Lake District. Stubbornly Victorian in its old-fashioned atmosphere; enough wood carvings to have kept 100 whittlers busy for 20 years; buckle-bending teas for hikers' appetites; 36 rooms and 20 baths; the Boathouse, the prime buy, is closed Dec. 8-Feb. 1. We like the garden and the kindness, but some pilgrims may find the decor as overpowering as a 3-week holiday in Hagia Sophia. Otherwise warmly recommended. (☎ *09663-2201.*)

### Low Wood

On the outskirts, and a fair bet for budgeteers; it has 141 bedchambers; bid for the newest ones. (☎ *0966-33338.*)

## CARLISLE

### Crown and Mitre

Reigns supreme at this key hub on the road to Scotland. Coffee shop for light bites; cranberry-colored Belowstairs Restaurant accurately named and adequately provisioned; Edwardian Peace & Plenty Pub; Jonesian Railway Tavern. The front singles were minuscule; others, however, were spaciously sized and flairfully outfitted. (☎ *0228-25491.*)

### Crest

A smart alternate choice and a bit more expensive. (☎ *0228-31201.*)

### Farlam Hall

Near Brampton, 9 miles from Carlisle and nestled in 4-1/2 acres of walled gardens. Distinguished dining salon facing a pond and meadows; superior English traditional furnishings in its 11 rooms, all with bath. A nice piece of Cumbria run by ingratiating people for surprisingly low tariffs. Odd closing times in winter, so be sure to reserve ahead. (☎ *06976-234.*)

## COCKERMOUTH

### Globe

On the main street with 30 nice units. (☎ *0900-822126*; FAX: *823705.*)

## CONISTON

### The Sun

This spot in Cumbria shines best. It's small and pleasant. (☎ *05394-41248.*)

# GRASMERE

### Michael's Nook Country House

Something rather special in the region. Reservations are an absolute must, and to be privileged to ingest even a morsel in its refined sanctum sanctorum you had better be a resident guest or reserve at least a meal in advance; stragglers are decidedly unwanted here. The 10 rooms are pleasant and rich with touches of Victoriana, especially the baths, which are studies in polished brass and nickel. A pompous period piece that is beautifully maintained but of dubious value to well-meaning travelers who might not be greeted warmly here. (☎ 09665-496.)

### Wordsworth

Very attractive in a more commercial way. (☎ 09665-592.)

### Prince of Wales

My next choice. (☎ 09665-666.)

# KENDAL

### Woolpack

In the middle of the town on Stricklandgate, with 53 rooms. (☎ 0539-723852.)

# KESWICK

### Armathwaite Hall

One of the most imposing sylvan retreats in the entire Lake District, but complaints have been arriving of late. Venerable estate 7-1/2 miles out of town, at the north end of Bassenthwaite Lake; beautiful green apron sloping to the water's edge; L-shape castle; baronial furnishings; closed Nov.-April. Let's hope it remains on top. (☎ 059-681551.)

### Castle Inn

Personally run year-rounder, also up at the Keswick end of the lake. Crossroads situation; clean, attractive appointments; modest rates. For motorists in search of a cozy 1-night hitching post.

### Lodore Swiss ☆☆☆

On the outskirts across the road from Bassenthwaite Lake, this hotel generates a younger, more spritely aura. Building in gray Borrowdale stone; heated swimming pool; 2 saunas; 2 gyms; sun lounge; masseuse; tennis court; dancing twice weekly; nursery with resident nanny. Fresh, well-appointed public rooms; cheerful bar; waterfront dining salon; La Cascade Grill; 73 comfortable accommodations and 65 baths. (☎ 059-684285; FAX: 684343.)

### Keswick

Smack-dab beside the old station. Lovely manicured garden; 75 bedchambers in a mansion that is again seeing better days. (☎ 07687-72020; FAX: 71300.)

### Royal Oak

Open year-round. Careful maintenance; basic but pleasant enough especially in its newer nests. (☎ *0596-72965.*)

### George

This hotel reeks with antiquity, among other things; nice people, however. (☎ *07687-72076.*)

### Derwentwater

An excellent position, but an invasion of bus tours spoils its peace. (☎ *07687-72538.*)

## PENRITH

### North Lakes Gateway

A viewful 85-room haven on Ullswater Rd. Prices are steep, but the rewards are fair. (☎ *0768-68111*; FAX: *68291.*)

### George

You can pay about half as much; it has fewer units; look for it on Devonshire St. (☎ *0768-62696.*)

## POOLEY BRIDGE

### Swiss Chalet

A small, moderately priced stop by this crossroads at the end of Ullswater Lake. (☎ *08536-215.*)

## ULLSWATER

### Sharrow Bay                                    ☆☆☆☆☆

On the quiet far side of Ullswater Lake—just beyond Pooley Bridge, this hotel commands sweeping vistas of water and hillscape that resemble the best of the Scottish highlands. Sleep is divided between the main Country House and neighboring outbuildings, all rather limited in the space of the accommodations but nevertheless comfortable if not somewhat prissy. In fact, throughout the various parts, a prodigious sneeze in the many porcelain-filled precincts could cause a crockery disaster of national significance. Dining rooms (smoking and non) are in the main house, with the cocktail hour and meal established at a set time. The delicate and variegated gastronomy is world famous—as prolific as that ordained for a 16th-century monarch's feast. Proprietors Francis Coulson and Brian Sack are the souls of professional skill and hospitality. A high spot among the fells. (☎ *08536-301.*)

### Leeming                                        ☆☆☆☆

On a hill overlooking the water at the far end of Ullswater, is one of the biggest catches in any of the lakes. Its front apron slopes down to a forest of cypress, fir, and pine trees; exquisite, refined regency dining room with French blue ceiling and gilt trim; viewful lounges with open fires for cooler days; elegant public rooms; 17 bedchambers, most with private bath; no telephones, but a call system and radio in each unit. (☎ *07684-86622*; FAX: *86443.*)

### Howtown

On the same lake beyond Sharrow Bay, lodge style, designed mainly for long-staying visitors. Dark woody bar; dining room with hearth, oils, and pewter plates; lots of horse brass, copper, stuffed foxes, antlers, and other hunt thematics. No private baths for its 16 units; a pair of 2-bedroom cottages for self-catering; reasonable rates. A 4-night hitch is par.

## WINDERMERE

### Miller Howe ☆☆☆☆☆

On a hillock above the somewhat busier Lake Windermere. In the local dialect "Howe" is similar to the French "chez"—and a lovely home it is, with its excellent antique furnishings, paintings, prints, and scenes of early lakeside life. Almost half of its 13 rooms face the greensward and waterfront, some with private balcony. Chef-Patron John Tovey produces a cuisine that rates among the finest in the land. An oasis of gentility, taste, and calm. (☎ *09662-2536.*)

### Belsfield ★★★

Sprawls scenically over the side of a gardened knoll facing the lake. (☎ *09662-2448.*)

### Old England

This hotel has slipped largely because of its convention trafficking. Nice terrace above the water overlooking the small boat docks; mixture of Victorian and Flash Gordon appointments; modern lakefront wing bringing capacity up to the 100 mark, the latest of which are the best. (☎ *09662-2444*; FAX: *3432.*)

### The Hydro

Big and rambling, but some regency touchups have helped; it specializes in group traffic. (☎ *09662-4455.*)

### St. Martin's

Across from Old England, a tiny, clean, economy stop.

### Beech Hill

A recommendable hideaway of about 50 rooms on the Newby Bridge Rd. (☎ *09662-2137*; FAX: *3745.*)

# DISCOVERING THE MIDLANDS— AND ON TO THE NORTH

*Old fashioned ways in England*

As if it were a contradiction in terms, there is no middle range, exact median, nor precise boundary for the Midlands. It's an amorphous central district composed of a mixed bag of counties, each and every one of them varying significantly in character, climate, customs, history, landscape, sightseeing lures, and distinctive buildings. As you might imagine, there are muscular industrial areas, some of the towns seeming rather dreary, especially in inclement weather—not too rare a commodity here. Shires like Cheshire and Lancashire, on the other glance, combine to offer you a glittering visit to remember. These regions boast the most beautiful and wild countryside, providing a dramatic backdrop for the delightful villages and traditional mill towns dotting the valleys. The region lives and breathes an exciting heritage, proud of its historic towns, museums, stately homes, and castles. Many thoughtless visitors probably bypass the area on their way to York, the Lake District, or Scotland. Yet there are several communities full of interest and areas of awesome scenery. Let's look at a selection of the Midland highlights.

## ANTIQUITY IN LINCOLNSHIRE

**Lincoln** is situated 135 miles north of London, its great Cathedral looking down from the banks of the River Witham. So much of regional history centers on this great house of worship; it would be a sin of omission to miss it. The site of this city was occupied by the Romans and later developed by the Normans as an administrative center. Today it is a hub of important heavy engineering, being vital to the British economy

**Newport Arch** is a remnant of early importance, one of the declarative statements of Roman design and building techniques in England. The great central arc was flanked by two smaller ones, one of which remains standing today at North Gate. An extensive collection of Latin antiques can be found in the **City and County Museum**. Most visitors see only the Cathedral, but try to include **St. Mary-le-Wigford** and **St. Peter-at-Gowts**, two fine old churches in the High Street. The town is in Saxon-Norman style, probably dating back to the 11th century. **Lincoln Castle**, west of the cathedral, was the bastion of William the Conqueror. There are a few remains of castles in this area; those of **Lincoln** and **Tattershall** are the ones most often toured by sightseers.

The crowning glory of Lincoln, of course, is its famous **Cathedral**, consecrated in 1092. It contains the earliest gothic style still in existence, with many adjustments from the massive Norman work on the west front to the late Norman expressions elsewhere in the towers. The three original spires collapsed in the 16th century; one was said to be the highest in the world at that time and was made of wood. The present central tower houses the enormous bell, **Great Tom of Lincoln**, weighing more than five tons. The Library was designed by Christopher Wren; scores of travelers troop in to see the original **Magna Carta**, which was signed by King John in 1215. It also houses first editions of *Paradise Lost*, *Don Quixote*, and *The Faerie Queene*.

Numerous attractive buildings can be found in the narrow medieval streets. In the close (**Minster Yard**) there is a **tithe barn** of 1440 and an ancient **Bishop's Palace**. As a change of faith, there is also the **Jew's House**, dating from the 12th century, and **Aaron's House**, which the local tourist

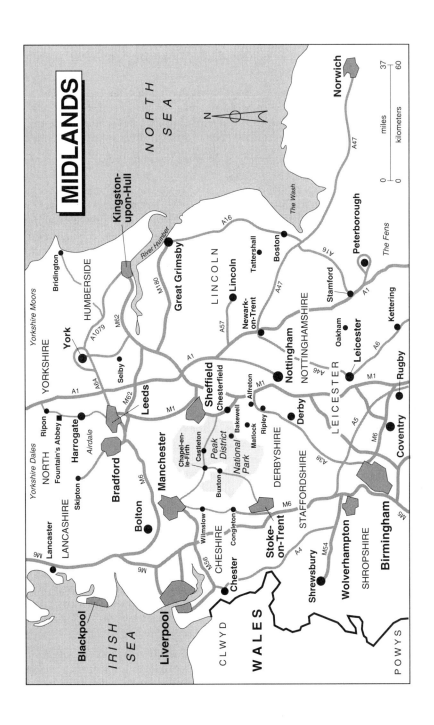

office sincerely avows is the oldest building in the nation that is still occupied—a record of some kind. High Street is lined with timber-framed 16th-century dwellings. To the south and east lies a fertile area of farmland and fens, the flat monotony of which is broken by pretty villages of honey-colored stone.

**Stamford**, a greystone market town, has resided for centuries on the River Welland, the handsome aquatic boundary between Lincolnshire and Northamptonshire. Its history is often tied in with the fortunes of the Cecil tribe.

Lord Burghley, the creator of **Burghley House** in 1577, was a powerful factor in the region. Its superb rooms shimmer with priceless works of art only to be outshone by its antique furnishings. Elizabeth I slept here, her bedroom preserved intact and unused since. The minarets and spires are simply silly; the landscaping by Capability Brown is everlastingly beautiful. **The Burghley Tombs** are located in **St. Martin's Church,** certainly worth seeing. The town, incidentally, seems filled with important religious buildings such as the Benedictine **Priory of St. Leonard**, built in the seventh century, **All Saints** and **St. Mary's** churches, a **Carmelite monastery,** and the fascinating almshouse known as **Browne's Hospital.** Don't miss any of these.

The **George Hotel** was originally a coaching inn of the 14th century. Part of the Old Town wall can be seen at the Baskan in West Street. St. George's Square is the noble showcase of several old houses, including one which has been constantly occupied since 1350. (So argue with Aaron in Lincoln, if you don't believe me.)

**Spalding** is famous as the U.K.'s "Netherland." From the fields of tulips, swampy marshland, and fens in the southeast of the country, you might feel as if you've stepped over into Holland. The abundance of windmills adds to this impression. Early April is best for the daffodils; from then until mid-May is the time for tulips—provided the season is normal.

Tracking your way farther north, you'll come to the town of **Boston**, the home of the Pilgrim Fathers. Browsing around its **Guildhall,** you can sense even today the mood of oppression felt by America's ancestors in 1607. Another fascinating experience is the climb to the top of the **Boston Stump** in **St. Botolph**; the church's lantern tower provides extensive views of the countryside. Not far away is **Belvoir Castle,** from the 11th century; it was destroyed by fire and rebuilt in 1816. Within are great works of art—Holbeins, Reynolds, Gainsboroughs, and some of the finest tapestries in the country. Be sure to see the elegant State Room, its remarkable Regimental Museum, and the surrounding gardens, which are outstanding.

**Leicester**, a university town, is on the Soar River, 96 miles above London. The troops of Latium seem to have employed a lot of their energy here. Roman occupation is in evidence at the **Jewry Wall** as well as the grand **Public Baths.** Modern tourism—bless its heart—might have been born in this city. In 1841, Thomas Cook organized the first excursion by rail from Leicester to Loughborough and back. Things took off after that.

Of the town's prominent sights, **Chantry House** dates back to 1511, the **Guildhall** is late 14th century, while the **Court Houses** were active in the 17th century. **Charnwood Forest** is northwest of the city; higher parts of it are barren due to the slate and volcanic ash of the past. This same action created a rich valley full of marvelous flora. A short drive up the B-5327 brings you to the beautiful 850-acre Bradgate Park. **Bradgate House,** now unfortunately in ruins, was the birthplace of Lady Jane Grey, who was eventually executed by Mary Tudor. Both her neck and her crown got the chop.

**Oakham** is the heartland of the British hunt—rolling hills, **Rutland Water** (a linkage of lovely man-made lakes), and nonstop communion with the totally bewitching environment. In the village you'll find the **Buttercross** (a covered market), the ominous **Stocks**, and an engaging museum of old farm implements. **Oakham Castle** features a pedigree harking to the 12th century. The **Great Hall** is merely a shell of secular architecture, but peculiar in that every peer who has passed through the parish has always left a horseshoe—some gilded, some colossal in size, some beautifully fashioned—to decorate its walls as a gesture of good fortune.

## ROBIN HOOD'S NOTTINGHAMSHIRE

**Nottingham** is an industrial old-timer fed by the abundant waters of the Trent. **St. Mary's Hill** was an early British earthwork, the caves having been used as dwellings. These grottoes—part man-made, part natural—were hewn and fashioned out of the easily worked Bunter sandstone of **Castle Rock**. The most popular hollow is called the **Trip to Jerusalem Inn**, crafted in the year 1189. Most of it is inside Castle Rock, together with a whole brewery that has been operating for centuries. The rock on which the castle stands is in the south of the city upon a cliff, which looms over far more conventional earthlings below.

**St. Mary's Church** is Perpendicular in style, the tower rising gracefully into the skies to be seen and admired for miles. **St. Peter's** is the oldest one in the city, going back probably to the 12th century while the cathedral, **St. Barnabas**, is almost a Johnny-Come-Lately—arriving as recently as 1844. Other interesting targets might include the **Costume Museum**, **Brewhouse Yard**, and **Shire Hall**. The 16th-century **Wollaton Hall and Park** today serve as the Natural History Museum. The first machine for making looped and knitted fabrics was developed in Nottingham. Later came spinning frames. Out of these inventions grew its fame as a lace-making and hosiery town. The original location of the colorful lace market is today a zone of bars and restaurants, but related textile industries spread throughout the region.

To the north, **Newstead Abbey** beckons romantics to the ancestral home of Lord Byron. Housed within are relics of a very poetic past and tributes to Dr. Livingstone, who stayed here in 1864. The only parts of the original building that have withstood time are the West Front, the Cloisters, and Chapter House.

South of Nottingham at **Radcliffe-on-Trent** is **Holme Pierrepont,** a brick medieval manor and courtyard garden. Within there is a fine assemblage of 17th-century English oak furniture and other collections running from the 16th to the present century. The grounds surrounding the Hall and its estate are extensive. This is a pleasant excursion from the city hubbub. Conservationists can applaud how beautifully a once ugly gravel quarry could be resurrected as an asset to nature.

**Southwell** draws most visitors to admire its **Minster,** with origins going back to the seventh century. What you will see today, however, was started only about 800 years ago. The carvings are splendid. Look at the 14th-century stone rood screen and the flower work on the doors of the Chapter House. The precision has remained clear even till today. You'll also note twin spires that feature unique pyramidal roofs. Pause for a pint at the **Saracen's Head** in town; Charles I spent his last night as a free man under its roof.

**Newark** is a market town that was once owned (way back in 1055) by Lady Godiva. It lies on the navigable River Trent. The original **Castle** was started in 1123 and replaced about half a century later. The Gate House and West Tower stand today, but most of the fortification was destroyed by Cromwell. The cathedral-like church of **St. Mary Magdalene,** one of the grandest in the country, is composed of several architectural expressions from various periods. It boasts one of the largest 14th-century brasses in the country and a much admired 16th-century oak screen. If you are in the cobbled market square, the **Town Hall** (18th century) was the castle where King John expired—of overeating. Also of interest in this immediate vicinity are the **White Hart Inn** and the **Clinton Arms,** where overindulgence is not unknown either.

**Eastwood** was the birthplace of the author D.H. Lawrence. You will see his humble beginnings—an ordinary miner's home—as it was in 1885.

## PILGRIM'S REGRESS

American visitors frequently are interested in tracing the origins of early settlers to the New World. These might involve visiting some of the villages where the Separatist Movement took root. William Brewster, for instance, one of the pillars of the Pilgrim Movement, began his adventure at **Scrooby**. William Bradford, the governor of Plymouth Colony, was born in a manor house at **Ansterfield**. **Blyth**, **Bawtry**, and **Babworth** are other hamlets with connections to the beginnings of a new republic.

**Sherwood Forest** sheds its leaves to the north of Nottingham. The legendary domain of Robin Hood and his exploits against the Sheriff of Nottingham, made this part of the shire both famous as well as formidable. In the **Dukeries**—so-called because several dukes purchased estates in this area—portions of Sherwood Forest are still preserved. The **Visitor's Center** is housed at **Edwinstowe**, where you'll find models and miniatures of the esteemed outlaw and his merry band. A ramble along many of the marked walks is rewarding; you can also visit the **Major Oak** (Robin Hood's tree). Legend has it that Robin married Maid Marion in the local church.

Two other targets in the area could include **Thoresby Hall** and **Rufford Abbey**. The former comprises 29 suites and 78 bedrooms, which could probably be classified as the biggest Victorian house in England. Moreover, the interior is splendid and the great structure is set in majestic parks with lakes; chestnut trees abound and there's even a model village. Rufford Abbey was Cistercian until the Dissolution in the 1530s, which then saw the building of a massive timbered estate, now embraced by beautiful parkland for strolling and contemplating the erosion of history.

## AROUND AND ABOUT IN DERBYSHIRE, CHESHIRE, AND STAFFORDSHIRE

Surrounded by the industrial sprawl of the busy-busy Midlands and the bustling northern cities, the 542 square miles of the **Peak District National Park** offer some of the wildest, most rugged, fully captivating—and unexpected—scenery in England.

The southern part, near Matlock Bath, is perhaps the more gentle topography. The undulating limestone hills are intersected by the picturesque Darwent Valley. **Darwent Dams**, built between the turn of the century and the 1930s, hold the waters of the three huge reservoirs—Ladybower, Darwent, and Howden—creating a miniature Lake District. The pine-fringed lakes, overlooked by high moorland, are surrounded by footpaths and streams teeming with trout. Dip a line and see for yourself.

**Chatsworth**, 8 miles north of Matlock, offers the sightseer **Chatsworth House**, set in the soft leafy folds of the Darwent Valley. It is the estate of the Duke and Duchess of Devonshire, containing one of the nation's prestige private art collections, magnificent state apartments, and grounds with impressive waterworks. Chatsworth was built between 1686 and 1707 for William Cavendish; extensive additions were applied in the 19th century. Richly furnished and expensively decorated throughout, the library is even more lavish in its treasury of paintings, sculptures, silver, porcelain, and curiosities. The 100-acre garden is enhanced with cascades, spectacular fountains, tall chestnut trees, and secluded walks. The surrounding park of 1000 acres was landscaped by Capability Brown. Attractive villages and historic homes abound in this area. Haddon Hall, a fortified manor house (see below), is an excellent example.

**Bakewell** is an ancient market town, famous for its delightfully fattening Bakewell Tarts or Puddings. You can walk off a trial sampling on the fine riverside pathways surrounding the village. It is rightly proud of its 12th century church and its enduring Saxon Cross. A medieval five-arch bridge adorns the riverscape; many of the houses date back to Tudor and Stuart days, and the 17th-century Bath House has connections to Roman plumbers of a much earlier time. Nearby on the Wye is **Haddon Hall**, a medieval manorial home belonging to the Duke of Rutland. It was begun in the 11th century and looks, even today, like a forbidding greystone storybook fortress. Terraces stair-step down to the banks of the riverside.

**Cheshire** (just off the A-34 southwest of Congleton) is best known for **Little Moreton Hall**. Surrounded on all four sides by its own moat, here is a beautifully kept "black & white" house, a superb example of English half-timbered architecture that is almost entirely medieval in style. Happily for today's visitors it has remained largely unchanged since the middle of the 16th century. What you will see in your visit these days was begun in 1480 consisting of two wings; a second stage of building was rendered in 1559 and finalized in 1580. The Great Hall says it like it is; it's great, indeed. The Withdrawing Room with its panelled ceiling of molded beams is one of the originals from which we take the term "drawing room," being the chamber to which visitors would "withdraw" after the meal in the dining salon. The Parlour, with its fine paintings, is an added attraction. One of the most impressive features is the Long Gallery (68 feet) with its brocade of delicately patterned windows. Also worth noting is its Chapel fitted manfully with stout oak furniture.

**Capesthrone Hall,** a Jacobean manor, is on the A-34 between **Alderley Edge** and **Congleton**, about 7 miles south of **Wilmslow**. You'll soon see the imposing shape of the hall across the Cheshire fields, its unusual turrets and distinctive architecture enchantingly discernible through the trees. This stately home was begun in 1722; it was nearly razed by fire in the next century, and now stands proud again, retaining parts of the original building. The graceful facade is even longer than that of Buckingham Palace. As you approach the house, a glittering silvered chain of small lakes spanned by a picture-book bridge is on the left. Jodrell Bank (see below) rises up above the fields and hedges in the distance. You'll come to it soon, so budget your time. A collection of art treasures from across Europe is on display. Have a look, too, at the American Room, containing furniture crafted by Yankee cabinetmakers in the 18th century.

Though it may sound like a television series, **Mow Cop** is actually a rather splendid ruin of a castle built on the higher ground of Mow Cop, the name of a rocky outcrop with commanding views from its dramatic and desolate heights. From this lofty pinnacle you can aim your modern-day Canon (or Nikon or Leica) over at least seven of the surrounding counties.

The single most impressive feature of the Cheshire countryside is also one of its most recent—the massive Mark IA radio telescope at **Jodrell Bank,** between Withington and Goostrey. There are very few places on the Cheshire Plain where its huge white bowl, measuring 250 feet in diameter, cannot be seen. It was completed in 1957 and for more than a decade was the largest radio telescope in the world, being almost the same height as St. Paul's Cathedral in London. The Concourse Building nearby offers an exhibition of explanatory diagrams, photographs, and working models describing the techniques used. Once the visitor's appetite for galactic discovery has been whetted, the Planetarium, with its 40-foot projection dome, provides a visual display of celestial interplay.

Among the more enchanting villages in this area are **Rowley** and **Ashford-in-the-Water**. **Bakewell** (previously mentioned) is the largest town, however, and **Buxton**, the highest town in Albion, is one of the loveliest of the larger settlements. Buxton, like Matlock, owes its existence to the celebrated thermal springs. The 5th Duke of Devonshire entrusted the design of the elegant Georgian Crescent and the Great Stables to architect John Carr of York. To give you an idea of how the English love their horses, the **Great Stables** (built in 1780) were later converted into the **Royal Hospital,** with a gigantic 164-foot dome. Today many visitors continue to be lured to Buxton for its medicinal waters; these can be sampled in the **Pump Room**. Brought up from a depth of one mile, it maintains a constant temperature of 82 degrees F. Southwest of Buxton in the direction of **Congleton** you'll see some high craggy peaks, sentinels that survey the bleak empty moors below. Look for signs to **The Cloud** (3 miles east of Congleton), offering breathtaking vistas. The highest point is **Axe Edge** at 1810 feet. An interesting side-trip is to **Rudyard**, after which Rudyard Kipling was named; his parents met and got engaged there—and perhaps a little bit more.

**Castleton** brings you geographically into the north of England. In fine weather, miles of country walks are inviting. A favorite one is to the 900-year-old **Peveril Castle**, now in ruins, which overlooks the village. The keep has associations with a work by Sir Walter Scott. If the skies are unfriendly, the local caves provide shelter and fascination. These include **Treak Cliff, Blue John Cavern** (producing an attractive stone of the same name), **Peak Cavern,** and **Speedwell**. The last is the most spectacular, while Peak Cavern is the largest. **Chapel en le Frith**—the name is derived from the Norman-French for "Chapel in the Forest"–is surrounded by excellent walks to the attractive town market place and to **Combs** village and reservoir. The broad and green **Edale Valley** spreads out under the high Kinder Park. On the opposite side of the valley, **Mam Tor,** a 3-mile ridge, separates Edale from the Hope Valley. In this district you'll also pass **Shivering Mountain** and the dramatic **Winnats Pass**. In 1665 **Eyam** village was struck by the Great Plague, obliging its inhabitants to isolate themselves to escape its spreading. The story to this day demonstrates the impact the disease had on the people at that tragic moment. **Hathersage** is closely associated with the Bronte family. Here also there is a grave that is claimed to be that of Little John, one of Robin Hood's jovial hoodlums.

## YORKSHIRE FROM PEAKS TO DALES

Don't be put off from visiting the northern counties of England by the label "The Industrial North." Though it was the birthplace of the Industrial Revolution with all that those holdovers imply, there is a beauty in the shouldering countryside that readily rewards the visitor—glorious wild scenes of peaks and moorland. The reason why the manufacture of cloth moved here from the south is simple: beneath this rugged and at times awe-inspiring landscape lie veins of coal and iron. But its towns are built around and surrounded by fascinating vestiges of history such as Roman settlements, towering Norman churches, castles, stately homes, and modest but romantic villages. And, of course, there is the inimitable city of York.

## YORK

At the epicenter of its four counties is this superb metropolis that is simultaneously reverent, jolly, handsome, and muscular. The York resident has a special lilt in his speech and a twinkle in his eye. Jovial banter is a way of life up here and treating people as equals is a golden mean. There's little of the snobbery that you occasionally meet in the more southerly shires and there's a welcome that is sincere and heartwarming to the traveler. Its history is zesty and rich, having been the capital of northern Britain for the Romans when its name was Eboracum. Later the Vikings made it their southern hub. In Anglo-Saxon times Christianity spread out from York, which though effectively destroyed by the Normans, was rebuilt as the important and lovely city that can be seen today. Naturally, **York Minster** is the crowning glory. It is the largest medieval church in England—created, fashioned, and loved during the 13th to 15th centuries—in a mixture of architectural expressions. The nave is perhaps the best example of the Decorated style in Britain, while the transepts (the oldest parts) are in the Early English mode. The choir is Perpendicular. Its original 14th- and 15th-century stained glass evokes infinite (and well deserved) local pride. In the north transept are the beautiful "Five Sisters" (slim lancet apertures); behind you in the south is the splendid Rose window. The east face of the choir boasts the most extensive unitary assemblage of stained glass on earth. In particular, the Chapter House should not be missed as it is regarded as England's prime example of the Decorated style for such a building. Recent excavations under the central tower cast a new light on York's earlier history. Archaeologists determined that the site has been inhabited since Roman times, almost 2000 years ago. It is not the **Undercroft Museum**. Also in the grounds of the Minster are several other noteworthy buildings such as **St. Mary's Abbey** (founded in 1098), the 16th-17th-century **King's Manor**, and the **Treasurer's House** (mainly 17th century).

On the shoulder of the river stands the **Guildhall,** the only one in England to have been in continuous use since its construction in the 15th century. As you walk through the city, you may notice many street names that end in "gate." This is the old Scandinavian word for street. The best example of a medieval street is **Stonegate,** containing a 12th-century house. A walk along the original city wall, three miles in all, would repay the effort. Four of the medieval gates (real gates, not "streets" this time) still stand, each with its forbidding portcullis. Also have a browse along the **Shambles,** the ancient meat market and now an enchanting walk into the past, with plenty of antique and art shops worth exploring.

There are three impressive museums, though the first is more than the name suggests. This is the immensely popular **Jorvik Viking Center**—Jorvik was the nordic name for the capital—that allows you to experience the sights, sounds, and even the smells of Viking York, circa A.D. 950. You are taken through each of the various scenes of life (as it then was) on a "time train." **York Castle** is another time capsule, the oldest part being the 13th-century Clifford's Tower. For steam enthusiasts, the **National Rail-**

**way Museum** in Leeman Road is a full head of enjoyment; don't be derailed into doing anything else if choo-choos are your pleasure.

Throughout the city of York are many wonderful old churches. Two good examples are **Holy Trinity** (which dates from the 13th century and has interesting pew boxes) and **All Saints** or **St. Martin-cum-Gregory,** with fine medieval glass windows still intact.

The **Vale of York** is north of the city—an area of fertile farmland watered by the River Ouse. One object of the excursion should be to visit the famous **Castle Howard,** one of the most spectacular Palladian homes in Britain. Surrounded by its scenic park, which contains a domed temple and the family tombs, the ornate estate itself is more than 300 years old—but it is not a castle. It was, however, built on the site of one. On display inside is a much publicized collection of paintings, statuary, and furniture, as well as displays of 18th to 20th-century costumes. Vanbrugh, the architect of the awful Blenheim Palace, did this one, too, and far better, in my opinion.

Still have some time to spare? There are the towns of **Beverly** and **Selby,** each with interesting churches, or perhaps a trip to the coast. The resorts of **Scarborough** and **Bridlington** are nearby. But the most typical and possibly the most rewarding will be trips to the Dales and the Moors.

## *YORKSHIRE DALES AND BRONTE COUNTRY*

A convenient base from which to see this area is from the cathedral city of **Ripon**. (The British definition of a city is a town with a cathedral.) This 12th-century example has a Saxon crypt, a fine, Early English west facade, an intricate 15th-century screen, and delicate woodcarvings. The oldest of the city's many historic buildings is **St. Anne's Hospital** (14th century). A good example of half-timbered construction is the 13th-century **Wakeman's House**, which is connected to a time-honored ceremony that is practiced to this day—this evening, rather. Each night, as he has for a thousand years—not the same chap, of course—the official Hornblower (Wakeman) sounds his horn at dusk in the city's market square. Some wags declare that citizens either sleep very late here or have the fellow confused with the Sandman.

Before heading off into the Dales proper, two particular visits are recommended. The first is **Newby Hall**, a classic Queen Anne house with exceptional tapestries, sculpture, and well-kept grounds. The second is **Fountains Abbey**, with religious architecture boasting three centuries of tasteful growth. It was begun by the Cistercian monks in the 12th century and though in ruins now, it still emanates power and respect.

**Fountains Hall,** which is in the vicinity, was created in the 17th century from stones taken from the monastery—a common practice in those days. (And not unheard of today if you can get away with it.)

Head next for **Pately Bridge**, perhaps on the route passing the Foster Beck Flax Mill (now a restaurant), which still sports a huge wooden 17th-century waterwheel. From here move on to **Lofthouse**, from where you can explore **How Steam Gorge**, a 70-foot cleft with two deep caves. Return to the B-6265 and aim for **Grassington**. En route is the **Stump Cross Cavern,** where a relaxing quarter-mile walk reveals oddly shaped ice and rock formations. The whole area has several Iron Age barrows. You are now in beautiful Warfedale. Rising high above the valley are great limestone spires such as **Kilnsey Crag** and **Yew Cogar Scar**.

Next, turn the steering wheel toward **Malham**, a wee village set gemlike into magnificent scenery. From here you can walk to **Malhorn Cove,** a huge natural amphitheater fringed by a spectacular 240-foot cliff. Feeling energetic? Then hike to the moorland above to **Malham Tarn,** home of numerous species of wildlife. A 1-1/2-mile trail leads you to **Gordale Scar,** with its waterfalls and rushing cascades. Passing through Malham is the 250-mile footpath called **The Pennine Way**. For the very fit this leads to **Pen-y-Ghant,** which, at 2273 feet, is one of the three main peaks in the Dales. (Don't attempt this rugged trek if the weather is not good.)

As you drive toward **Skipton**, the trilogy of **Kirkby**, **Malham**, and **Airton**—you are now in Airedale—are worth a pause to see the outstanding examples of 17th-century village life. Ruskin loved Kirkby and the Vale of Lune. As the epoch's arbiter of good taste, it would be worth your time to study the reasons for his judgment. I think you'll feel rewarded. At **Gargrave** you cross the **Leeds-Liverpool Canal** (127 miles long). Here a boat trip easily can be arranged; it will take you through breathtaking scenery. At Skipton are the remains of a castle, a museum, and an old corn mill that also houses a museum.

At **Bolton Abbey** there's the 12th-century Augustinian priory, now in ruins but beckoningly situated in a bend of the river. There is still a lot to see of it, however. You can stroll along the banks and witness (or arrange) some of the best angling in Britain. Here the river noisily forces its way through a narrow gorge. Farther north is the shell of **Barden Tower,** a 12th-century fort that is in remarkably good nick for its age.

If you are returning to **Ripon**, you could turn in via **Harrogate**, an attractive former spa where coaching horns are still used to greet the arrival of guests. There are many lovely houses and gardens embracing the town center, and a museum is located in the 19th-century Pump Room. Then at **Ripley** there is a castle set in a wonderful natural park.

Another optional circuit: **Richmond** can serve as your base this time. This historic town is dominated by a huge 11th-century Norman fort with a keep that you may enter. The reminder of this defense permeates the mood of all below it. Within the town from the cobbled Market Place you can tour through the narrow streets with their ancient Greyfriars Tower, the Little Theatre of 1788, and many Georgian and Victorian dwellings.

To the north is **Barnard Castle.** Like many another product of the Middle Ages, the cottages, shops, and inns developed at the fringes and provide further interest and recreation for today's visitor. Nearby is **Bowes Museum,** which has one of the noteworthy art collections in Britain. The ruins of **Egglestone Abbey**—though only a few walls remain—are charmingly sited by the River Tees, and near **Bowes Castle** are the remains of a

Norman fort that were built upon the foundations of yet another bastion from the Roman occupation.

Driving south through Stang Forest and then the lovely Arkengarthdale brings you to **Swaledale,** a severe incision on the Yorkshire skin that cuts west from Richmond following the River Swale. At **Grinton** is a superb Norman church and down in the valley are relics of the lead mining exploited actively in the 18th-19th centuries.

South again following your nose on the A-6108 brings you redolently to **Wensleydale**. This is the home of the well-known Yorkshire cheese. You'll sniff it out before you arrive.

**Middleham** is an attractive hamlet for a pause; the castle is worth a look, and if you happen to be into horses, it is also an important breeding and training center. Farther south is **Jervaulx Abbey,** a Cistercian ruin harking back to the 12th century. The religious buildings on the river's banks evoke a mood of communal monastic endeavor that is almost palpable. You can then return to Richmond via Masham. (Calterick Bridge, which is on your way, was opened 70 years before Columbus left for the New World.) There is also horse racing on the local oval.

Access to the western Dales is from **Settle**, a charming market town with narrow streets. Looming over the town is **Castleberg Crop.**

To the north is **Ribblesdale,** a long wide valley with varied landscape that is ideal for hiking or casual walking. And don't forget the Iron Horse. The railway line to Carlisle runs through here, surely one of the most talked-about train rides in the nation for its awesome beauty. To the east is mighty **Pen-y-Ghent**.

Beyond **Hawes** (one source of Wensleydale cheese) are **Hardrow Scar** and **Force,** spectacular cascades that plunge nine stories from the Scar into a well-watered glen.

To the west of Settle is **Ingleton**. This is also a fine terrain for walking. There are several beauty spots in the area, such as **Thornton Force** and **Pecca Falls.** A circular 2.5-hour route takes you through riverside landscape—but pick your weather. **Ingleborough** is another of the Three Peaks (2373 feet). It is very popular with seasoned potholers.

Twenty-one miles west of Leeds is the stoneclad village of **Haworth,** famous as the home of the talented Bronte sisters. The power of such novels as *Jane Eyre* and *Wuthering Heights* and the story of the three Bronte sisters makes Haworth second only to Stratford-upon-Avon in popularity for literary pilgrimages. But there's a price to pay for the casual observer since it lacks any of the excitement and panache of The Bard's home territory. Charlotte and Emily are buried below the local church. Their father's parsonage is now a museum. A short walk takes you to **Withens,** the "Wuthering Heights" of the novel; on the moor a couple of miles west of Haworth stands **Pondon Hall,** the likely model for "Thrushcross Grange." You can stay here since it's now a bed-and-breakfast retreat for such Bronte disciples who care to immerse themselves in the lore of this family; for lunch try Haworth's **Black Bull,** a lackluster pub where Branwell Bronte knocked back a few too many. In general, unless you have an uncontrolla-ble passion to be on stage for the novels' settings, you can probably live very comfortably without the gloomy, windswept wasteland and lugubri-ous edifices that attach to such talented people. Haworth can be reached by bus or train from Leeds.

## THE NORTH YORKSHIRE MOORS

Within its borders, the **National Park** contains 553 square miles of heather-dappled savannas and fertile valleys. To the west rise the uplands of the Cleveland and Hambleton Hills; spreading east there's the rugged loneliness of the Yorkshire coast, and to the south, the lush woodlands of the **Vale of Pickering**.

A good starting point is **Pickering**, which is 25 miles from York. Mainly Georgian and Victorian in composition, there are also some older houses plus the antiquated castle, now in ruins, from the 12th century. The **church** offers some interesting 15th-century wall paintings, and the town's **museum** is located in a lovely Georgian structure.

If you are motoring, be sure to include the **Dalby Forest Drive**, a wood-land that is alive with a wide variety of wildlife, including the rare red squirrel. Birdwatchers also are drawn to this region. When you are in the district of **Goathland** you can walk on the open moor where numerous streams form highly talkative waterfalls. To the south is a more taciturn section of reticent Roman road, still a proud emblem of the world's best civil engineers.

Several villages are situated high on the moors and command superb views of the vales below. One such candidate is **Newton-on-Rawcliffe**—the name says it all—with its awesome lower canyon rimmed by crags and sav-age (or "raw") cliffs.

**Lockton** is another. Across the moor is the **Hole of Horcum,** a vast decliv-ity suggesting perhaps an ancient meteorite strike. Saltersgate Inn, once the haunt of smugglers, is an amusing stop in the neighborhood. The view is reminiscent of a Yorkshire version of the Ngorongoro Crater.

A drive to the coast brings you to salty old **Whitby,** with its long mari-time traditions. Captain Cook once worked on the coal barges along this strip; his house is in Grape Street. Then, way up in the town, **St. Mary's Church** is a worthwhile climb for noting the exquisite interior. Above Whitby are the grim ruins of an abbey founded in A.D. 657, but the harbor views for me are the most rewarding since this waterway is teeming with ac-tivity even today.

Now if you nip down south, you'll come to **Robin Hood's Bay**, a be-witching coastal hamlet with dubious associations with the jolly brigand of Sherwood Forest. It did, however, have a sinister bloodline. Once the lair of smugglers, its snailway of steps and crooked hive of casbah–like houses in darkened lanes easily evoke images of those swashbuckling epochs. The town is worth seeing by any measure of visual truth or utter fiction.

One of Yorkshire's high-season redoubts is **Scarborough**, with its modest-size mountain behind the town offering the interesting remains of a 12th-century fortress. This high ground also serves as a panoramic eagle's nest for getting away from the summer throng below and enjoying the best of the Old Town from afar. In fringe seasons, the middle of the urban center can be pleasurable and diverting, however. (The medieval section was dollied up in the 18th-19th centuries as Scarborough took on a "fashionable" glitter in the eyes of its devotees.)

From here you can take the fast highway southeast through the Vale of Pickering and the magical **Yorkshire Wolds**, and in about an hour you have left the coast behind you and returned to the noble inland city of York.

See if you don't agree that on your journey you have met some of the most agreeable human beings on earth. That's one of the county's best hidden assets.

# WHERE TO STAY

## BAKEWELL

**Rutland Arms**
Offers 36 units on the Market Square at moderate prices. (☎ *062981-2812.*)

## BIRMINGHAM

**Plough & Harrow**                                                     ★★
More color and charm than the big-city institutions; about 45 rooms, so you must reserve ahead. (☎ *021-4544111*; FAX: *4541868.*)

**Midland**                                                                  ☆
Twice as large, comfortable, centrally located, and fairly costly. (☎ *021-6432601.*)

**Albany**
More than double again in capacity, is at Queensway. A major hostelry with all that implies. (☎ *021-6438171*; FAX: *6312528.*)

**Le Biarritz** (148 Broomsgrove St.) is one of the more refined continental restaurants in town. (☎ *6221989.*)

**Barton Arms** (out of the center) is an excellent Edwardian pub.

Many Chinese and Indian establishments are in this city. I like **Ho Tung** (*308 Bull Ring Centre*) and **Rajdoot** (*12 Albert St.*) respectively. Good reports of **Sloan's** (*27 Chad Sq.*), but I haven't tried it personally. **Adil** (*148-50 Stoney Lane, Sparbrook*) offers a local favorite: balti, which may have come from the Himalayas. The flavors as well as the service are distinctive while the prices follow the pattern of being highly digestive. (☎ *021-449-0335.*)

## BUXTON

**Lee Wood**
On the Manchester pike with 40 rooms and fine hospitality. (☎ *0298-3002.*)

**Palace**

Larger than Lee Wood and more expensive. (☎ *0298-22001*; FAX: *72131.*)

## CASTLETON

**Castle**

Small, cozy, and fun. (☎ *0433-20578.*)

## CONGLETON

**Lion & Swan**

On Swan Bank—preening, of course. Nice and not expensive. (☎ *0260-273115.*)

## LEICESTER

**Holiday Inn**

A worthwhile 200-room Yankee import. Prices are reasonable. (☎ *0533-531161.*)

**Embassy Grand**

A bit more expensive and a bit more grand. (☎ *0533-555599*; FAX: *544736.*)

**Leicester Forest Moat House**

Pleasantly located, small, and agreeable for travelers. (☎ *0533-394661.*)

**Stapleford Park**

Near **Melton Mobray** (northeast of Leicester), is the hyper-ambitious project of Bob Payton, an American who made a fortune with his Chicago Rib Shack and pizza enterprises. He then gave free reins and blank checks to numerous designers to individually decorate their own "signature bedrooms" within the vast country house that formerly was a hunting lodge. Prices can run to £500 per night without pausing for breath. If you've got it and don't mind flaunting it, you certainly can't help being impressed. (☎ *057-284-522.*)

## LINCOLN

**White Hart**

A well-loved old timer facing the cathedral, offers 50 comfortable rooms and the best location in town for sightseers. (☎ *0522-26222*; FAX: *531798.*)

**Eastgate Post**

In the same management group as White Hart, is a bit larger and also is a reliable stop. (☎ *0522-520341*; FAX: *510780.*) Don't fail to visit **Harvey's** and/or **Troffs** beside the cathedral arch for refreshment—by bottle or platter.

## MATLOCK

**Riber Hall**

A bewitching stone Elizabethan manor edging the Peak District. A dozen half-timbered bedrooms are cozy and well decorated in period furnishings. Cuisine is fine traditional fare. (☎ *0629-2795.*)

## NEWARK-ON-TRENT

**Robin Hood**
Provides 20 rooms for your merry band; midtown location. (☎ *0636-703858.*)

## NOTTINGHAM

**Albany**
Usually the first choice among big hotels. (☎ *0602-470131*; FAX: *484366.*)

**Stakis Victoria**
Would be second choice after Albany. (☎ *0602-419561.*)

**Strathdon Thistle**
A good choice on Derby Rd. (☎ *0602-418501.*)

## OAKHAM

**Hambleton Hall**
Very much in the 20th century but carefully nurtured in manoristic grace by its enthusiastic proprietors, Stefa and Tim Hart. Their 15 rooms are as fine as any tasteful traveler could desire; so is the notable cuisine in Franglais style; and so is the friendly greeting of the credo carved above its portal: *"Fay ce que voudras"* ("Do as you like.") (☎ *0572-56991.*)

## SOUTHWELL

**Saracen's Head**
Right on the market place and near the Minster. Very handy; small and reliable. (☎ *0636-812701.*)

## STAMFORD

**The George**
The old reliable house here on St. Martins. (☎ *0780-55171*; FAX: *57070.*)

**Garden House**
Also at St. Martins, is a slightly cheaper and reliable alternative. (☎ *0780-63359.*)

**Ye Old Barn**
In a mews, is good for snacks.

**Scotgate**
Known for ploughman's fare in a Victorian setting.

# ON TO THE NORTH

## BEVERLY

**Beverly Arms**

The bigger choice. (☎ *0482-869241.*)

**Rowley Manor**

16 rooms at Little Weighton, is possibly more fun. (☎ *0482-848248.*)

## BOLTON ABBEY

**Devonshire Arms**

As comfortable as an old shoe, a bit run-down (in a nice way), with good country food, and a fine English atmosphere. The site is delightful; prices are reasonable. (☎ *075-671441.*)

## BRIDLINGTON

**Monarch**

A pleasant stop on South Marine Dr. (☎ *0262-674447*; FAX: *604928.*)

## HARROGATE

**Majestic**

A good choice for position and comfort. While the lobby, bar, 2 elevators, and carpets have been renewed, my inside bedchamber seemed to face more tubing than might have been seen at an Apollo launching pad. (☎ *0423-68972.*)

**Old Swan**

Hatched in 1679, fun for antiquarians. Ancient bar; skylighted Bramham dining room; book only the newer rooms here. (☎ *0423-500055.*)

**Crown** ☆

Follows the Old Swan; the public rooms are very attractive; bedchambers are routine. (☎ *0423-67755.*)

**Pool Court** ☆☆

At *Pool-in-Wharfedale.* A worthy hideaway in West Yorkshire. The hospitality is noteworthy. There are only a handful of gemlike accommodations. The restaurant is perhaps more well known than the luxurious inn, but both earn extensive praise. (☎ *0532-842288.*)

## LEEDS

**Hilton**

I prefer the International Hilton on Neville St. (☎ *0532-442000*) to the **National Hilton** in outlying Garforth (☎ *0532-866556.*)

**Crest**

Smaller, more select, and more expensive. (☎ *0532-826201.*)

### 42 The Calls
I've heard good things about this hotel in a converted warehouse, but I've not yet called in personally.

### Bryan's
(*9 Weetwood Lane*). Try sparkling Jan Fletcher's for a true fish-and-chips meal, often declared to be the best in Britain. This talented and glamorous businesswoman gave new meaning and stature to the lowly food of the commoner. The secret: top quality at sea-floor prices.

### Olive Tree
(*Rodley Lane*). Offers Hellenic undertones to its refined international fare.

### Box Tree ☆☆☆☆
The luxury dining spot in nearby Ilkley still is supreme. While the modern approach to gastronomy has been shelved under its new management, the fine quality of more traditional cuisine is greatly appreciated locally. It's still almost as expensive as in the past. (☎ *0943-608484.*)

## LIVERPOOL

### St. George's ☆☆
On Lime St. in the St. John's district. Rather large (155 rooms) but good. (☎ *051-7097090;* FAX: *7090137.*)

### Atlantic Tower
Much bigger, on Chapel St. (☎ *051-2274444;* FAX: *236-3972.*)

### La Grande Bouffe
(*48A Castle St.*) You can dine fairly well here.

**Mayflower** (*48 Duke St.*). An unexpectedly Chinese repast is served here. The hotels produce more English fare.

## MANCHESTER

**Crowne Plaza** is a Holiday Inn with Edwardian pretensions. A large house and business oriented. (☎ *061-2363333.*)

### Grand
Should soon reopen after a total renewal. Check first. (☎ *061-2369559;* FAX: *2368349.*)

### Willow Bank ★
A nice personality. It's out on Wilmslow Rd. at Fallowfield. (☎ *061-2240461.*)

### Blinkers French
(*16 Princess St.*) Dining is a sophisticated experience in the contemporary mood.

### Yang Sing

( *34 Princess St.* ) A splendid Chinese restaurant, predominating in Cantonese cooking.

## MIDDLEHAM

### Miller's House

A Georgian-style re-creation in hotel form with flowered wall coverings and country-house decor. Ample comfort and flair; uninspired but adequate cookery in a slightly pretentious mood.

## PICKERING

### Forest and Vale

This warmhearted 21-room hostelry is on Malton Rd. (☎ *0751-72722*; FAX: *75132.* )

### Old Brewery House

Another small lodging on its own Market Sq. (☎ *0603-870881.* )

## RICHMOND

### Frenchgate

An ideal base for seeing the local Norman ruins; only about a dozen rooms. (☎ *0748-2087.* )

## SCARBOROUGH

### Royal

My first choice is on St. Nicolas St. (☎ *0723-364333.* )

### St. Nicolas

Located on St. Nicolas Cliff. (☎ *0723-364101.* )

## SELBY

### Londesborough Arms

An agreeable haven on Market Pl. (☎ *0757-707355.* )

## SHEFFIELD

### Grosvenor House

Seems to command Charter Sq. (☎ *0742-720041.* )

### Hallam Tower

On the Manchester Road at Broomhill. This and the above are in the same management group. (☎ *0742-670067.* )

## WHITBY

### Royal

On West Cliff, has a good view of the harbor. (☎ *0947-602234.* )

## YORK

### Middlethorpe Hall ★★★★★

In 26 acres of park, one of England's finest Queen Anne hotel-homes. Top-rank British cuisine by a chef who has trained with the best kitchen masters in France and England; 3 separate dining salons for greater intimacy. Splendid atmosphere combined with ingratiating hospitality. (☎ *0904-641241.*)

## The Grange ★ ★ ★

A Regency town house close to all the major sites; excellent furnishings and textiles; cozy but elegant Ivy Restaurant plus the brick-vaulted Brasserie for informal dining. The cookery is straightforward English with abundant finesse; prices very good for the quality. A charming country house in middle York.

## Royal York

A midtown alternative. (☎ *0904-653681.*) Both of the above set excellent tables.

## Bilbrough Manor

If you wish a Gallic accent in your gastronomy, try this handsome retreat with post-nouvelle creations. The price is determined by the number of selections chosen from a set menu. (☎ *0937-834002.*)

# NORTHUMBRIA

*Hadrians Wall*

North was the operative word, and it stood as a buffer against the tribes that continuously attacked the southern counties. It was a kingdom, and that realm today is divided into Durham, Northumberland, Cleveland, and the unit known as Tyne and Wear. As an Anglo-Saxon entity it had enormous power, and its tentacles spread from the Humber and the Ribble over the Scottish countryside to what is now called the Firth of Forth and extensively along the Ayrshire coast of what is present-day Scotland. A lot of blood has been spilled on this soil, a recorded history that goes back to A.D. 547 when the residents called this land Norpanhymbre. Nowadays, how-

345

ever, those battles are forgotten, and a peaceful coastline, quiet countryside, and a few bustling cosmopolitan towns beckon visitors to enjoy their comforts.

Cleveland is one of the nation's smaller counties; industrial Teesside makes its money, but there are areas of great beauty along the coast and the North York Moors, its best features for sightseers.

**Guisborough** is one of its more pleasant hubs (southeast of Middlesborough), and it snuggles in the cup of the Cleveland Hills. Most visitors come to see the 12th-century **Priory** that today can provide only a few sectors that are intact sufficiently to be enjoyed. These areas (such as the Gatehouse) are open to you. While here, see the 15th-century church that is in better shape than the Augustinian institution.

For a marvelous overview of the hills, moors, and coast, drive to **Rosebery Topping**—topping out at more than 1,000 feet in altitude. It is south of Guisborough toward another charmer called **Great Ayton**.

As soon as you see the imposing **Durham Cathedral**, you will immediately recognize the one-time wealth of this region and the willingness of its God-fearing citizens to spend their prosperity on a lavish praise to Heaven. Both industry and agriculture have found their appropriate moments in history. The abundance of coal in the region fed the furnaces of the eastern sector of the county of Durham, while in the west the fields were plowed in the shadowed folds of the Pennine hills.

For purity of rustic scenery, you'll also certainly want to wander out to **Weardale** and **Upper Teesdale**. Apart from **Durham Castle** and the **University**, the cathedral alone could occupy a good morning or afternoon for viewing. It was begun late in the 11th century following the Roman conquest by William of St. Carilef and stands as one of the major ecclesiastical monuments in the Christian world. It grew slowly so you'll find evidence of numerous periods of architectural stylization within its stones.

Surrounding this majestic centerpiece are the **Durham Dales**, composed of the Upper Pennines, which spread toward Northumbria and create an area of almost unexpected natural beauty—unexpected because the neighboring commercial center seems so heavily obligated to commerce as well as to a degree of industrial pollution. But here in the Dales are heather patchworked blankets blending with the green of the valleys. It is an area of waterfalls and rushing streams.

Drive over the moors to **Barnard Castle**, a worthy target town that has been running its market beside the babbling River Tees for centuries. The **castle** itself was constructed by and named for Bernard Balliol, obviously not the best of spellers. After you have scrambled over the ancient fortress, make time for a visit to **Bowes Museum**, an ornately French-style edifice from the 19th century. Connoisseurs and scholars from all over the world come to view its outstanding art collection. While here you are within close driving distance of **Egglestone Abbey**, the frequently photographed **Greta**

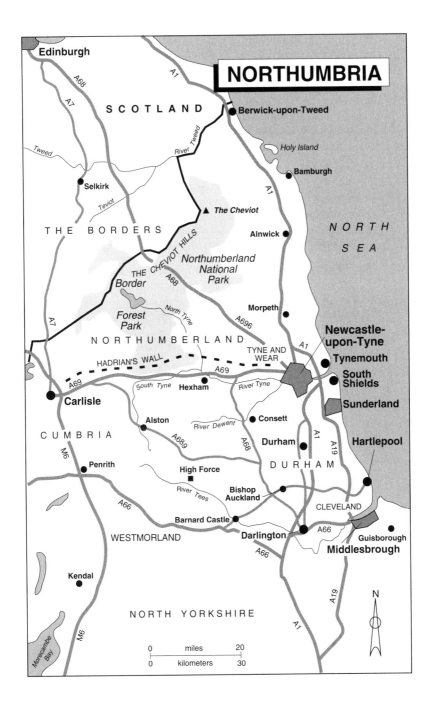

# NORTHUMBRIA

Edinburgh

SCOTLAND

Berwick-upon-Tweed

*River Tweed*

*Tweed*

Holy Island

Selkirk

Bamburgh

*Teviot*

▲ *The Cheviot*

THE BORDERS

Alnwick

N O R T H

S E A

THE CHEVIOT HILLS

*Northumberland National Park*

Border

*North Tyne*

Morpeth

Forest Park

NORTHUMBERLAND

Newcastle-upon-Tyne

HADRIAN'S WALL

TYNE AND WEAR

Tynemouth

*South Tyne*   Hexham   *River Tyne*

South Shields

A69

Carlisle

Sunderland

Alston

*River Derwent*

Consett

CUMBRIA

Durham

Hartlepool

Penrith

High Force

DURHAM

Bishop Auckland

CLEVELAND

*River Tees*

Barnard Castle

Darlington

WESTMORLAND

Guisborough

Middlesbrough

Kendal

NORTH YORKSHIRE

N

*Morecambe Bay*

| 0 | miles | 20 |
|---|-------|-----|
| 0 | kilometers | 30 |

**Bridge**, **Bowes**, the interesting sights of **Staindrop**, and possibly one of the most impressive fighting houses of the ancient world, **Raby Castle**.

The object at **Brancepeth** is to see the **Church of St. Brandon**, with its varied history and architecture to match. It is located within the fortification walls. Gothic moods predominate, but no single style commands your attention. The outstanding 17th-century woodwork and splendid artistic fillips are a credit to Bishop Cosin, Rector of Durham Cathedral, who ordered the work. A scholar in the decorative arts, however, might howl in agony over the duel between the faithful and the faithless, an artistic reflection of clerical vs. temporal values as portrayed on the building's surfaces.

**Consett's** attraction to outdoor types is a unique walk in the woods—unique because you'll be strolling along the abandoned railway line that runs from Blackhill to Swalwell. This 10-mile stretch is called the **Derwent Walk**, and it must be one of the most attractive pieces of real estate in Durham County. It can be joined in several places along the trail, so don't despair if you don't feel like making the full 10-mile trek.

**Tan Hill Inn** could be the perfect setting for an Alfred Hitchcock movie. If you are crossing the moors, the dales, or taking a safari along the Pennine Way, you would surely see this rise in the topography that commands an incredible view over the flats. The Romans came through it here heading for Stainmore Gap. Drovers, packmen, colliers, and smugglers all used the several paths that came to this pinnacle in the moors. As in centuries past, it is a natural place to pause.

If you are looking for spectacular footage for your still or video cameras, then you need search no further than **Upper Teesdale**. The river network has sliced innumerable incisions into this exquisite valley. As the lead mining in the area gradually subsided, the sense of nature has become more and more visible. Within the skein you'll find **Low Force Waterfall** and, about 2 miles away, **High Force**, which drops from an altitude of nearly seven stories in height. The power of the water drives through the volcanic, cubistic rock formations and settles in the valley beneath the Whin Sill, a limestone band common to this area. The roar of the water is again heard less than five miles away, where it funnels to the **Caldron Snout**, the highest cascade in the U.K., which drops nearly the height of a 20-story building!

For a rest from your hiking, why not enjoy the calmer waters of **Cow Green Reservoir**? And if you're hiking along the Pennine Way, here is an ideal bivouac. Pennsylvanians may feel nostalgic for their Quaker State since so many members of that faith occupied this terrain, especially **Middleton**, when it was a successful mining center.

**Weardale** itself was once an elitist hunting area for the Prince Bishops of Durham. Wildlife abounded and rushing streams etched their way along slopes to contribute effusively to the River Wear. There are tempting moments for sportsmen by the trout-and-salmon-filled pools. At the western edge of the vale is **Burnhope Reservoir**, with marvelous vistas of the meadows below. **Tunstall Reservoir**, north of Welsingham, has become the address of many feathered critters who fly in these skies; some of them are rare breeds, and all are protected.

For man-made sights, you might try the lead mining center at **Killhope**, where there is a restored and working waterwheel just waiting to be used as a photographer's prop. There is a weavers' exhibit at **Ireshapeburn**, or you could watch local artisans at work at **Bootherlee**. West of Stanhope is **Heathey Burn Cave**. Bronze Age weapons and artifacts used in the early domestication of horses in England have been found here. The graceful outline of **Egglestone Abbey**, a 12th-century ruin, stands clear against the Durham sky—and only an outline remains. But just from the size of its windows, you can easily conjure up the image of an important institution of its day. Its location along the Tees suggests that the abbey had considerable influence politically.

Situated a mile north of **Staindrop**, is **Raby Castle**, a 14th-century structure, one of the largest of its kind in Britain, second only in size to Windsor. It was built by the Neville tribe, and one of the towers is said to date back to the 11th century. Many a sinister plot was hatched in its corridors, such as one to establish Mary Queen of Scots on the throne of England. The collection of English, Dutch, and Flemish paintings as well as the period furniture are major assets. There is also a handsome display of horse-drawn carriages.

Farther north is **Hamsterley Forest**, with both motoring as well as walking trails. These follow the enchanting meanders of **Bedburn Beck**. Most of the paths are simply for strollers, but there's a more ambitious half-day journey (if the weather is nice) that leads to **High Acton Moor**, a wonderful forest excursion. Thoughtfully, the rangers have included a special trail for children, where youngsters can identify plants and animals.

**Durham City** stands tall on a sandstone peninsula. It was founded when monks fled from Lindisfarne in A.D. 875, fearful of the irascible raiding Danes. Here at "Dun Holm" they settled and built a shrine to St. Cuthbert, whose bones they had packed and brought along with them for the outing. Pilgrims began to visit Cuthbert over the years, and the town developed apace. The shrine can still be seen in the **cathedral**. Adjoining is the **Norman castle**, home of the Prince Bishops for 800 years (until 1832). It is now part of the university. The narrow medieval streets survive, and the wooded riverbanks provide the setting for an exhilarating walk.

**Northumberland** was always a buffer zone. At first during military campaigns and now touristically and economically, it is often neglected. Many a motorist rips through this county on the way to Scotland, missing the beauty and historic interest of this "land in between." Its central zone contains the Cheviot Hills, mostly in the **Northumberland National Park**. Few roads pierce this remote and unspoiled landscape, which is wedged between Hadrian's Wall and southern Scotland. The **Border Forest Park** soughs in the winds of its western flank. There is only one pike, the A-68, running through **Redesdale** on its lonely way from **Otterburn** to **Carter Bar**. For walkers the region offers the moody atmosphere of the **Simonside** and **Cheviot** ranges. The most comprehensive route follows the well-known and oft-trodden **Pennine Way Long Distance Footpath**, which also takes in an impressive length of the Roman Wall before swinging north toward **High Cheviot** (2674 feet), the park's loftiest summit.

The coast is a gloriously uncluttered strand between two celebrated salmon rivers, the **Tweed** and **Coquet**. For the most part, it's a low profile of dunes and open bays with only a few cliffs at **Bamburgh** and **Dunstaunburgh**. Sturdy Northumbrian fishing cobles put out from the village harbors; you can book on for a sea trip to observe the grey seals and fowl colonies of the **Farne Islands**. When you develop a hunger, **Craster** is famous for oak-smoked kippers. The most romantic spot on the entire coast is **Lindisfarne**—that's for pure beauty of the landscape.

**Hexham**, above the Tyne River, is a historic, expanded village with narrow streets, an unthinkably ancient Market Square, a fine abbey church, and its Moot Hall. The abbey had its day in Saxon times; hereabouts are period relics, the Saxon font, the misericord carvings on the choir stalls, Acca's Cross, and St. Wilfred's Chair (unoccupied by Wilfred).

No one can pass this way without stopping almost in awe to look at the poetry in stone known as **Bamburgh Castle**. It stands upon a rocky ridge in perfect storybook fashion. Here the Normans built a great bastion, and earlier the site had served a military and political function as the focal point for the kingdom of Northumbria. The fishing village of Bamburgh itself is interesting, and you may wish to take a look at the handsome 13th-century church in the town. Across the dunes and out to sea, the small grouping of salt-and-pepper rock dots are the Farne Islands.

**Blanchland** is the prime attraction in the Derwent Valley, known as one of the earliest planned settlements in England. Most of what you will see is a product of the last two to three centuries, but this, too, grew out of the efforts of the enterprising Premonstratensians, who among other forms of religious devotion also seemed to love syllables. There are extensive traces of their 13th-century occupation on this lonely spot. The most distinguished building is probably **The Lord Crewe Arms**, formerly a manor house that also includes some of the earlier property, notably the Abbot's Lodging, the Guest House, and the kitchen. The inn is reputed to be haunted, and I was told the nocturnal wraith is a gorgeous, libidinous woman. (Next morning at breakfast there were a lot of doubtful red-eyed gentlemen brooding over their smoked kippers. Consultation with a few indicated that the ghost does not appear on a nightly basis.) Incidentally, Britain has about 10,000 "haunted houses." **Blanchard** is about a 20-minute drive from Hexham on the B-6306, which takes you across wonderful moorlands.

**Border Forest Park**, itself a gigantic area comprising 145,000 acres, is enhanced by the **Northumberland National Park**, which makes the entire natural preserve almost as large as a small country. The "Border," of course, refers to Scotland, and the protected zone knows no boundary but splits with beautiful abandon into the Caledonian territory. The Dukes of Northumberland exploited this gift as an official hunting zone. **Kielder Castle** served as a shooting lodge for these privileged members of aristocracy. The estate was built in the 18th century. As a curiosity of language, the English often refer to palatial estates used for this purpose as "shooting boxes," a classic of English understatement.

If you take the road heading west across the fells to Morpeth, you'll soon come to the community of **Cambo**, site of **Wallington Hall**, which was begun late in the 17th century by William Blackett. The surroundings reflect the landscape tastes of the period and combined with this 13,000-acre spread are 16 farms, which were added to the total and given to the National Trust for eternal protection. In this spacious wildlife parkland district, the dimensions are almost Texan in scope. Within several hours' driving time you have **Northumberland National Park**, **Kielder Forest**, and the adjoining **Kielder Reservoir System**, the **Border Forest Arch**, **Newcastleton Forest**, **Kirshope Forest**, **Tinnisburn Forest**, and slightly to the south, the **Spadeadam Forest**.

From **Bellingham** in the east—a good springboard for your rovings—to the **Scottish Border** in the west and from the **Cheviot Hills** on the northern border to **Hadrian's Wall** in the south, this huge area affords lovely motoring, walking, pony-trekking, and fishing. In the eastern section there are inviting river valleys; more centrally high rugged moorlands provide superb vistas, and in the west are huge forests. The enormous **Kielder Reservoir** provides a lakeside ambience.

Not far from **Rothbury**, which is about half-an-hour southwest of **Alnwick**, you come to **Cragside**, the home of the armaments dealer and inventor Lord Armstrong, who had this eccentric estate concocted in the late 1800s by the famous Norman Shaw. Obviously, Armstrong, a whimsical sort, took an active part in the folly of its design. The house might more aptly have been called Armstrong Village, because that is what it appears to be from a distance with its variegated chimneys, gables, towers, eaves, and multitude of roof levels. The same toyland mood prevails in the interior, so do plan to spend a little time at this unusual sightseeing target.

**Hermitage Castle** (across into Scotland) is well worth the short excursion. It was here that Mary Queen of Scots is said to have had secret meetings with her lover. This gloomy fortification stands on the desolate moorland landscape, its four ominous towers and grim walls complementing perfectly the forlorn surroundings.

Stop at the attractive village of **Newcastleton**, which provides a rewarding sight of the beautiful **Liddesdale**, which spreads like a carpet around you. Then, after **Newcastleton Forest**, are the 1678-foot **Larriston Fells**.

For those who prefer the A-1 route, there are many options. Seven miles west of Morpeth on the B-6343 is **Meldon Park**, a fine late Georgian house built in 1832 for the enterprising Cookson family and still occupied by them today. The ornate staircase and an elegant Hall are the focal points inside; the gardens also are noteworthy.

**Alnwick** is about an hour's drive north of Newcastle, occupying a strategic outlook across the Aln river. The hilly district was useful as a fortification site near the sea, and above the town there's an early 14th-century

**castle** that has been extensively renovated; it contains a museum in the postern tower as well as a library. A gateway from about 1350 with stone figures on the battlements and a fine Norman arch of the middle 12th century are among its more ancient portions. Generally, too, remains of the Old Town are still visible; one of the four gates, **Bondgate**, with its Hotspur Tower, still stands. The Perpendicular **St. Mary** and **St. Michael** churches were founded at the beginning of the 14th century, and there's a 15th-century **Chantry** in Walkergate, so there is no shortage of history about for the scholar. Alnwick, in fact, boasts the second-biggest castle in England (after Windsor). This is the home of the Duke of Northumberland. It dates back to the 12th century, a grand example of medieval fortification architecture as restored by Salvin. The interiors are richly decorated. The main apartments are open to visitors; fine paintings, furniture, and historical heirlooms are on display.

**Berwick-upon-Tweed** is the most northerly town in England. As a fickle frontier settlement it changed allegiance 13 times in 300 years. There are three lovely bridges crossing the Tweed; on the northern bank is the Old Bridge, with 15 arches built between 1610 and 1634; the Royal Border Bridge was finished by Robert Stephenson around 1850. Tweed Road Bridge is from early in this century. Some of the more popular attractions are the muscular town ramparts enclosing Berwick on the east and on the north. These were flexed on the orders of Elizabeth I to protect the burghers from a threatened invasion by the French. While the five bastions are unique in Britain, only a few fragments of Berwick Castle itself survive.

# TYNE AND WEAR

This is a thriving, active, urban sprawl linking the hubs of Newcastle and Sunderland. The port of Newcastle has been vital economically for centuries. The scenic beauty of the moors and the indigo hills as well as the rugged coastline are enchanting. Americans are often drawn here because of their interest in the ancestral home of George Washington.

**Newcastle** provides a dramatic change from the peaceful country tours and walks up to now. This is a hustling, modern industrial town, graced with fine streets, parks, and some old buildings. One enters the city by its famous landmark, the **Tyne Bridge**. A lot of coal used to pass under it, but those prosperous times have fled even though the expression of carrying coals to Newcastle has remained in our language.

In Roman times Newcastle served as a fort on Hadrian's Wall, and during the Saxon period it was baptized **Monk Chester**, due to the large number of religious settlers who constructed hostels here. Though religious, it still had a military character. The name that stuck is derived from the New Castle, which began life in the 12th century. George Stephenson was the one to stoke up the steam locomotive here in 1823, and within one generation the **university** was founded. This really marked the city's christening of the Industrial Revolution locally and from then onward it has been the home of some of Britain's busiest and most hospitable people.

As you approach Newcastle, your first view will be the **three bridges**: High Level is the oldest, then you have the steel railway span spun up by Robert Stephenson to serve his burgeoning locomotive affairs, and the Swing Bridge between the two just mentioned. Each is distinctive, and it is a unique experience to see three separate epochs and functions side-by-side-by-side. **St. Nicolas** is the cathedral, and while it remained merely a church for nearly 600 years, it was finally promoted to its present exalted rank late in the last century. The delay is curious. A brief stroll through is convincing evidence of the importance this building must have enjoyed for local Christians since the 14th century, when it was begun.

Just a few miles south of Newcastle is **Beamish Museum**, an open-air and vivid re-creation of northern life in the 1920s. A tram rumbles down the cobbled street, and you will surely want to visit the shops, pubs, houses, and the old station. At **Home Farm** you can watch the animals, sample home-baked bread, and descend into a "drift" mine. (This is signposted from the A-1 near Chester-le-Street and from the A-68 at Castleside.)

**Washington Waterfowl Park** and its neighboring **Washington Old Hall** has appeal simultaneously for students of Americana as well as for naturalists, who will obviously enjoy the 110 acres of protected lands, ponds, and hides for viewing the migratory birds that come to settle here or rest here en route to other grounds. The house, which is a Jacobean reconstruction, served as the Washington family home for nearly 500 years, being first occupied in 1183. As a complement to the "American connection," the ornithological authorities have brought in quite a number of birds from the New World. There's a wonderful wader lake plus refuges for wilder birds of the hillsides. Viewing is made easy through the provision of blinds from which you may watch the animals and trails that pass a multitude of feeding stations. For both historians as well as nature lovers this morsel of Northumbria can, indeed, be a rewarding experience.

# WHERE TO STAY AND EAT

## ALNWICK

**White Swan**
A reasonable stop in the midtown area. (☎ *0665-602109;* FAX: *510400.*)

## BERWICK-UPON-TWEED

**Kings Arms**
Three-dozen agreeable rooms in this colorful ancient town. (☎ *0289-307454.*)

## BLANCHLAND

**Lord Crewe Arms**
A comfortable, somewhat spooky haunted hotel in the moor. Fun for a change. (☎ *043475-251.*)

# DURHAM

**Royal County**
The biggest hotel, with 116 rooms—and with almost the top tariffs too. (☎ *091-3866821;* FAX: *3860704.*)

**Lumley Castle**
About half the size of Royal County and adequate. (☎ *091-3891111.*)

# HEXAM

**Royal**
Boasts merely 2-dozen rooms, but the comfort and caring are substantial. Its midtown location is convenient. (☎ *0434-602270.*)

# NEWCASTLE

**Gosforth Park**                                                    ☆☆☆
Overlooks the racecourse, romps over the finish line by at least several lengths. Handsome Brandling Grill; adjoining Silver Ring Bar; fitness center and wonderful sport and leisure facilities, plus barber and beauty salons, a sauna, boutiques, and a riding school. (☎ *091 2364111.*)

**The Waterside**
A new-ish contender at **The Quayside** (see below); 18 rooms of moderate price, lively bar, and outstanding restaurant. (☎ *091-230 0111.*)

**Swallow**
94 doorkeys at Newgate. Prices are easy to digest. (☎ *091-2325025;* FAX: *2328428.*)

**Copthorne**
In **The Close** at a district called **Quayside**. It's a good hotel but best of all it's near a clutch of fun diners and pubs such as the **Cooperage**, **Crown Posada**, **Offshore 44**, **Flynn's**, and the hyperactive **Hanrahan's** (☎ *091-2220333.*)

The city also offers a **Chinatown**, the **Bigg Market**, and **Jesmond** for dining and late snacks. **Fisherman's Lodge** is especially recommended for sea fare. **Francesca's** and **Santana's** for Italian cookery and flair. **Royal Station** is a modest midtowner. (☎ *091-2320781.*)

# OTTERBURN

**Percy Arms**
A nice location in the hamlet. Okay for a pause in one of its 30 rooms. (☎ *0830-20261.*)

# THE MARCHES— ENGLAND AND WALES CONSORT

*Cottage at Shrewsbury*

"The Marches" is an age-old label for the soft and misted border land linking England and Wales. A. E. Housman described the interface thusly: "A country for easy livers, the quietest under the sun." The atmosphere of both is combined into a puzzling yet charming mix, neither completely Welsh nor wholly English.

Though the name itself is not too promising, there is ample variety of landscape throughout the area; it stretches from the Dee estuary

355

in the north to the mighty Severn network in the south. A noteworthy and somewhat contradictory feature of the Marches is the several ranges of hills and mountains, standing green and brown against the skyline. They enclose or give way to shallow valleys, meadows, and orchards. In the south, for instance, the bracken-clad Black Mountains look down upon a spectacular wooded vale, deep-cut by the River Wye. Farther north this becomes gentler, containing vast pastures along the river banks. To the east is the Royal Forest of Dean, always romantic and dazzling in autumn. North of Shrewsbury, the contours contrast sharply with those of the south. Here is a wide plain of cultivation edged by extensive meres providing sanctuary for wildlife.

Some of Britain's finest rivers flow through the Marches. Originating in the storied mid-Welsh mountains, they create gentle valleys as they meander to the sea. The Severn is Britain's longest river, the Wye one of its most beautiful. There are others too: the Teme, the Dee, and the Usk.

Much of the area has been bypassed by modern industry and as a result, rural and urban life have a rich quality gratifyingly unchanged over the centuries. The villages are close-knit, full of cozy privacy engendered by the half-timbered cottages and houses. Some of the smaller towns have tremendous character, each with particular specialties. But it is to the main towns you should go for the full panoply of past and present. Here you can find some of the best preserved examples of architectural styles.

Constantly as you travel over today's peaceful Marches—so secure and ordered—you see huge reminders of a turbulent past: the castles. The Dark Ages offers us vivid recollections of defense in the vast earthworks of **Offa's Dyke**. This was the visible divide between Mercian dominance and Celtic attack. Under the advancing Normans, control was established and maintained through a great line of "fighting houses" thrown up swiftly by the Marcher Lords. The remains of these glorious and ruined fortifications dot the high ground throughout the countryside. This interrupted line was the rough separation between England and Wales for centuries.

Wales used to be known for its coal; today only four pits are in operation while the steel industry has been modernized and scrubbed clean. Copper, lead, and zinc are minerals of the past. In their place are food processing, pharmaceuticals, electronics, and a wham-bang entry into important financial services and merchant banking. Sleepy and lovely in spring or autumn, South Wales in summer becomes a popular holiday region, with many overpacked seaside resorts bristling with caravans and campers along the coast and hills, and beautiful valleys farther inland. North Wales offers a hardier variety of scenery with its spacious beaches and rugged cliffs. The once-sooty highstack Welsh industrial zones are rapidly being converted to high-tech environmentally friendly communities. Finally, fine roads now knit together the entire land.

## THE WYE VALLEY

Here is lowland England, nudging the mountain uplands such as they be, and the Malverns, its first foothills. The country offers the fast-running Wye, the orchards of Evesham, the cathedral cities of Hereford and Worcester, and Offa's Dyke.

The **Forest of Dean** stretches eastward toward the Severn. It is one of England's few remaining expanses of original untouched woodland. It was a royal hunting preserve under the Normans and has remained Crown property ever since—beautiful at all times, but autumn is ideal. The area was once a center of industry for coal-mining, iron-making, and charcoal burning, which still continue at some sites today. Several places are worth a stop. **St. Briavels** has a church built in 1089. In addition, there is a **Castle** (presently a youth hostel), augmented by a magnificent 13th-century **Gatehouse** and an even earlier **Great Hall**. There are numerous other villages and towns, each full of character. The **Dean Heritage Center** depicts the life of foresters and miners through the centuries.

**Ross-on-Wye** is seen standing on a platform of red sandstone. While the skyline is punctuated by the 208-foot spire of **St. Mary's Church** (mainly 13th century), the centerpiece of the attractive High Street is the pink-toned arcaded **Market Hall** (1670). There are several other important ancient buildings, including some wonderful **almshouses**, the 16th-century **Wilton Bridge**, and **Wilton Castle**. The **Prospect** is a marvelously tended garden overlooking the river. **Penyard Woods** are nearby, and the Roman armament hub called "Ariconium" is also a worthy excursion point locally.

**Shobdon** is worth a trip to see **Church of St. John the Evangelist**, known for its gracious 18th-century drawing room and the lightness of the sculpturing in its interior. The details on these walls are some of the best to be found in the county. It is out of sync in two respects: the 20th-century East Window and rather raw looking Norman font, both okay in their own respective periods but less than faithful to the whole.

**Teme Valley** requires a day's drive out into this 50-mile loop covering **Bromyard**, **Clee Hill**, and **Newham Bridge**. It's a composite of English countryside dotted with charming hamlets along the route. It threads through hops yards, gardens, farms, and orchards; spring, when the fruit blossoms are flowering, is the time to go.

At nearby **Goodrich**, look in on what's left of heroic **Goodrich Castle**. Of the original, only the 13th-century keep has been kept, but that and the

Outer Walls can keep you busy for hours. It was held by the Earls of Shewsbury for nearly 300 years from the mid-14th century.

**Symond's Yat** attracts shutterbugs to its beautiful bend in the River Wye. Climb up to Yat Rock (one of the evergreen tourist attractions locally) for a birds-eye perspective of the waterway.

**Monmouth** was the scene of many a fuss and feud. Evidence of this is seen in the ruins of a massive fort and a fine stone bridge blocking a strategic approach to the city, made more important because of its situation at the confluence of the Monnow with the Wye. The bridge and the stronghold hark back to the 12th century. Later epochs produced handsome religious buildings—the **Priory** is one—as well as distinctive homes of Georgian and Tudor styles. **Great Castle House** is from the 17th century and can be visited by the public. If you would like to see the entire region to obtain a feeling of its military importance, look at it from **Kymin Hill** on the outskirts. It's worth the climb.

On the way to **Chepston** you pass beside **Offa's Dyke**, which was a defense rampart against the Welsh raids during the eighth century. The dyke (walls and ditches) is so long and formidable that once upon a time it successfully divided the combatants for a distance of nearly 170 miles. Chepstow itself is prettily situated on the little Wye and the mighty Severn. Due to its strategic position, the Normans built a castle on a crag above the town. **Chepstow Castle,** with a low profile along the Wye's nether banks, is very well preserved and has a Norman keep begun around 1120. A walnut tree in the courtyard is said to be more than 600 years old.

**Tintern Abbey** is often called Britain's truly consummate Cistercian abbey—complete, however, without the blessings of a roof. Nevertheless, you can see a lot and guess how life was in ancient times. It was founded in 1131 by Walter de Clare and made immortal by Wordsworth. It is so impressive that it once motivated a spiritual movement to construct future churches open to the heavens.

**Cwmcarn** is the place to begin a half-hour motoring trip outlined by officials who are trying to direct your attention to **Ebbw Vale.** Stopping lay-bys (a term used by the British for rest areas), picnic zones in the forest, and well-marked trails follow a 7-mile course of absolute natural beauty. You'll have to pay a small sum to enter the area, but its well worth it to enjoy the sun-dappled paths and the glimpses of the distant Bristol Channel and Brecon Beacons.

**Lower Wye Valley** is rambling country, by car or by foot. The River Wye itself rambles as it searches for a path to the sea. Over the centuries it has cut dramatic gorges, which you can follow. The water has provided heavy foliage for the banks, shade for hot summer days, and ponds for cooling off. One of the best target zones for such exploration lies between Goodrich and Parkend, vaguely following Offa's Dyke. Here again you are near the Royal Forest of Dean, or the England of yore. The canopy of leaves is said to resemble what must have been common across the nation many years before "civilization" and before extensive forestry—50 square miles of marvelous protected park. Have a picnic anywhere. Her Majesty's Government provides the back drop. Take it perhaps along the splendid **Abbotswood Forest Trail,** where you can contemplate the entire range of Black Mountains across to the Severn outwash. You can even see the Cotswolds Hills from here. **Clearwell Caves** is in this forest zone. It contains a museum of mining, once an active industry here. It's a fascinating (if not spooky) experience.

**Snowshill** could be a Cotswolds settlement. The stone is the same, and the fine snuggle of cottages is similar in style. The rise provides an excellent view into the Vale of Evesham. The **Elizabethan Manor** is the chief sightseeing target, the attractions being a collection of musical instruments, some antique toys, early timepieces, and a lovely terraced garden.

**Tewkesbury**, tucked in at the spot where the Severn and the Avon join hands, is a town you must see if you enjoy the mood of Old English community living. It's like a jumble game of toy houses, roofs askew, curved lanes, the water rushing through the town, and even an antique watermill. **The Bell** is just one of the numerous inns here, this one serving the church in antiquity as a resting place for pilgrims. The **Hop Pole** has warmhearted connections with Charles Dickens. As in all towns of this nature, the church is the centerpiece—and like most important ones in this part of the English realm, it is of Norman construction. The tower can be climbed; the panorama will give you a graphic demonstration of the handiwork effected on the topography by the Avon and Severn rivers over the eons.

**Uley** is generally not visited in and for itself, but because it is near the **Uleybury Hillfort**, which reveals the cunning defenses of early people in this district. If you can believe it, the fort is more than 30 acres in size. In the same district is the amusingly labeled **Hetty Pegler's Tump,** possibly the name of the land owner's wife. Her "Tump" is one of the distinctive long barrows so frequently seen as defense mounds in this militant landscape. The official name, however, is the much more prosaic **Uley Tumulus** (which also sounds a bit anatomical).

**Cardiff,** down on the coast and tucked into a protective corner of the Bristol Channel is the Welsh capital. It is a muscular port city that prospered mightily during the coal era and is now too large to suit my own personal taste. It is attractive in parts and certainly one of those parts is the moated **Cardiff Castle**, which stands a bit impishly on a mound within a walled compound. This, of course, is very old indeed, but not far away are the 19th-century monuments to the wealth and imagination of one of the city's most charismatic benefactors, a gentleman named Bute. You can visit the ornate surroundings of the Bute homestead and come away with a new appreciation of conspicuous consumption. Then after you've visited the **Cathedral**—a separate division of the Church of England—you can take the southern coastal pike past the resort hubbubs of **Barry Island** to **Llantwit Major** where the **St. Illtud Church** reveals a heritage dating back almost 1600 years. In fact, it is two churches (both are fascinating) that time has linked into one. Here you'll also find one of the pigeon cotes described earlier in introductory material, a kind of architectural folly that also generated food for the Norman table.

Now if you continue to drive west, the coast turns north to **Swansea,** which should be a lesson to students of industrial wastelands. It was further crushed by ceaseless Luftwaffe bombing and is now enjoying a certain recuperation. Swansea is proud to be the second city of Wales, the metallurgical victim of a bygone time seeking to regain its youth. Trees have been planted everywhere, the Maritime Quarter is alive with salty life, and a marina contains 600 yachts. The Picton Sea Eagle is a rebuilt man-o-war where you can lift a pint with many another seafront hardy. There's a shopping center and the **Dylan Thomas Theatre.** Going to the Uplands, where the poet lived, you sense his love for "the still house over the mumbling bay." (Never missing an opportunity for a pun, the poet also would have been referring to the lower seaside resort known as **The Mumbles,** which leads to **Bracelet Bay.**) You'll quickly tire of Swansea, but its adjacent **Gower Peninsula**, in contrast to the town that industry felled, is one of the most enchanting preserves in Wales. The southern beaches, when not overrun, are delightful, as are the dunes of the **Oxwich** shore, where stark white bungalows glower under tonsures of thatching.

## SOUTH-CENTRAL BORDERLANDS

**The Wye**—and probably **Hereford's** wherefore—runs through this ancient town, which is set amid prolific orchards and productive pastureland. It is esteemed for both its cider—more than half the total output of England comes from here—and for its prominent cattle. This colorful birthplace of lusty Nell Gwynne, also has—as if in moral counterpoint—for its main attraction, the 12th-century **Hereford Cathedral**. Different styles of architecture, from Norman to Perpendicular, adorn it. An outstanding feature is the Library of chained books with more than 1,600 copies and the 14th-century *Mappa Mundi,* one of the oldest maps of the world, as it was known to 13th-century scholars. The Cloisters that lead to the Bishops Palace offers a rare 12th-century timbered hall, rare because it in itself is so handsome and because so many of England's ancient wooden structures have been destroyed by fire over the eons. Other buildings of interest in the town include **St. Peter's Church**, **Old House** (an early 17th-century building converted into a Jacobean Museum), and **St. John Coningsby Museum**; the last contains a 12th-century chapel and a Hall incorporating almshouses that are nearly four centuries old.

Ten miles southwest of Hereford, **Kilpeck** is visited because of its rather two-faced Norman church, often hailed as one of the best the French ever contrived. The interior is what you might expect in Celestial religious sculpture, but the exterior is rampant with genre renditions of life in its most basic earthly forms. The Victorians did not appreciate such vulgar piffle, and it was their rage and not age that worked hardest on the preservation of the house of worship. It's an amusing detour. If you have more time, the **castle** next door is receiving.

**Ledbury** is on the other side (east) of Hereford, a town jacketed with high-contrast black-and-white timbered buildings so often noted in this area. Generally, however, you only see one or two per village and here you have the entire theater scene complete. The local **Heritage Center** can fill you in on the history of the market origins, the **Norman church,** and many of the individual centuries-old dwellings. Ask also about **Eastnor Castle,** built by the First Earl of Somers. It features armor, tapestries, fine paintings, and antique furniture. The **castle** is more modern (19th century) than the Ledbury scene.

## GOLDEN VALLEY

Driving westward and following the Wye, you'll soon arrive at the gateway to the lush Golden Valley. Here are several villages, many of them with excellent churches or ruined castles. Bibliophiles will rejoice in the browsing at **Hay-on-Wye** with its numerous bookshops dotted along the narrow streets.

**Dorstone's** local church was founded by Thomas de Brito, implicated in the murder of Thomas Becket in Canterbury Cathedral. And a mile out of Dorstone is **Arthur's Stone**, a tomb dating from 2000 B.C. Drive along the Golden Valley and you will reach the Norman-influenced **Peterchurch** with its impressive **Wellbrook Manor**, one of the finer examples of a 14th-century hall house to be found throughout The Marches. The placid valley of the River Dor is a bucolic realm of narrow country lanes, hills, and meadows. Follow the route that runs through Dorstone, Peterchurch, Vowchurch, and Abbey Dore, and you will mine 24-carat Golden Valley scenery. **Dore Abbey**—you see the French influence in its name—is really a product of the 12th century and probably was richer in farmsteads than Tintern. Hard-working Cistercian monks converted the forest wilds into rich farmland that is as good as gold for the Golden Valley of today. For very specialized botanical tastes, the **Abbey Dore Court** is probably the capital of ferns.

**Haugh Wood**, not far from the Welsh border, is about a quarter of an hour's drive southeast of Hereford. It's a lovely stop—the "wood" in its name referring to the oaks and larches that abound. Between them you can see the purple flush of the Welsh hills. If the picnic ants misbehave or the weather is not kind, you can drive down to Fownhope's leading pub and have a tot at **The Green Man**.

The **Norman church** here, incidentally, boasts a tower composed of 22,000 oak shingles—a statistic that has never been challenged since the days of William the Conqueror.

Between Hereford and Worcester are the **Malvern Hills,** made famous by the soft mellow mineral water that issues from its fonts and is distributed worldwide. This is rural, scenic England at its best. The lofty sharp ridge of 18 humps and saddles rises abruptly from the broad, flat valley of the River Severn. The highest point is **Worcestershire Beacon** (1395 feet). You can walk the 9 miles of the spine to enjoy absolutely stunning views over about a dozen counties. On Herefordshire Beacon (1114 feet) is an Iron-Age fortification. It is still called **British Camp** and was the locale that inspired a work by Edward Elgar, who lived in the region.

The main center from which to tour the area is **Great Malvern**, where people once came to take the waters. Mineral water is still bottled at **Holy Well,** and you can visit **St. Anne's Well** to sample the clear, full-bodied beverage. The town itself clusters around the ancient **Priory Church** (15th century), which has excellent stained glass and tiles. Edward Elgar, the composer who was knighted by the Crown, is buried at **St. Wulfston's Church** on the Ledbury road. His home, now a museum, is at **Upper Broadheath**. It is simple but engaging.

**Leominster** (pronounced Lemster) is an old market town of Saxon origin on the River Lugg. In medieval times it prospered because of its fine quality wool. It is surrounded by hop gardens and orchards, also suggesting it made a penny or two from agriculture. Part of the town is tightly packed with narrow streets and timber-framed houses. The greystone **Priory**—no place for feminists—is proud of showing off its medieval ducking stool employed to dip nagging wives into the river; it was last used as late as 1809, more recent requests having been denied. **Orange Court** is a noteworthy and oft-visited "portable" dwelling going back to 1633. It was picked up two centuries later and plunked down where you see it today. In general most of the houses are more stable, but this town does appear to have a dual personality. Part of it is crammed into narrow, sharply angled streets while another part is more spacious owing to its development during the highly organized Georgian period.

Three miles north of Leominster is **Berrington Hall.** Henry Holland began his mansion in 1778, and the green thumb of "Capability" Brown was responsible for the grounds. The garden, as you might expect, is splendid and mature, while the house itself is an attraction for the finesse and richesse of design and materials.

**Croft Castle** is 5 miles northwest of Leominster, on the Welsh border. The namesake Croft family have inhabited it for 900 years. It's a perfect architectural statement of a Marcher castle set in a well-forested surround. If you continue on to Ludlow, you will pass **Richard's Castle,** a pre-Norman antique that is really only a foundation of its glorious past. It probably was at its full height just before the Battle of Hastings.

## A RING AROUND "BLACK & WHITE" COUNTRY

**Ludlow**, situated between Hereford and Shrewsbury, is a muscular settlement of the Middle Ages with a high-rise fortress standing smartly over the Teme, its lifeblood river. Later a town was constructed within the embrace of a stalwart protective wall. Wander among its streets and see if you can identify the various periods that developed under its safe custody. The **St. Lawrence Church** is a good starting point.

This patch of England is known affectionately as "black and white" country because of the vivid contrast of darkened timbers against white

walls. In this region are many such two-toned villages capturing the enduring mood and pace of Old England.

Once in the district, try to see **Eardisland**, one of the most diverting
niches of Herefordshire, prettily situated on the river Arrow. The citizens
seem devoted to flowers since hardly a dwelling is without some sort of floral display. Stroll over to the 14th-century **Yeoman's Hall**; also visit **Staick
House**, built around 1300. Another stake is not so appealing; that's the
whipping post, where the townspeople punished their fellow sinners.

A few minutes to the west of Leominster is **Burton Court**, a fine 18th
century house with a neo-Tudor front. The **Great Hall** with its remarkable
timber roof goes back to the 1300s.

Another charmer is **Weobley** (pronounced Webbley), which began official life as early as the seventh century. It was listed in the *Doomsday Book*,
the first major tax document of England. Charles I tucked in at **The Crown**
after the battle of Naseby in 1645. The **Red Lion** is yet another antique that
will catch your eye. The houses probably looked the same for him as they
will for you. It's a storybook village just made for painters, for fairy-tale authors, and, of course, for princes and kings.

**Pembridge** is just down the pike on an old coaching road from London
to South Wales, but the timbered **New Inn** was already quite old by the
time the first coaches called. It dates from the 15th century and was once
used by wool traders. Opposite is an ancient covered **Market Hall.** The
**Church** is mainly 14th century, accented by a huge detached bell house of
pyramidal design. There are also some very attractive residences around the
skirts of the town.

Continue along the A-44 to arrive at **Kington**, so named to flatter the
sovereign, Edward the Confessor. The original population lived on the hill
above the present main street—**St. Mary's Church,** as you might expect,
being the focal point. Nearby are the 1632 buildings of a school. The town
is protected by Hergest Ridge and Rushock Hill, the former offering the
best views of the surrounds.

Follow the pike from Kington and 6 miles farther on you will find yourself in Wales. The first town is **Presteigne**, just 12 miles west of Leominster. The ancient **Radnorshire Arms** is a stout timbered house that became
an inn in 1792 and a posthouse sometime later. Presteigne was the administrative seat of the former county of Radnorshire. Being so close to its
neighbor, English themes meld here with Welsh expressions in a curious
but handsome architecture. **Burfa Camp,** an Iron Age bastion, is just a few
minutes south of this town. It was a castle that served as the extended fortification known as Offa's Dyke.

At **Knighton** you can turn back toward **Ludlow**. En route you'll come to
**Brampton Bryan,** an ambitious 13th-century fortress, built by (who else?)
Bryan de Brampton. Then, at **Adforton** there is an **Augustine Abbey** founded in 1179 that is worth a stop. Then you cross the River Teme to climb
up the banks again, make a loop, and arrive once more in the town of Ludlow in Shropshire (Salop), a fine base for your explorations. The River Sev-

ern divides this historic border county of Shropshire, where ridge upon ridge of wild hills roll westward into Wales and **Ludlow Castle** still broods above the Teme.

## A SHROPSHIRE EXCURSION

**Shrewsbury** is the capital of the county of Shropshire, or Salop, as it was renamed in 1973. This is hilly country over which many bloody battles were fought to establish territorial possession. The town lies on a strategic horseshoe bend of the River Severn. This is one of the finest Tudor showcases in the entire nation. Be sure to see **Abbot's House**, which dates back to 1450, and the tall, gabled **Ireland's Mansion** from 1575 in High Street. Georgian and Regency homes, well preserved ancient bridges, and handsome churches all mingle together, forming a rich townscape.

Roger de Montgomery started to build the **castle** in 1083, choosing a position that dominated the whole town. Today the **Shropshire Regimental Museum** occupies it, representing more than 300 years of proud service. Shrewsbury is also a town of great churches, some of which are Saxon or Norman in origin. The most graceful spire you'll spy rises from **St. Mary's**; the beautiful stained glass comes from Germany.

Edward VI decreed the opening of **Shrewsbury School**, which put in order the gray cells of Charles Darwin and Samuel Butler; novelist Mary Webb is buried in the churchyard. Other areas of outstanding interest include the **Old Market Hall** and **Owen's Mansion** (both late 16th century), **Rowley's Mansion** (1618), and the most colorful antique street of the town called **Butcher Row**.

Shrewsbury became fashionable in a rush toward 18th-century gentrification. As the country squires acquired town houses, numerous Georgian facades blossomed, flanking the lovely gardens in Belmont.

About a half-hour's drive west from **Wolverhampton** is the dramatically arranged market town of **Bridgnorth** by the Severn. It is divided into Low Town and High Town. These are joined by a severely vertical funicular, a ride that provides breathtaking views of the shire. Capping this is another engineering feat—the drunken tower of a Norman castle, which leans at almost three times the tilt of its Pisa cousin. In fact, the town seems to be playing games with the law of gravity, if not scorning it altogether. The great engineer Telford designed the **St. Magdalene Church,** a rather conservative but attractive building. East Castle Street is full of engaging examples of 18th-century architecture.

**Ironbridge** is a page from the Industrial Revolution if not the birthplace of British industry. The name of this city (and the one above) are really boasts of bridge building prowess at a time of breakneck technical development. The Severn Gorge was sort of an early Rhur Valley in the heyday of English prosperity. Everything was happening, and busy engineers could hardly contain their enthusiasm to utilize new materials. Numerous changes were wrought through civil projects, but today the area is again sleepy and soothingly arresting for its natural beauty. There is a lot to see. For starters, try the stimulating **Blists Hill Open Air Museum.**

Within 30 minutes' driving time is **Long Mynd**. If you are vigorous, you can walk the 10-mile **Port Way** trail, which is ideal for ridgerunners. Quieter types may prefer an afternoon at the **Coalbrookdale Museum,** which captures the activity of the area in a more lazy fashion. Not far from here you'll find the **Stiperstones,** which is another spine of rock, some of it in white quartzite that glistens magically in the sunlight. You are now looking into the heartland of Old Roman lead sources, which provided plumbing for aristocratic Latium.

**Wenlock Edge** is recalled in the poetry of Housman's *A Shropshire Lad.* This is the source of the tons of limestone that are found in so many of the local village churches and dwellings. Those in **Hop Dale** or the Tudor estate called **Wilderhope** are good examples in the region. While you are doing the upland reel don't overlook a spot called the **Wrekin,** which stands quite high above the groundlings of the Severn Vale. Today it is a beacon. Yesterday it was an Iron Age fortress. **Stockesay Castle** is an exceptional 13th-century great house of the region with all that you expect in towers, walls, parapets, gates, a vast hall, and, of course, a moat. Try to see it—with plenty of film. Then drive over to the **White House,** which features a 14th-century hall and 16th-century cross wing. It contains a museum of country life.

**Church Stretton** offers a mixture of Victorian red brick and older black-and-white buildings. **Much Wenlock** is a charming market town with many fine old buildings.

## TO CHESTER IN THE NORTH

While in this district and if time permits, take the worthwhile detour to **Powys**, a severely landlocked parcel of Wales; this could be termed the "Castle Route." Landlocked, yes—but not without water. The Severn, the Wye, and the Usk all feed through and beautify the zone, which is possibly at its most enchanting within the **Brecon Beacons National Park**. In many places you will see the defense network of Offa's Dyke. Sidewalk adventurers may prefer the city of **Brecon**, with its outstanding **cathedral**.

Not exactly en route but well worth the search is **Welshpool**. Although the town itself has much to remind us of the past, the main purpose of this side trip is to visit **Powys Castle**. Built in the 13th century but much changed over the centuries, it has an excellent refined and lived-in interior as well as a splendid 18th-century garden. As you then head northward, you can tarry in **Oswestry**, near which is a massive Iron-Age hill fort, and visit **Chirk**, a pleasant small town where a Telford aqueduct (see below) carries a canal across the valley. Nearby is **Chirk Castle**, an excellent example of a border stronghold; give yourself plenty of time because there is much to see inside.

**Llangdlen** is home of the famous **Eisteddfod** (Music Festival) in July. Along this way look for the spectacular 1,007-foot-long aqueduct at **Pont**

**Cysyllte**, built by Thomas Telford in 1805 and still used today. The four-arched medieval bridge is majestic in concept. **Plas Newydd** is a handsome, much admired (and photographed) black-and-white timbered house. Overlooking the town is a 13th-century ruined castle that is set in an Iron Age bastion. Here the centuries fly by like will- o-the-wisps.

Nearby are the Cistercian-Welsh ruins of **Valle Crucis Abbey** ("Valley of the Cross"), destroyed by order of Henry VIII. The **Pillar of Elisey** is a pre-Norman survivor recording a battle against the Saxons in 603. Now take the high road over the spectacular **Horseshoe Pass** with its extraordinary views across the verdant Dee Valley.

You come out into the rich farmland of the **Vale of Clwyd** dominated by cheerful **Ruthin**, with its hospitable castle. An old market town encircled by wooded hills, Ruthin has a number of attractive 16th- and 17th-century timbered houses, products of a wool-rich community. Finally, after covering the Clywdian Mountains, you arrive in **Chester**, standing on the edge of England like the medieval guardian it once was.

**Chester**, as old as Christianity itself, was founded by the Romans, who called it Deva. Under the Normans it was the area's capital. The medieval town was also a port until the River Dee became too silted in the 15th century. The walls have survived intact, and the views they afford are worth the two-mile walk around the perimeter of the Old City.

There is an abundance of well-preserved black-and-white buildings. The pick of these is **The Rows,** the famous galleries or tiers of shops in midcity. Other sites worth visiting are **God's Providence House, Bishop Lloyd's House,** and **Old Ladies House.** The **cathedral** is mainly 14th century, and incorporates Benedictine monastic remains. **St. John's Church** is Norman, and, therefore, quite handsome. The Agricada Tower of the **castle** is a product of the 13th century whereas the sterner portions were added or reformed during the following 600 years. If children are in tow, a trip to **Chester Zoo** is a must. Some discerning people—and perhaps a lot of its four-footed residents—consider it the top zoo in the nation.

## OTHER WELSH HIGHLIGHTS

After exploring the great divide where the Marcher Lords defended their territories and after briefly pausing in the only two cities in the principality—**Cardiff** and **Swansea**—there are numerous spots of beauty to be enjoyed and historical monuments in the interior. I've already mentioned the attractions of the Gower Peninsula that have been incorporated into the Swansea picture. In the north, one of my favorite stops in the off-season period, when the crowds are absent, is **Conwy**, near where you can board the ferry at **Holyhead** for Ireland. It's a fortified compound built by Edward I overlooking the river's mouth. When the tide is out vessels with twin keels snub their noses at the law of gravity and sit gracefully on the estuary floor, rising to enormous heights on long mooring lines when the sea runs in. Three splendid bridges—one with turrets—form a coronet around **Conwy Castle** while the emerald-blue Welsh hills serve as backdrops. It's a little confusing selecting the right bridge for visiting the castle so I suggest parking in one of the town lots and walking in. It's everything you always wanted in an ancient fort, so don't pass it up if you're in the neighborhood.

Not far away are the twin beaches of **Llandudno**, a resort worth seeing, with numerous hostels and boarding houses (which are jammed from June to early Sept.). Up in the hills there are some excellent hotels such as **Bod-ysgallen**. Incidentally, if you are asking directions, the Welsh language can be a tongue-twister. Double Ls come out as "t-h," so the town is pronounced "Than-dun-yo" and the hotel is "Bodess-gathlin." Spellings also can be confusing and village names may appear differently on local signposts from the moniker applied by English cartographers. Never think for a minute that you are anywhere else but in a separate nation. I once stupidly mailed a letter to a friend living in Anglesey and the envelope was returned with angry red crosses through the "England" that I had thoughtlessly given as the address. They are very proud and jealous of their idiom in Wales so your attention to it will be appreciated by the locals. Incidentally, you can take a language lesson on this same island of Anglesey simply by visiting the village of **Llanfairpwllgwyngyllgogerychwyrndrobwyllllantysiliogsogo-goch**, called **Llanfair PG** for short. All those syllables translate into the following: "Church of St. Mary in a hollow of white hazel near to a turbulent whirlpool and St. Tysilio Church, which is close to a red cave."

Go up the river (south from Conwy) to **Bodnant** and visit one of Gwynedd's finest gardens. East of here is **Denbigh,** with the remains of another fortification commissioned by Edward I. The gatehouse is of unusual construction. You can browse through a friary that was similarly a product of the late 13th century, albeit less warlike. Have you ever considered yourself "all thumbs"? Well, the poor chap who started this religious institution is believed to have manicured two thumbs on each hand. Within the town is **Leicester's Folly,** which was begun as an annex of the relocated **Cathedral** of neighboring **St. Asaph**. The trouble is, St. Asaph never was moved, as projected, to the Denbigh site and thus remains a relatively small house of worship— which thereby bestows the title of "city" on the hamlet. (By definition, you'll remember, only a community with a cathedral can be called a city in the U.K.) Here you are again in an ancient military zone.

Going toward the coast you pass **Rhuddlan** with more muscle flexed by Edward I and a great deal of Welsh history associated with its turf. Then, as if to mock the soldiers of yore, there's an overblown ersatz castle at **Gwrych**, which is only from the last century—a bit of Early Epcot put to use nowadays as a recreation ground that you can well avoid in winter, spring, fall, and especially in summer.

In the vast county of **Gwynedd** you'll find some of the most beautiful countryside in Britain. Within its generous boundaries is **Bala,** with its long cobalt lake that nourishes one flank of the glorious **Snowdonia Park,** a national preserve that covers almost 1000 square miles and sprawls over deep green mountain ranges into the darker-yet forests of **Aberhirnant.** If you want an eyeful of this impressive terrain, take the backroad from **Dinas Mawddwy** to **Bala**. There's also a rail route along the eastern shore of the lake—all of four miles long!

Out at **Caernarfon** (same county), which faces **Anglesey**, across the silvered **Menai Straits**, there is the castle from which the town takes its noble name. It, too, was a part of Edward I's defense network, but now overlooks a peaceful waterfront dotted by fishing smacks and dinghys racing round the buoys on regatta days.

Mainers might enjoy a quick hop up to **Bangor** for sentimental reasons, or to see its university, but if you want more action, go on to **Penrhyn Castle,** where very little is authentic but a big effort is made to impress the vernal rubberneckers who rush in by the busload. Also, if you can avoid the throngs of tourists by starting early in the morning, arrange a trip on the **Snowdon Mountain Railway.** It's a cog line that covers a wondrous stretch of raw Welsh beauty and grinds its way to a viewful ridgetop at a height of more than 3,500 feet. From here you can look down upon the lake at **Llyn Peris**, over the **Dinorwic Quarry,** or back to the reflected surface of **Crib Goch.**

Finally, if you are going on to the west, you come down from the Welsh heights to cross the flat mounds of **Anglesey** and meet the ferry point at the busy port of **Holyhead**. Next stop, **Dun Laoghaire.** That's pronounced "Dun Leery," and it's in the nation called *Poblacht na hEireann*, the Republic of Ireland.

# WHERE TO STAY

## *GREAT MALVERN*

### CHESTER

**Grosvenor**
Smart public rooms, the leather-padded Arkle Bar, fully carpeted bedrooms, and a giant parking garage behind the hotel. (☎ *0244-324024;* FAX: *313246.*)

**Blossoms**
Slightly smaller and slightly less expensive. Also reliable. (☎ *0244-323186;* FAX: *46433.*)

**Post House**
Also in town (☎ *0244-680111.*)

**Gables**
A nice guesthouse on Vicarage Rd., Hoole. (☎ *0244-23969.*)

**Chester Court**
On Hoole Rd. (☎ *0244-20779.*)

**Ye Olde King's Head**
Near the Row, dating from the early 16th century. (☎ *0244-24855.*)

## Soughton Hall
At **Northop**, about 15 minutes from Chester and residing in a park of 150 acres of beautiful North Welsh terrain. An imposingly noble house, it offers a dozen sumptuous accommodations, open hearths, antique furnishings, and cuisine that is said to be noteworthy. (I haven't tried it personally.) The Rodenhurst family are dedicated hosts. (☎ *035-286-207/484/ 265*; FAX: *035-286-382.*)

## GREAT MALVERN

### Cottage in the Wood
On Holywell Rd. in neighboring Malvern Wells. (☎ *0684-573487*; FAX: *560662.*)

## HEREFORD

### Green Dragon
Substantial and colorful. (☎ *0432-272506*; FAX: *352139.*)

### Moat House
A link in a popular chain of hotels. Not central, so a car is essential. (☎ *0432-354301*; FAX: *275114.*)

## LEOMINSTER

### Talbot
Small and nicely sited. (☎ *0568-6347.*)

### Broadway Lodge
More modest. (☎ *0568-2914.*)

### Royal Oak
A few bedrooms; the farmhouse cookery is good and inexpensive. (☎ *0508-2610.*)

## LUDLOW

### The Feathers
One of the most fetching of "signature" hotels in England. Half-timbered facade; superb oak-and-brick restaurant; antiquity and finesse oozing from every pore. (☎ *0584-875261.*)

### Angel
Also a charmer full of old-world flavor; the pride of Broad Street. (☎ *0584-2581.*)

## ROSS-ON-WYE

### Pengethley Hotel
Georgian ambience in a country setting. (☎ *0989-87211.*)

### The Royal
Built under the shadow of the church spire, looking at a greensward and a watery scene. Reliable. (☎ *0989-65105*; FAX: *768058.*)

# SHREWSBURY

### The Lion

Roars with moderate pride just a bit out of town. (☎ *0743-53107*; FAX: *52744.*)

### Lion & Pheasant

Located in the middle of the city, and about half the Lion's price, even with the plus of a pheasant. (☎ *0743-236288.*)

# WORCESTER

### The Elms ☆☆☆

Out at neighboring **Abberley**, with handsome grounds and an imposing bearing. One of the nicest in the region; only 27 rooms, so reserve ahead. (☎ *0299-896666.*)

### Southcrest

At **Pool Bank** and much more moderate in price. (☎ *0527-41511.*)

### The Giffird

The conventional High Street choice. (☎ *0905-726262*; FAX: *723458.*)

# *WALES*

# ABERGAVENNY

### Llansatffraed Court

Well sited for viewing the best of **Gwent**. Now Georgian in shape, the building has been around since the 16th century. Proud house and superb grounds. (☎ *0873-840678*; FAX: *840674.*)

# ABERSOCH

### Porth Tocyn

A bit out of town and very attractive. (☎ *075881-2966.*)

# BALA

### Pale Hall

The High Victorian dowager queen of North Wales (close to **Llandderfel**). Built in 1870 for an engineer, the 22,000-acre estate was later taken over by the Duke of Westminster as a shooting ground. Ornately carved oak interior; magnificent 19th-century furnishings; vast rooms overlooking some of the finest wooded hillsides of Gwynedd. Hospitality by Tim and Jain Ovens. (☎ *067-83285.*)

# CARDIFF

### Angel

Uplifted from a fallen spirit of yore. All the traditional values have been retained and polished. (☎ *0222-32633.*)

# DOLGELLAN

**Bontddu**
Near the steam rail center called Ffestiniog; a place for train nostalgists. (☎ *0341-49661.*)

# LLANDUDNO

**Bodysgallen**                                    ★ ★ ★ ★ ★
(Pronounced "Bodessgathlin") wins my bid for the top spot in Wales. It's near the Holyhead ferry point for Ireland. A country home and garden at their finest. The gastronomy is cultured without being prissy and still rates among Britain's top tables. The people are especially warmhearted. (☎ *0492-584466*; FAX: *582519.*)

**St. Tudno**
In **Llandudno**, facing the waters below the Victorian pier; 21 cheery rooms and interesting food; moderate prices. (☎ *0492-874411.*)

**Llangammarch Wells Lake Hotel**                    ★
An attractive country house on 50 acres of Mid Welsh nature. Easy to take if you're big on peace and tranquility. (☎ *05912-202.*)

# LLANWRTYD WELLS
## (Abergwesyn)

**Llwynderw**                                    ☆☆
Looks better inside than on the exterior. In the central highlands with vast Welsh panoramas. Very tranquil. (☎ *05913-238.*)

# LLYSWEN

**Llangoed**                                    ☆☆☆
Not far from the Brecon Beacons, a creation of Sir Bernard Ashley, the Laura Ashley fabric-ator. The 17th-century manor is a reflection of their country taste.

**Bear**
At **Crickhowell** and within the B-B National Park. Very atmospheric, especially in the bar/lounge. (☎ *0873-810-408*; FAX: *811696.*)

# MONMOUTH

**Kings Head**
In midtown with a few dozen inviting bedchambers and dining facilities. (☎ *0600-2177.*)

# PENRHYNDEUDRAETH

**Portmerion**                                    ★ ★
A delightful coastal stop built in village style. It was the fantasy creation—almost Mediterranean in mood—of Sir Clough Williams-Ellis, a whimsical architect who went public with his dreams. (☎ *0766-7704228*; FAX: *771331.*)

# RUTHIN

### Ruthin Castle

Famous for its medieval banquets. Not by the sea, but a fortress of some magnitude in the Clwyd Valley. (☎ *08242-2664*.)

# ST. DAVIDS

### Warpool Court

Broods over the waves from a lovely site near the cathedral. (☎ *0437-720300*.)

# TALYLLYN

### Minffordd

A bright spot in the Tywyn area. Only 7 rooms but very pleasant. (☎ *0654-73665*.)

# VALE OF GLAMORGAN

### Coed-Y-Mwstwr

The name may not be easy to pronounce, but it's easy to take under the mindful kindness of Michael and Barbara Taylor. Secluded pastoral setting; fine Victorian manor; tennis and golf; top cuisine. It's close to **Coychurch** and **Bridgend**. (☎ *0656-860621*; FAX: *863122*.)

### Egerton Grey

At **Barry**, is a bit farther south toward **Porthkerry**. The imposing stone house is filled with antiques and period furnishings. Well-kept grounds. A good country choice for luxury living. (☎ *0446-711666*; FAX: *711690*.)

# NORTHERN IRELAND

*Feeding the ducks, Ulster*

The "troubles" with the Irish of the southern counties have greatly reduced tourism to Ulster. And what a pity that is, because this is a charming little slice of Great Britain. Around the frontier you may note security measures to counteract IRA activities. Farther inside there are few traces of the ongoing disturbances. A good time to avoid it is July 12 when bonfires and demonstrations sometimes boil over in an ardent celebration of the ancient Battle of the Boyne. (Memories are paid overtime in this part of the world.)

For the visitor who wanders across the border into the land of the Orangemen, you'll discover a tidy, prosperous, humming little land with a flavor all its own, and with little or no resemblance to its southern neighbor. The people, the architecture, the customs have a Scottish or British stamp; the Scottish influences so far outweigh the Hibernian that outsiders find it hard to believe the two live on the same island. Ulster, the traditional name, is generic but inaccurate. The reapportionment of 1920 gave Eire three of Ulster's nine counties; while the name persists, its correct term is Northern Ireland.

The population is roughly 1,250,000, of which Belfast, the capital, claims nearly a quarter. Smack in the center is **Lough Neagh**, 153 square miles of lake; around this hole in the doughnut are strung the counties of **Down**, **Antrim**, **Derry**, **Tyrone**, **Fermanagh**, and **Armagh**.

The climate is mild for the latitude, thanks to the Gulf Stream; the scenery is a study in contrasts. Derry and Antrim have wonderful bays and headlands; the Mourne region in Down has a rugged grandeur; the western part of Fermanagh is studded with islands of enchanting beauty; inland, there are glens, mountains, lakes, rivers, and an ever changing landscape. The least interesting region is the middle.

There's a Parliament for local legislation, and representation in the Houses of Parliament in London. Living habits are British. Industrially, the traditional enterprise was devoted to shipyards, linen factories, rope works, and tobacco factories, but in later years the diversity into high-tech industries has helped it pull through some slumps.

Don't plan to stay in Belfast. It is an historic city, with plenty of antiquities, but most of the accommodations are uninspired and the city lacks the charm of the outlying districts. Try to see the **Giant's Causeway,** one of the geological wonders of the world. Run out to **Antrim Castle,** or to **Enniskillen**, or stroll along **Londonderry's** town walls (the best preserved in Britain) or climb the rolling **Mountains of Mourne.**

There is not one single compelling target for the sightseer, but the countryside itself is lovely, and there's scarcely a hint of unrest.

# WHERE TO STAY

## BELFAST

### Europa
A reasonable choice on Great Victoria St. (☎ *0232-74491*; FAX: *327800.*)

### The Conway
A reliable base with 82 comfortable rooms. (☎ *0232-61210*; FAX: *626546.*)

# BALLYGALL

**Ballygally Castle**
Outside of the town and worthwhile for an overnight. (☎ *057483-212.*)

# BANGOR

**Ballyhome**
A nice seafrontage and three-dozen rooms. (☎ *0247-472807.*)

# ENNISKILLEN

**Killyhevlin**
Out on the A-32, a few minutes from town. Small and agreeable. (☎ *0365-23481.*)

# LONDONDERRY

**Everglades**
This hotel may not remind you of Miami, but the people are warm-hearted. It's on the A-5, west of town. (☎ *0504-46722.*)

# PORTSTEWART

**Carrig-Na-Cule**
On The Promenade in the middle of the port. (☎ *026583-2016.*)
**Edgewater** offers 31 pleasant units on the strand. (☎ *026583-2224*; FAX: *3314.*)

# SCOTLAND

*Edinburgh Castle and Princes Street*

For a postcard nation roughly the size of West Virginia—only 375 miles long and 150 miles wide—Scotland's influence in British history, economy, and politics has been titanic. Today, a good many lads and lassies are considering political separation from England. The process is called "devolution" and is commonly debated across the land. The notion is fundamentally a Labour Party concept, so after the 1992 win at the polls by the Conservatives, independence has gone back up on the shelf for another one to three years at least. Independent or not, Scotland remains one of the more blessed spots on earth for beauty, and its people reflect the hospitality of their lovely terrain. In all your travels it will be hard to find more kindness per capita than you will discover among the friendly Scots. Their roads are blissfully uncrowded. There's always time for a chat—and, certainly, a wee tot. There's plenty to see, so let's get started.

You can absorb a lot in a relatively short span. Scotland offers everything from icy alpine lakes to palm trees warmed by a Gulf Stream climate. There are bogs, snowcapped mountains, rills, heaths, waterfalls, moors, glens, and prairies. When you look at a map you'll note that the topography forms three natural divisions and several clusters of islands. The Southern Uplands, a wedge between the English border and the Edinburgh-Glasgow line, stretch in a number of moorlike ranges from south to north—the Lowthers (or Leadhills), Moorfoots, Cheviots, and others. Sheeprearing and woolens keep these hardworking folk out of mischief; the fishing is extra fine, because the Clyde, Tweed, and other rivers rise here. The Central Lowlands, that narrow band that belts the waist of the nation, contains three quarters of Scotland's 5 million inhabitants and nearly all its heavy industries. Edinburgh, certain Clyde lochs and resorts, and the handful of its better attractions shouldn't be missed. The Highlands are among the most glorious holiday areas in the world. These granite mountains and plains, split across the center by Loch Ness and Loch Lochy, sprawl over more than half the country's terrain. Grouse, deer, salmon, trout, ptarmigan, and hare abound in the purple moors, flashing streams, turquoise lakes, and cool forests. The once sleepy Shetland and Orkney island groups have grown richer as petroleum investments burgeon. The Hebrides, Skye, Arran, Bute, and other tranquil isles—each different, each fascinating to the off-trail explorer—round out the picture.

## AUTHOR'S OBSERVATION

*This year and next you may be vexed with us over the telephone numbers within this chapter. I'm afraid it can't be helped because the area codes and combinations are gradually changing. Your hotel hall porter probably will have the new numbers as they apply.*

All the **British Tourist Authority** (BTA) sources that were recommended for England and Wales apply for Scotland. Go to them in the planning stages or for details on specific places that interest you while you are composing your journey. Once you arrive in the capital, the helpful **Scottish Tourist Board** (23 Ravelston Terrace, Edinburgh) can open many new doors and dimensions of adventure for you. They can find you living space with Scottish crofters, tell you where and how to fish for salmon or trout, guide you to a ski slope, a hunt, a horse, a sailboat, or a hang glider. Phone

# SCOTLAND

Nairn

Inverness

Grantown-on-Spey

*Loch Ness*

Aberdeen

Braemar

Fort William

Pitlochry

Dunkeld

Dundee

Iona

Oban

Perth

NORTH SEA

ATLANTIC OCEAN

Dunblane

St. Andrews

Stirling

Glasgow

Edinburgh

Peebles

Prestwick

N

N. IRELAND

ENGLAND

or write STB's **Information Department** (P. O. Box 705, Edinburgh EH4 3EU; ☎ *(031) 332-2433*. They can also advise you on discount cards for your visit.

The **National Trust of Scotland** (5 Charlotte St., Edinburgh) helps guide visitors to the top treasures of the nation. These may include hardware (castles) or software (cultural events and sites). The selection is vast and varied. Best of all, the Trust rents self-catering accommodations right in the historic buildings or near such properties. Write to them or phone ☎ *(031) 226-5922* for advice. Package trips with shelter in such areas can be supplied by the Stakis Hotels chain, which is moderate to upper-moderate in price and quality. The number to phone is ☎ *03552-49235*. Another useful private source is Mrs. J. Ball, who runs a company called **Tours and Travel Promotions** (25 Brunstane Dr., Edinburgh EH15 2NF; ☎ *(031) 669-5344*). Her specialty is luxury bookings, hunting parties, golf, fishing reservations, and the like.

## A CAPSULE JUNKET

To savour all of Scotland could take several lifetimes. Farther along are some detailed itineraries, but if time is short and you are combining Scotland with an English roundelay, then perhaps I can help you by suggesting a two-day capsule excursion that can be stretched to three very full days in the country.

**Edinburgh** is the beginning and end of your loop, and **Inverness**, capital of the Highlands, is your midway stop. One day before departure, if you've never tried a real Scottish haggis (see "Where To Eat"), ask your porter to telephone the **Station Hotel** in Inverness and arrange that this traditional treat be waiting; 24-hour notice is generally required. Then on the following morning, leave Edinburgh at 8:30 a.m., point the nose of your car toward **Stirling** (gateway to the Highlands), and get the lowlands along the Firth of Forth behind you as briskly as you can.

**Doune** has an unthinkably ancient fortress-castle plus a sport- and racing- car collection of the 1920s and 1930s—but perhaps you'd rather push on to **Gleneagles**, Scotland's most fabulous hotel, for a coffee break; this baronial country estate is something special. Then proceed to the Dewar's White Label town, **Perth**, for a friendly aperitif in the Highlander Bar of the Station Hotel, followed by lunch in the dining room here (the food is the best in the area).

Now cut northwest along the river valley through **Pitlochry**, **Blair Atholl**, along glorious **Glengarry**, through **Drumochter Pass** and the **Forest of Atholl** down to **Dalwhinnie**, and onward. (Mid-April to early-October, the **Pitlochry Festival Theatre** draws crowds to its competent performances. Six plays ranging from Shakespeare to Chekhov to Jean Anouilh to Noel Coward are presented Monday through Saturday.)

By teatime, **Carrbridge** should loom up, and the simple, fishing-and-sporting Carrbridge Hotel should break out homemade dainties. You might want to take in the **Landmark Visitor Center,** which capsulizes Highland history and lore. It has its own restaurant, plus shops. One hour after you're roadbound again, you'll be in Inverness, where the austere but adequate Station Hotel—and your haggis, I hope!—is waiting.

The second day you take a different, even more spectacular route. Start no later than 8 a.m. After leaving the "Ceud Mile Failte!" sign (Gaelic for "100,000 Welcomes!") behind at the city limits of Inverness, you loaf along the **Caledonian Canal** until it opens into **Loch Ness**—and as you parallel the 24 miles of this landmark, keep every eye in the car peeled for "Nessie," the fabled Loch Ness Monster! **Loch Lochy** is next—and then, 2 miles before **Spean Bridge**, you'll pass the famed **Commando Memorial**, a stirring sight in a stirring location.

Now it's time for coffee in the Milton Hotel in **Fort William**. Refreshed, stretching your legs almost in the shadow of Britain's highest peak, Ben Nevis, you next take the bridge crossing at Ballachulish, then swoop across the magnificent **Rannoch Moor** and **Black Mount**. After the turn-off at **Crianlarich**, there's an interesting ride down **Glen Falloch** to the northern tip of **Loch Lomond**, and you now view this loch of song and story in its entirety all the way down to its termination at **Balloch**. Tea at **Buchanan Arms** at **Drymen** will then be yours for the asking—and home you go to Edinburgh, in time for a well-earned dinner. Fewer than 400 miles, round-trip—with about 4000 miles' worth of scenery!

For the 1-day extension, on the second morning of the trip, instead of driving to the Caledonian Canal, continue west and north from Inverness to **Beauly**, **Muir of Ord**, **Garve**, and **Braemore Forest**; turn off on A-832 around **Braemore Lodge**, go through **Dundonnell**, follow along the south shore of **Little Loch Broom** (not to be confused with Loch Broom and Ullapool to the north), and then sweep in a U-shape hook through **Aultbea**, **Poolewe**, **Gairloch**, and back along the lovely shores of **Loch Maree** to **Kinlochewe**.

Turn southwest on A-890 at **Achnasheen**, and follow it to the turn-off for **Kyle of Lochalsh**, your destination. This is the ferry point for the **Isle of Skye** and its capital, **Portree**. (If you want unspoiled rural flavor and untouched scenic magnificence, this is it.) Round-trip bus excursions from Inverness, encompassing the enchanting Isle of Skye, operate selected days between May and September.

On the third morning, take off early for the Kyle of Lochalsh ferry and continue along A-87 through **Dornie**, **Invershiel**, **Cluanie Br. Inn** and **Tomdoun** to **Invergarry**. At Invergarry, pick up the route down Loch Lochy described in our 2-day tour (to Spean Bridge, Fort William, Loch Lomond, and eventually to Edinburgh). The only thing you'll miss is Loch Ness, but honest to goodness, you'll never miss it.

These are fairly stiff hauls—but in 48 or 72 hours, you'll have a better cross section of the real Scotland than most travelers can get in a week.

**Oban**, a lovely little port, is one of the most convenient jumping-off points for scouting the Hebrides. Day excursions may be made to the islands of **Mull**, **Lismore**, and **Iona**. (The last is the birthplace of Scottish

Christianity, where St. Columba preached, and where the first abbey has been restored.) Aboard the RMS *Columbia* you can take 3-day minicruises or hop on a car-ferry for a visit to the islands. Even shorter skims aboard 12-passenger motor launches leave at scheduled intervals from the *Oban Times* slip and glide out to **Seil Island**. There you may stroll the beach and actually pet the animals for which the isle was named. Caledonian Mac-Braynes' Steamer Services also run comfortable year-round circuits through both Inner and Outer Hebridean points; these include 2 or 3 day minicruises or a (ho-ho-ho!) Island Hopscotch program in which you pick the places and the time ashore. Cars can be ferried, too. The vessels are solid; the comfort is sound; the food is hardy and substantial; the price is right. Local wags who thirst for a sea voyage remark that MacBraynes' steamers are all beautifully equipped "with quite a few engines" (local parlance for "bars")—and that they are, mon!

## *TRANSPORTATION*

**Airlines** • Scotland is in with Britain regarding its flying services (see "England"). Glasgow Airport is the intercontinental terminus, while Edinburgh Airport handles much of the European work.

**Taxis** • You'll pay about £2 for the first mile, and there's no supplement for baggage unless it rides in front with the driver. The tip should be about 10% of the fare.

**Trains** • Since Scotland is crosshatched by the ScotRail network, see the appropriate section on England. All facilities and equipment are pooled throughout the U.K. The popular Thrift-Tour Tickets and other bargains include the noted Circular Tours of Scotland, and Caledonian Mac-Braynes' Steamer Services in the West Highlands and Western Isles. Most of these are sold only in North America.

Scotland has its own version of the Orient Express—a luxury train called the Royal Scotsman. The scenery alone is worth the price. A 6-day chuff begins in Edinburgh and covers the nation for something like £1200 per person in a State Cabin. Lower rates for simpler accommodation or shorter trackage; meals and drink are included for all on board.

## *FOOD*

The Scots love the table, and their approach to it bears little resemblance to that of the English. Specialties: *Haggis* (see below); Scotch broth; *Cock-a-leekie* (Chicken and leek soup); roasted or stewed grouse or ptarmigan; fresh trout, salmon, haddock, cod, or sole; Arbroath Smokies; kippers; fried herring in oatmeal batter, or grilled herring with mustard sauce; Findon *Haddock* (finnan haddie) with poached egg; scones; pancakes; oatcake; shortbread; heather honey; *Black Pudding* (oatmeal, blood, and seasonings); *White Pudding* (oatmeal and onion base); *Black Bun* (chewy with raisins and ginger); marmalade; and many, many more. When you see the "Taste of Scotland" sign at a restaurant, it indicates participation in a program to offer many of the above specialties, as well as an extra dollop of Scottish hospitality.

Meal hours: lunch, 12:30-2 p.m.; tea, 3:30-5 p.m.; dinner, 7-9 p.m. or later in summer, but 6-8 p.m. in winter. Chinese, Indian, and Italian restaurants usually operate until or shortly after midnight, providing the only late-hour fare on any main street.

**NOTE**: No visitor can say he knows the real Scotland until he has gone through the **Haggis Ceremony**. This national festival dish of oatmeal, assorted chopped meats, and spices must be specially prepared, but that's easy; just call any good hotel on your itinerary a day before you plan to arrive, and ask them to serve a Haggis for your dinner. Be sure to order hot mashed turnips on the side, and be doubly careful not to forget what the Scots call the "gravy"—straight Scotch whiskey (or malt) sipped between bites, the only liquid that complements this fascinating dish. Maybe you'll love it, or maybe you'll loathe it—but I'll guarantee you'll find it sufficiently intriguing for the low-cost gamble of buying it.

## *DRINKS*

For nearly 500 years, distillers all over the civilized world have tried to imitate Scotch whiskey. But even with identical ingredients and methods—for reasons that are unclear—no foreign-produced product has ever come within hat-tipping distance of the original.

This Most Seraphic of Solaces of Gentlemen, as Samuel Johnson put it, is classified into 5 types—4 geographical (Highland, Lowland, Islays, and Campbel towns) and the 5th chemical (grain spirits for processing). North Americans overwhelmingly prefer the Highland category, because its peat-fire-dried malt adds the distinctive smoky tang to which they are accustomed. After it is matured in casks for at least three years (usually four or five), blending formulae are applied by each producer. There are about 3000 blends! The scotch we drink usually contains from 17 to 45 different whiskies. The Royal Family of this Kingdom are the pure Pot Still Malt runs, which are not blended but remain in their virgin glow. Of these there are fewer than 100. Many Scots sip theirs with water; personally, I prefer it neat on a cold day and not at all on a hot day; soda is universally considered to be a sacrilege, and ice is also not quite cricket. Islay (pronounced Eyelay) is mysteriously rich in peat, lacking in sweetness, and firmly in a class by itself; so is the smoky two-fisted 10-year-old Laphroaig (pronounced Laff-royg); Glenmorangie, at the other end of the scale, is one of the smoothest, softest, and most delightful elixirs I know. Glenlivet, Glen Grant, and Glengarry are all better known and fine. Ironically, it's sometimes a chore to find your familiar proprietary brand in the nation of its birth—too much is exported. Bartenders, however, know their fluids intimately, so if you tell them the name of your usual back-home favorite, they will pluck a similar choice off the shelf for you.

Drambuie is nectar from the Isle of Skye. Its base, of course, is Scotch, but the rest, except for mountains of sugar, is a secret. For saving his life during his attempt to regain the throne, Bonnie Prince Charlie gave the Laird of Mackinnon the recipe, and it's been guarded as carefully as the crown jewels since 1745.

Scottish brewers build brass knuckles into many of their products. "Prestonpan's 12-Guinea Ale" (delicately referred to, when ordered, as "a wee heavy" or "a dump") is one of the strongest ales made; it's dark, thinnish, and somewhat cloying. McEwan's, the most popular export ale, and Younger's, the leading beer, are on draft in the better pubs.

## AUTHOR'S OBSERVATION

*When you drink with a Scotsman, say "Slans-Jey-Vah!" (phonetic spelling) instead of "Cheers!"–and watch his eyes sparkle with surprise at hearing his traditional Gaelic toast from the lips of an outlander.*

## A TOTTER DOWN THE MALT WHISKEY TRAIL

Don't tell another living soul, but it was an Irishman (with the unlikely name of Coffey) who gave us the Scotch we enjoy today. His was the catalyst that allowed malt to shake hands with grain in a distilling process that resulted in blended whisky. "Blended" is still the heavyweight seller from Scotland, created in part from the original single malts. Since its beginnings as more or less a cottage trade serving the blended market, malts themselves have become an area of connoisseurship. Masters, it is said, got so persnickity that when they finally changed their copper stills for new ones, they incorporated "old" dents and bulges so as not to risk changing the delicate nuances of flavor.

As a measure for comparison in your testing explorations in Scotland, order a wee tot of 12-year-old Macallan, which many consider the most noble of malts. It is soft, mellow, and warmly sentimental. Those who do not enjoy it criticize it for exactly those same qualities, but once you try it you will at least have a starting point from which to gauge all others.

Perhaps the most comprehensive distillery tour can be had at the famous **Glenfiddich** works at **Dufftown** in the Grampian range, which is the heartland of malt. The hour's free stroll takes place weekdays from 9:30 a.m. until 4:30 p.m. and even on weekends in summer. It's a big operation at the fall of the Fiddich River, tranquil because after the waters contribute their purity, the young spirits must sleep in sherry casks for many years before being decanted into their distinctive three-cornered bottles and going out to the world for appreciation.

**Edradour** Quite the opposite of the Glenfiddich giant, is the tiny signature distillery at **Moulin**. A trio of craftsmen turn out only 600 gallons of malt per week and manhandle just a dozen casks in the process. But what results is an elixir that has been a beverage of the privileged classes since early in the 19th century. Here you will see the same wort-to-wash process and similar oaken barrels from which the impurities, known as foreshots and feints, have been banished. But if a liquid can have a designer label, then the house of Edradour is among the most noteworthy. It has visiting hours close to those of Glenfiddich, but since Edradour is so small you'd better phone first (☎ *0796-2095*). The chaps may have gone fishing for the day.

**Blair Athol** is known the world over and remains a major contender in the Pitlochry zone. Here you can even sign up for an evening of high spirits in another Scottish form. It's called the ceilidh (pronounced "kay- lee") and resembles a tartan version of a Tennessee barn dance—probably the Appalachian capers came from Scotland in the first place.

If you don't wish to amble far from the main hubs, then **Glenkinchie** is at **Pencaitland**, near Edinburgh, and **Glengoyne** is at **Kellearn** at Stratchclyde, close to Glasgow. Both distillers keep their portals open throughout the year, but like most industry in Scotland, August is a go-slow period; that's when many workers are on holiday. If one can make any generalizations at all about such an individualistic trade, the key ingredient is water and the softest of it probably trickles into and around the Spey, whereas the more muscular tones are flavored by streams such as those fed by bogs on Islay and similar Hebrides outposts.

Finally, after you've sampled the big-city distilleries, the talents of the Speyside magicians from Glenlivet to Cardhu, the handiwork of the gnomes of the Grampians and the Lowlands, you can strike out for the kippery islands of **Talisker**, **Laphroaig**, **Lagavulin**, and the like, where the peat smoke permanently permeates the air and its drink is guaranteed to cure and preserve your tonsils forever.

## *GOLFING GUIDELINES*

If you yearn to win a passel of Scottish pounds, bet some patsy that Edinburgh is farther north than Moscow. Then if you need a follow-up, challenge your opponent to guess within 50% of accuracy how many golf courses there are in the capital area. There are eighteen 18-hole circuits within the city limits (located no farther than 5 miles from Holyrood Palace) plus five 9-hole rounds. And if that doesn't zap them hard enough, you can open the Edinburgh phone book and rattle off at least threescore more just for the record.

There are few things that can make you feel quite so "foreign" as teeing up on Scottish turf and not knowing the lore of the links. Soon enough you'll learn that Scots play golf with quite another style. In this windswept country, the high arc of a beautifully lofted ball is seldom observed—it might land behind you on a breezy day. Courses are seldom overwatered as in North America; either they are in a natural state or the wind dries off the rain, providing an added feature of a long bounce rather than our hit-and-stick techniques. I've even entertained a notion that entire tournaments could be played with only a two iron and a putter!

Here are some tips that refer specifically to the nation's most noteworthy circuit, the Old Course at St. Andrews. The same form more or less applies to all the more famous courses, according to my Scottish friends. (I have never had trouble getting a tee time on short notice.) Anyone with a reasonable handicap rating can play, but you must obtain a tee-off time; in peak seasons this should be done 2 to 6 months ahead, offering several preferences (8 minutes between parties). September is difficult, when the Royal & Ancient has its own club games (usually second and third weeks). The cost for "putting in your ballot" is £20 per round and when you show up you get back £10; the playing fee is £20 for 18 holes to the starter (☎ *0334-73393*) or Links Manager Alec Beverage ☎ *(44) 334-75757*, FAX: *77036*). These exalted personages are often mistaken for deities. One wintry morning I watched as a neat, handsomely sweatered American golfer was scolded at Muirfield for not appearing in front of His Grace (read Club Secretary) with a tie and jacket. It is a waste of time to beg for space before such ridiculous pomposity, so this is why a detailed account here might be helpful.

## OTHER TIPS

Use only a few clubs stuck into a pencil bag. Generally, links courses (seaside ones) are windy, so the less lofted numbers are preferable. You will, however, find pull-carts, but there are all too few caddies nowadays. Cars on the courses are not too popular.

Be prepared for the worst weather and pack along rain gear even on the brightest days.

Don't display colorful sartorial fashions appropriate for Palm Springs. Dress like a grouse—in drab shades, tweeds, or worn plus-twos. Un-chic is proper.

Women are restricted—often to play on certain days or certain hours. They also may not enter certain clubhouse areas in particular locales.

On those blustery courses, don't speak loudly—unless you want to be overheard by someone at the next downwind hole.

Don't believe Scottish handicaps; they're either too high or too low. (Only 3 scores are turned in each year!) Scots, however, are very proper sportsmen and women, so you can count on them to portray their playing correctly.

Play with dispatch; 2-1/2 hours is par for 18 holes.

There are no "Mulligans" in Scotland. That's an Irish term. Instead, ask for a free drive on the first hole and be surprised if you get it.

In Scotland a "foursome" means two balls and four players. To convey the American concept of a quartet of players teeing off together, you should refer to "four-ball" play.

A "scratch" player is one who regularly makes par. Par and scratch are used almost interchangeably.

Here are some don'ts at the 19th hole: No ice with your malt—and no soda either.

Never display cash for bets at private clubs. Resist any urge ever to discuss business at the clubhouse.

Most clubhouses prefer men to wear a blazer and tie at lunch.

And now that you are armed with those disarming hints, here are some choices of links around the nation by category. Most are by the sea.

**Public Courses** • Gleneagles is inland (often considered the best), Turnberry (my pick for beauty), Gullane, Carnoustie, Dornoch, Cruden Bay, and St. Andrews (four other fine circuits available besides the famous Old Course, where golfing was born). In the Aberdeen region, tee off at Auchmill, Balnagask, Haylehead, or King's Link.

**Private Courses** • Muirfield, Prestwick, Troon, Blairgowrie, Brunstfield, Deeside, Murcer, Royal Aberdeen, Royal Burgess (oldest club in the world), and Western Gailes.

**Quaint Golfing (all public)** • Braids, Boat of Garten, Machrihanish, Stonehaven.

# EDINBURGH

Like Rome, this Scottish capital is situated on seven hills, but by far the dominating one is where its earliest inhabitants decided to build a fortress, now Edinburgh Castle. And from here at the pinnacle of its crown all of its history seems to flow along a path called the Royal Mile to Holyrood Palace. Duneadain, as it was called in ancient times, was not only a hilltop stronghold but it provided protection and security so that culture and education could flourish within the shadow of its mighty custody. Within its embrace are schools, fine shops, museums, splendid hotels, interesting restaurants, proud pageants and, of course, the world-famous Edinburgh Festival every year in late summer.

Your Scottish reel is likely to begin and end here, so you will need a little orientation to the major sights to see. About three days are ample for most visitors since so many holidaymakers are desirous of getting free of metropolitan fetters and heading off to the captivating countryside. Nevertheless, Edinburgh is one of Europe's most comfortable, scenic, and engaging capitals, so don't leave without enjoying some of its charms. Following are the bare bones of our basic anatomy lesson:

### Edinburgh Castle

Easily the most striking structure in the city, it stands majestically above the town on a huge jutting rock. At a height of about 270 feet, the castle walls offer the best panorama of the city and surrounding hills and coastline. There has been a fortress of some sort on this site since before the 7th century. When King Malcolm moved here in the 11th century, the castle was greatly enlarged. The tiny chapel on the east side of the castle grounds was dedicated to Malcolm Canmore's wife, Queen Margaret, and is now Edinburgh's oldest building; this explosive lady—and simultaneously a saint—also inspired **Mons Meg**, a 15th-century cannon. Today, the castle houses the **Scottish Regalia** (crown, scepter, sword, and jewels) as well as the **Scottish War Memorial**, with a fine collection of historical weapons and costumes.

### Royal Mile

As I've just mentioned, this is the road that runs down the hill from Edinburgh Castle to Holyrood Palace, through the oldest part of the city and comprising Castle Hill, Canongate, High Street, and the Lawnmarket. Since the entire early population of "Old Town" lived along these four streets, the "mile" is positively packed with wonderful historic places: The High Kirk (Church) of Edinburgh, with its beautiful crownshaped spire, many fascinating museums, the John Knox residence, and enchanting 16th- and 17th-century houses.

### Gladstone's Land

*483 Lawnmarket.* Something of a fancy 17th-century tenement building, this is one of the many arcaded structures that once lined the streets of the Royal Mile. Some of these buildings stood as high as 14 stories. Gladstone's Land was built in 1620, and is one of the few with its arcades still intact.

### Parliament House

*Upper High St.* King Charles I had this building constructed in 1623 to replace the Collegiate buildings of St. Giles Cathedral as home to the Scottish Parliament. Today, Parliament House is used by Scotland's supreme court. In the Great Hall you will find an excellent collection of portraits by famous Scottish artists, including Raeburn. In the square: the equestrian statue of Charles II, the city's oldest.

### Lady Stair's House

*Off Lawnmarket, through Lady Stair's Close.* Built in 1622, this house has been turned into a monument to 3 great Scottish writers: Robert Burns, Robert Louis Stevenson, and Sir Walter Scott. Collections of letters, pictures, and interesting memorabilia of the authors are displayed here.

### St. Giles Cathedral

*Upper High St.* One of Edinburgh's greatest historical sanctums, the High Kirk of Edinburgh has not always been here as such, having boasted of cathedral status for only five years of its controversial history. For more than 1000 years a church has been standing on this location, earlier efforts having been burned, pillaged, and rebuilt. Here you will also find the extraordinary Chapel of the Most Ancient and the Most Noble Order of the Thistle, Scotland's lofty order of chivalry.

### Anchor Close

*Off High St.* This is a fine example of the many such tiny alleys that once led to the quaint inns and public houses characteristic of the 18th century. Many of these taverns date back to the 16th century. If

SCOTLAND

389

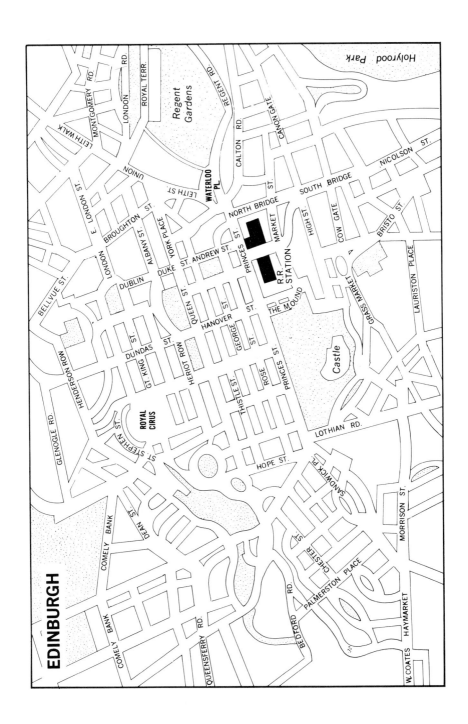

you ramble over to Grassmarket, you'll see the **White Hart Inn**, a writ-ers' retreat that rings with echoes of Burns and Wordsworth.

### Museum of Childhood

*38 High St. opposite John Knox's House.* Here is a fascinating assem-blage of toys, games, dolls, books, and costumes. Although most of the collection is from the mid-19th century, there are some primitive toys that predate the Christian era, as well as a few early 20th-century knickknacks. This museum is as much fun for adults as it is for children.

### Canongate Tollbooth

*Canongate.* Constructed in 1591, this is now a trades union museum. Several turreted towers with outside steps characterize the medieval structure.

### Acheson House

*140 Canongate.* Sir Archibald Acheson, secretary of state to King Charles I, built this courtyard mansion in 1633, the same year Charles was crowned. The peak of elegance for its first 100 years, thereafter it became a huge brothel, then a home for approximately 15 families. It now houses the **Scottish Craft Center** where you can buy all sorts of beautiful handmade articles.

### Holyrood Palace

*At bottom of Canongate.* Originally undertaken in the early 15th cen-tury as a guesthouse for the now ruined Abbey of Holyrood, the struc-ture was elaborately expanded to its present state by Charles II in 1671. Before Charles, Mary Queen of Scots lived here for six years of her exciting reign. The old part of the Palace still contains her bed-room and the room in which David Riccio, the Queen's supposed lover, was murdered. Holyrood Palace is where Queen Elizabeth II stays when in Edinburgh. Tours of the palace are fascinating for their colorful details.

### Royal Museum

*Chamber and Queen Sts.* This is a vast and comprehensive museum, with exhibits covering a huge range of subjects including natural his-tory, geology, archaeology, medieval war history, and cultural arts and crafts. A visit will require a fair bit of time.

### National Gallery

*The Mound.* A breathtaking collection of paintings by British and European masters from the 1300s to the early 20th century. A sepa-rate section houses the great Scottish artists.

### Scottish National Portrait Gallery

*Queen St.* Definitely one of the most interesting galleries in the city, here you will find lifelike portraits of Scotland's most famous and important citizens from the 16th to the 20th centuries. You'll become familiar with John Knox, father of Presbyterianism; poet Robert Burns; Sir Walter Scott; Mary Queen of Scots; and many more.

## Georgian House

*7 Charlotte Sq.* Completely furnished in period decor, it offers a rare view into the lavish lifestyle of the rich during the late 18th century. Don't miss the kitchen, which is packed full of obsolete but interesting culinary objects. Audiovisual presentations on the topography and history of New Town are included in the admission fee.

### EXCURSIONS

**Linlithgow Palace** • About 55 minutes outside the city by bus; as spellbinding for the history buff as it is for the average tourist. Mary Queen of Scots was born here in 1542, and Bonnie Prince Charlie stayed here between attempts to seize the English throne. In 1646 the last Scottish parliament was held at Linlithgow. The surrounding 16th- and 17th-century houses are worth noting, as are the Cross Well and the Castle fountain. Also situated here is the 15th-century St. Michael's Church, the largest parish church in Scotland to escape damage during the Reformation.

**Dunbar** • A snug old fishing village situated 35 minutes north of Edinburgh by train. The surrounding Lammermuir Hills and the beautiful Firth of Forth are the setting for the ruins of a castle where Mary Queen of Scots was brought after her reputed lover, David Riccio, was murdered. Enjoy a stroll along the beautiful pebble beach and through the charming town streets.

## WHERE TO STAY

**Balmoral** ☆☆☆☆☆

Formerly called the North British (N.B.) and well situated on the main boulevard of the city. A total renovation program was completed not long ago, providing the city with one of the most distinguished hotels in all of Britain. It is simultaneously grand and welcoming, with tall galleries, comfortable lounges, spacious rooms, and a well-trained, cosmopolitan staff. The quality, location, and history of this fine house bode well for continuing prestige. (☎ *(031) 556-2414*)

**The Sheraton** ☆☆☆☆☆

Stately design in vaguely postmodern motif; fresh lobby in light tones; Cafe Beaumont glass-faced and dotted with foliage and palms; Atholl Bar with piano tinklings. You'll find a heated pool, sauna, and gym; well-furnished accommodations with uninspired textile selections (in this land of weavers); extrafine suites. I suspect it will mellow like a heritage dram. (☎ *(031) 229-9131*; FAX: *228-4510*)

**Caledonian** ☆☆☆☆☆

Facing Edinburgh Castle, this hotel glows with sparkle and interior grace. Many visitors feel this is the most luxurious hotel in the downtown area. I would argue that the area itself is not the ideal choice while the establishment is excellent. Some impressive accommodations (the quietest rooms front the abandoned station, not the castle), some only so-so; 5th floor with dormer windows. The popular Pompadour features excellent Scottish fare; light meals are served in the Gazebo; attractive courtyard patio for summer. (☎ *(031) 225-2433;* FAX: *225-6632)*

### George                                                   ☆☆☆☆

A dramatically improved example of the finest neoclassical decor; in other words: Adam architecture. The rehabilitation not only includes revisions in the current facilities, but the grafting of extra bedchambers that join the main building. Chambertin dining room and wonderfully antique self-service Carver's Table restaurants; the Clans Bar; typical Scottish entertainment in High Season. (☎ *(031) 225-1251;* FAX: *226-5644)*

### Carlton Highland                                          ☆

Up the bridge from the Balmoral. Apart from the extensive comforts for creatures, those same creatures can huff-and-puff in an extensive sports complex that adjoins. (☎ *(031) 556-7277.)*

### Hilton National                                          ☆☆

This hotel perches not beside but over the Water of Leith, a millstream that dances through the hotel and separates one of its bars from the restaurant. Two other bars also cater to raging thirsts. (☎ *(031) 332-2545;* FAX: *332-3805)*

### Post House                                               ☆☆☆

One of the most appealing modern addresses in the nation if you have a car. It's a 5-minute drive from the center on the Corstorphine Road to Glasgow, backing onto the Zoo, raised above the highway and looking across rolling meadows toward the Pentland Hills. Dining and imbibing corners galore; superb comfort in its well-appointed bedchambers. (☎ *(031) 334-0390;* FAX: *334-9237)*

### Royal Scot

Five minutes from the airport, and physically more daring in concept. Wood has been handsomely melded into a modern interior design; pool and health club. Many business travelers use it. (☎ *(031) 334-9191,* FAX: *316-4507)*

### King James

In town, an unusually busy host, is packing 'em in. Attractive Brasserie St. Jacques and Dunedin Suite. The smallish accommodations are thoughtfully outfitted. Okay as an up-to-date midtowner. The Scottish Dinner Show known as Jamie's Cabaret is one of the best acts in town. (☎ *(031) 556-0111)*

### Roxburghe                                                ★★★

Tranquilly situated, it retains far more of a family air than its busy-busy colleagues. Traditional tones with Adam highlights preserved; light, airy downstairs a la carte dining room; captivating ground-floor cocktail bar (which you might prefer for light dining) in

Le Consort; self-serve luncheon buffet; staffers extremely cordial throughout. (☎ *(031) 225-3921*; FAX: *220-2518*)

### Royal Terrace

After undergoing a renewal in a Georgian country house mood, the results now make this an attractive choice for lodging. (☎ *(031) 573-2222*; FAX: *557-5334*)

### Howard

Bristling with renewed vigor. All 40 units freshened and provided with private baths. (☎ *(031) 557-3500*)

### Dalhousie Castle ☆☆☆☆

A noble address outside the city proper. The neighboring Jacobean Feast (at Dalhousie Courte, a few miles distant; see "Where to Eat") is a highly bruited publicity come-on, but its soft-spoken luxury accommodations in the quiet isolation of the fortress are absolute charmers. Henry IV held the castle in siege for 6 months and many a modern traveler might happily bivouac here for a lifetime—or at least a fortnight. All 25 units are truly superb, but I'm especially fond of the Bridal Suite in the Tower or #22 up on the battlements (no elevator). Something unique and spectacularly rewarding for 20th-century day-and-knight-hood. The official address is Bonnyrigg, a short haul from Edinburgh. (☎ *0875-20153*)

### Greywalls ★★★★★

*Muirfield, Gullane, 17 miles from Edinburgh, overlooking the golfing shrine of Muirfield.* A masterpiece of architecture by Sir Edward Lutyens, Britain's preeminent Edwardian designer and my favorite housebuilder from any period. It is a joyful blend of coziness, elegance, and solidity. (Only the dining salon seems out of style; the cuisine, however, is excellent.) Gardens laid out by Gertrude Jekyll; engaging hearthside library; cheerful rooms. The "walls," incidentally, are not "grey" but a tweedy beige. It's Mecca for golfers: 10 courses in the immediate area, 4 of which are championship grade. Open Apr. to Oct. (☎ *0620-842144*; FAX: *842241*)

### Houstoun House ☆☆☆

At Uphall, about 20 minutes by car from the bright lights—another tranquil dreamland! This one is a converted mansion embraced by green lawn, guarded by a rolling 18-hole golf course. Handsome, refined dining salon on the 1st floor; glass-lined, linkside lounge; vaulted whitewashed bar with deep, soft divans and crackling fire in the chimney; 19 bedchambers with private bath (or one immediately adjoining); added wing with modern conventional decor. For reservations, write to Houstoun House, Uphall, West Lothian, or if you want to telephone to book a table, the number is ☎ *Broxburn 3831*. One of the warmest recommendations in this book, but not at all for seekers of the fancy, the ritzy, or the pretentious.

### Johnstounburn House

*40 minutes or 15 miles from the city at Humbie.* One of Scotland's brightest gems, having gotten back into business after a period of closure. Wonderful gardens and park; 17th-century mansion tone; splendid lounges; richly paneled dining room. Surely (and happily) on the comeback trail. (☎ *0875-33696*)

### Borthwick Castle

*20 minutes from the capital at Gorebridge.* A product of the early 15th century where 10 rooms are available to paying guests. Candlelit dinners are served by the log fire in the Great Hall beneath a 40-foot Gothic arch and minstrel's gallery. Today you'll find a cozy snuggery from which Mary Queen of Scots once escaped custody. Had she waited until it was refashioned, she would have changed her mind. From step number one of the spiral staircase to turrets, here's a tidy tower of taste and comfort.

### Prestonfield House

*Out on Priestfield Rd.,* this hotel mentioned under "Where To Eat," the category on which its esteem is more properly based. The hotel part is excellent provided you receive one of its few prized rooms incorporating a private bath.

### Donmaree

*21 Mayfield Gardens.* This hotel also can be recommended as a restaurant, but the gardens, the score of large, comfortable, homespun rooms with handmade duvets, and the delightful hospitality of the Galts, who own it, urge me to list it primarily as a hotel. Go for either purpose and you won't be disappointed.

### Forth Bridges Moat House

At the headland of the famous firth, casts a commanding sweep over the wind-chafed waters. Efficiency-style bedchambers; 107 rooms with bath; some with TV (who could watch it with that magnificent sea outside your window?); each unit with its own teamaker set and all the fixin's; fitness center and pool. For motorists and wide-eyed wanderlusters. Especially useful if you are playing golf courses on that side of the firth. Rush-hour traffic across the bridge can ruin composure and tee time. (☎ *(031) 331-1199;* FAX: *319-1733*)

### Hawes Inn

*Nearby at South Queensferry,* down by the water opposite the old pier. Here is where (room #13 to be exact) Robert Louis Stevenson blocked out the plot for *Kidnapped* and began writing the novel; it is also where Sir Walter Scott penned his *Balfour.* Only 7 bedchambers, 3 baths, a darned good dining room, and a cozy cocktail lounge and bar. For nostalgists, excursionists, and overnight adventures, but not for long stopovers.

### Crest

*3 miles north of Edinburgh.* Six floors of 120 lookalike cells; 6 so-called suites; 2 levels of public rooms; wide windows that don't allay the narrowness of the dimensions. Sheltering arms, but uninspired ones.

### Braid Hills ★

*South of town on Braid Road,* weaves much more flair. Total of 70 units split equally between singles and twins; reasonable rewards; pleasant as a suburban address. (☎ *(031) 447-8888)*

### Ellersly House

*About 2 miles from the center on Ellersly Rd.* Updated very recently and remains a worthy choice for tranquillity seekers. Garden situation and croquet green enhancing the converted private home. (☎ *(031) 337-6888)*

### Dalmahoy ☆☆☆☆

*A combined hotel, country club, and golfing center at Kirknewton,* 3 miles from Edinburgh just off the A71. Space for about 225 guests in a luxurious greystone Georgian mansion that was built in 1725 for the Earl of Morton. Two 18-hole courses, heated pool, saunas and steam, fitness hall, beauty salon, squash and tennis, plus a thousand acres of parkland. It's new but already causing quite a stir in Scotland—and no wonder since no effort nor pound of Scottish sterling has been spared. (☎ *(031) 333-1845;* FAX: *335-3203)*

## WHERE TO EAT

Edinburgh brightens its gastronomic horizons a bit more each season. Young and daring entrepreneurs are making a noble effort to enliven the tablescape of their capital town, but it remains to be seen whether the crusted Old Guard will support those gallant whippersnappers. Perhaps the tourist traffic alone will be enough to keep them alive—and indeed they do merit the outlanders' attentions. Let's hope they keep up their inspired kitchenwork. Hotels, in the meantime, are redoubling their efforts and the results are heartening.

### Cousteau's ☆☆☆

*Hill St. Lane N.,* As if you hadn't guessed, this restaurant is a breath of sea-fresh air. Outside hang colossal iron swimfins and a giant diving mask suggesting a link with the great French naturalist (which doesn't exist except for the proprietors' esteem for the deep). Downstairs bar and dining above. Well-made cane furniture with leaf-green upholstery. Main dishes in the £6-17 range; excellent mussels; splendid grilled fish. But the showstopper is the spectacularly attractive cold seafood platter served in a rugged scoop of cork bark almost a foot long and radiant with marine critters. Closed Sundays; dinner only. Very good.

### Vito's

*55A Frederick St.* A bright touch of Tuscany in the heart of the city. (You'll probably prefer this Vito to the original one at 109 Fountainbridge, which is hued in gray and brown.) Down a few steps to a bewitchingly colorful cellar; unusual heavy white-pine tables and chairs with red backing; terra-cotta floors; gaily painted tiles; front wall composed of beehive wine racks; two small rooms plus a bar and lounge. Amiable Italian waiters; muscular seasonings in the ample selection of Latin dishes; sweets rolled out on an amusing trolley carved as a wooden horse. Different and uplifting.

### Caledonian                                               ☆☆☆

Known for excellent standards of cookery at the Pompadour (dancing nightly except Sun.).

### Balmoral                                                ☆☆☆☆

As previously mentioned, this hotel has been completely redone. It has always been noted for its superior gastronomy amid gracious surroundings and, indeed, those attributes continue.

### George                                                   ★ ★ ★

Turns droves of visitors into calorie-counters (see "Where to Stay"). Have drinks in the colorful Clans Bar, which is a living history of Scotland. Chambertin caters to continental tastes. The Carver's Table combines turn-of-the-century decor with 20th century self service in an amiable and economic way. All segments recommended.

### Cafe Royal & Oyster Bar

*17 W. Register St.* This cafe/bar has always prided itself on its seafood. The place itself is a period piece to be savoured.

### Doric Tavern

*15-16 Market St.* A friendly sort of haven having only 9 tables with blue-and-white-checked cloths; cozy, informal, "family" aura; food superior.

### Hunter's Tryst                                           ★ ★ ★

*Oxgangs Rd.* A delightful former coaching inn, once hosted Scott and Stevenson—and if their roast beef was as good as mine, they must have been regular customers. The name aptly embodies its romantic candlelit mien. A lover's tryst, too.

### Beehive Inn

Abuzz with a loyal colony of diners. A nice couple are the drones who supervise the steak and seafood fare (which is superb).

### Pierre Victoire

*10 Victoria St.* An equally animated stop in an enjoyable old district of town. Here's the place to tuck in to a heaping plateful of delicious coldwater scallops; pork with mango is also good. Hardy fare at low prices; plenty of hub-bub every day but the Lord's. Open for lunch and dinner. (☎ *(031) 225-1721*)

### Houstoun House

*At Uphall.* One of the top tables in the British Isles.

### Prestonfield House
10 minutes from your midtown doorstep, this hotel has been the prestige oasis. Here's a beautiful converted estate gentled by somnolent grace, fanning peacocks, Highland cattle, grazing lambs—and, gulp, fleets of buses on summer evenings with tourists trooping into the neighboring festival center. (Only the idea is disturbing, but still it affects the mood generally.) Fireside bar for friendly persuasions; a few bedrooms for visitors with lingering ambitions; large menu and generally excellent cuisine; chic clientele who find it wiser to reserve in advance. Open all year for lunch and dinner.

### Cramond Inn
8 miles (20 minutes by #41 bus) from the center, where the River Almond meets the Firth of Forth at Cramond. This 300-year-old village tavern and adjoining pub lost its popularity for a while, but now it's back on track. I think you'll like it.

### La Potiniere
*At Gullane*, bordering the golfing shrine of Muirfield. This restaurant has only about a half-dozen tables, but its fame goes well beyond its capacity so be sure to book if you're going this way.

### Howgate Inn
(30 minutes out of the center) The tiny Scandinavian-minded inn is another winner; rich dining on copper service; medium tabs for superior rewards.

### Jacobean Feast
*Out at Dalhousie Courte, (3 miles from the castle) in Bonnyrigg.* Eat with your fingers or a hunting knife; lusty singing by medieval troubadours; free double-decker bus service from Edinburgh Monday through Thursday; find your own way out and back Friday and Saturday; always book ahead. Inclusive banquet, serving about 170 vassals, for about £15, and no tipping.

### Royal Mile Banquets
*(9 Victoria St.).* If you've got an abiding love for humanity, you might try it. These robust spectacles have become pretty popular all over—but not with gastronomes.

### Pride of the Union
A 60-foot barge that ambles along the Union Canal, leaving Bridge Inn jetty at Ratho (near the airport) before (7:30) sunset and returning around 11 p.m. An accordionist adds a few more notes of charm. The minicruise and galley-works cost about £16 per passenger; teatime voyaging also available. Reserve by ☎ *3331320* and allow about 30 minutes (and £10 or so) for the taxi run from midtown.

## *NIGHT LIFE*

Weeknight dancing at some of the better hotels, but no strip or girlie cabarets. Folk singing and dancing are pervasive as family entertainment.

When the sun goes down in Scotland, you've got your choice of hotel dancing, pub crawling, the handful of casinos in Edinburgh and Glasgow, or washing your drip-drys 5 or 6 times. Edinburgh offers a few discotheques: **Buster Brown's**, the **Red Hot Pepper Club**, **The Century 2000**, **The Network**, **Citrus Club**, **Club Sandino**, and **Calton Studios**. They are responsible for most of the next-day red-eye in the capital.

## PUBS

As in London and Dublin, the pub of yore is rapidly being replaced here by a hybrid that is part saloon and part discotheque. Today it's rare to find a thoroughbred stall where hairy-chested males gather for purposeful drinking. The oldest and best examples, physically unchanged for decades (when you can find one today), are rich with color, flavor, and charm. Routine neighborhood corner-tavern examples, on the other hand, are often painfully plain and colorless.

Edinburgh offers several enchanting establishments. For the authentic feel of the Old City, try one or more of the following:

### The Abbotsford

*(3 Rose St.)* This pub will transport you to mellow Victorian days. You may lunch here or nibble its snacks; noon to 2:30 p.m. and 5-11 p.m., jam-packed on Saturday night; delightful. Upstairs it provides traditional Scottish fare. Equally beguiling is

### The Volunteer Arms

("Canny Man's"), about a 15-minute taxi ride from the center at 237 Morningside Road. Its Public Bar is stuffed with mementos accumulated over nearly a century. Go between 7 a.m. (if your liver functions at that hour) and 8 p.m.; Saturdays are best.

### Scott's

*(202 Rose St.)* A family institution with a loyal following. Drinks only; an exceptionally amiable spot.

### The Golf Tavern

*10 minutes out at Brunstfield Links.* This tavern faces the pitch-and-putt course of one of the world's oldest golfing centers. Sporting clientele; friendly Public Bar and higher-toned Cocktail Bar. Lunch or beverages from noon to 2:15 p.m.; evenings from 5-11 p.m.; go Saturday, if possible.

### The Laughing Duck

Specializes in German beer and Saxon moods—in decidedly gay surroundings.

# WHERE TO SHOP IN EDINBURGH

## SHOPPING HOURS

Generally speaking: 9 to 9:30 a.m.-5:30 p.m., Mon.-Sat., Thurs. till 7:30 p.m. in Princes St., George St., and the Waverley Market-St. James Centre.

## PUBLIC HOLIDAYS

Jan. 1, Jan. 2, Good Friday, first Mon. and last Mon. in May, Aug. Bank Holiday, Dec. 25-26.

## SHOPPING AREAS

Princes St., Rose St. running parallel behind it and now partially a pedestrian zone, George St., Royal Mile, Grassmarket, and the Waverley Market.

## THINGS TO BUY

Scottish clothes, tartans, traditional jewelry, and other national items, Scottish handicrafts, silver, thistle glass, bagpipes, sheepskin-lined suede coats, deerskin fashionings, sporting equipment, antiques, River Tay pearls.

In '76 the weavers of Harris tweed—the vegetable-dyed, hand-spun and woven cloth known throughout the world—voted overwhelmingly to continue their age-old manufacturing methods instead of converting to mass production. In this increasingly shoddy merchandising culture, these gallant individualists demanded adherence to the venerable tradition that their product is a "tweed made from pure virgin wool originating in Scotland, spun, dyed and finished in the Outer Hebrides, and handwoven by the islanders in their own homes on the Islands of Harris, Lewis, Uist, Barra, and their several purtenances and all known as the Outer Hebrides." Salutes!

Yet another island group has been heard from:

*The Shetland Knitwear Trades Association* is identified by its logo of a lady knitting. Only articles produced on these 100 Scottish rock dots will sport the label. It is estimated that almost a half million items are produced by about 2,000 cottage "outworkers." These include thick sweaters called "gansies" as well as other accessories. Since so many low-grade knockoffs of Shetland and Fair Isle knitwear are flooding the market—the names have become generic—the islanders are now determined to protect their cherished image. Both styles incorporate patterns rooted in Scandinavia as well as in textiles found in the flotsam of the Spanish Armada. Shetlands are chiefly monotone while Fair Isles blend various hues. For a guarantee of quality, look for the lady in the logo.

## ANTIQUES

**Wildman Brothers** *(54 Hanover St.)* is dependable for silver, china, mirrors, and the like. **McIntosh's** *(60 Grassmarket)* offers mixed pieces; it's small. Most zealots look for Portobello pottery jugs and brass candlesticks, reputedly blue-ribbon choices. **Alexander Adamson** *(48 St. Stephen's St.)* specializes in Georgian furniture among other things. **Cavanagh-The Collector's Shop** *(49 Cockburn St.)* has oddments of coins, postcards, medals, and other militaria. **Dunedin Antiques** *(4 North West Circus Pl.)* is known for its furniture, metalwork, and antique fireplaces. **Whytock and Reid** *(Sunbury House, Belford Mews)* can supply church furnishings, rugs, carpets, and British 18th- and 19th-century furniture. **Carson Clark Gallery, Scotia**

**Map Sellers** *(173 Cannongate)* speaks for itself. **John Nelson** *(22 Victoria St.)* is a mecca for print collectors.

**Antique Fairs:** One takes place at the **Roxburghe Hotel** July 26-30 and Nov. 18-22. (These dates could differ slightly from year to year.) Another venue is the **Assembly Rooms**, (June 20 and 27, July 4, 25, Sept. 5 and 26). The annual **Antique Dealers Fair of Scotland** is in full cry Oct. 9-11. We recommend you check all these dates before-hand.

## BAGPIPES

**Clan Bagpipes** *(13A James Court, Lawnmarket)* announces its skirl on that most Scottish of Scottish real estate, the Royal Mile. The basic model sells for about £300, puffing on up to the finest silver and ivory adornments, which command around £1350. Make your neighbors into enemies with the £50 kit, providing a practice chanter, an instruction book, a cassette but, alas, no earmuffs. Joseph Hagan is the clan master here.

## BRASS RUBBINGS

**Scottish Stone & Brass Rubbing Centre** *(Trinity Apse, Chalmer's Close, High St., opposite Museum of Childhood)* is for do-it-yourselfers. They'll show you how and equip you, and then you may choose from their copies of Pictish stones, Scottish brasses, and Medieval church brasses to work on. An inexpensive way to solve the problem of a gift or enhance your own home.

## CRYSTAL

Glass has been produced in Scotland since the 16th century. Pride of the nation is **Edinburgh Crystal**. The factory is located at Penicuik—10 miles south of the capital.

## DEPARTMENT STORE

**Jenners** *(Princes St.)* is an all-purpose address.

## HANDICRAFTS

**The Living Craft Centre** *(Royal Mile)* sells baskets, pottery, knitwear, jewelry, printed textiles, and stone carvings. Another possibility is the **Tartan Gift Shop** *(96a Princes St.)*. They stock more souvenir-type merchandise, much of which, in my opinion, sadly lacks in quality.

## JEWELRY, GOLD AND SILVER

**Hamilton & Inches** *(87 George St.)* an 1835 interior that itself is an architectural showpiece by David Bryce) has represented the apogee of Scottish traditional jewelry (both old and new), gem set ensembles, silverware, and globally famous Edinburgh crystal since 1866. If you're looking for Highland Dress accessories, here is probably the international center for this specific skill, following a history of distinction that is as proud as the clans they serve. **R. L. Christie's** *(18 Bank St.)* is also highly respected.

## PURE MALT SCOTCH WHISKIES

**Justerini & Brooks** *(39 George St.)* is a paradise for connoisseurs of this most glorious of national dews. As you are probably aware, while the overwhelming majority of scotches are made of perhaps 30 to 40 different blends, this light, super-fine type is the product of one single distilling run. On these premises you will find what surely must be the largest assemblage in the world. **The Whisky Shop** *(Waverly Market, Princes St.)* also stocks an extensive range.

## SHOPPING CENTER

**Waverley Market** *(Princes St.)* spreads out over three floors. There's a craft center as well as the usual varied stores found in a mall. The lower floor is a veritable United Nations of fast-food counters. Open Mon.-Fri. 9 a.m. -6 p.m., Thurs. till 7 or 7:30 p.m., and Sun. 11 a.m.-5 p.m.

## SPORTING GOODS

Dip your line first at **Country Life** *(229 Balgreen Rd.)* or at **F&D Simpson** *(28 W. Preston St.)*, both specialists in angling and hunting.

## TARTANS AND TWEEDS

Both **Geoffrey (Tailor)** next door to the **John Knox House** (*57-59 High St.*) and **Angus Young** *(515 Lawnmarket)* are held in great esteem locally. **Kinloch Anderson** (*4 Restalrig Dr.*, ☎ 031-6617241, out of the center) is the venerable firm, founded in 1868, which specializes in superior quality men's and women's clothing—tartans (a range of over 400 available), tweeds, cashmere, silk, and cotton. For your convenience, shopping possibilities elsewhere in the nation are included here so that you can plan your purchases from an Edinburgh base. Hotels and dining options are included in the subsections titled "Where To Stay and Eat."

# WHERE TO SHOP IN GLASGOW

While it draws far fewer travelers than Edinburgh, the demand for first-line merchandise is equal and the quality is identical. Princes Square offers an international luxury showcase. Elsewhere you'll find the extrafine **Frasers** *(Buchanan St.)* for furnishings and bric-a-brac, **Burberrys Ltd.** *(64 Buchanan St.)* for rainwear, sports clothes and cashmeres, and **National Trust for Scotland** *(Hutchesons Hall, 158 Ingram St.)* for gift ideas and myriad publications. The headquarters store of **R. G. Lawrie** *(110 Buchanan St.)* is also here, for souvenirs.

## *ELSEWHERE IN SCOTLAND*

### *ABERDEEN*

## ANTIQUES

**John Bell & Co.** *(Bridge St.)* probably has one of Scotland's most worthy collections. Six floors fully stocked. Proprietor Bell and his son are impeccably candid and honest in their dealings; sometimes shudderingly costly.

## FISHING RODS

**Fishing Tackle Ltd.** *(35 Belmont St.)* is now the acknowledged laird of the streams.

### AUCHTERARDER

## TEXTILES

**R. Watson Hogg Ltd.** has been extolled for its top quality, guaranteed mailing, recorded updating of sizes, and a handsome variety of textiles.

### DUNKELD

## DEERSKIN PRODUCTS

**The Jeremy Law Collection** of bags, belt, shoes, and gloves can be seen at the Highland Horn & Deerskin Centre. It's a wee detour off the A-9 Perth-to-Pitlochry road.

### FORT WILLIAM

## TWEEDS AND WOOLENS

**Highland Homespun** *(High St.)* is about the best in town, but come autumn the pickin's are slim.

### GALASHIELS OR HAWICK

## MILL SHOPS

Bargain hunters who pass through these two manufacturing centers of the well-known "Border knitwear," are urged to stop at their mill shops for this specialty, as well as for fine tweed skirt lengths at factory prices.

### INVERNESS

## KNITWEAR

Give priority to **Hector Russell House** *(4/9 Huntly St.*, beside the River Ness). It purports to have any registered tartan, either in-the-bolt or tailored. Ladies' knits start at around £80, "full" models are £175 or so, and children's versions are a bit less. Clan chiefs have been patrons here for decades.

### LOCH LOMOND

## SUEDE COATS AND JACKETS, SHEEPSKIN LINED

The well-known **Antartex factory** is located near here, about 30 minutes from Glasgow at Alexandria, on the Lomond Industrial Estate (☎ *Alexandria 52393*). Hand knits are also available for both men and women.

### OBAN

## HAND-MADE CELTIC JEWELRY AND OTHER SCOTTISH SPECIALTIES

**The Iona Shop** *(2 Queens Park Pl.)* creates gold and silver Celtic jewelry with semiprecious stones in its own workshop. It also purveys such national products as Scottish horns, Sgian Dubhs (Gaelic black daggers), Celtic table mats, staghorn cutlery, and Celtic wall plates by Spode. Here's far and away the best of its kind in the region.

## PERTH

### DESIGNER KNITWEAR

**The Scottish Pedlar,** (Mrs. Patrick Henderson, Lawton, Burrelton, ☎ 082-15219) is a delightful lady named Morag Henderson; she welcomes visitors to her historic Perthshire home, by appointment, to see a constantly updated selection from both established names in this field as well as talented newcomers. She has an eye for men's and women's fashion. Due to low overhead, her prices also are low. If she doesn't have your size, she'll order it and send it. Only 10 miles from Perth, this is an experience no shopper should miss.

### RIVER TAY PEARLS

**A. & G. Cairncross,** the 101% reliable jewelry leader here, offers the best selection of this fascinating curiosity. This freshwater variety is harder than the oriental type; because they're so rare, they are usually graduated. Interesting but expensive. They are genuine seed pearls, not to be confused with "seeded" pearls.

## PITLOCHRY

### WOOLENS

**Macnaughtons'** extra-large stocks of woolen machine-made products—skirts, coats, suits, ties, purses, and more—don't impress me with their styling, but perhaps you'll disagree.

## ST. ANDREWS

### KNITWEAR

The nation's best buy and most famous garment is knitwear. Of the scores upon scores of outlets I've perused, not one reaches knee-high to the **St. Andrews Woollen Mill,** adjoining the Old Course Pilmour Links here. Manager Jimmy Stuart warmly encourages visitors to wander through the rambling building, to view the Tartan Gallery (over 600 tartans) and the collection of knitting stitches. Shetland pullovers in the £16 bracket; top-name cashmeres in the £125 range, dipping for special bargains to £100 or so; tartan travel blankets, £20; sheepskins, £32; mohair throws at £30 and stoles for £11; many more choices, including cut-price ends-of-batches, factory seconds, discontinued lines, and a category amusingly dubbed "Frustrated Exports." Personal dollar checks accepted; V.A.T. refunded; packing and mailing provided; closed on the Good Lord's Day. If you're anywhere nearby, please don't miss it!

### CHINA AND POTTERY

**The St. Andrews' Pottery Shop** *(1 Ellice Pl., North St.)* features Buchan Thistleware, Dunoon Stoneware, the full Montrose line, and its own historic Scottish Castles designs in fine bone china plus displays of leading British china and crystal. They pack and post to any destination. No shipping, however, from its seconds shop (South St., corner of Abbey St.). Owners Mr. and Mrs. Dennis and their helpful staff will take good care of you.

---

**AUTHOR'S OBSERVATION**

*Watch out for phony "white heather" (it's 10 to 1 that it has been doctored to resemble this extreme rarity), and the typical tourist claptrap (worth about half what they ask for it, if that).*

## EDINBURGH TO THE SOUTHERN RIM SIR WALTER SCOTT'S BORDERLAND

From the capital you can run south passing **Borwith Castle** to **Stow**. There's a historic bridge near the church here, engineered to keep heavily laden packhorses from falling into the chilly Gala Waters, which rush beneath. Arthurian legend prevails, suggesting that the King sundered a Saxon band on this ground. To commemorate the victory he is said to have offered a place of worship that every villager avows was the beginning of civilization in Stow. The road continues to the wool center of **Galashiels**, which can be amusing in spring during the pageant that dramatizes the town's valiant history. Nearby is **Abbotsford House**, where Scott penned the *Waverley* series and where he seemed to love its built-in forlorn mood. You can experience this on your own visit. It remains as it was when the author lived in it, and a Scott descendant often conducts tours of the house.

**Selkirk** was even more militant than **Galashiels**, a bastion throughout most of its career against those persistent English who kept moving up angrily from the southern border. There are many bitter memories of those battles, possibly the most poignant being the fiery end of the settlement following the conflict at **Flodden**. You'll find more peaceful recollections out at neighboring **Bowhill House**, now a museum and focal point of the refined life of rural Scotland. This estate also has connections with Scott, who for three decades wore the badge of sheriff of Selkirk. (His courtroom is on display in the **Market Place**.)

Vast and imposing **Newark Castle** is farther west, guarding the Yarrow's banks; it had a brave past but is a ruin today. New Jersey readers might be interested to know that in 1423 it was called New Wark, not to be confused with neighboring **Auldwark** (Old Wark) **Castle**, which has disappeared.

**Melrose** is where the heart of Robert Bruce was entombed in a once-glorious Cistercian Abbey. Now its best features are preserved in a museum in the town. Then drive into Kelso from the northern approach, passing **Floors Castle,** the home of the Dukes of Roxbourgh. The **Tweed Bridge** is impressive, but most come to see the Abbey (founded in 1128), which became a stronghold and where 100 men, including those of the cloth, were slaughtered. **Turret House** illustrates the history of this market town, which gained prosperity in the leather trade. Scott was very fond of Kelso.

Turning to the southwest to rejoin your route, you come to **Jedburgh**, which is proud of its **Abbey** built by David I in 1118; the rose window (**St. Catherine's Wheel**) and the **Norman Portal** are exceptional. Mary Queen of Scots is strongly linked to the town's history, which is depicted in the Visitor Centre.

**Peebles**, almost in the leafy midst of **Glentress Forest**, has been and still is a spa. Outdoor types come for the noble salmon that glide beside the banks of the buff-colored town. The Tweed reflects the spires and the hills in a fetching, civilized way. Go up to the bygone House of Fraser called **Neidpath Castle**, which overlooks the same waters that flow beside neighboring **Traquair House**; the latter is opined to be of the 10th century and possibly the oldest residence in Scotland. Traquair can be visited, an interesting interlude comprising wonderful art and mementos of the dozens of sovereigns who have dwelled under its roof. Ale is made in Traquair's brewery; you are invited to view the ancient methods and sample the results.

**Manor**, a few minutes southwest of Peebles, is only a wee hamlet but it is forever associated with Scott and *The Black Dwarf*, one of his major works. The excursion is rewarding, if only for the scenery. Another Scott excursion would be to Clovenfords, where one of his earlier homes is located. The residence, called **Ashiesteel House**, was the birthplace of the *Lady of the Lake* and other novels. As you approach Edinburgh, you'll pass through **Roslin**, so try to see the fine little **Rosslyn Chapel** on your way. Again, Scott included it in his works. Finally,

**Liberton** is almost at the fringe of the capital and is worth a pause if you have the time for its fortress view over the city.

## GLASGOW TO THE BORDERLAND GLENS
## ROBBIE BURNS AND BRIGADOON

Until recently **Glasgow** has seldom experienced a good press. It traditionally has been a tough, muscular, no-nonsense city with little time for the luxuries of the easy life. Then things began to happen. First of all it took a bath and scrubbed itself into a squeaky-clean appearance with fresh-faced buildings and refreshed parks. Then it went full-tilt for culture, and the city's dynamic Lord Provost (mayor) whipped up support from the business community and the citizens generally to give the town's very soul a retread. Those efforts have been startling, and the payoff resulted in Glasgow being annointed the title of "European City of Culture." It's been nonstop ever since. Tally-ho for the arts!

With nearly 725,000 inhabitants, Glasgow is the industrial capital of Scotland and the third largest city in Great Britain. Shipbuilding and engineering make the wheels turn; the famous **Cathedral** dates back to 1197, and the **University** to 1450. Yet there's a born-again sensation coupled with a vigorous civic drive hereabouts. Just look at the gleaming, glassy **St.**

**Enoch's Centre**, or the young-at-heart shopping enclave called **Prince's Square**. After 4 decades of searching for a proper showcase, the dazzling **Burrell Collection** now has a museum base at **Pollock Park**, 3 miles from midcity. It's an eye-opener because the 600 paintings—rivals of the Hearst trove—lay unseen in crates for so many years waiting for a window on the world. (Even so, only 40% of the works can be displayed at one time.) The **Kelvingrove Art Gallery, City Chambers, Hunterian Museum**, the engaging **Transport Museum**, the new and unique **St. Mungo Museum of Religious Life and Art** (its namesake was the first bishop of Glasgow), **Provand's Lordship 1471 House, Botanic Gardens**, and **Zoo** are among the attractions; the city has 50 public parks, 15 art galleries, nearly 2-dozen smart new office buildings, and 5 newspapers.

**Kilbarchan** (8 miles, off A-737) is the place to watch 200-year-old looms at work at **Weaver's Cottage**; *Tue., Thur., Sat.* in season. **Crookston Castle** predates Columbus. The airport is now second only to London's Heathrow in its traffic of British skywaymen. The hotels, drab and mercantile until recently, are improving; a rigidly enforced antismoke campaign has dispelled the one-time grim, grimy franchise on smog; the city's beautiful antiquities are now being revealed in a more flattering light. (Convenient jump-off point for many interesting excursions.)

**Ayr** is your first stop along the southwest coast after passing the exceptional golfing center of **Troon**. (This flank of Scotland, incidentally, boasts almost 25 miles of continuous links to catch any duffers who stray out of Prestwick looking for a round.) Burns put poetry on the map for the Scots and it was at Ayr's **Auld Kirk** that he was christened. He later wrote lyrically of the townspeople:

> *Ayr, wham ne'er a toon surpasses*
> *For honest men and bonnie lasses.*

Cross the **Twa Brigs** over the Ayr, visit **Loudon Hall**, then browse through the Burns lore at **Tam O'Shanter Museum**. Or if you wish to visit the misted Isle of Arran, Caledonian MacBrayne runs a 120-car ferry over to its shores.

Then turn away from the sea to neighboring **Alloway**, the charming, humble birthplace of the poet; his parents' whitewashed, thatch-roofed cottage is open to the public, and the ancient bridge over the quiet Doon is still here to be admired. William Burns, Robert's father, is buried at **Alloway Kirk**, and it was from here that Tam glimpsed the evil spirits cavorting outside the church window.

The route through the **Doon Valley** takes you via Hollybush and Patna to Dalmellington, which is near the cascades of **Lambdoughty Burn**. Backtracking to the east you come to **Straiton**, where the road follows the southern path of the Girvan River to the **Falls of Tairlaw**. Then the forests begin in earnest: First, **Carrick**, then **Galloway** and, finally, **Glentrool** on the hills above the **Loch of Trool**. Man has made these woodlands, but God has given them his blessing. Limitless walks around the lake can occupy days of leisure. Robert Bruce battled against the English here in the early 14th century. His victory is noted in stone.

Your trail leads northwest out of the rich glens to the open brooding moors, beside the Dusck to **Pinwherry**. From here northward toward **Turnberry** (back on the coast) and **Maybole** (inland a few miles), the Kennedy clan were all-powerful for generations.

**Turnberry** is one of Britain's great golfing sites. The situation is peaceful, the hotel is splendid, and the prices are astronomic. There's a belief that Robert Bruce was born at **Turnberry Castle**, and while it is not certain, at least it is known that he won an important skirmish at this point. The playful seals that receive stray missiles from the golf course represent the only conflict on these shores today.

Just up the lane enroute to Glasgow you will pass **Culzean Castle**, which is open to public view. This reveals—possibly at its best—the architecture of Adam, who has had such influence on decoration the world over since the 18th century. The edifice and vast surrounding parkland can easily absorb a full morning or afternoon. A presentation focused on Eisenhower reveals the general's fond memories of this estate.

# BALLOCH AND THE LOMOND LOOP

By far, the choice of every tour-package operator is **Loch Lomond**. And why not? It is lyrical country. But if you wish to avoid the throngs of competing rubberneckers, set off early in the morning. In summer Scotland has days almost as long as those in Scandinavia, so there is ample daylight at 4:30 a.m. If that's too tough, then during early spring and from September onward the traffic is much diminished. And even in high season if you drive a few miles farther north or west, the lochs are just as captivating, and you'll hardly ever see a bus tour.

You depart from Glasgow by leaving the Firth of Clyde on your left. Immediately after the city is behind you, **Dumbarton Rock** rises to command the important waterway. Almost since the beginning of man's occupation of the coastal area, this spot has been the obvious choice for a fortification. Today there are remnants of all periods, from a recently built barracks to a 12th-century portal to a dungeon to traces of its 5th-century might. There is even a sundial donated by Mary Queen of Scots—if you arrive after the sun comes up, that is.

By the time you are approaching **Balloch**, the water system of **Lomond** is in motion. This is a boating center and at its fringe is a **Wildlife Park**. The region is sometimes called "The Henley of Scotland"; you can take a steamer for a 2-1/2 to 3-hour voyage on the loch with return to Balloch. If you drive, take refreshment at **Drover's Inn** at the northern junction of four counties. Rob Roy's mum was born in the kitchen; it's been a favorite nip-inn since the 17th century. And it seems not to have changed since the first mug of ale and platter of herring and oatmeal were set before a herdsman. Today the drovers of yore are hikers and nature lovers. In fact, several of the islands and the shore belong to the **Lomond Nature Reserve**. This drive takes you along 23 miles of the nation's largest inland lake and provides you with an excellent view of **Ben Lomond**, which soars higher than 3000 feet. At **Tarbet** the loop begins its return via **Arrochar**, a town that caters to nautical pastimes of Loch Long's saltwater sailors. From here you can wind your way up to **Strachur** for the wild, lonely beauty of **Loch Fyne**, cross to the yachting center of **Sandbank** on **Holy Loch**, or slip into Glasgow via **Gairlochead**, which is also a watery playground for boating types.

## NORTH BETWEEN THE MIGHTY FIRTHS OF FORTH AND TAY

**Edinburgh** is about a third of the way out on the southern flank of the Firth of Forth. Before the great bridge was built that spans this body of water just west of town, traveling to the north meant hours of periphery driving before you really got going. Now in a few minutes you are first awed by the engineering feat and then grateful to be immediately in the country and cruising rapidly away from the city.

If you veer east, a morning's drive will bring you to **St. Andrews**, an enchanting ancient university town, probably more well known as the Shrine of Golf than for its respected position in academe. Basically, it is composed of several parallel streets running along the beautiful coast. The scholastic activities are at one end and the golf links are at the other—the international centerpiece of the sport being the all- powerful stone-faced **Royal and Ancient Golf Club** (aka "R & A"), which stands at the start-finish apron of the Old Course. There is now a well-researched museum at the Royal & Ancient for dedicated disciples of the sport. The town offers the sacrosanct **Old Course, The New, The Eden, The Jubilee,** and the recently added **Strathynum**. Throughout Fife there are dozens more, and beyond this county the galaxies of fine courses seem endless. Golf, by legend, may have begun at St. Andrews, but it certainly doesn't end there. (See Golfing Guidelines.)

For coastal browsing, take the road to lovely **Crail** (another golfing wonderland and a fishing village of great character that used to host smugglers) and then on to the herring port of **Anstruther**. Neighboring **Pittenweem** is another active fishing haven augmented by some worthwhile architecture (the **Priory, Church,** and **Kellie Castle**).

**Elie** has a golf course with a submarine's periscope towering above the starter's box. It monitors the "blind side" of a hill so that your splendid drives don't cause an international incident with a fellow player.

Incidentally, ladies, you are not really welcome in most parts of the Clubhouse here, and there is a separate entrance for you that you must take. (To be fair, this or similar ukases apply at many English and Scottish clubs. Even—or should I say especially—the R & A in St. Andrews forbids women ever to pass through its portals.)

**Leven**, also for golf, is quite a way from **Loch Leven** (farther west), where Mary Queen of Scots escaped from an island fortress. The lake area is laced with wonderful paths for walking.

From here I would suggest turning northwest toward **Auchterarder**, where the **Gleaneagles Hotel** and sporting complex is located. Here, no doubt, is one of the sensational beauty spots of Scotland and of golfdom, the **King's** course being a mecca for devotees. The **Queen's** is also a challenge; the **Monarch** is the newest. The **Mark Phillips Equestrian Centre**, with a splendid indoor arena for training in inclement periods, is also part of the scene as well as pools, a gym, and dozens of pastimes.

If you turn southwest nearing the 12th-century **Cambuskenneth Abbey**, you will soon see the greystone pinnacles of **Stirling Castle**, which obviously marks the gateway to the Highlands. Numerous Scottish sovereigns based here and, of course, the city of **Stirling** became a Royal Burgh. It was captured and recaptured many times, but its full noble story can be absorbed at the Visitors Centre, which is open the same hours as the Castle on a daily basis.

If you wish to pause, **Callender** is a more tranquil locale than Stirling, a place enjoyed by Sir Walter Scott during his frequent travels. From here you'll want to see **Brig O'Turk, Leny Pass**, and, of course, **the Trossachs**, which are also known as "Rob Roy" and "Lady of the Lake" Country. The opportunities for exploring nature at its best are here, including that "lake" itself. In summer, you can glide over the waters of **Loch Katrine**, visit the birthplace of Rob Roy, and relive the poetry Scott left behind.

# HIGHLANDS, LAKES, AND COAST

Combining one or two of the previously described circuits with this more northerly route can greatly enhance your appreciation of Scotlandscape. For lakes you have **Lochs Linnhe**, **Leven**, **Lochy** and **Ness**; for firths you have **Lorne**, **Inverness**, and **Moray**; for glens and moors you have **Etive**, **More**, **Coe** and **Rannoch**; for Highlands you have the **Grampians** themselves, with **Ben Nevis** the loftiest mountain in the land. And that's just for starters. You could branch out to the Hebrides (see later), the Western Isles, the Shetlands or the Orkneys. They, indeed, are compelling for off-track exploration, but, as you will read further along, the distances are time-consuming, the connections are sometimes complicated, the accommodations are limited, and the season is short for welcoming visitors.

**Oban** faces the Inner Hebrides dotted with isles such as **Mull**, **Coll**, **Rum**, **Eigg**, **Uist**, (the latter in the Outer Hebridean group), and the beckoning romance of **Iona**, where St. Columba landed, established a place of worship, and then began Christianizing Europe in the 6th century. (From Oban, a hydrofoil can whisk you there in 1-1/2 hours for a marvelous day excursion.) Oban itself is the gateway to the islands, an enchanting greystone port hugging the generous curve of the coast.

As you begin the northern journey you'll pass **Dunollie**, a castle owned by the MacDougalls, who once controlled a third of Scotia. While you cannot visit this compound, very soon you come to heroic **Dunstaffnage Castle**, which Robert Bruce won from the MacDougalls. The **Stone of Destiny** was guarded here before it went to **Scone** to become the coronation altar of Scotland. Flora MacDonald was held prisoner here, and much of Scottish history pivots on this ancient and legendary morsel of real estate.

Still on the castle route, **Barcaldine** is at a junction just before the fortress of the same name; it has stood majestically over **Loch Creran** since the 1500s, fell to near ruin, and early in this century was restored to become a private residence. With permission it can be visited. Also at the outskirts of the village is **Sea Life Centre**, with a wonderful collection of critters from the deep. As you are heading back toward the open waters of Loch Linnhe after having come to Portnacroish, there's yet another fighting home known as **Castle Stalker**, aptly named because James IV put it to royal use as a hunting lodge. Today you can climb among its parapets and twisting staircases for magical evocations of a dauntless past.

The road aims north to **Ballachulish**, an attractive settlement overlooking the interface of Lochs Linnhe and Leven and facing the forested and haunted hills of **Glencoe**, where the Campbells swiftly and conclusively dispatched their clan rivals, the MacDonalds. The brutal event remains as fresh in the minds of Scots today as was the shock to the local tribal world in the 17th century. It's a vast package of scenery to take in but as yet an added bonus, you should try to see the **Folk Museum** in the town of Glencoe, which goes beyond the odious conflict to display the more peaceful aspects of life in the glens. Think about it as you climb the trail up to Glencoe Pass to view the expansive **Moor of Rannoch**, the largest in Scotland. At places the bogs are deep enough to cover a two-story house.

Because the moor is so vast and the scenery is a repeat of this first impression from the Pass, I suggest you return on the same road but take the loop around Loch Leven via Kinlochleven and rejoin the Lochaber route to **Fort William**. This seems to be the happy hunting ground of bus tours. There are several restaurants, package-oriented hotels, some reasonable shopping for tweeds and wool, and throngs of milling trippers stretching their legs after a highland roll. It's a place of extremes—the highest mountain in Britain being Ben Nevis with its deepest sea loch (and the freshwater **Loch Morar**), plus the shortest river in the U.K. The **West Highland Steam train** chugs happily through the area.

On a sunny day, hop a sightseeing vessel to **Seil Island**; the scenery is wondrous and the seals offer excellent fellowship (even if they can't spell their own name, which derives from Middle English and Celtic roots). Boat trips and connections to the west (via **Mallaig**) are handy. If you want to follow your whims to Skye, Mallaig is a convenient ferry port; you'll pass the mighty **Inverlochy Castle** at the junction of the two lochs. Otherwise, the main road continues north to the ruins of **Invergarry Castle**, which was headquarters of Bonnie Prince Charles around the time of the Battle of Culloden.

Below is the glistening mirror of **Loch Oich**, which leads to the mysteries of **Loch Ness** via the Caledonian Canal. The area is replete with lore surrounding its camera-shy resident, Nessie. The hulk has been impossible to snare over the decades, but scientists and creature buffs are still hard at it with their traps, recording devices, in-place cameras, and the latest sophis-

ticated monster-catcher gear. No luck to date, but everyone agrees that
Nessie certainly wears a sinister, albeit fleeting smile. If you want to set up
your photo session, try the view from **Orquhart Castle**, about half way up
the loch toward Inverness. The handsome ruin stands out on a knoll well
into the lake, and some locals avow that after sunset you may note mon-
sters nibbling at the luscious grassy banks. (Be sure to use a quick shutter
setting.)

   **Inverness** is one of the main cities of the Highlands, but if you are coming to see the countryside, a busy town may not be your bidding. You
might wish then only to pause, perhaps visit **Queen Mary's House** or the
stalwart **Victorian Castle**, have a meal in one of the better hotels, and push
on to the more casual atmosphere of **Nairn**, with its lovely sand beaches
tipping into the cold shallows of the **Moray Firth**. Golfers will love it as a
base. The scenery is engaging, and the climate is usually delightful in summer. Take a side trip southwest to nearby **Cawdor Castle**, which was the
seat of the Thanes until the early 16th century. It provides a good picture
of life during the time of Macbeth.

   Another military target in the region is **Fort George**, built around 1748
but still occupied by the Queen's Own Highlanders; you can visit the museum within. Its history has always been associated with artillery. Its position is ideal for photography—and howitzers. The road turns inland a bit
as you move toward **Forres**, a bewitching little village in every sense. Macbeth was to learn of impending "toil and trouble" from the trio of hags
who conjured up his fortunes from a boiling cauldron. Duncan, an influential regional liege who achieved formidable stature in Shakespeare's play,
ruled here nearly a thousand years ago. Today there is no trace of such past
glories, but the town still can cast its spell on the passerby.

   **Elgin** is about a half-hour farther northeast. (**Lossiemouth**, with its wide
sandy beaches and caves to **Covesea** is due north 12 miles. Unless you are
looking for coastal features you can skip it.) The **Cathedral**, begun in the
13th century, is a major attraction, and geologists of any stripe are drawn
to the wonderful and comprehensive **Elgin Museum**, which focuses on fossils of the Old Red Sandstone, Permian, and Triassic epochs.

   **Buckie** is noteworthy for its **Maritime Museum**. Within the shadow of its
yardarms, you have some attractive salty village ports and waterside hamlets such as **Portessie**, **Findochty**, **Portknockie**, **Cullen**, and **Portsoy**—all of
them more or less involved with sea activities or the special, subtly hued
marble hewn from local quarries.

   **Banff** and **Macduff** are towns made for postcard promoters. **Banff Museum** is big on its namesake silver, as well as on arms and armor. You'll also
probably wish to see **Duff House**, a beauty of Georgian Baroque style by
William Adam. The views from both townlets are breathtaking. Drive over
to **Cruden Bay** (wonderful golf) and see **Bullers O'Buchan** and the clifftop
ruins of **Slains Castle**, which inspired Stoker's Dracula.

   From this point, you can start a southward vector through the historic
market town of **Turriff** (with a side trip here to **Delgatie Castle**) and on to

**Aberdeen**, the feverishly prospering petro-king of the North Sea coast. Apart from the black-gold rush, it is also a year-round flower center and a seasonal resort. Commerce and art are mated in creating better theater, more music, and a far more active cultural scene. Discerning admirers of whiskeys may stagger along the **Malt Whiskey Trail**, which incorporates the glens of **Livet**, **Fiddich**, and a half-dozen more greats in the distillery realm, plus some of the most beautiful countryside of Europe.

Additional trailblazers can troop the **Castle Trail** in the historic Gordon district, running north and west of Aberdeen. Hotels are jammed with business visitors, and petrodollars have caused local prices to skyrocket. The expanding limits spread along the banks of the **Don** and the **Dee** rivers and not far from the off-shore oil fields that are being developed by the nation. Between the mouths of these waterways, a 2-mile sandy beach has been dedicated to holidaymakers—perfect for Polar Club bathers who sprout walrus hair on limbs, back, and shoulders. Outstanding university, 15 lovely parks, numerous arts projects supported by the oil companies, venerable **St. Machar's Cathedral; Bridge of Dee** (built 1500); don't miss the **Fish Market**, one of the most interesting in the United Kingdom.

You next drive along the Dee to the bustling (summer only) town of **Banchory**. You can headquarter here for wonderfully scenic excursions into the hills or roll on to one of my favorite Scottish havens called **Ballater**. This captivating townlet might be called "the gemstone of the castle belt." Down the pike a few miles is the queen's own **Balmoral**, where the gardens are open to public inspection (when she is not in residence). A bit farther is magnificent **Craigievar**, which was lived in until very recently and was left totally intact and furnished when the owners shifted to other digs so that everyone could share the beauty of their ancestral estate. Of course, **Braemar Castle** is next door and is viewable; the lecture tour here is superb. In the same region are **Crathes Castle and Gardens, Dunideer Castle, Drum Castle,** and you might drive back a short distance to browse through the engaging **Banchory Museum**. There's the Z-plan **Castle Fraser** with its extensive **Castles of Mar** exhibition. (The Z-formed structure was once widely acknowledged as the most modern defense system architects could devise.) This area is so sylvan and so enchanting that unless you have compelling reasons for settling in nearby busy Aberdeen, I would overwhelmingly urge you to bunk here.

From any of these beautiful hamlets, the return route leads through captivating country and handsome towns. It descends into the dramatic **Spital of Glenshee** (possible side trip to Kirriemuir, Arbroath, the golfing magic of Carnoustie, to Dundee) and passes **Blarigowrie** on its way to Perth. This is in the region of Blaire Castle (Pitlochry) for a further detour. At this point the pike to Edinburgh or Glasgow is easy, open, and swift.

## "OVER THE SEA TO SKYE," ETC.

Don't tell that untraveled songsmith, but the fabled isle referred to in the ballad is really only a stone's throw "over the sea" from the Scottish mainland. Standing downwind of **Skye** you can even smell the heathered

shore at **Kyleakin** and see the serrated **Cuillin Hills**. There are two main
ferry crossings. The chief reason for doing the southern cross from **Mallaig**
to **Armadale** would be if your name happens to be Donald (or Mac-
Donald), since the handsome white **Clan Donald Center** is here and features much of the dramatic feuding lore between this tribe and the more
northerly MacLeods. (As far as I know, the golden arches of another Mac-
Donald descendant do not yet adorn these skyeways.) Most likely you'll arrive on the easier route from **Kyle of Lochalsh**, where the ferry sails from
its slipway at Kyleakin and your auto rolls off to start you on your way. If
you were in a rush (no cases listed to date), you could traverse Skye from
north to south in a couple of hours, not passing more than a dozen cars in
your cross-country passage. Sheep might wander aimlessly across the roads;
the vistas are vast with pockets of shimmering lochs sparkling in the soft
baize emerald landscape. On Sundays even the sheep seem to slow down.
Sabbatarians—active on the islands of Harris and Lewis—remain a stern
voice on the Hebridean scene, so most of the tranquility on the Lord's Day
hereabouts can be blamed on, or credited to, these staunch keepers of the
faith. Skye, however, is not affected, nor are many other isles. Because of
this influence you would do best to schedule island hops to Harris or Lewis
on any days other than the sabbath.

**Portree**, at the island's midriff and facing the isle of **Raasay**, is the capital. It is held in a fractured cup of rocks looking bayward. Here are several
hotels of modest size and numerous whitewashed cottages that serve the
bed-and-breakfast trade very hospitably. On the tour to the north, pass by
the **Quiraing**, a queer arrangement of stone formations, as you head for the
**Flora MacDonald Monument**. This historical figure spent some years at **Flo-
digarry** and is honored in many places of the world—North Carolina is one
of them—for her cunning in saving the life of Bonnie Prince Charlie. In the
same area is a "Black House" containing the **Skye Cottage Museum**.

Most of the island dwellings are white now, so as a curiosity of earlier
days when there was a predominance of black houses, you will probably
enjoy a pause here. The ring road around the coast passes the ruins of heroic **Duntulum Castle**, a fine stop for photographs with a view to the isle of
**Harris**, of tweed fame. A great deal of this textile, however, is marketed
through **Uig**, which lies just south of here and is a gateway to the Outer
Hebrides. **Port-na-Long** is also known for this weaving specialty.

**Dunvegan Castle** is an evergreen tourist attraction, especially if you are
in the MacLeod family, which made this their stronghold for almost four
centuries. It stands three stories tall on a rocky rise above the loch, looking
toward Harris. The higher square tower, turrets, and crenels, indeed,
evoke a noble bearing, and the artifacts within are worth viewing. And if
you are needing a wee tot of single malt to lift your spirits, the famous Talisker elixir is distilled patiently and masterfully in the nearby settlement of
**Carbost**. Why not stop by for a dram?

All within this reach of enchanting sea and shore are the lonely He-
brides—**Rhum**, **Muck**, **Canna**, **Eigg**, **Coll**, **Tiree**, with **Mull** and tiny **Iona** to
the south tucked in below Skye and running around the peninsula rim to

Oban farther east. Across a westerly stretch of water called **The Minch** lie
the more remote misted isles of the Outer Hebrides.

From Uig (on Skye) you can take passage for **Lochmaddy** on **North Uist**
or for **Tarbert** on the much larger island of Harris. On the northern flank
of **Lewis** there's a splendid castle at **Stornoway**. Then come **Barra**, at the
lower end, and **South Uist**—or the tiny rock-dot of **Eriskay**, where 24,000
cases of spirits tragically went down to the ocean floor—and were salvaged
merrily by the islanders who inspired the hilarious film *Whisky Galore!* In
any case, the tight little island may not be worth a special trip, but this, as
others, can be seen in private vessels that leave the piers of the major ports
at any time that suits the skipper's digestion.

For those major ports or islands, talk to the **Caledonian MacBrayne** ferry
people, who are represented on almost any wharf in these ports. (**Caledonian MacBrayne** is really the glue that holds the Hebrides together.) Otherwise, any travel agent can do the task of putting together a trip of very
reasonable outlay. As a guideline, providing you have the time and don't
expect fireworks, I'll suggest a sampler. Begin at **Oban** on the early morning boat. By midnight you have passed **Barra**, with its **Kissimul Castle** at
the harbor entrance, and finally tied up at **South Uist**, in the sleepy port of
**Lochboisedale**. Though you yourself may be drowsy, there is still a suggestion of midsummer light in the sky—and dawn is not long in coming.

**Iona** is the rockdot where St. Columba landed and began to christianize
the north of Britain in the 6th century. Macbeth also found his final resting
place here. You can hop to Mull by boat, take an overland transfer, and
cross to Iona at the western extremity. Within easy walking distance of the
small dock is the ancient Abbey, the Nunnery, a coffee shop and, naturally,
a golf course. Of the 2 tiny hotels, I prefer the **Columba** to the **Argyle**, but
both afford reasonable comfort and restful vistas of the Sound and Fionn-
phort on the Ross banks. Shoppers can visit charming "Fiona of Iona,"
mistress of **Iona Scottish Crafts** where woolens, jewelry, and pottery of the
isles are purveyed.

If riding on the waters is not to your liking but looking at them is, there
is an enjoyable option for landlubbers. It's the rail link referred to as **The
Hebridean**, which runs between **Inverness** and **Kyle of Lochalsh** and peers
out upon some of the most captivating land-and-seascapes available in all
of railroading. The observation car is comfortable and focused on what
you've come to see; it also includes a lass to serve as your guide. If you can,
choose a north-facing seat by the windows.

There's a wonderful stretch west of **Dingwall** penetrating **Blackwater** and
edging past the deer-dotted hillsides that feed **Loch Garve**. Farther along,
**Loch Luichart** is larger but no less wild and beautiful.

After the romp across **Strath Bran**, keep your eye open for **Glencarron
Lodge**. The Scots are great storytellers, and from this dwelling hangs the
tale of the quirky Lady Cobbold, its long-deceased proprietress. In her global roamings she had managed to enter the forbidden city of Mecca. So impressed was she that she became a Moslem then and there. And to confirm

her devotion well into the next world, she left orders that when she passed on, she should be planted so as to face the sacred Middle Eastern shrine forever from a standing position. Now it is not known whether kneeling would have been more correct for this ceremonial posture or the gravediggers simply did not go deep enough to completely cover Lady Cobbold. In any case, it is said that she suffered some undignified pats on the head with the spades before she properly fit into the accommodation provided. A tip of your chapeau (or Tam O'Shanter) will be appreciated as you pass.

This is about the midway point between Dingwall and the ferry point for Skye. Only an hour remains of the rail journey, but it is a rewarding one as you begin a lochside run from **Strathcarron** past **Strome Castle**, into the severe rock cuttings passing **Plockton**, and finally to the watery junction that is **Kyle**.

A typical trip to an island can be a test of one's passion for tranquility, if not solitude. Take the rolling isle of **Colonsay**, for example. There's one hotel and 14 miles of paved road to cover all of its 10,000 acres. There are 120 residents, a few boarding houses, 620 plant species, and enough fowl to keep your nose in a bird book all day long. In fact, that's what most people who visit the **Colonsay Hotel** come to do. Ornithology is the evergreen topic hereabouts, as it is on many of the isles. The seals have a great sense of humor, and the feral goats are handsome creatures. The latter are not angry, even if they glare at you harmlessly along the rocky shore. Departures from **Oban** on the *Caledonian MacBrayne* ferry, usually three times a week; the passage takes a little over two hours and costs under $25. Take along plenty to read, some binoculars for the wildlife that you'll witness in flight, and some insect repellant for the unseen airborne attacks by midges (the name Scots have given to the voracious "teeth with wings" that also occupy the great outdoors).

# WHERE TO STAY

## *EDINBURGH TO THE SOUTHERN RIM*

### BRAMPTON

**Farlam Hall**                                                    ★ ★

This hotel actually is in England, but it is just at the border and convenient for exploring **Hadrian's Wall**. Only a dozen rooms; a country house with connections to John Wesley and steamy George Stephenson. Excellent cuisine. (☎ *06976234*; FAX: *06976683.*)

### GALASHIELS

**Woodlands House**

A cozy spot with a few rooms and a mighty heart. Nice. (☎ *0896-4722.*)

**Kingsknowes**

Much bigger (11 rooms!) and is also a worthy stop; you'll find it on the Selkirk Rd. (☎ *089658375.*)

# KELSO

### Marlefield Country House
Known more as a restaurant, but it does have a few ingratiating bed-chambers. (☎ *0573-561.*)

### Ednam House
More of a conventional hotel, and convenient if you are visiting **Flodden Battlefield** and **Floors Castle**. (☎ *0573-24168.*)

### Woodside
Very reasonable in price; 11 rooms. (☎ *0573-24152.*)

# MELROSE

### George & Abbotsford
Near to the memory of Sir Walter Scott. (He's at rest at nearby **Dryburgh Abbey**.) Fishing rights on the Tweed. Take a room facing the abbey. (☎ *089682-2308.*)

### Waverley Castle
Big by comparison (100 rooms) and prices are lower. (☎ *089682-2244.*)

# MUIRFIELD (GULLANE)

### Greywalls                 ☆☆☆☆

The legendary golfing shrine east of Edinburgh. If you don't play the sport, you might feel out of place. If you do, however, it is excellent and geared to precisely this audience. Be sure to check well in advance to learn if you can obtain starting times on the superb course (see "Golfing Guidelines") and be sure to bring your handicap certificate. (☎ *0620-842144;* FAX: *72294.*)

### Open Arms
At nearby **Dirleton**, composed of a half-dozen small stone houses and catering to a more general audience. The cookery is noteworthy.

# NORTH BERWICK

### Marine                          ☆☆
In the same area is a stalwart upper-crust candidate with views to the links course and the Firth of Forth. Some units quite expensive. (☎ *0620-2406;* FAX: *4480.*)

# PEEBLES

### Peebles Hydro
A bulky old-timer that has been in the spa biz for generations. There's a comfortable feeling about it. (☎ *0721-20602;* FAX: *22999.*)

### Tontine
More refined, smaller and maybe not as much fun. Still, it's very good and recommended. (☎ *0721-20892.*)

# SELKIRK

### Philipburn House
Only 16 rooms, but it is the last word in hospitality. Travelers love it—and so do I. (☎ *0750-20747*; FAX: *21690.*)

# GLASGOW TO THE BORDERLAND GLENS

## AYR

### Embassy Caledonian
The largest hotel in the area, with 114 rooms on the Dalblair Rd. which is convenient for Prestwick Airport. (☎ *0292-269331*; FAX: *610722.*)

### Fairfield House
On Fairfield Rd., more intimate with a couple of dozen units. (☎ *0292-267461*; FAX: *261456.*)

## ALLOWAY

### Balgarth
Another small hostelry in the southern area serving Prestwick and the coast. (☎ *0292-42441.*)

## DRYMEN

### Buchanan Arms
Long a favorite of Stirlingshire, being 5 miles from Lomond's shores. Colorful lounge and enclosed dining terrace; so-so cuisine; comfortable rooms. (☎ *0360-60588*; FAX: *60943.*)

## GLASGOW

### One Devonshire Gardens
At the same address as its name, the discerning choice for non-hotel types. Only 8 accommodations and each a gem; superb refined cuisine. (☎ *041-3392001*; FAX: *3371663.*)

### Albany
Boasts 250 units that are comfortable but uninspired. (☎ *041-2482656*; FAX: *2218986.*)

### Holiday Inn
Even larger than Albany. The food spreads are tempting, but the place is vast. Basically quite good (☎ *041-2265577*; FAX: *1.*)

### Hospitality Inn
Located at the Convention Centre, with all that implies. It's well managed for a giant. (☎ *041-3323311*; FAX: *3324050.*)

### Excelsior
Placed handy to Glasgow Airport, about 10 miles from the city center and useful if the weather socks in your flight. (☎ *041-8871212*; FAX: *8873738.*)

### The Ubiquitous Chip

(12 Aston Lane), In a warehouse down an alley away from midtown. The game is excellent in season; prices are reasonable. (☎ 041-3345007.)

### October

(128 Drymen Rd., Bearsden) Another noncentral choice where careful cookery is offered at not too costly tabs. Sample the monkfish if it's on the menu. Cuisine is mainly French. (☎ 041-9427272.)

## PRESTWICK

### Carlton

On the Ayr Rd. (see also Ayr for other choices). Very comfortable after a long transoceanic journey. (☎ 0292-76811.)

### Towans

On the Powermill Rd., moderate in price, and adequate for a brief stay. (☎ 0292-77831.)

## TROON

### Marine Hotel                                          ☆☆☆☆

A quick skip from Prestwick Airport and 26 miles from Glasgow, offers an unprecedented 25 miles of golf courses in a row. (At the Royal Troon Club, women may play only on certain days.) Almost 2 dozen units in attractive decor; dining room with sea and links panorama; handsome cocktail bar. Heaven for golf bugs, but becoming a frequent target for short-stay excursionists and package trippers. (☎ 0292-314444; FAX: 316922.)

## TURNBERRY

### Turnberry Hotel                                      ☆☆☆☆☆

Situated in Ayrshire 50 miles south of Glasgow and 15 miles from Ayr—a the favorite of the "Burns Country" excursionist, as well as many dyed-in-the-Shetland golfers. Now that it is under Japanese ownership, many Far Eastern guests sign the register and occupy starting times on the links. (Hence, be sure to fix your golf dates when you make your hotel booking.) Each of its 115 units with private bath or shower plus TV sets; color-matched textiles to offset the stark-white walls; fresh bar; spacious and viewful lounges, dining room, and bedchambers. The selected grounds sanctified for British Open Golf Championships; tennis courts; indoor pool; dancing and movies; snooker room; minibus service to Prestwick and other getaway points; smoothly operated. (☎ 0655-31000; FAX: 31706.)

## *BALLOCH AND THE LOMOND LOOP*

## DUMBARTON

### Travelodge

Offers 32 routine units. You will have to dine out since food is not served. (☎ 0389-65202.)

# DUNBLANE

**Cromlix House** ★★★

This hotel resides on a hunting estate of some 5000 wooded acres about 4 miles north of the picture-postcard town. The Victorian mansion, with a heritage reaching to the dawn of Scottish history, has its own private chapel, antiques of museum quality, and heraldic needlepoint that enthusiasts cross the Atlantic just to view. Meals—and superb they are—are likely to be your most memorable dining experiences in Scotland. The 14 bedrooms (with private baths) are in the grand tradition of a great country house. Rates are high, but so is the quality for the rare privilege of visiting such a home. (☎ *0786-822125*; FAX: *825450.*)

# LOCH LOMOND

**Lomond Castle**

A suitable choice if you wish to overnight in the Lomond district. Its 21 rooms are reasonably priced. (☎ *038985-681.*)

**Tarbert**

Close to Arrochar, a lovely part of the lake (western side). It's quite a bit bigger and still lower in price. (☎ *03012-228.*)

# KILCHRENAN

**Ardannaiseig** ☆☆☆

Residing on a small bluff beside Loch Awe (a bit west of Dumbartonshire). This is Scotland's Garden Belt, warmed by the Gulf Stream effect. All of the main public rooms are viewful, and the bedrooms for its 28 guests, each with its own bath and telephone, are comfort-oriented but not fussy. The hotel supplies boats for fishing in the Loch—both rainbow or brown trout—and a picnic hamper, if desired. Also on the grounds are facilities for tennis, croquet, clay pigeon shooting; a liaison has been made in the neighborhood for golf, rough-shooting, or deer stalking. Closed from Oct. through the winter and so remote that you should be sure to reserve ahead. (☎ *08663-333*; FAX: *222.*)

## *NORTH BETWEEN THE MIGHTY FIRTHS OF FORTH AND TAY*

# ANSTRUTHER

**Craws Nest**

A reasonable stop out on this coastal littoral. It's in the heart of the great golfing terrain of Fife. (Crail is very close.) (☎ *0333-310691.*)

**The Cellar** ★★

Draws many discriminating diners who drive out from Edinburgh. Warmhearted atmosphere provided by Peter and Vivien Jukes. Reserve ahead. (☎ *0333-310378.*)

# AUCHTERARDER

### Gleneagles                                              ☆☆☆☆

An entertainment institution with 220 rooms, some of the greatest golfing facilities in the world (Kings Course is only one of 5 courses), an equestrian center, pools, a country club, squash, fishing—almost anything related to sport and leisure. It's expensive and perhaps too organized for many. (☎ *0764-62231*; FAX: *62134.*)

# AUCHTERHOUSE

### Old Mansion House                                      ☆☆☆

On the Tay near Dundee. Merely a half-dozen rooms in a dwelling that goes back 5 centuries. The kitchen is one of the most highly regarded in Angus; the mood, too, is highly appealing. (☎ *082626-366*; FAX: *400.*)

# CUPAR

### Peat Inn                                               ☆☆☆☆

At a crossroads called *Peat Inn*; it's close to nothing much but not far from Cupar, Dundee, or Perth. The Inn is really 8 reasonably priced suites next to a restaurant of considerable fame locally. The effort, the kindness, and the results are all rewarding.

### Ostler's Close

At **Bonnygate**, well known to gourmets of Scotland. It has long been one of the nation's leading restaurants. Closed Sun. and Mon. (☎ *0334-55574.*)

# CALLANDER

### Roman Camp

Formerly a hunting lodge of the Dukes of Perth. Library, lounge, and magnificent gardens within the 30-acre estate. Maintenance a bit spotty, but perhaps the owners believe this is its homespun aura. (☎ *0877-30003*; FAX: *0764.*)

# DUNKELD

### Dunkeld House                                          ★★

(Perthshire) resides on one of the most romantic Tayside stretches you're likely to find in all of Scotia. Entrance via an arched stone gate; a mile's drive through forest and garden to the ocherhued mansion; lawns of Karastan neatness and lush vegetation; pitch-and-putt golf course; all facilities for fishing in that glorious river. (☎ *03502-771.*)

# KINROSS

### Windlestrae

A small hotel with an outstanding restaurant. If it is toward evening try to pause for dinner; it will be worth a stopping over for the night. (☎ *0577-63217*; FAX: *64733.*)

# LEVEN

**Old Manor**,
On the Leven Rd., is handy to a very good golf course. Limited accommodations, but okay if you are drawn mainly for the sport. (☎ 0333-320368.)

# PERTH

**Royal George**
This hotel has been around for a long time, and it is fairly comfortable. (☎ 0738-24455; FAX: 30345.)

**Station**
My next choice, but neither this nor Royal George is too thrilling. (☎ 0738-24141; FAX: 39912.)

**Coach House**
More fun for dining than either of the above hotels, which are too austere.

# ST. ANDREWS

**Old Course**                                          ☆☆☆☆☆
Stands in modernistic splendor at the edge of Scotland's prime golfing real estate, is easily the leader. Glorious views from the Swilcan Lounge and new restaurant; expanded suites and bedroom facilities in brown, peach, white, and blue; patchwork quilts; dozens of ingratiating touches such as silent valets, flowers, fruit, and even (sometimes) whiskey. Excellent pro shop and tiptop porters who can get golfers onto any course in the nation with only a phone call. Don't forget to tip for this service. (☎ 0334-74371; FAX: 77668.)

**Rusacks**                                                   ☆☆☆
Bordering the links and recently given an entirely new tone while maintaining its enviable traditional atmosphere. It boasts lockers and changing rooms so that "outsiders" may play the local courses without struggling into or out oftheir wardrobes beside their parked cars. Beautiful high-ceilinged lounge; upgraded cuisine; excellent comfort; a delightful 19th hole. (☎ 0334-74321; FAX: 77896.)

**Rufflets**                                                  ★★★
Offers only 21 bedchambers; naturally they are almost always booked. Outskirts situation about 10 minutes by car to the tee; substantial cookery; homespun rewards, but inhospitable reception. (☎ 0334-72594.)

**Scores**
On a hillock overlooking the course, is ideally situated; now that the maintenance has improved, I think you'll enjoy it. (☎ 0334-72451; FAX: 73947.)

### Argyle

Good for budgeteers; it provides bed and breakfast only. (☎ *0334-73387.*)

### St. Andrews Golf Hotel

With the same sea-and-course view as Scores, has undertaken some updatings and is an adequate shelter for golfers nowadays. (☎ *0334-72611*; FAX: *72188.*)

When the golfing is done and evening light lingers in these northern skies, the **Old Course** is lovely. At lunch the lounge is fun or outside by the course wall, have a sandwich at the rough and ready **Jigger Inn**, only a simple pub but with plenty of atmosphere. In town, the **Vine Leaf** on South Street (an alley entrance) is especially good for its vegetables. **Merchant's House** is also worth a try. **Littlejohns**, on the main street, is kitsch in every respect. An electric train runs around the top of the room. Food is unusual, abundant, and worthwhile as a change of pace from sedate places.

### The Grange Inn

At an outskirts address used a lot by sporting types, appealing for atmosphere. The open fires and antique intimacy conspire nicely at the end of the day.

Outside of town, both **The Cellar** at **Anstruther** (excellent sea fare) and the **Peat Inn** (also described earlier) are intimate and upmarket. For shoppers, the St Andrews Woollen Mill, adjoining the Old Course Pilmour Links, is the knitwear outlet for me. See my shopping section appended to the Edinburgh report for further details on this great opportunity.

## STIRLING

### Park Lodge ☆

A charming Georgian retreat with lovely antique furnishings in its handful of rooms. (☎ *0786-74862.*)

### Golden Lion

In the center of town and more of a conventional hotel with 85 rooms and, happily, a tranquil location. (☎ *0786-75351.*)

## *HIGHLANDS, LAKES, AND COAST*
## ABERDEEN

### Caledonian

The old stalwart here on Union Terrace. Space for about 150 guests; reliable restaurant. (☎ *0224-640233*; FAX: *641627.*)

### Royal

A midtowner with a fine Scottish tradition; agreeable dining. (☎ *0224-585152*; FAX: *583900.*)

**Treetops**

Out on the Springfield Rd. in the west end. Nice lounge and bar; fitness and leisure center. (☎ *0224-313377*; FAX: *312028.*)

**Skean Dhu**

A large house out on the Souter Head Rd. (**Altens**). If you like big enterprise here it is—and well done, too. (☎ *0224-877000.*)

**Acharacle Glenborrodale Castle**

A handsome site on 1000 acres of Western Highlands beside the north shore of Loch Sunart. Many of its 16 rooms with fourposter bed, baths en suite; a kitchen that thrives on the produce of the estate and regional pickin's. Ideal for quiet times. (☎ *097-24266*; FAX: *24224.*)

## ADVIE

**Tulchan Lodge**

This luxury spot is writing a deluxe chapter in the Spey River anthology. Shooting and angling rights plus all the comfort and convenience that humanity can divine will cost you close to £1250 per week per person. It is so special that more space can't be devoted to it except to recommend it to the sporting set. (☎ *08075-200*; FAX: *235.*)

## APPIN

**Ardsheal House**

The quiet domain of resident-proprietors Jane and Bob Taylor, eager Americans who open their 12 rooms (8 with private bath) and their great hearts to tranquillity seekers. Casual and homespun, it's on the shores of Loch Linnhe and has roots reaching back to the 16th century. Clearly, the greenhouse dining salon is one of its most arresting blossoms; the cuisine is interesting in choice and wins orchids locally for execution; ask to see some of the stunning locally made sweaters that are sometimes shown here for sale. There's a tennis court; boating nearby. For more information, write Kentallen, Appin, Argyll PA38 4BX. (☎ *063174-227.*)

**Airds**

At Port Appin, a cozy tie-up at what was an early ferry point and is now a 14-room inn. You receive a wondrous view of Loch Linnhe, warm hospitality, and excellent cooking. (☎ *063-173.*)

## BALLACHULISH

**Ballachulish**

Mentioned because this is an important junction and a springboard for the Glencoe rovings. Nothing very much, but okay in a pinch. (☎ *08552-606.*)

## BALLATER

**Tullich Lodge**

Fit for a baron. This 10-bedroom noble mansion sits tall in its own park overlooking the rushing Dee. Antiques and fine furnishings fill the twin first-floor lounges and spaciously comfortable accommodations. When they are at their best, resident-proprietors Hector Macdonald and Neil Bannister create an atmosphere of cheerful bonhommie; they also can produce some of the finest cuisine in Scotland and present it in one of the liveliest salons in Aberdeenshire. A beguiling retreat. (☎ 03397-55406; FAX: 55397.)

### Kildrummy Castle

Not too distant, surrounded by 15 acres of park and water gardens. Great fishing along 3 miles of the Don. The original fortress dates from 1245, but comforts are modern and ample. (☎ 03365-71288; FAX: 71345.)

### Raemoir House

A 28-room noble mansion for sporting and relaxing types, backed by the 1500-foot Hill of Fare plus legions of supporters who sing its praise from all quarters of the globe. The landscape around this hostelry is a chapter from *Field & Stream*. Excellent. (☎ 03302-4884; FAX: 2171.)

### Craigendarroch

A lovely tawny-rose, towered structure with blissful Deeside scenery, ample luxury in its 23 accommodations, and local game, beef, or seafood in its Oaks restaurant. Pool, children's room, beauty salon; golfing nearby at the Ballater Club. (☎ 03397-55858; FAX: 55447.)

### Invery House

At *Banchory*, almost midway between Ballater and Aberdeen (on A-93). It resides on 40 acres on the west bank of the River Feugh, a white mansion with stately home appointments and the grace of ages. Only 30 guests tuck in, many of them devoted to sports and outdoor pursuits of the region. (☎ 03302-4782; FAX: 4712.)

### Mar Lodge                                                                        ☆

A former royal hunting manse, and judging from the clientele observed on a recent visit, its chief appeal is still for nimrods and anglers. If these are not your primary interests, you might be happier in one of the above establishments.

## BANFF

### Banff Springs

On a lonely bluff overlooking a magnificent stretch of sea and coast. The modern lines suggest a suburban grade school; nevertheless its comfort is abundant. Snack facilities plus full restaurant; 30 nice rooms. (☎ 02612; 2881.)

### County

Homelike and cozy, in Banff proper. It offers only 7 units. (☎ 02612-5353.)

### Fife Lodge

Overlooking the River Deveron, a worthy stopover. (☎ 02612-2436.)

Two additional hotels of note in the region are the 100-room **Waterside Inn** (☎ *0779-71121*; FAX: *70670*) at **Peterhead** and the park-surrounded **Saplinbrae House** near **Old Deer**. **Pennan** has the waters-edge **Pennan Inn** (☎ *03466-201*).

# BRAEMER

### Braemer Lodge
Offers only 8 rooms, but the atmosphere is pleasant; just the evening meal is served (and usually pretty early). (☎ *03383-627.*)

### Invercauld Arms
Noteworthy cuisine; offers about 60 accommodations and is used frequently by package tours. (☎ *03383-605.*)

# BUCKIE

### Cluny
A cute little spot to stop for the night. Ask about dining at the nearby **Old Monastery**, which is very attractive.

# ELGIN

### Mansion House
Offers a dozen rooms, good food and warm hospitality. (☎ *0343-548811*; FAX: *547916.*)

# ERISKA

### Isle of Eriska
This stately home has stood above the Firth of Lorne since 1884 and is reachable via a modern bridge today. (Eriska is a flat, water-girt island about 15 minutes by car from Oban.) A personable, hard-working couple, Robin (he) and Sheena (she) Buchanan-Smith, have wrought wonders in providing such a discriminating panoply of enticements in so remote a clime. Crackling fires, oak panels, deep snooze-away chairs, a well-stocked bar, restful vistas, books, books, and more books all conspire to giving up thoughts of ever wearing a wristwatch again. The exceptions are just before mealtimes when telltale cooking fragrances hint of grand things to come. Rooms are named for Hebridean Islands, and my own favorite twin mooring is "Skye," with vast vaulted wooden roof, rich antique appointments, color-keyed linens, excellent carpeted bath, and its own large skylight in the ceiling. Closed winters; distinguished and costly. (☎ *063172-371.*)

# FORRES

### Ramnee
A useful stop on the Victoria Rd. (☎ *0309-72410.*)

# FORT WILLIAM

### Inverlochy Castle
Steals not only all the local innkeeping thunder but, to an ever-grow-

ing number of devotees, it is now considered one of the brightest lightning bolts in the national welkin. Exquisitely appointed baronial estate surrounded by 50 acres of garden within 500 acres of farmland; only 14 supersumptuous luxury accommodations; skilled skilletry with predinner drinks in the richly outfitted salon; coffee and libations in the lounge; billiards in the trophy room; blue-ribbon price tags; open May through Oct. normally, but they will welcome special parties throughout the year if requests are made. Please reserve way, way, w-a-y in advance with personable young director Michael Leonard. Wonderful. (☎ *0397-2177*; FAX: *2953*.)

### Milton

A solid bet   but not for the victuals. (☎ *0397-2331*.)

### Croit Anna Motel

3 miles out, has become a close contender, with solid comfort and cookery in a ranch-style motif. (☎ *0397-2268*.)

### Alexandra

Much improved since it spent a packet on modernizations. (☎ *0397-2241*.)

## GRANTOWN-ON-SPEY

### Grant Arms                                                              ☆☆

Elegance has marched smartly to the fore. White leather furniture commanding attention in the parade-ground-size lounge. Winter-garden restaurant reconnoitering the Cromdale Hills; elaborate menu forecasting superior fare. You'll also discover a licensed snack bar, a sauna, and a beauty parlor. (☎ *0479-2526*.)

### Muckrach Lodge

At *Dulnain Bridge*, a haven for sportsmen, walkers, and anglers. The Sunday evening meal is so enriching that you'll pick up your ergs for the week right here—and delicious they are.

### Craiglynne Hotel                                                         ☆

Pure Walden for the nature lover, the sportsman, or the world-weary. Tumbling, salmon-full Spey only a toddle from your doorstep; daily (or overnight, if you wish) pony trekking across fells and mountain slopes; shooting parties arranged; hardy tartan bar with peat fire usually smoldering; friendly, home-style service. (☎ *0479-2597*.)

### Nethybridge Hotel

15 minutes south along the river at the hamlet of the same name, offers less zing in its more ancient amenities. But fishermen go into ecstasies over its 6-mile reach of private Spey. Strictly for dedicated anglers. (☎ *047982-203*; FAX: *686*.)

## INVERNESS

### Caledonian

Offers 100 units with private bath; swimming pool, sauna, and fitness center. Modern rather than traditional tone. Peppy, fun-filled atmosphere. (☎ *0463-235181*; FAX: *711206*.)

### Mercury
Recently expanded, now provides 118 latchkeys to contemporary dwelling space. (☎ *0463-239666*.)

### Kingsmills
A mile from the center; its ways are traditional while its amenities are modern. The mood is youthful; golf available. (☎ *0463-237166*; FAX: *225208*.)

### Culloden House ★
2 miles out, takes its name from the battleground nearby where Bonnie Prince Charlie was defeated in his attempt to capture the British throne for the Stuart kings. Never mind. It will capture your heart and soul more than 2 centuries later. Everything about it bespeaks the easy comfort of country life. (☎ *0463-790461*; FAX: *792181*.)

## IONA

**Columba** and **Argyle** are the only two stopping places on the island. A nice adventure for one night.

## KYLE OF LOCHALSH

### Lochalsh Hotel
80 miles west of Inverness at the ferry point to the Isle of Skye, features an admirable view across the strait; modern appointments and genuine Scottish flavor and color. Well-supplied bar; 40 rooms, about half with bath; service spare; book long, long, long in advance because this minihouse is always crowded. While it is open all year, the biggest crush comes during high season when visitors are heading Skye-ward. Here is the most important way station en route. (☎ *0599-4202*.)

### Balmacara
Six miles south of Kyle. A viewful and a worthy alternative.

## LOSSIEMOUTH

### Stotfield
Closely linked to its golf links. The accommodation is fair but no rave. (☎ *034381-2011*.)

## NAIRN

### Newton ☆☆
30 minutes northeast of Inverness on the Moray Firth, was described to me by a good Scotsman as "a civilized place"—and that it is. Here is a favorite quiet hideaway of prime ministers, industrial colossi, and Very Old Families. Vintage 1850 structure surrounded by 35-acre parkland; castle architecture; 2 championship golf courses; tennis courts; trout and salmon fishing; central heating and open peat hearths; numerous lounges; cocktail bar oriented (or is it "occi-

dented"?) toward the most glorious sunsets in the Highlands. The cuisine is above average for Scotland. Not posh, but deeply satisfying. (☎ 0667-53144; FAX: 54026.)

### Golf View

Bigger, more modest, and less expensive. Waterside situation; also with tennis facilities, and near the links; commendable cookery; attentive service; the best corner units are Nos. 106, 207, and 307. (☎ 0667-52301.)

### Royal Marine

With 47 kips, most with private plumbing, kept in fine trim. Recommended, and open all year. (☎ 0667 53381.)

## OBAN

### Caledonian

Offers a midtown waterfront situation just a toot from the Hebridean ferry slips; old exterior; spacious public rooms; vista-oriented dining salon. Coming up with gratifying speed. (☎ 0631-63133.)

### Park

Ready after a reconstruction spree with fresh amenities and a beckoning mien. Lots of work and many rewards. (☎ 0631-63621.)

### Great Western

Beautifully perched on the Esplanade, an imposing gray and white Georgian building with a viewful lochside command. Glass-fronted terrace and adjoining bar; excellent position. (☎ 0631-63101.)

### Manor House

Fewer than a dozen rooms and a reliable kitchen. (☎ 0631-62087.)

### Alexandra

Less appealing for comfort, boasts a better down-the-loch panorama; it is older in tone, despite recent refurbishings. (☎ 0631-62381.)

## PITCAPLE

### Pittodrie House                                          ★★★

North of Braemar, is one of the most historic and well-appointed estates in the nation. The antiques are collector's items (please don't) and the library is superb (it can be used for private dining). By contrast, there is color TV in every bedchamber. Superior homelike comfort with an elegance that only time and grace can provide. (☎ 04676-444.)

## SKYE

### Skeabost House

A pleasant 21-room country place outside of Portree. (☎ 047032-202.)

### Rosedale

In town with a waterfront view and 23 units. (☎ 0478-3131.)

## Kinloch Lodge

Half the size of the above pair and with cozy-corner charm.

## Isleornsay

(☎ *04713-333.*) The island is very seasonal, so don't go without a reservation.

.

# INDEX

# Introducing the 1994 Fielding Travel Guides— fresh, fascinating and fun!

## The travel guide series that started truth in travel is back.

An incisive new attitude and an exciting new look! All-new design and format. In-depth reviews. Fielding delivers travel information the way frequent travelers demand it—written with sparkle, style and humor. Candid insights, sage advice, insider tips. No fluff, no filler, only fresh information that makes the journey more fun, more fascinating, more Fielding.

| | |
|---|---|
| **Australia 1994** | **$16.95** |
| **Belgium 1994** | **$16.95** |
| **Bermuda/Bahamas 1994** | **$16.95** |
| **Brazil 1994** | **$16.95** |
| **Britain 1994** | **$16.95** |
| **Budget Europe 1994** | **$16.95** |
| **Caribbean 1994** | **$16.95** |
| **Europe 1994** | **$16.95** |
| **Far East 1994** | **$16.95** |
| **France 1994** | **$16.95** |
| **The Great Sights of Europe 1994** | **$16.95** |
| **Hawaii 1994** | **$16.95** |
| **Holland 1994** | **$16.95** |
| **Italy 1994** | **$16.95** |
| **Mexico 1994** | **$16.95** |
| **New Zealand 1994** | **$16.95** |
| **Scandinavia 1994** | **$16.95** |
| **Spain & Portugal 1994** | **$16.95** |
| **Switzerland & the Alpine Region 1994** | **$16.95** |
| **Worldwide Cruises 1994** | **$16.95** |
| **Shopping Europe** | **$12.95** |

To place an order: call toll-free
**1-800-FW-2-GUIDE**
add $2.00 shipping & handling, allow 2-6 weeks.

## For Travel Insiders Only!

# FIELDING'S
# TRAVEL
# SECRETS

FIELDING'S TRAVEL SECRETS is the insider's travel guide, available only to travel professionals and a very limited number of Fielding Travel Guide readers. Created by Fielding's experienced staff of writers and released in six bi-monthly installments per year, the insider's report is packed with timely travel information, trends, news, tips and reviews. Enroll now and you will also receive a variety of significant discounts and special preview information.

Due to the sensitive nature of the information contained in these reports, subscriptions available to non-travel industry individuals are limited to the first 10,000 subscribers. The annual price for all six installments is $60. This offer also comes with an unconditional money-back guarantee if you are not fully satisfied.

To Reserve Your Subscription
## 1-800-FW-2-GUIDE

# Favorite People, Places & Experiences

| ADDRESS: | NOTES: |
| --- | --- |

**Name**

**Address**

**Telephone**

**Name**

**Address**

**Telephone**

**Name**

**Address**

**Telephone**

**Name**

**Address**

**Telephone**

**Name**

**Address**

**Telephone**

**Name**

**Address**

**Telephone**

**Name**

**Address**

**Telephone**

# Favorite People, Places & Experiences

| ADDRESS: | NOTES: |
|---|---|

**Name**

**Address**

**Telephone**

**Name**

**Address**

**Telephone**

**Name**

**Address**

**Telephone**

**Name**

**Address**

**Telephone**

**Name**

**Address**

**Telephone**

**Name**

**Address**

**Telephone**

**Name**

**Address**

**Telephone**

# Favorite People, Places & Experiences

| ADDRESS: | NOTES: |
|---|---|

**Name**

**Address**

**Telephone**

**Name**

**Address**

**Telephone**

**Name**

**Address**

**Telephone**

**Name**

**Address**

**Telephone**

**Name**

**Address**

**Telephone**

**Name**

**Address**

**Telephone**

**Name**

**Address**

**Telephone**

# Favorite People, Places & Experiences

| ADDRESS: | NOTES: |
|---|---|

**Name**

**Address**

**Telephone**

**Name**

**Address**

**Telephone**

**Name**

**Address**

**Telephone**

**Name**

**Address**

**Telephone**

**Name**

**Address**

**Telephone**

**Name**

**Address**

**Telephone**

**Name**

**Address**

**Telephone**

# Favorite People, Places & Experiences

| ADDRESS: | NOTES: |
|----------|--------|

**Name**

**Address**


**Telephone**

**Name**

**Address**


**Telephone**

**Name**

**Address**


**Telephone**

**Name**

**Address**


**Telephone**

**Name**

**Address**


**Telephone**

**Name**

**Address**


**Telephone**

**Name**

**Address**


**Telephone**